Iron Ball Paint
Ferrite Balls
absorbs Radar

TO THE STUDENT: A Study Guide for this textbook is available through
your college bookstore under the title STUDY GUIDE for BUSINESS
COMMUNICATIONS, NINTH EDITION by William C. Himstreet and
Wayne Murlin Baty. The Study Guide can help you with course material
by acting as a tutorial, review, and study aid. If the Study Guide is
not in stock, ask the bookstore manager to order a copy for you.

BUSINESS COMMUNICATIONS

KENT Series in Business Education

BUSINESS COMMUNICATIONS

PRINCIPLES AND METHODS

NINTH EDITION

William C. Himstreet

Wayne Murlin Baty

PWS-KENT Publishing Company

B O S T O N

PWS–KENT
Publishing Company

20 Park Plaza
Boston, Massachusetts 02116

PWS-KENT Publishing Company is a division of Wadsworth, Inc.

Library of Congress Cataloging-in-Publication Data

Himstreet, William C.
   Business communications: principles and methods / William C.
Himstreet, Wayne Murlin Baty. — 9th ed.
      p.   cm.
   ISBN 0-534-91983-9
   1. Commercial correspondence.   2. Business report writing.
3. Business communication.   I. Baty, Wayne Murlin.   II. Title.
HF5721.H5   1990
658.4′5—dc19   89-22829
                                                CIP

Cross-Cultural Communications photo essay
Developmental Editor: Robine Andrau; *Photo Researcher:* Ann Rahimi-Assa;
Designer: Julia Gecha
Photo Credits: p. xvii (T) The Bettman Archive; p. xvii (M) The Bettman Archive; p. xvii (B) Historical Pictures Service, Chicago; p. xviii (T) Eddie Hironaka/The Image Bank; p. xviii (M) Donald Dietz/Stock, Boston; p. xviii (B) © Frank Siteman/The Picture Cube; p. xix (T) © Jeffry W. Myers/Stock, Boston; p. xix (B) Comstock, Inc.; p. xx (T) John Henebry; p. xx (B) © Tony O'Brien/Picture Group; p. xxi (T) courtesy Tjona Storm van Leeuwen; p. xxi (M) © James D. Wilson/Newsweek; p. xxi (B) © Rob Nelson/Picture Group; p. xxii (T) courtesy Environment Canada; p. xxii (B) Alex Webb/Magnum Photos, Inc.; p. xxiii (T) courtesy NASA; p. xxiii (M) Aram Gesar/The Image Bank; p. xxiii (B) courtesy Ricoh; p. xxiv (T) Pierre Perrin/Sygma; p. xxiv (B) courtesy Cray Computers

Editor: Rolf A. Janke; *Production Coordinator & Cover Designer:* Robine Andrau; *Manufacturing Coordinator:* Marcia Locke; *Interior Design:* Julia Gecha & Quadrata, Inc.; *Typesetting:* Bi-Comp, Inc.; *Cover Printing:* New England Book Components & Blackbourn, Inc. *Printing and Binding:* Arcata Graphics/Halliday

Printed in the United States of America

91 92 93 94 — 10 9 8 7 6 5 4 3 2

PREFACE

Reviews from users of the eighth edition of *Business Communications* and frequent discussions with our peers in education led to many of the changes in this ninth edition. Writers of textbooks in business communication tend to add chapter after chapter to demonstrate broad coverage and to incorporate new material. This tendency has led to a proliferation of tiny chapters rather than to an integration of new developments within the structure of business communication courses.

In this ninth edition, we have reorganized content in fewer chapters without sacrificing important concepts. The content of this book is organized in 18 chapters divided into 6 parts; the prior edition contained 21 chapters divided into 7 parts.

• Organization of the Text

A review of the new organization reveals how the reduction of three chapters was accomplished.

Part 1, Communication Foundations and Oral Communication, is a reorganization of four previous chapters into three. The three current chapters cover (1) organizational communication, (2) interpersonal communication and listening, and (3) public speaking and oral reporting. Listening formerly constituted a separate chapter as part of a section on speaking and listening. Because it is so much a part of interpersonal communication, listening is now covered earlier in the course in a foundation chapter. Public speaking and oral reporting have also been moved forward to Part 1. At the same time, both listening and speaking receive further attention in sections on employment and reports.

Part 2, Using Words and Style Effectively, concentrates on word choice and writing style. Content is organized in two chapters that have been rated highly by users for several editions. Noteworthy by its absence is a chapter on keyboarding and dictating. That material has been condensed and is included in the appendix. For courses in which dictating and keyboarding receive considerable classroom attention, the appendix also includes written communication formats and organized grammar and mechanics reviews.

Part 3, Communicating Through Letters and Memoranda, contains four chapters. Material on memorandum preparation, formerly a separate chapter, is now integrated in the basic letter chapters. In this way, we have tried to treat letters and memoranda as similar means of communicating in writing but with one serving external and the other internal communication needs of organizations.

Part 4, Communicating About Work and Jobs, has been revised to include both functional and chronological (factual) résumés, a variety of employment messages, and employment interviewing. Although we are convinced the functional résumé represents a creative, new approach, we do recognize the need for chronological résumés to meet some application requirements and to serve the needs of those who may not have acquired sufficient experience to take advantage of the functional style.

Part 5, Communicating Through Reports, continues to have four chapters, including the familiar and effective chapters on process and research methods and on managing data and using graphics. Significantly greater emphasis is given to proposals in the chapter on short reports and proposals. A new complete report provides the focus for the chapter on formal reports. This chapter also includes an expanded discussion of contemporary documentation methods.

Part 6, Communicating Electronically and Cross-Culturally, provides an appropriate concluding section for the text. We are grateful to Jean Gonzalez of Cypress College for her assistance in the preparation of the material on electronic tools in business communication. The emphasis is on what electronic tools can accomplish in manipulating, presenting, and sharing business information. The final chapter on cross-cultural communication introduces problems created when Americans must work for foreign management or must manage labor forces composed primarily of people with varying cultural backgrounds.

Therefore, former chapters containing material on the memorandum and on listening have been integrated into existing, closely related chapters; and material on keyboarding and dictating, formerly a separate chapter, has been moved to the appendix. We believe the new organization and the support materials contribute to a much sounder teaching–learning package.

• Features Retained from Previous Editions

A new edition of a textbook builds on the past edition. After several editions, you might expect the new one to look little like its early ancestors. Yet, some concepts, theories, and methods of presentation have moved through nine editions of *Business Communications*. Some of the things we have retained include the following:

1. The sentence-by-sentence analysis of messages provides the rationale for idea sequences and word choices. We believe this approach, used in the first edition of the text, is superior to one that consists of long, step-by-step checklists that seem to stifle creativity and regiment student production. At

the same time, we have included several broad summaries to provide principles.

2. The pleasant-routine, unpleasant, and persuasive message plans were also included in the first edition. These plans—often called good news, bad news, and persuasive—are effective and were proposed by Professor Sherwin Cody in his book *Success in Letter Writing, Business and Social*, published in 1906. We've retained this approach to planning because psychologically it makes sense as the best way to "get through" to recipients of messages.

3. Marginal comments throughout the text were first used in our third edition and proved popular. These comments were in question form until this edition. Now the comments take the form both of questions and statements. They add a little more emphasis to highlight content; and in some cases, they may promote class discussion.

4. A mix of end-of-chapter assignments ranges from simple and familiar consumer and personal writing tasks to rather sophisticated business problems. This mix permits students to follow a simple-to-complex learning pattern. People seem to write and talk most effectively when using themselves and their affairs as subjects.

5. About Language and Usage was introduced as a feature of the eighth edition. It provides an interesting vocabulary and usage lesson in each chapter. However, the items should be looked on as providing "learning for learning's sake" and not as an integral part of course content that will appear on examinations.

• Instructional Resources

Instructional resources complement the textbook and offer materials and activities for classroom use. The instructional resources elements were designed to simplify and strengthen the study of business communication. We believe their use can make both in-class and out-of-class time more effective. The faster the turnaround time between submitting homework and receiving feedback, the better the learning:

- *Instructor's Manual and Test Bank*. The manual contains teaching suggestions, test and quiz items with answers, and solutions to end-of-chapter questions. Extensive coverage of grammar, writing style, and usage is included.

- *Transparencies*. Although any of the material in the Instructor's Manual may be reproduced as transparencies by adopters of the text, an additional package of fully developed overhead transparencies is available on adoption. The package is keyed to the text and includes many solutions to the end-of-chapter problems and cases.

- The *Study Guide*, a supplementary book for student use, is designed to reinforce learning. It includes these sections:

1. *Check Your Knowledge:* short-answer items covering chapter content.
2. *Communication Glossary:* matching exercises for terms used in each chapter.
3. *English Review:* short review exercises of English usage and grammar in each chapter.
4. *Spelling Checkup:* spelling exercises covering frequently misspelled words.
5. *Case Problems:* a case built around one company and calling for written solutions runs throughout the guide.

Answers to all but the case problems are provided in the Study Guide to assure immediate reinforcement of learning.

- *Computerized Interactive Practice Set* diskettes are attached to the back cover of this text. CIPS provides students with an inductive review of grammar principles. User instructions are in an appendix. If backup diskettes are needed, refer to the Instructor's Manual for order forms.

• To Students

Although the preceding discussion seems as though it were written mainly for instructors, it is intended for you also. Sometimes you can develop a greater appreciation for a book when you know about the concerns that went into its preparation. We didn't write this book only for teachers. We wrote it for you. In fact, we wrote the first edition years ago just as we taught the course; we thought we could write a book our students could appreciate, use, and perhaps retain as a later reference. You won't find many so-called real-world examples with business letterheads in our model letters. We want our examples and your letters to be better than that.

From our own teaching and corporate experience, we know that good writing and speaking are often the only ways in which a young person's ability is brought to the attention of top executives. Learn to write and speak well. When you do, you'll find little competition.

People succeed in careers for a variety of reasons. They fail mostly, however, because of their inability to speak, write, and interact with others adequately. Your study of business communication might be your most important and valuable undertaking.

• Thank You

Authorship of nine editions of a textbook almost makes a career. To us, the labor and time seem like a small price to pay for the friendships made, the recognition received, and the satisfaction felt. At the same time, our spouses, Maxine Himstreet and Maxine Baty, and our children, now grown and on their own, probably recall the difficult times more readily than we. A part of each of them is in this book.

We must also acknowledge the help, support, and advice of the publisher's staff. Those who worked with us look on each publication as a team accomplishment. We're glad to be included on the team.

Additionally, to the many faculty members with whom we have worked and the many, many professional educators who have reviewed, critiqued, and made significant contributions to each edition, and particularly to this one, we will always be gratefully indebted. For recent editions, we extend our thanks to the following truly professional faculty:

R. Jon Ackley
Virginia Commonwealth University

Suzanne T. Allen
Columbus Technical Institute

Sherrill Amador
Southwestern College

Lena Ampadu
Towson State University

Vanessa Dean Arnold
University of Mississippi

Edward R. Bagley
Essex Community College

Bonita L. Betters-Reed,
Simmons College

Linda Bloom
Pensacola Junior College

Vicki Lynn Boeder
Madison Area Technical College

Ed Borgens
San Diego City College

Deborah Bosley
Millikin University

George Boulware
Belmont College

Mary Ellen Bowe
Front Range Community College

Carl H. Boyer
University of Toledo

Linda H. Brody
Towson State University

Jenelle M. Brooks
DeKalb Community College

William J. Burling
Pennsylvania State University

Jeannette Caggiano
Suffolk Community College

Diane Calaway
Surry Community College

Eugene Calvasina
Troy State University

Gloria Campbell
Wartburg College

Joseph Cantrell
Foothill College

Catherine Carlson
North Hennepin Community College

Sharon Chase
San Jose State University

James L. Clark
Pasadena City College

William Clemente
University of Oregon

J. R. Cole
University of Akron

Carol J. Cozan
University of Guam

Beth Crabtree
Guilford Technical College

Sheila Criger
Mohave Community College

Moyne Cubbage
Rhode Island College and Providence
    College

Earl L. Dachslager
University of Houston

Ann Davert
Rancho Santiago College

Frankie T. Davis
Palm Beach Junior College

Rodney Davis
Ball State University

Jane L. Dawkins
Clark College

Janette Day
Fullerton College

Wanda DeBoer
University of Northern Colorado

Christie Steiger Delfanian
North Dakota State University

Marcia Dier
Clackamas Community College

Earl A. Dvorak
Indiana University

Margaret Ehrhart
Fairleigh Dickinson University

Les Ellenor
Okanasan College

Gwendolyn M. Ellis
Grambling State University

Noel Falkofska
University of Wisconsin-Stout

Nancy Fann
Middle Tennessee State University

Alton Finch
East Carolina University

Pat Garner
Golden Gate University

David H. Gigley
Ohio University—Chillicothe

Lee Goddard
Bowling Green State University

Berta Gramling
Phillips County Community College

Carmen Griffin
Rio Salado Community College

Mary Ellen Guffey
Los Angeles Pierce College

David J. Hamilton
Bemidji State University

Ellen G. Hankin
Rider College

Margaret Hebert
University of Houston

Donna Heilman
Fullerton College

Paulette Henry
Howard University

Rovena L. Hillsman
California State University

Beverly Holmskog
Tabor College

N. LaRue Hubbard
Glendale Community College

Edna-Marie Hudson
Chesapeake College

Jennie Hunter
Western Carolina University

Thomas H. Inman
Southwest Missouri State University

Betty Jacquier
American River College

Marcia L. James
University of Wisconsin—Whitewater

Heidi Janes
St. John's, Newfoundland

Fannie E. Johnson
Western Oklahoma State College

Tommy G. Johnson
University of Southwestern Louisiana

Fred Jordan
Barry University

Debra K. Kellerman
St. Cloud State University

Elree Kellog
University of Utah

Erna Kemps
North Central Technical Institute

Leon F. Kenman
American Graduate School of
    International Management

Rebecca F. Kifer
University of Pittsburgh

Morgan Kjer
North Hennepin Community College

David Kok
Kolej Damansara Utama, Malaysia

Margaret Kortes
Lake Tahoe Community College

Craig LaClair
California State University–Sacramento

Barbara Lea
West Valley College

Dorothy Leavitt
Sul Ross State University

Peggy E. C. Lee
Virginia State University

Patricia Lehrling
Kankakee Community College

Lee Lemon
University of Nebraska—Lincoln

Mary E. Leslie
Grossmont College

Judy Leusink
Aims Community College

Jewel Linville
Northeastern Oklahoma State
   University

Terry L. Long
Ohio State University

Barbara Loush
Oakland Community College

Loretta C. Lowles
Pensacola Junior College

Dona Walton Luse
University of New Orleans

Cynthia Lyle
Texas Tech University

Margaret McCue
SUNY—Morrisville

Joan L. McCullough
Cosumnes River College

Harriet McIntosh
University of New Orleans

Frederick E. McNally
California State University

C. R. McPherson
Louisiana State University—Shreveport

Thomas B. Mack
Mesa College

Mary Louise Meeh
Delta College

Peter F. Meggison
Massasoit Community College

Zonell Webster Miller
Rose State College

Linda S. Munilla
Georgia Southern College

Beverly H. Nelson
University of New Orleans

Athyleen F. Nicholson
Fort Steilacoom Community College

Gerald R. O'Donnell
Niagara University

Pallavi Pandit
Pennsylvania State University

James G. Patterson, III
Jackson Community College

Susan Pehl
Modesto Junior College

Doris D. Phillips
University of Mississippi

Lois Pigford
Community College of Denver

Merton E. Powell
Ferris State College

Marlene S. Putnam
Fresno City College

R. David Ramsey
Southeastern Louisiana University

Maurice E. Ransom
Pikes Peak Community College

Bernard J. Reilly
Oakland Community College

Elizabeth L. Reynolds
St. John's, Newfoundland

Elizabeth Robertson
Tennessee State University

Patricia Rush
Indiana Vocational and Technical
   College

A. Ray Rustand
Pensacola Junior College

Joan Ryan
Lane Community College

Charlotte W. Sargeant
Southern Connecticut State University

Marguerite Shane-Joyce
McNeese State University

Larry Smeltzer
Louisiana State University

Clara J. Smith
North Seattle Community College

Carleen Spano
Miami-Dade Community College

Goldie Sparger
Surry Community College

Florence Staggs
Saddleback College

Sharon D. Steigmann
Indiana University of Pennsylvania

Skaidrite Stelzer
University of Toledo

Marilyn Stinson
St. Cloud University

Jacqueline Stowe
McMurry College

Lois Sullivan
Bergen Community College

Alden S. Talbot
Weber State College

David S. Terrell
Camoson College, B.C.

Billy E. Thompson
Austin Peay State University

W. B. Turner
Golden State University

Beulah Underwood
San Diego Mesa College

June Underwood
Portland State University

Robert Underwood
Ball State University

Anne C. Utschig
University of Wisconsin—Fox Valley

Palmina Uzzolino
Montclair State College

George Walters
Emporia State University

Douglas F. Warring
Inver Hills Community College

Max L. Waters
Brigham Young University

Suzanne W. Wegman
Nazareth College

Judy F. West
University of Tennessee—Chattanooga

Leonora F. West
San Diego City College

James J. Weston
California State University—
    Sacramento

Jane F. White
Georgia Southern College

Roberta Whitney
University of Nevada—Las Vegas

Jerry L. Wood
Northern Montana College

Barry E. Woodcock
Tennessee Tech. University

Sandra Woodward
Portland Community College

Eugene D. Wyllie
Indiana University

Sandra A. Young
Jones Junior College

Donald Zahn
University of Wisconsin—Whitewater

Adelle W. Ziemer
Lehigh County Community College

CONTENTS

COMMUNICATING THROUGH REPORTS

COMMUNICATING ELECTRONICALLY AND
CROSS-CULTURALLY

CROSS-CULTURAL COMMUNICATION

◀ Egyptians used hieroglyphs as a pictorial writing system from about 3000 B.C. until the time of the Roman Empire. Also throughout this time, they developed and used a more cursive script, written with reed pens and ink on papyrus. Hieroglyphic script not only conveyed a message but also formed part of the decoration of monuments. Because of the preservation of hieroglyphs, we have seen ancient culture and history transmitted through several centuries.

▼ Advances in technology, from movable type in the sixteenth century to high-speed presses in the nineteenth, created conditions for widespread literacy. Along with books and newspapers, the telegraph and telephone (pictured here in the 1897 version) were the foundations for modern communications, accelerating the speed and frequency of intercultural contacts, now a permanent part of our environment.

▲ Centuries of war and commerce in the lands bordering the Mediterranean Sea left remnants of Egyptian, Greek, Roman, Arabic, and Norman French culture throughout the area. In the Age of Exploration, beginning in the fifteenth century, Portuguese, Spanish, Italian, and English explorers carried European culture to Africa, Asia, and the Americas by conquest and settlement. Communications, however, remained relatively slow. Not until the nineteenth century would railroads and telecommunications exceed the speed of horses and ocean-going vessels.

▶ San Francisco's China-town, founded during the California gold rush of the 1840s, is now one of the largest Chinese communities outside Asia. Although the community preserves its language, religions, and customs, second-generation residents participate in both American and Chinese cultures and serve as a link between the two.

◀ Miami's Little Havana has grown rapidly since the 1960s, with the influx of Latin American immigrants and political refugees. The Hispanic community is a dynamic presence in the larger society, giving rise to communications challenges, including controversy about the role of the Spanish language.

▶ New arrivals from Asia and Latin America have enriched the older mosaic of predominantly European immigrants. As in the past, Americans rely on the educational system, among all our institutions, as the best means of building cultural bridges.

Despite advances in technology and high-speed communications in the later twentieth century, cross-cultural differences show no signs of vanishing. Essential to effective communications in an era when political and economic relations among nations often have global impact is the recognition, understanding, and respect of the customs, beliefs, and values of other cultures.

▲ Americans shake hands and say "How are you?" ◄ Japanese bow upon meeting and say "Ikago desuka." These greeting rituals are just one example of different national customs. The same action can have different meanings: In America, a circle formed with the thumb and forefinger means "everything is okay"; in France, it means zero; in Japan, money; and in Brazil, a vulgarity.

Although United States imports have exceeded exports in recent years, U.S. direct foreign investment exceeded $300 billion in 1989, almost $50 billion more than direct foreign investment in the United States.

◄ With such widespread operations as the familiar "golden arches" of a McDonald's fast-food outlet in Tokyo

► and an American Express office in Mexico, American investments have introduced U.S. business practices and customs in more than 50 countries.

In the context of a global economy, effective communications between owner-managers from one culture and employees from another are essential to success. American fast-food outlet managers must understand local food preferences and taboos; and supervisors in Japanese auto factories in the U.S. must deal with the customs of the American workplace.

▶ The United States's leading trade partners are Canada, Western Europe, and Japan. Franchises selling foreign automobiles, such as this BMW/Ferrari/Alfa-Romeo dealership in Massachusetts, are found in most medium and large cities.

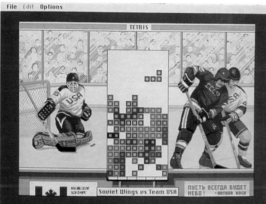

◀ Americans can now play the Russian computer game Tetris, evidence that, despite cold war rivalry, trade between two long-time adversaries is possible.

▶ Japanese T.V. sets dominate the U.S. market. The overwhelming imbalance of Japanese exports over imports in U.S.–Japanese trade has led to strained communications between these two economic superpowers in recent years.

◀ Normally friendly neighboring countries occasionally develop strains in their relationship. Canadians blame careless or uncontrolled industrial practices in the United States for the spread of acid rain beyond national borders and subsequent damage to Canadian forests. Neighbors with open borders may also disagree on trade policies, but solutions are more easily reached with a history of mutual goodwill.

▶ The United States also enjoys an open border with Mexico, but illegal Mexican immigration has been a troubling issue. Cultural differences and language barriers have further complicated this continuing challenge to constructive resolution of a problem between friendly neighbors.

▶ Technology binds the international community. Satellite communications, which became widespread in the 1980s, make possible almost instantaneous transmission of news events—from sports contests to political revolutions—around the globe.

◀ The few supersonic Concorde planes in service make a round-trip Atlantic crossing in about six hours, less time than the ordinary jet flies one way.

▶ Facsimile reproductions using fax machines and telephone lines are among the most recent features in station-to-station communications. Over three million were in use in 1989; and projections indicate the total growing at the rate of about a million a year, perhaps for the next decade. Printed material sent from a fax machine is reproduced almost instantly at the receiving machine.

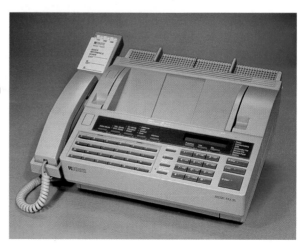

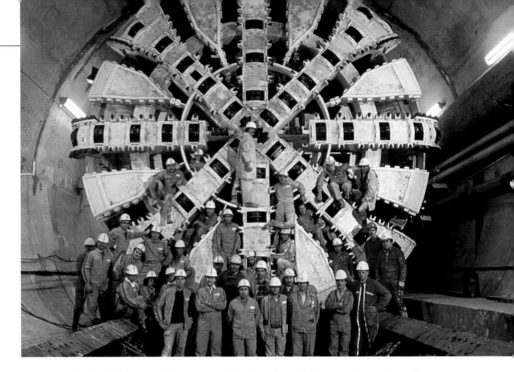

▲ The English Channel between England and Europe has long been one of the world's most difficult waterways to cross. The big news now is the Chunnel, a 30-mile underground (and underwater) link between Dover, England, and Sangatte, France, to be completed in 1993.

◀ Computers, such as the Cray-2 super-computer, continue to amaze us with their speed and multiple uses. Technology provides new *means* of transmitting information, but only people can determine the *content* of communications that will reduce cultural barriers.

O B J E C T I V E S

When you have finished studying Part 1, you should be able to

- Recognize and analyze four levels of communication.
- Understand the interrelated characteristics of organizations.
- Use effective methods of interpersonal communication.
- Put good listening habits into everyday use.
- Prepare and deliver public speeches.
- Deliver quality oral reports.

COMMUNICATION FOUNDATIONS AND ORAL COMMUNICATION

Organizational Setting for Business Communication

Communication problems grow much faster in any organization than the organization itself grows.

The Morris Maxim, JOHN O. MORRIS

D uring your income-producing years, you'll probably spend most of your communicative time within an organization. As a manager in business, government, or other industry, you'll have a variety of responsibilities. You'll be required to motivate, to instruct, and to control people in ways that will contribute to the success of your organization. This success depends greatly on the ability to communicate.

Purposes of Communication

We could choose any one of the many definitions of communication for our study of communication in business. The most suitable, in our opinion, is that communication is a process by which information is exchanged between or among individuals through a common system of symbols, signs, and behavior. As a process, communicating has synonyms such as expressing feelings, conversing, speaking, corresponding, writing, listening, and exchanging.

Communicating is a pervasive process.

People communicate to satisfy needs in both their work and nonwork lives. People want to be heard, to be appreciated, and to be wanted. They also want to accomplish tasks and to achieve goals. Obviously, then, a major purpose of communication is to help people feel good about themselves and about their friends, groups, and organizations.

Communicating informs, persuades, and entertains through verbal and nonverbal messages. Verbal means "through the use of words," either written or oral. To be precise, speakers and writers should avoid using "verbal" when they mean "oral." In this book, *oral* and *spoken* will identify speech communication; *written* will identify writing tasks.

Might a person send verbal and nonverbal signals simultaneously?

Nonverbal means "without the use of words." People constantly send nonverbal messages through body motions, appearance, aromas, clothing, uniforms, facial expressions, jewelry, automobiles, and a variety of other symbols, signs, and behaviors.

Four Levels of Communication

Information, as a communication term, is the property of a word, symbol, or sign to convey meaning. An example is "ouch!" People form messages by combining several pieces or bits of information. When a person "talks to herself or himself" mentally as a way of processing information being received, *intrapersonal communication* is occurring. Intrapersonal communication is the way in which individuals process information based on their own life experiences. Therefore, communicating may be difficult when a sender of a message has significantly different life experiences from the recipient of the message.

Interpersonal communication, a second level, takes place primarily when two people are involved in the process. As mentioned, they have two goals: (1) They want to accomplish whatever task confronts them, and (2) they want to feel better about themselves as a result of the exchange. These two goals are commonly referred to respectively as task goals and maintenance goals, and they exist side by side in varying degrees in most of our daily activities.

A third level of communication is *group communication.* A group includes more than two people: a committee, a club, or all the students enrolled in a class. Groups are formed usually because the combined efforts of a number of people result in greater output than the individual efforts of the same number of people. In other words, groups can do more for the individuals than the individuals can do for themselves.

Another level of communication arises when groups discover that they are unable to accomplish their goals without some kind or organization. Thus organizations as we know them are really combinations of groups ordered in such a way that large tasks may be accomplished. This fourth level is *organizational communication.*

Despite the differences in size and complexity, each of these levels of communication continues to have task and maintenance goals. But the idea of maintenance goals can be expanded, or divided, into two distinct goals: (1) a self-maintenance goal that describes the individual's need to maintain his or her personal worth or psychological well-being, and (2) a group-maintenance goal that describes the group's need to maintain its *esprit de corps*—the nontask relationships they have established by interacting with one another as a team.

The study of organizational communication is a subject on which entire books have been written, but a brief review of communication in the organization should help us understand the role of management in the organizational communication process.

What is the motivation for forming groups?

How is an organization different from a group?

What is the difference between a task goal and a maintenance goal?

Communicating in Groups

Most of your oral communication in business will occur in one-to-one relationships, which receives major emphasis in Chapter 2. You will probably also make oral reports and speeches. Your second most frequent oral communication activity, however, will likely occur when you participate in groups—primarily groups within the organizational work environment. Group and committee work have become crucial in most organizations. Group meetings can be productive when members understand something about groups and how they operate.

• Purposes of Groups

What is meant by "synergism?"

Groups form for synergistic effects; i.e., through pooling their efforts, group members can achieve more collectively than they could individually. At the same time, the social nature of groups contributes to the self-maintenance goals of members. Communication in small groups leads to group decisions that are generally superior to individual decisions. The group process can motivate members, improve thinking, and assist attitude development and change. The emphasis that groups place on task and maintenance activity is based on several factors in group communication.

• Factors in Group Communication

As you consider the following factors in group communication, try to visualize their relationship to some groups you have belonged to through school, church, athletics, and social activities.

Leadership The ability of a group leader to work toward task goals while, at the same time, contributing to the development of group and individual maintenance goals is often critical to group success.

Longevity Groups formed for short-term tasks, such as to arrange for a dinner and program, will spend more time on the task than on maintenance. However, groups formed for long-term assignments, such as an audit of a major corporation by a team from a public accounting firm, may devote much effort to maintenance goals.

Could maintenance goals be served during task activities?

The House Banking Committee has over 50 members.

Size The smaller the group, the more its members have the opportunity to communicate with each other; conversely, large groups often inhibit communication because the opportunity to speak and interact is limited. When broad input is desired, large groups may be good; when expert opinion is the goal, smaller groups may be more effective. Interestingly, large groups generally divide into smaller groups for maintenance purposes, even when the large group is task oriented. Although much research has been conducted in the area of group size, no optimal number of members has been identified. Groups of five to seven members are thought to be best for decision-making and problem-solving tasks. An odd number of members is preferred because deciding votes are possible and tie votes are infrequent.

Perception and Self-Concept   People who are invited to join groups have perceptions of how the group should operate and what it should achieve. The member also has a self-concept that dictates fairly well how the member will behave. Comics try to preserve their images, those known as aggressive attempt to preserve that reputation, and those who like to be known as moderates will behave in moderate ways by settling arguments rather than initiating them. When expectations and satisfaction of self-concepts fall short, groups will probably be ineffective.

Status   Some group members will appear to be better qualified than others. Consider a group in which the chief executive of the organization is a member: when the chief executive speaks, members agree; when members speak, they tend to direct their remarks to the one with high status—the chief executive. People are inclined to communicate equally with peers, but they tend to speak upward to superiors and downward to subordinates. As a generalization, groups require balance in status and expertise, not homogeneity.

Group Norms   A norm is a standard or average for behavior, and all groups possess norms. A teacher's behavior helps establish classroom norms. When a teacher is generally late for class, students will begin to arrive late. When the teacher permits talking during lectures, the norm will be for students to talk. People conform to norms because conformity is easy and nonconformity is difficult and uncomfortable. Conformity leads to acceptance by other group members and creates communication opportunities.

Thus the performance of groups depends on several factors, but none is more important than leadership. The leader can establish norms, determine who can speak and when, encourage everyone to contribute, and provide the motivation for effective group activity.

What is the preferred pronunciation of "status"?

Characteristics of Formal Organizations

What elements distinguish a formal organization from a group? Both are made up of individuals, and both have goals. Some groups may exceed the size of some organizations in terms of individuals.

Essentially, formal, large organizations are characterized not by a single factor but by a combination of

Four critically related characteristics

1. Goal orientation
2. Specialization of individuals and units
3. Interdependence of individuals and units
4. Formalized hierarchy

• Goal Orientation

Organizations can accomplish some things individuals and groups cannot do by or for themselves. The task goals, for example, of individuals and groups may generate such complicated and sizable endeavors that more complex entities are necessary to accomplish them. Take the example of the small-business person whose business expands beyond the personal ability to cope with it.

Try to visualize the one-druggist pharmacy that concentrates on filling prescriptions. Ultimately, the pharmacist's son or daughter graduates from college with visions of taking over the family business and developing it into something big. Soon, greeting cards, confections, toiletries, and a variety of other items fill the shelves. Business is good. More space is needed. As a result, a larger building is leased in a more desirable location. Additionally, more employees are needed to handle the expanded business. In fact, it isn't too long before the store is handling clothing, housewares, toys, stationery, food, beverages, garden supplies and the great variety of things available in many modern drugstores. The prescription department is now far at the rear of the store—so those customers using it must pass all the impulse items on the way to pick up their prescriptions—and it occupies only a small portion of the total space. Thus, the goal orientation of the store has changed to the point where individuals or groups could not achieve those goals by themselves.

• Specialization of Individuals and Units

Does specialization eliminate or increase the need to communicate?

The new drugstore calls for more employees and for some skills not available within the family. Purchasing merchandise for resale, maintaining inventories, maintaining accounting and other office records, developing displays, and exercising control over a variety of activities have all required some specialization. Business has become so good that management—the family—is thinking of expanding the business into a branch or chain operation. They add to all those other jobs a specialist in market research and a consultant for site selection.

To exercise the necessary control over the wide range of activities, management has also organized its personnel into functional units called departments: purchasing and marketing, finance and accounting, warehousing and inventory control, prescriptions, and planning. Within these departments, specialization of labor further occurs. Purchasing and marketing have specialists in cosmetics, paper products, outdoor products, clothing, and so on. Obviously, as the complexity of the undertaking increases, greater specialization is required. This specialization leads to the next characteristic of the large organization.

• Interdependence of Individuals and Units

Because of specialization in the large, formal organization, each of the departments is dependent on each of the others to some extent. Sales efforts on the part of the marketing staff are very much dependent on a steady and uninterrupted flow of merchandise provided by the warehousing and inventory-control department. Regular reports from these units to finance and accounting provide the basis for an efficient record-keeping system that can, in turn, provide information to assist management in planning and decision making.

Within each of these departments, too, specialization of people leads to interdependence of individuals. Therefore, the dependence of units on one another in the large organization is also a characteristic of the internal structure of the smaller units. The large organization is now composed of smaller units, and these units are composed of individuals. All, however, are organized so that the goals of the organization can be achieved. The organization grew or matured in step with changes in goals. Keep in mind, however, that in the everyday work of the organization the task goals of the total organization exist side by side with the group-maintenance goals of the departmental units and the self-maintenance goals of the individuals involved. The interdependence characteristic of units and individuals applies equally to both task goals and maintenance goals.

Does *interdependence* mean "mutual dependence"?

• Formalized Hierarchy

To achieve its goals, the organization needs to direct and coordinate the interdependence of units and individuals toward a desired end. Formal organization structure results from efforts to achieve coordination. As

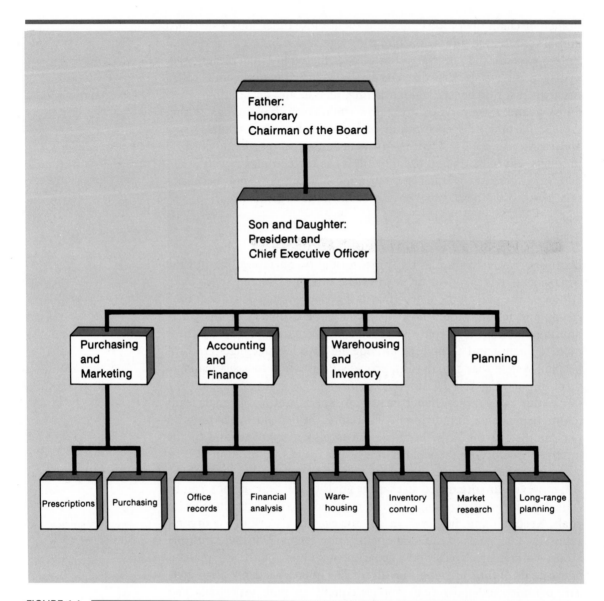

FIGURE 1.1

Organization chart: The Super Drugstore.

shown in Figure 1.1, the original pharmacy has grown into a sizable super-drugstore operation with a formalized hierarchy.

The formalized hierarchy ensures that communication occurs effectively as an element in coordination. Coordination, in turn, results from effective communication and well-organized programs or systems.

These four characteristics are acquired as the organization develops, and they are probably acquired in the order listed. As goals expand beyond the capacity of the current organization, additional specialization is necessary to achieve them. As specialization increases, interdependence also increases. And as interdependence of individuals and units increases, the need for formalized structure or hierarchy to ensure communication and hence coordination becomes greater.

Organizational Structure and Communication

Almost any knowledgeable person can sketch an organization chart similar to the one for The Super Drugstore. But not everyone can describe what the chart represents. Traditionally, organization charts have been used to describe the authority structure of the organization. People in higher positions in the chart appear to have greater authority than those at lower levels. If used to describe communication in the organization, however, the chart may be entirely inadequate. Many people talk only to those immediately above or below them, employees whose positions on the chart are connected to theirs by an uninterrupted line? Is each department on the chart autonomous and shielded from relationships with other departments? If units and individuals depend on one another, the chart does not define the communication structure.

Nor does the chart necessarily define the role structure—the relative importance of each department or individual participating in the organization. The honorary chairman of the board occupies the highest spot on the chart, but the actual role may have little to do with the success or failure of the organization. Someone in the lowest level on the chart—in financial analysis, for example—may play a role of considerably greater importance than the position's status on the chart would indicate.

Organization charts help define the scope of the organization and assist people in getting a total view. Because people generally occupy roles and perform functions in all those spaces in the organization chart, the pictured structure could seldom be considered a final answer. At the same time, the organizational structure is much easier to talk about when everyone uses the same graphic presentation.

The organizational structure does affect the behavior of individuals and units within it. Most organizations are pyramid shaped. The higher

Are most organizational charts pyramid shaped?

Does position on the organization chart indicate one's impact on an organization?

a person is on the pyramid, the greater are the apparent authority and rewards. Most people probably strive for a higher position on the pyramid; this striving may determine relationships with peers, subordinates, and superiors. Competition has become a characteristic of the American way of life. People and organizations compete for a greater share of scarce resources, for a limited number of positions at the top of organizations, and for esteem in their professions. Such competition is a healthy sign of the human desire to succeed; and in terms of economic behavior, competition is fundamental to the private-enterprise system. At the same time, when excessive competition replaces the cooperation necessary for success, communication may be diminished, if not eliminated.

Might competition for promotion be a likely barrier to effective communication?

Just as we want to look good in the eyes of our peers, superiors, and subordinates, units within organizations want to look good to one another. Behavior may then take the form of "I win, you lose" and replace cooperative behavior, which could be characterized by "I win, you win." As a result, excessive competition may have a negative influence on the performance of the organization—everybody loses.

At the same time, the organization may change behavior when effective communication takes place. Most conflict among people and groups results from a lack of understanding. When one unit is uninformed about the importance or function of another, needless conflicts may occur as groups attempt to better themselves at the expense of others. Interestingly enough, groups engaged in competition tend to solidify and become more cohesive with great internal group morale. As a consequence, the competitive spirit of the group may intensify and lead to further deterioration of communication with other groups. It's easy to visualize what such activity may do to cooperative efforts in the total organization. Therefore, although competition is appropriate and desirable in many situations, management must take steps through open communication to reduce competition and to increase cooperation. When the competitors have an understanding of others' importance and functions, cooperation is more likely. This statement is as true of cooperation among individuals as it is of cooperation among groups within organizations.

Within the groups that make up an organization, what is usually the basis for conflicts?

Organizational structures are designed by management as a means to control members' and units' behavior. Some of the previous comments have pointed to problems introduced by rigid organization structures, but other problems occur when individual- or group-maintenance goals mix with the task goals of the organization.

External and Internal Systems

Two systems of organizational communication simultaneously influence human behavior. The *external* system is typified by the formal organization chart, which is created by management to control individual and group behavior and to achieve organization goals. Essentially, the external system is dictated by the technical, political, and economic environment of the organization. Within this external system, people are required to behave in certain ways simply to get the work done. Because it is dictated by environmental forces existing outside the needs of the individuals in the organization, the system is called external.

External systems are imposed on people.

The *internal* system develops as people interact within the formal, external system and certain behavior patterns emerge—patterns that accommodate social and psychological needs. To distinguish between the two systems, return to The Super Drugstore and its organization chart. The owner/pharmacist works full time in the prescription department, which is subordinate to and apparently has a reporting relationship to the purchasing and marketing department. Quite likely, however, the people in the purchasing and marketing department don't give the owner a bad time. Their behavior in the external system is minimal and just enough to get the work done. In the internal system, however, their behavior is adapted, depending on their personal perceptions of the owner.

Internal systems are developed within people.

• Systems in Action

As another example, if the work hours for office staff are 8:00 A.M. to 5:00 P.M., that is part of the external system. But if one office employee begins at 4:50 to clear the desk, put on outdoor clothing, and get ready to run for the door promptly at 5:00, this behavior may spread to all others in the office and become a part of the internal system. The external system, then, requires certain behaviors to get the work done, nothing more. The internal system develops from emergent behaviors and assists in achieving maintenance goals. These two systems operate concurrently but to varying degrees in all organizations, and management must recognize and work with both.

Is automobile driving behavior subject to external systems?

When participants rely almost entirely on the formalized external system as a guide to behavior, the system might be identified as a *bureaucracy*. Procedures manuals, job descriptions, organization charts, and other written materials dictate the required behavior. Communication channels are followed strictly, and red tape is abundant. Procedures are generally followed exactly; terms such as *rules* and *policy* serve as sufficient reasons for actions. But even the most formal of organizations cannot function long without an internal system emerging. As people operate within the external system, they must interact on a person-to-person basis and create an environment conducive to satisfying their personal emotions, prejudices, likes, and dislikes.

Take the college classroom, for example. The student behavior required to satisfy the external system is to attend class, take notes, read the text, and pass examinations. On the first day of class, this behavior probably is typical of almost all students, particularly if they did not know one another prior to attending the class. As the course progresses, however, the internal system emerges and overlaps the external system. Students become acquainted, sit next to people they particularly like, engage in horseplay, and may even plan ways to beat the external system. Cutting class and borrowing notes is an example. Soon, these behaviors become norms for class behavior. Students who do not engage in the internal system may be looked on with disdain by the others. Obviously, the informality of the internal system is good for people because it helps satisfy maintenance goals. At the same time, it affects communications.

• The Grapevine as an Internal System

The grapevine is perhaps the best known informal communication system. It is actually a component of the internal system. As people talk casually during coffee breaks and lunch periods, the focus usually shifts from topic to topic. And one of the topics most certainly would be work—job, company, boss, fellow employees. Even though the external system calls for very definite communication channels, the grapevine tends to develop and to operate within the organization.

Why call this informal system "the grapevine"?

As a communication channel, the grapevine is reputed to be speedy but inaccurate. If the building is on fire, the grapevine may be the most effective way, in the absence of alarms, to let occupants know of the problem. It certainly beats sending a written memorandum.

As an inaccurate channel, the grapevine may be mislabeled. Even formal communication may become inaccurate as it passes from level to level in the organizational hierarchy. Perhaps the inaccuracy of the grapevine has more to do with the message input than with the output. For example, the grapevine is noted as a carrier of rumor, primarily because it carries informal messages. If the input is rumor, and nothing more, the output obviously will be inaccurate. But the output may be an accurate description of the original rumor.

For the college student, the grapevine carries much valuable information. Even though the names of the good teachers may not be published, students learn those names through the grapevine. How best to prepare for certain examinations, teacher attitudes on attendance and homework, and even future faculty personnel changes are messages traveling over the grapevine. In the business office, news about promotions, personnel changes, company policy changes, and annual salary adjustments are often communicated via the grapevine long before being disseminated by formal channels.

A misconception about the grapevine is that the message passes from person to person until it finally reaches a person who can't pass it on—the end of the line. Actually, the grapevine works through a variety of channels. Typically, one person tells two or three others who each tell two or three others, who each tell two or three others, and so on. Thus, the message may spread to a huge number of people in a very short time. Additionally, the grapevine has no single, consistent source. Messages may originate any place and follow various routes. More will be said about sources and routes later in this chapter.

Do you ever participate in the grapevine?

Management must recognize that an informal, internal system will emerge from even the most carefully designed formal, external system. To ignore this fact is to attempt to manage blindfolded. Yet, some managers do try to work exclusively with the external system. For them, the achievement of organizational goals must be extremely difficult. As long as people interact, the organization will have both systems.

Communication Flow in Organizations

The flow of communication within the organization may be upward, downward, or horizontal. Because these three terms are used frequently in communication literature, they deserve some clarification. Although the concept of flow seems simple, direction has meaning for those participating in the communication process.

• Downward Communication

Downward communication flows from superior to subordinate, from policy makers to operating personnel, or from top to bottom on the organization chart. As messages move downward through successive levels of the organization, they seem to get larger. A simple policy statement from the top of the organization may grow into a formal plan for operation at lower levels.

Is a college class an
example of
downward
communication?

Teaching people how to do their specific tasks is an element of downward communication. So, too, are orientation to a company's rules, practices, procedures, history, and goals. Employees learn about the quality of their job performance through downward communication.

Downward communication normally involves both written and oral methods and makes use of the following guides:

1. People high in the organization usually have greater knowledge of the organization and its goals than do people at lower levels.

2. Both oral and written messages tend to become larger as they move downward through organizational levels. This expansion results from attempts to prevent distortion and is more noticeable in written messages.

Why do messages
seem to get longer
as they move
downward?

3. Oral messages are subject to greater change in meaning than are written messages.

The reaction of receivers to messages received is called *feedback* and is a technical term in communication theory. When a superior sends a message to a subordinate who then asks a question or nods assent, the question and the nod are signs of feedback. Feedback is considered in detail in Chapter 2 on interpersonal communication. In organizational communication, feedback may flow both downward and upward.

• Upward Communication

Communication upward, while necessary and valuable, does contain risks. As a general observation, upward communication is feedback to downward communication. When management requests information from lower organizational levels, the resulting information becomes feedback to that request. Employees talk to superiors about themselves, their fellow employees, their work and methods of doing it, and their perceptions of the organization. These comments are feedback to the downward flow transmitted in both oral and written form by group meetings, procedures or operation manuals, company news releases, and the grapevine.

Accurate upward communication keeps management informed

COMMUNICATION FLOW IN ORGANIZATIONS

about the feelings of subordinates, helps management identify both difficult and potentially promotable employees, and paves the way for even
more effective downward communication. At the same time, upward
communication is often misleading because employees generally will tell
management what they believe management wants to hear rather than
what it should be told. Employees reporting upward are aware that their
communications carry the risk of putting them on the spot. They might
commit themselves to something they cannot handle, or they might
communicate incorrectly.

    These factors, then, are important to consider when upward com-
munication flow is involved:

1. Upward communication is primarily feedback to requests and
   actions of superiors.
2. Subordinates often tell the superior what they think the superior
   wants to hear even though their messages might contradict their true
   observations and perceptions.
3. Upward communication is based on trust in the superior.
4. Upward communication is frequently a threat to the subordinate.

    How is feedback from subordinates helpful to managers?

• Horizontal or Lateral Communication

Horizontal or lateral communication is often used to describe exchanges
between organizational units on the same hierarchical level. This description is one of the major shortcomings of organization charts.
Charts really don't leave much room for horizontal communication
when they picture authority relationships by placing one box higher
than another and define role functions by placing titles in those boxes.
But horizontal communication is the primary means of achieving coordination. In The Super Drugstore, for instance, the chart implies that
people in finance and accounting can't communicate directly with people in purchasing and marketing without going through the president.
Obviously, that would be a rather difficult way to operate a complex
organization.

    In fact, horizontal communication would probably exist as part of
the internal system even though it is not defined by the formal chart.
Workers at the same level tend to talk with one another about their
work, their superiors, and their working conditions. No doubt, they also
talk with one another about various personal, nonwork problems. As a

result, horizontal communication can contribute to self-maintenance goals as well as to task goals.

Coordination: the most important goal of lateral communication

In this respect, management must recognize that informal horizontal communication takes place in any system or organization where people are available to one another. The informal communication and behavior that is not task oriented develops alongside formal task communication and behavior, contributing to morale, to improvements in ways to accomplish tasks, and to clarification of upward and downward communication. Formalized horizontal communication serves a coordinating function in the organization. Units coordinate their activities to accomplish task goals just as adjacent workers in a production line coordinate their activities.

Summary

Groups and organizations exist because people working together can accomplish more and make better decisions than can the same people working individually. In other words, the total is greater than the sum of the parts.

As tasks increase in size and complexity, specialization is required and interdependence of people and units is critical. These elements are organized to achieve goals and the resulting entity is an organization. Communication helps control and coordinate the work of the organization through a formal, external system and an informal, internal system. The external system exists to accomplish tasks, and the internal system serves a personal-maintenance purpose that results in people feeling better about themselves and others. Because these systems operate simultaneously, a modified system emerges that combines qualities of both.

"Great communicators" tend to succeed.

Communication flows upward, downward, and horizontally or laterally. These flows often defy the ability of management to describe them graphically. To cope with communication problems in organizations, management should (1) attempt to balance the external and internal systems, (2) use the systems for effective task accomplishment and maintenance purposes, and (3) indicate by example their concern for effective communication.

Organizations are strengthened when people have a knowledge of and skill in interpersonal communication, which we discuss in Chapter 2.

About Language and Usage

Most people use "viable" to mean able to live, to take root and grow, to be workable, to survive and have real meaning. An organization is described as viable when it is workable and capable of surviving and growing. The following word family members are tied together by the root "organ." (Definitions are not comprehensive.)

Organ: a tool, an implement, a special part of animals or plants adapted to a special function.

Organic: having the characteristics of, or derived from, a living organism.

Organism: an animal or plant having diverse organs that function together to maintain life and activities.

Organize: to provide with an organic structure; to make into a whole with unified and coherent relationships.

Organization: a unified, consolidated group of elements; a systematized whole.

Exercises

Review Questions

1. Synergy results from group work. What is synergy?
2. What are the two forms of verbal communication?
3. What is the difference between interpersonal and intrapersonal communication?
4. What are the two major goals of both interpersonal and group communication?
5. How does the longevity of a group task affect its attention to maintenance efforts?
6. Why is an odd number of group members frequently desirable?
7. Why do people conform to norms?

8. Four factors combine to characterize large, formal organizations. What are they?

9. How might an organization chart fail to indicate the relative importance of positions or individuals on the chart?

10. What is a possible cause of most conflict between or among groups?

11. How might the pyramid shape of an organization chart affect individual and group performance?

12. What is the system of organizational communication called when it relies on rules, procedures, and formalities?

13. What is the system of organizational communication called when it is characterized by maintenance activities?

14. Does the grapevine lend itself to easy tracking? Why?

15. Why do downward messages tend to become larger as they travel through successive organizational levels?

16. Is organizational control achieved through lateral communication or through upward–downward communication?

17. What technical term describes the receiver's reaction to a message?

18. How might upward communication be threatening to a subordinate?

Activities

1. Be prepared to describe the communication in an organization with which you are familiar. Your description should use the terminology of this chapter.

2. Be prepared to describe the communication in a group with which you are familiar.

Interpersonal Communication and Listening

The deepest principle in human nature is the craving to be appreciated.

WILLIAM JAMES

S cholars and researchers have long sought, in their own ways, to define communication and to advance theories about what goes on in this amazing process that consumes almost all of our awake time. No doubt you have your own notions about communication and how it takes place. For other than the intrapersonal communication that takes place within ourselves, your personal definition of communication would probably include the ideas that someone must put together a message, transmit it in some way to a receiver, and hope that the receiver would understand it. That description is essentially correct, but the process is fraught with personal elements that make it a constant problem for all of us.

Communication involves risk.

The Human Communication Process

A major advance in communication theory came with Claude Shannon's 1949 publication of his mathematical theory of communication. He and other information theorists at the Bell Telephone Laboratories were concerned with the process of transferring signals accurately from sender to receiver. Their concern was not with words or word meanings but with sending coded material from one machine to another: a message from a satellite (of which none existed) to earth or from one computer to another, for example.

At about the same time, behavioral scientists were putting together a theory of human communication from accumulated research. This general theory has much in common with the work of the information theorists. Even though one was concerned with machine-to-machine communication and the other with people-to-people communication, both groups were talking and writing about a similar process. The process is presented in simplified form in Figure 2.1, and the following definitions help describe the process.

Information is the property of a signal or message enabling it to convey something the recipient finds both unpredictable and meaningful. Loosely defined, information is the inside interpretation of an outside event. For example, when we touch a hot surface, our inside interpretation of this outside event may be "Ouch!" This interpretation is information and can be measured in bits. On command, the computer is capable of recalling one or a combination of bits. In proper combination, bits form meaningful messages. In human communication, bits of information are words or other communicative symbols used to describe

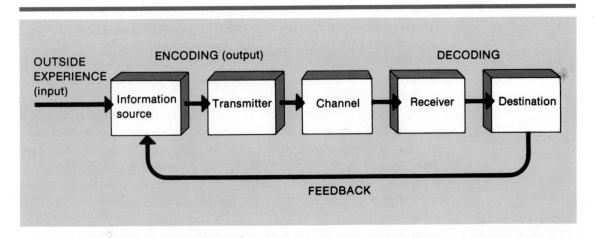

FIGURE 2.1

The communication process.

a person's reaction to events or inside interpretation of an external happening. Information is the stuff of which messages are made.

A *message* is a transmissible combination of bits of information. Messages are composed of language symbols, machine or human.

Encoding is the process of selecting and organizing bits of information into transmissible message language. Encoding takes place in the *information source,* a computer or human mind.

Decoding is the process of interpreting a message. Decoding takes place at the *destination,* the receiver's computer or mind.

Feedback is a message or part of a message that the recipient returns to the sender so that the message may be modified or adjusted to make it clearer to the recipient. When one person responds to another's message, the response is called feedback. Feedback is the reaction of the receiver to the message received.

Input is the sum of the experiences that build up the supply of bits of information in an information source such as a computer or a human mind. In other words, information fed into storage or memory for use in communication is input. Input may be likened to psychological stimuli that cause people to take action.

Output is the total information released from the information source for transmission.

Today, three strategically placed communication satellites 22,300 miles above the earth and traveling at the speed of the earth's rotation monitor every square inch of the earth's surface. A single satellite can

> Why is a decoded message sometimes different from an encoded one?

> Satellite communication is a growth industry.

cover the entire North American continent, transmitting wire-service photos to newspapers, live radio and television broadcasts to audiences, and up-to-date business data and reports to offices. The information sent from the satellites to earth is *feedback* to the messages received by the satellites. We, of course, haven't seen the ultimate in machine-to-machine communication!

In human communication, the communication process affects our every waking moment in ways ranging from a friendly "Good morning" or "Hi" to classroom presentations, medical reports, world and local news, and intimate relationships. When you realize that you are both a sender and a receiver simultaneously, you can understand the complexities of human communication. To "Good morning," you probably react (provide feedback) by saying, "Good morning. How are you?" or "Hi." Your response to the good morning wish leads to a reaction from the other person and perhaps a conversation then occurs. During your conversation, you alternately listen and speak; but when you are listening, you are also encoding the message you will send when it's your turn to speak again. If you and your friend do not run into communication barriers, you'll probably have a mutually satisfying conversation.

Communicating may lead to good feelings.

Some Behavioral Factors in Communication

As long as humans are involved in communication, the process will not be perfect. Human frailties such as prejudice, ego involvement, subjectivity, and varying reactions to the environment contribute to problems of communicating. Additionally, differences between senders and receivers in vocabularies, educational and occupational backgrounds, age, appearance, cultural elements, and a host of other factors create barriers to effective communication.

When the industrial revolution of the nineteenth century led to large-scale industries, giant companies, and labor unions, management had to be concerned about better ways to cope with these significant changes. Management theorists looked to the behavioral sciences for patterns of human social activities and guides to human behavior to provide a framework for management in the industrial age. These same patterns have proved fruitful to managers in our sophisticated high-technology environment. As we change from manufacturing to a service and technological industrial base, the classical foundations undergo modification to cope with change.

For those of you who are interested in pursuing these classical foundations, see the following works:

Berne, Eric. *Games People Play*. New York: Ballantine, 1964.

Leavitt, Harold J. *Managerial Psychology*. Chicago: University of Chicago Press, 1958.

McGregor, Douglas. *The Human Side of Enterprise*. New York: McGraw-Hill, 1960.

Maslow, Abraham H. *Motivation and Personality*. New York: Harper & Row, 1954.

Nichols, Ralph, and Stevens, Leonard A. *Are You Listening?* New York: McGraw-Hill, 1957.

Ruesch, Jurgen, and Bateson, Gregory. *Communication, the Social Matrix of Psychiatry*. New York: Norton, 1951.

Taylor, Frederick W. *Scientific Management*. New York: Harper, 1911.

• Theory of Human Communication

Various contributions to a theory of human communication emphasize that difficulties in communication lie not so much with what we say or write but with what goes on in our own minds and in the minds of those with whom we are communicating. Briefly, the theory of human communication stresses the importance of such factors as social situation, role, status, rules, and instructions in understanding social action and personal intent.

A *social situation* is established when people enter into a communication exchange and their behavior is organized around a common task. Then, participants assume individual *roles* that arise from their parts in the activity. They also have *status,* which is their position based on the "organization chart" or other prescribed functions. Role is an informal part; status is a formal position. College seniors assume authoritative roles; freshmen play submissive roles. The administrative assistant to an executive, because of position in the executive office, may play a role considerably more authoritative and powerful than prescribed by the organizational structure.

Are role and status always equal for a person?

Within the business world, of course, such symbols (status symbols) as job titles, uniforms, office decor, and support staff help us identify status. Actions, time with the firm, work habits, and proximity to authority lead to roles higher than status. Good communicators can differentiate role and status.

All games are played by *rules*. In business, the unwritten rules come from the internal system and maintenance activity. Written rules are formal company policies and procedures. The rules help determine who

Does your campus have any unwritten rules?

may talk with whom, what or what not to say, how long a session may last, and how to present a message. As people live and work, they learn the rules of the game, as they must, to create places for themselves. *Instructions* assist receivers in understanding message meaning and intent. Nonverbal signs such as facial expressions, bodily motions, perspiration, and posture give clues about the sender's feelings and intentions.

• Human Needs

Abraham Maslow developed the concept of a hierarchy of needs through which people move. In our society, most people have reasonably satisfied their lower-level physiological and security and safety needs for food, shelter, and protection from the elements and physical danger.

Beyond these two basic need levels, people progress through a series of three higher need levels: (1) social needs for love, acceptance, and belonging; (2) ego needs to be heard, appreciated, and wanted; and (3) self-actualizing needs, including the need to achieve one's fullest potential through professional, philanthropic, political, educational, and artistic channels.

As people satisfy needs at one level, they move on to the next. The levels that have been satisfied still are present, but their importance diminishes.

Effective communicators are able to identify and appeal to need levels in various individuals or groups. Advertising is designed to appeal to need levels. Luxury-car ads appeal to ego needs, breath freshener ads appeal to social needs, and fire alarm ads appeal to security and safety needs. In business, efforts to help people satisfy needs is essential. A satisfied worker is generally more productive than a dissatisfied one.

When a need level is satisfied, does it go away?

• Management Styles

Douglas McGregor attempted to distinguish between the older, traditional view that workers are concerned only about satisfying lower-level needs and the modern view that production can be enhanced by assisting workers to satisfy higher-level needs.

Under the older view, management exercised strong control, emphasized the job to the exclusion of concern for the individual, and sought to motivate solely through external incentives—a job and a paycheck. McGregor labeled this management style Theory X. Under the modern style, Theory Y, management strives to balance control and individual

Theory Y is people oriented.

freedom. By treating the individual as a mature person, management lessens the need for external motivation—treated as adults, people will act as adults. Combining Maslow's and McGregor's ideas leads to the conclusion that "The right job for the person" is a better philosophy than "The right person for the job."

Recent efforts to develop greater job satisfaction have involved workers in "team" and "quality circle" programs. Rather than relying on single-task, production-line approaches, the "team," as used in some automobile and other heavy-manufacturing industries, builds the product from beginning to end. Each team member is capable of performing most of the production jobs.

"Quality circles" are voluntary groups of workers who meet with supervisors or management periodically to identify production problems and propose solutions. The external motivation characteristic of McGregor's Theory X is replaced by intrinsic motivation provided by involvement, cooperation, and opportunities to be heard and appreciated.

• One-to-One Communication

Several years ago, transactional analysis was developed and often practiced as a means of analyzing behavior patterns in interpersonal relationships. One of the most important contributions of transactional analysis is the concept of *stroking*.

Research indicates that babies left unattended or ignored for extended periods can develop physical as well as psychological problems. Babies require coddling, patting, and loving; in transactional analysis terms, these actions are called stroking. Adults also require stroking for mental health—but of a different sort. Saying "Good morning" to another person is a stroke. The reply, "Same to you" is another stroke. Although this exchange may seem incidental and unimportant, imagine the reactions if the two were friends and no exchange took place.

Stroking applies human relations principles.

A pat on the back from the boss, a congratulatory phone call or letter, and taking the time to listen to another person are examples of everyday stroking. By paying attention to giving strokes, managers can greatly improve communication and people's feelings about their work.

People engage in communication with others in the hope that the outcome may lead to mutual trust, mutual pleasure, and psychological well-being. The communication transaction is a means of sharing information about things, ideas, tasks, and selves. Before two strangers meet,

FIGURE 2.2
Knowledge about each other is nil.

what they know about each other might be depicted by the two circles shown in Figure 2.2.

John and Jane apply strokes.

After an introduction—"Hello, I'm John Green"; "Hello, I'm Jane Smith"—they know something about each other, if only each other's name and gender. They probably also gain an impression about each other through appearance and dress. At this point, the two circles begin to overlap, as shown in Figure 2.3, to indicate the surface things they know about each other.

As the transaction progresses, the overlap becomes greater and they learn more and more about each other. Green may ask, "Care for a cup of coffee?" and Smith may answer, "Oh, I hate coffee, but I'd love tea." As a result of this exchange, Green learns a little more about Smith.

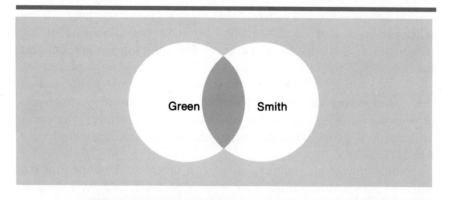

FIGURE 2.3
Knowledge about each other increases.

Additionally, Smith may have gained some information about herself—that she was appealing enough to be invited to share coffee. Green must have felt encouraged, too. He invited Smith, and she accepted.

Stroking pays
dividends.

As the relationship between Smith and Green develops, they continue to learn more about each other. Their behavior leads to trust, and this trust leads to freer conversation.

• Johari Window

The nature of sharing is that people learn not only about others but also about themselves. Two simple circles do not provide for this concept, but the Johari Window, shown in Figure 2.4 (named for its creators, *Jo*seph and *Harri*ngton), does. The upper left-hand area, labeled "I," or "free area," represents what we know about ourselves and what others know about us. Area II designates those things others know about us

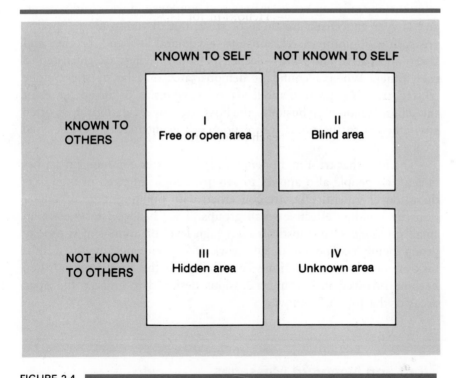

FIGURE 2.4

The Johari Window. Adapted from *Of Human Interaction* by Joseph Luft, by permission of Mayfield Publishing Company. Copyright © 1969 by the National Press.

Everyone has hidden area items. What are yours?

but that we don't know about ourselves; for example, you are the only person who can't see yourself as you really are. Mirror images are reversed. Things we know about ourselves but that others don't know about us occupy the hidden or secret area, III. Area IV includes things we don't know about ourselves and others don't know about us.

Each of these areas may vary in size to the degree that we can learn about ourselves from others and to the degree that we are willing to disclose things about ourselves to others. Only through reciprocal sharing can people learn about themselves and about others. In communication practice, such sharing occurs only when people develop *trust* in each other. Of course, trust is something that must be earned. We are usually willing to tell people about our school records, our jobs, and other things that aren't truly personal. But we share personal thoughts, dreams, and inner feelings only with selected others—with those whom we have learned to trust. Trust is a quality we develop from experience with others. Through performance, we earn the trust of others. The relationships existing between boss and employee, doctor and patient, and lawyer and client are those of trust, but of trust only in specific areas. In more intimate relationships—wife and husband, brother and sister, and parent and child—deeper, personal feelings are entrusted to each other. When a confidant demonstrates that he or she can be trusted, trust is reinforced and leads to an expansion of the open area of the Johari Window. In business, the boss–employee relationship is often strengthened to the point where nonwork elements can be discussed freely.

Good friends listen; listeners become good friends.

The idea that trust and openness lead to better communication between two people also applies to groups. People engaged in organizational development, OD, are concerned with building large organizations by building effective small groups. They believe effectiveness in small groups evolves mostly from a high level of mutual trust among group members. The aim of OD work is to open emotional as well as task-oriented communication. To accomplish this aim, groups often become involved in encounter sessions designed to enlarge the open areas of the Johari Window.

Word and Nonword Messages

Although most concern in communication study is given to verbal messages, nonword messages and meanings other than those expressed in words are all around and bombard us regularly.

• Intrapersonal Communication and Decoding

In the discussion of human communication theory, we mentioned the need to be sensitive to nonverbal elements of communication. Nonverbal communication includes any communication occurring without the use of words. Gestures, body motions, clothing, grooming, uniforms, aromas, facial expressions, and hundreds of other factors bring messages to people from all angles at any time. What we do with this bombardment of messages depends very much on our past experiences and our perceptions of ourselves and of the world around us. Probably no two people are identical in these respects.

Intrapersonal communication is perhaps the purest and most basic form of communication. The role we play in communicating with others depends on how we communicate with ourselves. We process incoming messages—received by our eyes, ears, skin, nose, or tasting organs—by selecting, evaluating, and interpreting them in terms of previous experiences. Additionally, we generate messages internally, either physically or psychologically. And we process those messages in the same way we process messages arising from external stimuli.

How do you react when a police car follows yours?

As you study communication, consider how you perceive yourself in various situations. Do you see yourself the same way in all situations? Or do you perceive yourself a little differently in your various roles as student, friend, citizen, employee, brother or sister, son or daughter, or parent? Self-concepts are composed of all the things we know about ourselves either consciously or subconsciously. We each have a physical perception of ourselves—how we look to others; how we walk, smell, sound; and how we perform in physical activities.

How do others perceive you? Is that your own perception?

Additionally, we each have perceptions about ourselves as social creatures. We have ideas about how we appeal to others, how we interact socially, how we handle emotions, and how we communicate in large or small groups. And certainly we have perceptions about our intellectual selves: how we study, how we fare in terms of grades, and how deeply we become interested in intellectual things.

The simple schematic of the communication process presented earlier in this chapter becomes inadequate when we complicate the process by introducing the concept that each human will process incoming messages in different ways depending on previous experiences and self-perceptions.

• Messages Without Words

A *metacommunication* is a message that, although *not* expressed in words, accompanies a message that *is* expressed in words. For example,

"Don't be late for work" gives that admonition (communication); yet the sentence may imply (but not express in words) such additional ideas as "You are frequently late, and I'm warning you," or "I doubt your dependability" (metacommunications). "Your solution is perfect" may also convey a metacommunication such as "You are efficient," or "I certainly like your work." Whether we are speaking or writing, we can be confident that those who receive our messages will be sensitive to the messages expressed in words and to the accompanying messages that are present but not expressed in words.

A *kinesic* communication is an idea expressed through nonverbal behavior. Messages can be conveyed through winks, smiles, frowns, sighs, attire, grooming, and all sorts of bodily movements. The science of kinesics seeks to gain knowledge about the impact of bodily movements on communication. Some examples of kinesic messages:

Action	Possible kinesic message
A wink follows a statement.	"Don't believe what I just said."
A professor is habitually late for class.	"I am busy." "I don't care much for students."
The boss starts to dial a number while a subordinate is talking.	"We're finished with our conversation; go away."
A group leader sits at a position other than at the head of the table.	"I want to demonstrate my equality with other members."
A receptionist offers a magazine to a client who must wait for a while.	"I want you to have something interesting to do while you wait."

Would a refusal to answer a question classify as a kinesic communication?

The list could go on and on. These unworded ideas (kinesic communications and metacommunications) have characteristics that all communicators should take into account:

1. *Unworded messages cannot be avoided.* Both written and spoken words convey ideas in addition to the ideas contained in the words used. All actions—and even the lack of action—have meaning to those who observe them.

2. *Unworded messages may have different meanings for different people.* If a committee member smiles after making a statement, one member may conclude that the speaker was trying to be funny; another may conclude that the speaker was pleased about having

made such a great contribution; another may see the smile but have no reaction to it.

3. *Unworded messages may be intentional or unintentional.* "You are right about that" may be intended to mean "I agree with you," or "You are right on *this* issue, but you have been wrong on all others discussed." The sender may or may not intend to convey the latter and may or may not be aware of doing so.

4. *Unworded messages may get more attention than worded messages.* If an interviewee stamps out a cigarette on the floor while making a statement, the words may not register on the mind of the interviewer. Or, an error in basic grammar may get much more attention than does the idea that is being transmitted.

5. *Unworded messages provide clues about the sender's background and motives.* For example, excessive use of big words may suggest that a person reads widely or has an above-average education; it may also suggest a need for social recognition or insecurity about social background.

6. *Unworded messages are influenced by the circumstances surrounding the communication.* Assume that two men (Ward and Wood) are friends who work for the same firm. When they are together on the job, Ward sometimes puts his hand on Wood's shoulder. To Wood, the act may mean nothing more than "We are close friends." But Ward becomes a member of a committee that subsequently denies a promotion for Wood. Afterward, the same act could mean "We are still friends"; but it could also arouse resentment. Because of the circumstances, the same act could now mean something like, "Watch the hand that pats; it can also stab."

7. *Unworded messages can actually contradict the accompanying worded message.* "We appreciate your writing to us when you have a problem" may be taken to mean the opposite when nothing has been done to solve the problem or to explain the lack of action. When actions and words appear to be in conflict, receivers place more confidence in the message communicated by action. And keep in mind that when police discover that a suspect's words and actions are incongruent, suspicion about the suspect becomes stronger.

8. *Unworded messages may be beneficial or harmful.* Words or actions can be accompanied with unworded messages that help or hurt the writer's purpose. Metacommunications and kinesic communications can convey something like, "I am efficient in my business and considerate of others," or they can convey the opposite. They

What unworded messages might accompany "Drive carefully"?

cannot be eliminated, but they can be made to work for communicators instead of against them.

Although no one can give a set of rules for interpreting unworded messages, awareness of their presence and impact will improve chances of choosing correct words and encoding messages effectively.

Listening as an Interpersonal Skill

Want to get a job? Want to keep a job? Want to get promoted? If so, become a good listener! Good listening habits pay off in several ways:

Listening is an example of stroking.

1. Good listeners are liked by others because they satisfy the basic human needs of being heard and being wanted.
2. Job performance is improved when downward oral messages are received and understood.
3. Accurate feedback from subordinates provides confidence for management about job performance.
4. Superiors and subordinates both may acquire greater job security from fewer mistakes or ignored messages.
5. People who listen well are able to separate fact from fiction, to cope effectively with false persuasion, and to avoid having others use them for personal gain. In other words, good listeners don't "get taken" very often.
6. Listening opens doors for ideas and thus encourages creativity.
7. Learning will be enhanced; listening is the missing "L" in learning.
8. Job satisfaction increases when people know what is going on, when they are heard, and when they participate in the mutual trust that develops from good communication.

As a skill, listening depends on our abilities to receive and decode both worded and unworded messages. The best devised messages and sophisticated communication systems will not work unless people on the receiving end of oral messages actually listen. Senders of oral messages must assume their receivers can and will listen, just as senders of written messages must assume their receivers can and will read.

Can you detect when another is not listening?

Most managers spend a major part of their day listening and speaking with subordinates, superiors, customers, and a variety of business or industry colleagues and associates. In business, government, and education, listening is a part of face-to-face communication. It constitutes an interpersonal skill as critical as the skill of speaking.

Keep in mind, however, that the need for listening occurs in two types of situations: (1) face-to-face situations of an interview nature, and (2) formal situations in which an audience listens to a speaker. One is intimate, the other impersonal.

In interview situations for example, while I am speaking, you supposedly are listening. As the listener, you interpret my message and plan what you will say next. I watch you for some form of feedback and, if necessary, adjust my message. This interaction typifies the classic communication process pictured earlier in Figure 2.1.

In the formal speech–listening situation, the speaker intends to provide the audience with information in such a way that listeners will accept the message and perhaps act in a way the speaker intended. The primary difference between face-to-face interview listening and speech listening is the limited opportunity for the speech maker and the audience to provide feedback and to adjust to it. Formal speakers obtain broad but limited feedback from audiences, which may enable speakers to adapt their messages to the feedback. At the same time, the audience receives little speaker feedback short of interrupting the speech for clarification.

Hearing is not listening.

We engage in formal listening to varying degrees when listening to a speech, sermon, or lecture. We engage in interview-type listening when we are in face-to-face, two-person situations or in small group discussion. For many people, face-to-face meetings consume most of their working time.

Bad Listening Habits and Practices

Physicians can't cure people of ailments unless their diagnoses reveal the nature of the ailment. In the same way, you can't improve your listening unless you understand some of the nonphysical ailments of your own listening. One way to begin is to examine a few common listener ailments, to identify those that may affect your own listening, and to work on cures for them. Most of us have developed bad listening habits in one or more of the following areas.[1]

Do any of the following habits apply to you?

Faking Attention   Have you ever had an instructor call on you to respond to a question in class only to find you weren't listening? Have you ever had a parent, friend, or fellow worker ask you a question and

---

[1] Ralph G. Nichols and Leonard A. Stevens, *Are You Listening?* New York: McGraw-Hill Book Company, 1957.

find you weren't listening? Have you ever left a classroom lecture and later realized that you have no idea what went on? Have you ever been introduced to someone only to find that thirty seconds later you missed the name?

If you had to answer "yes" to any of these, join the huge club of "fakers of attention." It is rather large because almost all people belong. Isn't it wonderful that we can look directly at a person, nod, smile, and pretend to be listening! We fake giving feedback.

Welcoming Disruptions   Listening properly requires both physical and emotional effort. As a result, we welcome disruptions of almost any sort when we are engaged in somewhat difficult listening. The next time someone enters your classroom or meeting room during a lecture, notice how almost everyone in the room turns away from the speaker and the topic to observe the latecomer. Yielding to such disruptions begins early in life. Perhaps it is a form of curiosity.

Watch for this event
to happen soon.

Overlistening   Overlistening occurs when listeners attempt to record in writing or in memory so many details that they miss the speaker's major points. Overlisteners "can't see the forest for the trees." Typical of this type of bad listening habit is the old story about the college freshmen who, on the first day of class when the professor begins with, "Good morning," put it in their notes.

Stereotyping   Most people use their prejudices and perceptions of others as a basis for developing stereotypes. As a result, we make spontaneous judgments about others based on their appearances, mannerisms, dress, speech delivery, and whatever other criteria play a role in our judgments. If a speaker doesn't come up to our standards in any of these areas, we may simply turn off our listening and assume the speaker can't have much to say.

Can you think of any
occupational
stereotypes?

Dismissing Subjects as Uninteresting   People tend to use "uninteresting" as a rationale for not listening. Unfortunately, the decision is usually made before the topic is ever introduced. A good way to lose a teacher's respect is to ask, "Are we going to have anything important in class today?" when you have an opportunity or need to do something else. Lord Chesterton once said we have no such thing as an uninteresting subject, only disinterested listeners.

Failing to Observe Nonverbal Aids   Good listening requires use of eyes as well as ears. To listen effectively you must observe the speaker. Facial expressions and body motions always accompany speech and contribute much to messages. Unless you watch the speaker, you may miss the meaning. Bad habit: looking out the window while someone is speaking.

Should classrooms be windowless?

In addition to recognizing bad listening habits and the variety of barriers to effective listening, you should also recognize that listening isn't easy. Many bad listening habits develop simply because the speed of spoken messages is far slower than our ability to receive and process them. Normal speaking speeds are between 100 and 150 words a minute. The human ear can actually distinguish words in speech in excess of 500 words a minute, and many people read at speeds well beyond 500 words a minute. Finally, our minds process thoughts at thousands of words a minute.

We just can't speak fast enough to challenge the other's human listening equipment, which means listeners have the primary responsibility for making oral communication effective. We do seem to listen to gifted speakers, but they are rare. In our everyday activities, good listening requires considerable mental and emotional effort. Note the barriers that create communication problems between speakers and listeners, as shown in Figure 2.5.

Most people run out of breath at 200 to 250 words a minute.

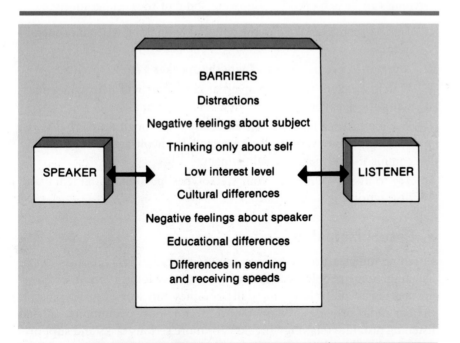

FIGURE 2.5
Barriers That Create Communication Problems Between Speakers and Listeners.

Listening for Positive Results

Listening involves much more than hearing. People's physical ability to hear is generally excellent; and if a disability affects hearing, mechanical aids are available. Hearing is only the first step in the listening process. Once received, the message must be interpreted. Interpretation is a mental, not a physical, process. A final step is for the receiver to determine what action should be taken. The message might be stored for later use, as is done with educationally learned material, or it might be dismissed as is often done with insignificant messages.

Casual "chit-chat" usually goes unstored.

We listen to (1) receive information, (2) solve problems, (3) share with others, and (4) persuade or dissuade. Each reason may call for a different style of listening or for a combination of styles.

• Intensive Listening

When we listen to obtain information, solve problems, or persuade or dissuade (as in arguments), we listen intensively. Intensive listening requires that we marshal all our listening forces to be successful. Intensive listening can be achieved by following some of these suggestions:

1. Try to become involved in the material by making written or mental notes.
2. Attempt to predict or anticipate the speaker's future points.
3. Watch speakers for any nonverbal clues that will help you understand the speaker's point of view and emotional state.

Involvement improves listening.

4. Provide listener feedback either orally or through nonverbal nods, facial expressions, or body movements to encourage further speaker comments and behavior adjustment.
5. Try to avoid yielding to your stereotypes, personal judgments, and distractions.

• Casual Listening

Listening for pleasure, recreation, amusement, and relaxation is casual listening. Some people have the radio on all day long; it provides background music and talk during daily routines and work periods, just as the car radio provides "companionship" for most commuters. Casual listening provides relaxing "breaks" for more serious tasks and supports our emotional health.

An interesting concept about all listening, but particularly true of casual listening, is that people are selective listeners. We listen to what we want. In a crowded room in which everyone seems to be talking, you can block out all the noise and engage in the conversation you are having with someone.

Casual listening doesn't require much emotional or physical effort, which is one of the reasons people engage in "small talk" and "chit-chat."

• Listening for Feelings with Empathy

Empathy occurs when a person attempts to share another's feelings or emotions. Counselors attempt to use empathic listening in dealing with their clients. Good friends often provide empathic listening for each other. Empathy is a valuable trait developed by people who are skilled in interpersonal relations. The interesting thing about empathic listening is that it more often than not results in reciprocal listening. When we take the time to listen to another, the courtesy is generally returned. Empathy leads to sharing.

Empathic listening is strong stroking.

Many people in positions of authority have developed excellent listening skills that apply to gaining information and to problem solving. However, just as many have failed to develop good listening practices that work effectively in listening for feelings.

For example, a meeting between a boss and employee might go something like this: "Boss, I really have a problem." "That so, George? Well, take a seat and let me hear about it," the boss says in a friendly tone. As George takes a seat, the boss continues, "George, you think you have a problem, eh? How would you like to have the ones I'm faced with now? First, I'm right in the middle of union negotiations for the new three-year contract, I've had several problems with our supervisory crew in the Midland plant, and somebody has screwed up our inventory procedure so we're running short and will have to back-order with several customers." The boss finishes with, "George, I have another appointment now. If you'd like, we can continue our discussion tomorrow. I want to be of help, and my door is always open to you." George leaves completely frustrated, his problem still on his mind and unresolved.

The boss either failed to interpret what George said or was too self-centered to take the time to listen. George probably feels worse after the meeting with the boss than he did before he entered the office. In addition, the boss learned nothing from the exchange. What if George's

Why can't perfect empathy be achieved?

problem were company related? Good listening might have resulted in information helpful to solving the boss's own problems.

Total empathy can never be achieved simply because no two people are exactly alike, and one can never really become the other person. The more similar our experiences, however, the better our opportunity to put ourselves in the other person's shoes. Two people who have been skydiving, for example, can appreciate how each other felt the first time. Listening with empathy involves some genuine tact along with other good listening habits. Remember that listening for feelings normally takes place in a one-to-one situation. Close friends who trust each other tend to engage in self-disclosure easily. Empathic listening is enhanced when the participants exhibit trust and friendship. Here are some suggestions:

1. Get in step with the speaker. Try to understand the speaker's background, prejudices, and points of view.
2. Try not to interrupt the speaker. Wait for an indication that you should enter the conversation.
3. Encourage the speaker to continue by giving indications that you understand. You can do this by developing your own repertoire of encouraging signs such as a nod of the head, a throat-clearing sound, a smile, and even an encouraging grunt.
4. Take advantage of your speaking opportunities to express your understanding of what has been said up to that time. Your skill in summarizing will protect you against misunderstandings of terms used.
5. Use questions and paraphrases to your advantage in understanding the other's feelings. When the speaker says "I really hate that old so-and-so" you might add "He really isn't a nice person?" Then the speaker might say something like "Oh, I don't hate him as a person; it's just that he can be so demanding at times that I get all upset." Your question elicited an answer that helped reveal the true source of the problem. A paraphrase is simply a restatement in your own words of what the other person has said—this is called *active listening*. Using your own words helps both you and the other person to get in step toward understanding. Paraphrasing and questioning also clarify language problems.

Practice provides experience and skills.

Frequently you may have to combine listening intensively and listening for feelings. The interviewing process, for example, may combine the two. Job interviewers must try to determine how someone's personality, as well as skill and knowledge, will affect job performance.

• Listening for Information

Listening for information should be restricted to the search for data or for material to be learned. In the classroom, for example, the instructor usually has a strategy for guiding the class to desired goals. The instructor will probably stress several major points and use supporting evidence to prove or to reinforce them. When engaged in this type of listening, you could become so engrossed with recording every detail that you take copious notes without using an outline. The end result is a set of detailed notes without any organization.

Understand the outlining process. When you take notes, use a logical system such as the Roman-numeral outline that uses I-A-1-a schemes to carry an outline to four different levels—one major item with three degrees of subitems. If you find yourself with a lot of information beyond I-A levels, you are probably making notes from detailed information that is not essential to your success in the course.

Listen for principles and methods—not minor details.

In the process of listening for information, watch the speaker. Most speakers have developed a set of mannerisms composed of gestures and vocal inflections to indicate the degree of importance or seriousness they attach to portions of their presentation. Above all else, listening for information requires that listeners be able to separate fact from fiction, comedy from seriousness, and truth from untruth.

• Listening for Problem Solving

Unlike listening for information, problem-solving listening involves greater use of your analytical ability to proceed through problem-solving steps. You should have an understanding of the problem, recognize whatever limitations are involved, and know the implications of possible solutions. Watching some talented top executives in situations calling for problem-solving listening reveals some interesting methods and approaches to this kind of listening, such as

1. A pen or pencil often becomes an ally in the analytical process. Jot down items that should be introduced as feedback to the speaker.
2. If you are a "modeler" in the computer sense, you might find doodling can help you assemble your ideas for drawing a meaningful picture.

Many "great minds" were doodlers.

3. Listen not only with the speaker but also try to think ahead at times. Thinking ahead can help you develop a sense of the speaker's logic.

4. Become a good summarizer. When your turn comes to respond, trace the development of the discussion and then take off from there with your own analysis.

5. Don't be hesitant about "tailgating" on the ideas of others. Creative ideas are generated in an open discussion related to problem solving.

Creativity results from good listening habits applied in a free-wheeling discussion. Most of our ideas emanate from external stimuli rather than silent introspection. When we listen effectively, we increase our capacity to create.

Suggestions for Effective Listening

From the communication process, we know that the availability of feedback and the opportunity to observe the nonverbal signs that accompany worded messages are the critical factors in effective communication. Face-to-face, interpersonal communication is the most effective level of communication because both factors are present. A telephone conversation, providing for instant feedback but not nonverbal signs, is the second level of effectiveness. The least effective level, the written message, provides neither for instant feedback nor nonverbal signs. Because it is the least effective level and is used so widely and so frequently, written communication receives major attention in the study of business communication.

The two critical factors in face-to-face communication: feedback and nonverbal signs.

Because of the availability of both feedback and nonverbal signs, you can enhance the effectiveness of your face-to-face listening by following these suggestions:

1. *Watch the speaker.* Gestures, facial expressions, and eye movements can add much to the words used and the meaning intended. If the speaker can't look you in the eye, the sincerity of the remarks made may be questioned. Of course, the opposite is probably true: Firm eye contact may be interpreted as added sincerity or firmness.

2. *Provide feedback.* You can acknowledge understanding, agreement, disagreement, and a variety of other feedback responses through facial expressions, sounds, and gestures. In this way, the speaker can either provide whatever restatement or added information may be necessary or continue with the discussion.

3. *Take the time to listen.* Because people in a communication transaction are simultaneously serving as both senders and receivers, you may become occupied with thoughts about what to say when it's your turn to speak and may fail to listen.

4. *Use your knowledge of speakers to advantage.* In most jobs, face-to-face oral communication occurs between people who already know each other. Through experience, you will begin to recognize others' speaking and organizing traits. Some people simply seem to run on and on with details before ever making their point. Ask them what they had for dinner, and in reply you'll probably be given recipes for each item and a description of the dining room's decor. With this type of speaker, you'll learn to anticipate the major point but not pay much attention to the details. Other speakers give conclusions first and perhaps omit support for them. In this case, you'll learn to ask feedback questions to obtain further information.

> Use feedback to get the meaning.

Summary

People engaged in communication encode and decode messages simultaneously while playing roles as both senders and receivers. In the communication process, feedback helps people resolve possible misunderstandings and thus improve communication effectiveness. Feedback and the opportunity to observe nonverbal signs are always present in face-to-face communication, the most effective communication level.

From the behavioral sciences and the work of several pioneering management theorists, we know that people

1. Want to be heard, to be appreciated, to be wanted.
2. Like to be treated as adults and to know that their ideas and suggestions have been considered.
3. Require "stroking" for their personal well being.
4. Process messages based on their own life experiences and not necessarily the way others might anticipate.

Listening, the most used communication skill, is crucial in interpersonal communication. Additionally, the quality of listening affects organizational communication, helps determine success in education and in careers, and provides evidence of listener empathy. Perhaps the most important suggestion for developing good listening habits is "Take the

---

About Language and Usage

The nature of communication is sharing and having "in common." Note how some selected dictionary definitions for the following words support the sharing concept:

Common: belonging to and shared by all or many.

Commune: to share communion; to share; to think, as in "commune with nature;" a group of people living together and sharing equally.

Communicate: to impart, share, make common; to be connected; to have a significant, meaningful relationship.

Communicative: giving information readily; talkative.

Community: a social group or group of nations having interests and traditions in common; i.e., the business community, the European Economic Community, a community of scholars.

Communism: any economic theory or system based on ownership of all property by the community as a whole.

---

time to listen." Good listening methods will then become habit, and you will find them of great value in job interviews, which we discuss in Chapter 12.

Exercises

Review Questions

1. What is the difference between information theory and a theory of human communication?
2. What is the relationship between information and messages?
3. What is your description of feedback? How does it work in communication?
4. What types of differences between sender and receiver create barriers to communication?
5. How does *role* differ from *status*?

6. Is the uniform of a police officer a status symbol? What quality or qualities does it add to the officer's messages?

7. What is the relationship between written and unwritten rules in business communication and the external and internal systems in organizations?

8. School clubs, groups, and societies help people satisfy which of Maslow's need levels?

9. What is meant by "stroking"?

10. What are three reasons why people engage in one-to-one communication?

11. The willingness of a person to self-disclose depends on what factor in a relationship?

12. When a family member leaves for work in the family car and another says, "Bye-bye; drive carefully," what are some possible metacommunications?

13. What are some payoffs for effective listening on the job?

14. What is a primary cause of bad listening habits?

15. What is meant by "people listen selectively"?

16. Good listening for feelings depends on what listener trait?

17. How does "overlistening" occur?

18. Why is face-to-face communication more effective than telephone communication? Than written communication?

Activities

1. In groups of three, develop a list of 12 to 15 annoying listening habits of yours or of others. Be prepared to present the list to the class.

2. Compile a list of situations during the next two days that (a) provide evidence of bad listening habits and (b) provide opportunities for metacommunication.

3. Prepare a record of your listening, speaking, reading, and writing activities and time spent in each during the hours of 8 A.M. to 5 P.M. for the next two days. You should attempt to record the time distribution for each one-hour time block in such a way that you obtain a total time for each activity for each day.

Public Speaking and Oral Reporting

If all my possessions were taken away from me with one exception, I would choose to keep the power of speech, for with it I would soon regain all the rest.

DANIEL WEBSTER

S urvey findings reported in *The Book of Lists* reveal that death provides people's second greatest fear; the first is having to speak before an audience. Nervousness, even fear, before speaking is not unusual. Edward R. Murrow, a famous newscaster and commentator of early television days, echoed the feeling of many talented speakers when he said, "I always develop some nervousness before speaking. The moisture in the palm of my hands is the sweat of perfection." If you learn about voice control, development of speeches and oral reports, and delivery methods and techniques, you may become a member of the much sought-after, elite group of speakers who relish the opportunity to address audiences and who, incidentally, are well rewarded.

Additionally, throughout your career, you'll be judged by the effectiveness with which you communicate orally in your daily activities. On one occasion, you might make a presentation to your peers in committee work, to subordinates as part of a training or information program, or to superiors at a board of directors' or shareholders' meeting. In any case, your reputation is on the line. When you are effective, you gain status, you earn respect, you find managing others easier, and you become promotable to increasingly higher levels. You may even take on a more attractive personal appearance as a by-product of your speaking ability.

Do these comments apply to anyone you know?

Controlling Vocal Qualities

Knowledge about and skill in three important qualities of speech—phonation, articulation, and pronunciation—are necessary to the development of effective speaking habits. Let's briefly look at each.

• Phonation

Phonation involves both the production and variation of the speaker's vocal tone. We project our voices and convey feelings—even thoughts—by varying our vocal tones. Such elements as pitch (how high or low the tones are), intensity (how loud the tones are), and duration (how long the tones are held) are factors in phonation. These factors permit us to recognize other people's voices over the telephone. Anyone who studies oral communication should also remember that changes in vocal quality occur with changes in emotional moods.

Identify someone with a good voice.

In general, good voices have medium or low pitch, are easily heard but not too loud, carry smooth sounds, and are flexible in conveying emotional moods. Weak or poor voices generally have a very high or monotonous pitch, are too soft or too loud for comfortable listening, are jerky and distracting, or may lack flexibility.

Practicing the following exercises can be helpful to anyone trying to achieve good voice qualities:

1. *Breathe properly and relax.* Nervousness affects normal breathing patterns and is reflected in vocal tone and pitch. The better prepared you are, the better will be your phonation. Although relaxing may seem difficult to practice before a speech, a few deep breaths, just as swimmers take before diving, can help.

2. *Listen to yourself.* A tape recording of your voice reveals much about pitch, intensity and duration. Most people are amazed to find their voices are not quite what they had expected. "I never dreamed I sounded that bad" is a common reaction. Nasal twangs usually result from a failure to speak from the diaphragm, which involves taking in and letting air out through the larynx where the vocal cords operate. High pitch may occur from the same cause, but it may also be a product of speaking too fast.

3. *Develop flexibility.* The good speaking voice is somewhat musical, with words and sounds similar to notes in a musical scale. Read each of the following sentences aloud and emphasize the underscored word in each. Even though the sentences are identical, emphasizing different words changes the meaning.

I am happy you are here.	Maybe I'm the only happy one.
I am happy you are here.	I really *am*.
I am happy you are here.	Happy best expresses my feeling.
I am happy you are here.	Yes, *you* especially.
I am happy you are here.	You may not be happy, but I am.
I am happy you are here.	Here and not somewhere else.

• Articulation

An articulate speaker produces smooth, fluent, and pleasant speech. Articulation is the way in which a speaker produces and joins sounds. Faulty articulation is usually caused either by (1) organic disorders of the teeth, mouth, tongue, lips and other speaking equipment; (2) lack of education; or (3) personal carelessness. *Snoo* for *What's new* is an example of carelessness. *Dis, wid,* and *dem* for *this, with,* and *them* may result from a lack of knowledge and education. Various forms of lisping

Good articulation means clear speech.

may result from organic disorders. These examples should not be confused with *dialect,* which people informally call "an accent." A dialect is a variation in pronunciation, usually of vowels, from one part of the country to another. Actually, everyone speaks a dialect; and speech experts can often identify, even pinpoint, the section of the country from which a speaker comes. In the United States, people often describe dialects as New England, New York, Southern, Texan, Ozark, Midwestern, Mountain, and Western. Within each of these, minor dialects may arise regionally or from immigrant influence. The simple fact is that when people interact, they influence each other even down to speech sounds. Yet, many prominent speakers have developed a rather universal dialect that seems to be effective no matter who the audience is.

To improve your articulation, most authorities suggest that you become aware of common errors. Make your tongue, lips, and teeth do the jobs they should to produce proper sounds. Next, understand the speech sounds. Vowels, for example, are always sounded with the mouth open and the tongue clear of the palate. Consonants are responsible primarily for the distinctness of speech and are formed by an interference with or stoppage of outgoing breath.

• Pronunciation

The dictionary provides the best source to review pronunciation. People may articulate perfectly but still mispronounce words. The best rule to follow, perhaps, is to pronounce words in the most natural way. The dictionary often gives two pronunciations for a word. The first one is the desired pronunciation and the second an acceptable variation. To adopt, for example, a pronunciation commonly used in England such as *shedule* for *schedule* or *a-gane* for *again* could be considered affected speech. In other cases, the dictionary allows some leeway. The first choice for pronouncing *data* is to pronounce the first *a* long, as in *date;* but common usage is fast making pronunciation of the short *a* sound, as in *cat,* acceptable. Good speakers use proper pronunciation and refer to the dictionary frequently in both pronunciation and vocabulary development.

Learn the vowel sound symbols used in dictionaries.

When your voice qualities combine to make your messages pleasingly receptive, your primary concerns revolve around knowing your audience and developing appropriate messages.

Knowing Your Audience

Because all audiences are not the same, speakers must be able to identify characteristics common to each audience. A research scientist should not deliver a speech to a lay audience in highly technical terms. A speech about acid rain to a farm group should address the farmers' problems, for example, and not focus on scientific causes of acid rain. People listen to speeches about things of interest to them. "What's in it for me?" is the question most listeners ask. Here are some important facts you can obtain about most audiences: age, gender, occupations, educational levels, attitudes, values, broad and specific interests, and needs, if any.

We all ask this question.

Your analysis of most of these factors enables you to gear your speech specifically to your audience. In addition to these factors, you should also consider certain things about the occasion and location. Patriotic speeches to a group of military veterans will differ from speeches to a group of new recruits, just as Fourth of July speeches will differ from Memorial Day speeches. Seek answers to the following questions when you discuss your speaking engagement with someone representing the group or audience:

Is retirement planning a good topic for an audience of 25-year-olds?

1. How many will be in the audience?
2. Will I be the only speaker? If not, where does my presentation fit in the program? What time of day?
3. How much time will I be permitted? Minimum? Maximum?
4. What are the seating arrangements? How far will the audience be from the rostrum? Will a microphone be available?
5. Is the audience required to attend?

Answers to these questions reveal whether the speaking environment will be intimate or remote, whether the audience may be receptive and alert or nonreceptive and tired, and whether you will have to develop additional motivational or persuasive devices.

As a general observation, audiences *do* want to be in tune with a speaker. A well-prepared speaker can establish audience rapport easily. Your speaking goal is to have the audience react favorably to you and to your message. Keep in mind that your success will be judged by only one group: the audience. From planning your speech to practicing its delivery, focus your preparation on the audience.

Well-known speakers are generally well prepared.

Selecting a Topic

Good public speaking doesn't usually just come naturally. Good speakers spend far more time preparing than giving their speeches. If you have taken a public speaking class, you will recall some of the problems of selecting a topic of interest not only to you but also to your audience. . . .

Tom:	I have to give a speech in class, but I don't have anything to talk about.
Jan:	I've never known you to be speechless before!
Tom:	Don't joke around; I have a real problem.

Tom: I have to give a speech in class, but I don't have anything to talk about.

Jan: I've never known you to be speechless before!

Tom: Don't joke around; I have a real problem.

Jan is empathic.

Jan: You mean a problem of selecting a topic. Why don't you talk about your main interest?

Tom: That's just it. Since I've gotten involved in the program to help elderly people with their tax returns, I haven't had much time to play around or take part in social activities.

Jan provides feedback.

Jan: I see what you mean. You really don't have many accounting students in your class.

Tom adjusts to feedback and finds a topic.

Tom: You don't have to be an accounting student to help others. I think we should all take an interest in and participate in things off campus that might help others. Helping others might be a good way to strengthen our educations.

Jan: I think you've just selected a great topic!

Tom now has a topic that meets a major criterion for speech success. *Select a topic that is of interest to you!* If you can't show interest, how can you expect your audience to do so?

In selecting speech topics, these suggestions might help:

Speaking is better when you use specific personal incidents.

1. In addition to topics of personal interest, try to narrow the selection further by concentrating on topics about which you can display enthusiasm.

2. Because speaking about yourself is easy, talk about your work, your hobbies, your special educational pursuits, your politics, or your views on current problems for which you are especially qualified by experience or study.

3. For young groups, use inspirational or motivational messages. You must analyze mature audiences using the criteria discussed under "Knowing Your Audience."

4. Attempt to select topics about which you know more than the audience and that tend to complement the interests of the audience.

In making your topic selection, remember that your speech must have an objective:

1. What reaction or action do you want from your audience?
2. What idea do you want them to accept?
3. What would you like them to learn?

Whatever you select as a topic, you should keep in mind your objective. Any speech you might give will ultimately aim to persuade, entertain, instruct, inform, or a combination of these. When you attempt to integrate more than two of these objectives in one speech, your job becomes very complicated.

Planning Your Speech

The process of planning your speech evolves from your speech objective or objectives. The traditional purposes of speeches are

1. *To entertain.* After-dinner speeches are generally designed to entertain. Although these speeches may have a secondary objective of informing or persuading through their messages, the content and delivery is developed with entertainment in mind.

   Hint: Don't take yourself too seriously.

2. *To inform.* When your major objective is to have the audience understand a body of information, concentrate on the logical presentation of content.

3. *To persuade.* Political speeches fall in the persuasive category because they attempt to influence or change the attitudes or actions of an audience.

Entertaining and informative speeches use the following expository types of organization:

1. *Narrative—telling a story.* Autobiographical stories and tales of adventure are examples of narration.

2. *Descriptive—describing a situation.* Speeches about how certain companies or industries handle problems of personnel, competition, new-product development, and similar topics are common at trade and industry association meetings and fall in the descriptive classification.

   These organizational types are easy to prepare and easy to follow.

3. *Explanatory—using a logical sequence.* Explanation is the basis for many talks within organizations. The talks are designed to explain existing or new policies and procedures to staff members.

Persuasive speeches succeed only when audiences react as the speaker intended. To obtain desired reactions, speakers must convince listeners of the benefits the desired action holds for them. Appeals to reason or to emotions such as pride, fear, love, economy, safety, health, and quality motivate human action.

Although persuasive speeches may also use narration, explanation, and description, speakers seldom achieve their expository speech objectives by relying on the appeals of persuasion. Too much persuasion may lead the audience to distrust the factual material in expository speeches. The distinction between expository and persuasive speeches is helpful in planning and outlining your speech.

• Planning Your Strategy

With an understanding of the purpose of your speech—why you are giving it, what you hope to achieve—and a conception of the size, interest, and background of the audience, you should arrive at the best type of speech organization to use.

Make a few written notes about your purpose and about the makeup of the audience, keeping in mind the time of day and the probable attitudes and mental alertness of the audience. These notes should assist you in selecting content for your speech.

• Outlining Your Speech

Assume you are a successful business executive and are well known as the chairperson of the local "Say No to Drugs" campaign. You have been invited to speak at a major session of an all-day conference of the Key Clubs from high schools in your community. Key Clubs are service clubs similar to Kiwanis Clubs, and members are generally above-average academically and oriented to community service. You speak at 10 A.M., and you'll have thirty minutes to present your message. About 300 students—both men and women—will be your audience.

For once, you won't have to worry about raising money for the campaign. Your audience analysis indicates it is the age and community-oriented group that could benefit from a talk about the long-range effects of drug use and addiction. In return, it could spread your message among youth throughout the community.

Your analysis indicates that a simple message about the widespread use of drugs—a topic suitable for adult groups—isn't what is needed. You want the audience to react in two ways: (1) say "no" to drugs and

(2) carry the message to their peers and younger people. How can you convince this audience that they will benefit by taking active roles in the fight against drugs? You should appeal primarily to their already deep sense of service. Your supporting appeal should be developed around their own health and welfare. Yours must be a motivational speech.

To build the foundation for an emotional appeal, you may draw from several examples, methods, and techniques first to ensure audience understanding and then to reinforce it. These examples, methods, and techniques might include any of the following items:

1. *Use statistical support.* Are statistics or other quantitative measures available to lend authority and believability to your points? Surely you can find material on numbers of addicts, ages, dollars spent on drugs, and the cost to society in lost work time and hospital treatment.

   Items 1, 2, and 3 may be read as part of the speech.

2. *Use anecdotes.* Anecdotes are stories having a relationship to the speech topic or a moral ending. As the speaker, you are expected to have qualifications to speak. Stories about prominent citizens or role-model athletes who support your program or who perhaps have had careers ruined by drugs have strong emotional appeal.

3. *Use quotes from prominent people.* Comments made by other authorities are always helpful. In the case of drug problems, the U.S. Surgeon General, the local chief of police, a hospital administrator, a border patrol administrator represent sources of quotations.

4. *Use jokes.* You know young people like humor, but you rule jokes out of this speech. You simply can't find any that are closely related to your topic, and you know this relationship must exist for any joke in any speech to be effective.

   Be careful with jokes.

5. *Use visual displays.* Slides, flip charts, and handheld objects are effective in many speaking situations. At this early stage try to think of visual displays that will complement your oral presentation.

In a typical talk of 30 to 45 minutes, you can plan on two things. First, time permits development of only a few major points. Second, your audience can absorb only a few major points regardless of the length of the speech. Thus, you might outline a presentation as follows:

I. Introduction
   A. Purpose
   B. Justification of or importance of the topic

Experienced speakers use simple outlines.

    II. Major point 1 with support
       A. Anecdotes
       B. Statistics
       C. Quotes of authorities
   III. Major point 2 with support
       A. Anecdotes
       B. Statistics
       C. Quotes of authorities
   IV. Major point 3 with support
       A. Anecdotes
       B. Statistics
       C. Quotes of authorities
    V. Summary and conclusion

Note how anecdotes, statistics, *and* quotations are used to support each major point. Making every statement in a talk into a major point—something to be remembered—is impossible, unless the talk lasts only 2 or 3 minutes. Consider a speaker who must get contributions to a highway safety campaign in the school system. The major purpose of the talk is to persuade people to give to the program. To develop this point, however, the speaker will probably build the talk around two or three major points:

Highway safety must be improved.

Young people are the most susceptible to effective safety education.

Highway safety is everyone's business.

Supporting statistics, stories, and quotes to support these points are plentiful. Accidents, injuries, and fatalities occur daily and records are maintained. Stories abound about the cost of accidents, increasing insurance rates, and the effects of alcohol and drugs on drivers. With this evidence the speaker might spend only a couple of minutes encouraging people to contribute.

Your speech on how to say "no" to drugs will draw on the same type of support for major points. Here are some ideas for your major points:

Case studies and incidents strengthen points.

Drugs are harmful to health.

Expensive drug habits lead to crime.

People who say "no" take pride in themselves.

Drug-testing practices may be harmful to your career.

Children of addicts are also addicted.

Community service is a good citizen's commitment.

Helping others rewards you with good feelings.

Once you have selected your major points, locate your supporting material. You may also reverse the process when you have a supply of major points from which to choose. In that case, use those for which you have a supply of supporting material. The best sources for supporting material will be those you use in your everyday reading and listening. The broader your reading, the greater will be your supply of material.

See Reader's Digest for ideas.

Although stories, statistics, quotations, and the like may seem trivial, they are critical to effective speaking. They retain listener interest, provide proof and evidence supporting major points, and often provide the humor and enlightenment that turn an otherwise dreary topic into a stimulating message. They are one of the professional speaker's most important inventory items. How does a speaker accumulate these items? Most obtain them from personal reading. When they come across something that seems worth remembering, they write it down.

Like any other kind of story, a speech has a beginning, a body, and an ending. Your content really constitutes the body of the speech, but the beginning and ending are very important. What you say at the beginning sets the stage for your entire performance and initiates your rapport with the audience. The speech on highway safety might well have begun with "Just last year fifteen young people from our community were taken from us in the prime of their years by automobile crashes that could have been avoided."

Such an opening certainly would get attention. So too would an opening such as this for your speech to young people on drugs: "I live in a quiet, middle-class, comfortable neighborhood. That is until just a few months ago when four young people from three different families were killed in an automobile accident following a party at which drugs were used." What people hear first in a speech has much to do with how they will accept your message.

Following the body of your presentation, you must end the talk effectively. Work hard to develop a closing that will leave the audience with your major thrust. If the ending can relate to your opening, so much the better. "So my friends, let's make our community drug free so you and our other young citizens may grow up to enjoy the benefits of health, education, family, and freedom" would close the "no" to drugs speech strongly. In fact, you wouldn't have to say "Thank you." Simply stand back and accept the applause.

Applause is a speaker's reward.

Delivering Your Speech

All speeches fall into one of the following categories of delivery style:

1. *The impromptu speech.* Impromptu speaking may be frightening to most people because the speaker is called on without forewarning. In some cases, speakers can anticipate the request and formulate thoughts. In any case, impromptu speaking style should be direct and frank. Someone not properly informed can simply say, "Thank you," for being called on and explain why the opportunity is being declined.

Scary?

2. *The extemporaneous speech.* Extemporaneous speeches are planned, prepared, and rehearsed but not written in detail. Professionals use extemporaneous style. Simple cues written on 3 × 5, or smaller, cards may provide enough material for the speaker to talk meaningfully for long periods. Familiarity with the material makes this style effective. Teachers use it because material may be adapted to different class situations, just as public speakers may adapt their material to different audiences.

3. *The memorized speech.* Of the speech styles, memorization has the greatest limitations. Speakers are almost totally unable to react to feedback, and—as everyone who attended elementary school knows—the speaker who forgets a point and develops a mental block may lose the entire speech. Memorized speeches tend to sound monotonous, restrict natural body gestures and motions, and lack conviction. For short religious or fraternal rites, however, the memorized presentation is often impressive.

This never happened to you, did it?

4. *The written-and-read speech.* For complex material and technical conference presentations, written-and-read speeches ensure content coverage. Additionally, this style protects speakers against being misquoted and also fits into exact time constraints, as in television or radio presentations. Written-and-read speeches often prevent speaker–audience rapport, particularly when speakers keep their eyes and heads buried in their manuscripts. If you use this method, write in large letters, avoid using difficult words that might cause you to stumble, and underscore in color items that need particular emphasis.

Watch political speeches.

Electronic devices now make it possible to project manuscripts on transparent screens on each side of the speaker's podium. Thus, the speaker may read the manuscript and appear to the audience to be speaking extemporaneously.

Using Style in Speeches

Although the following suggestions are all appropriate for formal public speaking, most apply to speaking styles and to speaking situations generally:

1. Expect a few "butterflies" before you speak. A touch of nervousness probably means you'll be a success.

2. Once you are standing, try to select a few friendly faces in the audience. Speak to them because it is easier to speak to a few than to the audience as a whole. A sea of nondescript faces is a difficult audience. When you make eye contact with a few as shown in Figure 3.1, you'll appear to be speaking to each person in the audience.

3. Use gestures naturally. Body motions really can't be practiced. But try to be conscious of overusing your hands and arms. Remember the snide observation that "Some people wouldn't be able to speak at all if they couldn't use their hands."

4. At least until you gain some confidence and experience, use a lectern to hold your notes and to steady a shaky hand. Keep in mind, though, that weaning yourself from the lectern will eliminate a physical barrier between you and the audience. You'll also appear to speak naturally.

5. Use jokes or humor appropriately. If you can't tell a joke well, don't use one or you may be the joke! Humor must be related to your speech content. Good speakers tell jokes primarily about themselves. Because of expanding multinational involvement, refrain from any humor that may reflect negatively on race, color, religion, the opposite gender, and nationality. Poor-taste humor can destroy an otherwise good speech.

6. Watch your audience. They'll tell you how you're doing and whether you should shorten your speech. Be attentive to negative feedback in the form of talking, coughing, moving chairs, and other signs of discomfort.

7. Work particularly hard on your closing remarks. A good closing serves to leave the audience in a good mood and may help overcome some possible mistakes during the speech.

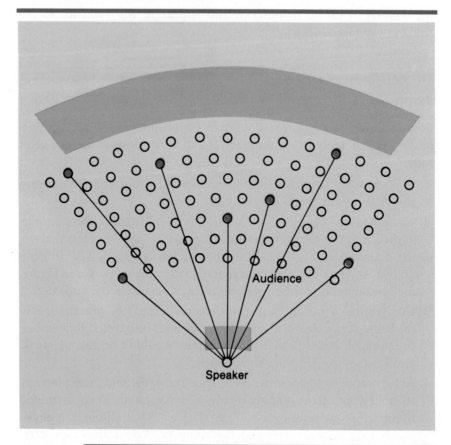

FIGURE 3.1

Selecting listeners for eye contact.

8. Dress carefully and tastefully. Appropriate clothing and good grooming affect audiences positively.

9. Appear confident and appear to enjoy making the speech.

10. Avoid annoying speech habits. Clearing your throat or uttering a soft cough constantly will shift audience attention from the speech to the speaker. Additionally, avoid the following words and phrases:

You know	After each statement
Well,	Before each statement
Like I said	
Myself	For me or I

Between you and I	Between you and me is correct.
What I hear you saying is	
Near miss	It was a miss; use "near hit."
Basically	Before many statements that aren't basic
Idiomatic redundancies such as bare naked, visually eyeball, overcrowded, senseless murder, visual view, and others	

Some Comments on Public Speaking

Public speaking is both an art and a skill. Careful planning and practice cannot be overemphasized as the means to build skill in speaking. If you feel more confident when reading from a manuscript, do so. A poor extemporaneous speech will not compare favorably to a properly delivered written-and-read speech.

Your status lends credibility to your speeches. If the audience doesn't know much about you, insist on a proper, impressive introduction. Professional speakers prepare their own introductions. You should do the same.

Why prepare your own introduction?

Making an Oral Report

Oral reporting differs from public speaking in that it isn't "public." Within organizations, oral reporting is an important means of obtaining and exchanging information for decision making and for policy development. Oral reporting is an efficient way to communicate because several people receive the message at the same time rather than individually at different times. It also constitutes an effective means of communicating because the audience is able to provide immediate feedback for clarification. As a result, oral reporting can significantly reduce message distortion and misunderstanding.

You may be surprised at how soon you'll be called on to make an oral report after you join an organization. This method of communication is used far more frequently than you might imagine. Because you

Good oral reporters get promoted.

make oral reports primarily to peers and superiors, you have an opportunity to present yourself in a favorable way.

• Planning Your Presentation

Oral reports differ from stand-up, public speeches in at least these respects:

1. Much more is usually known about the audience for an oral report, and the speaker is probably known by most members of the audience. The oral report is normally given *within* the organization.
2. Because the audience is smaller, the setting for the oral report will be more intimate than the setting for a formal speech.
3. Questions are more likely to be asked during the oral report.
4. The time allotted for an oral report tends to be short. Thus, you must plan your presentation carefully so it covers the topic fully, yet concisely.
5. The primary purpose of an oral report is to inform, not to entertain.

Oral reports should be expository, that is, narrative, descriptive, or explanatory. Appeals to emotion should not be used. Even a salesperson should not use emotional appeals when addressing a group of company officers about ways to solve problems and benefit the organization. Persuasion is an outcome of logical topic development. A broad outline for an oral report should include

Persuasive reports differ from used-car sales pitches.

1. Purpose of the report as an introduction
2. Discussion, including
    a. Method of research and background material
    b. Presentation of findings
3. Conclusions and implications as an ending

Among the reports that can be planned around this outline are reviews of economic conditions; summaries of new methods, practices, or policies; periodic reports of progress; studies of personnel; analyses of financial problems; and reports of research.

Unlike a written report, your oral report does not have chapter headings and subheadings to guide the reader. Thus, you should plan to use topic sentences to indicate when you change from one part of the report to another. Statements such as "Next, I will describe the two major problems to be faced when making a change such as the one proposed," are helpful. You can also make a longer than normal pause between the end of one section and the beginning of the next. You may even indicate a change from topic to topic by changing your body position noticeably.

Another outline technique is to have a list of major topics on a posterboard or flip chart so you can simply point to each one as you begin to talk about it. By using techniques that indicate a topic change, you will help your audience follow your presentation. If they make an effort, most will have a mental outline of your presentation.

As a general observation, an oral report audience will have a built-in interest in the presentation. This interest gives the speaker an advantage over the public speech in which the speaker must build audience interest as the talk develops. Now we'll look at some features of the oral report; many of these features distinguish reporting from public speaking.

Introduction   In both oral reports and speeches, the speaker should thank the one who made the introduction. "Thank you, Mr. Chairman" after the introduction for an oral report and "Thank you for your kind introduction, Ms. Garcia" for a speech are adequate. Then you follow with your own introduction to your presentation. The public speaker uses the opening as an effort to capture the attention of the audience. Startling statements, jokes related to the topic, famous quotations, and anecdotal stories are familiar speech openings.

For the oral report, you might use one of those speech openings if you believe it appropriate; but because your purpose is to report—not to entertain—you should seek to stay with your subject. An opening statement such as "When we were granted the approval to open a new branch office in Watson, we assigned a team to select the best possible inner-city location" introduces the subject immediately and sets the stage for the rest of the report. If you want to organize your report in a direct sequence, you might begin with "I want to inform you about why and how we selected the corner of Main and First in Watson as the location for our newest branch office."

Body   You'll recall from the discussion of speech organization that major points are supported by anecdotes, statistics, and quotes. As you prepare your oral report, however, you'll have to support your major points with factual information. Persuasive, emotional talk is out— unless, of course, you want to give the board of directors the idea that you'd make a good used-car salesman. The design of your paragraphs will become readily apparent to your listeners if you begin with a topic sentence and follow with the supporting material. For example, "Three possible sites for the branch were available—Main and First, the Rose-

Three parts: introduction, body, concluding summary

burg Mall, and the City National Bank building at Main and Twelfth. As this chart shows, pedestrian foot traffic is . . ." uses the topic sentence and follows with an introduction to the factual data to be presented.

Summary   In a public speech, the ending is often an urgent plea for the members of the audience to take some action or to look on the subject from a new point of view. In the oral report, the terminal or summary section is like that of the written report. First, state your conclusion and support it with the highlights from your supporting evidence; i.e., "In summary, we selected the Main and First location because it had. . . ." As we discuss the use of visual aids in oral reports, try to picture not only how effective they can be in conveying your message but also how much easier they can make your own job of planning your report.

• Using Visual Aids

Visual aids are developed from the variety of graphics discussed in Chapter 14 and are important to oral reports because they reinforce the spoken word. Through the use of visuals, a speaker hits the listener (receiver) with doubled impact—through the eyes and the ears. An ancient Chinese proverb says, "Tell me, I'll forget. Show me, I may remember. But involve me and I'll understand." Thus, the use of visuals approaches desirable audience involvement. Additionally, graphics provide the audience with a means of resolving possible communication problems with the speaker by providing answers in advance of questions.

Skilled speakers generally develop a set of graphic aids before they determine exactly what to say about each one. Graphs, tables, and pictures are the most-used items. Here are some guides for using them:

1. Make the graphic large enough to be seen by everyone in the audience. Either large paperboard displays or overhead transparencies are effective. In some organizations, great care is taken in the preparation of 35-millimeter slides, which can be used with a carousel projector and controlled by the speaker with a hand-held slide changer. This is an expensive method, but it may be desirable because of your analysis of the audience or the number of times the materials might be used.

2. Keep the graphics simple. Too much detail may lead the audience to concentrate on unimportant items and often makes letters and figures too small to be effective.

3. Use a small file card to record what to say about each graphic. Then, as you proceed from one graphic to another, simply move to the next file card. Sometimes you may write notes lightly in pencil directly on paperboard materials and refer to them without the audience's seeing them.

4. During the presentation, step to one side of the graphic so the audience may see it. Use a pointer if necessary. In any case, direct your remarks to the audience, not to the graphic—maintain eye contact.

Let's examine some of the visual devices available to speakers. The most common are posterboard graphs and outlines, overhead transparencies and projectors, flip charts, blackboards (chalkboards), and 35-millimeter slides.

Posterboard Displays   Posterboard can be purchased in a variety of sizes, colors, and weights from most bookstores, art supply stores, and stationers. Size and weight determine the price, but you should know that the lighter-weight boards have a tendency to bend and fall forward when placed on easels or chalk trays. It is embarrassing to have one begin to sway and then fall loudly to the floor during your presentation.

You can use poster paints to develop your visual, and you can also purchase paste-on letters if you are not a good letterer. Perhaps most important in terms of your presentation is to make sure your visual is large enough to be read by the entire audience.

Small notes not visible to the audience may be placed on posters.

Note visuals in Figure 3.2 (a) and (b), which could be effectively presented on posterboard. Incidentally, they are the type of graphic that can be displayed for quite a long time, providing an outline for the items to be covered in all or part of a presentation. For an audience of about a hundred, graphics should be on posterboard at least 16″ × 22″ and in large lettering. During the presentation, the speaker simply points to each item as it comes up.

Make certain that you do point accurately even if you have to touch the board with your finger or a pointer. Experience has shown that people will go to great pains to make a good visual and then fail to make effective use of it. Inexperienced speakers often fall into the habit of simply nodding their heads toward the visual. That isn't enough to keep the audience with you. You could lose your audience by failing to point to each bar in Figure 3.2 (c).

Overhead Transparencies   You have certainly been exposed to overhead transparencies during your education, but you may not have learned to prepare them. You can make a transparency of almost any-

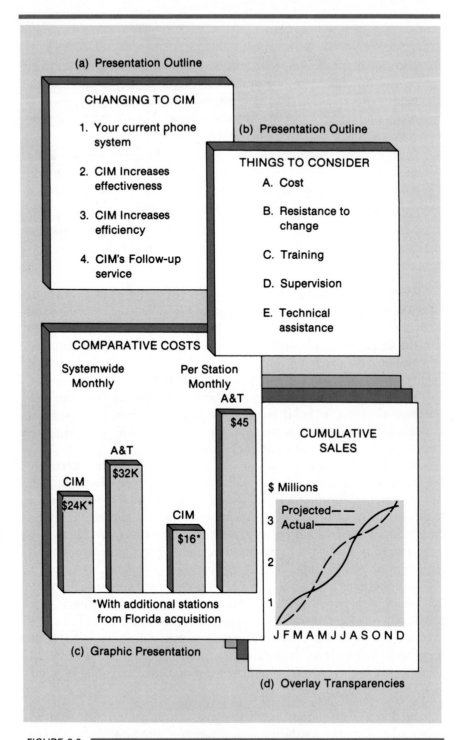

FIGURE 3.2
Visual aids in oral reporting.

thing from free-hand drawings to book pages simply by running your materials through a transparency-making machine, although some machines will not produce transparencies from anything but a photocopy.

Overheads: your most flexible visual support

During your presentation, you can refer to specific parts of the transparency by pointing specifically to the part either on the screen or on the overhead projector plate that holds the transparency. Additionally, you can quickly remove a transparency and replace it with another because the projector is usually within arm's reach. An advantage of the use of transparencies is their adaptability to overlay presentations. For example, visual (d) in Figure 3.2 consists of two transparencies. First, the speaker displays a transparency with only the headings and projected sales line; then the speaker places the second transparency, which contains only the actual sales line, over the first. This is an effective technique when you want to talk about projected sales before getting the audience involved in actual sales and the reasons for the discrepancies. Overlays are helpful when you want to show the step-by-step development of a procedure or a process, such as a flow chart or the manufacture of a product. Incidentally, you can write on transparencies with specially designed pens; in this way, a blank transparency serves the same purpose as a chalkboard.

Chalkboards   We are all familiar with chalkboards in the classroom and the varying degrees of teachers' ability to use them. For oral presentations outside the classroom, you can use portable chalkboards. Some of the major problems presented by chalkboards are the slickness and lack of cleanliness of some, poor penmanship of the user, and the failure of the user to erase items once they have been considered.

If you plan to use this method, practice beforehand and make certain the equipment is satisfactory. If your chalkboard display is sizable or complex, you'll find it helpful to place it on the board before your presentation. Most portable boards have two sides, thus permitting you to keep your material from view until you need it.

Flip Charts   Flip charts consist of a pad of paper with sheets about 2′ × 3′, fastened at the top, and mounted on an easel with a tray for crayons or colored pens. The speaker can prepare a series of visuals before the presentation and simply "flip" from one visual to the next as the talk progresses. Additionally, flip charts are often used to record ideas during a discussion. Although they serve many of the same purposes as a chalkboard, flip charts permit the speaker to use color to advantage and to prepare material in advance, a factor not always available when chalkboards are used.

Photographic Slides Presentations built around the use of 35-millimeter slides usually involve several visuals in a planned sequence and are displayed by means of a carousel or other slide projector. A major disadvantage is that the room should ordinarily be darkened.

For sophisticated presentations, however, slides add a great deal of impact. The slides are often prepared by graphic artists before being reduced to projector size, a process that can be very expensive compared with other visual methods. For presentations involving ordinary photography, of course, the slide method is most appropriate.

• Keeping Within Time Limits

If your presentation is part of a busy program, be prepared to complete the presentation within the allotted time. In many organizations, speakers have one or more rehearsals before making reports to groups such as a board of directors. These rehearsals, or dry runs, are made before other executives, critiqued, timed, revised, and rehearsed again. In some organizations, sessions are videotaped so participants can see how they come across.

Look to the meeting chairperson for additional time, if necessary.

Questions often disrupt carefully laid plans. At the same time, questions provide feedback, clarify points, and ensure understanding. More often than not, people ask questions that will be answered in a later part of the presentation. In these cases, you should say something like, "I believe the next slide will clarify that point. If not, we will come back to it." If the question can be answered quickly, the speaker should do so while indicating that it will also be covered later in the presentation. If necessary, the speaker might also indicate that questions will be answered following a certain portion of the presentation. In any case, rehearsal should include a session on questions that might be raised. Then, the talk may be altered to anticipate the questions.

The importance of oral reports cannot be overstressed. College students, for example, often wonder about why they should practice oral reports; yet, many find themselves called on early in their careers to make such presentations. Their futures may hinge on the effectiveness of their performance.

Summary

Oral communication plays an important role in the day-to-day conduct of business. Conversations and phone calls represent informal communication tasks. Speeches, talks, and oral reports make particular demands on people as formal communication tasks.

Public speaking differs from oral reporting in several respects but primarily in the nature of the audiences. The audience for an oral report as a rule is smaller, better known to the speaker, and more likely to create a less formal, more intimate speaking environment. An oral report audience probably demands more logical development and rejects emotional persuasion.

Oral report and public speaking methods and techniques are similar, of course, but they do differ in some respects. Although vocal qualities must be controlled in any speaking situation, public speakers must also be concerned about the physical setting, the need for eye contact with a larger audience, and perhaps wide variations in audience interest. The oral reporter makes greater use of visual aids and often must adjust to audience interruptions during the course of the presentation.

Skill in speaking before groups is a valuable quality that can be developed through training and practice.

About Language and Usage

Here are some foreign words and phrases commonly used in business and often in conversation:

ad hoc	for a special purpose
bona fide	in good faith
fait accompli	a thing already done
hoi polloi	the masses
per se	by itself
modus operandi	method of operation
sine qua non	essential condition; without which nothing
status quo	condition in which it is
vis-à-vis	face to face with; opposite
quid pro quo	something for something; an equivalent

Most dictionaries show pronunciation. Note that the preferred pronunciation of *status* is "stay-tus." *Data* is correctly pronounced "day-ta."

Exercises

Review Questions

1. Who is the best speaker currently on the national political scene? Why?
2. How do articulation and pronunciation differ?
3. What are some of the things a speaker should attempt to learn beforehand about the audience? What is the best source for this information?
4. Would you attempt to use jokes in speeches if the speech might be aided by a joke or two? What suggestions would you give to a prospective speaker about the use of jokes?
5. How does the scheduled time of a speech play a part in speech preparation?
6. Can you list two topics on which you believe you are qualified to give a five- or ten-minute talk?
7. What does narration mean? How does a narrative speech differ from a descriptive one?
8. What are the traditional purposes of speeches?
9. How might too much persuasion on the part of the speaker affect the audience when the purpose of the speech is to inform or to entertain?
10. What items, materials, or methods might a speaker use to assist or to reinforce audience understanding?
11. Why are the opening and closing portions of a speech so important?
12. Why is memorization a hazardous speech style?
13. What speaking style is most used by professional speakers?
14. In general, how does oral reporting differ from public speaking?
15. How is persuasion developed in oral reporting?
16. Why is oral reporting an effective and efficient way to communicate?
17. What is the key element in the opening of an oral report?
18. How might the ending of an oral report differ from the ending of a public speech?

Activities

1. Prepare a one-page analysis of the speaking skill of a well-known television newscaster or commentator. Pay special attention to speech qualities, audience eye contact and rapport, and objective versus subjective presentations.

2. List what you believe are your own speaking strengths and weaknesses. Discuss how you can work to eliminate the weaknesses.

3. Prepare a 2- to 3-minute speech on a business subject of your choice or other topic as assigned.

4. As part of a team of four, present a mock annual shareholders' meeting before the class. You should work from an annual report of a major company. One person should be the chief executive officer, one the chief operating officer, one the chief financial officer, and one the chief marketing officer. Each will speak for about 2 to 3 minutes. The CEO should be the presiding officer and introduce each of the others appropriately before each speaks. Included in your report will be a review of the year's activities, plans for the next year, and something about the firm's role in the community.

O B J E C T I V E S

When you have finished studying Part 2, you should be able to

- Select and use words best suited for your message.
- Use words based on the role they play in written and oral communication.
- Identify parts of speech.
- Prepare sentences, paragraphs, and composition for use in business writing.
- Avoid some common errors made by writers.

USING WORDS AND STYLE EFFECTIVELY

Using Words Effectively

Meanings receive their dignity from words instead of giving it to them.

PASCAL, 1670

or ultimate success, athletes begin by mastering the basics of their sport. Likewise, managers and employees who hope for success must master the basics of written and oral communication.

Usage exercises are to writers as physical exercises are to professional athletes—both groups must master their craft by constant reviews and drills. Regardless of their advanced status in school or business, those who already have the greatest command of writing basics are most appreciative of an opportunity to review. Those who have the poorest command sometimes are least appreciative and feel insulted by a study of elementary English-language principles. Just as athletes are not insulted by doing drills in basics, many high-level executives and many outstanding graduate students have acknowledged the need for more instruction in the fundamentals of writing.

Executives are spending more and more time at the keyboard. Because their errors in spelling, word usage, punctuation, and sentence structure can damage their credibility, many are taking refresher courses. Some major corporations now offer grammar-review sessions for their executives because they realize that principles taught in a basic English course really are applicable in business. Peter Drucker, a world-renowned authority on management, categorizes English as a *vocational* course because its principles can be *applied* on the job.

English is a *vocational* subject.

Because mistakes in word usage can confuse, distract, and mislead the reader, a brief review is in order. The principles selected for discussion represent the type of errors most frequently found in the writings of undergraduate and graduate students and business executives. If you already know these principles, a review will decrease the likelihood of forgetting to apply them. For those of you who don't know them, study them with the intent to use them in expressing ideas.

The discussion of word usage is not all-inclusive. It is limited to the most important considerations in word choice and in correct usage of words in certain categories.

Word Choice

Clarity and human relations are major concerns of communicators.

If words are well chosen, a reader or listener will (1) understand the message clearly and (2) react favorably to the writer or speaker. In other words, the major concerns are *clarity* and positive *human relations*, which we address by our choice of words. Each of the following factors is an important consideration in word choice: preciseness, simplicity and formality, repetition, and parallelism.

• Preciseness

Normally, specific words serve business writers better than general words. Specific words are more vivid:

We need a <u>truck</u> for this job.	General
We need a <u>pick-up</u> for this job.	Specific
The truck is <u>out of commission</u>.	General
The truck has <u>two flat tires</u>.	Specific
Congratulations on <u>your recent honor</u>.	General
Congratulations on being named <u>employee of the month</u>.	Specific

Sometimes, though, general words serve better than specific words:

Thank you for the explanation of your <u>financial status</u>.	General	**General words are sometimes preferred.**
Thank you for writing to me about your <u>problems with creditors and the possibility of your going bankrupt</u>.	Specific	
Frank told me about <u>what happened last week</u>.	General	
Frank told me about the <u>tragedy in your family</u>.	Less general	

In getting along with others, general statements can be useful; they can keep negative ideas from getting more emphasis than they deserve. Of course, writers who don't have specific information or for some reason don't want to divulge it will employ general words. *For vivid business communication use specific words.*

• Simplicity and Formality

Just as attire for the evening is dictated by the nature of the social event and others who will attend, the degree of formality in writing is dictated by the nature of the message and backgrounds of those who will read it. The writing in dissertations, theses, legal documents, and high-level government documents is expected to be formal. Business memoranda, letters, and reports are expected to be informal. Business writers prefer words from the left-hand column:

Informal	instead of	**Formal**
chew		masticate
end		terminate
get		procure
home		domicile
pay		remunerate

Why not use big words to impress people?

Simple, informal words (such as those listed) are readily understood, easier to spell, require less time in keyboarding and less space on a page, and are less likely to draw attention away from the idea being expressed. If a reader stops to question the writer's motive for using words similar to those in the right-hand column, the impact of the message may be seriously diminished. Likewise, the impact would be diminished if the reader stopped to question a writer's use of simple, informal words. That distraction is unlikely, however, if the message contains good ideas that are well organized and well supported. Under these conditions, simple words enable a reader to get the message clearly and quickly.

The caution is not against use of words that have more than two or three syllables; rather it is against habitual use of a long, infrequently used word when a simpler, frequently used word has the same meaning. Of course, people who communicate with others in their same profession or occupation would be expected to use the terminology to which they are accustomed.

Why build a good vocabulary?

Having been encouraged to use simple words, you may question the value of building a vocabulary. People who have large vocabularies have a better chance of finding just the right word for expressing an idea, they have a better chance of understanding what others have written, and they have a better chance of making a good score on college-entrance and certain employment tests. Moreover, some studies have found a high correlation between vocabulary and executive success. Although the research does not necessarily show that vocabulary was the *cause* of executives' movement up the promotional ladder, it does suggest that for some reason top executives have broad vocabularies. Perhaps the personal qualities that resulted in a broad vocabulary were the same qualities that resulted in promotion.

Students of business should build their vocabularies, but the purpose of business messages is not to advertise a knowledge of infrequently used words. Rather it is to transmit a clear and tactful message. For the informal writing that is practiced in business, *use simple words instead of more complicated words that have the same meaning.*

• Redundancies

A redundancy is a phrase in which one word unnecessarily repeats an idea contained in an accompanying word. In each sentence, which phrase constitutes a redundancy?

> We need to review the basic fundamentals of law.
> Consensus of opinion is that a promotion is warranted.
> We have a free gift for you.

Since "fundamentals" are "basic," both words are not needed. Since "consensus" means "survey of opinion," both are not needed. Since a gift by definition is without charge to the receiver, "free" is not needed; "gift" is sufficient.

The following redundancies are common:

But nevertheless	But *or* nevertheless
Exact same	Same
Exactly identical	Identical
Full and complete	Full *or* complete
Other alternative	Alternative
Past history	History
Personal opinion	Opinion
True facts	Facts *or* truth
Whether or not	Whether

Redundancy is not to be confused with repetition. In a sentence or paragraph, we may need to use a certain word again. Repetition serves a purpose and *is not* an error. Redundancy serves no purpose and *is* an error. Because such an error wastes words and risks distracting from the idea presented, *avoid redundancies.*

• Parallelism

In the following pairs of sentences, the ideas are the same. Which is stated better and why?

> We have three stated goals: to increase production, to expand our market, and recruiting skilled workers.

In a paragraph, does use of a certain word for the third time constitute redundancy?

Redundancy is taboo, but repetition can be very useful.

We have three stated goals: to increase production, to expand our market, and to recruit skilled workers.

Mark received a superior rating in hitting, fielding, and the technique of stealing bases.
Mark received a superior rating in hitting, fielding, and stealing bases.

The *what* and *why* of parallel construction

In each pair, the second sentence is better. It presents similar ideas in a similar way grammatically—"to increase," "to expand," and "to recruit" in the first pair, and "hitting," "fielding," and "stealing" in the second pair. In both pairs, reexamine the first sentence. Because one of the three elements is presented in a form different from the others, that element looks as though it does not belong. In addition, the variation in construction suggests inconsistency on the part of the writer or speaker.

When people get together for a certain purpose, they tend to have commonality in dress. A group attending a wedding would dress differently from a group attending a picnic. A person who is dressed for a wedding but attends a picnic appears to be out of place. When ideas appear together for a certain purpose, they should have commonality in grammar. If one of the ideas is presented in a different way grammatically, it also appears to be out of place. Commonality in grammatical presentation is called *parallel construction*. Just as geometry employs the word *parallel* to identify lines that run in the same direction, English employs the word *parallel* to identify ideas that are presented in the same way grammatically.

The principle of parallel construction applies not only to elements of a series that appear in a sentence, but also to major units in an outline, to subunits that appear under a major unit, and to headings that appear on typewritten pages. If one major heading appears in complete-sentence form, so should the others; if one subheading appears in question form, so should other subheadings under that division, etc. *Present multiple units in the same way grammatically.*

• Tone

Tone is the way a statement sounds. The tone of a message conveys the writer's or speaker's attitude toward the message and the receiver. Chances for achieving good human relationships are diminished when the tone of a message is overly negative, condescending, too formal, demeaning, or overly euphemistic.

Positive and Negative Tones   Negative words are associated with unpleasant tone; positive words are associated with pleasant tone. In each pair of sentences, which sounds better?

We cannot pay until September 1.
We can pay on September 1.

Construction will not begin before January 1.
Construction will begin soon after January 1.

You made a failing score.
Your score was 63; passing scores were 69 and above.

The first sentence in each pair contains a negative word—"cannot," "will not," and "failing." In each pair, both sentences are sufficiently clear; but the positive words in the second sentence make the message more diplomatic. It sounds more pleasing and does a better job of promoting human relations. For good human relations, rely mainly on *positive words—words that speak of what* can *be done instead of what* cannot *be done, of the* pleasant *instead of the* unpleasant.

Positive words are *normally* preferred, but sometimes negative words are more effective in achieving the twin goals of *clarity* and positive *human relations.* For example, addition of negative words can sharpen a contrast (and thus increase clarity):

Accentuate the positive.

Use an oil-based paint for this purpose; <u>do not use</u> latex.
Manuscripts are to be typewritten; handwritten material is <u>not</u> accepted.

When pleasant, positive words have not brought desired results, negative words may be justified. Assume, for example, that a meat cutter has been told with positive words that T-bone steaks are to be cut a certain way. Discovering later that the cutter has reverted to the wrong way, the butcher may use such negative words as "*No, that's the wrong way,*" demonstrate once more, and explain. Further discovery of incorrect technique would justify use of even stronger negative words. The cutter could have needed the emotional jolt that negative words can provide. *When the purpose is to sharpen contrast, or when positive words have not evoked the desired reaction, use negative words.*

But don't forget: negative words can be useful.

Condescending Tone   Condescending words seem to connote that the communicator is temporarily coming down from a level of superiority to join the receiver on a level of inferiority. Note these examples:

Condescension—a reminder of inequality

As a retired editor of best sellers, I could assist you in editing your PTA newsletters.

With my Ph.D. and your GED, we should be able to work out a suitable set of by-laws for the new club.

Such reminders of inequality seriously hamper communication. *Avoid use of condescending words.*

Euphemistic Tone   A euphemism makes an idea seem better than it really is. For example, the idea of picking up neighborhood garbage does not sound especially inviting. Someone who does such work is often referred to as a *sanitation worker* or *sanitation engineer.* Contrasted with *garbage collector,* these words have pleasant connotations. As such, they are not objectionable. Other commonly used and accepted euphemisms are *passed away* for *died, allowed to resign* for *fired, senior citizen* for *aged, reprimanded* for *bawled out, cohabiting* for *shacking up,* and *customer service* for *complaint department.*

Some euphemisms are acceptable.

We generally recognize such expressions for what they are—distasteful ideas presented with a little sugar coating. Knowing that the sender was simply trying to be polite and positive, we are more likely to react favorably than unfavorably. Yet, euphemisms with *excess* sugar coating or those that appear to be deliberate sarcasm are to be avoided. For example, a secretary would probably rather be introduced as *secretary* than as an *amanuensis.* And the person to whom the secretary is introduced would probably prefer *secretary* also. To refer to a typist as *superintendent of the keyboard* is to risk conveying a negative metacommunication, such as "We wish this typist held a more respectable position, but we do the best we can by making it sound good." To the receiver (and to the typist), just plain *typist* would sound better. *Use euphemisms when the purpose is to present unpleasant thoughts politely and positively; avoid them when they will be taken as excessive or sarcastic.*

Flattering Tone   Compliments (words of deserved praise) normally elicit favorable reactions. They can increase a receiver's receptivity to subsequent statements. Yet, even compliments can do more harm than good if paid at the wrong time, in the wrong setting, in the presence of the wrong people, or when the motive might be suspect.

Compliments *can* be detrimental to good communication.

Flattery (words of *un*deserved praise) may be gracefully accepted, but the net result is almost always negative. Although flattery *can* be accepted as a sincere compliment, the recipient is more likely to interpret undeserved praise as an attempt to curry favor. Suspicion of motive makes effective communication less likely. *Use compliments judiciously; avoid flattery.*

Skip the flattery.

Demeaning Tone   Read the following pairs of sentences. Which sentence seems more appropriate and why?

Marie is a <u>stew</u>.
Marie is a <u>flight attendant</u>.

That suggestion came from the <u>grease monkey</u>.
That suggestion came from the <u>lubrication person</u>.

Julio is a <u>hog head</u>.
Julio is a <u>locomotive engineer</u>.

In each of the preceding pairs, the first sentence can be taken as a put-down of an occupation. Like words that put down races or nationalities, words that put down occupations work against a writer's purpose. An expression that is designed to make an idea seem negative or disrespectful (sometimes called a *dysphemism*) is a demeaning expression. Because such expressions divert attention from the real message to emotional problems that have little to do with the message, *avoid demeaning expressions.*

Ouch! It's a dysphemism.

Connotative Tone   Human relations can really suffer when connotative words are inadvertently used instead of denotative words. The denotative meaning of a word is the literal meaning that most people would ascribe to it. The connotative meaning is the literal meaning plus an extra message that reveals the speaker's or writer's qualitative judgment. Here is an example:

We rode in John's <u>car</u>.   Denotative
We rode in John's <u>foreign job</u>.   Connotative

The second message contains a denotative message and an additional message: the author of the sentence has a bias for or against foreign cars. The connotation may fruitlessly introduce thoughts about whether purchase of foreign cars is wise. While thus occupied, the mind may not pay sufficient attention to the statements that follow "foreign job."

Consider some further illustrations:

Let's meet in the <u>cafeteria</u>.   Denotative
Let's meet in the <u>mess hall</u>.   Connotative

I read it in the students' weekly <u>newspaper</u>.	Denotative
I read it in the students' weekly <u>smear sheet</u>.	Connotative

Note the commonality between connotations and metacommunications. Both involve messages that are implied. In the preceding illustrations, the connotations seem to be more harmful than helpful; but connotations can be helpful:

We rode in John's <u>flashy new sports car</u>.	Connotative but positive
Let's meet in the company's <u>five-star cafeteria</u>.	Connotative but positive

Compared with denotative words, connotative words invite a wider range of interpretation. Words that elicit a positive reaction from one person could elicit a negative reaction from another.

The appropriateness of connotations also varies with the audience to which they are addressed and the context in which they appear. For example, "foreign job" might be received differently by a group of teenagers and a group of senior citizens. The expression is also less appropriate in a research report than in a popular magazine.

Connotations are influenced by the passage of time. "May I pour you some more coffee?" may have a connotation of genuine desire to serve if asked during a meal. An hour later, the same words could connote: "Don't you think it's about time for you to leave?"

Avoid *all* connotations?

Business writers are encouraged to *rely mainly on denotative words or connotative words that will elicit a favorable reaction.* By considering the audience, the context, and the timing, a writer can usually avoid connotative words that elicit unfavorable reactions.

For most business writing, word choice is characterized by preciseness, informality, parallelism, and tone. Other considerations are best reviewed under "parts of speech" categories.

Word Categories

In a book that discusses a wide variety of communication problems, a complete discussion of word usage is hardly possible. The following discussion touches on a high percentage of word-selection problems encountered in business communication.

Just as using a big, unusual word may result in receipt of the wrong message, misusing a small, common word may also result in receipt of the wrong message. And, just as using big words for the purpose of impressing can cause human relations problems, using small words in the wrong way grammatically can also cause human relations problems. Even when the correct message is received, a detected grammatical error can get more attention than the message itself. Such an error can cause the recipient to wonder about the sender's educational background or respect for others. Word-selection problems exist in all parts-of-speech categories.

Consequences of making a grammatical error.

• Words That Label

Nouns—words that label people, places, and things—appear in all sentences. Pay special attention to the underscored words in each pair of sentences. Which do you prefer, the first sentence or the second?

> Cancellation of the requirement will occur in July.
> The contract will be canceled in July.

> That decision is to be made by the supervisor.
> The supervisor is to make that decision.

In both pairs, the first sentence employs an abstract noun as the subject; the second employs a concrete noun as the subject. Just as the star in a film is the most important character, the subject in a sentence is the most important noun. The more vivid it is, the better. Since "cancellation" and "decision" are abstract nouns, they are hard to envision. Since "contract" and "supervisor" are readily envisioned, the meanings of the second sentences come through more clearly. Using an abstract noun as a sentence subject is certainly not an error; in fact, when an idea needs to be included but does not need emphasis, using an abstract noun as the subject may be desirable. Usually, however, writers and speakers will convey clearer messages if they *use concrete nouns as subjects.*

Abstract nouns can sometimes serve well as sentence subjects.

• Words That Replace

In the following sentence pairs, note that a word used in the first sentence has been replaced by another word in the second:

> When Charles was 18, Charles entered law school.
> When Charles was 18, he entered law school.

> The motion was out of order; the motion was withdrawn.
> The motion was out of order; it was withdrawn.

Replacing "Charles" and "motion" (nouns) with "he" and "it" (pronouns) brings welcomed variety without decreasing clarity. Yet, sometimes careless use of pronouns can cause serious problems in human relations.

Pronouns with Gerunds Note the underscored words in the following pairs of sentences:

> I shall appreciate your <u>help</u>.
> I shall appreciate your <u>helping me</u>.

> We were concerned about his <u>telephone conversation</u>.
> We were concerned about his <u>talking on the telephone</u>.

In the first sentence of the first pair, "help" is used as a noun (it tells what is being appreciated). Likewise, in the second sentence, "helping me" is also used as a noun (another way of expressing "help"). Now, note the words that precede "help" and "helping me." Without a moment's hesitation, a receiver knows that the word preceding "help" should be in the possessive form ("your"). "I shall appreciate *you* help" would just not sound right. Since "helping me" serves the same purpose in the second sentence that "help" serves in the first, the word preceding "helping me" must be possessive also. In the second sentence of the second pair, note the use of the possessive form ("his") before "talking."

The expressions "helping me" and "talking on the telephone" are called *gerunds* (verbs used as nouns and characterized by an *-ing* ending). Each of the following sentences contains a gerund. Of the two words that precede the gerund, determine which one is correct.

Can a verb be used as a noun?

> She was annoyed by (<u>me, my</u>) whispering.
> I shall appreciate (<u>Tom, Tom's</u>) submitting an application.
> We were not aware of (<u>them, their</u>) joining the group.

Does a possessive pronoun precede a gerund?

In each sentence, the second choice is correct. *Before a gerund use the possessive form.* To a recipient who knows English well, failure to use the possessive form before a gerund is distracting.

Gender Pay special attention to the pronoun "he" in these sentences:

> When your auditor arrives, <u>he</u> is to go directly to the superintendent.
> A lawyer could probably solve the problem, but <u>he</u> would have to be a tax specialist.

The person who wrote these sentences was probably applying an age-old rule of English: When the gender of a noun ("auditor" in the first sentence and "lawyer" in the second) has not been revealed, use a masculine pronoun. When the English language began to emerge a few hundred years ago, women did not have the status they have today. In today's world, women can be auditors, lawyers, physicians, professors, and can practice other professions formerly restricted to men. Therefore, someone who uses the masculine pronoun runs the risk of conveying a between-the-lines message that says "Women don't serve in professions" or "I don't think women *should* serve in professions or have equal status with men."

When are masculine pronouns objectionable?

A high percentage of women are accustomed to the old masculine pronoun rule. They use it themselves, fully aware that it is not really intended to offend. Surely, the statement, "One small step for man, one giant leap for mankind" was not intended to exclude one of the sexes. Neither does the statement, "Man does not live by bread alone" intend to imply "But women do live by bread alone." However, some people are very sensitive to use of the masculine pronoun. To them, such usage can seriously interfere with correct reception of a message by inviting attention to a social issue instead of to the specific idea conveyed.

Because clear receipt of the message is so important, a writer or speaker can scarcely afford the risk involved in using a masculine pronoun that could be taken as an offense. Offensive pronouns can be avoided in a variety of ways:

How can offensive pronouns be avoided?

1. Avoid use of a pronoun completely.

   Original: When your auditor arrives, he is to go....
   Revised: Upon arrival, your auditor is to go to the superintendent.

2. Repeat the noun.

   Original: ...the courtesy of your guide. Ask him to....
   Revised: ...the courtesy of your guide. Ask the guide to....

3. Use a plural noun.

   Original: If a supervisor needs assistance, he can....
   Revised: If supervisors need assistance, they can.... (Because "they" can refer to men only, women only, or both, it avoids implying that supervisors can be men only.)

4. Use pronouns from both genders.

   Original: Just call the manager. He will in turn....
   Revised: Just call the manager. He or she will in turn.... (Occasional use of "he or she" may not be particularly distract-

ing, but repeated use can take attention away from the message.)

Although the English language has a common-gender pronoun *(they)* in the plural, it does not have such a pronoun in the singular (except for *it,* which is hardly appropriate for referring to people, and *one,* use of which is seldom advisable.) Until such a pronoun emerges and is accepted, *avoid use of masculine pronouns that may be considered offensive.*

First Person Sometimes, reaction to a message is strongly influenced by the choice of pronoun employed. If the first-person pronoun *(I)* is used frequently, the sender may impress others as being self-centered—always talking about self. When *I* is used, it appears as the subject, and the subject of a sentence gets emphasis. Knowing that overuse of *I* is discouraged, some people try to circumvent its use by inserting such words as *the undersigned, yours truly, this researcher,* or *this reporter.* Use of these expressions is just as bad as or worse than use of *I.* They may be taken as a devious way of inserting self into the message without use of the first-person pronoun. *Avoid overuse of "I" and other words that identify self.*

"Second person" designates the person *to* whom a remark is addressed.

Second Person Another pronoun that frequently interferes with correct interpretation is *you. You,* always referring to the person or persons being addressed, is called a *second-person pronoun.* In the following sentence, what does *you* mean?

You can't interpret these figures.

If the author of the sentence means *he* or *she* can't interpret, "you" should not be used. If "you" is intended to mean the specific person being addressed, it could be inaccurate or insulting. The person to whom the statement is directed *may be able* to interpret or be offended because ability to interpret has been underestimated. If "you" in the sentence means "no one" or "the average person," the message may be misunderstood. Because "you" in such sentences can be interpreted in three ways, *avoid "you" when the person it stands for is not clear.*

The following sentences employ the second-person pronoun. In which sentence is *you* less advisable?

You typed a perfect copy.
You made numerous mistakes on this page.

The first sentence contains a positive idea. The person to whom the sentence is addressed can hardly resent being associated with perfection.

The second sentence contains a negative idea. Sensitivity about the mistakes is heightened when the person addressed is directly associated with the mistakes. If the speaker's desire is to be diplomatic (at least to be no more negative than necessary), the second sentence could be revised to avoid the use of second person: "This page contains numerous mistakes." For better human relations, *use second person for presenting pleasant ideas and avoid second person for presenting negative ideas.* However, use of second person with negative ideas *is* an acceptable technique on the rare occasions when the purpose is to jolt the receiver by emphasizing a negative.

Normally, avoid second person in stating negative ideas.

Although use of "you" is discouraged when the antecedent is vague and when the idea is negative, the more common mistake is the failure to use "you" frequently enough. "You" (appropriately used) conveys to receivers a feeling that messages are specifically for *them.* Thus, its use heightens interest and increases vividness. Use of "you" thus contributes to clarity and human relationships.

For success in human relations, a "you attitude" is an essential. Thinking in terms of the other person's interests, trying to see a problem from the other's point of view, asking, "Under these circumstances, what would my viewpoint be?"—these habits not only assist people in getting along with others, they make communication more effective. Those who have the "you attitude" find use of "you" is natural and easy.

"You attitude" assists in using second person.

Third Person   Like second and first person, third person has an influence on human relations. Note the difference:

> You will be severely challenged by tomorrow's test.
> Students who took the test last semester said they were severely challenged by it.

Whether the first sentence is preferred over the second depends on the speaker's purpose. If the intent is to heighten concern over the test, to emphasize its difficulty, the second person is more effective. If the intent is to transmit the idea of difficulty with less emphasis, the third person is more effective. *Use second person to emphasize an idea and third person to de-emphasize an idea.*

Agreement   The following illustrations contain an error in pronoun usage:

> The recommendations arrived today; the judge checked it thoroughly.
> When the statement was first made, they were refuted.

Singular verbs with
singular pronouns;
plural verbs with
plural pronouns

As "recommendations" is the noun to which the pronoun refers, the pronoun "it" should be changed to a plural form. Since "statement" is the noun to which the pronoun refers, "they" should be changed to the singular form, "it." Recognizing the lack of agreement, a reader or listener wonders whether more than one noun is involved or whether the wrong pronoun has been used. To avoid this confusion, *make sure pronouns agree in number with their antecedents.*

Case   Pronouns may appear in almost any position in a sentence. Selecting the right form to use is seldom a problem when the pronoun is at the beginning. Without stopping to think about it, English-speaking people will say *I went* instead of *me went, they went* instead of *them went.* Pronouns that serve as subjects of sentences are called *nominative-case* pronouns; pronouns that serve as objects are called *objective-case* pronouns. Errors in pronoun usage are more likely to occur when the pronoun is at the end of a sentence:

> The report was intended for Maria and I.
> Send copies to Phil and I.
> This quarrel is between Tony and I.
> The flowers are from Ed and I.

Note: "Tom and *I* are
waiting," but "Wait
for Tom and *me.*"

In the four sentences, "I" should be changed to "me." If a question should arise about whether to use the nominative-case pronoun, the answer becomes obvious when the sentence is read without the words that accompany the pronoun. Since no one would say "was intended for *I*," no one should say "was intended for Maria and *I*." Coming after the preposition "for," the pronoun should be in the objective case, "me." Since "send copies to *I*" would not sound right, "send copies to Phil and *I*" is not right.

Because most errors in pronoun usage seem to occur in sentences involving two or more people, further illustrations are presented. In each pair of sentences, observe that objective-case pronouns follow the underscored prepositions (words that show relationships between nouns or pronouns and other words in a sentence).

> Wait for me.
> Wait for Neva and me.
>
> Send copies to us.
> Send copies to Dorothy and me.
>
> Give the difficult tasks to me.
> Divide the difficult tasks between Chester and me.

Take a picture of me.
Take a picture of my son and me.

In the preceding pairs of sentences, the first sentence has *one* object and employs an objective-case pronoun. The second sentence in each pair employs a *compound* object and also employs an objective-case pronoun.

Pronouns that serve as sentence subjects are *I, you, he, she, we,* and *they.* Pronouns that serve as objects are *me, you, him, her, us,* and *them.* Usually, those in the second group will appear near the end of a sentence; those in the first, at or near the beginning. *Use objective-case pronouns to follow prepositions.*

In the following sentences, observe that pronouns follow words that show action (verbs):

Mr. Shaw is taking me to the Harbor Club for lunch.
The systems analyst helped me.
The president encouraged us.
Georgia assisted them.
The officer stopped Tom and me.

Use of "Tom and *me*" does not mean that the objective pronoun is always used when two people are discussed. "Tom and *I* were stopped by the officer" uses a nominative pronoun because "Tom and *I*" serve as the subject of the sentence. *Use nominative-case pronouns as subjects of sentences, but use objective-case pronouns to follow verbs.*

Sometimes, reflexive (self) pronouns are incorrectly used instead of nominative or objective pronouns:

Incorrect:	Sue and myself will attend.
Correct:	Sue and I will attend.

Incorrect:	The note was signed by Jane and myself.
Correct:	The note was signed by Jane and me.

Reflexive pronouns (such as herself, himself, myself, themselves, and yourself) re-identify a noun or pronoun for emphasis:

I myself am not alarmed.	Calls special attention to "I"; inclusion of "myself" has about the same effect as would underscoring "I."
The supervisor herself made the rule.	Use of "herself" indicates that the preceding word is especially significant.

After verbs and prepositions, use objective-case pronouns.

"Myself" is a poor substitute for "I" or "me."

Reflexive pronouns also reflect action on or by a subject:

> Tim hurt <u>himself</u>.
> The visitor excused <u>herself</u>.

Use "self" words to (1) re-identify and thus achieve emphasis or (2) reflect action on or by a subject. Do not use them to replace nominative or objective pronouns.

• Words That Show Action

Because every sentence includes an action or linking verb, correct use of verbs is especially important.

Correct: "One of the tires *is* flat." Incorrect: "One of the tires *are* flat." Why?

Agreement   For those whose native language is English, correct use of verbs is almost automatic: *they are, he is, she was, we were*. Whether to use *is* or *are* depends on whether the subject is singular or plural. Yet, because people are accustomed to using a plural form of the verb to accompany a plural noun or pronoun, they sometimes use the wrong verb when a noun appears between the subject and the verb. Observe the misuse of verbs in these sentences:

> Only one of the officers <u>are</u> present.
> The typists, not the secretary, <u>is</u> responsible.
> Each of the following pages <u>have</u> been proofread.

In the first sentence, note that the subject is "one," a singular form. "Officers" is not the subject and therefore has no influence on the form of verb that is used: "Only *one . . . is* present." Likewise, "The *typists . . . are* responsible." "*Each . . . has* been proofread."

Because subject–verb agreement is a principle of English, such errors are especially distracting. Even though recipients may be able to understand exactly what is meant, the message will not come through with the impact it deserves. Instead, the error may generate thoughts about whether the error resulted from haste, lack of respect, or lack of knowledge. To avoid such possibilities, senders must *use verbs that agree in number with the subjects of sentences.*

Agreement in person is also a necessity. The verbs in the following examples are used incorrectly:

Does "She don't drive" illustrate lack of agreement in number?

> He <u>don't</u> like to travel.
> George <u>don't</u> make mistakes.
> You <u>was</u> notified.

Just as verbs must agree with subjects in number, they must also agree in person. "First person" describes a speaker or writer—*I* and *we*. "Second person" describes the one spoken or written to—*you*. "Third person" describes the one spoken or written about—*he, she, him, her, it, they, them*. In most usage, correctness is automatic: *I was* instead of *I were*, *she cooks* instead of *she cook*, and *they work* instead of *they works*. The most common errors are in the use of *don't* with third-person singular ("Alice don't live here any more") and *was* with second-person singular ("You was a kid once yourself"). Thus, the correct forms of the previously displayed sentences are "He *doesn't* like to travel," "George *doesn't* make mistakes," and "You *were* notified." To avoid all the communication hazards that accompany a grammatical error, *use verbs that agree in person with their subjects.*

Tense   In addition to revealing action, verbs reveal the *time* of action—past, present, or future. Observe the words that indicate time:

> We <u>received</u> your report last week, we <u>are studying</u> it, and we <u>will make</u> a decision tomorrow.

All three tenses are employed in this example. Using three tenses in the same sentence was *necessary* if events were to be properly placed in time. But sometimes, *unnecessary* changes in tense cause confusion and distraction:

> He <u>studies</u> (present) the proposal and <u>offered</u> (past) his reaction. John <u>offered</u> to pay but <u>fumbles</u> for his wallet.

Such sentences cause listeners or readers to wonder which is to be thought of—a present event or a past event. Each sentence should employ two present-tense verbs or two past-tense verbs, but not one of each. For consistency, *do not make unnecessary changes in tense.*

In English, two words are required for expressing verbs in infinitive form: *to be, to go, to write, to work, to study*. In other languages (French and German, for example), only one word is required for expressing infinitives: *aller* for "to go" in French, and *gehen* for "to go" in German. Even though the English infinitive is presented in two words, it is to be thought of as a unit. As a unit, it should not be split:

> Incorrect: He was trying <u>to</u> rapidly <u>complete</u> his report.
> Correct: He was trying <u>to complete</u> his report rapidly.

> Incorrect: We want you <u>to</u> seriously <u>consider</u> the proposal.
> Correct: We want you <u>to consider</u> the proposal seriously.

Although ideas in the incorrect sentences are not seriously distorted, a reader or listener could be distracted; the grammatical error may get more attention than the message itself. To avoid that possibility, *avoid splitting infinitives.*

Which is right: (a) avoid changes in tense, or (b) avoid unnecessary changes in tense?

An infinitive: *"to go"*; a split infinitive: *"to quickly go"*

Active and Passive Verbs   In the following example, the first sentence employs an active verb; the second, a passive verb:

> Charlotte <u>edited</u> the script.
> The script <u>has been</u> edited.

Both sentences employ the verbs correctly. In sentences in which the subject is the *doer* of action, the verbs are called *active*. In sentences in which the subject is the *receiver* of action, the verbs are called *passive*. When sentences employ active verbs, receivers get a sharp picture. Recall that the two essential parts of a sentence are the subject and the verb. When the subject is the actor, clarity of ideas is heightened. When sentences employ passive verbs, receivers get a less distinct picture. In the second sentence, a reader becomes aware that something was done *to* the script, but who did it is not revealed, and the reader or listener gets a less complete picture.

Some passive sentences reveal the doer; others do not.

Even when a passive sentence contains additional words to reveal the doer, the imagery is less distinct than it would be if the sentence were active:

> The script <u>has been</u> edited <u>by Charlotte</u>.

The word *"script"* gets the most attention because it is the subject. The sentence seems to let a reader know the *result* of action before revealing the doer; the sentence is less emphatic.

Because active verbs convey ideas more vividly, senders rely more heavily on active verbs than passive verbs. Passive verbs are useful, though, (1) in concealing the doer ("The script has been edited"), (2) in placing more emphasis on *what* was done and what it was *done to* than on who *did* it ("The script has been edited by Charlotte"), and (3) in subordinating an unpleasant thought. Both of the following thoughts are negative:

> You <u>failed</u> to fill in the form properly.
> You <u>have let</u> this machine become very dirty.

Use passive verbs with negative ideas.

Both sentences are active. Because the subject "you" is the doer, the sentences are emphatic. But, normally, negative thoughts should be deemphasized. Presenting an unpleasant thought emphatically (as active verbs do) makes human relations difficult. When passive verbs are used, the sentences retain the essential ideas, but the ideas seem less irritating:

> The form <u>has not been</u> filled in properly.
> The machine <u>has been</u> allowed to become very dirty.

Use active verbs with positive ideas.

Just as emphasis on negatives hinders human relations, emphasis on positives promotes human relations:

You <u>have filled</u> in the form perfectly.
You certainly <u>keep</u> this machine clean.

Because the subjects ("you") are the doers, the sentences are emphatic; pleasant thoughts deserve emphasis.

Sometimes, the expressions *past tense* and *passive verbs* are confused. *Past* and *passive* do have similar sounds, but they have different meanings. Passive verbs appear in sentences in which the subjects are acted upon; past-tense verbs appear in sentences in which events have taken place already:

Passive: The work <u>has been done</u>.
Active: John <u>has done</u> the work.

Note that such words as *have, had,* and *has* are frequently used when sentences are passive, but those words can be used also when the sentences are active—as in the second sentence. A passive sentence is not necessarily a sentence about a past event. In fact, a passive sentence can be in the future tense:

The job <u>will be completed</u> before tomorrow afternoon.

Since the subject is not a doer, the sentence is passive—regardless of whether the tense is past, present, or future. Out of concern for clarity and positive human relations, *use active verbs to present important points or to present pleasant ideas; use passive verbs to present less significant points or to present unpleasant ideas.*

"Passive" and "past" have different meanings.

• **Words That Describe**

A word used to describe a noun is called an *adjective*. Compared with nouns and verbs, adjectives play a less significant role in a sentence. Adjectives describe or give information about nouns. Compared with nouns and verbs, adjectives present fewer problems in usage. However, a common problem is using adjectives that are too strong or too frequently used:

Sales have been <u>fantastic</u>.
Mr. Jones presented a <u>ridiculous</u> plan.

Use of such adjectives can cause a receiver to wonder about a sender's objectivity. A person who wanted to report a highly satisfactory sales program would do well to avoid "fantastic" and, instead, give some details. Even though a plan may be worthy of ridicule, a person who comments on it would be better off to point out areas needing improvement. By labeling a plan "ridiculous," a speaker might risk being labeled biased or overly negative. Communication is normally more effective if writers and speakers *avoid using adjectives that are used too frequently by others, are overly strong, or are overly negative.*

Compound Adjectives   Sometimes, writers or speakers search in vain for the right adjective. Not finding one that presents the right shade of meaning, they can form an adjective by joining two or more words with a hyphen. At first, a writer may put down "We need *current* reports." Recognizing that "current" may be taken to mean "daily" or "weekly," the writer can use a compound adjective:

We need up-to-the-hour reports.

The compound adjective makes the description more precise. Note that "up-to-the-hour" is used in the same way as "current"—to describe the noun that immediately follows it. When two or more words are used to form a single-word describer of the noun that follows, a hyphen is used to join the words, and to present them as one. In spoken language, "up-to-the-hour" would probably be spoken a little faster than other words in the sentence. The speeding-up technique helps to demonstrate that they are used as one word. In written language, the hyphen serves the same purpose.

Using or failing to use the hyphen in a compound adjective is more than just a matter of mechanical correctness or punctuation. Improper use of the hyphen can cause serious differences in meaning:

All night seminars have been canceled.
All-night seminars have been canceled.

In the first sentence, "all" is describing some things—"night seminars." The sentence means that every one of the seminars meeting at night has been canceled. In the second sentence, "all-night" is describing "seminars." The sentence means that seminars lasting the entire night have been canceled. Here are some further examples:

A new car salesperson	The phrase means a new person who sells cars.
A new-car salesperson	The phrase means a person who sells new cars.
His two base hits won the game.	The phrase means two hits, but they could have been singles, doubles, triples, or home runs.
His two-base hits won the game.	The phrase means doubles, but the number of such hits is not revealed.

Hyphens are used to join descriptive words that *precede* a noun and are used as one-word describers. Hyphens are not used when describers *follow* nouns.

Difference in meaning? "Two-day seminars" and "Two day seminars"

> The boss made a spur-of-the-moment decision.
> His decision was made on the spur of the moment.

For accurate communication, writers must *use hyphens to join words that form a one-word describer of a noun that follows.*

Coordinate Adjectives   When nouns are described in more than one way, the hyphen is not employed. Observe the difference:

Hyphens for compound adjectives; commas for coordinate adjectives

> Jane was asked to fill out a long, complicated questionnaire.

The questionnaire is long; it is also complicated. Either word could be omitted and the sentence would still make sense. Such adjectives are called *coordinate* adjectives. They are alike in that each describes the following noun. Since each describes separately, they are not joined with a hyphen; rather they are separated with a comma. Careful writers and editors learn to *place a comma between coordinate adjectives.*

Superlatives   Messages are sometimes influenced negatively by another form of adjective—the superlative:

> This dryer is the best one on the market.
> The factory has the worst odor imaginable.

Superlatives are very useful words. Frequently, the extreme unit in a series needs to be identified—the *highest* or *lowest* score, the *latest* news, the *youngest* employee. But, when superlatives are totally unsupported—or even unsupportable—their use is questionable. Furnishing proof that no other dryer is up to the standards of this one would be extremely difficult. Proving that one odor is the worst imaginable is practically impossible. Knowing that such statements are exaggerations, the receiver may not believe them at all. In fact, someone who has used a superlative to transmit an *unbelievable* idea may not be believed when offering support for a *believable* idea. For the sake of credibility, *use only supported or supportable superlatives.*

Define *superlative.*

Avoid *all* superlatives?

Adverbs   Like adjectives, adverbs describe or modify. Adjectives describe or modify nouns; adverbs describe or modify verbs, adjectives, or other adverbs:

Tim writes rapidly.	"Rapidly" describes a verb.
Sue is an extremely efficient operator.	"Extremely" describes an adjective.
Juan works very rapidly.	"Very" describes an adverb.

Superlatives can be either adjectives or adverbs. They are adverbs when they modify or describe verbs:

Ernie types <u>fastest</u>.
This item sells <u>best</u>.

Whether a superlative is an adjective or an adverb, the same principle applies: *Use only supported or supportable superlatives.*

Like adjectives, adverbs can arouse skepticism or resentment if they are used without care:

> **When adverbs are too numerous or too strong, the message may seem subjective.**

Our prices are <u>ridiculously</u> low.
Our forecasts have been <u>fantastically</u> accurate.

For the sake of credibility, *avoid using adverbs that are used too frequently by others, are overly strong, or are overly negative.*

The position in which an adverb or adjective is placed can make a genuine difference in the meaning of the sentence:

<u>Only</u> John gets his vacation in summer.	"Only" modifies "John," meaning no other employee gets a summer vacation.
John gets his vacation in summer <u>only</u>.	"Only" modifies "summer," meaning John never gets a vacation at any other time.
John gets his <u>only</u> vacation in summer.	"Only" modifies "vacation," meaning John gets one vacation; it's in summer.
John gets <u>only</u> his vacation in summer.	"Only" modifies "gets," meaning John gets no other benefits.

For the sake of clarity, *place an adverb or adjective close to the word it describes.*

• Words That Join

Conjunctions assist in joining ideas. When the ideas are of about equal significance, *coordinate* conjunctions are employed:

Maria did the typing and duplicating, <u>but</u> Gus did the collating.
The reports are ready for editing, <u>and</u> the statements are ready for checking.

When the ideas are not of equal significance, *subordinate* conjunctions are employed:

The clerk checked out <u>when</u> the job was finished.
The reporter left <u>before</u> anyone could talk with her.

Note that the coordinate conjunctions "but" and "and" in the preceding sentences are preceded by a comma. The comma is sometimes appropriately omitted when the coordinating conjunction joins two ideas that are exceedingly short ("He left *but* I stayed.") Note that the subordinating conjunctions "when" and "before" are not preceded by a comma.

Punctuation of adverbial conjunctions is different from punctuation of coordinate conjunctions:

> The report arrived today, <u>but</u> it has not been evaluated.

Use a comma with conjunctions.

> The report arrived today; <u>however</u>, it has not been evaluated.

Use a semicolon with adverbial conjunctions.

The words *however* and *therefore* appear frequently in business communication. Although they come between two related ideas, their relationship is a little closer to the second idea. The comma, which is a weak mark of punctuation, separates the adverbial conjunction from the second idea; the semicolon, a strong mark of punctuation, separates it even more definitively from the first. For accurate punctuation, then, *place a comma before coordinate conjunctions; place a semicolon before adverbial conjunctions and a comma after them.*

• Words That Show Relationships

Prepositions are used to show a relationship between a noun or objective-case pronoun and some other word in the sentence. Some examples are

> The file is <u>in</u> the desk.
> The file is <u>on</u> the desk.
> The file was taken <u>to</u> the desk.
> The file is <u>under</u> the desk.
> The file is <u>beside</u> the desk.
> The file was taken <u>from</u> the desk.

Prepositions normally do not appear at the beginnings or endings of simple sentences. Sometimes prepositions are unnecessarily attached to the ends of sentences.

> Original: Where is the superintendent <u>at</u>?
> Revised: Where is the superintendent?

> Original: What did he do that <u>for</u>?
> Revised: Why did he do that?

Sidebar notes:

Equally significant ideas: coordinating conjunction, use a comma. Ideas of unequal significance: subordinating conjunction, don't use a comma.

Adverbial conjunctions: semicolon before, comma after

Which is better? "Where do you live at?" or "Where do you live?"

Yet, prepositions can be effectively placed at the ends of sentences.

> Jan was less concerned about what she was living on than what she was living for.
>
> Before you can take anything out, you must put something in.

For purposes of contrast, the key words "for" and "in" need emphasis. Last-word position affords that emphasis. *Place prepositions at the ends of sentences only when doing so serves a useful purpose.*

Prepositions are sometimes repeated for purposes of clarity. Do these sentences have the same meanings?

> All majors must attain at least a C average in accounting, law, and finance.
>
> All majors must attain at least a C average in accounting, in law, and in finance.

In the first sentence, one average is computed—an average of all grades made in the three disciplines combined. The single preposition implies a single average. In the second, three averages are computed—the average in accounting courses only must be at least a C; in law courses only, a C; and in finance courses only, a C. Three prepositions imply three separate averages. Under the terms of the second sentence, a student who had a D average in accounting, an A in law, and an A in finance would still not have satisfied the academic requirements. *Repeat the preposition before each word in a series if doing so conveys the precise meaning intended.*

For a more thorough treatment of word-usage problems, consult an English reference book. For a list of words frequently misused, see the Appendix.

Summary

Errors in word usage cause lost meaning, lost time, distraction, and concern about the writer's or speaker's background. The following principles summarize the discussion of effective word usage.

Precise, Informal Words

- For vivid business communication, use specific words.
- For the informal writing that is practiced in business, use simple words instead of more complicated words that have the same meaning.

Redundancies

• To save time and space and to avoid distraction, do not use redundancies.

Parallelism

• Present multiple units in the same way grammatically.

Positive and Negative Words

• Rely mainly on positive words—words that speak of what can be done instead of what cannot be done, of the pleasant instead of the unpleasant.
• When the purpose is to sharpen contrast, or when positive words have not evoked the desired reaction, use negative words.

Condescending Words

• Avoid using condescending words.

Euphemisms

• Use euphemisms when the purpose is to present unpleasant thoughts politely and positively.
• Avoid using euphemisms when they will be taken as excessive or sarcastic.

Compliments and Flattery

• Use compliments judiciously.
• Avoid using flattery.

Demeaning Expressions

• Avoid using demeaning expressions.

Denotative and Connotative Words

• Rely mainly on denotative words or connotative words that will elicit a favorable reaction.

Words That Label (Nouns)

• For clear, emphatic writing, choose concrete nouns as subjects of sentences.
• Before a gerund, use the possessive form of noun or pronoun.

Words That Replace (Pronouns)

- Avoid using masculine pronouns that may be considered offensive.
- Avoid overusing "I" and other words that unnecessarily call attention to the writer.
- Avoid using the word "you" when the person it stands for is not obvious.
- For better human relations, use second person for presenting pleasant ideas and avoid using second person for presenting negative ideas.
- Cultivate a "you attitude"; it assists in effective use of second person.
- Use second person to emphasize an idea and third person to de-emphasize an idea.
- Make sure pronouns agree with their antecedents.
- Use nominative-case pronouns as subjects of sentences; use objective-case pronouns to follow verbs and prepositions.

Words That Show Action (Verbs)

- Use verbs that agree *in number* with the subjects of sentences.
- Use verbs that agree *in person* with their subjects.
- Avoid splitting infinitives.
- Use active verbs to present important points or to present pleasant ideas.
- Use passive verbs to present less significant points or to present unpleasant ideas.

Words That Describe (Adjectives and Adverbs)

- Avoid using adjectives and adverbs that are used too frequently by others, are overly strong, or are overly negative.
- Use a hyphen to join words that form a one-word describer of a noun that follows.
- Place a comma between coordinate adjectives.
- To maintain credibility, use only supported or supportable superlatives.
- For clarity, place an adverb or adjective close to the word it describes.

Words That Join (Conjunctions)

- For accurate punctuation, place a comma before coordinate conjunctions.

- Place a semicolon before adverbial conjunctions and a comma after them.

Words That Show Relationships (Prepositions)

- Place a preposition at the end of a sentence only when doing so serves a useful purpose.

- Repeat the preposition before each word in a series if doing so conveys the precise meaning intended.

About Language and Usage

Formal English is used in most academic and literary prose, and informal English is used in everyday speaking and writing. Both are correct, but substandard English is never correct. The following types of expressions are informal and not substandard:

Idioms are expressions peculiar to a language. We learn them early in life and use them easily even though they may misuse grammar and seem illogical: *keep in touch, catch a cold, have a try at, drop in.*

Colloquialisms are expressions commonly used in conversation but usually avoided in writing: *aren't I?; who, me?;* using *so* rather than *so that.*

Slang expressions have meanings popular with certain groups and are usually worn out in a short time. Some— such as *rascal*—eventually become accepted parts of language and of good usage. Slang is also peculiar to some age groups. Some slang words growing weak from use are *pad, cool, awesome, uptight,* and *far out.*

Speakers may add vividness to their speeches, but they do run risks of audience alienation by offending or confusing some listeners.

Exercises

Review Questions

Word Choice   For each pair of sentences, *which* is preferred? *Why* is it preferred?

1. **a.** I had a *writing instrument* in my pocket.
   b. I had a *ball-point pen* in my pocket.

2. **a.** We heard about *your injuries.*
   b. We heard about *your broken arm and the multiple lacerations on your back.*

3. **a.** The patient was unable to *ambulate.*
   b. The patient was unable to *walk.*

4. **a.** We have a *gift* for you.
   b. We have a *free gift* for you.

5. **a.** Most of her time was spent in *negotiation* with suppliers, conducting seminars, and working with committees.
   b. Most of her time was spent in *negotiating* with suppliers, conducting seminars, and working with committees.

6. **a.** Both pipe fitters were *fired* last week.
   b. Both pipe fitters were *let go* last week.

7. **a.** I *can't help* you until this task is finished.
   b. I *can help* you just as soon as this task is finished.

8. **a.** I've been promoted twice since I did work like you are doing, but I'll be glad to help you for an hour.
   b. I'll be glad to help you for an hour.

9. **a.** Tom told me about your *recent success.*
   b. Tom told me about your *receiving the suggestion-of-the-month award.*

10. **a.** Every year during the Christmas season, the Joneses send us a copy of their *bragg sheet.*
    b. Every year during the Christmas season, the Joneses send us *a summary of their activities for the year.*

Word Categories   Each sentence violates a principle discussed in the preceding pages. Identify the error.

Example: I shall appreciate you helping me.
The Error: Does not use the possessive form before a gerund.

11. She was astonished by me accepting so soon.
12. If a lawyer calls, tell him I'll be away until Monday.
13. This writer is eager for an explanation.
14. I have finished reading the research report; you can't tell whether the conclusions are valid.
15. You put the wrong set of figures in this table.
16. The article is to include a picture of the driver and I.
17. The professor excused Fred and I from the room.
18. Only one of the orders have been filled.
19. He don't drive fast.
20. We tried to quickly establish friendship.
21. You failed to sign the agreement.
22. Evaluation of the proposal will be done by our personnel committee.
23. The bids were ridiculously high.
24. The coach is happy about the come from behind victory.
25. We had a fast comfortable trip.
26. Our cafeteria serves the best coffee in the world.
27. John conducts all the morning seminars; but Harry conducts all the afternoon seminars.
28. The project is to be completed three weeks earlier than originally announced, therefore we need to hire six additional operators.
29. The caller didn't say where he lived at.
30. Jim took advantage of a once in a lifetime opportunity.

Exceptions   Give your answer to each question. Answers need not be in complete-sentence form.

31. Business writing is normally informal, but when is formal writing acceptable?
32. Simple words are normally preferred; but when would a difficult, technical term be justified?
33. In most situations, positive language is recommended; but when is negative language more appropriate?
34. Euphemisms can make unpleasant ideas seem less unpleasant, but under what conditions would a euphemism be detrimental?

35. Generally, business writers are encouraged to use denotative words; but under what conditions would connotative words be acceptable?

36. Normally, concrete nouns serve well as sentence subjects; but under what condition would abstract nouns serve better?

37. For good human relations, use of "you" is encouraged; but under what condition should "you" be avoided?

38. Normally, active voice is preferred; but when is passive voice better?

39. Superlatives are useful words, but when is their use detrimental?

40. The practice of ending a sentence with a preposition is usually discouraged, but when is a preposition appropriately used as the last word in a sentence?

Activities

Compose a sentence that has the characteristic described:

1. Employs parallel construction in a series of items.
2. Illustrates a euphemism.
3. Begins with a concrete noun.
4. Begins with an abstract noun and thus de-emphasizes an unpleasant thought.
5. Illustrates correct use of a pronoun to precede a gerund.
6. Employs a third-person pronoun.
7. Employs a nominative-case pronoun.
8. Employs an objective-case pronoun.
9. Uses active voice to emphasize a positive idea.
10. Uses passive voice to de-emphasize a negative idea.
11. Illustrates correct punctuation of a compound adjective.
12. Illustrates correct punctuation of coordinate adjectives.
13. Illustrates acceptable use of a superlative.
14. Illustrates correct punctuation of a sentence that has a coordinating conjunction.
15. Illustrates correct punctuation of a sentence that has an adverbial conjunction.

Using the Techniques of Style

In composing, as a general rule, run your pen through every other word you have written; you have no idea what vigor it will give your style.

SYDNEY SMITH, 1855

T he subject of the preceding chapter was words. The subject of this chapter is progressively larger units of thought: phrases, sentences, paragraphs, and compositions. Success in studying this chapter is at least partially dependent on a reader's willingness to think. When invited to answer a question, stop to present a mental answer. This prior intellectual involvement will increase the likelihood that the answer (which appears soon after the question) will be meaningful.

Ideas contained in a message are commonly referred to as "content." The *way ideas are expressed* is referred to as "style." Style, then, involves choosing the right words to build effective phrases, sentences, paragraphs, and compositions.

Computer programs are now available to aid style improvement. The software is advertised in such publications as *Personal Publishing, Personal Computing,* and *Portable Computer.* Stores that sell computer software can be very helpful in selecting a suitable program. Typically, the writer (1) composes at the keyboard, (2) gives a command for the computer to analyze the writing, (3) studies the computer's analysis (which appears between the lines of the double-spaced composition), and (4) revises. For example, in the space beneath a sentence that says "Authorization of this procedure is recommended, . . ." the computer may say, "Sentence begins with a long, abstract noun and uses passive construction. In rewriting, try 'authorize' and. . . ."

Can computers actually analyze writing?

Such criticism can be extremely valuable, but those who *already* know the most about composition will benefit most from such programs. Obviously, a writer who has an effective style will need to spend less time revising and will be more likely to understand and appreciate the computer's suggestions. Knowing about the availability of such programs, you might think, "Why bother to learn now? The computer will solve my writing problems later." The computer, though, will do nothing more than suggest ways to improve. It may be friendly, but it won't do the work.

The more you already know about writing the more a computer can help you improve.

One writing-analysis program reportedly checks compositions against 3,000 principles of English! Compared with that number, this chapter presents very few—but they are the ones most frequently encountered. For those of you who already know these principles, reading the chapter will increase the likelihood that you will use them effectively. For those of you who don't know or may have forgotten them, these principles are worth learning. As a preliminary check to see whether you *already* know the stylistic principles discussed in this chapter, take the following pretest:

Instructions

Cover the answer to the first question with a sheet of paper, mentally form an answer to the question, slide the paper down, and read the answer. Does your criticism of the style employed in each of the sentences agree with the answers given?

Sample: Where is the boss at?	Unnecessarily employs a preposition as the last word. "Where is the boss?" is sufficient.
1. I am sure you will agree that the program was successful.	The expression of certainty is unjustified. If the author *can* be sure, the idea probably is known already and need not be expressed. If the author can't be sure, the statement is not true.
2. The pamphlet was sent under separate cover.	"Under separate cover" is a worn expression. Such words as "also," "yesterday," or "in another envelope," and so on could be substituted.
3. Your complaint has been evaluated.	"Complaint" sounds negative or accusing. "Request" would be better. Or perhaps the whole statement could be left to implication.
4. The writer appreciated your thoughtfulness.	"The writer" is a poor substitute for "I." It's longer and implies that the author wants to insert self into the sentence without being discredited for the use of first person.
5. If work is begun soon.	The words do not constitute a complete sentence.
6. While reading the paper, my dog disappeared.	The participial phrase dangles; that is, it isn't attached to the right noun. As is, the sentence

(continued)

	implies that the dog was reading. "While I was reading the paper, my dog disappeared" or "While reading the paper, I noticed that my dog had disappeared" are acceptable revisions.
7. There are two possible answers to that question.	The sentence begins with an expletive (the meaningless word "there") and thus presents the verb before presenting the noun. Better writing presents the noun first: "That question has two possible answers" or "The answers to that question are. . . ."
8. The purpose of school is to learn.	The idea in this sentence is known already. The reader could be insulted by this platitude.
9. A very important criterion (speed) was overlooked in the evaluation.	An appositive that deserves emphasis is de-emphasized through use of parentheses instead of dashes. That is, . . . criterion—speed—was. . . .)
10. I endorsed your check and deposited it.	The sentence conveys an idea that need not be stated in words. The check was obviously endorsed or it would not have been deposited. Thus, "I deposited your check."

Phrases

A phrase is a group of words that does not constitute a complete sentence. Texts in grammar have more complete discussions of phrases, but those selected for discussion here commonly present problems in business writing.

• Certainties

Read the following pairs of sentences, paying attention to the underscored phrases. Which—the first or the second—is better?

I <u>am sure</u> you will agree that the instructions are clear.
<u>Reexamine</u> the instructions to see whether they are clear.

I <u>know</u> you have read Chapter 10.
Chapter 10 was assigned last week.

In each pair, the author of the first sentence seems to be making a declaration of certainty when certainty is hardly possible. If through prior discussion the speaker *can* be sure of agreement, the first sentence is unnecessary. If the speaker really *knows* the chapter has been read, the listener is probably already aware of the idea contained in the sentence. When the phrases "I know" and "I am sure" *cannot* be true, the speaker or writer who uses them risks transmitting a between-the-lines message that warns the reader by saying "Watch out—some of my other ideas may be stretched, too."

The expression "as you know" is to be avoided for the same reasons: the receivers either already know that they know and the words are unnecessary, or the words are simply inaccurate. *Avoid expressions of certainty when certainty is hardly possible.*

What is your reaction when "As you know," precedes an idea you don't know?

• Clichés

Phrases that have become overused are called *clichés*. In each sentence, which phrase is well worn?

Please send a reply at your earliest convenience.
A booklet is being sent under separate cover.
Enclosed please find a copy of my transcript.

"At your earliest convenience," "under separate cover," and "Enclosed please find" have been used so much that they no longer appear original. Now, look at the same sentences without the clichés:

Please send a reply <u>as soon as you can</u>.
The booklet is being sent <u>in a larger envelope</u>.
<u>The enclosed transcript</u> should answer most of your questions.

Clichés can make reading monotonous, and they can make a writer seem like a copier. But they present a still more serious problem. Suppose Trisha is sitting in the waiting room of an office. A man enters and says to the receptionist, "I'm George; don't you look gorgeous today." After filling out forms, he takes a seat by Trisha and uses the same line. Because Trisha knows the line has been used before, she may not take it as any sort of a compliment. George has an expression he can use without thinking and possibly without meaning. Between the lines, a worn expression can convey such messages as these: "You are nothing

Do clichés boost a reader's ego?

special." "For you, I won't bother to think; the phrases I use in talking with others are surely good enough for you." Some more clichés are discussed on the following pages.

according to our records, our records indicate

Since everyone knows business firms keep records, the phrase "Our records indicate your last payment was due on January 5" is not necessary unless the person should contrast *his* or *her* records with others that are being discussed. If not, then the same idea is communicated more simply and directly by saying, "You. last payment was due on January 5." However, if the purpose is to contrast records, the phrases may be useful. ("According to the client's records, the account is paid; according to our records, it isn't.")

at an early date

The expression is vague. Be specific. *Soon* is an improvement. Giving the exact date is more helpful.

at this time

The expression means *now,* so why not say *now?* It is shorter and less overused. Also, the words may imply (without the writer's intent) that *another* time is being considered.

at this writing, at this point in time

When else could it be? Say now *if* an expression is necessary.

attached please find, please find enclosed, enclosed you will find

These expressions seem to imply that something has been hidden or that locating it may be difficult. In addition, they usually tell what is known already—that the letter accompanies other material. References to enclosures can be made in *sentences* that also say something else, such as "Refer to page 7 of the enclosed folder to see the basic steps of operation."

claim, complaint

In letters to customers, these words suggest negative thoughts. No one wants to learn that a letter asking for a legitimate adjustment has been branded as a *complaint*. And no one would be pleased to read a sentence that says, "You *claim* the cog was stripped when the drill was installed." To some people, the words *complaint* and *claim* suggest a request for something to which they are not entitled. "We appreciate your letter of March 18" is better than "We appreciate your complaint of March 18."

Avoid the word "complaint" with second person.

have a nice day

Imagine yourself as seventh in line at a grocery-store checkout counter. By the time you are ready to leave, the clerk has said "Have a nice day" to the six who preceded you. Now, it's your turn. Do the words have much meaning? Because the same expression is used for everyone, it may have little meaning for anyone. If the words are *not* really meant, the phoniness will probably be detected.

> hereto, herewith, hereby, said, above, same, thereof, wherein, hereinafter

All these words are overused law terms. They seem to convey an unneeded tone of legality and formality.

> I have your letter, your letter has been given to me for reply

These ideas will be understood without taking time to express them.

> I remain

Who would think of saying, "I remain," or "I shall remain," if the expression had not been learned from others? In business letters, the expression is useless and should be omitted.

> no problem

Although the words *deny* the existence of a problem, they are used in discussing something that *is* a problem. "If you don't have the cash, no problem; we accept credit-card purchases." Since a shortage of money is a problem, *no problem* is best omitted.

> permit me to say

Asking permission to make a statement is not necessary. Besides, asking permission and then immediately proceeding without it may imply that we are rude or are saying something that should not be said.

> please contact me if you have any further questions

If this sentence says exactly what is meant, and if the receiver has not encountered it frequently before, its use is not especially objectionable. However, it does have these disadvantages: (1) it implies doubt about whether other questions have been answered adequately, (2) it is especially out of place if the preceding discussion has not been about *questions,* and (3) it may actually encourage needless correspondence.

> pursuant to your request, referring to your request, in reference to your letter

These expressions often appear at the beginning of letters. Readers recognize them as coming from a person who would rather copy than

Even pleasant-sounding words can irritate.

Some clichés should be changed to words that sound more original; others should be eliminated.

think—someone who says the same thing at the beginning of all letters. Such beginnings can have meaning when they identify the reply with a specific piece of correspondence. But referring to previous correspondence is more smoothly done in an indirect manner. Instead of saying, "Pursuant to your January 21 request for a catalog, we are sending it to you today," say, "The catalog you requested on January 21 was mailed today."

recent date

Be specific. State the exact date.

take this opportunity

Save time by getting right into the subject.

the writer, the undersigned

Such expressions suggest that we are trying to give the impression of modesty. Using *I* too frequently is monotonous; it also places greater emphasis on the writer than on the reader. But obvious attempts to circumvent *I* are just as bad. Instead of "I found that sales and collection departments actually have common goals," or "The writer found that sales and collection departments actually have common goals," rephrase to "The survey showed that sales and collection departments actually have common goals," or "Sales and collection departments, according to the survey, actually have common goals."

Is "the writer" a good substitute for "I"?

thanking you in advance

The expression seems to say, "I know you will do as I have asked you to do. After you do it, I will be grateful. Instead of sending a note of gratitude later, I'll just save time (and a stamp) by expressing my thanks now." To express gratitude for expected or requested action, "I shall appreciate your (action)" or "If you will (action), I shall be grateful" are less worn than "Thank you in advance."

this letter is for the purpose of, this will acknowledge receipt of

These words are usually just space fillers that warm up to the real message. Omit them and get right to the point.

trusting you will, trusting this is, we hope, we trust, I hope, I trust

Not only are these expressions overused, they introduce the unpleasant idea of doubt. If we say, "We trust this is the information you wanted," we are suggesting our own doubts, and the reader may also begin to doubt. The expression should be omitted in most cases.

under separate cover

Instead of using this nebulous expression, we can be specific by saying that a package is being sent by express or parcel post.

wish to, would like to

These words may convey *no* meaning, or they may convey the *wrong* meaning. "We wish to say that we have considered the idea" probably means "We have considered the idea." "We would like to recommend Mr. Clark" may be taken to mean either "We recommend Mr. Clark" or "Recommending Mr. Clark would be a pleasure, *if we could.*"

you know

This expression is more common in spoken than in written expression. "The technique is, you know, complicated. It took us, you know, many weeks to develop." The "you know" is distracting, meaningless, or inaccurate—all of which make it objectionable.

The following list contains many other expressions that have become clichés:

Can you add to this list?

above (as in "if the above is")	in regard to
acknowledge receipt of	in terms of
along this line	in the event that
are in receipt of	in the near future
as a matter of fact	inasmuch as
as the case may be	kindly (as in "kindly fill out")
as to	meet with your approval
as yet we have not heard from you	party (as in "another party wants")
at all times	please be advised that
at an early date	previous to
avail yourself of the opportunity	prior to
contact (as in "please contact us")	relative to
due to the fact that	same (as in "have cashed same")
for your information	take the liberty
in accordance with	we feel
in due course	we regret to inform
	would say

From a writer's or speaker's point of view, some of the preceding phrases are convenient; they can be used easily and quickly. But to avoid monotony, to keep from seeming to have no originality, and to avoid possible human relations problems, *avoid clichés.*

• Brevity

Ideas that are sufficiently implied need not be stated. For example,

Are implications
connotative or
denotative?

> She took the test and passed it.

If she passed the test, she obviously took it. The sentence can be shortened:

> She passed the test.

Observe how the following sentences on the right have been improved by eliminating the words that can be implied:

The <u>auditor reviewed the figures and concluded</u> that they were accurate.	The *auditor concluded* that the figures were accurate.
The <u>editor checked the transcript and found</u> three spelling errors.	The *editor found* three spelling errors in the transcript.

Sometimes sentences can be shortened by using suffixes or prefixes and making any necessary changes in word form: *-ful, -ly, -ing, -iest, -ed, -less, -able, -ible, -ic, -ical, -ous,* or *-ious.* For example:

Prefixes and suffixes
can reduce
wordiness.

She was a typist <u>who took great care.</u>	*She was a careful* typist.
He waited <u>in an impatient</u> manner.	He waited *impatiently.*
Carpenters lose time <u>when they have to use</u> a standard hammer.	Carpenters lose time *by using a standard hammer.*
the work <u>that he had not finished</u>	his *unfinished* work
the machine <u>that made the most noise</u>	the *noisiest* machine
the workers <u>who have the most skill</u>	the *most skilled* workers
Omit the expressions <u>for which you have no use.</u>	Omit *useless* expressions.
Only half the material <u>could be used.</u>	Only half the material *was usable.*
a person <u>with a lot of energy</u>	an *energetic* person
<u>arranged according to the alphabet</u>	*in alphabetical order*
a speech <u>that was full of pomp</u>	a *pompous* speech
a person <u>of great industry</u>	an *industrious* person

The expressions on the right represent useful techniques for saving space. However, the ones on the left cannot be categorically condemned. Sometimes, their use provides just the right *emphasis*.

Using a *compound adjective* often helps to reduce the number of words required to express an idea.

He wrote a report that was up to the minute.	He wrote an *up-to-the-minute* report.
They were engaged in an enterprise that was first class.	They were engaged in a *first-class* enterprise.
His policy of going slowly was well received.	His *go-slow* policy was well received.

Compound adjectives appear *before* the nouns they modify.

By using the compound adjectives, we reduce the number of words required to express our idea and thus save the reader a little time.

- ## Surprise, Doubt, and Judgment

Phrases that reveal a writer's surprise about a reader's behavior can cause problems in human relations. Why are the following sentences risky?

I am surprised that you did not accept.
I just cannot understand your attitude.

"I am surprised" risks conveying something like "I am accustomed to normal behavior. Yours is abnormal and therefore bad or totally unjustified." "I cannot understand" takes the same risks. Such expressions are particularly offensive to receivers because they seem to place them in a position of recognized inferiority.

What would "I'm surprised you won" connote?

Similarly, expressions that reveal judgment of recipients' emotional balance are very risky. "I am so sorry you are upset" may be intended as a heart-felt apology, but the "I am sorry" can be completely overshadowed by "you are upset." It could mean "Your conduct is such that I recognize your lack of self-control. Because of your condition, you could not be thinking rationally." *Avoid expressions of surprise, doubt, and judgment when they would be interpreted as put-downs of individuals.*

Could "Sorry to upset you" add to (instead of allay) irritation?

Sentences

For a complete review of sentences, consult an English handbook. The following discussion identifies problems and techniques most likely to be encountered by business writers.

• Structure

All sentences have at least two parts: *subject* and *verb*.

Sally	retired.
(subject)	*(verb)*

The rains	came.
(subject)	*(verb)*

In addition to subject and verb, a sentence may have additional words for completion of their meaning. These words are called *complements:*

Sally	retired	in her twenty-fifth year.
(subject)	*(verb)*	*(complement)*

The grade	was changed	to a B.
(subject)	*(verb)*	*(complement)*

The children	played	baseball.
(subject)	*(verb)*	*(complement)*

Observe from the preceding examples that a complement may be expressed in one word (the third sentence) or more than one word (the first and second).

A group of words that does not express a complete thought (that isn't a sentence) is called a *phrase* or a *clause*. A phrase does not include a subject and a verb; a clause does. In the following examples, the phrases and clauses are underscored:

Phrases: One <u>of the workers</u> was absent.
The people <u>in that room</u> have voted.
The electrician fell <u>while replacing the socket.</u>

Clauses:

As the president	reported this morning...
(subject)	*(verb)*

If construction	is begun in January...
(subject)	*(verb)*

...if I	can pay the rent.
(subject)	*(verb)*

Could a dependent clause serve as a complete sentence?

Clauses are divided into two categories: dependent and independent. A dependent clause does not convey a complete thought. The preceding illustrations are dependent. An independent clause does convey a complete thought; it could be a complete sentence if presented alone:

As the president reported this morning,	sales increased in May.
(dependent clause)	*(independent clause)*

If work is begun in March,	the job can be completed in July.
(dependent clause)	*(independent clause)*

I can keep my apartment	if I can pay the rent.
(independent clause)	*(dependent clause)*

Although an independent clause can be stated as a separate sentence, a dependent clause cannot. Without the remainder of the sentence, "As the president reported this morning" does not convey a complete thought and should not be presented as a separate sentence. When a *sentence fragment* (a portion of a sentence) is presented as a separate sentence, readers become confused and distracted.

Sentences fall into four categories: *simple, compound, complex,* and *compound–complex:*

Simple:	The parents went to work.	
Compound:	The parents went to work, and the children went to school.	Two independent clauses
Complex:	As I expected, the parents went to work.	A dependent and an independent clause
Compound–complex:	As I expected, the parents went to work; but they plan to return before five o'clock.	A dependent clause and two independent clauses

In the preceding examples, note the use of punctuation to separate one clause from another. When punctuation is omitted or used incorrectly, the result is usually a *run-on* sentence. Run-on sentences also result from the use of too many clauses in one sentence.

Is a coordinating conjunction sometimes preceded by a *semicolon?*

Original:	New forms have been ordered they should be delivered next Friday.
Revisions:	New forms have been ordered. They should be delivered next Friday.

New forms have been ordered, and they should be delivered next Friday.

New forms have been ordered; they should be delivered next Friday.

The new forms, which were ordered last week, should be delivered next Friday.

Original: New forms were delivered today, the number of questions has been reduced from fifteen to five, this simplification will reduce office work by 25 percent.

Revision: New forms were delivered today. Because the number of questions has been reduced from fifteen to five, office work will be reduced by 25 percent.

• Misplaced Elements

Place pronouns close to the words for which they stand.

A common problem in sentence structure is the placement of words, clauses, or phrases in the wrong position:

Original: We have taken the check to the bank, which was unsigned.

The sentence is confusing (or amusing) because it seems to imply that the bank was unsigned. That impression is given because the "which" clause is placed closer to "bank" than to "check."

Revised: We have taken the check, which was unsigned, to the bank.

Similarly, the following sentences have very different meanings:

The questionnaire, which has some serious defects, is being returned to the committee.	This sentence means the questionnaire is defective.
The questionnaire is being returned to the committee, which has some serious defects.	This sentence means the committee is defective.

• Dangling Participial Phrases

The following sentences illustrate a very common (and sometimes very serious) type of error. What causes the confusion?

Being new to our city, I extend a welcome to you.
While taking an exam, the teacher noticed Sam was turning pale.
Typing at seventy-five words per minute, a few errors were made.

Reexamine all three sentences. Each is complex. Each begins with a dependent phrase. The dependent phrase speaks of action without revealing who the doer is. "Being new to our city" does not reveal *who* is new. "While taking an exam" does not reveal *who* is taking an exam. "Typing at seventy-five words per minute" does not reveal *who* is typing. Because the word *I* comes immediately after the idea of being *new,* the newness is attributed to the speaker. But, surely, the person being spoken to is the newcomer. The second sentence implies that "the teacher" was taking an exam. The third sentence implies that "a few errors" were doing the typing.

When a sentence begins by identifying action without revealing who the doer is, the subject of the independent clause gets credit for that action regardless of whether that credit is justified. Such sentences can be corrected in three different ways:

1. Change the introductory (beginning) phrase to a dependent clause:

   Since you are new to our city, I extend a welcome to you.
   While Sam was taking an exam, the teacher noticed he (Sam) was turning pale.
   While Jane was typing at seventy-five words per minute, she made a few errors.

   In these revisions, confusion is removed because action and actor in the dependent clause are close together.

2. Change the *subject of* the independent clause:

   Being new to our city, you are extended a warm welcome.
   While taking an exam, Sam turned pale and the teacher noticed his condition.
   Typing at seventy-five words per minute, Jane made a few errors.

   Confusion is removed because the doer of the action mentioned in the phrase is introduced immediately after the phrase.

3. Begin the sentence with the independent clause.

   I extend a welcome to you, being new to our city.
   The teacher noticed Sam was turning pale while taking an exam.
   A few errors were made because the paper was typed at seventy-five words per minute.

   In these revisions, confusion is removed because the subject of the independent clause is not placed close enough to action of the dependent phrase to merit association with it.

To "dangle" is to "hang loosely." A phrase dangles if it is not clearly attached to the appropriate noun or pronoun.

Why is a dangling participial phrase a more serious error than a redundancy?

The problem illustrated in the preceding sentences is the *dangling participial phrase*. "Being new to our city, I extend a welcome to you" is misleading because the introductory phrase dangles—is not properly attached to its doer. *When the introductory phrase identifies action without revealing the doer, present the doer immediately after the phrase.* In other words, the subject of an independent clause is presumed to be the doer of any action mentioned in a dependent phrase that precedes it.

• Expletives

By definition, an *expletive* is a meaningless word. Find the meaningless word in the following sentence:

> There is to be an addendum made to the policy.

Try to grasp the true meaning of "there." Since it is not being used in the sense of contrast with *here,* it does not mean "location." The same idea can be presented in fewer words:

> An addendum is to be made to the policy.

What are the disadvantages of employing expletives?

In addition to being shorter, the revised sentence has another advantage: It presents words in the normal sequence of the English sentence—subject, verb, complement. In the original sentence, a reader is exposed to the verb ("is") before knowing what the sentence is about. Being unusual, such sentences make reading a little more difficult.

Are expletives considered grammatical errors?

Expletive beginnings are not considered grammatical errors but are seldom advisable. Usually any sentence that begins with *There is, there are,* etc., can be improved upon. Also, sentences that begin with *It is* can usually be improved upon:

> Original: It is probable that our rules should be changed.
> Revised: Our rules probably should be changed.

> Original: It is encouraging to note that sales have increased this month.
> Revised: Sales have increased this month; the figures are encouraging.

As a sentence beginning, "It is" is sometimes recommended; sometimes, not.

Although each of the preceding original sentences does have a subject ("It") that precedes the verb ("is"), the subject is vague; only after having read the entire sentence do we become aware of what "It" means. The revisions employ fewer words, and they employ the more conventional subject–verb–complement pattern. Of course the word *it* can serve as a first word when the antecedent is in a preceding sentence:

> ...of this document. It is being revised....

Seeing "It" before the verb "is," we know that "It" stands for "document." Such a pronoun can serve well as a coherence technique, and its use is not to be discouraged at all. *Avoid expletive beginnings.*

• Platitudes

A platitude is a direct statement of an idea that almost anyone would know already:

> Employees like to be well paid.
> Team members should cooperate with one another.
> Music is different from noise.

Because the message in such a sentence is so elementary, a receiver is insulted. The negative reaction could interfere with reception of the message from other sentences. *Avoid platitudes.*

Do platitudes influence human relationships?

• Voice

If a sentence is in the *active voice,* the subject is a doer of action. If a sentence is in the *passive voice,* the subject is not a doer; rather the subject is acted upon. (See the discussion of active and passive verbs in Chapter 4.)

> Active voice: Angela wrote the report.
> Passive voice: The report was written by Angela.

The active sentence draws attention to Angela. The passive sentence draws attention to the report. Readers normally get more vivid imagery when sentences are active. The first sentence invites the reader to see a woman using a pen or a word processor. The second directs attention to a completed report. The choice of either active or passive voice is determined by the writer's purpose.

Active sentences are more vivid than passive sentences.

From the discussion of tone, recall that positive ideas should be emphasized and negative ideas should be de-emphasized. Which sentence places more accent on the *positive* idea?

> Jerry completed the job ahead of schedule.
> The job was completed ahead of schedule.

Since a person (Jerry) is the subject of the first sentence, and since people are easily envisioned in action, the first sentence is more vivid. *For presenting positive ideas, use the active voice.*

Normally, use active sentences for pleasant ideas; use passive sentences for negative ideas.

Which of the following sentences places greater emphasis on the *negative* idea?

Jerry completed the job two months behind schedule.
The job was completed two months behind schedule.

Again, the first sentence, which is active, is more vivid. But normally negative ideas should be toned down. Because the idea is negative, Jerry would probably appreciate being taken out of the picture. Because the second sentence is in the passive voice, it places more emphasis on the job than on who failed to complete it. *For presenting negative ideas, use the passive voice.*

• Mood

Sometimes, the tone of a message can be improved by switching to the subjunctive mood. Subjunctive sentences employ such conditional words as *if, could, would, might,* and *wish.* Subjunctive sentences speak of conditions contrary to fact, of doubt, or of possibility. In each pair, the second sentence is subjunctive. Which seems more diplomatic?

Does "We wish we could" *connote* "We can't," or does it *denote* "We can't"?

I cannot attend the convention with you.
I wish I could attend the convention with you.

I am unable to accept your invitation.
If I accepted your invitation, I would have to miss my parents' anniversary party.

I cannot pay until next month.
I wish I could pay this month, but I must pay my taxes instead.

In all three pairs, a negative idea is involved; but the second sentence transmits the negative idea in positive language. Positive language is more diplomatic. In the second and third pairs, the revised sentences include a reason. Because a reason is included, the negative idea seems less objectionable and tone is thus improved.

Tone is important, but clarity is even more important. The revised sentence in each of the preceding pairs sufficiently *implies* the unpleasant idea without stating it directly. If for any reason a writer suspects the implication is not sufficiently strong, a direct statement in negative terms is preferable. *For tactful presentation of an unpleasant thought, consider stating it in the subjunctive mood.*

• Emphasis

A landscape artist wants some points in a picture to stand out boldly and others to get little attention. A musician sounds some notes loudly and others softly. Likewise, a writer or speaker wants some ideas to be *emphasized* and others to be *de-emphasized*. Normally, pleasant and important ideas should be emphasized; unpleasant and insignificant ideas should be de-emphasized.

Normally, negative ideas should be subordinated.

About Language and Usage

As a matter of usage, people should use the prefix *ex* and the word *former* correctly when referring to a relationship that existed previously. When *ex* is attached to a term, the new term designates the person who held the title immediately before the current holder. For example,

President George Bush
Ex-president Ronald Reagan
Former presidents Jimmy Carter, Gerald Ford, et al.

A man or woman who has been married twice prior to the current marriage has a spouse, an ex-spouse, and a former spouse. In some fraternal organizations and service clubs, all former presidents are labeled *past* presidents and the ex-president is called the *immediate* past president.

Like clarity, emphasis is influenced by sentence structure. Which sentence places more emphasis on the idea of John's taking a job?

John took a job in insurance.
John took a job in insurance, but he really preferred a job in accounting.

The first sentence has one independent clause. Because no other idea competes with it for attention, its idea is emphasized. *For emphasis, place an idea in a simple sentence.*

Which sentence places more emphasis on the idea of John's taking a job?

For stating an important idea, is a simple sentence better than a compound sentence?

John took a job in insurance, but he really preferred a job in accounting.

Although he took a job in insurance, John really preferred a job in accounting.

Note that the first sentence is compound; the second, complex. In the first sentence, the idea of taking a job is in an independent clause. Because an independent clause would make sense if the rest of the sentence were omitted, an independent clause is more emphatic than a dependent clause. In the second sentence, the idea of taking a job is in a dependent clause. By itself, the clause would not make complete sense. Compared with the independent clause that follows ("John really preferred...."), the idea in the dependent clause is de-emphasized. *For emphasis, place an idea in an independent clause; for de-emphasis, place an idea in a dependent clause.*

Which sentence places more emphasis on the idea of *success*?

The mission was successful because of....
The mission was successful; this success is attributed to....

In the second sentence a form of "success" is repeated. *For emphasis of a word, let it appear more than once in a sentence.*

In each pair, which sentence places more emphasis on the words *success* and *failure*?

The project was a success; without your efforts, it would have been a failure.
Your efforts contributed to the success of the project; otherwise, failure would have been the result.

Success resulted from your efforts; failure would have resulted without them.
The project was successful because of your efforts; without them, failure would have been the result.

In the first sentence, "success" and "failure" appear as the *last* words in their clauses. In the third sentence, "success" and "failure" appear as the *first* words in their clauses. For attention, words that appear first compete only with words that follow; words that appear last compete only with words that precede. *For emphasis of a word, let it appear first or last in a sentence or clause.*

Sometimes, the sting of an unpleasant thought can be reduced by placing that thought in the same sentence with a pleasant thought:

Original: Another seven points and your overall score would have been considered passing.

Revised: Another seven points and your overall score would have

Should significant ideas be placed in dependent clauses?

Why place a negative idea and a positive idea in the same sentence?

been considered passing, <u>but your score in chemistry was in the ninety-sixth percentile.</u>

Original: Because of increased taxes and insurance, you are obligated to increase your monthly payments by $50.

Revised: Because of increased taxes and insurance, you are obligated to increase your monthly payments by $50; <u>but, from last year's figures, your home is increasing in value at the monthly rate of $150.</u>

For improved tone, place a positive idea in the same sentence with a negative idea.

In the following sentences, the ideas are the same; but the emphasis is different:

The problems have been narrowed into three categories: absenteeism, tardiness, and alcoholism.
The problems have been narrowed into three categories: (1) absenteeism, (2) tardiness, and (3) alcoholism.

> **What is the effect of placing a number before each unit in a series?**

In the second sentence, the words preceded by numbers get special attention. They are easier to locate when a page is reviewed. If the preceding and following sentences on the page contain no numbers, the words with numbers take on special significance. The significance can be magnified even further:

The problems have been narrowed into three categories: absenteeism, tardiness, and alcoholism.
The problems have been narrowed into three categories:
   a.   Absenteeism
   b.   Tardiness
   c.   Alcoholism

> **When other ideas are in paragraph form, tabulated ideas are emphatic.**

The preceding example employs a technique referred to as "tabulation." Units of a series are placed in a column and indented (instead of being placed side by side). Because each unit in the series is on a line by itself (where it does not have to compete for attention), and because the arrangement consumes more space on the page, a tabulated series is attention getting. On typewriter keyboards, a special "tab" key facilitates making the indention needed for keyboarding columnar (tabulated) items.

> **Enumerated ideas draw special attention.**

A letter assigned to a unit has the same effect as a number. In the second sentence, each of the three elements is emphasized because it appears on a line by itself, where it is not competing with other words for attention. *For emphasis of units in a series, precede each element by a number or letter; for still further emphasis, tabulate the series.*

Careful writers employ punctuation marks for emphasis and de-emphasis, particularly when sentences contain appositives. An *appositive* is a word that purposefully repeats or explains a preceding word. Upon reading each of the following sentences, try to decide whether the appositive ("Cal Thomas") is emphasized or de-emphasized.

Four ways to punctuate an appositive.

The job was completed in two days by one man (Cal Thomas).
The job was completed in two days by one man, Cal Thomas.
The job was completed in two days by one man—Cal Thomas.
The job was completed in two days by one man: Cal Thomas.

Parentheses label an idea as parenthetical; it could be left out. An idea that could be omitted is not thought of as particularly important. Use of parentheses is like saying "The name is not especially important, but just in case it is of interest, here it is." The comma in the second sentence implies neither emphasis nor de-emphasis. "One man" and who that man is are of about equal importance. The dash in the third sentence is considered a strong mark of punctuation. Requiring two strokes on the keyboard, the dash looks longer and stronger than a comma. In oral presentation, a word preceded by a long pause gets special emphasis. Likewise, a dash attaches special emphasis to an appositive. The colon in the last sentence serves the same purpose as the dash. Requiring two dots and two keyboard spaces after it, a colon is a strong mark of punctuation; it serves to magnify the appositive. *For appositives, use parentheses for de-emphasis, a comma for neutral emphasis, and a dash or colon for emphasis.*

Another way to emphasize or de-emphasize an idea is to include words that label it:

But most important of all....
A less significant aspect was....

For emphasis or de-emphasis, attach words that label ideas as significant or insignificant.

• Punctuation

Speakers use pauses and voice inflection to assist listeners in extracting meaning from sentences. Similarly, writers use punctuation marks. For both writers and readers, knowledge of punctuation is essential.

In the preceding pages, sentences used to illustrate *other* principles also illustrate principles of punctuation.

Place a comma before the conjunction in a compound sentence.

I wanted to pay this month, but I must pay my taxes instead.
The reports are ready for editing, and the statements are ready
for checking.

Place a comma after a dependent clause that precedes an independent clause.

As I expected, the parents went to work.
If work is begun in March, the job can be completed in July.

Place a comma before and after a parenthetical phrase.

The typist, not the secretary, is responsible.
Management does, as I learned today, plan to revise pay scales in
January.

Place a comma between coordinate adjectives.

Jane was asked to fill out a long, complicated questionnaire.
The system provides cold, dry air.

For appositives, determine the punctuation by the amount of emphasis desired.

We had one problem, weather.	Neutral emphasis
We had one problem (weather).	De-emphasis
We had one problem: weather.	Emphasis
We had one problem—weather.	Emphasis

Place a comma after the units in a series (except the final unit, which
is followed by a period).

All majors must attain a C average in accounting, law, and
finance.
Our primary problems are in absenteeism, tardiness, and
alcoholism.

Place a colon before a series if the series is preceded by a complete
thought.

The problems have been narrowed into three categories:
absenteeism, tardiness, and alcoholism.
Three items are essential: pencil, paper, and eraser.

Place a semicolon before an adverbial conjunction and a comma
after it.

The report arrived today; however, it has not been evaluated.
Your efforts contributed to the success of the project; otherwise,
failure would have been the result.

**Omitting a
conjunction is an
acceptable practice.**

Place a semicolon between independent clauses when the conjunction is omitted.

> Your score was 63; passing scores were 69 or more.
> The recommendations arrived today; the judge checked them thoroughly.

Place a semicolon before the conjunction in a compound–complex sentence.

> As I expected, the parents went to work; but they plan to return before five o'clock.
> The parents went to work; but, as I expected, they returned before five o'clock.

Use hyphens to join words that form a compound adjective.

> He wrote an up-to-the-minute report.
> Diana applied for a two-week vacation.

For a more thorough review of punctuation, see the Appendix.

Paragraphs

A paragraph is one or more sentences that discuss a single portion of a topic. For example, consider a leaflet written to accompany a telephone answering machine that has been purchased. The overall topic is how to get satisfactory performance from the machine. One portion of that topic is assembly. Sentences that list the steps can appear as one paragraph, perhaps with steps numbered. Another portion (paragraph) would discuss operation; another, maintenance. Within each paragraph, one of the sentences serves a special function.

• Topic Sentence

**A topic sentence *may*
be stated at the *end*
of a paragraph.**

Typically, paragraphs contain one sentence that identifies the portion of the topic being discussed and presents the central idea. That sentence is commonly called a "topic" sentence. For example, "To assemble your new answering machine, take the following steps in the order presented: Step 1. . . ." In this illustration, the topic sentence *precedes* details. Such paragraphs are called *deductive* paragraphs. When topic sentences *follow* details, the paragraphs are called *inductive* paragraphs. Readers appreciate consistency in the placement of topic sentences. Once they catch on to the writer's pattern, they know where to look for main ideas.

When the subject matter is complicated and the details are numerous, paragraphs sometimes begin with a main idea, follow with details, and end with a summarizing sentence. But the main idea may not be in the first sentence; the idea may need a preliminary statement. For a writer, composition is simplified if a basic pattern (inductive or deductive) is selected and employed. That consistency simplifies the reader's task as well.

Consideration of the reader determines whether to use the inductive or deductive paragraph. If a reader might be antagonized by the topic sentence in a deductive paragraph, antagonism can be avoided by leading up to the topic sentence (making the paragraph inductive). If a writer wants to encourage reader involvement (to generate a little concern about where the details are leading), inductive paragraphs are recommended. Inductive paragraphs can be especially effective if the topic sentence strikes the reader as confirmation of a conclusion the reader has drawn from the preceding details.

These suggestions hardly apply to the first and last sentences of letters. Such sentences frequently appear as single-sentence paragraphs. But for reports and long paragraphs of letters, *strive for paragraphs that are consistently deductive or consistently inductive.* Regardless of which is selected, topic sentences are clearly linked with details that precede or follow.

If a paragraph is inductive, might a reader know the content of the topic sentence before reading it?

• Coherence

Although the word *coherence* is used sometimes to mean "clarity" or "understandability," it is used throughout this text to mean "cohesion." If writing or speaking is coherent, the sentences stick together and each sentence is in some way linked to the preceding sentences. The following techniques for linking sentences are common:

What are some of the techniques for achieving coherence?

1. Repeat a word that was used in the preceding sentence.

   . . . to take responsibility for the decision. This responsibility can be shared. . . .

   The second sentence is an obvious continuation of the idea presented in the preceding sentence.

2. Use a pronoun that represents a noun used in the preceding sentence.

   . . . to take this responsibility. It can be shared. . . .

Because "it" means "responsibility," the second sentence is linked directly with the first.

3. Use such connecting words as *however, therefore, yet, nevertheless, consequently, also, in addition,* etc.

> ...to take this responsibility. <u>However</u>, few are willing to....

"However" implies, "We're continuing with the same topic, just moving into a different phase." Remember, though, that good techniques can be *over*used. Unnecessary connectors are space consuming and distracting. Usually they can be spotted (and crossed out) in proofreading.

4. Use words that are frequently found together.

> The <u>sophomores</u> rejected the idea. The <u>juniors</u> accepted, but with some reluctance.

The words "sophomores" and "juniors" are commonly found together. If *student* appears in one sentence, *teacher* can be used as a linking word in the following sentence by continuing with a discussion of people in academics. The same would be true of such word pairs as *employer* and *employee, summer* and *winter, state* and *federal*—any words that are thought of in pairs.

Careful writers use coherence techniques to keep readers from experiencing abrupt changes in thought. *Avoid abrupt changes in thought, and link each sentence to a preceding sentence.* Coherent writing simplifies reading.

• Readability

What qualities make a message difficult to read?

Even though sentences are arranged in a sensible sequence and coherence techniques have been employed effectively, reading can still be difficult or fruitless. Two factors that contribute to readability are (1) length of sentences and (2) size of words. In an effort to determine the school grade level at which a passage is written, Robert Gunning[1] developed a readability formula:

1. Select a passage of 100 words or more.
2. Find the *average sentence length* by dividing the number of words in the passage by the number of sentences. Count compound sentences as two sentences.

---

[1] Robert Gunning, *The Technique of Clear Writing* (New York: McGraw-Hill, 1968), pp. 38–39.

3. Find the number of *difficult* words per hundred. A *difficult* word is defined as a word with three syllables or more. Words are *not* to be counted as difficult if they (1) are compounded words made from smaller words, such as *however* or *understand;* (2) are proper nouns; or (3) are verbs that became three syllables by addition of *-ed* or *-es,* such as *imposes* or *defended.* Determine difficult words per hundred by dividing the number of words in the passage into the number of difficult words and multiplying the resulting figure by 100.
4. Add the average sentence length and the number of difficult words per hundred.
5. Multiply the resulting figure by 0.4, to arrive at the reading grade level at which the passage was written.

The following passage illustrates application of the formula: ("Difficult" words are underscored.)

Each successive development has changed society. Early writing freed oral societies from limitations of time and space. Their legacies were transmitted* in writing; therefore, anthropologists and historians have not had to rely on hieroglyphs, pottery, utensils, and religious artifacts to study our recent past.† However,‡ the world was essentially illiterate until the development of printing. Printing made literature available to other than the religious elite. Printing multiplied the dimensions of communication; those who weren't literate were encouraged to become so.†

High-speed printing and inexpensive newspress paper overcame‡ all previous limitations and led to mass communication. With the advent of the telegraph, telephone, radio, and television, the world became a smaller place and instant communication commonplace.‡ What a milestone we achieved when millions of Americans§ (plus millions throughout the world) saw and heard Neil Armstrong begin his walk on the moon.

The passage contains 141 words in 11 sentences. The number of "difficult" words is 33.

---

* Not a "difficult" word (because it is a verb that became three syllables by addition of "-ed").
† Counted as two sentences (because it is a compound sentence).
‡ Not a "difficult" word (because it is made from two separate words compounded into one).
§ Not a "difficult" word (because it is a familiar proper noun).

Average sentence length (141/11)   12.8
No. of "difficult" words per 100
   (33/141 × 100)   23.4
Add 12.8 and 23.4   36.2
Multiply 36.2 by 0.4   14.48

The reading grade level is between 14 and 15. The resulting grade level is referred to by Gunning as the *Fog Index*. For most business writing, the desirable Fog Index is in the eight-to-eleven grade range. A writer need not be overly concerned if the index turns out to be a little over eleven or under eight.

For students and business people who have access to a computer and the appropriate software, the grade level of your writing can be quickly ascertained. The computer does the counting and calculating for you.

Trying to write at the grade level of the actual recipient is inadvisable. The level may not be known, and even those who have earned advanced degrees appreciate writing they can read and understand quickly and easily. *For quick, easy reading (and listening), use small words and short sentences.*

In a letter to a Ph.D. in engineering, should the Fog Index be above 16?

• Variety

Although a short *average* sentence length is desirable, keeping *all* sentences short would be undesirable. The passage may sound monotonous, unrealistic, or elementary. A two-word sentence is acceptable; so is a sixty-word sentence—if it is clear. Just as sentences should vary in length, they should also vary in structure. Some complex or compound sentences should be included with simple sentences.

Variety is just as desirable in paragraph length as it is in sentence length. A paragraph can be from one line in length to a dozen lines or more. But, just as average sentence length should be kept fairly short, average paragraph length should be kept short.

Paragraphs in business letters are typically shorter than paragraphs in business reports. First and last paragraphs are normally short (one to four lines), and other paragraphs should normally be no longer than six lines. A short first paragraph makes a letter look more inviting to read than a long first paragraph. A short last paragraph enables a writer to emphasize the parting words.

In letters, what is the advantage of employing short first paragraphs?

In business reports, the space between paragraphs comes as a welcomed resting spot. Long paragraphs make a page look as if reading would be laborious. Paragraphs approach the danger point when they exceed eight to ten lines, depending on the subject matter.

Although variety is a desirable quality, it should not be achieved at the expense of consistency. Using *I* in one part of a letter and then without explanation switching to *we* is inadvisable. Using the past tense in one sentence and the present tense in another sentence is unwelcome variety at the expense of consistency. Unnecessary changes from active to passive voice (or vice versa) and from third to second person (or vice versa) are also discouraged. Generally, *strive for short paragraphs, but vary their lengths.*

Should consistency
be sacrificed to
achieve variety?

• Emphasis

In sentences, the first and last words are in emphatic positions. In paragraphs, the first and last sentences are also in emphatic positions. An idea that deserves emphasis can be placed in either position, but an idea that does not deserve emphasis can be placed in the middle of a long paragraph.

In sentences and
paragraphs, where
are the emphatic
positions?

In sentences that contain a series, each element in the series can be emphasized by placing a number before it. In paragraphs, sentences can be numbered and tabulated with the same effect. For example, a long report could close with a concluding paragraph that restates four supporting reasons for a conclusion. The reasons can be emphasized by preceding each reason with a number, by presenting each reason on a separate typewritten line that is about an inch shorter than other lines, and by leaving extra space between the numbered reasons. Note that the revised concluding paragraph attaches increased emphasis to the reasons:

Original: For our needs, then, the most appropriate in-service training method is computerized instruction. It is least expensive, allows employees to remain at their own work stations while improving their skills, affords constant awareness of progress, and lets employees progress at their own rates.

Revision: Computerized instruction is the most appropriate in-service training method because it
1. Is the least expensive.
2. Allows employees to remain at their work stations while improving their skills.
3. Affords constant awareness of progress.
4. Lets employees progress at their own rates.

Why should *I* be used sparingly?

In paragraphs, the first and last words are also in particularly emphatic positions. The word *I*, which is frequently overused in letters, is especially noticeable if it appears as the first word. It is still more noticeable if it appears as the first word in *each* paragraph. *However* and *but* are to be avoided as first words if the preceding paragraph is neutral or positive. These words imply that the next idea will be negative. Unless the purpose is to place emphasis on negatives, such words as *denied, rejected,* and *disappointed* should not appear as the last words in a paragraph. *Within paragraphs, emphasize a sentence by placing it first or last or by assigning it a number in a tabulated series.*

Compositions

Just as sentences are formed from smaller units (words), and paragraphs are formed from smaller units (sentences), compositions are formed from smaller units (paragraphs). Regardless of whether a composition is a letter, a report, or a speech, problems encountered in sentence and paragraph construction are also encountered at the composition level.

• Unity

What *is* unity?

If a letter has unity, it will cover its topic adequately but will not include extraneous material. It will have a beginning sentence appropriate for the expected reader reaction, paragraphs that present the bulk of the message, and an ending sentence that is an appropriate closing for the message presented.

If a report has unity, its introduction will identify the topic, reveal the thesis, and give a preview of upcoming points. The introduction may also include some background, sources of information, and the method of treating data. A unified report will also have a summary or conclusion that brings all major points together. Between the beginning and the ending, a unified report will have paragraphs arranged in a systematic sequence.

• Sequence

The typical business message (letter, memorandum, or report) has (1) a major idea and (2) some accompanying ideas that are less significant. Prior to beginning, the writer must answer two questions: Should the major idea be stated first or last? What is the best sequence for presenting the accompanying ideas?

When messages begin with the major idea, the sequence of ideas is called *deductive*. When messages withhold the major idea until accompanying details and explanations have been presented, the sequence is called *inductive*. The decision about whether to write deductively or inductively is vital. It has a strong influence on the extent to which the message will be understood clearly and reacted to favorably. Subsequent chapters discuss sequence-of-idea patterns more thoroughly. For now, simply remember that the most dependable guide is *anticipated reader reaction*. If the message will likely *please or at least not displease, write deductively*. If the message will likely *displease or understanding of the major idea is dependent on prior explanations, write inductively*.

For determining the sequence of ideas that accompany the major idea, the following bases for paragraph sequence are common:

1. *Time*. In reporting on a series of events or a process, paragraphs proceed from the first step through the last step.
2. *Space*. If a report is about geographic areas, paragraphs can proceed from one area to the next until all areas have been discussed.
3. *Familiarity*. If a topic is complicated, the report can begin with a point that is known or easy to understand and proceed to progressively more difficult points.
4. *Importance*. In analytical reports where major decision-making factors are presented, the factors can be presented in order of most important to least important, or vice versa.
5. *Value*. If a report involves major factors with monetary values, paragraphs can proceed from those with greatest values to those with least values, or vice versa.

Readers expect the first paragraph to introduce a topic, additional paragraphs that discuss it, and a final paragraph that ties them all together. If the ending can't be easily linked to some word or idea presented in the beginning, unity has not been achieved. The effect is like that of an incomplete circle, or a picture with one element obviously missing. *Make sure that compositions form a unit with an obvious beginning, middle, and ending and that in-between paragraphs are arranged in a systematic sequence.* If the sequence is logical, coherence is easy to achieve.

How can you determine whether to begin a letter with the main idea?

A good outline assists in achieving coherence and transition.

• Transition

Just as sentences within a paragraph must adhere, paragraphs within a composition must also adhere. Connecting words, pronouns, repeated words, and orderly sequence are helpful. Especially helpful at the composition level is the *transition sentence.*

Unless a writer (or speaker) is careful, the move from one major topic to the next will seem abrupt. A good transition sentence can bridge the gap between the two topics by summing up the preceding topic and leading a reader to expect the next topic:

> Cost factors, then, seemed prohibitive until efficiency factors were investigated.

This sentence could serve as a transition between the *cost* division heading and the *efficiency* division heading. Since a transition sentence comes at the end of one segment and before the next, it emphasizes the central idea of the preceding segment and confirms the relationship of the two segments. Since the two can be easily presented in one sentence, the next heading seems like a logical one to discuss next.

Transition sentences are very helpful if properly used, but they can be overused. For most reports, transition sentences before major headings are sufficient. Normally, transition sentences before subheadings are unnecessary. Having encountered the previous subheading only a few lines back, a reader may readily see its relationship to the upcoming subheading. Also, transition sentences typically summarize, and the discussion under a subheading of a report is seldom long enough to merit summarization. *Place transition sentences before major headings.*

• Emphasis

Just as emphasis is a critical factor in composing sentences and paragraphs, it is also critical at the composition level. The following techniques are commonly employed:

1. *Position.* Beginning and ending positions are emphatic. The central idea of a talk or report appears in the introduction and the conclusion. Good transition sentences synthesize ideas at the end of each major division.

2. *Repetition.* A central idea is emphasized by transition sentences that repeat the essence of a discussion.

3. *Space.* The various divisions of a report or talk are not expected to be of equal length, but an extraordinary amount of space devoted to a topic attaches special significance to that topic. Similarly, a topic that gets an exceedingly small amount of space is de-emphasized.

4. *Headings.* Ideas that appear in headings get more attention than ideas that don't. Ideas that appear in subheadings are less emphatic

Which is more likely to employ transition sentences: a *letter* or a *report*?

Should transition sentences be employed between *sub*topics?

By what techniques can parts of an entire composition be emphasized?

than ideas that appear in major headings—a factor that should be taken into account at the outline stage. *Talking headings* (headings that reveal the conclusions reached in the following discussion) are more emphatic than general topic headings. For example, "Costs Are Prohibitive" is more emphatic than "Cost Factors."

5. *Nonverbal devices.* Ideas presented in graphs, charts, tables, or pictures are emphatic. Some ideas are more clearly presented in such devices. Also, the contrast in appearance is appealing.

Within a composition, achieve emphasis through position, repetition, space, headings, and nonverbal devices.

• Grammar, Spelling, Punctuation, and Keyboarding

Errors in grammar, spelling, punctuation, and keyboarding can be harmful in many ways:

In what ways are grammatical and mechanical errors harmful?

1. They can cause a message to be completely misunderstood.
2. They can cause a reader to waste time.
3. They can cause distraction from the message.
4. They can cause a receiver to lose confidence in the sender—to wonder if the error resulted from haste, ignorance, or lack of respect.

Strive for perfection in grammar, spelling, punctuation, and keyboarding.

Editing and Rewriting

If writing and organizing are done simultaneously, the task seems hopelessly complicated. If questions about what the message is, what the reader's reaction will be, and whether to begin with the main point have been answered first, the writing is greatly simplified. Happy with those decisions, a writer can concentrate totally on *expressing* ideas.

Before writing, think about content and organization.

The thinking that precedes writing helps to stimulate the flow of words. Rapid writing (with intent to rewrite certain portions if necessary) is normally better than slow, deliberate writing (with intent to avoid any need for rewriting portions). The latter approach can be time consuming and frustrating. Thinking of one way to express an idea, discarding it either before or after it is written, waiting for new inspiration, stopping to read and reread preceding sentences—these time-consuming habits can actually *reduce* the quality of the finished work.

Why write rapidly?

Recall your own writing experiences. Which is the more pleasant time for you: (1) the time spent writing a sentence or (2) the time spent *between* sentences? Because the time spent between sentences can be so unproductive and frustrating, that time should be reduced or eliminated. For most people, writing rapidly (with intent to rewrite certain portions if necessary) is the better approach by far. A famous author was quoted as saying "There is no such thing as good writing, but there is such a thing as good *re*writing."

If composition is done on a word processor, editing and proofreading can be done easily on the screen. First, reread the message to see whether it is complete, accurate, and clear. Then, check grammar, spelling, punctuation, and format. In a letter or a memorandum, seemingly trivial errors can interfere with reception of the message. The author, not the keyboarder, is held responsible for such errors. The list of proofreader's marks in the Appendix (page 695) provides a good summary of errors to look for.

Summary

In a discussion of writing, "style" means "the way ideas are expressed." Even for those who can write well already, a review of basics can bring about improvement (just as professional athletes frequently improve by reviewing and drilling on basic movements). For writers, computerized style-improvement programs are available. They are most helpful to those who know basics best. This chapter discussed stylistic problems that recur frequently in business writing. Basic as they are, the principles are frequently violated by business executives and students seeking advanced degrees.

Phrases

- Avoid expressing certainty when certainty is hardly possible.
- Avoid using clichés.
- Be brief. (Avoid using wordy expressions.)
- Avoid expressing surprise, doubt, and judgment when they would be interpreted as put-downs of individuals.

Sentences

- When the dependent phrase identifies action without revealing the doer, present the doer immediately after the phrase.

- Avoid using expletive beginnings (sentences in which the verb appears before the subject is stated).
- Avoid using platitudes (direct statements of ideas that almost anyone would know already).
- For presenting positive ideas, use the active voice.
- For presenting negative ideas, use the passive voice.
- For tactful presentation of an unpleasant thought, consider stating it in the subjunctive mood.
- For emphasis:
  a. Place an idea in a simple sentence.
  b. Place an idea in an independent clause; for de-emphasis, place an idea in a dependent clause.
  c. Use an important word more than once in a sentence.
  d. Place an important word first or last in a sentence.
  e. Precede each unit in a series by a number or a letter; for still further emphasis, tabulate.
- To de-emphasize a negative idea, place it in a sentence with a positive idea.
- For appositives, use parentheses for de-emphasis, a comma for neutral emphasis, and a dash or colon for emphasis.
- For emphasis or de-emphasis, attach words that label ideas as significant or insignificant.
- For a summary of the most commonly used punctuation, see pages (130 to 132).

Paragraphs

- Avoid abrupt changes in thought, and link each sentence to a preceding sentence.
- For quick, easy reading (and listening), use small words and short sentences.
- Strive for short paragraphs, but vary their lengths.
- Strive for paragraphs that are consistently deductive or consistently inductive.
- Within paragraphs, emphasize a sentence by placing it first or last or by assigning it a number in a tabulated series.
- If a message will likely please or at least not displease, write deductively. If a message will likely displease, or if understanding of the major idea is dependent on prior explanations, write inductively.

Compositions

- Make sure that compositions form a unit with an obvious beginning, middle, and ending and that in-between paragraphs are arranged in a systematic sequence.
- Place transition sentences before major headings.
- Within a composition, achieve emphasis through position, repetition, space, headings, and nonverbal devices.
- Strive for perfection in grammar, spelling, punctuation, and keyboarding.

These suggestions can assist in presenting clear, tactful messages that should be easily understood and positively received.

Exercises

Review Questions

1. Who is more likely to benefit from a computerized program that evaluates writing style, the person who (a) is very familiar with the basics of grammar or (b) knows little about the basics of grammar? Explain.

2. Which group of words is a phrase and which is a clause? (a) Although I agree with you, . . . or (b) Under the circumstances, . . . What is the distinguishing feature?

3. What are the disadvantages of using expressions such as "I *know* you will want to. . . ." and "I am *sure* you have. . . ."?

4. What are the disadvantages of using clichés?

5. (a) What do compound adjectives and coordinate adjectives have in common? (b) How are they different?

6. If a client or customer is obviously upset, what is wrong with your saying, "I'm sorry you are upset"?

7. Which determines the form of verb that should be used in a sentence: (a) the subject or (b) the word preceding the verb?

8. What is the difference between a dependent and an independent clause?

9. What is the difference between a complex sentence and a compound sentence?

10. Which provides more emphasis for an idea:

    a. A simple sentence or a complex sentence?

    b. An independent clause or a dependent clause?

    c. Parentheses or dashes?

    d. Tabulated arrangement or paragraph arrangement?

11. Which is the more accurate statement about sentences that contain dangling participial phrases? The reader may be confused about (a) when action was taken or (b) who took action.

12. List two disadvantages of beginning sentences with expletives.

13. Do platitudes affect human relations in a positive way? Explain.

14. Which is better for presenting a pleasant idea: (a) active voice or (b) passive voice? Explain.

15. What is the advantage of using the subjunctive mood for stating a negative idea?

16. For a word that deserves emphasis, which position in a sentence is better? (a) Use the word as the first or last word in the sentence. (b) Place the word in the middle of the sentence.

17. Does tabulation assist in achieving emphasis? Explain.

18. List some techniques for achieving coherence (a) within paragraphs and (b) among major sections of a composition.

19. If the objective in revising a report is to reduce the readability level from 16 to 12, what editorial changes would you make?

20. Should paragraphs be uniform in length? Explain.

21. What is the difference between deductive sequence and inductive sequence?

22. A report stops abruptly, without a "wrap-up" paragraph. Which principle has been violated: (a) unity or (b) coherence?

23. What are the advantages of including transition sentences in a long report?

24. What is the advantage of trying to anticipate a reader's reaction to a message before beginning to write?

25. Under what conditions would you recommend: (a) deductive writing and (b) inductive writing?

Activities

Each of the following sentences illustrates a weakness discussed in Chapter 5. (a) Using terminology employed in the chapter, identify the weakness. (b) Rewrite the sentence in such a way as to eliminate the weakness. Item 0 illustrates the type of answers expected:

Sample: 0.   Where is the dictionary at?

Answers: **a.**   Ends with an unnecessary preposition.

                b.   Where is the dictionary?

1. I am sure you realize the consequences of delay.

2. At this point in time, we recommend cash purchases.

3. We would like to advise you that the opening date is June 1.

4. The agent will bring you a list of names that have been arranged according to the alphabet.

5. I am resigning to accept a once in a lifetime opportunity.

6. Since you are upset, we are revising the payment schedule.

7. Your proposal is being evaluated by our attorney, which was received today.

8. While waiting in the lobby, my name was called.

9. There is to be a meeting of committee members on April 10.

10. It is not likely that rules have been changed.

11. Time can be saved at three stages: keyboarding, proofreading, and distribution.

12. Only one of the machines are working.

13. We cannot supply the materials before March 15.

14. My tax forms were completed and mailed before April 15.

15. You failed to initial the pen-written changes.

Insert punctuation marks where needed.

16. The figures were received at headquarters on Thursday but they were not processed until the following Tuesday.

17. If the merchandise is shipped on March 1 it will be delivered before March 7.

18. The merchandise will be delivered before March 7 if it is shipped on March 1.

19. Sodium not potassium is to be added to the solution.

20. We rode all day in a crowded noisy bus.

21. The most important consideration (financing) will be discussed tomorrow.

22. The mixture is rich in vitamins minerals and fiber.

23. The new system has three advantages costs less to install needs less maintenance and meets higher quality standards.

24. The consultant recommended a new marketing strategy it works much better than the strategy we formerly used.

25. When I carried a credit card I kept getting deeper and deeper in debt but I still could not resist buying.

26. Several applicants have been interviewed but none has been extended a job offer.

27. Several applicants have been interviewed however none has been extended a job offer.

28. Tim requested a four week leave.

29. As was predicted Tim requested permission to be away from his job for four weeks.

30. The agent seemed to have a take it or leave it attitude.

Compose a sentence that

31. Employs a compound adjective.

32. Employs coordinate adjectives.

33. Begins with a dependent clause.

34. Begins with an independent clause and ends with a dependent clause.

35. Illustrates a dangling participial phrase.

36. Illustrates an expletive beginning.

37. Conveys a platitude.

38. Employs passive voice.

39. Employs active voice.

40. Expresses a negative idea in the subjunctive mood.

41. Includes an appositive.

42. Illustrates correct punctuation of an adverbial conjunction.

43. Illustrates correct punctuation of a compound–complex sentence.

44. Illustrates correct punctuation of a coordinating conjunction.

45. Employs a pronoun that is followed by a gerund.

O B J E C T I V E S

When you have finished studying Part 3, you should be able to

- Apply planning and writing techniques to the solution of business problems.

- Use understanding of human needs and desires in written communications.

- Adapt your skills and knowledge to such tasks as ordering, handling claims, working with credit, and selling by mail.

- Practice effective methods of writing letters and memoranda.

- Write a variety of goodwill and special messages.

PART 3

COMMUNICATING THROUGH LETTERS AND MEMORANDA

Writing About the Routine and the Pleasant

*It is well to remember that grammar is common speech
formulated.*

W. SOMERSET MAUGHAM

A s the final step in an intellectual process, writing or dictating can be a very satisfying experience. It can give the same exhilarating sense of satisfaction in completion experienced by a skilled craftsman, artisan, or athlete. To many, however, it is an unpleasant experience.

Those who do not enjoy writing (among whom are professors, graduate and undergraduate students, and business executives) all seem to have problems in common: (1) they don't practice empathy, and (2) they begin writing without having first taken an important preliminary step—organizing.

Empathy

Empathy is the mental projection of one person's consciousness into the feelings of another. Dale Carnegie (in *How to Win Friends and Influence People*) illustrated empathy with a story of a retailer standing behind a counter. To determine what to say to a customer who had just entered, the retailer would take an imaginary walk to the customer's side of the counter and mentally ask, "If I were this customer, what would I want a clerk to say to me?" This attempt at projection into the other's point of view enabled the retailer to advise clerks on how to communicate effectively and thus increase sales.

In an ancient fable, a horse had gone astray. No one in the village had been able to find it. Upon learning of the problem, a vagabond entered the surrounding forest and soon returned with the horse. Asked to explain his success, the old man said: "It was easy; I simply went where I would have gone if I had been a horse." Before beginning his search, the man evidently considered such questions as Would the horse seek out *other* horses that graze in the forest? What kind of grasses or plants would a horse prefer and where do they grow? Would the horse prefer to face the wind while grazing? Which way would the horse go for shelter or for water?

Empathy: an asset in organizing and expressing thoughts

Just as the search for the horse was simplified when the searcher looked at the forest from the point of view of the horse, communication is simplified when the writer looks at the message from the point of view of the reader—through empathy. The following suggestions should help in achieving empathy.

• Cultivating a "You" Attitude

To the recipient of the message you are about to write, what would be major concerns? Would the ideas seem fair and logical? Are they clearly and respectfully expressed? Would the message seem self-centered? For people who have practiced courtesy and consideration since childhood, the "you" attitude is easy to incorporate into a written message.

Buy a gift that fits the receiver; design a message that fits the receiver.

• Using Your Knowledge of the Receiver

Knowing the following information facilitates empathy:

1. *Age.* A letter answering an elementary-school student's request for information would not be worded like a letter answering a similar request from a parent.

2. *Economic level.* A banker's collection letter to a millionaire is not likely to be the same form letter sent to clients who have fallen behind on their payments for small loans.

3. *Educational level.* A questionnaire sent to college graduates may need revision if it is sent to high school dropouts.

4. *Expectation.* Because college students are expected to meet high standards, a letter from a college student would probably shock a receiver if it contained errors in grammar or spelling.

5. *Motivation.* A speaker known to charge high fees would hardly be motivated by a request for a free lecture.

6. *Occupational level.* A message to the president of a major corporation may differ in style and content from a message to one of its many supervisors.

7. *Rapport.* If tactful approaches have brought no results or tactless responses, more direct statements may be justified in the upcoming message.

• Striving for Timely Delivery

If a letter isn't delivered on the expected or promised date, the would-be recipient will react negatively. The letter then automatically has a barrier to overcome when it *is* delivered. With empathy for the receiver, the sender probably would not want to time a message for delivery soon after the receiver has had a well-publicized emergency. As an income-tax accountant, for example, you probably would not have much enthusiasm for an unsolicited sales letter delivered a few days before April 15.

An untimely message may not get the attention it deserves.

Is reader reaction to a message predictable, even when the reader is a stranger?

Although knowledge about the recipient assists writers in developing empathy, they can practice empathy in communicating with people about whom they know little or almost nothing. From their knowledge of themselves and from their experiences with others, writers can predict (with reasonable accuracy) recipients' reactions to various types of messages. To illustrate, ask yourself these questions:

Would I react favorably to a messages saying my request is being granted?

Would I experience a feeling of disappointment upon learning that my request has been refused?

Would I be pleased when an apparently sincere message praises me for a job well done?

Would I experience some disappointment when a memo reveals that my promised pay increase is being postponed?

Now, reread the questions as though you were another person. Because you know *your* answers, you can predict *others'* answers with a high degree of accuracy. Such predictions are possible because of commonality in human behavior. Of course, each individual is unique; but each has much in common with others. Otherwise, psychology, psychiatry, and sociology would not have survived as disciplines. Yet, specialized study in these disciplines is hardly essential for fairly accurate prediction of others' reaction to business messages. Simply ask yourself how you would react if you were in the other person's position. Asking that question *before* you write a message greatly simplifies your message-organizing task.

Organization

In a discussion of writing, the word "organize" means "the act of dividing a topic into parts and arranging them in an appropriate sequence." Before undertaking this process, the writer needs to be convinced that the message is the *right* message—that it is complete, accurate, fair, reasonable, and logical. If it doesn't meet these standards, it should not be sent. Good organization and good writing cannot be expected to compensate for a bad decision.

About Language and Usage

Because of their Latin roots, *alumnus, alumni, alumna,* and *alumnae* are frequently misused. According to Webster's New World Dictionary, an *alumnus* (the singular form) is a male who has attended or been graduated from a school, college, etc. *Alumni* is the plural form of the noun and is used to signify more than one male alumnus. It is also used properly when referring to a group which includes both males and females, such as "Phyllis and George are alumni of State College." "George is an alumnus of State."

The feminine forms use *alumna* to refer to a female who has attended or been graduated from a school or college and *alumnae* as the plural form. For example, "Phyllis and Mary are alumnae (pronounced 'alumnee') of State," but "Phyllis is an alumna." "Alumnis" is never correct as "alumni" is already the plural form.

Clearness

• Why Organization Is Essential

When a topic is divided into parts, one part will be recognized as a central idea; the others, as minor ideas (details). The process of identifying these ideas and arranging them in the right sequence is also known as "outlining." As used in this text, "outlining" and "organizing" have the same meaning. Typically, those who don't particularly enjoy writing care even less for outlining. Exposed to the topic in elementary school, they may feel insulted at re-exposure. Many confess to having written outlines *after* writing assignments have been completed! Of those who have previously learned *how* to outline, few have seen the *value* of outlining:

1. Encourages brevity. (Reduces the chance of leaving out an essential idea or including an unessential idea.)

2. Permits concentration on one phase at a time. (Having focused separately on (a) the ideas that need to be included, (b) the distinction between major and minor ideas, and (c) the sequence of ideas, the

What is gained by taking time to outline before writing?

writer is now prepared for total concentration on the next problem—expressing.)

3. Saves time in writing or dictating. (With questions about which ideas to include and their proper sequence already answered, little time is lost in moving from one point to the next.)

4. Provides a psychological lift. (The feeling of success gained in preparing the outline increases confidence that the next step—writing—will be successful, too.)

5. Facilitates emphasis and de-emphasis. (Although each sentence makes its contribution to the message, some sentences need to stand out more vividly in the reader's mind than others. An effective outline ensures that important points will appear in emphatic positions.)

The preceding benefits derived from outlining are writer oriented. Because a message has been well outlined, readers benefit, too:

When a message has been well organized, do *both* writer and reader benefit?

1. The message is more concise.
2. The relationship between ideas is easier to distinguish and remember.
3. Reaction to the message and its author is more likely to be positive.

Reader reaction to a message is strongly influenced by the *sequence* in which ideas are presented. A beginning sentence or an ending sentence is in an emphatic position. (For a review of other emphasis techniques, see Chapter 5.) Throughout this chapter and other chapters on letter writing, note that outlining (organizing) is an important factor. Knowing *why* messages should be organized before they are written is not enough; knowing *how* to outline is also important.

• How to Organize Letters and Memoranda

Outline serves a writer as a blueprint serves a builder, as a map serves a tourist.

When planning your writing or dictating, you should strive for an outline that will serve the composer in much the same way a blueprint serves a builder or a map serves a traveler. When the goal is to produce a map or blueprint, thought precedes action. The same is true of outlining. Before listing the first point of an outline, you should answer the following questions:

1. What will be the central idea of the message?
2. What will be the most likely reader reaction to the message?

3. In view of the predicted reader reaction, should the central idea be listed *first* in the outline or should it be listed as one of the *last* items?

To answer the first question, think about the *reason* for writing. Is the purpose to get information, to answer a question, to accept an offer, to deny a request, etc.? Or, if the letter were condensed into a one-sentence telegram, that sentence would be the central idea.

To answer the second question (predicted reader reaction), ask: "If I were the one receiving the message I am preparing to send, what would *my* reaction be?" Because *you* would react with pleasure to good news and displeasure to bad news, you can reasonably assume a *reader's* reaction would be similar. Recall the twin goals of a communicator: clarity and effective human relations. By considering anticipated reader reaction, a writer facilitates achievement of the second goal. Almost every letter will fit into one of four categories of anticipated reader reaction: (1) pleasure, (2) displeasure, (3) interest but neither pleasure nor displeasure, or (4) no interest.

Four categories of reader reaction

After a letter or memorandum has been classified into one of the preceding categories, the next question is "Should the central idea be placed in the beginning sentence?" If so, present the message *deductively;* if not, present the message *inductively* (as discussed in Chapter 5).

Because the distinction between deductive and inductive writing is vital to an understanding of this and subsequent chapters, let's briefly recap what was said in Chapter 5. As messages in each category are discussed, these recommendations will be amplified:

Write Deductively (big idea first)	Write Inductively (details first)
When the message will *please* the reader.	When the message will *displease* the reader.
When the message is *routine* (will neither please nor displease).	When the reader may *not* be *interested* (will need to be persuaded).

Should you *always* begin with the central idea?

Although the principal focus is on *writing,* the same sequence-of-idea patterns are recommended for *oral* communication. These patterns are applicable in memoranda and reports as well as in letters.

Because deductive messages are easier to write, and because *pleasant* and *routine* messages follow similar outlines, they are discussed in the same chapter. (Inductive messages are discussed in more detail in Chapters 7 and 8.)

Business Letters

Letters that convey pleasant messages are referred to as "good news" letters. Letters not likely to generate any emotional reaction are referred to as "routine" letters. As depicted in the following lines, both outlines follow a deductive arrangement—the major idea is presented first, followed by supporting details. In both, the third point (closing thought) may be omitted without seriously impairing effectiveness; however, including it unifies a letter and avoids abruptness.

"Routine" letters are not likely to evoke an emotional reaction.

Good-news letter	Deductive pattern	Routine letter
Pleasant idea	_____	Big, important idea
	_____	
Details or explanations	_____	Details or explanations
	_____	
Closing thought	_____	Closing thought
	_____	

This sequence-of-idea arrangement has these advantages:

1. The first sentence is easy to write; it can be written with very little hesitation. After it, the details follow easily.
2. The first sentence is likely to attract attention. Coming first, the major idea gets the attention it deserves.
3. When good news appears in the beginning, the message immediately puts readers in a pleasant frame of mind; in this state, they are receptive to the details that follow.
4. The arrangement may save readers some time; once they get the important idea, they can move rapidly through the supporting details.

What are the advantages of the deductive arrangement for good-news and routine letters?

This basic plan is applicable in several business-writing problems: (1) routine claim letters and "yes" replies, (2) routine requests and "yes" replies, (3) routine requests related to credit matters and "yes" replies, and (4) routine order letters and "yes" replies.

• Routine Claims

Should a routine claim letter *begin* with the main idea?

A *claim* letter is a request for an adjustment. When writers ask for something to which they think they are entitled (a refund, replacement, exchange, payment for damages, and so on) the letter is called a *claim* letter.

Claim Letter   These requests can be divided into two groups: *routine claims* and *persuasive claims*. Persuasive claims, which will be discussed in a later chapter, assume that the request will be granted only after explanations and persuasive arguments have been presented. Routine claims (possibly because of guarantees, warranties, or other contractual conditions) assume that the request will be granted quickly and willingly, without persuasion. When the claim is routine (not likely to meet resistance), the following outline is recommended:

1. Request action in the first sentence.
2. Explain the details supporting the request for action.
3. Close with an expression of appreciation for taking the action requested.

Ineffective and effective application of this outline is illustrated in the sample letters that follow. To see the proper arrangement of letters on a typewritten page, turn to the Appendix, pages 704–707. In this chapter and those that follow, the peculiar arrangement on the page is designed to facilitate discussion. With sentences numbered and typed on shortened lines in the left-hand column, you can look at the commentary in the right-hand column (with the corresponding number) and easily see how principles are applied or violated.

Typically, a rather poorly organized and poorly written example is followed by a well-organized and well-written example, which is shaded in blue. In studying the commentary on poor examples, you can readily see why certain techniques should be avoided. In studying the commentary on well-written examples, you can see ways to avoid certain types of mistakes. The well-written examples are designed to illustrate the application of principles discussed in Chapters 4, 5, and 6. They are not intended as models of words, phrases, or sentences that should appear in letters you write. At the conclusion of this chapter, you should be able to apply the principles you've learned, while supplying your own words when you write.

The following letters illustrate first an inductive and then a deductive treatment of a routine claim letter.

① Late yesterday evening, I stopped by the construction site of the apartments you are under contract to build for me. ② At the present rate, you

① Begins with detail that will lead to the main idea.

② Makes an observation that could be omitted (although

appear to be well ahead of schedule.

3 According to our agreement, all requests and complaints are to be made in writing. 4 I noticed that water heaters had been installed in two of the apartments. 5 The units are 30-gallon heaters, but the "specs" call for 50-gallon heaters in each of the 12 apartments.

6 For some families, the smaller size may be sufficient; but others may need the larger size. 7 Since the larger size is specified in the agreement we signed, I respectfully request that the two 30-gallon units be removed and that 50-gallon water heaters be installed in all the apartments.

8 Thank you for your consideration in this matter.

9 I am enthused about the progress you have made.

Does the main point deserve emphasis?

it does show that the writer is willing to give credit where credit is due).

3 States directly that which is already known.

4 Moves toward the main idea.

5 Continues with detail.

6 Presents a reason for making the up-coming request.

7 States the main point of the letter. Stating the claim in such a long sentence keeps the request from receiving the emphasis it needs.

8 Employs a cliché.

9 Does close on a positive note but employs "enthused"; "enthusiastic" should be used instead.

Written inductively, the preceding letter does transmit the essential ideas; but it is unnecessarily long and the main idea is not emphasized. Surely, the builder intended to install 50-gallon heaters; otherwise, the building contract would not have been signed. Because a mistake is obvious, the builder would not need to be persuaded. Since compliance can be expected, the claim can be stated without prior explanation:

1 Please replace the two 30-gallon water heaters

1 Emphasizes the main idea

> (installed last week) with 50-gallon units.
>
> ② Because the larger units are essential for families that include children, the contract specifies a 50-gallon heater for <u>each</u> of the 12 apartments.
>
> ③ The project appears to be well ahead of schedule; thanks for your efforts.

by placing it in the first sentence.

② Follows with explanation.

③ Ends on a positive note.

Without showing anger, disgust, suspicion, or disappointment, the preceding claim letter asks simply for an adjustment. The major point receives deserved emphasis. Reader response to it should be favorable.

Favorable Response to Claim Letter Businesses *want* their customers to write when merchandise or service is not satisfactory. They want to learn of ways in which goods and services can be improved, and they want their customers to receive value for the money they spend. With considerable confidence, they can assume that writers of claim letters think their claims are valid. By responding favorably to legitimate requests, businesses can gain a reputation for standing behind their goods and services. A loyal customer may become even more loyal after a business has demonstrated its integrity.

An "adjustment" letter is a response to a claim letter.

Since the subject of an adjustment letter is related to the goods or services provided, the letter can serve easily and efficiently as a low-pressure sales letter. With only a little extra space, the letter can include resale or sales-promotional material. *Resale* is used in a discussion of goods or services already bought. It either reminds customers and clients that they made a good choice in selecting a firm with which to do business, or it reminds them of the good qualities of their purchase. *Sales-promotional material* is used in a discussion of *related* merchandise or service. For example, a letter about a firm's wallpaper might also mention its paint. To mention the paint is to use sales-promotional material. Subtle sales messages that are included in adjustment letters have a good chance of being read, but direct sales letters may not be read at all.

Include a sales message in an adjustment letter?

When the response to a claim letter is favorable, present ideas in the following sequence:

1. Reveal the good news in first sentence.
2. Explain the circumstances.
3. Close on a pleasant, forward-looking note.

Although the word *grant* is acceptable when talking *about* claims, its use *in* claim letters is discouraged. Such an expression as "Your claim is being granted" unnecessarily implies that the writer is in a position of power.

Ordinarily, a response to a written message is also a written message. Sometimes, people write letters to confirm ideas they have already discussed on the telephone. Before reading a well-written deductive response, study the commentary on each sentence in a poorly written inductive response:

Should the main idea be subordinated?

① Thank you for your letter of May 6. ② It has been referred to me for reply.

③ Looking at our contract, I see that it does specify 50-gallon heaters. ④ Therefore, we are complying with your request that the 30-gallon heaters be removed and that 50-gallon units be placed in <u>all</u> your apartments.

⑤ Thank you for calling this matter to our attention.

① Employs a well-worn beginning.
② States the obvious.

③ Leads to main idea.

④ Presents main idea.

⑤ Employs a sentence that seems polite but is well worn.

The preceding letter does reveal compliance with the request, but the main idea is not emphasized. In the absence of an explanation for the initial installation of 30-gallon heaters, the reader could become suspicious of the builder's intent. Although explaining is not obligatory, a builder who is honest and efficient would find out what happened. By investigating and explaining, the builder may impress the reader as being a manager who takes corrective and preventive measures.

In the revised letter, notice the deductive treatment and the inclusion of an explanation:

① Each of your apartments will have a 50-gallon water heater.

② The two 30-gallon units are being removed today.

① The good news (main idea) receives emphasis.

② Action is being taken already.

③ Thank you for reporting the problem before additional heaters were installed. ④ Clearly, "50-gallon" appears on the specs; clearly, "30-gallon" was keyboarded on the warehouse request form. ⑤ Some office personnel are embarrassed and determined to do better proofreading!

③ Reaction to the report is positive.

④ Explanation is presented.

⑤ Efforts to prevent recurrence of such errors are being exerted.

Confident that a routine request for an adjustment will be granted, the writer simply asks for it (in the first sentence and without seeming to complain). Knowing that the recipient will be glad to learn that a request has been granted, the writer simply states it (in the first sentence and without apparent reluctance). The details and closing sentence follow naturally and easily.

• Routine Letters About Credit

Normally, credit information is requested and transmitted by form letters or simple office forms. When the response to a credit request is very likely to be favorable, the request should be stated at the beginning.

Request for Information   The network of credit associations across the country has made knowledge about individual consumers easy to obtain. As a result, exchanges of credit information are common in business. Study the following outline for an effective letter request for credit information about an individual:

What is the outline for a credit-information request?

1. Identify the request and name the applicant early—preferably in the opening sentence or in a subject line.
2. Assure the reader that the reply will be held confidential.
3. Detail the information requested. Use a tabulated-form layout to make the reply easy.
4. End courteously. Offer the same assistance to the reader.

The following request letter applies the outline:

May we have credit information about Willard F. Jackson?

When he applied for credit with us, he gave your business as a reference.

Please fill in the blanks on this page. For any additional information you care to provide, please use the other side of the page. Your reply will be held in strict confidence.

We appreciate your help. When we can be of similar assistance, please call on us.

Sincerely,

Length of time sold on credit _____
Highest credit extended _____
Credit limit _____
Balance now due _____ Past due _____
Normal paying habits _____
Remarks _____
_____

The preceding letter showed another desirable arrangement for a credit request, which is to place the complete letter at the top of the page and to arrange the fill-in items at the bottom of the page.

Just as a theme or report is given a title, a letter can be given a title also. In a letter, the title is referred to as the "subject line." The following subject lines are typical:

SUBJECT: REQUEST FOR CREDIT INFORMATION ABOUT
        MR. WILLIAM C. WARD

SUBJECT: CREDIT INFORMATION, JONES-ANDERSON CO.

Requests for credit information are acceptable either with or without a subject line. The subject line does provide quick, emphatic identification of what the letter is about. Printed forms on which the names of the reference and applicant can be filled in are certainly desirable when the volume of credit requests is great.

Economize by using form letters.

Response to Request for Information Replies to requests for credit information are usually very simple—just fill in the blank and return it. If the request does not include a form, follow a deductive plan in writing the reply—the major idea followed by supporting details.

① We considered Mr. Willard F. Jackson, about whom you requested confidential credit information on May 26, as a very good credit risk.

① Presents the major idea. Reminds reader of the confidential nature of the letter.

2 During the ten years in which we sold building materials to him on credit, his highest balance was $70,000. His payments were always prompt. He reduced his balance to zero before moving away from Springerville.

2 Gives the information requested.

3 We found Mr. Jackson a pleasant customer and enjoyed doing business with him.

3 Ends courteously.

In credit letters, writers have an obligation to themselves, as well as to the addressee and the credit applicant. Good advice is to stick with facts, as this letter did. Why say "I'm sure he will pay promptly," when "His payments were always prompt" is a strong recommendation? Is there any need to say he *is* a good credit risk when all we know is that he *was* so considered when he bought from us?

To whom is the person who gives credit information obligated?

Request for Credit   When people want to begin buying on credit and assume credit will be willingly granted, they can place their request in the first sentence and follow with details:

1 Will you please fill the enclosed order on a credit basis?

1 Presents the major idea.

2 If you need information other than that given on the enclosed financial statements, please write to me.

2 Gives details.

3 Current plans are to place a similar order every two weeks.

3 Closes with a look to the future.

This approach is recommended only when the writer's supporting financial statements are assumed sufficient to merit a "yes" response.

Favorable Response to Request for Credit   Effective "yes" replies to requests for credit should use the following outline:

What ideas are included in a letter that grants credit?

1. Begin by saying credit terms have been arranged; or, if an order has been placed, begin by telling of the shipment of goods, thereby implying the credit grant.
2. Give some idea of the foundation upon which the credit grant is based.
3. Present and explain the credit terms.
4. Include some resale or sales-promotional material.
5. End with a confident look toward future business.

Before credit managers say "yes" to a request for credit, they must answer two basic questions: (1) Will this potential customer have the money to pay when the bills become due? (2) Will the customer be willing to part with the money at that time? To answer the first question, they consider the would-be customer's financial status and earning power. To answer the second question, they consider character. Ordinarily, they get information from the following sources: (1) the potential credit customer; (2) credit-rating associations; (3) those who are presently selling, or have previously sold, to the potential customer; and (4) others who may have some knowledge of the potential credit customer's ability to pay.

Why use form letters when replying to credit requests?

Most letters that say "Yes, you may purchase on credit" are *form letters*. If a firm uses word-processing equipment, an operator gives the machine instructions identifying the specific form to be typed. Stored in the memory of the machine, the message will be typed automatically. Firms receive so many requests for credit that the costs of individualized letters would be prohibitive. Typically, the form messages read something like this:

> We are pleased to extend credit privileges to you. Temporarily, you may purchase up to $2,000 worth of merchandise on time. Our credit terms are 2/10, n/30. We welcome you as a credit customer of our expanding organization.

Although such form messages are effective for informing the customer that credit is being extended, they do little to promote sales and goodwill. Whether to say "yes" by form letter or by individualized letter is a problem that each credit manager has to settle individually. If the list of credit customers is relatively short and few names are being added, individualized letters may be practical. A credit manager may also choose to use individualized letters if the workload in the department is such that letters can be sent without overworking present personnel or adding new workers. But even when credit grants are tailor made to fit the individual, they often fall short of their capacity to promote profitable business. Although the following letter is probably more effective than a form letter, it can still be improved:

1 Thank you for your order for 6 Unicook microwave ovens.	**1** Delays the answer to the reader's question, "May I pay for them later?"
2 They are being shipped today.	**2** Implies the answer to the question of credit extension—if they are being shipped, credit must have been granted.
3 We are pleased to report that your credit rating was investigated and found to be satisfactory.	**3** "Pleased" and "investigated" could have been taken for granted. The applicant may feel under suspicion.
4 Our credit terms are the usual 2/10, n/30.	**4** As this letter is to a dealer, the explanation of terms is probably sufficient. In letters to consumers, more detailed explanation and interpretation are helpful.
5 Welcome to our growing list of satisfied customers.	**5** Uses a cliché. As the dealer has read this many times before, it may be meaningless. By sending an individualized letter that explains what the dealer wants to know, the writer could *imply* the welcome.
6 We trust that this will be the beginning of a long and profitable business relationship.	**6** A good credit manager would not have ended his letter with a standard remark that was worn out long ago.

What impression does a cliché make?

In spite of its drawbacks, the preceding letter sounds about as good as the average credit letter that passes through the mail. It was not intended as a horrible example; it does, however, leave room for improvement.

From our discussion, we know why we should tell of the shipment and credit grant in the first sentence, we can see the wisdom of using

Why discuss the
basis for granting
credit?

resale and sales-promotional material, and we know the advantage of writing as if we expect future orders. But why should we discuss the foundation upon which we based our decision to grant credit? To prevent collection problems that may arise later. Just as lawyers work to prevent courtroom litigation and doctors work to prevent sickness, credit managers should work to prevent collection problems. Indicating that we are granting credit on the basis of an applicant's prompt-pay habits with present creditors encourages continuation of those habits with us. It recognizes a reputation and challenges the purchaser to live up to it. When financial situations become difficult, the purchaser will probably remember the compliment and try to pay us first.

Why would we discuss the credit terms? To stress their importance and prevent collection problems that may arise later. Unless customers know exactly when payments are expected, they may not make them on time. Unless they know exactly what the discount terms are, they may take unauthorized discounts. Furthermore, the mere fact that we take time to discuss terms in detail suggests that terms are important and that we expect them to be followed. The following revision applies these principles:

1 Six Unicook ovens should reach your store in time for your weekend shoppers.	**1** Present good news. Indicates that the writer has some consideration for the problems of a dealer. Implies the credit grant.
2 Because of your very favorable current rating and your prompt-pay habits with your other creditors, we are sending the shipment subject to the usual credit terms--2/10, n/30. **3** By paying this invoice within 10 days, you save almost $150.	**2** Gives the dealer recognition for having earned the credit privilege. Gives a reason for the credit grant; it was not granted haphazardly. Introduces the credit terms. Addressed to a *dealer*, the letter does not need to explain what "2/10, n/30" means.
	3 Encourages taking advantage of the discount. Talks about the discount arrangement in terms of profits for the dealer.

> ④ Unicooks are known for uniform cooking without a rotisserie.
>
> ⑤ Turn knobs in previous models have been replaced by pushbuttons--a feature that homemakers really seem to appreciate. ⑥ For other kitchen items on open account, use the enclosed order form.

④ and ⑤ Present resale.

⑥ Looks confidently forward to future orders.

Although the foregoing example was written to a dealer, the same principles apply when writing to a consumer. Of course, we have to talk to each in terms of individual interests. Dealers are concerned about markup, marketability, and display; consumers are concerned about price, appearance, and durability. Also, consumers may require a more detailed explanation of credit terms. But be careful. Don't present an elementary lecture. For example, don't use such an expression as "EOM" and then follow it with, "This means 'End of the Month.'"

The preceding example performed a dual function: it said "yes" to an application for credit, and it also said, "Yes, we are filling your order." But because of its importance, the credit aspect was emphasized more than the acknowledgment. In other cases (in which the order is for cash or the credit terms are already clearly understood), the primary purpose of writing may be to acknowledge an order.

What is the principal difference between a credit letter to a dealer and a credit letter to a consumer?

• Routine Letters About Orders

Like routine letters about credit, routine letters about orders put the main idea in the first sentence. Details are usually tabulated, especially when more than one item is ordered.

Order Letter   Order letters create one half of a contract. They constitute the offer portion of a contract that is fulfilled when the shipper sends the goods, thereby creating the acceptance part of the contract. Therefore, if we seriously want to receive shipment, we should make our order letter a definite offer. The outline for order letters is deductive:

What outline should be used for an order letter?

1. Use order language in the first sentence. Say, "Please ship," "Please send," "I order," or use some other suitable language that assures

List two possible interpretations of "I would like to order. . . ."

the seller of the desire to buy. Avoid phrases like "I'm interested," "I'd like to . . . ," or similar indefinite statements.

2. Carefully detail the items ordered. Be specific by mentioning catalog numbers, prices, colors, sizes, and all other information that will enable the seller to fill the order promptly and without the need for further correspondence.

3. Include a payment plan and shipping instructions. Remember that the shipper is free to ship by the normal method in the absence of specific instructions from the buyer. Tell when, where, and how the order is to be shipped.

4. Close the letter with a confident expectation of delivery.

In addition to the application of the outline principles, note the physical layout in the following order letter:

Please ship the following items, which are listed in your current catalog:

6	#W30X4817 double-roll bolts @ 17.98	$107.88
10	#T31X3816 double-roll bolts @ 23.98	239.80
4	#V27X2917 double-roll bolts @ 18.49	73.96
		421.64
	Tax	4.22
	Transportation	18.50
	Total	$444.36

Unless you normally use some other means, please ship by Highway Express.

In large companies, the normal procedure is to use purchase-order forms for ordering. And most consumers buying from mail-order houses use the order forms enclosed with catalogs.

The most important thing we can do as customers is to make sure our order letter or form is complete in every detail. If we sell by mail, we'll want to use every work-simplification technique within our means to make the order system foolproof.

Favorable Response to Order Letter   When customers place an order for merchandise, they expect to get exactly what they ordered as quickly as possible. For most orders, we can acknowledge by shipping.

No letter is necessary. But for initial orders or for orders we cannot fill quickly and precisely, we need to send *letters of acknowledgment*. Senders of initial orders like to know that they are going to receive what they ordered, they like to know their business is appreciated, and they need some information about the firm with which they are beginning a business relationship. If a regular customer's order is not being filled immediately, some form of explanation is expected. The explanation usually takes the form of a duplicated or printed sheet, similar to this:

What is the purpose of an acknowledgment letter?

Dear Customer:

    We appreciate your order for _____ .

    You should receive it within _____ days.

            Sincerely yours,

Forms like this are often sent as a matter of routine when orders can be filled immediately but will require considerable time in transit. Although the form is impersonal, it is appreciated because it acknowledges the order and lets the customer have some idea of its disposition.

    Nonroutine acknowledgments, however, require an individualized letter. And although initial orders can be acknowledged through form letters, the letters are more effective if individually written. Most people who write letters have no difficulty in saying "yes." But, because saying "yes" is easy, they can fall into the habit of making their letters sound too cold and mechanical:

Sometimes, *form acknowledgments are inappropriate.*

❶ Thank you for your order, which we are very glad to have.	❶ Begins with a cliché.
❷ We extend to you a sincere welcome to our ever-growing list of satisfied customers.	❷ Says to this customer the same thing that has been said already to thousands of customers.
❸ We were delighted to send you a dozen Sure-Alarm clock radios.	❸ Sounds exaggerated and, thus, insincere.
❹ They were shipped by express today.	❹ Presents information that should have been presented earlier.

⑤ We are sure you will find our firm a good one with which to deal and that our electronic units are unmatched in quality.

⑤ Includes an unsupportable statement of certainty.

⑥ Our latest price list is enclosed.

⑥ States the obvious.

⑦ Thank you for your patronage.

⑦ Ends with a cliché.

If a firm is truly grateful for clients' patronage, why not use "Thank you for your patronage" as the last sentence in all letters to clients?

Is this letter good enough to increase business? Let's see how the same letter sounds when it confirms shipment of goods in the first sentence, includes concrete resale on the product and business establishment, and eliminates business jargon:

① A dozen Sure-Alarm clock radios were shipped by Fastway air-express today.

① Sufficiently implies that the order has been received and filled. Refers to specific merchandise shipped and reveals method of shipment.

② The red ticket attached to each unit explains how the wake-up alarm works perfectly--even if the electric power fails.

② Points out a specific quality of the merchandise (uses resale).

③ See the enclosed folder for price lists and forms for ordering additional radios or other high-quality electric units.

③ Implies expectation of additional orders. Refers to enclosures without using an entire sentence to reveal their presence. Mentions related merchandise (uses sales-promotional material).

A major purpose of the acknowledgment letter is to encourage future orders. An effective technique to achieve this goal is to state that the merchandise was sent, include resale, and imply that future orders will be handled in the same manner. Don't expect to encourage future business by just filling the page with words like *welcome* and *gratitude*. They are overused words, and many people whose merchandise and service are poor overwork them. Appropriate action implies both gratitude and welcome. We can emphasize our appreciation by both action *and* words, but we should be careful. We should strive to make the words sound sincere and original.

• Letters About Routine Requests

Notice how routine requests and favorable responses to them employ the same sequence-of-idea patterns. Compared with persuasive requests (discussed in Chapter 8), routine requests are shorter.

Routine Request   Most business people write letters requesting information about people, prices, products, and services. Because the request is a door opener for further business, readers accept it optimistically; at the same time, they arrive at an opinion about the writer based on the quality of the letter. The following outline can serve as a guide in the preparation of effective requests that are expected to be fulfilled:

1. Make the major request in the first sentence.
2. Follow the major request with the details that will make the request clear. If possible, use tabulations.
3. Close with a forward look to the reader's next step.

What outline should be used for a routine request?

Let's take a look at a vague request letter:

① Last night's <u>Daily News</u> included an article about your speech to a local investor's club. The reporter presented some of your thoughts on state and municipal bonds, but I would appreciate more details than were printed in the paper.

② Do you have a copy of your speech? I'm sure some of the handouts you may have provided would be interesting.

① Delays the real purpose of the letter.

② Presents the request rather vaguely.

Now let's see how the request could be handled more efficiently:

① May I have a copy of your March 1 speech to the Investor's Club?

② Last night's <u>Daily News</u> included excerpts, just enough to whet the appetite for your complete discussion of state and municipal bonds.

③ As a potential investor, I would certainly appreciate a copy of your speech and any printed materials you may have distributed.

① States request.

② Presents details.

③ Expresses appreciation and alludes to action.

Note that the letter starts with a direct request for specific information. Then it follows with as much detail as necessary to enable the reader to answer specifically. It ends confidently with appreciation for the action requested. The letter is short; but if it conveys enough information and has a tone of politeness, it is long enough.

Favorable Response to Routine Request   "Yes" is so easy to say that many people say it thoughtlessly. The following letter accedes to a request, but it reports the decision without much enthusiasm:

① We have your letter in which you request an interview for the purpose of research in marketing.

② As I interpret it, the person you need to talk with is Mr. Rudolph Smith, who is in charge of our suggestions program.

③ Right now, he has a busy schedule indeed, but he has so arranged his work as to leave a half-hour open for you--1:30 to 2:00, November 20.

① States the obvious.

② Suggests "We had a good deal of difficulty in deciphering your message."

③ Hints that the favor was difficult to grant and, therefore, granted reluctantly.

What is the most likely reaction to a statement that suggests sacrifice on the part of the writer?

④ May we take this opportunity to assure you of our interest, and we wish you great success in your endeavors.

④ Uses too many words, is too general and perfunctory.

With a little planning and consideration for the candidate's problems, the following letter could have been written just as quickly:

① Yes, our Suggestions Supervisor, Mr. Rudolph Smith, can talk with you from 1:30 to 2:00 on November 20.

② After he leaves for his two o'clock meeting, you may enjoy looking through our files of accepted and rejected suggestions.

③ Mr. Smith thinks they will be of special interest to you since they have research implications.

④ After you have finished compiling the results of your study, we would like to see them.

① Answers the question in the first sentence.

Why grant a request in the very first sentence?

② Reminds the reader that one half-hour is all that can be spared. The offer to show the files is a polite gesture.

③ Reminds the reader that Mr. Smith does have some interest in the project.

④ Anticipates conclusion of the study (a pleasant thought!) and hints that the conclusions will be worth reading.

Occasionally, successful business or professional people are asked special favors. They may receive invitations to speak to various social or school groups. If they say "yes," they might as well say it enthusiastically. Sending an unplanned, stereotyped acceptance suggests that the talk will be in the same style:

① I was pleased to have your letter of November 14 in which you invited me to talk to your students in Insurance 302.

① Assumes that the expression of pleasure is of more interest than his indication of acceptance.

Why avoid beginning most sentences with *I*?

2 In reply, I wish to state that I have been in the insurance business for almost 25 years, having spent a good deal of time on the road as a life-insurance salesperson and some time in the home office as an actuary.

2 Talks about self in language that was trite long ago.

3 I have a talk that I could give on "Insuring your Career by Insuring your Friends," and I could supplement it with an 8-minute film on insurance careers.

3 More talk about self.

Was this letter written inductively?

4 I therefore consider it an honor and a pleasure to accept your invitation. I shall look forward to seeing you promptly at nine o'clock on Tuesday next.

4 Finally accepts after having indirectly indicated acceptance. The eighth *I* in the letter. The sentence indicates that he may be a stuffy speaker.

The following revision accepts the invitation graciously, presents an idea of the contribution to be made, and ends with a reference to the event at which the speech is to be given:

1 Yes, I accept your invitation to talk with your students in Insurance 302 about a career in insurance.

1 Accepts immediately. Reader is relieved. Now some other person won't have to be asked.

2 Your students are probably interested primarily in the selling aspects; but the talk can include actuarial careers, too, if any should indicate interest.

2 Employs a *you* attitude.

3 As a supplement to the discussion, they can see an 8-minute film. I'll bring the projector; please arrange to have a screen in the room.

3 Presents necessary details.

4 I plan to see you in Owens Hall at nine o'clock next Tuesday morning.

4 Ends by referring to the next step in the chain of events—linking present and future states the expectation pleasantly.

If responses to invitations were frequent, the preceding letter could be stored in the memory of a personal word processor, recalled, adapted, and used when the next invitation arrives. To communicate quickly and efficiently with clients or customers, large businesses are almost forced to use word-processing or form letters.

Form Letters for Routine Responses   Governmental agencies, savings and loan companies, banks, public utilities, and other organizations that serve a multitude of people use forms on which a variety of messages appear. To communicate a routine message, an office worker simply places a check mark (or marks) beside the message that applies. The company's letterhead usually appears at the top of the form; and space is left for keyboarding in the date, name and address, and account number:

Dear _____

We appreciate your inquiry about the late charges assessed against your account. After checking your record of loan payments, we have the following report:

✓ The late charge has been waived because it resulted from circumstances beyond your control.

___ Since the late charge appears to be valid, please add the amount to your next monthly payment.

___ A late charge of $_____ has been waived; however, the following unpaid late charge remains on your account: $_____. Please add the amount to your next monthly payment.

___ Other _____

_____

If your records should disagree with ours, please use the enclosed envelope for sending us copies of receipts or checks (both front and back).

Form letters can save time and money.

Instead of using forms similar to the preceding letter, office personnel could employ form sentences or paragraphs that have been stored in a word processor. It could be instructed to print the initial paragraph and the other sentence or sentences that apply.

Form letters are a fast and efficient way of transmitting frequently recurring messages to which reader reaction is likely to be favorable or neutral. When a form is designed for check marks in front of applicable sentences (as in the preceding example), the first sentence is of necessity introductory. Because the *main* idea is the one by which a check mark appears, the letter isn't in a strict sense deductive (as are the other letters illustrated thus far). For most "good news" and routine *letters,* though, deductive writing is preferred. The same is true of *memoranda* that contain routine information or messages that will evoke a favorable reaction.

Memoranda

Because letters go to people *outside* a firm and memoranda go to people *within* a firm, their formats are different (see pages 704–710 in the Appendix). A memorandum needs no return address, inside address, salutation, and complimentary closing. Instead, a typical memorandum presents (on separate lines) (a) name of the person *to* whom the message is addressed, (b) the name of the person *from* whom the message comes, (c) the *date,* and (d) the *subject.* When a memorandum is addressed to more than one person, all their names appear on the "To" line. If the list is long, a common practice is to write "Distribution" on the "To" line. Then, beneath the last line, write the word "Distribution" and follow it with an alphabetized list of the names. In addition to simplifying interoffice mailing and reference, alphabetizing eliminates the risk of having someone on the list wonder whether names appear in order of importance.

Is jargon okay in memoranda?

Principles of *writing* (see Chapters 4 and 5) that apply to business letters also apply to memoranda. Technical jargon, though, is more likely to be useful in memoranda. Since people doing similar work are almost sure to know the technical terms associated with it, jargon will be understood, it will not be taken as an attempt to impress, and it will save time. For the same reasons, acronyms and abbreviations are more useful in memoranda than in letters.

Outlining principles that apply to letters also apply to memoranda.

Principles of *organizing* that apply to letters also apply to memoranda. In both, empathy is the basis for deciding whether to proceed deductively or inductively. In addition, memoranda may employ other bases for determining the sequence of ideas: time (reporting events in the order in which they happened), order of importance, and geography are examples.

Although *graphics* may be used in letters, they are more likely to be useful in memoranda. Tables, graphs, charts, and pictures may be either integrated into the content of a memorandum or attached as supporting material. Tabulation is as useful in memoranda as it is in letters.

In memoranda, is tabulation acceptable?

The *subject line* (1) tells the reader what the following message is about and (2) sets the stage for the reader to understand the message. The following suggestions should be helpful in preparing subject lines:

1. Make the subject line as long as necessary to do the job. Some people tend to look at subject lines as though they were titles of books and so try to make them as short as possible. If, for example, your subject is the report of a meeting, "Report of Meeting" is a poor subject line. "Report of June 10 meeting on the relocation of Plant X" is a better subject line. In addition to aiding understanding, subject lines provide information helpful to file clerks.

2. Take a suggestion from newspaper writers: Think of the five Ws to give you some clues for good subject lines: *Who, What, When, Where,* and *Why*. Key words help in the development of good subjects.

3. Even though you may write a complete subject line, you should not assume the reader will remember it while reading your memorandum. Opening sentences should not include wording such as "This is . . ." and "The above-mentioned subject. . . ." The body of the memorandum should be a complete thought in itself and should not rely on the subject line for elaboration; a good opening sentence might very well be a repetition of most of the subject line. Even if the subject line were omitted, the memorandum should still be clear, logical, and complete.

4. Keyboard the subject line in all-capital letters if additional emphasis is desired.

As you have learned to do in writing letters, write memoranda deductively when they contain good news or neutral information; write inductively when they contain bad news or when they are intended to persuade. (Inductive memoranda are discussed in greater detail in Chapters 7 and 8.)

• "Good News" Memoranda

The following message would, of course, have a heading and be arranged on the page as illustrated on page 710. To facilitate analysis, it is arranged on this page in the same two-column format used in the discussion of letters.

SUBJECT: ADDITIONAL VACATION DAY	Gets attention by placing good news in the subject line.
① The Board of Directors has approved one additional vacation day for every employee.	① Begins with the good news. Good news deserves the emphasis that first-sentence position provides.
② This decision is our way of expressing gratitude for the most productive and profitable year in the history of the Wiggins Company. ③ With the approval of your department head, you may select any day between January 2 and June 30.	② Follows with an explanation. ③ Continues with details.
④ This day of vacation is in addition to year-end bonuses you will receive soon.	④ Adds additional detail.
⑤ Thank you for all you have done to make the year memorable, and best wishes for a healthful and happy new year.	⑤ Closes on a pleasant note.

As a good news message, the preceding memorandum presented the main idea in the first sentence, as do routine messages.

• Routine Memoranda

The memorandum is the most frequently used method of communicating about itineraries; procedures; personnel, marketing, and financial matters; and other matters of which a written record is needed.

Itinerary Memorandum   Before leaving on a long trip, an executive would probably list the itinerary in a memorandum. It would be distributed to the people who would most likely need to communicate before the journey ends. Such a memorandum would read as follows:

① From August 21 to 28, I will be away from the office.

② August 21: Leave LA at 8:15 A.M. by TWA. Arrive in St. Louis at 2:30 P.M.

③ August 21 to 24: St. Regis Hotel, St. Louis. Phone (314) 444-5555. Checkout: August 24, 8:00 A.M.

④ August 24: Leave St. Louis at 10:00 A.M. by TWA. Arrive in Detroit at noon.

⑤ August 24 to 28: Riverfront Inn, Detroit. Phone (313) 245-6711. Checkout: August 28, 8:00 A.M.

⑥ August 28: Leave Detroit for LA by TWA at 10:00 A.M. and arrive at 11:15 A.M.

⑦ I expect to return to the office by 1:00 P.M. on August 28.

① Begins with main idea. Leads to specifics.

② Begins by listing departure. (For easy reading and good appearance, the itinerary would be tabulated.)

③–**⑥** List dates, names of hotels, phone numbers, and departure times.

⑦ Provides useful information as well as a logical ending.

How would tabulation help?

Policies and Procedures Memorandum   When a proposed change is not controversial, or when some prior discussions indicate a reader's approval, a memorandum suggesting change is preferably written deductively:

① The ad hoc committee in charge of developing a procedure for handling payroll advances makes the following proposal:

① Introduces the main idea.

(2) Policy: All full-time employees may request payroll advances of up to 80 percent of their normal net pay for a payroll period in case of emergency.

(3) Advances are limited to one every two months for any employee.

(4) Procedure: Employees applying for advances take the following steps in the order presented:

Construct all items in the same way grammatically.

1. Obtain Form PR-7 from your supervisor.

2. Fill in all blanks in the Employee section of the form.

3. Obtain approval by having your supervisor sign on approval line.

4. Take the approved form to the receptionist in the Payroll and Benefits office, Room 1620.

5. Pick up your check at the time designated by the receptionist.

6. Sign the receipt form in the presence of the payroll receptionist when you pick up your check.

(5) With your approval, we will incorporate this material in the Personnel Manual.

---

(2) and **(3)** State the proposed policy.

(4) Introduces the upcoming list of steps.

1–6. Note that *time* is the basis for sequence. Note parallelism—all six steps begin with a verb. Each is a complete sentence (subject "you" understood). Appearing in tabulated form with space before and after, each step gets attention. Enumeration both emphasizes and reinforces the desired sequence.

(5) Seeks approval for inclusion in the manual. Because "this material" refers to the preceding statement of policy and procedural steps, its use adds unity to the message.

Memoranda About Personnel Changes   Although the following memoranda about personnel changes are short, each would be keyboarded in single-spaced form on a full-size sheet of paper:

Why use standard-size paper for a short memo?

1 Employment of Robert Justice as assistant marketing manager was terminated as of June 30. 2 We plan to announce a replacement by July 15.

3 In the meantime, please give Susan Wolfe your full support should she ask for your help.

4 I appreciate your help and understanding during this period of change.

1 Begins with major idea. Who did the terminating is either understood, not worth revealing, or to be kept a secret; so passive voice is employed.
2 Reveals plans for replacement.
3 Seeks to assist in getting the firm's work done and also to help the temporary replacement in getting cooperation.
4 Expresses gratitude.

On or before a newly hired person's first day on the job, an introductory memorandum assists in getting the new relationship off to a good start:

1 I'm pleased to announce the appointment of Robert T. White as assistant head of the marketing department. 2 He will fill the position vacated by Marvin Broad, who recently moved to Seattle.

3 Bob comes to us from Gynco Industries where he was in charge of all direct-mail advertising.
4 His duties with us will include direct mail, long-range planning, and

1 Begins with the main idea.

2 By referring to the one being replaced, gives a general idea of the new employee's responsibilities.
3 – 5 Relate background and duties. Use of "Bob" suggests that Mr. White probably prefers to be addressed by that name instead of "Robert" or "Mr. White." Revealing

liaison with our ad agency, Smith and Moore. **5** He has college degrees in art and business.

6 He certainly merits your full cooperation and support. **7** We wish him much success and extend a sincere welcome to our organization.

previous responsibilities and educational background could add to the new employee's initial credibility.

6 and **7** Encourage present employees be cooperative and seek to make the new employee feel appreciated.

Memorandum "To the File"   When information needs to be converted into written form and filed for future reference, the record may be made in memorandum form:

1 By telephone today, I confirmed with A. J. Anderson and Sons' chief engineer, Harvey Milstein, that nothing less than 1-3/4-inch reinforcing rods be used in the support wall of the truck lane on Conjeo Grade. **2** An on-sight inspection will be made to substantiate this agreement.

1 Records details that may be needed when the subject is discussed later. The record will be useful, and the act of writing the memo will assist the writer in remembering and using the information.

2 Includes additional information that affects future plans.

Memorandum reports of financial and marketing activities are illustrated in the Appendix on pages 709 and 710. Especially in memoranda that contain many paragraphs, headings may be helpful. Straight right margins tend to improve overall appearance. Electronic machines achieve straight right margins by varying the amount of space between words. Most words are followed by one space, but some are followed by two or three. This extra space appearing between certain words is distracting to some people. Although the format of memoranda differs from the format of letters, memoranda and letters employ principles of style and organization that are basically the same.

Summary

Success in communicating is strongly influenced by a person's empathy. Before beginning to express ideas, the writer (or speaker) needs to answer several questions. What, exactly, is the message going to be? In view of what the message is, how will it affect the receiver? In view of its effect on the receiver, which sequence of ideas is best?

When the receiver can be expected to be *pleased* because of what the message is, the main idea is presented first and details follow. Likewise, when the message is routine and not likely to arouse a feeling of pleasure or displeasure, the main idea is presented first (as illustrated in the letters and memoranda of this chapter). When the receiver can be expected to be *displeased* or not initially interested, explanations and detail precede the main idea (Chapters 7 and 8).

From a writer's point of view, the task of writing is simplified if a prior decision has been reached about whether the message should be deductive (main idea first) or inductive (explanations and details first). From a reader's point of view, well-organized messages are easier to understand and they promote a more positive attitude toward the writer.

The deductive approach is appropriate for the following types of letters: routine claim letters, routine letters about credit, routine letters about orders, and routine requests; and favorable responses to all of them.

The deductive approach is also appropriate for the following types of memoranda: any memorandum that contains good news as the central idea; other memoranda that transmit such nonemotional information as itineraries, changes in policies or procedures, personnel changes, and various types of short reports.

The writing principles that apply to letters also apply to memoranda. Both are written informally; but memoranda normally make greater use of jargon, abbreviations, acronyms, and graphics.

Check Your Writing

Routine and Pleasant Messages

Content

_____ Major idea is clearly identified.

_____ Supporting detail is sufficient.

_____ Facts or figures are accurate.

Organization

_____ Major idea is in the first sentence.

_____ Supporting details are in most appropriate sequence.

_____ Final sentence (in a letter) seems appropriate for an ending.

Style

_____ Words will be readily understood.

_____ Syntax is acceptable.

_____ Sentences are relatively short.

_____ Variety appears in sentence length and structure.

_____ Significant words are in emphatic positions.

_____ Significant or positive thoughts are stated in simple sentences or in independent clauses.

_____ Grammar is acceptable.

_____ Active voice predominates.

_____ First person is used sparingly or not at all.

_____ Ideas cohere (changes in thought are not abrupt).

_____ Expression is original (sentences are not copied directly from the definition of the problem or from sample letters in text).

Mechanics

_____ Keyboarding, spelling, and punctuation are perfect.

_____ Paragraphs are relatively short.

(continued)

Letters

_____ Format is consistent (block, modified block, simplified, or personal).
_____ Margins are consistent.
Letter parts are in appropriate vertical and horizontal position.

   _____ return address (if letterhead is not used)
   _____ date
   _____ inside address
   _____ salutation (if used)
   _____ subject line (if used)
   _____ complimentary close (if used)
   _____ keyboarded name
   _____ reference initials (if used)
   _____ enclosure notation (if appropriate)

Memoranda

_____ To, from, date, and subject lines are filled in.
_____ Margins are consistent.
_____ Courtesy titles are omitted.
_____ Blank space appears between paragraphs.
_____ No indentions are used for paragraphs.
_____ Lines are single spaced.
_____ Tabulated sentences or columns are indented.
_____ Handwritten initials are placed by name on the "From" line.

Exercises

Review Questions

1. What is your definition of _empathy_?
2. How does empathy assist in the organization of letters and memoranda?

3. To a writer, what are the advantages of outlining before beginning to write?

4. What is the distinction between deductive and inductive writing?

5. What questions should be answered before a writer decides whether to write deductively or inductively?

6. For a letter or memorandum that transmits good news, what are the advantages of placing the good news in the first sentence?

7. In the text, what word is used to label messages that are essential but neither convey bad news nor good news?

8. Are the outlines recommended for *written* messages applicable to *oral* messages?

9. What term is used to label responses to claim letters?

10. What is the difference between *resale* and *sales-promotional* material?

11. In which is tabulation more likely to be used: (a) a claim letter or (b) an order letter?

12. Why is business jargon more likely to be useful in memoranda than in letters?

13. What purpose is served by writing memos "to the file"?

14. Do principles of organizing applied in the writing of letters also apply in the writing of memoranda?

15. Are acronyms more likely to be useful in memoranda than in letters?

Activities

In composing solutions to the problems in this and the remaining chapters about letters and memoranda, proceed in the following manner:

a. Before composing, study the preceding chapter. Look primarily for principles that can be applied (not for expressions or sentences that might possibly be paraphrased or used word for word in the letter to be composed).

b. Study the writing problem until you understand the facts.

c. Assume you are the person facing the writing problem.

d. Anticipate reader reaction, and jot down on scratch paper the outline you will employ.

e. Compose rapidly without looking at the definition of the problem and without looking at sample letters from the preceding chapter. (A sentence written to *define* a letter-writing problem may not be appropriate in a letter designed to *solve* the problem. Practice in adapting and paraphrasing is not needed; rather, the purpose of the assignment is to give practice in planning and expressing in such a way as to achieve clarity and to promote good human relations.)

f. Before keyboarding the letter, refer to the definition of the problem for such specifics as names, addresses, and amounts.

g. Unless otherwise instructed, keyboard the letter in one of the letter-format arrangements illustrated in the Appendix.

h. If the nature of a problem is such that a letter is written by a consumer who would probably not have letterhead paper, use one of the formats illustrated in Figure A.6 or A.7, which include a typed return address. If the letter is from someone in a business organization: (1) Leave 2 inches of blank space at the top of the page (the space that would be taken up by the firm's letterhead); (2) select the arrangement illustrated in Figure A.3, A.4, or A.5, and (3) begin by keyboarding the date in its appropriate position.

i. Remember that the assignment was designed to give you experience in applying *principles* that can be used in offices. However, the mechanical *processes* of preparing a school assignment and producing an actual business letter are different. In a business office, the letter that you have written would probably have been dictated into a machine, transcribed in the word-processing center, edited and corrected on the screen, printed in letter-perfect form at speeds up to 600 words per minute, and stored in the machine (if desired) for subsequent use as a form letter.

j. Before handing in an assignment, refer to the checklist that precedes the letter-writing problems. By checking your letter against the list, you will either (1) gain confidence that your letter meets high standards, or (2) identify some changes that need to be made.

Thoughtful use of the checklist has the short-range effect of improving the grade on *the assignment being handed in*. Its use with all assignments has the long-range effect of indelibly stamping in your mind the four qualities that *all your subsequent writing* should have: (1) the *right ideas* with sufficient support (content), (2) the best *sequence* of ideas for clear understanding and human relations (organization), (3) the most appropriate ways to *express* ideas in words and sentences (style), and (4) high standards in putting words *on paper*—keyboarding, spelling, and punctuating (mechanics). At the end of each letter-writing problem appears the name and address that is to be used as an inside address on the keyboarded letter. Names and addresses are strictly fictitious. Unless otherwise instructed, keyboard your own name as the sender.

Claims

1. Albert Waterson, a WW II veteran, responded to a magazine ad by placing an order for a 24-volume set of World War II encyclopedias. When they were delivered, Volume 18 was missing. Surely, the publisher will want to send Volume 18 as soon as the omission is called to its attention; no persuasion is necessary. Write a letter to the publisher. In the letter, refer to an enclosed copy of the shipping invoice, which was received with the other volumes. It will provide needed details of the transaction. (Attempting to construct the invoice is not part of the assignment; assume that you have it ready for attaching to the letter.) Include Mr. Waterson's return address (see Figures A.6 and A.7 for placement): 412 East Jefferson Street, Wellsville, IA 50116. Address the letter to Heritage House Publishers, Inc., 432 Edgewood Plaza, Meade OH 43543.

2. Heritage House Publishers (preceding activity) had not included Volume 18 because it had not been released from the printer. Because of its complex graphics, it had required more production time than other volumes. A note of explanation (which Mr. Waterson had apparently overlooked) had been included in the shipment. The missing volume will be shipped within four weeks. Write a short letter, with which you plan to include a brochure about a soon-to-be-completed volume about the history of the U.S. Cavalry. Use your name as manager of the shipping department. Mr. Waterson's address: 412 East Jefferson Street, Wellsville, IA 50116.

3. In response to a TV commercial, you ordered a set of three cassettes—"Eddie's Best Songs." Cassettes 1 and 2 were exactly what you wanted and expected; Cassette 3 was totally blank! Return the blank cassette and request Cassette 3. The invoice accompanying the cassettes was numbered EBS-3-1785. The inside address: Eddie's Best Songs, Musi-Pro, Inc., 345 North Central, Centerline, TX 76543.

4. Upon receipt of the blank cassette (Activity 3), Musi-Pro mails Cassette 3. Although the recipient would probably be content to get it with or without an accompanying letter, Musi-Pro decides to send a short letter. It includes these ideas: the opportunity to correct an error was appreciated, a replacement cassette is being mailed promptly, a search for an explanation was fruitless, Musi-Pro tries

to be extremely efficient and regrets the inconvenience, and an accompanying pamphlet lists related recordings in which the recipient may be interested. Karl Worthy, 432 West 15th Street, Sylvester, OK 65362.

Credit

5. Within three months, you will receive your degree in construction engineering. You plan to begin constructing new homes in a city 100 miles from your school. On your most recent trip to that city, you picked up credit-application forms from one of its building-supply stores. After filling out the forms, you are confident you will be granted credit privileges. Write a letter to accompany the forms you are mailing to the store. Home Building & Supply, P.O. Box 21, Baxterville, KS 67891.

6. The construction engineer's credit application (Activity 5) has been approved. Initially, the engineer's credit limit is $100,000. As her construction projects expand, the limit can be raised if necessary. Home Building & Supply has prepared a pamphlet that gives details of the credit terms. As an official of the firm, write a letter conveying the good news. Call her attention to the enclosed credit-terms pamphlet. (Constructing the pamphlet is not part of your assignment; assume that it has been prepared already.) Ms. Carol S. Goodman, Room 347 Irish Hall, Southstate University, Woodland, NE 68451.

Order

7. Nancy Welch, mother of five and a health-food enthusiast, buys most of her vitamins, minerals, and related products from Western Biologics. By letter, she places an order for the following items: 2 bottles of lecithin capsules (100 per bottle) at $5.79 per bottle; 1 bottle of Special B-Complex with vitamin C (100 capsules per bottle) at $9.48; 3 bottles of brewers yeast tablets (300 per bottle) at $5.48 per bottle; and 2 bottles of Papayazyme (100 per bottle) at $5.79 per bottle. Her check ($55.58) includes $6.50 for tax and handling. For Mrs. Welch (whose return address is 792 West 22nd Avenue, Mineside, CO 81304), write the order letter to Western Biologics, P.O. Box 1442, Chula Vista, CA 90021.

8. When Mrs. Nancy Welch placed one of her largest orders for health-food products, one item ($49.50) was unavailable for shipment. Western Biologics credited her account for that amount. Knowing her credit balance was $49.50, she did not include a check for her

next order ($31.29); instead, she asked that it be charged against her current balance. Two weeks after the shipment was received, Mrs. Welch received a statement requesting payment for the $31.29 order. Actually, she owes the firm nothing; it owes her $18.21 (which would be her account credit if the transaction had been properly recorded). For Mrs. Welch, write a letter of explanation: Western Biologics, P.O. Box 1442, Chula Vista, CA 90021.

Other Routine Letters

9. Assume Elda Smith has asked you to write a letter for her about her late husband's deferred compensation plan. She has already called the office in which the plan is administered. Elda has a choice: (1) leave the money on deposit and let it earn interest until her husband would have reached 65 (about 10 years from now); or (2) accept a check now for the current value ($17,586). Elda expressed preference for the first choice, but the office needs *written* authorization with Elda's signature. Address: Charles Edwards, Manager, Missouri Deferred Compensation Plan, P.O. Box 1310, Jefferson City, MO 65314.

10. In response to an ad in a financial journal, George Wilson called a toll-free number and asked that a prospectus be sent to him. As one of the vice-presidents in charge of the Yield-Right Fund, you have decided to include a personalized letter in the envelope with the prospectus. (The letter is stored in the word processor and used in response to all requests for this prospectus.) Although the prospectus contains complete details of the proposed investment, one point is selected for inclusion in the letter (a point that deserves great emphasis): The *Delphi Money Fund Report* has rated Yield-Right as the top performer of all money-market funds (with similar investment criteria) for the 12-month period ending October 31 of the current year. George Wilson, 454 North 37th Avenue, Weston, PA 13342.

11. Before Edith went away to school, her parents called the Charge-Bank Credit Card Company and asked that she be issued a credit card with the parents' number on it. With this card, she could make purchases that would be paid for by the parents when they paid their monthly Charge-Bank bill. On the phone, Charge-Bank assured the parents that such arrangements could be made, but the request must be in writing. Write a letter authorizing Charge-Bank to issue a card to Edith. Charge-Bank Credit Card Company, P.O. Box 1227, Phoenix, AZ 85334.

12. Assume you are a personnel director. As much as possible, you prepare form letters for routine correspondence that frequently recurs. The letters are stored in the computer. When a letter is to be sent, the keyboarder enters the inside address; the automatic typewriter produces the desired letter. Prepare a form letter (just the paragraphs) that would be appropriate for responding to someone who has written an unsolicited letter of application. The form will acknowledge receipt of the letter and request the applicant to fill out and return the firm's standard application form. (Date, inside address, etc., are not to be included in your form; just compose the essential paragraphs.)

13. A recent publication has a picture of a product in which you have a special interest. If you had appropriate answers to certain questions, you might order the product. Write a letter to the manufacturer. Ask at least three questions. (For suggestions on format, see Figure A.6.)

14. The service department of an automobile agency has a plan for expanding and improving its service. It will send a short questionnaire to car owners who have had their cars serviced more than five times during the preceding year. Only five questions are asked; four of them require only a check-mark response and the fifth invites a written comment if a respondent chooses. A postpaid envelope is included, and respondents are invited to tear off a coupon good for a 20 percent discount on the next oil change. Compose a form letter that invites car owners to fill out and return the attached questionnaire. (Assume the questionnaire is already prepared; it's not a part of the writing assignment.)

15. The local public utility firm in your city is rumored to have plans for selling some tax-exempt bonds. If a prospectus is available, you would like to have a copy. Otherwise, you would like answers to some specific questions about the denominations available, limits on the number of bonds one person would be allowed to buy, maturity dates, yield rates, etc. The "zero-coupon" bonds are of special interest to you. Write to LaClede Electric, P.O. Box 1730, Lebanon, MO 63451.

Memoranda   In Chapter 6 and those that follow, all memorandum exercises are written for the same company: Markens Art Company. It sells sculpture, paintings, and folk art. With the sculptor, it has an exclusive arrangement: MAC is the only source through which his work is sold, and each item of sculpture in the MAC stores came from this artist only. One of the stores is in Santa Fe (where the main office is); others are in Ashland, Scottsdale, and Eureka Springs.

The stores are owned by the George Markens Family. George is president; other family members constitute the board of directors. The chief of operations is Vinita Clark; personnel manager, Paul Adams; accountant, Charles Atwood; sales manager, Henry "Hank" Appleton; and purchasing manager, Ruth Hutchinson. The store managers: Santa Fe, Calvin Worth; Ashland, Pauline Welch; and Eureka Springs, Wilma Snyder.

6·23

16. In the Ashland store last season, business was exceedingly good— especially during the months in which theaters were open for staged productions of famous plays. This year's productions promise to be even more appealing. Many who come to see the plays will have an interest in art. In preparation for the busy season, Pauline has requested permission to hire two additional sales people and an additional record keeper. She included convincing data about the workload, the amount of money spent for overtime last season, and so on. As if you were Paul Adams, write a memo to Pauline Welch. Let her know that her request is approved, that the new employees can be placed on the payroll as soon as the theater season begins, and that the guidelines for selection (of which she has a copy) are still in effect.

17. Although the sculptor is now famous (some of his pieces have sold for more than a quarter of a million dollars), some of the officers and managers have not met him. As though you were George Markens, write a memorandum to all officers and managers. On a Tuesday evening six weeks from now, the sculptor (Maynord Jenkins) will be attending a dinner with the Markens family, the officers, and the store managers. After showing some films that illustrate his artistic techniques, he will preview some of the units on which he is now working. He will devote about a half hour to questions and answers. The standard practice is for the firm to pay for managers' travel expenses, so they need not be mentioned. The dinner is at 7:30 P.M. in the Pima room of the Plaza Hotel, next door to the main office.

18. On the morning after the store managers have had a chance to meet the sculptor, Vinita Clark would like to spend an hour with them in her office—from 9:00 A.M. to 10:00 A.M. She wants to share ideas with them (and get ideas from them) on the subjects of safety and security in the stores. Insurance claims against the firm have been increasing, and thefts (especially thefts of folk art) have doubled in the last year. Prepare a memorandum to send to the managers.

19. Vinita Clark has decided MAC should participate in an art exhibit that will be seen by thousands of convention attendees in New Orleans. She has reserved space (for which she has paid the $900 fee). The exhibits will be on the mezzanine floor of the Roosevelt Hotel in New Orleans. The three-day showing is to begin on March 1, but displays will have to be set up on the evening of April 30. A few lightweight pieces of sculpture are to be included, but the primary emphasis is to be on folk art. Partly because Wilma Snyder was so successful in conducting a similar exhibit in Chicago last year, and partly because her store in Arkansas is closest to New Orleans, Wilma is to be in charge of the display booth. Wilma sent a detailed report of the Chicago convention; Vinita would appreciate a similar report after the New Orleans convention ends. As though you held Vinita's job, write a memorandum to Wilma Snyder.

20. Wilma Snyder's booth at the New Orleans convention was much more successful than she expected it to be (Activity 19). More than 800 people visited the booth. Some of them returned for a third or fourth look. Even the Europeans who stopped by were already familiar with Maynord Jenkins' sculpture. Sales of the book illustrating his works were brisk, as an attached list of direct sales and orders indicates. Wilma's expenses for meals, lodging, and travel were $937; receipts are enclosed so Vinita can reimburse her. Wilma had been able to attend a jazz concert and enjoy some of the famous New Orleans cuisine. Write Wilma's memo to Vinita. In it, refer to an attached report of sales and orders (which is not part of your writing assignment; assume that the figures compared very favorably with the figures from the Chicago convention).

Writing About the Unpleasant

A man does not know what he is saying until he knows what he is not saying.

G. K. CHESTERTON, 1927

Two assumptions permeate this chapter: (1) writers have valid support for their negative messages, and (2) readers are reasonable. Important in *all* messages, empathy is especially important when writing refusals or other types of bad news. The same is true of writing *style*.

Empathy

Like a selfish player on a team, a selfish person in business operates under a severe handicap. The person's actions and words reveal the trait. It makes cooperation hard to get, friends hard to keep, and decisions hard for others to accept. *Empathy* (as contrasted with selfishness) assists in escaping such hazards. Yet, those who *have* genuine empathy for others often forget to ask themselves, "If I were the receiver of the message I am about to transmit, how would I react?" The answer to that question has an impact on the *sequence* in which the ideas are presented and the *style* in which they are expressed.

• Sequence of Ideas

Why avoid putting bad news in the first sentence?

Just as good news is accompanied with details, bad news is accompanied with supporting details (reasons, explanations). If the bad news is presented in the first sentence, the reaction is likely to be negative: "They never gave me a fair chance," "That's unfair," "This just can't be." Having made a value judgment on reading the first sentence, readers are naturally reluctant to change their minds before the last sentence—even though the intervening sentences present a valid basis for doing so. Having been disappointed by the idea contained in the first sentence, readers are tempted to concentrate on *refuting* (instead of *understanding*) supporting details.

From the writer's point of view, details that support a refusal are very important. If the supporting details are understood and believed, the message may be readily accepted and good business relationships preserved. Because the reasons behind the bad news are so important, the writer needs to organize the message in such a way as to emphasize the reasons. The chances of getting the reader to understand the reasons are much better *before* the bad news is presented than *after* the bad news is presented. If presented afterward, reasons may not even be read.

People who are refused want to know why. To them (and to the person doing the refusing) the reasons are vital; they must be transmitted and received. The writer can simplify the process by employing the following outline:

1. Begin with an introductory paragraph that leads to the reasons for refusing the request.
2. Present the facts, an analysis, and the reasons for refusal.
3. State the refusal.
4. Close with a related idea that shifts emphasis away from the refusal.

This four-point outline is applied in letters and memoranda illustrated in pages that follow. But, before reading them, consider the reasoning that supports each point.

Point 1: Introductory Paragraph   Of course, the *first* paragraph in any series is in a sense "introductory." The first paragraph in a good-news letter contains the good news, but the introductory paragraph in the bad-news or refusal letter has a different function. It should (1) let the reader know what the letter is about (without stating the obvious) and (2) serve as a transition into the discussion of reasons (without revealing the bad news or leading the reader to expect good news). If these objectives can be accomplished in one sentence, that sentence can be the first paragraph.

Point 2: Facts, Analysis, and Reasons   Properly introduced, the essential information will be seen as related and important. If the bad news had preceded, (1) the message might have been put aside before this important portion was even read, or (2) the disappointment experienced upon reading the bad news might interfere with comprehension or acceptance of the supporting explanation. Compared with explanations that *follow* bad news, those that *precede* have a better chance of being received with an open mind. By the time a reader has finished reading this portion of the message, the upcoming statement of refusal may be foreseen and accepted as valid.

Point 3: Refusal Statement   Because preceding statements are tactful and seem valid, the sentence that states the bad news may arouse little or no resentment. If the writing were strictly inductive, the refusal statement would be last. Yet, placing a statement of refusal (or bad news) in the last sentence or paragraph would have the effect of placing too much emphasis on it. Preferably, *reasons* (instead of the bad news) should remain uppermost in the reader's mind. Also, placing bad news last would make the ending seem cold and abrupt.

Marginal notes:

In refusal letters, do reasons deserve emphasis?

What does the first paragraph seek to accomplish?

Putting bad news in the first sentence would de-emphasize reasons.

Why not save the bad news for the final sentence?

What does the final
paragraph seek to
accomplish?

Point 4: Closing Paragraph   A closing paragraph that is about some aspect of the topic other than the bad news itself helps in several ways. It assists in (1) de-emphasizing the most unpleasant part of the message, (2) conveying some useful information that should logically follow (instead of precede) bad news, (3) showing that the writer has a positive attitude, and (4) adding a unifying quality to the message.

Although the preceding outline has four points, a bad-news letter may or may not have four paragraphs. More than one paragraph may be necessary for conveying supporting reasons, and placing the statement of refusal in a paragraph by itself would give it too much emphasis. It's best placed near the end of the last explanatory paragraph. In the illustrations that follow (as well as examples in the Appendix) note that first and final paragraphs are seldom longer than two sentences. In fact, one-sentence paragraphs (as beginnings) look more inviting to read.

The *sequence* of those paragraphs is strongly influenced by human empathy. So is the manner of expression.

• Style

In messages that convey bad news, three stylistic qualities merit special attention: emphasis/de-emphasis, positive language, and implication.

What are some
stylistics of
subordination?

A basic of human relations is: "Emphasize the positive; de-emphasize the negative." For a review of *emphasis and subordination* techniques, see Chapter 5. The outline recommended for bad-news messages puts the statement of bad news in a subordinate position. Likewise, stylistic techniques work toward the same goal: subordinate bad news by placing it in the dependent clause, using passive voice, expressing in general terms, and using abstract nouns or things (instead of the person written to) as the subject of a sentence. Although a refusal (bad news) needs to be clear, subordination of it allows the reasoning to get deserved emphasis.

Positive language accents the good instead of the bad, the pleasant instead of the unpleasant, what can be done instead of what can't be done. Compared with a negative idea presented in negative terms, a negative idea presented in positive terms is more likely to be accepted. When you are tempted to use the following terms, search instead for words or ideas that sound more positive:

Think of some other
words that could be
added to this list.

chagrined	disregard	ignored
complaint	error	inexcusable
disappointed	failure	insinuation
disgusted	ignorant	irresponsible

lied	nonsense	ridiculous
misinformed	obnoxious	underhanded
mistake	overlooked	upset
neglect	regrettable	wrong

To business people who conscientiously practice empathy, such terms may not even come to mind when communicating the unpleasant. Words in the preceding list evoke feelings that contrast sharply with the positive feelings evoked by words such as

accurate	durable	health
approval	energetic	peace
assist	enthusiasm	pretty
cheerful	fragrance	productive
commend	freedom	prosper
concise	generous	recommendation
cordial	gratitude	respect
correct	happy	true

To increase the number of pleasant-sounding words in your writing, practice thinking positively—strive to see the good in situations and in others. Will Rogers professed to be able to see *some* good in every person he met.

Implication is often an effective way of transmitting an unpleasant idea. For example, during the noon hour one employee says to another, "Will you go with me to see this afternoon's baseball game?" "No, I won't" communicates a negative response, but it seems unnecessarily direct and harsh. The same message (invitation is rejected) can be clearly stated in an *indirect* way (by implication):

Must refusals be stated directly?

I wish I could.	Other responsibilities forbid, but the recipient would *like* to accept.
I must get my work done.	By revealing the necessity of working instead, the worker conveys the "no" answer.
If I watched baseball this afternoon, I'd be transferred tomorrow.	By stating an unacceptable consequence of acceptance, the worker conveys the idea of nonacceptance.
I'm a <u>football</u> fan.	By indicating a preference for another sport, the worker conveys nonacceptance.

Which of the preceding sentences illustrate use of the subjunctive mood?

By *implying* the "no" answer, the foregoing responses (1) use positive language, (2) convey reasons or at least a positive attitude, and (3) seem more respectful. These implication techniques (as well as emphasis/de-emphasis, positive language, and inductive sequence) are illustrated in letters that follow.

Saying "No" to an Adjustment Request

Assume a seller of oriental furniture receives the following request for reimbursement:

Please reimburse me for the amount of the attached bill.

When I ordered my oriental chest (which was delivered yesterday), I paid in full for the price of the chest and the transportation charges. Yet, before the transportation firm would make delivery, I was required to pay $144. Recalling that our state does not collect sales tax on foreign purchases, and holding a purchase ticket (Sh-311) marked "Paid in full," I assumed an error that you would be glad to correct.

The $144 was a *federal* tax (import duties). Before placing the order, the purchaser had been told that purchasers were responsible for import duties that would be collected at the time of delivery. In addition, a statement to that effect was written in bold print on the buy–sell agreement of which he was given a copy. Maybe he didn't listen; maybe he lost or did not read his copy. Even though the purchaser is clearly at fault, the seller's response could be more tactful than the following letter is:

1 I have your request for a $144 reimbursement and am sorry to say it cannot be made.

1 Begins with an idea that is not needed (receipt of the request could be taken for granted). Apologizing for a justified decision hardly seems appropriate. Refusing in the first sentence places emphasis on the refusal.

2 Clearly, the charge is for import duties.

3 In the discussion that preceded the purchase and in the documents you signed at the time, it was clearly pointed out that you would be responsible for import duties. 4 Duties are not collected at the time of sale because they cannot be accurately predicted.

5 I am sure you can understand my position in this matter. 6 Thank you for doing business with us; and if you have any further questions, do not hesitate to call or write.

2 Offers explanation that may not receive the emphasis it deserves, especially if reaction to the first sentence has been "They're crooks," or "It's totally unfair."

3 Presents needed information, but if the reader is still smarting from reaction to the first sentence, the point may not register with sufficient impact.

4 Commendably presents a reason for the method of operation.

5 Employs a cliché.

6 Employs a cliché. The words may seem polite but insincere. If taken literally, they could lead to unnecessary correspondence.

In the following revised letter, note that the first sentence reveals the subject matter of the letter and leads into a presentation of reasons. Reasons precede the refusal, the statement of refusal is subordinated, and the final sentence is about something other than the refusal.

1 Your hand-carved, monkeywood chest was delivered about a month sooner than we had predicted when purchase papers were signed.

2 Your copy does show prepayment of cost and transportation.

1 Reveals the subject matter of the letter. Leads to a discussion of reasons. Includes a reminder of a positive quality (it's hand carved).

2 Begins explanation.

3 Because the amount of import duty cannot be calculated until the shipping date, the tax is paid when shipment is received.

3 Presents reason for the procedure followed.

4 Before sales contracts are written, buyers are told of their responsibility to pay for import tax. 5 The sales ticket has a bold-face statement to that effect--on our copy and on yours.

4 and 5 Complete the explanation.

Are simple sentences best for stating refusals?

6 Responsibility for the tax, then, is yours; but you have reason to feel good about your purchase.

6 Reveals the refusal, which is stated in a compound sentence. The positive idea in the second clause takes some emphasis away from the you-must-pay idea in the first clause.

7 By ordering directly from the factory, you saved about 40 percent. You now have a beautiful chest that is exquisitely hand carved.

7 Employs resale in the final sentence.

The outline for an adjustment refusal

As we have seen, adjustment letters that say "no" follow a general sequence of ideas: (1) begin with a neutral or factual sentence that leads to the reasons behind the "no" answer, (2) present the reasons and explanations, (3) present the refusal in an unemphatic manner, and (4) close with an off-the-subject thought. Naturally, the ending should be related to the letter or to the business relationship; but it should not be specific about the refusal. Although the same pattern is followed in credit, order, and favor refusals, those letters are sufficiently different to make a discussion of each helpful.

Saying "No" to a Credit Request

Once we have evaluated a request for credit and have decided "no" is the better answer, our primary writing problem is to say "no" so tactfully that we keep the business relationship on a cash basis. Since requests for credit are often accompanied with an order, our credit refusals may serve as acknowledgment letters. And, of course, every business letter is directly or indirectly a sales letter. The prospective customers may be disappointed when they cannot buy on a credit basis. However, if we keep them sold on our goods and services, they may prefer to buy from us on a cash basis instead of seeking credit privileges elsewhere.

In a letter that refuses credit, what is a good counterproposal?

When the credit investigation shows that applicants are poor credit risks, too many credit writers no longer regard them as possible customers. They write to them in a cold, matter-of-fact manner. They don't consider that such applicants may still be interested in doing business on a cash basis and may qualify for credit later.

In credit refusals, as in other types of refusals, the major portion of the message should be explanation. We cannot expect our reader to agree that our "no" answer is the right answer unless we give the reasons behind it. Naturally, those who send us credit information will expect us to keep it confidential. But if we give the reasons without using the names of those from whom we obtained our information, we are not violating confidence. We are passing along the truth as a justification for our business decisions. Both writers and readers benefit from the explanation of the reasons behind the refusal. For writers, the explanation helps to establish fairmindedness; it shows that the decision was not arbitrary. For readers, the explanation not only presents the truth to which they are entitled, it also has guidance value. From it they learn to adjust habits and as a result qualify for credit purchases later.

Why discuss reasons for a credit refusal?

Resale is helpful for four reasons: (1) it might cause credit applicants to prefer our brand, perhaps being willing to buy it even on a cash basis; (2) it suggests that the writer is trying to be helpful; (3) it makes the writing easier—negative thoughts are easier to de-emphasize when cushioned with resale material, and by using resale material we sound confident of future cash purchases; and (4) it can confirm the credit applicant's judgment—suggesting the applicant made a good choice of merchandise is giving an indirect compliment.

Why use resale in a credit refusal?

Assume a retailer of electronic devices has placed an initial order and requested credit privileges. After examining financial statements that were enclosed, the wholesaler decides the request should be denied. The following letter would be substandard:

1 Your order of July 6 has been received, and your request for credit privileges has been given to me for evaluation.

1 States ideas that could have been left to implication.

② At this time, we do not believe it is in our best interest to sell to you on a credit basis.	② Reveals the negative decision before revealing the basis for it.
③ As you may be aware, many leaders in the field of finance recommend that businesses maintain a 2-to-1 ratio of current assets to current liabilities.	③ Presents an explanation, but unnecessarily raises doubts about the applicant's knowledge of financial matters.
④ Since your current ratio is approximately 1 1/4 to 1, your orders will need to have payment attached.	④ Continues with figures that should have preceded the statement of refusal.
⑤ We trust you will understand.	⑤ Reveals that the writer has doubts about the strength of the explanation.
⑥ An envelope is enclosed for your convenience in sending your check for $1,487.53, after which your order will be shipped.	⑥ Employs worn expressions in referring to the enclosure.
⑦ For a look at the latest in video games, see the enclosed folder.	⑦ Does make a commendable effort to encourage additional orders.

Contrast the tone of the preceding letter with the tone of the one that follows:

① The items listed in your order of July 6 have been selling very rapidly in recent weeks.	① Implies receipt of the order. Leads to an explanation.
② Supplying customers' demands for the latest in electronic technology is consistent with sound business practices.	② Introduces explanation. Implies approval of *one* of the applicant's practices (supplying most recently developed items).
③ One sound practice is careful control of indebtedness, according to specialists in accounting and finance.	③ Leads to discussion of *another* practice that is the basis for subsequent refusal.

If an application has both strengths and weaknesses, should any of the strengths be mentioned in the credit-refusal letter?

④ Their formula for control is to maintain at least a 2-to-1 ratio of current assets to current liabilities. ⑤ Experience has taught us that, for the benefit of all concerned, credit should be available only to purchasers who meet that ratio.

⑥ Because your ratio is approximately 1 1/4 to 1, you are encouraged to make cash purchases.

⑦ By continuing to supply your customers with timely merchandise, you should be able to improve the ratio.

⑧ Then, we would welcome an opportunity to review your credit application.

⑨ To send your check ($1,487.53) for your current order, just use the enclosed envelope; your order will be shipped promptly.

④ Provides further detail.

⑤ Continues with the explanation.

⑥ Employs positive language in expressing the refusal. Conveys "no" to credit purchases by recommending *cash* purchases. If a writer thought the statement of refusal should be more direct, the sentence could be expanded: "Because your ratio is approximately 1 1/4 to 1, the order will not be filled on a time-payment basis; but you are encouraged to make cash purchases."

⑦ Looks confidently to the future and reminds the applicant of the commendable practice discussed in the second sentence.

⑧ Encourages subsequent application and thus implies expectation of continued business relationship.

⑨ Reminds the merchant of the desired action.

In a credit refusal, would "buy for cash" be classified as a "counterproposal"?

> ⑩ Other timely items (such as the most recent in video games) are shown in the enclosed folder.

⑩ Employs sales-promotional material as a closing sentence. Uses "timely" as a reminder of the applicant's commendable business practice and as a technique for developing unity.

The preceding credit refusal explains, refuses, and offers to sell for cash. Although credit references have been checked, it says nothing about having conducted a "credit investigation." It does not identify referents, and it makes no apology for action taken. Similar writing challenges occur in refusing orders.

Saying "No" to an Order for Merchandise

Why might you refuse to fill an order?

For various reasons, we may not be able to send the merchandise that people have ordered from us.

1. We may be able to send it, but there will be a waiting period. (At such times we would acknowledge the order and write a letter saying "Yes, you will receive the . . . by. . . .")
2. We may not sell directly to consumers. (We would tell the customer where to buy the merchandise.)
3. We may not have what the customer ordered, but we have something that will serve his or her needs better. (We would hold the order until we have made the customer understand that we have something better.)

For orders that cannot be filled, the inductive approach recommended for all "no" letters is preferred. The following request has to be refused because the manufacturer to whom it is addressed does not sell directly to consumers:

> Please send a valve for my Sunex solar heater. According to the Manufacturer's Installation Guide, the part number is S-54. Since I don't have a price list, just send it COD.

If a manufacturer received many similar requests, they would very likely be answered by form letter. But even form letters do not have to be so cold and indifferent as the following letter:

① We have your recent request that we ship you a _____ .

② Unfortunately, we do not sell direct to consumers. ③ Your nearest dealer is _____ whose address is _____ . ④ May we suggest that you place your order there.

⑤ Thank you for your interest in our merchandise.

① The receipt of the order could have been implied.

② Distribution through dealers has advantages; it isn't necessarily "unfortunate." ③ Giving the exact name and address of a local dealer is commendable. ④ This suggestion misses a chance for resale.

⑤ The ending seems perfunctory.

People understand the practicality of form letters. They don't object to them because they are *forms;* but they do object to indifferent, matter-of-fact language. When stored in the memory of word-processing equipment, form letters can be individually keyboarded. They look like letters written specifically for a certain person. The general plan of the following revised letter is to make customers' desire for the merchandise so strong that they will be willing to wait for it and to purchase it through conventional merchandising outlets:

Why use form letters for refusing orders?

① When we began the manufacture of solar heaters, the valves (like the one you ordered) were made of plastic.

② They are now made of a copper alloy, which gives much longer and more dependable service.

③ As manufacturers, we devote all our efforts to experimenting on, making, and improving the Sunex.

④ Because we concentrate solely on these efforts (and leave selling and servicing

① Introduces the subject and leads to an explanation.

② Provides resale on the item ordered.

③ Begins the explanation.

④ Reveals—in positive language—that sales are not made directly to

to retailers), we have been able to develop one of the most efficient solar units available anywhere.

⑤ Your nearest retailer of Sunex parts is Western Supply Company, 217 N. 24th Street, Albuquerque, NM 75341.

consumers. Lets the reader see an advantage in the manufacturer's not selling to consumers directly.

⑤ Closes by providing needed information.

If the merchandise involved in the preceding letter had been expensive, or if orders sent directly to the manufacturer were rare, it would have been better not to use a form letter. Both form letters and individual letters can benefit from applying the following suggestions:

1.   Imply receipt of the order and confirm the customer's good choice of merchandise.
2.   Wherever appropriate in the letter, use resale to make the customer willing to reorder through the proper channel.
3.   Give reasons why sales are through dealers. Suggest or spell out how advantageously customers can buy through a dealer.
4.   Use positive language to explain that the order is not being filled.

Sometimes, customers *order* one item when they can more profitably *use* another, as in the following order letter:

Will you reload the casings in the box to which this letter is attached?

In each casing, put 1 1/4 ounces of No. 8 shot with 32 grains of SR7625 powder.

Continuing our arrangement of last year, charge the total bill to my MasterCard No. 5302 1826 0520 X120.

The individual has ordered reloads that are inappropriate for the casings returned. Filling the order as submitted would be a mistake. Injury, or at least dissatisfaction, could result. The following letter seeks to convince the recipient that the type of refill ordered is not the type of refill needed:

① The casings you sent to us have been received.

① Begins with an idea that could have been left to implication.

② However, we do not think it advisable to fill them as requested.

③ The load requested is too heavy for the shells.

④ In view of the condition of the shells, do we have permission to load them with 26 grains of powder and 1 ounce of shot?

⑤ Your order will be held until we hear from you.

② Reveals the refusal before presenting the explanation. After a neutral statement, "However" immediately lets the reader know that negatives follow.

③ Explains in general terms.

④ Needs more specific explanation. Commendably, seeks approval to send that which is usable.

⑤ Presents needed information, but the idea of "holding" the order seems a little negative. "Hear from you" is worn and literally implies oral communication.

Although letters such as the preceding may get the desired results, the following letter applies sound writing principles more effectively:

① The casings you sent to us can be filled with a variety of reload combinations.

② The copper portion of each casing is only 5/8 of an inch, and the plastic portion shows signs of wear. ③ They appear to have been reloaded once or twice previously. ④ If the requested load (32 grains of

① Implies receipt of the casings and the request that they be reloaded. Use of "variety" serves as an easy transition into a discussion of *two* of those combinations: the one requested and the one recommended.

② Begins the explanation. Presents some specifics.

③ Continues with explanatory details.
④ Continues with explanation. Uses specific

Should refusals be
stated in short
sentences?

powder behind 1 1/2 ounces of No. 8 shot) is used, portions of the plastic casing can become lodged in the barrel. ⑤ The result could be at least a nuisance and at most a serious accident.

numbers to tailor make the letter to this receiver; they serve to confirm the specific request. The receiver may not remember (and have no record of) what was ordered.

⑤ Gives further evidence that the item ordered was not the item needed.

⑥ Instead of filling your order as requested, we would like your permission to reload with 28 grains of powder behind 1 1/8 ounces of No. 8 shot.

⑥ *Implies* refusal for de-emphasis. Offers details of an alternative.

⑦ The extra safety would more than compensate for the slight decrease in range. ⑧ Your choice of the SR7625 powder is ideal; we recommend it because it burns so cleanly.

⑦ Reveals a disadvantage of the alternative, but de-emphasizes it by putting it in the sentence that states the primary advantage.

⑧ Includes resale by confirming the sportsman's choice of powder.

⑨ To authorize reloading according to our suggestions, just check the appropriate square on the enclosed card and return the card in the enclosed envelope.

⑨ Seeks confirmation of permission to send what is needed instead of what was ordered. Makes response easy. On the card, one of the squares (the options) could be to return the empty shells. Mentioning that option in the letter would give it undesired emphasis, so no reference is made to it.

The preceding letter involved no difference in price between the ordered item and the needed item. If the needed item should cost more, its advantages should be pointed out and then the extra cost stated.

Taking the time required for writing such a long letter to a customer may at first seem questionable. The preceding letter (as is so often true) is about a circumstance that recurs frequently. With one good draft in the file or in the word processor, the next letter can be adapted and reproduced quickly and with very little effort.

> Foreign Models Incorporated handles carburetors and other parts for European cars only.
>
> If you will place your order (which we are returning) with Pacific Motors at 1301 South Jackson Street in San Pedro, you should have your carburetor in a short time.
>
> When you need to trade cars, come in and see our selections. We have 14 different makes--from low-priced economy cars to the most expensive European sports cars.

Remember, the sales-promotional material didn't cost anything so far as paper and postage are concerned—we had to write anyway. And it's almost sure to be read—something we can't say of all sales messages.

What is an advantage of including sales-promotional material in an order refusal?

When people say "no" in a letter, they usually do so because they think "no" is the better answer for all concerned. They can see how recipients will ultimately benefit from the refusal. If the letter is based on a sound decision, and if it has been well written, receivers will probably recognize that the senders did them a favor by saying "no."

Saying "No" to a Request for a Favor

When a request for a favor must be denied, the same reasons-before-refusal pattern is recommended:

> ① You are to be commended for your efforts to identify principles that apply to the insurance field.
>
> ② One of our primary concerns has been preservation of confidentiality. Each policyholder is assured that information provided will be seen by insurance officials only.

① Introduces the subject without revealing whether the answer will be "yes" or "no."

② Gives reasons.

③ These confidentiality requirements must be strictly honored, but we do want to be helpful.

④ If you would like to see some of our blank policy forms, we can supply them.

③ Uses positive words in stating the refusal. Subordinates "no" by placing it in a long sentence that contains a positive idea.

④ Closes on a more positive note by offering an alternative.

The preceding letters—all of which are *responses* to prior correspondence—employ the same principles of sequence and style that are recommended for letters that *initiate* communication about unpleasant topics. The same principles apply, regardless of whether the communication is a letter or a memorandum.

Initiating Communication About the Unpleasant

The following memorandum to all employees is from the personnel director; the subject is a change in insurance premiums:

① Effective August 1, your payroll deductions for your Valley HMO Group health-insurance premiums will be increased between $15 and $30 per month. ② This increase, although regrettable, is unavoidable.

③ Premiums for our Group policy have risen drastically in the last 24 months. ④ Matco Enterprises was able to absorb the smaller increases of previous years, but this is no longer possible.

⑤ We considered reducing other fringe benefits as an

① Begins with the bad news.

② Employs negative language.

③ Begins the explanation.

④ Employs negative language and a pronoun (this) that has an indefinite antecedent (the noun for which "this" stands is not employed).

⑤ and ⑥ Begin with "We" and thus emphasize the

alternative to raising premium deductions, but the final conclusion was that such action would be unfair. ⑥ We <u>had</u> to raise premiums.

⑦ To more precisely estimate the amount of your monthly deduction, we have attached a booklet. ⑧ On page 3, you will find a table from which your deduction can be determined.

⑨ I trust you will understand this situation and assure you of our continued efforts to provide the best in health-care insurance.

writer. As the final word in a long sentence, "unfair" is emphasized. ⑥ Emphasizes the negative idea—simple, short sentence; first person, active voice.

⑦ Employs third consecutive sentence with "we" as the subject. Includes a split infinitive. ⑦ and ⑧ could be combined and stated more concisely—"we have attached" and "you will find" could be left to implication.

⑨ Introduces some doubt about whether the message will be clear. Unnecessarily shifts from use of "we" to "I." Commendably, includes a positive idea.

Now, contrast the preceding memorandum with its revision:

① For six years, Matco has been able to point with pride to its employee-benefits package, especially its Group health insurance.

② Overall, feedback from health-care institutions, physicians, and employees has been very favorable. ③ They like the speed and fairness with which claims are processed by Valley HMO. ④ To remain competitive and continue its high standards, Valley had to charge higher premiums

① Introduces the topic (health insurance). Employs positive language—"pride" and "benefit."

② and ③ Employ coherence techniques—"feedback" is about the "insurance" in (1), and "They" in (3) has antecedents in (2). *Before* the bad news (increased premium deduction) is presented, the paragraph reminds employees that experiences with their Group policy have been last year; Matco Enterprises was able to absorb the cost.

⑤ This year, Valley (like most other HMO's) has had to increase premiums again, but this time Matco must ask employees to share the cost. **⑥** The amount of your monthly deduction (which begins on August 1) can be determined from the table on page 3 of the attached booklet. **⑦** It also summarizes other important features of Matco's complete employee-benefits package.

very favorable. **④** Uses "high standards" (that from which employees *benefit*) in the same sentence that uses "higher premiums" (that for which employees will have to *pay*). In the same sentence with a positive, the negative is subordinated.

⑤ Achieves coherence by repetition of "year" in sentence (4). Presents bad news ("share the cost") in a compound sentence—for subordination. **⑥** Refers directly to the attached booklet without such unnecessary words as "attached is a booklet" and "you will find a table." **⑦** Achieves unity by using "employee-benefits package," which appeared in the first sentence. Assists in subordinating the premium increase by closing on another idea that is positive.

In rereading the two preceding memoranda, note that the revision is more concise, it uses language that is more positive, and it presents explanations before bad news. In the following memorandum, the boss informs the recipient of having done a poor job:

In subject lines, negatives are emphatic.

① Your Substandard Presentation.

② Your presentation to XYZ Company representatives this morning was below our standards. **③** The following

① As a subject line, these words immediately put the reader on the defensive.

② Emphasizes a negative thought by placing it in the first sentence and using negative language.
③ Emphasizes negatives

weaknesses were apparent:

1. Too technical.
2. Participants had no chance for hands-on experience.
3. Failure to get participants to respond to questions for fear that they would look foolish.

④ I insist that the presentation be revised before the same firm sends another group of representatives to visit us next week.

⑤ You might check to see whether our training consultant can be helpful.

with negative words (weakness and failure). Emphasizes unpleasant points by using tabulation and enumeration. Needs parallelism. (Point 2 is a complete sentence; 1 and 3 are phrases.)

④ Seems unnecessarily demanding ("I insist").

⑤ Seems unnecessarily weak in referring to action ("You might check").

Tabulation and enumeration highlight negatives.

The following revision would be more effective:

① Next Week's XYZ Presentation.

② Your presentation to XYZ Company representatives this morning was thorough and clear to me.

③ Because you were so well informed and organized, participants who

① As a subject line, these words assist in achieving a positive tone. A discussion of qualities desired in *next* week's presentation can have a much more positive tone than a discussion about the weaknesses of *this* week's presentation.

② Uses positive language in introducing the subject. Use of "to me" assists in the transition to a discussion of others in the next paragraph.

③ Lets compliment precede criticism. By recognizing positive qualities, the boss were already somewhat familiar with our system could benefit greatly. **4** Most of them, though, would have gained more from a less technical discussion that involved hands-on experience and encouraged spontaneous questions.

5 Before next week's presentation, ask our training consultant (Carol Ried) for suggestions. **6** She has excellent ideas and access to the latest in audio-visual equipment.

establishes objectivity and reduces the sting of comments about negatives. **4** Identifies ways in which improvement can be made.

5 and **6** Close with a helpful recommendation.

These analyses of letters and memoranda have highlighted most of the critical problems encountered in writing unpleasant messages. However, a few remain.

Special Problems in Writing About the Unpleasant

While studying the preceding pages, you may have thought about the following questions:

- Is an inductive outline appropriate for *all* letters that convey bad news?

When would a deductive presentation of bad news be appropriate?

It is for *almost* all. Normally, the writer's purpose is to convey a clear message and retain the recipient's goodwill. In the rare circumstances in which a choice must be made between the two, clarity is the better choice. When the deductive approach will serve a writer's purpose better, it should be used. For example, if you submit a clear and tactful refusal and the receiver resubmits the request, then a deductive presentation may be justified in the second refusal. Apparently, that refusal needs the emphasis provided by a deductive outline.

Placing a refusal in the first sentence can be justified when

a. the letter is the second response to a repeated request;
b. a very small, insignificant matter is involved;

c. a request is obviously ridiculous, immoral, illegal, or dangerous;

d. a writer's intent is to "shake" the reader;

e. a writer–reader relationship is so close and longstanding that satis-factory human relations can be taken for granted; or

f. the writer *wants* to demonstrate authority.

In most writing situations, the preceding circumstances do not exist. When they do, a writer's goals may be accomplished by stating bad news in the first sentence.

• Don't readers become impatient when a letter is inductive, and won't that impatience interfere with understanding reasons?

Concise, well-written explanations are not likely to make readers impatient. They relate to the reader's problem, they present information not already known, and they help the reader to understand. (Naturally, explanations that are unnecessarily long, irrelevant, wordy, or platitudinous would generate impatience.) Even if readers do become impatient while reading well-written explanations, that impatience is less damaging to understanding than would be the anger or disgust that often results from encountering bad news in the first sentence.

• In inductive letters or memoranda, in which portions are mistakes most likely to be made?

The most important portions are the first paragraph, the statement of bad news, and the last paragraph.

• First Paragraph

The introductory paragraph should let the reader know the topic of the letter without saying the obvious. It should build a transition into the discussion of reasons without revealing the bad news or leading a reader to expect good news. The following introductory sentences do reveal the subject of the letter, but they have weaknesses:

I am writing in response to your letter requesting....	The letter is obviously a response; omission of this idea would shorten the message. An "I" beginning signals that the letter may be writer centered.
Your letter of the 14th has been given to me for reply.	Obviously, the writer—instead of someone else—had the job of responding.

I can understand how you felt when you were asked to pay an extra $54.	Having requested a refund, a reader may be led to expect it. In the receiver's mind, the empathy displayed in the first sentence would be sufficiently strong to reveal the disappointment of subsequent denial; surely the request is to be granted. When a preceding statement has implied that an affirmative decision will follow, a negative decision is all the more disappointing.
Although the refund requested in your letter of May 1 cannot be granted, . . .	Immediate emotional reaction may cause the letter to be put aside at this point, or it may interfere with understanding of the explanations that follow.
Your request for an adjustment has been considered. However, . . .	The statement is neutral—doesn't reveal whether the answer is "yes" or "no." When "however" or "but" follows immediately after a "good news" or neutral statement, the reader learns—before explanations have been presented—that the answer is "no." Such a beginning has about the same effect as an outright "no" beginning.

The following introductory paragraphs (1) identify the subject of the message and (2) serve as a transition into the discussion of reasons for a denial. (To illustrate transition/cohesion, the first words of the second paragraph are also presented.)

The double-indemnity feature of your policy has two provisions. In each, the key words are "natural" and "accidental." "Natural causes" are defined as . . .	To a policyholder who has submitted a double-indemnity claim, the topic of the letter is recognized immediately. "In each" relates the second sentence to the first; "natural" provides the transition from the introductory paragraph to the second paragraph, which begins the explanations.

Your application was reviewed separately by two loan officers. Each officer considered ...	To a would-be borrower who has applied for a loan, the subject of the letter is quickly established. Use of "officer" in the second paragraph is a coherence technique—an idea introduced in the first sentence is continued in the second. In the second paragraph, discussion of the officers' reviews will satisfy an expectation aroused in the first sentence.
After your request for permission to pick up leftover potatoes, we reviewed our experiences of recent years. Last year, two incidents....	An officer of a food-for-the-hungry mission would immediately recognize the letter as a response to a request that the mission be allowed to enter a grower's field and harvest potatoes left by the mechanical pickers. Note that repetition of "year" ties the second paragraph to the first and that the second paragraph intends to present details of the "experiences" mentioned in the introductory paragraph.

The preceding sentences illustrate effective introductory paragraphs that introduce a discussion without stating bad news or leading the reader to expect good news. Additional ideas can be incorporated into effective beginning paragraphs:

1. *A compliment.* A letter denying a customer's request could begin by recognizing that customer's promptness in making payments.

2. *A point of agreement.* If the letter being answered makes a statement with which you can agree, a sentence that reveals agreement could get the letter off to a positive discussion of other points.

3. *Some good news.* When a letter contains a request that must be refused and another that is being answered favorably, beginning with the favorable answer can be effective.

4. *Resale.* If the subject of correspondence is a product that has been bought, a refusal could begin with some favorable statement about the product.

5. *A review.* Refusal of a current request could be introduced by referring to the initial transaction, or by a review of certain circumstances that preceded the transaction.

6. *Gratitude.* Although an unjustified request may have been made, the reader may have done or said something for which you are grateful. An expression of gratitude could be used as a positive beginning.

• Bad-News Sentence

In a sense, a paragraph that presents the reasoning behind a refusal at least partially conveys the refusal before it is stated directly or indirectly. Yet, one sentence needs to convey (directly or by implication) the conclusion to which the preceding details have been leading. The most important considerations are *positive language* and *emphasis.*

Your request is therefore being denied. Or We are therefore denying your request.	Being negative, the idea is not pleasant. Stated in negative terms, the idea is still less pleasant. Both sentences seem to heighten abrasiveness through use of emphasis techniques. The simple sentences are emphatic. "Denied" stands out vividly in the first sentence because it is the last word. The second sentence is in first person and active voice, which are emphatic.
The preceding figures do not justify raising your credit limit to $3,000 as you requested, but they do justify raising the limit to $1,500.	The sentence employs negative language, but it does employ two commendable techniques of subordination: it places the negative in a long, two-clause sentence, and it includes a positive idea in the sentence that contains the negative idea.

To soften the impact of a negative idea, a very helpful technique is *implication*—an indirect statement, metacommunication. The following sentences illustrate commendable techniques for *implying* a refusal:

Although the Bell Road property was selected as the building site, nearness to the railroad was considered a	Reveals what was *not* done by stating what *was* done. Note also the passive construction and the complex sentence, both of which

plus for the Hampton property. [Statement made to the owner of Hampton.]	de-emphasize. "Bell Road property was selected"—the bad news—appears in the dependent clause, which is less emphatic than an independent clause. Inclusion of a positive—nearness to the railroad—assists in de-emphasizing the negative.
If the price were $15,000, the contract would have been accepted.	States a condition under which the answer would have been "yes" instead of "no." Note use of the subjunctive words "if" and "would."
By accepting the arrangement, the ABC Company would have tripled its insurance costs.	States the obviously unacceptable results of complying with a request.

• Last Paragraph

Having presented valid reasons and a tactful refusal, a writer needs a closing paragraph that includes useful information and demonstrates empathy. It cannot do so by including statements such as these:

We trust this explanation is satisfactory.	Could be taken as a confession of doubt about the validity of the decision.
We hope you will understand our position.	May imply doubt about the receiver's ability to understand. Use of "position" seems to heighten controversy; positions are expected to be defended.
We are sorry to disappoint you.	Risks a negative retort: "If it made you feel so bad, why did you do it?" Can be interpreted as an apology for the action taken. If a decision merits apology, its validity is questionable.
Thank you for your interest.	This well-worn statement is often used thoughtlessly. Some refusals are addressed to people who have apparently *not* been interested

	enough to listen, read, or remember; otherwise, they wouldn't have made the requests. For them, the sentence is inappropriate. For others, it may seem shallow and perfunctory.
When we can be of further help, please don't hesitate to call or write.	This sentence is well worn and negative. *Further* help may seem especially inappropriate to someone who has just read a denial. The writer may see the *explanations* as helpful, but the reader may think the *denial* is being labeled as "helpful."

The final paragraph is usually shorter than the preceding explanatory paragraphs. Sometimes, a one-sentence closing is enough; other messages may require two or three sentences. The final sentence should seem like an *appropriate* closing; that is, it will bring a unifying quality to the whole message. Repetition of a word (or reference to some positive idea) that appears early in the letter serves this purpose well. Restatement of the refusal (or direct reference to it) would only serve to emphasize it. Possibilities for the final sentence include: reference to some pleasant aspect of the preceding discussion, resale, sales-promotional material, an alternative solution to the reader's problem, some future aspect of the business relationship, or an expression of willingness to assist in some *other* way. Consider the following closures, which use the preceding suggestions:

Your addition of the home-mortgage rider to your policy last year was certainly a wise decision.	Refers to something pleasant from the preceding discussion. "Home-mortgage" and other provisions had been mentioned in the early part of a letter to a client who was refused a double-indemnity settlement.

According to a recent survey, a four-headed VCR produces sound qualities that are far superior; it was an ideal choice.	Uses resale, a reminder that his four-headed VCR has a superior feature. His request for without-cost repair had been denied.

Mini-sized compacts and adapters are now available; see the enclosed folder.	Includes sales-promotional material. Request for without-cost repair had been denied.
Our representative will show you some samples when she calls next week.	Looks to a future event. The samples had been proposed as a possible solution to the recipient's problem.
If you would like to see the orientation film we show to management trainees, you would be most welcome.	Seeks to show a good attitude by offering to do something else. The student had been refused permission to interview certain employees on the job.

In general, the same principles that apply to first, middle, and final sentences of a *written* message also apply to an *oral* message. The same principles that apply to all the letters in this chapter also apply to memoranda.

Summary

Letters and memoranda in this chapter employ an inductive outline that places the main idea near the end of the letter. This sequence of ideas has the following advantages:

For conveying bad news, what are the advantages of an inductive outline?

1. It sufficiently identifies the subject of the letter without first turning the reader off.

2. It presents the reasons *before* the refusal, where they are more likely to be understood.

3. It emphasizes the reasons by letting them precede the refusal.

4. It avoids a negative reaction. By the time the reasons are read, they seem sensible, and the refusal is foreseen. Since it is expected, the statement of refusal does not come as a shock.

5. It de-emphasizes the refusal by closing on a neutral or pleasant note. By showing a willingness to cooperate in some other way, the writer conveys a desire to be helpful.

About Language and Usage

The word *benevolent* conjures images of kindness to others. It comes from two Latin roots: *bene* meaning "well" and *volens* meaning "wishing"; hence, "well wishing" or "wishing others well."

benefit	benediction	voluntary
beneficiary	benefactor	volunteer
benevolence	volition	volunteerism

In French and Spanish *bene* and its variations relate to "well" or "good." *Volens* has changed somewhat to connote free will as well as wishing, and this is evident in the preceding list of words.

The Greek *misos* means "hatred," the opposite of *philos*, meaning "love."

misanthrope	hater of humankind (*anthro*)
misogynist	hater of women
philanthrope	lover of humankind
philology	love of knowledge
philatelist	lover of stamps (a stamp collector)
philosophy	love of wisdom or knowledge (*sophy*)

Check Your Writing

Unpleasant Messages

Content

_____ Major idea is clearly identified.
_____ Supporting detail is sufficient.
_____ Facts or figures are accurate.

Organization

_____   First sentence introduces the general subject

      _____   without stating the bad news,

      _____   without leading a reader to expect good news,

      _____   without making such an obvious statement as "I am replying to your letter," or "Your letter of May 1 has been received."

_____   Details or explanations precede bad news.

_____   Main idea (unpleasant idea) emerges from preceding discussion.

_____   Closing sentences are about something positive (an alternative, resale, or sales promotion).

Style

_____   Words are readily understood.

_____   Sentences are relatively short.

_____   Variety appears in sentence length and structure.

_____   Principal idea (the unpleasant idea, or the refusal) is sufficiently clear.

_____   Some techniques of subordination are employed to keep the bad news from emerging with unnecessary vividness; such as,

      _____   bad news appears in a dependent clause,

      _____   bad news stated in passive voice,

      _____   bad news revealed through indirect statement, or

      _____   bad news revealed through use of subjunctive mood.

_____   First person is used sparingly or not at all.

_____   Ideas cohere (changes in thought are not abrupt).

_____   Expression is original (sentences are not copied directly from the definition of the problem or from sample letters in the text).

Mechanics

_____   Letter format is consistent (block, modified block, simplified, or personal business).

_____   Letter parts are in appropriate vertical and horizontal position.

_____   Margins are consistent.

_____   First and last paragraphs are short.

_____   Keyboarding, spelling, and punctuation are perfect.

Exercises

Review Questions

1. What is the antithesis of "empathy"?
2. List the four points that would appear in an outline for a letter that conveys bad news. (List them in the best sequence.)
3. In planning a message, with which should a writer be concerned *first*: (a) the *organization* of the ideas or (b) the manner of *expressing* the ideas?
4. One disadvantage of stating a refusal in the first sentence is that the reader may stop reading at that point. State another disadvantage.
5. As a beginning sentence, what is wrong with "I am responding to your letter of the 25th"?
6. What would be the disadvantage of waiting until the last sentence to convey bad news?
7. List some stylistic techniques for achieving subordination.
8. Which will make a refusal stand out more vividly in a reader's mind? (a) A direct statement (b) Implication
9. Which is the more emphatic way to state a refusal? (a) Positive language (b) Negative language
10. In which part of a refusal letter would sales-promotional material be most appropriate?
11. Under what condition should a memorandum be written inductively?
12. In the final paragraph, should a writer strive to achieve unity by referring to the statement of refusal? Why?
13. List some conditions under which a writer would be justified in stating bad news in the first sentence.
14. How can writers reduce the risk that readers will become impatient while reading explanations that precede bad news?
15. Should the closing sentence apologize for action taken?

Activities

Adjustments

1. Charles Dawson had insured his home with Security Insurance Company. During the Christmas holidays, a neighborhood child

practiced marksmanship with a BB gun he had received as a present. Two shots went through Mr. Dawson's front window. Knowing that such damages were covered by his policy, he had the window replaced and paid the $81.45 statement. Then, he sent the statement to Security asking for reimbursement. Security cannot reimburse because the policy has a $100 deductible clause. He had chosen to include the clause because it made his premium payments lower. Possibly, the child's parents may have a policy that covers liability for such incidents. As a claims manager at Security Insurance, address an appropriate letter to Mr. Charles Dawson, 321 West 4th Street, Wilbur KS 67543.

2. Lt. Andrew Johnson wrote a letter to the manufacturer of an electric blanket, asking that it be replaced under the terms of its two-year guarantee. It was given to him as a wedding present 28 months ago. It was used one season. Then, it was washed and stored for the next season while he was overseas. It was guaranteed for two seasons, but it had been used for only one. When he returned, the blanket would not heat; he returned it to the manufacturer.

   Although the washing instructions that were attached to the blanket stipulated that it be tumble washed, it had apparently been squeezed (either by wringer or by hand). The damaged wires will not permit current to flow. The guarantee has expired anyway. It was not for two years of use; rather, it was for two years from the date it was purchased by a consumer. The blanket is to be returned. Write a letter to Lt. Andrew Johnson, P.O. Box 1234, Westview OR 97654.

   [handwritten margin note: Modifies open-ended Block]

3. George Brandt bought a personal computer from one of the retail stores of a large computer-distribution center. He noticed its ninety-day warranty for materials and workmanship and returned the manufacturer's certification-of-purchase form. Relatively unfamiliar with personal computers, he studied portions of the operator's manual and the first few frames of a tutorial cassette. He accidentally erased most of the tutorial cassette. And, when he tried to get "Menu" to show on the screen, the machine refused the command. He could not find help in the manual. In panic, he took off the cover (with the use of a screwdriver) and looked inside the monitor for possible causes of the problem. No luck. The retailer refused an adjustment under terms of the warranty; an unauthorized attempt at repair had invalidated the warranty. George wrote the main office of the distribution center requesting permission to bring the unit in for repair without charge. In all probability, George had not given

the machine appropriate instructions and had ignored the bold-faced instructions on his manual: **"Do not remove cover; only factory-trained specialists are authorized to do repair work."** As repair manager in the distribution center, write a letter refusing the repair-for-free request. Offer to inspect it and provide an estimate of the repair cost. George Brandt, 981 North Hickory Lane, Scottsdale, AZ 85143.

4. When Southtown Drug Store bought Halloween candy, it overestimated the amount that could be sold. The manager asked the wholesaler's representative about taking back the unsold portion. Not satisfied with the representative's "no" answer, she wrote to the wholesale firm. Candy wrapped or packaged for special events is delivered to the store with special-colored forms. The forms (as well as catalogs of the wholesaler's merchandise) have vividly stated notices to the effect that the merchandise cannot be returned. As the wholesaler, write a refusal letter. Mr. John Baxter, Manager, Southtown Drug Store, 874 South First Street, Wells, IN 32117.

Credit

5. Having decided to build a swimming pool, George and Sandra Rustow made an application for a $15,000 loan from a personal finance company. The company's credit check revealed a consistent record of slow pay. On more than one occasion, they paid only after forceful attempts at collection. As manager of the local branch of the finance company, write a refusal letter. Mr. and Mrs. George Rustow, P.O. Box 432, Baxter, WI 54321.

6. Ernestine Bagota left an application for credit at your department store and was told that she would be informed by letter about the results of her application. From the application, these facts are apparent: The family's income last year was $21,000. The family has four children, two of whom are in high school. The father is temporarily out of work but hopes to resume within three weeks. Obligated payments each month are $900. Additional obligations now would be a severe strain on her finances. Write a letter refusing her credit application, but encourage her to take full advantage of the seasonal sales your store offers. Some sales markdowns are as much as 50 percent. Ernestine Bagota, 917 West Hermosa Street, Wellville, TX 78540.

7. As though you were credit manager for a major oil company, prepare a form letter to be stored in the computer and sent to underage

applicants for credit cards. Students who are not yet old enough to vote can either reapply after reaching the legal age or ask an adult to sign a form guaranteeing that charges against the account will be paid. In the letter, refer to a guarantee form attached to the letter. (Preparing the guarantee form is not part of the assignment.) After the signed form is returned, the request will be reconsidered.

8. Suppose that you are the credit manager for a manufacturer-distributor of sports equipment. The proprietor of a small retail store seeks permission to make credit purchases. Although her financial statements appear to justify credit purchases, other reports list her as negligent about meeting payment deadlines. Perhaps a little resale and sales-promotional material would assist in getting her business on a cash basis, but her credit-purchase request is to be declined. Ms. Linda Rinehart, 684 East Broadway, Elmwood, NV 91342.

9. Thomas Greene, who installs and repairs refrigeration units for homes and businesses, has placed a $1,000 order from the Refrigerator Warehouse. The record shows he owes $3,000, which is 45 days overdue. As credit manager, refuse the order until the $3,000 is paid in full. Thomas Greene, Route 2-B, Box 21, Baxter Springs, TN 45678.

Order

10. A firm that specializes in the sale of electrical appliances and plumbing fixtures received an order from a man in a rural community. The order is for a 3-hp electric pump, which he plans to install on the pressure system that supplies water to his household. He indicated that his well was 95 feet deep, but the pump he has ordered is good for wells no deeper than 60 feet. Almost certainly, he will need a 5-hp motor, which will cost $42 more. It is just like the one ordered, except bigger and more powerful. As manager of the store, you decide to hold the order and the check. You will write an explanatory letter. The customer has three options: (1) send a check for $42 and authorize shipment of the larger pump, (2) ask for shipment of the smaller pump in spite of the information supplied, or (3) ask for a return of his check. Gordon Atwood, RR 3, Box 14, Hillview, TN 45677.

11. Mr. and Mrs. Edward Jones bought a couch that had been marked down from $400 to $120. Rather than pay delivery charges, they asked their son to haul it home for them in his truck. Upon delivery, two problems became apparent: There was a large stain on the back

side and a spring on the bottom was not anchored. They called the store about the problem and learned the couch could not be returned. Neither would the store fix it free of charge. Thinking a letter to the manager might get results, they wrote. The purpose of the sale had been to move out damaged merchandise or items from broken sets. Boldly displayed in the store were signs stating that the items were being sold on an "as is" basis and could not be returned. Tags attached to each item bore the same information. In refusing the request, you, as the manager, send the name and phone number of a small, independent operator who does good work. Mr. and Mrs. Edward Jones, 1133 East Fourth Street, Alton, TN 45116.

12. A certain mail-order house can no longer supply catalogs free of charge. The costs of designing, printing, and distributing have increased rapidly in recent years. The charge is now $5. For storage in the computer (and use when needed), write a form letter for sending to people who have requested a catalog but have not included a check.

Request

13. For several years, you as a civic-minded accountant have conducted some free seminars on investments for retired citizens. This year, the local Association of Retired Citizens has asked you to conduct a three-hour workshop on the filing of tax returns. You can select the specific date, but it is to be in the last two weeks of March—a time in which the topic is of most interest to retirees. For you, March is a most inconvenient time; you need every hour of available time that month if you are to satisfy the needs of your clients. Write a letter refusing the request. Association of Retired Citizens, P.O. Box 419, Oakwood, IA 63981.

14. Computers, Incorporated sold a computer to a dentist. The sales agreement provided that an operator in the dentist's office would be admitted free to a five-day training class conducted on the seller's premises. Within a week after completing the training, the operator took a new job. The dentist now requests permission to enroll another operator for five days of free training. The dentist had bought the computer at a big discount, seats in the training sessions are scarce, and the cost of providing the free training classes is excessive. Write a letter refusing the request for *free* training, but offer to provide it for $200. Dr. Anne Quinn, Room 302, Professional Building, Graham, UT 84312.

15. As a college professor, you are the advisor for twenty students. Today, a letter came from an advisee's parent. It requested that you sign a "good student" form—a form that would, if properly signed and returned to the insurance company, reduce an insurance premium by $70. To qualify for the reduction, a student must have earned a B average or higher on the grade report from the preceding semester. Because the student's average for the preceding semester was a C−, you cannot sign. The parent's letter had pointed out that insurance firms "don't check out the facts anyway" and that a signature would be very much appreciated. Because of obligations to yourself, your advisee, the school, and the insurance company, you must return the form unsigned. Mr. Sam Smith, 789 West Elm Street, Common City, SD 56491.

Bad News

16. Assume you are the owner of the buildings in a twenty-store retail center. Since the center opened two years ago, costs have risen so much that next year's rent is to be raised 15 percent. Compose a letter that gives your tenants the bad news. It is to be used as a form letter. Just compose the paragraphs; other parts can be inserted when the letter is keyboarded.

17. A manufacturer of fiberboard boxes needs a form letter that can be mailed to its customers. The purpose: reveal that, effective two months from now, prices on fiberboard boxes will be raised 10 percent. A revised price list is being prepared and will reach customers within two weeks. To hold prices down, the firm has tried every cost-cutting technique it can think of (such as labor-saving machinery, employee training, time-and-motion studies, merit-rating systems). These efforts did help, but the increases are still necessary. Compose the paragraphs that would be stored in the computer and mailed later.

Memoranda

18. Vinita Clark, chief of operations at the Markens Art Company (see introduction to Activity 16 in Chapter 6) has received a memorandum from Ruth Hutchinson. Orally, Ruth had discussed the possibility of a year's leave of absence. Vinita had asked that the proposal be presented in written form. Ruth wants to be paid her salary for the year. The leave will allow her time to complete a book on which she has worked part time for five years. About famous sculptors of

America, the book will devote considerable space to the work of Maynord Jenkins (the sculptor with whom MAC has an exclusive arrangement).

By the time her leave is completed (and her book finished), Ruth will have reached the retirement age of 65. She plans to retire at that time.

Unquestionably, Ruth's background (both before and after coming to work for MAC 15 years ago) has prepared her well for writing the book she describes. Until about a year ago, her work as purchasing manager had been outstanding. Lately, she has seemed preoccupied; much of her work has been passed on to her subordinates. Instead of "working" on the book part time for five years, she has probably been merely thinking about it. If her work of recent months is a valid indicator, Ruth would not complete the book. If it were completed, it would probably assist in the sale of Jenkins' work; but the advertising value would be far less than the cost of her year's salary.

After discussing the proposal with George Markens (who says there is no precedent for paid leaves), Vinita decides to refuse the request and offer early retirement instead. According to the MAC retirement policy, Ruth would be able to retire now at 60 percent of her base pay—only 2 percent less than she would receive if she retired at 65.

Assume Ruth and Vinita have discussed the leave and the possibility of early retirement, but (as Vinita required Ruth to do in making the request) Vinita provides a *written* response. As though you were Vinita Clark, write the memorandum.

19. Paul Adams, personnel manager for Markens Art Company, has decided to attend a national convention of personnel managers. Estimated cost of travel, registration fee, and lodging is $1,100, which he wants his employer to pay. Precedent for paying such expenses is well established—for those who plan far enough in advance. In his five-year tenure with MAC, Paul has not previously attended such a meeting. If he had such intentions, he should have responded last year when the accounting department sought estimates of each department's expenses for the coming year. Since the budget does not allow for such an expenditure this year, Paul will have to pay his own expenses—if he goes. His personal accountant will probably confirm that the expense is deductible on his income-tax return. As Vinita Clark, write the refusal to Paul Adams.

20. Pauline Welch, manager of MAC's Ashland store, has been promoting a series of weekly lectures on various art topics. The topic for October 27 (7:30 P.M.) is History of American Sculpture. Knowing of Ruth Hutchinson's background and her plans to write a book on the subject, Pauline invites Ruth to participate. Ruth's granddaughter is getting married on that date, and this is one task Ruth cannot delegate. Attending the lecture is impossible. Write the memorandum Ruth would send to Pauline.

21. Three weeks from the current date, the paved parking lot MAC has been leasing for its employees will close. In its place, a multistory parking garage will be erected. Construction will require about four months. During that time, MAC employees will be able to park in the Third Street Parking Lot. That means a three-block walk to and from the office. When the new structure is completed, cars will be parked under a roof—shielded from the sun in summer and harsh weather in the winter. A covered walkway will be erected between the lot and the company's offices. As though you were George Markens, write a memorandum addressed to all employees.

22. As a standard procedure, applicants for jobs in MAC stores are interviewed by the manager and other selected employees. The home office has recently received some complaints from applicants who were not hired. True or not, the applicants have pointed out some possible violations of the Equal Employment Opportunity Commission's guidelines (which prohibit discriminatory hiring based on color, gender, race, creed, handicap, age, or national origin). In interviews, or in the "small talk" that precedes them, such topics are to be avoided. Questions about marital status, intent to have children, possible arrests (and many others described in the guidelines in each store manager's office) are not to be asked. Store managers need to review the guidelines themselves and make sure others who talk with job applicants are also familiar with the guidelines. Otherwise, MAC could be severely embarrassed. As personnel director Paul Adams, write a memorandum addressed to the store managers.

Writing to Persuade

All the achievements of mankind have value only to the extent that they preserve and improve the quality of life.

CHARLES LINDBERGH

B ecause persuasion is a broad topic, this chapter is divided into two parts. Suggestion: study Section A, read and mentally answer the review questions, and put the text aside; study Section B later.

• **Section A:**   ## Sales Letters

A "sale" (exchange of goods or services for money) may or may not be preceded by prior discussion. Most grocery shoppers, for example, make their selections and pay without first discussing quality and price with the grocer. For most car shoppers, however, a discussion will precede the transaction. A transaction will take place only after the shopper is *convinced* that the exchange is favorable or at least equitable. This *act of convincing* is most commonly called "persuasion" or "selling." Selling (persuasion) is not an attempt to trap someone into taking action favorable to someone who exchanges goods or services for money. Rather it is an honest, organized presentation of information upon which a prospective buyer may choose to act.

For those who will earn their living in a marketing-related field, knowledge of sales writing is especially beneficial. It is also beneficial for those in all other fields. The principles applied in selling a *product* are very similar to the principles applied in selling an *idea*. Typically, accomplishment requires the setting of *goals*. Achievement requires *cooperation*. Cooperation seldom results without exchange and acceptance of *ideas*. In all occupations and professions, rich rewards await those who can persuade others to accept their ideas or buy their products. Those rewards seldom go to those who rely on a "gift of gab" for success in persuasion. Instead they go to those who are well informed and well prepared.

Getting Ready

Preliminary planning is vital.

Success in *writing* is directly related to success in preliminary *thinking*. If the right questions have been asked and answered beforehand, the writing will be easier and the message will be more persuasive:

What strong features does the product (or idea) have?
How is it different from its competition?

Who are the people to whom the message is directed and what are their wants and needs?

What specific action is wanted?

Which writing principles will be especially helpful?

• Knowing the Product

You cannot be satisfied with knowing the product in a general way; you need details. Get your information by (1) reading all available literature, (2) using the product and comparing it with others, (3) conducting tests and experiments, (4) watching others use the product, (5) observing the manufacturing process, and (6) soliciting reports from users. Before you write, you need concrete answers to such questions as these:

What questions must be answered before writing a sales letter?

1. What will the product do for people?
2. From what materials is it made?
3. By what process is it manufactured?
4. What are its superior features in design and workmanship?
5. What is its price?
6. What kind of servicing, if any, will it require?

Answers to these questions about the product are not enough; similar questions must be answered about competing products. Of particular importance is the question, "What is the major difference?" People are inclined to choose an item that has some advantage not available in a similar item at the same price. For example, some people may choose a brand of bread because it is made from a formula developed by fourteenth-century monks; others may choose bread because it contains no preservatives; still others may choose bread because it is wrapped in two-layer paper.

Why is the major difference so important?

• Knowing the Reader

Is a sales letter to be written and addressed to an individual? Or is it directed to a group? If it is addressed to a group, what characteristics do the members have in common? What are their common goals, their occupational levels, their educational status? To what extent have their needs and wants been satisfied? (See the discussion of Maslow's needs hierarchy in Chapter 2.)

Envision yourself as the person receiving the letter.

Some may respond favorably to appeals to physiological, security, and safety needs (to be comfortable, to be healthy, to save time and money, or to avoid danger). People with such needs would be favorably impressed with a discussion of such features as convenience, durability, efficiency, or serviceability. Others may respond favorably to appeals to their social, ego, and self-actualizing needs (to be loved, entertained, remembered, popular, praised, appreciated, or respected). Appeals to the second group of needs are usually referred to as "psychological" appeals. Because most Americans' lower level needs have been satisfied, appeals to psychological needs are more common. The more that is known about the reader, the more accurately an appeal can be selected.

What is an "appeal"?

• Knowing the Desired Action

What do you want your reader to do? Fill out an order form and enclose a personal check? Return a card requesting a representative to call? Write for more information? Whatever the desired action, you need to have a clear definition of it before beginning to compose the letter.

Using an Attention Getter

Various techniques have been successful for getting recipients to put aside whatever they are doing or thinking about and consider an unsolicited letter. Some commonly used methods:

The first sentence should arouse desire to read sentences that follow.

1 A ball-point that writes every time!

2 Top-quality golf balls at $9 a dozen!

3 A penny saved is a penny earned.

4 INCOME TAXES WILL GO UP 10 PERCENT, the papers are saying. You know what that means for those in our business.

5 Our city spends more for alcohol than for education!

6 It's "sale-ring" day at the local stockyards. Come along. Let's see what goes on.

1 A solution to a problem.

2 A bargain.

3 A proverb.

4 A news announcement.

5 An astonishing fact.

6 A story.

7 "We have met the enemy and they are ours," cabled Commodore Perry. We get the same report from those who use our termite killer.

8 Whetstone--the Cadillac of sterling silverware!

9 What if the boss came to your desk and said, "We're going to increase production by 13 percent this week"?

10 Gasoline that will not knock! We have it.

11 A young sophomore approached his professor's desk at the end of the first class period of the semester and said, "Sir, I had this class last semester, but I flunked because the teacher was so brilliant. I think I can make an 'A' under you."

12 Why does Oriental wool make the best carpets?

13 Feel the piece of gingham attached to this letter. Notice....

14 Here's a silver-plated spoon for your new baby. Accept it with our sincere compliments.

15 The Latest Summer Styles
Have Just
Arrived Today,

Mr. Smith:

16 You should see....

how easy it is to operate a tractor with power steering.

7 A quote from a famous person.

8 An analogy.

9 A what-if opening.

10 An outstanding feature of the product.

11 An interesting anecdote.

12 A question.

13 A comment on an attached gadget.

14 A gift.

15 A fake inside address. (These lines would be arranged in the inside-address position, getting attention by location.)

16 A split sentence.

Regardless of the attention-getting technique we choose for any letter, we should ask ourselves some pertinent questions: (1) Is the attention getter related to the product and its virtues? (2) Does the first sentence introduce a central selling feature? (3) Is the attention getter addressed to the reader's needs? (4) Does the attention getter sound interesting? (5) Is the attention getter original? (6) Is the first paragraph short?

• Starting with the Product

The beginning sentence must suggest a relationship between recipient and product. It must pave the way for the remainder of the sales letter. The sentences that follow the first sentence should grow naturally from it. (See the discussion of coherence in Chapter 5.) If readers do not see the relationship between the first sentences and the sales appeal, they may react negatively to the whole message—they may think they have been tricked into reading.

Ordinarily, we have no difficulty in thinking of some way to get attention. But the main problem is getting attention in an appropriate manner. Is the following attention getter related to the product and its virtues?

When the first sentence exaggerates or seems to mislead, the remaining sentences may not be read.

> Would you like to make a million?
>
> We wish we knew how, but we do know how to make you <u>feel</u> like a million. Have you tried our latest mentholated shaving cream?

The beginning sentence is short and, being a question, it's emphatic. But it suggests that the remainder of the letter will be about how to make a million, which it is not. All three sentences combined suggest that the writer is using high-pressure techniques. Since the mentholated cream does have virtues and these virtues are important, one of them could have been emphasized by placing it in the first sentence.

• Focusing on a Central Selling Feature

Almost every product will in some respects be superior to the products of competitors. If it is not, such factors as favorable price, fast delivery, or superior service may be used as the primary appeal. This primary appeal (central selling point) must be emphasized, and one of the most effective ways to emphasize a point is by position. An outstanding feature mentioned in the middle of a letter may go unnoticed, but it will stand out if mentioned in the first sentence. Note how the following

Select a major feature of the product or a primary user benefit; emphasize it throughout.

sentence introduces the central selling feature and leads naturally into the sentences that follow:

> Your Gazette delivery van brings your paper at almost exactly the same time every day. You can almost set your watch by it.
>
> And the news stories are just as timely as it is punctual. For example....

• Addressing the Reader's Needs

Few people will buy just because doing so will solve a problem for someone else. How would a student react to the following sales opening?

> After years of effort and expense, we have developed an electronic dictionary.

With the emphasis on the seller and the seller's problems, the sentence isn't particularly appealing. Revised, the beginning paragraph is changed to focus on a problem the reader has:

> Your first draft is complete. Time is short and your spelling must be perfect. You can use "Right-Spell" (an electronic dictionary) to meet your term-paper deadline.

Emphasize the reader, not the writer.

Empathy—important in *all* communication—is especially important in persuasive communication. Before you begin writing, and while doing it, think in terms of reader interests.

• Using an Original Approach

All the preceding attention-getting devices (and others, too) are useful. We can use any one of them without being copyists. For example, beginning a sales letter with an anecdote is all right, but we should not use one with which many people are already familiar. Good sales writing often shows in the very first sentence how a product can solve a reader's problem. However, when mentioning the feature, don't use the same peculiar combination of words other people are known to use. That's bad sales technique; it's also poor composition. People like to read something new and fresh; it gets their attention and interest. And writers should enjoy creating something new.

• Some Principles

Return to Chapter 5 for a quick review of coherence and emphasis.

The principles of unity, coherence, and emphasis are just as important in sales letters as in other letters. In addition, some other principles seem to be especially helpful in sales letters:

1. *Use concrete nouns and active verbs.* Concrete nouns and active verbs help readers see the product and its benefits more vividly than do abstract nouns and passive verbs.

Why are sales letters usually longer than other letters?

2. *Use specific language.* General words seem to imply subjectivity unless they are well supported with specifics. Specific language is space consuming (saying that something is "great" is less space consuming than telling what makes it so); therefore, sales letters are usually longer than other letters. Still, sales letters need to be concise—they should say what needs to be said without wasting words.

3. *Let readers have the spotlight.* If readers are made the subject of some of the sentences, if they can visualize themselves with the product in their hands, if they can get the feel of using it for enjoyment or to solve problems, the chances of creating a desire are increased.

4. *Stress a central selling point.* Few products have everything. A thorough product analysis will ordinarily reveal some feature that is different from the features of competing products. This point of difference can be developed into a theme that permeates the entire letter. Or, instead of using a point of difference as a central selling point, a writer may choose to stress one of the major satisfactions derived from using the item. A central selling point *(theme)* should be introduced early in the letter and should be reinforced throughout the remainder.

5. *Use an inductive outline.* Well over eighty years ago, Sherwin Cody summarized the basic steps in the selling process.[1] The steps have been varied somewhat and have had different labels, but the fundamentals remain relatively unchanged. The selling procedure includes four steps:

What are the four steps in the selling procedure?

   a. Getting the prospect's attention.

   b. Introducing the product and arousing interest in it.

   c. Presenting convincing evidence.

   d. Encouraging action.

---

[1] Sherwin Cody, *Success in Letter Writing, Business and Social* (Chicago: A. C. McClurg, 1906), pp. 122–126.

These steps constitute the basic outline for sales letters. Trying to devote one paragraph to each point in the outline would be a mistake. Points (a) and (b) *could* appear in the same sentence. Point (c) could require many paragraphs. This four-point outline is appropriate for *unsolicited* sales letters.

Unsolicited sales letters differ from solicited sales letters in that the latter have been invited by the prospect; the former have not. For example, a letter written to answer a prospect's questions is a *solicited* letter; a letter written to someone who has not invited it is *unsolicited*.

Someone who has invited a sales message has given some attention to the product already; an attention-getting sentence is hardly essential. Such a sentence is essential, however, when the recipient is not known to have previously expressed an interest. The very first sentence, then, is deliberately designed to make a recipient put aside other thoughts and concentrate on the rest of the message.

Why are unsolicited sales letters more difficult to write than solicited sales letters?

• Keeping Paragraphs Short

The spaces between paragraphs serve three purposes: (1) They show the dividing place between ideas. (2) They improve appearance. (3) They provide convenient resting places for the eyes. What is your psychological reaction to a fifteen-line paragraph? Doesn't reading it seem an arduous physical and mental chore?

A reader is encouraged to take that first step if it's a short one. If possible, hold the first paragraph to three or fewer lines. A one-line paragraph (even if a very short line) is perfectly acceptable. You can even use paragraphs less than one sentence long! Put four or five words on the first line and complete the sentence in a new paragraph. Of course, be careful to include key attention-getting words that either introduce the product or lead to its introduction.

Should the first paragraph be the longest?

Introducing the Product

A persuasive message is certainly off to a good start if the first sentences cause the reader to think "Here's a solution to one of my problems," "Here's something I need," or "Here's something I want."

We may lead the addressee to such a thought by introducing the product in the very first sentence. If we do, we've succeeded in both getting attention and arousing interest in one sentence. Good sales writ-

Should a sales letter have four paragraphs—one for each phase of the selling process?

ing does not require that we have separate sentences and paragraphs for each phase of the letter—getting attention, introducing the product, giving evidence, and stimulating action. To follow such a plan would be to place our writing style in a straitjacket. But, if our introduction of the product is to be effective, we need affirmative answers to the following questions: (1) Is the introduction natural? (2) Is the introduction action centered? (3) Does the introduction stress a central selling point?

• Being Cohesive

If the attention getter does not introduce the product, it should lead naturally to that introduction. One sentence should grow naturally from another. Note the abrupt change in thought in the following example:

> Strained eyes affect human relationships.
>
> The Westview Association of Office Managers has been conducting a survey for the last six months. Their primary aim is to improve lighting conditions.

"Strained eyes" as first words of the first sentence are related to "lighting conditions"—the last words of the third sentence. But the thoughts are too far apart. No word or phrase in the first sentence is readily identified with the words of the second sentence. The abrupt change in thought is confusing. The writer may have sought diligently for an attention getter; this one is not particularly related to the sales message that follows. Has the relationship between the two sentences been improved in the second example?

Let one sentence lead smoothly to the next.

> Strained eyes affect human relationships.
>
> That's one thing the Westview Association of Office Managers learned from their six-month survey of office lighting conditions. For light that is easy on the eyes, they're switching to BA's Kold Kathode. When you flip on your Kold Kathode lights, you get. . . .

The second sentence is tied to the first by the word "that's." The "light" of the third sentence refers to the "lighting" of the second. And the Kold Kathode is introduced as a solution to the problem of strained eyes.

• Being Action Oriented

If we want to introduce our product in an interesting way, we won't simply bring it into the view of the reader and begin describing it.

Remember, active voice is more emphatic than passive voice. Action is eye catching—it holds attention and interest more readily than does description. Remember, too, we normally expect *people* to act and *things* to be acted upon.

Place the product in your readers' hands and talk about their using it. They will get a clearer picture when they read about something happening than when they read a product description. And the picture is all the more vivid when the recipient is the hero of the story—the person taking the action. If we put readers to work using our product to solve problems, they will be the subject of most of our sentences.

In some sentences, use the *reader* as the subject.

A small amount of product description is necessary and natural; but too many sales writers overdo it, as in the following excerpt:

> This VM600 Komcord is housed in a die-cast aluminum case. It has a 750-watt bulb, pitch-control knob, and easy-to-use, swing-out film gate.

See how each sentence has a *thing* as the subject. We're looking at a still picture. Now let's turn on the action. Let's let a *person* be the subject and watch that person *do* something with our projector.

> Lift this Komcord. See how easy it is? That's because of the lightweight aluminum case. Now, swing the film gate open and insert the film. All you have to do is keep the film in front of the groove embossed on the frame. See how easily you can turn the pitch-control knob for the range of sound that suits you best. And notice the clear, sharp pictures you get because of the powerful 750-watt projection bulb.

In a sense, we don't sell products—we sell what they will do. We sell the pleasure people derive from the use of a product. Logically, then, we have to write more about that use than we do about the product.

Let readers see the *benefit* they derive from using the product.

• Stressing the Central Selling Point

If the attention getter doesn't introduce a distinctive feature, it should lead to it. We can stress important points by position and by space. As soon as readers visualize our product, they need to have attention called to its outstanding features; the features are therefore emphasized because they are mentioned first. And if we are to devote much space to the outstanding features, we have to introduce them early. Note how the attention getter introduces the distinctive selling feature (ease of operation) and how the following sentences keep the reader's eyes focused on that feature:

> Your child can see vivid moving pictures of this year's
> birthday party--and from a machine so easy to use that your
> child can operate it.
>
> Watch the child lift the Komcord combination video recorder.
> See how easy? We kept the weight down to four pounds by
> using an all-aluminum case. Let the youngster set it on a
> coffee table, chair, or kitchen table--easily.
>
> Now, swing the film gate open and insert film. All you have to
> do is keep the film in front of the groove embossed on the
> frame. See how easily you can turn the pitch-control knob for
> the range of sound you like best. And notice the clear, sharp
> pictures you get because of the powerful 750-watt bulb.

Does stressing one point mean excluding other points?

By stressing one point, you do not limit the message to that point. For example, while *ease of operation* was being stressed, other features—pitch-control knob, swing-out film gate, 750-watt bulb—were mentioned. Just as a good film presents a star who is seen throughout most of the film, just as a good term paper presents a central idea that is supported throughout, just as a school yearbook employs a theme throughout, so should a sales letter stress a central selling point.

Presenting Convincing Evidence

After we have made an interesting introduction to our product, we have to present enough supporting evidence to satisfy our reader's need.

• Emphasizing the Central Selling Point

We should keep one or two main features uppermost in the recipient's mind. When we present evidence, we should choose evidence that supports this feature or features. For example, it would be inconsistent to use appearance as an outstanding selling feature of compact cars while presenting abundant evidence to show economy of operation.

• Using Concrete Language

Why should we avoid unsupported generalities?

Few people will believe us if we make general statements without supporting them with factual evidence. Saying a certain machine is efficient is not enough. We have to say *how we know* it's efficient and present some data to illustrate *how* efficient. Saying a piece of furniture is durable is not enough. Durability exists in varying degrees. We must present information that shows what makes it durable; we must also define *how* durable.

Especially in the convincing-evidence portion of the sales letter, we need all the information we have gathered about our product. We can establish durability, for example, by presenting information about the manufacturing process, the quality of the raw materials, or the skill of the workers:

Why are facts and figures important in the evidence section?

> How can we guarantee your NCC carpet to last for 10 years? Because we use Oriental wool exclusively--every fiber of wool is at least 12 inches long. And the longer the raw wool, the greater the strength of the yarn. Count the number of knots per square inch. Our carpets have 400 knots in every square inch. Conventional carpets, which have an average life of about 5 years, have fewer than 100.

Evidence presented must not only *be* authentic; it must *sound* authentic, too. Facts and figures help. Talking about wool fibers of twelve inches and carpets with 400 knots to the square inch suggests the writer is well informed. These figures increase reader confidence. Figures are even more impressive if the reader can get some kind of internal verification of their accuracy. For example, the following paragraph not only presents figures, it gives their derivation:

> We insulated 30 houses in Mesa last year. Before the insulation, we asked each homeowner to tell us the total fuel bill for the four coldest months--November, December, January, and February. The average cost was $408, or $102 a month. After insulation, we discovered the fuel bill for the same four-month period was $296, or $74 a month--a saving of $28 a month, or 25 percent.

• Being Objective

We must use language that people will believe. Specific, concrete language makes letters sound authentic. Unsupported superlatives, exaggerations, flowery statements, unsupported claims, incomplete comparisons, and remarks suggesting certainty all make letters sound like high-pressure sales talk. And just one such sentence can destroy

What are some signs of subjectivity?

confidence in the whole letter. Examine the following statements to see whether they give convincing evidence. Would they make a reader want to buy? Or do they merely remind the reader of someone's desire to sell?

> These are the best plastic pipes on the market today. They represent the very latest in chemical research.

The way to tell which pipes are best is to gather information about all pipes marketed and then choose the one with superior characteristics. We know that the writer here is likely to have a bias in favor of the product being sold. We don't know whether the writer actually spent time researching other plastic pipes, and we also don't know whether the writer would know how to evaluate this information. And, lastly, we certainly don't know whether the writer knows enough about chemistry and chemical research to say truthfully what the very latest is.

> Gardeners are turning handsprings in their excitement over our new weed killer!

Might an unsupported superlative in one sentence reduce confidence in subsequent statements?

Really? Doesn't that statement seem preposterous? And, if we don't believe in the handsprings, can we believe in the weed killer?

> Stretch those tired limbs out on one of our luscious water beds. It's like floating on a gentle dreamcloud on a warm, sunny afternoon. Ah, what soothing relaxation!

The adjectives in every sentence suggest subjectivity. Even though some people may be persuaded by such writing, many will see it as an attempt to inveigle them.

Note the incomplete comparison in the following example:

> Go farther on Duratread tires.

Can incomplete comparisons be misleading?

With which tires are Duratreads being compared? *All other* tires? With *most* other tires? With *one* unnamed brand? With *a few other* brands? Unless an additional sentence identifies the other element in the comparison, we can't tell. Too often, the writer of such a sentence hopes the reader will assume the comparison is with *all* others. Written with that intent, the incomplete comparison is unethical. Likewise, statements of certainty are often inaccurate or misleading:

> We are sure you will want to order the complete set of encyclopedias; but even if you don't, this first volume is yours to keep.

Can the writer be sure? "If you don't" conveys a connotation that the writer is *not* sure.

• Interpreting Statements

Naturally, your readers will be less familiar with the product and its uses than you will be. Not only do you have an obligation to give information, you should interpret it if interpretation is necessary. Point out how the information will benefit the reader. For example:

> And the new Karns refrigerator is frostproof as well as economical to operate.

Some prospects may not fully comprehend what "frostproof" means for them. If we make the most of this feature, we have to say *what* makes it frostproof and suggest *how* a frostproof refrigerator is superior to one that is not. The economy-of-operation feature need not have been introduced until the frostproof feature was fully discussed. The following revision interprets this feature:

Why should we bother to interpret statements?

> Open the door to the frozen-food compartment of your Karns. No frost anywhere--even if the door has been opened several times during the day. The moment you open the door, a small fan concealed in the back wall begins to circulate the air. The air isn't still long enough to deposit frozen particles of moisture. Take frozen strawberries or juice from the new Karns and open the cans without first having to remove frost.

The following excerpt from a sales letter uses a pocket calculator as the subject of the sentence. Note how it states dimensions in cold figures without interpretation:

> This calculator weighs 1/2 ounce. Its dimensions are 3 1/4 by 2 1/4 by 1/16 inches. It comes in black or ivory.

In what respects is a $\frac{1}{2}$-ounce unit superior to a 9-ounce one? Or is a 9-ounce unit actually better? If there is any advantage in having a calculator of these dimensions, what is it? What would be the disadvantage if it were twice as big?

Now see how interpretation makes the letter more convincing:

> Compare the weight of this calculator with the weight of a credit card. The credit card may be heavier than the calculator's 1/2 ounce. See how easily it fits inside a billfold. That's because its dimensions are 3 1/4 by 2 1/4 by 1/16 inches--about the size of a playing card.

Let readers see the relationship of features and benefits.

The revision shows what the figures mean in terms of reader benefits. It also makes use of a valuable interpretative technique—the comparison. We can often make a point more convincing by comparing something unfamiliar with something familiar. As most people are familiar with the size of a playing card, they can now visualize the size of the calculator. The playing-card comparison can also be used to interpret prices. For example, an insurance representative might write this sentence:

> The annual premium for this 20-year, limited-payment policy is $219.00, or 60 cents a day--not much more than a cup of coffee.

• Talking About Price

Why should we introduce price late in the letter?

Most sales letters should mention price. They should either tell what the price is or say something to assure the reader that the price is not unreasonable. Logically, price should be introduced late in the letter—after most of the advantages have been discussed. Few people want to part with their money until they have been shown how they can benefit by doing so.

People are inclined to react negatively to price. They may think it's too high, even when it is actually low. So we have to find ways to overcome price resistance:

1. Introduce price only after having presented the product and its virtues.

2. Keep price talk out of the first and last paragraphs—unless, of course, price is the distinctive feature.

3. Use figures to illustrate how enough money can be saved to pay for the expenditure. (For example, say that a $70 turbo-vent that saved $7 per month on summer electric bills would save approximately $70 in two 5-month summers, and that the vent would last for many summers.)

4. State price in terms of small units. (Twelve dollars a month sounds less than $144 a year.)

5. If practical, invite comparison of like products with similar features.

6. If facts and figures are available, use them to illustrate that the price is reasonable.

Why state price in a long sentence that is compound or complex?

7. Mention price in a complex or compound sentence that relates or summarizes the virtues of the product. In the sentence where price is mentioned, remind readers of what they get in return. The positive

aspects (satisfaction from using the product) should be put beside the negative aspects (giving up money). If we have given convincing evidence, the positive features should remain uppermost in a recipient's mind; therefore, the emphasis is taken off the negative features. Illustrations:

> Small enough to fit in the palm and big enough to record a three-hour lecture, the voice-activated Minicord sells for $70 during the month of March.

> For a $48 yearly subscription fee, _Medisearch_ brings you a monthly digest of recent medical research that is written in nontechnical language.

> Purigard saves the average pool owner about $10 in chemicals each month; thus, the $150 unit completely pays for itself in 15 months.

8. Let the figure representing price appear in some position other than the first or last word of a sentence. (See the preceding illustrations.) First and last words are emphatic; but, unless price is the central selling point, it should be subordinated.

Of course, one letter probably would not utilize all of the preceding techniques for de-emphasizing price. They are not to be employed when the central selling point is a very favorable price. Under that condition, _emphasis_ (instead of _de-emphasis_) techniques would be appropriate.

• Giving Evidence

If we can present research evidence to support our statements, we have a good chance of convincing:

Results of research add to conviction.

> We asked 100 farm laborers to wear our Worth white dress shirts for 60 days. We asked 100 other farm laborers to wear white dress shirts manufactured by Goodwear. Each night both groups of shirts were run through automatic washers and dryers, ironed, and supplied to the workers the next morning. After 15 days, only 3 Worth shirts had frayed cuffs and collars; 51 Goodwear shirts had frayed cuffs and collars. See the difference in the pictures on the enclosed folder.

Relating the experiment takes more space and time, but it is well worth the effort. Experimental facts are much more convincing than general remarks about superior durability and appearance.

• Using Enclosures

Why avoid introducing the enclosure in the first paragraph?

Ordinarily, the enclosure is less significant than the letter itself. The letter should make the recipient want to read the enclosure. Thus, the preferred technique is to refer to the enclosure late in the letter—only after the major portion of the evidence has been given. Since readers have already seen the enclosure, we should not call attention to it by saying "Enclosed you will find" or "We've enclosed a brochure." An enclosure is easily referred to in a sentence that also says something else:

> Please compare the pictures on the enclosed folder.

• Using Testimonials

If our product is really beneficial, some people are likely to report their satisfaction. If they don't write voluntarily, we can invite their comments through questionnaires or by attaching cards to the merchandise—cards the users are urged to fill out after they have used the merchandise for a certain time. One way to convince prospective customers that they will like our product is to give them concrete evidence that other people like it. Tell what others have said (with permission, of course) about your product's usefulness.

• Offering a Guarantee

Guarantees and free trial convey both negative and positive connotations. By revealing willingness to refund money or exchange an unsatisfactory unit if necessary, a writer confesses a negative: the purchase could be regretted or refused. However, the positive connotations are stronger than the negatives: the seller has a definite plan for ensuring that buyers get value for money spent. In addition, the seller exhibits willingness for the buyer to check a product personally and to compare it with others. The seller also implies confidence that a free trial will result in purchase and that a product will meet standards set in the guarantee. If terms of a guarantee are long or complex, they can be relegated to an enclosure.

Motivating Action

Regardless of the kind of evidence we give, we give it for the purpose of motivating action. If preceding paragraphs have been unconvincing, a well written final paragraph has little chance of success.

Our chances of getting action are increased if we (1) state the specific action wanted, (2) allude to the reward for taking action in the same sentence in which action is encouraged, (3) present the action as being easy to take, (4) provide some stimulus to quick action, and (5) ask confidently.

What are some characteristics of the action ending?

• Mentioning the Specific Action Wanted

Unless specific instructions are included, such general instructions as "let us hear from you," "take action on the matter," and "make a response" are ineffective. Whether the reader is to fill out an order blank and return it with a check, place a telephone call, or return an enclosed card, define the desired action in specific terms.

• Alluding to the Reward for Taking Action

For both psychological and logical reasons, readers are encouraged to act if they are reminded of the reward for acting. If our letter has been well written, we will have chosen a distinctive selling feature (the reward for using our product). We will have introduced it early—perhaps in the very first sentence—and we will have stressed it in the following paragraphs. The distinctive selling feature is the big idea we've tried to put across. We want it to stick in the recipient's mind. Thus, we should also work it into our parting words—where it will be emphasized.

Why allude to the reward for taking action?

A distinctive selling feature is to a sales letter what a theme is to a speech. It's a thread of continuity running through every paragraph. A public speaker, for example, introduces a theme, follows it with analysis and interpretation, and ends with a final reference to the theme. A sales letter follows the same pattern. To end without a final reference to the selling feature (theme) would be like ending a speech without summarizing remarks. The picture must be complete. Something in the ending should remind the reader of the beginning and the middle.

• Presenting Action as Being Easy to Take

What is one way to reduce the likelihood of procrastination?

People naturally hesitate to attempt something that is difficult or time consuming. Instead of asking readers to fill in their names and addresses on order forms or return cards and envelopes, do that work for them. If action is easy or consumes little time, they may act immediately; otherwise, they may procrastinate.

• Providing a Stimulus to Quick Action

We want action, fast or slow; however, we prefer fast action because it's more certain. The longer the reader waits to take action on our proposal, the dimmer our persuasive evidence will become. Reference to the central selling point (assuming it has been well received) helps to stimulate action. Here are some commonly used appeals for getting quick action:

1. Buy while present prices are still in effect.
2. Buy while the present supply lasts.
3. Buy before a certain date approaches—Christmas, Father's Day, the end of the season.
4. Buy now while a rebate is being offered.
5. Buy quickly to get product benefits quickly.

Prospects will not necessarily act because we tell them to act. The following expressions seem to shout *too* loudly for action:

Act today.	Do it now.	Don't delay.
Hurry, hurry, hurry.	Why wait?	Don't wait another minute.

• Asking Confidently for Action

Why avoid *hope* and *if* statements in the action ending?

Sales writers who have a good product and have presented evidence well have a right to feel confident. Instead of "*If* you want to save time in cleaning, fill in and return . . . ," writers can demonstrate confidence in favorable action by stating "To save time in cleaning, fill in and return. . . ." Of course, writers will make a mistake if they sound overconfident. And conversely, statements suggesting lack of confidence, such as "If you agree . . ." and "I *hope* you will . . . ," should be avoided. (Recall the discussion of doubtful expressions in Chapter 5. "I *hope* you will" also connotes "In view of my weak presentation, I recognize that you *may not*.") Between the lines, such thoughts convey, "I have some doubts about my product or my selling ability." If such doubts exist in the mind of the writer, they are generated in the mind of the reader.

For good appearance and proper emphasis, the last paragraph should be kept relatively short. Yet the last paragraph has a lot to do—it must suggest the specific action wanted, refer to the distinctive selling feature, present action as being easy to take, encourage quick action, and ask confidently. Observe how the following closing paragraph accomplishes these tasks:

What ideas should appear in the final paragraph?

1 For perfect legal-document copies in six seconds or less, **2** initial the enclosed order blank and mail it by January 1. **3** Those who order by January 1 will receive 1,000 free sheets of the specially treated copy paper.

1 Final reference to the central selling feature.
2 Action made easy. Definite action defined.

3 Stimulus to quick action.

The following version is an improvement because it places the central selling feature in the very last line:

Initial the enclosed order blank and mail it by January 1, and we'll ship you 1,000 free sheets of the specially treated copy paper along with the machine. And from now on, you'll get perfect copies of multipage legal documents in six seconds or less.

Now that we have examined the major problems encountered in writing the various parts of sales letters, let's read and analyze some complete letters. Note the inductive sequence of ideas.

Writing a Complete Sales Letter

The following letters illustrate the principles discussed in the preceding pages. Although they may seem long, each can be typed on a single page of letterhead paper. Typically, sales letters are longer than letters that present routine information or convey good news. Specific details (essential in getting action) are space consuming.

The following sales letter is unsolicited:

① How to increase the range of the Hughes 500D without decreasing safety--for three years Jefferson Aviation worked on this problem.

① Seeks to gain attention by identifying a problem in which the recipient will almost surely be interested.

② The effort paid off in January 1978, when our range-extension fuel tank was awarded the official STC by the FAA.

② Introduces the product.

③ With the crash-resistant tank installed under the rear seat, the Hughes 500D can still be licensed in the "normal" category.

③ Begins presentation of evidence.

④ By the time the tank had met these high standards, it had gone through experiment after experiment.... Demand is heavy. Orders are being received daily.

④ Discusses evidence in three paragraphs of detail not included here.

⋮

⋮

⑧ For additional information, or for an appointment to discuss our award-winning, crash-resistant tanks, call (613) 966-9040.

⑧ Encourages action and alludes to the tank's main feature.

The following letter employs similar techniques of style and organization:

① When the doctor gives you instructions, how often have you thought, "I wish you had time to explain" or "On medical matters, I wish I were better informed"?

① Seeks to gain attention by introducing an experience the recipient has probably had. Presents "informed" as the central selling point.

2 To inform people on such topics as home care of patients, first aid, or detection of illness, Medical Publishers is introducing the Handbook of Health.

3 In it, you can read about symptoms before calling at the doctor's office. **4** Having done some reading first, you are informed--you have improved your chances for effective communication with your doctor.

5 From the Handbook of Health, you can become even better informed after calling at the doctor's office. **6** If the doctor used words unfamiliar to you, you can turn to the 3,000-word encyclopedia of medical terms that appears in the back of the book.

7 If you really don't understand why a certain treatment was recommended, just look it up. **8** Whether you want to be better informed on such topics as infectious diseases, skin disorders, pregnancy, laboratory tests, or operations, you can turn immediately to one of the handbook's 30 chapters.

2 Introduces the product as a solution to a problem. Employs "inform" to achieve transition from the preceding sentence and to reinforce the central selling point.

3 Begins presentation of evidence. Employs a pronoun for coherence with the preceding sentence. Uses reader as subject in an active-voice sentence. **4**–**11** Continue with presentation of evidence. Note especially that the reader is the subject of the sentences, the sentences are active, and "informed" receives considerable stress.

5 Includes reminder of the central selling point.

6 Supports central selling point.

7, **8**, and **9** Continue to point out ways in which a user can become better informed. Throughout, note that the reader is the doer in the sentences; the verbs are active.

9 You can read and understand quickly because each chapter author (a medical specialist in the subject discussed) took great care to write in language that intelligent, concerned patients can understand.

10 And for concrete illustrations of points discussed, you can see vivid diagrams and three-color pictures (more than 1,000 such illustrations appear in the 1,212-page Handbook). **11** See the enclosed excerpts of sample pages.

12 Handbook of Health (which will keep you informed and able to converse easily with your physician) sells for $18--about 1 1/2 cents per page.

13 To get the informative Handbook of Health, you have but to initial the enclosed card (see instructions printed on it). **14** By mailing the card before March 1, you will also receive a complimentary copy of our 74-page booklet "Physical Fitness and You."

10 and **11** Keep the reader involved through active sentences and references to enclosures.

12 Presents price in a sentence that reinforces the primary reward for paying that price.

13 and **14** Associate action with reward for taking action, identify specific action desired, make action easy, and reward quick action.

Some sales letters have no attention getters.

The preceding letter is an illustration of an *unsolicited* sales letter. The same principles apply in writing a *solicited* letter, with one exception: because the solicited letter is a response to a request for information, an attention-getter is not essential.

Because one sales letter is sometimes reproduced and mailed to thousands of people, careful proofreading is imperative. Large firms generally have their sales letters written by professionals. Before a letter is sent, it may have gone through several drafts and have been discussed by the firm's sales executives. Like content, organization, and style, mechanics are also important.

Printing and Mailing

A sales message (even though extremely well written) is ineffective if the would-be reader reacts negatively to the envelope in which it arrives or the paper on which it is printed. Such mechanical matters are less challenging than composing paragraphs, but they deserve careful attention. Some vital questions about paper and printing:

What is the most appropriate size, color, and weight of paper?

What size print is best? Would a different color be appropriate for words that deserve special emphasis?

Would some underlining that appears to have been done by hand be appropriate?

Should a personalized inside address be included?

Some vital questions about the envelope:

Was the letter solicited?

What is the most appropriate color and size? (If an enclosure is to be included, the envelope will have to be large enough to accommodate it.)

Is a window envelope appropriate? Should any of the message be visible through the window?

Should the return address appear on the front or on the back?

Should first-class postage be attached, or would metered postage be better? Can this letter be sent bulk rate?

Should addresses be keyboarded on envelopes, or would glued-on mailing labels be better?

Should such words as "Important" or "Immediate Attention Required" appear conspicuously on envelopes?

Answers to such questions vary, depending on the nature of the business, the people to whom letters are addressed, and cost. Help is always available from an advertising department, or specialists in direct-mail advertising. Again, empathy is helpful: "If I received an envelope that looks like this one, would I react negatively? Would I open it?" In general, the envelope should be consistent with the message, it should not violate principles of good taste, and it should not be misleading. Putting "Personal" on an envelope when the letter is not personal, labeling it as urgent when it isn't, or arranging to have "Pay to the order of" appear through the window preceding the addressee's name (on a check that turns out to be phony)—such gimmicks are to be condemned. A would-be reader who has been tricked into opening an envelope is almost sure to react negatively, even though the letter applies every principle previously discussed.

Summary: Sales Letters

The first step in selling is to become informed—particularly about the product, about competing products (if any), and about the prospective buyer. The sequence of ideas in a sales presentation is inductive: get attention, introduce a product, give evidence, and encourage action. Effective sales letters employ a central selling point, just as a report employs a theme. Good sales letters let the reader, rather than the product, serve as the subject of many of the sentences. Readers can thus envision themselves using the product to satisfy their needs. Consistency, good taste, and costs are key factors in printing letters and preparing envelopes for mailing.

• Section B: Requests and Collection Letters

The preceding discussion of sales letters assumed the product was sufficiently meritorious to reward the buyer for taking action. The discussion of persuasive requests assumes requests are reasonable—that compliance is *justified* when the request is for an adjustment, that compliance will (in some way) be *rewarded* when the request is for a favor.

Writing a Persuasive Request for Action

Typical among persuasive requests are claim letters and letters that request special favors. Although their purpose is to get favorable action, the letters invite action only after attempting to arouse a *desire* to take action.

• Writing a Persuasive Claim

Claim letters are often routine because the basis for the claim is a guarantee or some other assurance that an adjustment will be made without need of persuasion. However, when an immediate remedy is doubtful, persuasion is necessary. In a typical large business, the claim letter is passed on to the claims adjuster for response.

In modern businesses, any reasonable claim will probably be adjusted to the customer's satisfaction. Therefore, venting strong displeasure in the claim letter is of little value. It can alienate the claims adjuster—the one person from whom cooperation is sought. Remember, adjusters are human beings, too. And very likely, they have had little or nothing to do with the manufacture and sale of the product. They did not create the need for the claim letter.

From the point of view of the claims adjuster, claims should be welcomed. Only a small percentage of claims are from cranks; the great bulk are from people who believe they have a legitimate complaint. The way in which the adjuster handles the claim determines, to a large extent, the goodwill of the company. For the adjuster, granting a claim is much easier than refusing it. Because saying "no" is one of the most difficult writing tasks, the writer of a persuasive claim letter has an advantage over the adjuster.

Like sales letters, persuasive claim letters should employ an inductive sequence. Unlike routine claim letters, persuasive claims do not begin by asking for an adjustment (as the following letter does):

> I respectfully ask that you reimburse me for $105, the amount of the attached work order.
>
> When my 510 hatchback failed the state's emission control test, I took it to your service department. Four hours later, the office called and informed me that the car was ready to be picked up.
>
> Stopping at the cashier's window a few minutes before closing time, I paid the $105 your clerk said was due and received the keys. Then, I noticed the mechanic's comments on the work order. I needed a new carburetor. The cost new, I found out, was $516.
>
> Talking with the service manager, I discovered that the $105 was for labor—all for taking the carburetor apart and putting it back together. He said a previous owner had evidently replaced

Why do businesses appreciate claim letters?

the original with one of inferior quality, that it could not be fixed, and that the car would still not pass the state's inspection.

I pointed out I had purchased the car new from your agency and the carburetor had never been repaired or replaced. For $105, I had received no value at all.

He pointed out that the mechanic had spent three hours working on my car at $35 per hour. He insisted his charge was in line with company policy.

Is it in line with your advertising? "Integrity is the bottom line." After spending $105, I still have my emission-control problem. Where is all that integrity? Please refund. I'll try to solve my problem some other way—without buying a carburetor that is almost as expensive as a used car.

Two major changes would improve the preceding letter: (1) writing inductively (to reduce the chance of a negative reaction in the first sentence), and (2) stressing an appeal throughout the letter (to emphasize an incentive for taking favorable action). In a persuasive claim letter, an *appeal* serves the same purpose that a *central selling feature* does in a sales letter. Both serve as a theme; both remind the receiver of a benefit that accrues from doing as asked. Note the application of these techniques in the following revision:

① When I bought my 510 hatchback from ABC Auto four years ago, I had been influenced by your advertising: "Integrity is the bottom line." **②** After the car failed this year's emission-control test, I took it to ABC's service department. **③** It had serviced the car for four years, and I had confidence that the job would be done right—with integrity.	**①** Seeks attention by using the firm's name and slogan. Reveals the subject of the letter (the writer's car). Introduces a central appeal. **②** Employs "car"—the 510 in (1)—for cohesion and transition. Begins explanation. **③** Includes a further reminder of the central appeal. Adds emphasis to the appeal (integrity) by placing it last in the sentence and paragraph. Refers to the length of the business relationship (four years)—the customer has demonstrated confidence in

the firm and contributed to the firm's profits.

④–**⑦** Continue with needed details.

④ Four hours later, I received a call; the car was ready for me. **⑤** After paying $105 at the cashier's window, I noticed the mechanic's comment on the work order: "Needs a new carburetor." **⑥** The charge on the work order was totally for labor—the three hours spent in taking the unit apart and reassembling it. **⑦** The service manager said a previous owner had evidently replaced the original with one of inferior quality, it could not be fixed, the car would still not pass inspection, and a new carburetor would cost $516.

⑧ While he explained, I was thinking "Are these statements congruent with 'Integrity is the bottom line'?"

⑧ Makes further reference to the central appeal (slogan seems to contradict actions).

⑨ Except ABC, from which I purchased the car new, it had no previous owner. **⑩** Beyond normal servicing, it had needed no repairs at all. **⑪** ABC would not have exchanged carburetors before selling the car new—because of concern for integrity.

⑨–**⑪** Present further reasoning (if an inferior unit had been installed, ABC is responsible). Make further reference to the central appeal. Place "integrity" in an emphatic position.

⑫ Yet, the service manager firmly and politely explained that ABC was justified in charging for the employee's working time.

⑫ and **⑬** Continue to lead up to the request for a refund.

⓭ But that effort was fruitless. Shouldn't the car owner have some consideration?

⓮ Money was spent; no value was received. ⓯ Please refund $105 and demonstrate that integrity is your bottom line.

⓮ Continues to lead up to the request for a refund.
⓯ Connects the request with ABC's need to make actions and advertising consistent.

Knowledge of effective claim writing should never be used as a means of taking advantage of someone. Hiding an unjustifiable claim under a cloak of untrue statements is very difficult and strictly unethical. Adjusters are fair-minded people who will give the benefit of the doubt, but they are not give-away specialists who will satisfy a grumpy customer simply to avoid a problem. An ethical business follows the Golden Rule.

• Asking a Favor

Occasionally, everyone has to ask someone else for a special favor—action for which there is not much reward, not much time, or not much inclination. Consider an invitation extended to a prominent person to be the speaker at a professional meeting. Assume that we have no money to offer. Will a deductive letter be successful? The following letter illustrates a direct request in what is really a persuasive-request situation:

What are some common errors in writing invitations?

❶ The Society of Real-Estate Appraisers will hold its annual seminar and dinner at the Tilton Hotel on May 23.

❷ We would like very much to have you join us and be the principal speaker at the dinner meeting, which will begin at 7 p.m.

❶ Begins with an announcement that may be of little interest to the recipient.

❷ Extends the invitation before letting the person see any reason for accepting.

3 Spouses of the members will be guests at the dinner meeting; and we, of course, invite your spouse to attend. I'm sure your background and writing in the field of real estate will enable you to select a subject of interest to us.

3 Fails to suggest a topic, but instead implies that the chosen topic might not be of interest to the group.

4 Will you let me know promptly that your busy schedule will enable you to accept our invitation?

4 Risks refusal because "busy schedule" provides an excuse.

Now note the contrast between that letter and the one that follows:

1 Your recent article "Are Appraisers Talking to Themselves?" in the Appraisal Journal has drawn many favorable comments from local real-estate appraisers.

1 Begins on a point that is related and of interest to the receiver.

2 The Southeast Chapter of the Society of Real-Estate Appraisers, in particular, has felt a strong need for more information about appraisal report writing from the point of view of a specialist in real-estate education. About 200 members will be attending our annual seminar dinner meeting. They would be very glad to meet you, and they would be especially interested in hearing you discuss "Appraisal Report Writing."

2 Presents details before making the request. Revealing membership enthusiasm for the topic before making the request helps to increase the reader's enthusiasm for the proposal.

What is the advantage of presenting some details before making the request?

Why put the request
in a paragraph that
mentions a reader
benefit in granting it?

③ By accepting this invitation to be the featured speaker, you'll be able to assist the appraisal profession. You'll also have the opportunity to meet several new members of our group.

④ You are also invited to bring a guest to the meeting. It will be held at the Tilton Hotel on Thursday, May 23, at seven o'clock. We can promise you a pleasant evening and an attentive audience.

⑤ We would appreciate having, with your acceptance, a photograph of you for display purposes.

③ Presents the invitation and attaches it to the advantages of acceptance.

④ Provides details that will be useful if the reader accepts.

⑤ Seeks specific action.

Note that the preceding letter employs an inductive approach. When a deductive approach is employed in a persuasive situation, chances of getting cooperation are minimal. For example, what might be a probable reaction to the following beginning sentence?

Please send me, without charge, your $350 computerized instructional software package on office safety.

If the first sentence gets a negative reaction, a decision to refuse may be made instantly. Having read "no," the reader may not read the rest of the letter or may hold stubbornly to that decision in spite of a well-written persuasive argument that follows the opening sentence.

What outline should
be used for a
persuasive letter?

The following letter employs an inductive approach. (Note the extent to which it applies principles encountered earlier.)

The participants in our management-training program need to know more about office safety, and they need to become familiar with computerized instructional software.

Each year, about 50 new employees enter the training program. Eventually, each is to assume a position of responsibility at the home office or at one of our 39 branch offices. Many will at some time be responsible for in-service training within their departments.

Their present training provides some instruction in safety, but not to the extent to which it is treated in your CIS package. Many in the program have yet to experience any form of computerized learning. They need to learn from direct experience about its potential.

If they could actually use your CIS-ST (the one described in the current issue of Today's Office), they could begin to appreciate the advantages of planned reinforcement. And, they could become real boosters of CIS as an alternative in in-service training.

In return for the opportunity to acquaint this select group with your CIS-ST, would you send a complimentary package? Every trainee would have an opportunity to use it and become sold on its advantages in training employees. Your sending the package will enable us to enrich our training and give your CIS-ST some well deserved promotion.

Assuming that the preceding paragraphs adequately emphasize a receiver's reward for complying, the final paragraph need not shout loudly for action.

In business, requests for information are very common; and information for research reports frequently is obtained by questionnaire. Validity and reliability of results are strongly influenced by the percentage of return. If the letter inviting respondents to complete the questionnaire is written carelessly, responses may be insufficient. The following letter has serious weaknesses:

① Please complete the enclosed questionnaire and return it to me in the envelope provided.

② I dislike having to impose on the valuable time of a busy executive such as you, but in order for me to complete the research for my thesis at the university,

① Invites action without having first given any incentive.

② Puts writer and reader on different levels by suggesting humility. Use of "impose" could serve as a reminder that the request *is* an imposition and

Do not apologize for taking a reader's time.

I must seek first-hand information from business leaders.

③ The study deals with the attitudes of purchasing agents toward vendor gratuities. ④ As I believe you know, gifts from sellers to executives who do the buying for companies pose a problem of great concern.

⑤ The questionnaire seeks information about practices in your firm and about your own opinions. ⑥ Responses will be kept confidential, of course. ⑦ Please return the questionnaire to me by April 18.

therefore should be denied.

③ Does reveal the nature of the research—a point that should have been introduced earlier. ④ Risks alienating by introducing doubts about the reader's knowledge.

⑤ and ⑥ Do let the reader know what to expect but need to include some incentive for responding. ⑦ Employs an action ending, but it seems a little demanding—especially when no incentive has been introduced.

The most serious weaknesses of the preceding letter are asking too quickly for action and providing no incentive for action. It is reminiscent of an ancient poet who wanted his calf to go through an open barn door. The calf refused and the poet hit it repeatedly with a stick. It still refused, until the maid let it drink milk from a pail. While it drank, the maid walked through and the calf followed. The maid provided incentive. Sometimes the reward for taking action is very small, but somehow the letter needs to make it evident. Note the reward in the following revision (it appeals to the higher order of needs discussed by Maslow):

Even when the reward for taking action is small or intangible, point it out.

① What if vendors continue making more and larger gifts to purchasing agents?

① Seeks purchasing agents' attention. Use of "purchasing agents" establishes the letter as being related to the recipients' work. Since the topic is current in the literature, agents may have already become interested.

2 For ethical and economic reasons, this question is of vital importance to purchasing agents. **3** Yet it has not been answered in the literature, and recent purchasing journals have emphatically called for answers based on research.

4 As a student who plans a career in purchasing, I am seeking opinions from selected purchasing managers. **5** Results will be shared with participants soon after the results are interpreted.

6 So the study will be complete and authoritative, please participate by completing the enclosed questionnaire and returning it to me in the envelope provided.

7 Your answers, which can be indicated quickly by making check marks, will be confidential and reported only as part of group data.

8 To get a report of the findings to you and other participating managers before school ends in early

2 Calls attention to the importance of the topic. At this point, the reader may think "I've often wrestled with this problem, but I wish I could have found an answer."

3 Leads to an introduction of the questionnaire as one step toward finding answers.

4 Introduces the questionnaire.

5 Reminds managers of the *reward* for taking action. Professional managers who now have (or already had) an interest in the problem would see the sharing of results as a positive. Thus, they would be more inclined to say "Yes" when the specific request is made.

6 Makes the request for action in a complex sentence that contains an additional idea that is positive.

7 Presents some needed assurance. With "quick marks," the effort is pictured as consuming little time.

8 Mentions a deadline—in a sentence that reminds managers of the reward for complying.

Provide incentive before making the specific request for action.

Make response easy.

Express gratitude.

> June, I need to receive the enclosed forms by May 1.
>
> ❾ I shall appreciate your help and am eager to share with you a summary of what I learn about vendors and gratuities.

❾ Expresses gratitude, alludes to the reward for participating, and adds unity by using the words "vendors" and "gratuities"—words that tie in with the first paragraph.

Are routine requests shorter than persuasive requests?

Persuasive messages are usually longer than routine messages. To provide enough information on which to base a decision, and to provide incentive for action, persuasive messages require more space. To a person whose interest has been aroused in the first paragraphs, a long letter is more likely to be welcomed than resented. Some extremely effective sales letters have been as long as five pages (single spaced).

Use inductive approach to overcome resistance.

Like persuasive letters, persuasive memoranda need extra space for developing an appeal. The memo in Figure 8.1 *could* have been written deductively, but the production manager recalled an experience of the preceding year. The president had implied his opposition to a change in work schedules. Therefore, the subject line does not reveal *how* reduction in congestion is to be achieved. (If the president read "change in work schedule" in the subject line, the memo would be off to a bad start.) Knowing the president's concern about morale, and recognizing the problem's impact on morale, the production manager uses morale as an appeal. The word "morale" is used in the first sentence and near the end—as the last word in a paragraph where it gets emphasis. It also appears in the second and third paragraphs.

Select an appeal *before* beginning to write.

Organization, though, is the same: the specific request for payment comes *after* an attempt to make the debtor see an advantage in paying. Collection letters are shorter than most persuasive messages.

Writing a Collection Letter

What are the two goals of a collection letter?

As in other persuasive letters, the primary purpose of a collection letter is to get action (payment). A secondary goal is to maintain a customer's goodwill.

MEMORANDUM

To: H. B. Smith, President
From: George Adams, Production Manager
Date: March 1, 1990
Subject: Proposal to reduce parking congestion at peak hours

Although employee morale is already high, we can do something to make it still higher.

Almost 1,000 of our employees come to work and leave at the same time. With more than 600 cars in our parking lot, about 30 minutes are required to clear it each evening. Having worked hard for eight hours without wasting any company time, employees experience a challenge to their morale when a half hour of their time is wasted.

Many employees, especially production workers, begin their day with a negative pull on their morale: they must arrive at the parking lot a half hour early so they can begin work on schedule.

The following schedule changes would go a long way toward solving the problem (without cost to Smith Manufacturers):

Production and Plant Staff

Change work hours of production and plant staff. Instead of beginning at 8 a.m. and leaving at 4:30 p.m., begin at 7:30 a.m. and leave at 4:00 p.m. This change would affect about 700 employees. It has support from the Employee Council.

Office and Management Staffs

Make no change in work hours for office and management staffs. By the time they arrive at the parking lot, production and plant workers would be already settled in their parking spaces. By the time they leave, traffic lanes should be clear for fast departure.

By making these changes, Smith Manufacturing would again demonstrate its concern for employees' problems. They would be appreciative, and we could detect a positive influence on their morale.

After you have considered this change, I would be pleased to survey production and plant personnel about their willingness to begin and leave work a half-hour early.

FIGURE 8.1

Persuasive memorandum.

**Why are collection
letters shorter than
other persuasive
letters?**

Like other persuasive letters, collection letters are written inductively. However, collection letters are shorter. Normally, customers know that they owe (no need to devote space to informing them). They expect to be asked for payment (no need for an attention getter and no need for an apology). If a letter is short, its main point (pay is expected) stands out vividly. Compared with a long letter, a short letter has a greater chance of being read in its entirety. In a long letter, the main point could end up in the skipped-over portion or have to compete for attention with minor points.

Knowing that slow-to-pay customers may not respond to the first attempts at collection, businesses that use collection letters normally use a series (if the first letter doesn't bring a response, a second letter is sent; then, a third; etc.).

• Collection Series

**What are the four
characteristics of an
effective collection
series?**

An effective series of collection letters incorporates the following characteristics: timeliness, regularity, understanding, and increasing stringency.

1. *Timeliness.* Procrastination is a bad habit for anyone. For the collection writer, putting off until tomorrow is an especially bad practice. The longer debtors are given to pay, the longer they will usually take. Most people react favorably to deadlines. Deadlines stick in our minds, put our world out of balance, and provide the motivation to act. Thus, effective collection efforts should be made promptly, and they should encourage payment by certain dates.

2. *Regularity.* We should never let the obligation out of the debtor's mind. Although we can't send a collection letter every day, we can base the time lapse between letters on our previous experience with debtors and on a knowledge of the overall effectiveness of our collection practices. A regular system for mailings impresses on debtors the efficiency of collection practices.

3. *Understanding.* Understanding involves adaptability and skill in human relations. The collection series must be adaptable to the nature of the debtor. Good-pay risks should probably be given more time to pay than debtors with poor-pay reputations. We should recognize that many debtors have very good reasons for not having paid on time. They should be given every opportunity to meet their obligations or to explain why they are unable to do so.

   Understanding also influences the regularity of the collection series. Letters should not be sent so close together that the debtor won't have a chance to pay before the next letter arrives. No one likes to receive a collection letter after the bill has been paid. Some collection letters paradoxically accuse the debtor of trying to avoid payment and then end with a sentence that says, "If you have already paid, please ignore this letter." This notation is appropriate on friendly, printed reminders only.

4. *Increasing stringency.* The fourth characteristic of the collection series is increasing stringency in letter tone as the seriousness of the delinquency increases.

Most collection authorities classify the letters in the series according to names descriptive of the seriousness of the problem. We can call these classes the *collection series.*

How many letters are in a collection series? The number of letters varies with the collection philosophy of the company and the nature of the debtor. We will have to write as many letters as necessary to collect the money or until collection is hopeless and must be attempted through legal action. For our study purposes, the following stages are used: (1) reminder, (2) inquiry, (3) appeal, (4) strong appeal or urgency, and (5) ultimatum. (See Figure 8.2.)

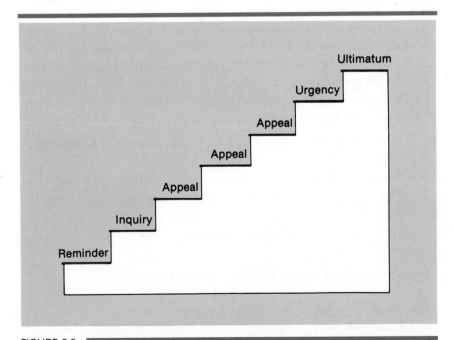

FIGURE 8.2
Stages in the collection-letter series.

The reminder is not
a letter.

1. Reminder Many people will pay promptly when they receive a bill. Shortly after the due date, a simple reminder will usually bring in most of the remaining accounts. The reminder is typically a duplicate of the original statement with a rubber-stamped notation or printed statement saying "second notice," "past due," or "please remit." To send a collection letter at this stage would be risky, indeed, for goodwill. The assumption is that the obligation has been overlooked and will be paid when the reminder is received. Very often, companies will use two or three reminders before moving to the letter-writing stage. Remember, letters cost money. They should be used only when we are reasonably sure collection is going to be difficult.

Colored gummed stickers may be attached to the statement for their attention-getting qualities. Or the duplicate copies of statements may be prepared on colored paper. The aim at the reminder stage is to make sure the reader recognizes the reminder element. But this step should be accomplished as though the reminder were a routine procedure (which it is). Under no conditions should the debtor feel singled out for special attention. For that reason, initialed handwritten reminders should be avoided at this stage.

Why should a
reminder letter look
routine?

2. Inquiry After sending the normal number of reminders without success, we must resort to letters. In some cases these are form letters; in other cases they may be form letters individually keyboarded to emphasize the personal touch. In all letters at the inquiry stage, though, the assumption must be that something has prevented the debtor from paying. The aim is to get some action from the customer, either in the form of a check or an explanation. These are the guideposts to follow in writing effective inquiry letters:

What is the desired
action of an inquiry
letter?

a. Because reminders have failed to bring payment, something is wrong.

b. Action on the part of the debtor is necessary. Either a payment or an explanation is expected.

c. With empathy, think and write positively.

d. Make it easy for the debtor to reply, but do not provide excuses for nonpayment.

The following letter effectively demonstrates the inquiry technique:

❶ Your January payment has yet to reach us, and

❶ Reveals the subject of the letter.

your February payment will be due next week.

2 Because prior payments have been on schedule, we wonder whether you have encountered an unusual circumstance.

3 If you have, please send an explanation. **4** Otherwise, please send a $94 check to cover January and February payments.

2 Recognizes prior prompt-pay habits. With empathy, shows awareness that the debtor may have a special problem.

3 Provides a choice: explain or pay. **4** Requests action. Indicates specific amount owed.

That letter did not provide an excuse for nonpayment. Nor did it mention that the customer had merely overlooked paying. These are two very important principles the inexperienced collector often violates. Frequently, too, inquiry letters mistakenly ask whether something is wrong with the goods purchased or service provided. If people are attempting to avoid payment as long as possible, they will be glad to tell us something was wrong with our product or service.

One letter of helpful inquiry is sufficient because any additional ones will only give the debtor the idea we will continue to wait. The increasing-stringency characteristic is best incorporated by reducing the proportion of helpful talk as we proceed from one stage to the next. Helpful talk can be used in the appeal and ultimatum stages, but it should not predominate as it does in the inquiry stage.

Why should we avoid mentioning possible excuses for nonpayment?

3. Appeal   By writing a short letter restricted to one appeal, a collection writer (1) increases the chances that the entire letter will be read, (2) places emphasis on the appeal employed, and (3) reserves something new to say if an additional letter is needed. Typically, collection letters employ appeals selected from the following list:

Should a collection letter list *three* reasons why the debtor should pay?

a. *Fair play*. Cooperation, loyalty, and honesty.
b. *Closure*. According to the closure principle in Gestalt psychology, people gain satisfaction from concluding that which they have begun; that is, from taking the final step—paying—in a business transaction.
c. *Pride*. Reputation, prestige, accomplishment, and ownership.
d. *Fear*. Loss of credit privilege, loss of possessions, and the possibility of litigation.

Does "... or your
account's condition
will be reported to a
credit-rating agency"
constitute a threat?

Each of the preceding appeals can be used to help a customer see the advantage of paying, but certain appeals should not be used. A threat of physical violence is outside the scope of rational behavior and is illegal. A statement of intent to destroy a credit reputation (by telling friends, relatives, employers, etc.) is also inadvisable and illegal. However, creditors are normally within legal limits when they provide facts about an account to firms or individuals entitled to receive such information. Appeals to fear, being negative, should be employed only after more positive appeals have been given a chance to solve the collection problem.

Several avenues are open when the indebtedness reaches the rather crucial appeal stage. For those debtors who have ignored the notices, reminders, and inquiries, the collection writer must (1) select the appeal most suitable for the individual case and (2) determine the best method of developing that appeal. The delinquent customer whose account has reached this stage must be persuaded to pay.

Going back to the basic appeals, we know a person can be persuaded to act when a challenge has been made to ambition, security, or reputation. Character, of course, is the most cherished part of reputation. People want to be known for their honesty, loyalty, and cooperativeness. Ambitions are usually achieved through the attainment of some position or the ownership of some valued possession. Security, as an appeal, must be approached indirectly. In the typical family, the head of the household provides the family with the necessities and luxuries of life. The threatened loss of any of them is a challenge.

Retailers who are in debt are probably most concerned about staying in business, making a profit, achieving ambitions, and building good reputations. Retail consumers, on the other hand, are not so concerned about the profit motive as about squaring their accounts and maintaining personal security. Knowing these traits, the collection writer can vary appeals, increase their sensitivity, and get at the heart of the problem. The appeal letter involves the area of human emotions. It must appeal, collect, preserve goodwill, and leave the door open for further business.

We can establish these two guides, then, for the appeal letter or letters:

1. Keep in mind the personal nature of the appeal. It is written for one person or for one company. We could personalize the letter by calling the reader by name if the use of the name falls naturally into place as we compose.

2. Write the letter from the reader's point of view. We shouldn't plead our own poverty as a reason why payment should be made. Instead, we should select an appropriate appeal and drive it home. We should concentrate on one appeal. Multiple-appeal letters don't provide time or space to develop any single appeal properly.

Should the writer's need for money be used as an appeal?

In the following example of an *appeal to fair play,* note how the debtor is encouraged to pay primarily because it is the right thing to do:

❶ Two months ago we shipped 24 dozen Amazon Golf Balls to you as the first purchase charged to your new account.	❶ Reviews the situation as an agreeable way to begin.
❷ The contract we mutually entered into was based on two things. The first was our ability to make delivery as agreed. The second was your ability to pay as agreed--an ability, incidentally, that was apparent in comments we received about you from your credit references.	❷ Informally reviews the nature of a contract to establish the basis for the fair-play appeal; also establishes ability to pay.
❸ You'll have to agree that we kept our part of the bargain. You'll have to agree, too, that the only way to complete the agreement is for you to send a check for $156 today.	❸ Develops the fair-play appeal by describing the necessary action.
❹ Slip the check in the enclosed envelope now--while this letter is before you.	❹ Requests action.

In *appeals to pride,* words such as *mutual, fair, cooperative, agreed,* and *bargain* point to the two-sided nature of the credit transaction. These words are useful in appeals to pride as well as to fair play. Appeals to pride can, of course, incorporate appeals to fair play. However, our emphasis in the pride appeal should deal primarily with reputation,

How are pride and fair-play appeals similar?

prestige, accomplishment, or ownership. In the following examples of appeals to pride, note how talk about a product can be related to the pride variations. The first letter is a typical form appeal to pride:

1 "Excellent" and "good" were the reports we received when we ran our routine check on your credit rating. As a result, we were pleased to open a credit account for you.	**1** Reviews the circumstances as a wedge for developing the appeal.
2 You must be proud of such a rating. Let us help you retain that pride by keeping your account in our "preferred" file, Miss Wright.	**2** Introduces the pride element. And develops the appeal.
3 All you have to do is pay your 30-day-past-due balance of $17.86 promptly.	**3** Requests action.

The following letter is a personalized appeal to the customer's sense of pride:

1 As a prominent lumber dealer in Ashton, you know the advantages of a good credit reputation. It can help bring business success, positions in local government, and prominence in community affairs.	**1** Establishes basis for the appeal and adapts the letter to the debtor.
2 I think you'll agree, Mr. Johansen, that your credit reputation helped you achieve these things--achievements of which you should be rightfully proud.	**2** Begins the appeal talk.

> ③ We are proud of the part we may have played through the years by extending you credit.
>
> ④ So that neither your pride nor ours will be shaken, won't you sit down right now and make out a check for $300 to balance your account.

③ Builds additional appeal by talking about what he owes us.

④ Requests action while emphasizing the appeal.

So far, our appeals to fair play and pride have intimated only lightly, if at all, that the debtor might lose some tangible possession or be forced to become involved in a distasteful credit or legal entanglement. Typically, these are fear appeals reserved for the strong-appeal or ultimatum letters.

4. Strong Appeal or Urgency   The strong-appeal letter emphasizes urgency. It says, in effect, "We must have the payment by return mail." By developing the basic appeals and insisting on payment for the debtor's own good, the writer adds stringency. Partial payments may be satisfactory, offers to accept time notes may be made, or full payment may be demanded. Comments about the cost of a lawsuit are common in urgency letters.

To emphasize the crucial status of the delinquency, the strong-appeal or urgency letter may be signed by a top executive rather than by a member of the collection staff.

Although implications about the loss of credit or possessions may be used, the best psychology is to let the reader know we are still willing to square things without undue embarrassment, as the following letter does:

What is the advantage of having a vice-president's signature on an urgency letter?

> Just in terms of interest earned, the $1,267.50 you have owed us for the past 60 days could have earned $24.00. We are concerned about the interest, but we are more concerned about retaining your goodwill and collecting the money rightfully due us.
>
> Neither of us looks forward to expensive litigation, nor does either of us relish the implications of submitting your

> account as "nonpay" to the Wholesale Furniture Dealers
> Association. Yet both things can happen.
>
> We certainly want your check within the next 5 days; but as
> a courtesy to you, we will accept your 60-day note at 9
> percent so that you can retain your credit.
>
> You must do one of these things, Mrs. Jenkins. The action
> you take now is extremely important to you and your
> business.

The appeal stages—both mild and strong—must of necessity be involved with human sensitivity, perhaps more than any other letter-communications issue. The deftness with which the writer handles the collection problem determines which customers are retained for the firm. At the same time, the account has reached a rather critical stage at which our assumption is that the customer will definitely pay only after a persuasive challenge to a sensitive point.

Some ways to make later-stage letters more stringent.

To develop the strong appeal from the mild appeal, follow these suggestions:

a. Change the appeal from one of challenging the debtor's *retention* of a favorable credit rating, a good reputation, or a prized possession to definitely implying that the debtor is about to *lose* something of value or *face a distasteful dilemma*.

b. Decrease the persuasive tone. Become more demanding.

c. Instead of talking about why the debtor *doesn't* pay, talk about why the debtor *must* pay.

d. Offer the debtor a choice between two or more things, none of which enables the debtor to get off the hook.

e. Let the debtor know clearly that the weight of evidence and the legal aspects definitely favor us and not the debtor.

If inductive letters fail, try deductive letters.

f. Consider using the deductive approach.

Recall from Chapter 7 that *sometimes* bad news is appropriately placed in the first sentence. Late in the collection series, nothing (including the inductive approach) has worked. At this stage, the creditor may be justified in "shaking" the debtor or demonstrating some authority. Someone who has waited unusually long to pay a debt may respond to unusual treatment. By beginning with a direct request for payment or setting a time by which payment *must* be made, a deductive letter could get results when preceding inductive letters have failed. The action beginning is very emphatic. If it shocks a debtor into payment, good. If it doesn't, little is lost by trying the deductive approach.

5. Ultimatum   When strong appeals fail to do their work, the collection writer must take the only remaining course of action: a letter that says, "You must pay now of your own volition or we will use every possible legal means to enforce collection." The debtor has only one choice. He or she must pay or face the consequences. Whatever recourse we have to final collection must be mentioned in the letter. We must make the most of the fact that we use the courts, a collection agency, or an attorney to enforce collection. Unfortunately, accounts getting to this stage may be as costly to the lender as they are to the borrower. Furthermore, if payment is not made, we're sure to lose the customer; if payment is made, we'd probably be hesitant about extending further credit to the customer.

Despite this dilemma, our letter should not use language that will make us susceptible to legal recourse by the customer. We must keep our self-control, show some impatience, and stay above the name-calling level. Any effort we can make to retain goodwill is worthwhile. Above all, we should avoid preaching because debtors who get to this stage do not react favorably to advice about how they should have acted. In the following ultimatum letter, the tone has changed from "must pay" to "now or else."

> When we agreed some three months ago to ship automotive supplies, you agreed that you would pay the $1,265 within 30 days. Yet the 30 days went by, then 60. Now more than 90 days have elapsed.
>
> During this time, we have sent you several overdue notices and letters--all without a single word of reply from you. Because our overdue notices and letters have gone unanswered, our patience is exhausted; however, our interest in you and your welfare is not.
>
> As members of the National Retail Credit Association, we are compelled to submit your name as "nonpay" unless we receive your check for $1,265 by June 6. The effect of a bad report could very well restrict your ability to purchase supplies on credit. In addition, our legal department would be forced to bring suit for collection.
>
> We have every right to enforce legal collection. You have until June 6 to retain your good record and to avoid legal embarrassment.

What is the basic message contained in an ultimatum?

Why avoid giving a lecture on credit?

Note how the ultimatum letter reviews the sequence of events, past and future, to indicate the seriousness of the matter. At this late stage, deductive writing is an option. To emphasize the ultimatum, in the preceding letter, we *could* use the third paragraph as the beginning paragraph. If the ultimatum letter does not result in collection, our only recourse left is to tell the debtor we are taking the steps promised. The account is no longer in our hands.

Why not send a *second* ultimatum letter?

• Form Letter

Under what conditions are form letters appropriate?

Many organizations use form letters to handle nearly all collection problems. The following principles establish the framework for companies planning to use a form-letter series:

1. The collection problem must be frequent. Personal finance companies, department stores, banks, and savings and loan associations are examples of organizations that can make good use of form letters.
2. Secured loans made by financial institutions such as banks, savings and loan associations, and finance companies give the lender the advantage of repossession or foreclosure if payment is not made.
3. The collection problems must be uniform. All letters must apply to the same types of problems.

Frequently the letters in the series are coded to indicate the collection stage at which they are to be used. In a finance company, for example, there is likely to be a complete series for debtors who have failed to make the first payment, another for those who have made the first payment but missed a later one, and still another series for those who have made all payments but the final one. One major oil company has a book of over 200 form collection letters, each covering a particular collection problem.

Except for the most routine early stages in the collection process, even form letters should be individually keyboarded so they can be personalized with names, amounts, and dates. One rule holds true: If the letter is an obvious form, don't try to camouflage it.

How does word-processing equipment simplify collection work?

Present-day word-processing equipment greatly simplifies use of form letters in collecting overdue debts. Having keyboarded an inside address, an operator has but to give the machine instructions on which form to type. It will print the remainder of the letter.

• Collection-Related Letters

The purpose of previously discussed letters was to get the debtor to *pay;* some letters, however, are designed to get the debtor to *conform.* For example, the following letter is an inquiry in which the debtor is asked whether another due date for payment would be desirable:

> Thank you for your March 1 payment, which was received yesterday, March 15.
>
> We are certainly satisfied with the regularity of your payments, but we do wonder if a different due date is advisable. Your payments are usually made around the 15th of each month.
>
> If a change to the 15th would enable you to meet your payments on time, make a notation to that effect at the bottom of this letter and return it to me promptly. Otherwise, please make your payments on the first as scheduled.

In the following case, the debtor pays exactly one month late and as a result will eventually cost the lender a month's interest income. Therefore, the writer attempts to extend the time limit by one month and also attempts to extract the additional interest.

> Your June 1 payment was received today, July 1. Although we thank you for this payment, we are concerned about the July payment which is now due.
>
> To avoid collection problems, please make this payment promptly. If payment is difficult at this time, we suggest that you request a one-month extension on the payment period of your loan. This would put your payments back on schedule and enable us to put your account back in the good-pay file. To do this, you should attach the late charge of $5, covering the interest payment for one month, to this letter and return it to me promptly.

The problem of collecting unearned discounts is one that plagues many businesses. For example, one furniture dealer pays his accounts some thirty to fifty days after they are due. And when he pays, he deducts whatever discount terms were given for prompt payment. On a $500 bill due on June 1, with terms of 3/10, n/30, he might pay on July 15 with a check for $485—the bill less the prompt-pay discount of 3 percent. Obviously, a business with several debtors employing the same tactics could lose a considerable sum unless it did something about it. Fair play, of course, is the primary appeal in such letters. "Do unto others" is an effective approach. Some of the furniture dealer's creditors sent printed notices (such as the one that follows) along with the next billing:

> The additional amount on your bill represents the discount that you may have inadvertently deducted when you paid your last bill after the discount period.

Persistent deduction of the discount then brings a letter something like this:

> The business you have brought our way is certainly appreciated. In fact, we are pleased to list you among our most prominent retail outlets.
>
> We are not so pleased, however, about your handling of your discount privilege. The 2 percent is given for prompt payment within 10 days of the first of the month. The money we receive early by offering the discount enables us to take similar discounts on our own obligations. Were it not for these savings, the cost of our product would have to be increased by 2 percent. Thus the increase would have to be passed on to you and our other customers.
>
> Because our business is based on either receiving full payment in a month or a discounted payment within 10 days, we ask that you help yourself and us by fairly observing the discount terms. In a mutually cooperative spirit, will you please send your check for $37.86 to balance your account.

• Language of a Collection Letter

Throughout the discussion of collection problems, we have noted that certain words are particularly effective. The mutuality of business problems and the resultant appeal to fair play have made *mutual, fair, cooperative, agreed,* and *bargain* good words to use in collection letters. The adverb adds stringency to collection language. Instead of being *important,* a problem has become *very important* or *extremely important.* Words and phrases such as *must, compelled,* and *no other alternative* are important in the strong-appeal and ultimatum letters.

Late-stage letters employ more forceful language.

When collection is by letter, the goals are to collect money without adversely affecting goodwill. When collection is by other means, the goals are the same.

Collecting by Telephone and Telegram

In recent years, use of the telephone in collecting has vastly increased. For large department stores with branches in many states, collection calls usually originate at the *home* office. Even though the calls are not local, they may be more cost effective than letters. The telephone has these advantages in collecting:

Why collect by telephone?

1. Saves time.
2. Makes a stronger impression on the debtor. Compared with one letter that is probably opened at the same time other letters are, a call at seven in the evening makes a stronger impact.
3. Gives debtors an opportunity to explain immediately. The caller may discover that payment has been made already, merchandise has been returned, or a request for an adjustment is pending. Under such conditions, payment cannot be expected. Customers appreciate the chance to explain.
4. Gives creditors an opportunity to demonstrate *consideration* (for those with serious problems that prevent payment now) and *firmness* (to those who offer weak explanations). By showing genuine understanding when a customer is trying to cope with serious problems, a firm may merit that customer's lasting loyalty.

Much depends on the caller's personality and capacity for empathy. Principles that apply in *written* attempts at collection also apply in *oral* attempts (positive thinking, positive language, understanding, timeliness, regularity, and increasing stringency, for example). On the second or third call to a customer, the words can be more negative and the tone more forceful than in the first call. Demeaning words (even in response to demeaning words) are self-defeating (and illegal). Sentences that even *imply* threats are to be avoided. Platitudes and elementary lectures about ways people should conduct their lives are best avoided.

When businesses decide whether to use the telephone or letters in collecting, the major considerations are cost and efficiency. In an effort to control costs, some businesses are using *recorded* telephone messages in their collection efforts. Such calls do remind debtors of their

What are the pros and cons of computerized collection calls?

obligations—and they save time and money—but they seem impersonal. Any resentment to a recorded call from a computer is somewhat lessened if the computer invites the debtor to make a statement, which it indicates will be recorded.

State laws govern collection by phone.

Those who use the telephone for collecting should become familiar with applicable state laws. Some states have restrictions on the *number* of calls about a debt and the *times* at which such calls can be made. And, of course, conventions of courtesy apply. Legal or illegal, a call at 3 A.M. is not advisable.

Telegrams should be used only in the last stage of collections. They are more expensive than either local telephone calls or letters, and appeals are necessarily limited because of the high rates for additional wording.

Registered mail has much the same urgency effect as telegrams. When any of these rapid means of communication is used, the debtor is sure to feel the urgency of the matter, and chances of collection are increased.

Summary: Requests and Collection Letters

The purpose of a persuasive message is to get action. People are not inclined to act because they are *told* to do something, but they will do something if they *want* to. The technique of persuasion, then, is to arouse desire.

When a writer's purpose is to sell a product or to request a special favor, ideas should appear in the following sequence: get the reader's attention, introduce the product or request, present evidence that the reader gains by buying or complying, and ask for action. The typical persuasive message is longer than the typical routine message; evidence of reader benefit is necessary and space consuming.

Compared with other persuasive letters, collection letters are shorter. Debtors already know that they owe money. A short letter that presents one good reason for paying has a better chance of success than a long letter that presents many reasons. In the collection series, each letter presents one appeal. If no response results, the next letter presents a different appeal. Collection by mail is often done by form letter. If a business has word-processing equipment, the letters are typed by computer. Collection by telephone or telegraph is sometimes more effective than collection by letter.

About Language and Usage

When something is not important, some people can only use the phrase "small potatoes" as a synonym. A little research reveals several synonyms they might use to add the spice of variety to their speaking and writing styles. They might use: *petty, insignificant, inconsequential, of little account, paltry, small, minute, trifling, minuscule, irrelevant, flimsy, puny, worthless, immaterial, second-rate, meager, picayune,* and even *nugatory!* Someone once defined a synonym as a word used when you can't spell the one you want!

Check Your Writing

Sales Letters

Content

_____ Writer is convinced that the product or service is worthy of consideration.

_____ Letter includes sufficient evidence of usefulness to the purchaser.

_____ Price is revealed (in the letter or in an enclosure).

_____ Central selling point is apparent.

_____ Specific action desired is identified.

Organization

_____ Sequence of ideas is inductive.

_____ First sentence is a good attention getter.

_____ Central selling point is introduced in the first two or three sentences and reinforced throughout the rest of the letter.

_____ Price is introduced only after reader benefits have been presented.

(continued)

_____ Price (what the reader gives) is associated directly with reward (what the reader gets).

_____ Final paragraph mentions (a) the specific action desired, (b) the reader's reward for taking the action, and (c) an inducement for taking action quickly. It also presents the action as being easy to take.

Style

_____ Language is objective.

_____ Active verbs (instead of passive verbs) predominate.

_____ Concrete nouns (instead of abstract nouns) predominate.

_____ Sentences are relatively short.

_____ Sentences vary in length and structure.

_____ Significant words are in emphatic positions.

_____ Ideas cohere (changes in thought are not abrupt).

_____ Through synonyms or direct repetition, the central selling point is frequently called to the reader's attention.

_____ Unity is achieved by including in the final paragraph a key word or idea (central selling point) that was introduced in the first paragraph.

Mechanics

_____ Letter parts are in appropriate positions.

_____ First and last paragraphs are short (no more than two or three lines).

_____ All paragraphs are relatively short (a paragraph of more than six lines is on the verge of being too long).

_____ "Enclosure" is typed on the letter if a brochure or pamphlet is to be enclosed.

_____ Keyboarding, spelling, and punctuation are perfect.

Persuasive Letter or Memorandum

Content

_____ Writer is convinced that the idea is valid, that the proposal has merit.

(continued)

_____ Reader will benefit, and the way or ways in which the reader will benefit are pointed out.

_____ A primary appeal (central selling feature) is incorporated.

_____ The specific action desired is identified.

Organization

_____ Sequence of ideas is inductive.

_____ First sentence gets attention and reveals the subject of the message.

_____ The major appeal is introduced in the first two or three sentences and reinforced throughout the rest of the message.

_____ Reader benefits are pointed out.

_____ Desired action is associated with the reader's reward for taking action.

_____ Final paragraph includes a reference to the specific action desired and the primary appeal. The action does not appear difficult to take, and (if appropriate) includes a stimulus for quick action.

Style

_____ Language is objective and positive.

_____ Active verbs and concrete nouns predominate.

_____ Sentences are relatively short but vary in length and structure.

_____ Significant words are in emphatic positions.

_____ Rules of grammar are applied effectively.

_____ Ideas cohere (changes in thought are not abrupt).

_____ Primary appeal is frequently called to the reader's attention— through synonyms or direct repetition of a word.

_____ Unity is achieved by including in the final paragraph a key word or idea (the primary appeal) that was employed in the first paragraph.

Mechanics

_____ Letter parts are in appropriate position. In memoranda, the "To," "From," "Date," and "Subject" lines are properly filled in.

(continued)

_____ In memoranda, courtesy titles are not employed.

_____ Paragraphs are relatively short but vary in length.

_____ "Enclosure" is typed on the letter if a folder, brochure, or pamphlet is to be enclosed.

_____ Keyboarding, spelling, and punctuation are perfect.

Collection Series

Content

_____ Inquiry letter simply asks for explanation, may include resale or sales promotion, states amount due.

_____ Each appeal letter is limited to one appeal.

_____ Each appeal letter is a little more forceful than the preceding one.

_____ Each appeal letter states amount due.

_____ Urgency letter is signed by a higher official than the one who signed the appeal letters, reveals seriousness of delay, states amount due.

_____ Ultimatum letter leaves the way open for payment by a certain date and time, states amount due.

_____ Compared with other persuasive letters, a collection letter is relatively short.

Organization

_____ Employs the inductive sequence.

_____ Inquiry leads up to request for explanation.

_____ Appeal letter reveals in the first sentence that letter is about the debt, introduces *one* reader benefit (appeal) for paying, requests payment, and mentions exact amount due.

_____ Urgency letter (from a higher official) reveals that letter is about the account, gives a very brief summary of the attempts to collect, urges payment, and states exact amount due.

_____ Ultimatum letter sets a date by which payment is expected and states action that will be taken if payment is not received, states exact amount due.

(continued)

Style

_____   Verbs are active.

_____   Nouns are concrete.

_____   *Mutual, fair, cooperative,* and *agreed* represent appropriate words at the appeals stage.

_____   Adverbs are used to make language stronger at urgency and ultimatum stages (*very* important, *extremely* critical, etc.).

Mechanics

_____   Letters, though short, are well balanced on the page.

_____   Letters are consistent in the format employed (block, modified block, simplified, or personal business).

_____   Spelling, keyboarding, and punctuation are perfect.

Exercises

Review Questions

Sales

1. What is the text's definition of "selling"?
2. Sales letters are normally longer than routine letters. Why?
3. What is the difference between a physiological appeal and a psychological appeal?
4. What are the characteristics of a good attention getter?
5. Define "central selling feature."
6. List the four points in the outline recommended for sales letters.
7. Which has more need for an attention getter in the first sentence? (a) a solicited letter or (b) an unsolicited letter.
8. In a well-written sales letter, which pronoun would be used more frequently? (a) first person or (b) second person.
9. Which is more accurate? (a) The first paragraph should be one of the *shortest* in the letter. (b) The first paragraph should be one of the *longest* in the letter.

10. In sales letters, which is ordinarily the better technique? (a) Use *things* as subjects of sentences. (b) Use *people* as subjects of sentences.

11. In selecting a central selling feature, what questions must be answered?

12. Under what condition would use of superlatives be acceptable in sales letters?

13. a. Compose a sentence that includes an incomplete comparison.

    b. In sales letters, why are incomplete comparisons to be avoided?

14. Ordinarily, which is the better spot for introducing the price of a product? (a) *Before* discussing worthy features. (b) *After* discussing worthy features.

15. Ordinarily, which is the better way to reveal the price of a product? (a) in a simple sentence or (b) in a complex sentence.

16. Which is the better way to call a reader's attention to an enclosure? (a) "Enclosed you will find a brochure." (b) "For additional features, see page 3 of the enclosed brochure."

17. List some characteristics of a good action ending.

18. Under what condition would it be appropriate to refer to the product's price in the final paragraph?

19. Are such expressions as "Act today," "Don't delay," and "Hurry, hurry," appropriate for inclusion in the final paragraph?

20. List some considerations in the preparation of envelopes that will carry sales letters.

Persuasive Requests and Collection Letters

21. What is the principal difference between a persuasive claim and a routine claim?

22. In a persuasive letter, what is meant by an "appeal"?

23. In the first paragraph of a persuasive request, what ideas should be included?

24. In a persuasive request, which should receive more emphasis? (a) the action desired or (b) the reward for taking action.

25. What would be the disadvantage of including "If you agree, please. . . ." and "I hope you will be able to. . . ." in the paragraph that asks for action?

26. In a letter that introduces a long questionnaire and encourages the

recipient to complete and return, should the writing be persuasive? Explain.

27. Ideally, should a persuasive request for action be stated in a simple sentence? Explain.

28. Why are collection letters normally shorter than other persuasive letters?

29. At the appeals stage in a collection series, how many appeals should each letter have?

30. Should an inquiry letter ask whether merchandise and service have been satisfactory?

31. In a collection series, how many letters should include an invitation to give reasons for the delay in payment?

32. Does the creditor's need for money serve well as a collection appeal? Explain.

33. One letter sets a date. If payment is not received by that date, the account will be turned over to a collection agency. After the date arrives and no payment is received, should a new date be set? Explain.

34. Which would have greater justification for use of negative terms? (a) an inquiry letter or (b) an ultimatum letter. Explain.

35. Compared with collection by letter, what are the advantages of collection by telephone?

Activities

Unsolicited Sales

1. Select a product that you own, assume you are its distributor, and write a sales letter addressed to others who are your age. Regardless of whether you select an item as expensive as your car or as inexpensive as a small pocket calculator, choose a product on which you yourself are "sold." You have pride in it, you have benefited greatly from its use, you are well informed about it, and you could heartily recommend it to others. You may assume an accompanying picture, folder, or pamphlet is included in the envelope. Just compose the paragraphs that you would use (date, inside address, etc., are not part of the assignment).

2. Select an unsolicited sales letter you (or a friend) received. On one sheet, list (a) the principles it applies and (b) the principles it vio-

lates. On another sheet or sheets, rewrite the letter (retaining its strengths and correcting its weaknesses).

3. From a newspaper or magazine, clip a picture of an advertised product. Using principles presented in this chapter, write an unsolicited sales letter. Attach the picture to the letter.

4. Prepare an unsolicited sales letter to be sent to professional people who subscribe to your state wildlife conservation department's monthly publication *Hunt for Pleasure.* Assume you are the owner of "Big Wing," a shooting preserve. You raise pheasants, quail, and chuckers. From November 1 through March 1, hunters come to your preserve (map enclosed) to shoot. Birds are released into surrounding fields. Hunters may bring their own dogs, guns, and ammunition; or these will be provided. Hunters pay $10 for each pheasant taken, $5 for each chucker, and $3 for each quail. No hunter goes away without a bird, even if it has to be supplied from the frozen-meat locker! As the enclosed brochure indicates, limited facilities are available for hunters who may want to spend the night and shoot the following day.

5. Zero-2 is a small trampoline. The frame is round, 44 inches in diameter. The bouncing surface (heavy nylon that simply will not wear out or break) is 11 inches above the floor. It is supported by six legs plated with high-quality chrome. Forty-four springs (of high-quality, 12-gauge steel) attach the bouncing surface to the frame. A 250-pound person can bounce comfortably without fear of breaking the springs. A decorative plastic cover, available in black, green, tan, or blue, conceals the springs. The Zero-2 is an ideal exercise device for retired people: It's only one step above the surface of the floor, it can add color to a room (some place it in front of a couch in place of a coffee table), it provides cardiovascular exercise without the necessity of getting dressed and leaving the house, it allows a person to exercise while watching TV, it is inexpensive ($129) and its benefits are supported by research. The Zero-2 was developed by a former college athlete after months of research on why trampoline artists had more strength than other athletes of comparable size. The conclusions: At the apex of a bounce, the trampolinist momentarily experiences *zero* gravity; upon returning to the canvas and continuing downward as far as the springs will permit, the trampolinist momentarily experiences *double* gravity. These movements from zero gravity to double gravity are very beneficial for every cell in the body. Because cells are gently massaging one another, they more

readily release their wastes and toxins to the blood stream. The cells can then more efficiently process oxygen delivered by the bloodstream; bodily strength is increased. The sales letter you write will be a form letter. Address to Chris Johnson, Madison Retirement Center, 49 Scottsville Road, Wilford, WV 26543.

6. Assume you are the owner of a local photo shop. This year you have an especially good offer on Christmas cards that include a family picture. You prefer to take four shots of a family and impose the best one on a card (family selects the picture and card), or you can use a picture that has been taken already. Although processing will probably require only a few days, a family should allow a whole month for delivery—to make sure its cards will be mailed in plenty of time for before-Christmas delivery. Prices are shown on an enclosed sheet. (Write the paragraphs only. As a form letter, date, inside address, etc., could be added later.)

7. Assume you have been asked by an association of retired persons to write a letter promoting a motoring plan similar to some other auto-club plans. It provides road and towing service plus several additional benefits. The cost is $32.50 per year. When a member needs emergency help, a call to an 800 number brings help quickly. Aided by a computer, a dispatcher locates the nearest service provider quickly. A service provider can change a tire in the driveway or on the highway at no charge to the member. Towing service is free. Routing service is free—regardless of how many times it is requested. The club pays up to $40 for services of a locksmith when keys are lost. The plan includes a Guaranteed Arrest Bond certificate (police in most states will accept it—instead of holding a driver's license to guarantee a court appearance after a traffic violation). If a traffic violation involves a legal fee, the club pays as much as $500 for certain types of violations. Members have a 10 percent discount at hotels listed on an attached folder. The club pays as much as $250 for treatment in an emergency room when treatment is more than 100 miles from home. Membership is effective immediately upon signing and returning an enclosed card; customers will be billed later for the first year's membership fee. Georgia Nagoski, McEldo Retirement Center, Rockport, PA 18765.

8. As a college student who cannot get the courses you want during the coming summer session—and having no summer job—you have decided to initiate a lawn service for professors who will be out of town during the summer. Service includes watering grass and

shrubs, mowing, trimming, and edging. Prices (described on an accompanying sheet) vary, depending on the size of lot, length of time of service, and amount of work to be done. Estimates are free and without obligation. Assignment: compose the paragraphs that would appear in your letter.

9. In an effort to expand its credit-card business, National Investors Trust Company wants you to write a letter to a select group of people who have outstanding credit ratings. Each respondent is invited to sign and return a form. Within a few days, the company will send a credit card that is good for credit purchases up to $3,000. Facts you may choose to include: The $25 annual fee will not be charged until the card is used. If the monthly statement is promptly paid in full, no finance charge is made. The annual percentage rate on a finance charge is 17.7 percent. Purchases can be made locally or in many countries of the world—at restaurants, hotels, motels, specialty stores, department stores, etc. With the card, you can get cash at airports, banks, shopping malls, universities, etc. Each cardholder receives a checkbook. When one of the checks is used to pay for a purchase, only the writer is aware that a credit-card account is involved. When the card is used for purchasing an airline ticket, the traveler is automatically insured for $250,000. Arthur Sanderson, Box 123, Woodford Heights, MI 48765.

10. As owner/operator of a house-cleaning service, you have decided to send a sales letter to homeowners. You are mainly interested in providing regular, weekly service; for example, your cleaners expect to work in a certain house every Tuesday morning. But, for a higher hourly rate, you can provide service on short notice whenever it is requested. The service includes window washing, sweeping, dusting, waxing, cleaning shower stalls, etc. State your prices and include any appropriate additional information.

Solicited Sales

11. Study the following request for information about one of your products:

Please send me some information about the shotgun in the attached picture, which appears in an article of this week's Land and Stream.

   a. What is its price? I am especially interested if the price is not more than $200.

b. How long is the barrel? For convenience in handling, I've always liked a gun with a 26-inch barrel.
c. Is this a 12-gauge gun? I strongly favor a 12-gauge for the duck hunting we do here.
d. How many shells does the magazine hold? I would like a magazine with 5-shell capacity and a 3-shell removable plug.

Since Land and Stream's article was about the man in the picture (not the gun), I learned only that the gun was a Trueshot. From the picture, it looks like a gun that impressed me at a shooting match two years ago. I shall appreciate your answers to these questions.

Incorporate the following information into your solicited response: Price, $249; highly polished steel barrel that will not rust; 30-inch barrel; adjustable choke; double safety lock; at annual shooting match in Westbrook, it put 10 percent more shot in the bull's eye than did any other gun; 5-shell capacity with removable plug; 12-gauge, which most hunters prefer for ducks; famous hunter Cal Phillips, who was pictured with the gun, got his limit of ducks with only one shot per duck. Clinton Gordon, Box 187, Route 4, Eastlake, MN 56543.

12. As manager of a tour-service agency, you receive the following letter:

Fifteen members of my literary-study group would like to take a tour of Europe next summer, preferably in the last half of July.

We envision a trip of about two weeks' duration. Although we can't expect to see all of Europe's countries, we are especially interested in England, France, and Switzerland.

Please send us whatever information you can about your service--prices, itineraries, accommodations, etc.

Although July is a busy month, the letter was received well in advance. A tour can be arranged for the last two weeks in July. Prices (listed on an enclosed folder) are based on a round trip from Denver, but any members who join the group in New York will receive a corresponding reduction. The tour includes Italy in addition to the three countries listed in the letter. All travel between countries is by air. A multilingual guide is provided. Tourists will stay in first-class hotels only. Other information (including suggestions about passports and visas) is included in an enclosed folder. Carolyn Allison, Box 121, Viewpoint, WY 83210.

Persuasive Requests

13. Assume you work in the computer department of a savings and loan association. The association wants to send you to an advanced data-processing seminar in San Francisco. The seminar begins on June 10 and continues for eight weeks. Your monthly paycheck will continue as usual, and you will be reimbursed for all expenses connected with the seminar—travel, food, and lodging. Since you have decided to take your wife and six-year-old son with you, housing is a problem. From a friend at San Francisco State College, you have learned the name and address of a teacher who plans to be in Australia for the summer. She would very much like to rent her house to a couple who have *no children*. Write a letter in which you try to persuade the teacher to rent her house to you—even though you will have a child with you. Professor Ruth Webster, P.O. Box 1351, San Francisco, CA 90123.

14. Assume you are in charge of various recreational programs conducted by your city's department of parks and recreation. In response to demand, you are offering an after-school program in playwriting and acting. About 20 children (ages 9–12) will enroll. They will compose and present plays. On the final night, parents will be invited to see performances. The group will meet each Tuesday evening from 4:30 to 5:30, beginning a month from now, for 10 weeks. The enrollment fee for each child is $20. You know of one person—a retired English teacher—who might be willing to direct the program. You can pay her a token $100 for assuming responsibility for the entire program. Jessica Wilson, P.O. Box 231, your city.

15. Carl West planned a trip a few weeks in advance and took advantage of airline discounts. One segment of his trip was a shuttle flight from an East Coast city to New York City. The ticket, purchased the first week in October, was for a flight on November 22. Price: $29. On shuttle flights, tickets are surrendered (or fares paid for) during the flight. The ticket agent on Carl's flight announced, "The price of this flight is $54. You may pay with cash, check, or credit card. If you have a ticket for less than that amount, just pay the difference when the agent comes to your seat." Recognizing the futility of arguing with a harried agent who would barely have time to finish making collections before the flight landed, Carl paid the additional $25 by credit card. Upon his return home, he wrote a letter to the airline. His reasoning: at the time of purchase, the ticket represented

a valid contract; offer and acceptance had taken place. The airline had agreed to provide transportation on a certain date for a certain price. He had paid the price, and the airline had had use of his money for six weeks before the service was provided. Announcing withdrawal from a contract *during flight* hardly seemed fair or legal. If Carl had known beforehand that the fare would be $54, he would have taken the train. As if you had the same problem experienced by Carl West, write a letter in which you request a $25 refund. Crossland Airways, P.O. Box 300, Kentwood, MA 01234-4321.

16. Louise Armstrong specialized in dental hygiene. Upon receiving her four-year college degree, she took her state's certification exam for dental hygienists. It consisted of answers to written, objective questions, and performance (cleaning a patient's teeth). When results were reported a month later, Louise discovered she had failed. The accompanying letter explained that she could take the exam again three months later and that (for guidance in preparing) she should call the certification office to discuss her test scores. She had missed the passing score by three points. On the written exam (which consisted of a seven-page, multiple-choice test), she had skipped one page completely. She attributed the oversight to pressure that normally exists when passing is extremely important. The page skipped included twenty questions; for each question, she was to select the best of four choices. If she had guessed at answers without even reading the questions, laws of probability indicate that she would have had five correct answers—enough to pass. On one of the six pages to which she responded, all twenty answers were correct. Taking the test again would mean waiting three months without a job (in a community in which the demand for dental hygienists is high), finding another patient for the performance portion of the exam, and paying transportation and lodging expenses for herself and the patient. The exam is given in a city 150 miles away. Louise wrote a letter to the certification board (a group of dentists) and requested that a certificate be issued on the basis of her previous test. It was issued. Write the letter you think she would have written. Western States Dental Association, P.O. Box 917, Albuquerque, NM 87654.

17. When Wilson Atherton attended an accounting association's convention in a distant city, he had the hotel laundry clean one of his suits. Wilson did not remove the suit from its transparent bag until he returned home. A large brown scorch (the shape of an iron) was

on the back of the jacket. The scorch obviously could not be removed; the $350 suit (which he had worn twice) had been destroyed. As Wilson Atherton, return the suit to the hotel and write a letter asking for $350. As a used suit, it would not really be worth that much; but you feel justified in asking the full price. Because of the damage, you also have to spend time shopping for a new suit. Hotel Clarkton, 15 Main Street, Jasper, IL 61234.

Memoranda

18. When Ruth Hutchinson (purchasing manager for the Markens Art Company) decided to ask for a year's leave of absence, she needed to be persuasive. As an effective manager should, Ruth had for years practiced the art of delegation. Two assistants are very familiar with all phases of her work, and they are acquainted with the people from whom most of the folk art is purchased. Ruth requests that her salary be paid to her during her absence, but she thinks MAC will be well rewarded. The book she has already begun will devote about 20 pages to the work of Maynord Jenkins. It should increase sales of his work (which is *all* sold through MAC), and because it should increase demand, prices should go up. That means more profits for MAC. Because of her long years of interest and study of American sculptors and because she has given many lectures in the United States and Europe, the market for the book would be very good. As though you were Ruth Hutchinson, write a persuasive memorandum to Vinita Clark. Ask for a leave beginning two months from now.

19. For years, Markens Art Company has paid its employees twice each month—on the 1st and the 15th. Occasionally employees (particularly those who are paid by the hour) have expressed a preference for checks every other Friday. When the matter was mentioned briefly last year, Charles Atwood (MAC accountant) expressed opposition. In his mind, the change would not be cost effective; besides, it would not affect the total paid to each employee yearly. Of course, such a change would need support from George Markens and Vinita Clark; but without Atwood's approval, it has little chance. As though you were Paul Adams (personnel manager), write a memorandum to Mr. Atwood. Try to get his support for paying employees every two weeks—on Friday.

20. Hank Appleton (sales manager at Markens Art Company) is responsible for finding speakers for the monthly meetings of a civic club to

which he belongs. Knowing of Ruth Hutchinson's background and interest in the history of American sculpture, he thinks she would be an ideal speaker. Yet, he knows how busy she is on her job at MAC; and he knows how much she cherishes her weekends. The club meets on a Friday night. Speakers receive no fee. Several members of the club have backgrounds rich in art and literature. As Hank Appleton, write a memorandum to Ruth inviting her to give a presentation (30–45 minutes) on a Friday evening two months from now. Dinner at the Forum Club begins at 7:00; her presentation would follow.

Collection Letters

21. Mrs. Kelley Matthews received an unexpected bill ($120) from a physician of whom she had never heard—Dr. Jerry Andrews. Evidently, he had been in the operating room as an observer while the family physician performed an appendectomy on her son Butch. Assuming the bill was a mistake or even a fraud, she returned it unpaid. She did not know that standard practice for major operations is that the performing surgeon be accompanied by another surgeon. In that capacity, Dr. Andrews was present—to assist, to render an opinion when asked, or to continue with the operation should the operating surgeon become unable to continue. Although the operation went smoothly and Dr. Andrews had little to do, his service was valuable and time consuming. The $120 fee is standard in the area. As if you were Dr. Andrews, write to Mrs. Matthews and collect. Mrs. Kelley Matthews, 221 North Fifth Street, Briarwood, NM 78341.

22. When Stan Watson was campaigning for election as county sheriff, he had $1,500 worth of signs printed. He paid $1,000, and the printing shop agreed to accept the remaining $500 after the election. After losing the election, Stan paid $100—his first of what was to be five monthly payments. Two weeks have passed since his second payment was due, but no check has arrived. Write an inquiry letter. Stan Watson, P.O. Box 121, your city.

23. A month has passed and Stan (Activity 22) has paid nothing. He now needs to pay $200. Write an appeal letter.

24. It's two weeks after you sent the appeal letter (Activity 23), and Stan has not yet responded. Write another letter with a different appeal.

25. It's now two weeks since you sent the second appeal, and you've still

received no response. Write another letter with a stronger appeal. (See Activities 22–24.)

26. Two weeks after sending the final appeal letter (Activity 25), write Stan an ultimatum.

27. You are the manager of an automobile supply company. When the Mansfield Service Station sent its most recent order, you checked the account before filling the order. The past-due balance is $950, and the credit limit placed on the account is $1,000. The owner of the station has placed the new order for $600 in tires and batteries. Write to the owner seeking some action on his part. You want to keep the account open by collecting for the present order before shipping the merchandise. Mr. Roy Swartz, Mansfield Service Station, 314 North Broadway, Central City, MI 34112.

28. Prepare a letter to send to Mr. Thomas Kaas. You, as the credit manager of a finance company, notice that he pays every month; but his payments are exactly a month late. Each month, you figure you lose a month's interest on his $200 account. Mr. Thomas Kaas, 784 North Elm Street, Independence, MO 73159.

29. You manage the Tune-of-the-Month Club. You sell stereo records to club members who contract for four records a year at eight dollars a record. A bill accompanies each record mailed. Because of the small amount involved in each sale, collection costs can be excessive. You decided that just one collection letter will be mailed to delinquent accounts. If payment is not received, the account will be sold to a collection firm for 20 percent of its value. Prepare a form letter that will be stored in your word-processing equipment for repeated use.

30. You are the manager of an appliance store. Prepare a form letter that will be sent to customers who have made their payments regularly and have now made the final payment on their accounts.

Writing Special Letters

A person without a sense of humor is like a wagon without springs—jolted by every pebble in the road.

HENRY WARD BEECHER

E very business person occasionally faces circumstances that vary from the usual day-to-day operations. Many of these situations require letters that provide an opportunity to create goodwill for both the business and the individual. This chapter discusses these situations and provides examples of these letters and messages. The purposes of the chapter are to provide (1) a modified handbook for unusual-circumstance letters and (2) an opportunity to develop a sensitivity about communication opportunities often overlooked by business people. In many cases, of course, the problem is not overlooked but simply avoided because of the business person's insecurity about social etiquette or procedures.

Condolences

A letter of sympathy to the family of a friend or business associate who has died should be written promptly. Yet, the sympathy message presents a difficult writing problem, with the result that these messages are often put off until too late or are not sent at all. One way to solve the problem, although a little impersonal, is to send a card (called an *informal*), which may be purchased at any stationery store, and include a short handwritten message: "Deepest Sympathy." Telegrams may also be used with messages such as "Deeply saddened by your loss. Sympathy to you and your family." Although etiquette now allows typed messages to be sent when the deceased is a business associate, a handwritten message provides a much more personal tone than does any other kind.

For condolences, are informals acceptable?

The simplest plan for such messages is (1) start with a statement of sympathy, (2) follow with sentences about mutual experiences or relationships, and (3) close with some words of comfort and affection. The following letter is to the widow of a deceased acquaintance:

> I was deeply sorry to hear of your sad news. Jim was a fine man with whom I spent many enjoyable and constructive times. He will be greatly missed by all of us who knew him and who worked with him in building a better community. Please accept my warmest sympathy and best wishes.

When a close relative (spouse, son, daughter, mother, or father) of a close friend dies, we should write the friend a letter of sympathy. Printed sympathy cards may also be used; but, in general, the closer the relationship, the greater the need for a personal written message of condolence.

Congratulations

Because the subject matter of congratulatory letters is positive, they are easy (and enjoyable) to write. Normally, they should receive a response.

• Writing Congratulations

All too often we read about the election, promotion, or other significant achievement of a colleague or acquaintance and think that a note or telephone call of congratulations would be in order—only to procrastinate until it is too late. The successful executive takes advantage of the situation to build goodwill for the company and for herself or himself. Some executives accomplish this goodwill gesture by using one of a supply of note cards, which is always available. Although handwritten messages are acceptable, typed ones permit more to be said. The thoughtfulness of sending letters of congratulations is genuinely appreciated. And when the letter is the only one the person receives, it really stands out.

In addition to promotions and elections, such events as births, weddings, and engagements call for acknowledgment. We should always acknowledge the events when those involved are employees of our firm.

Here is an example of a short letter of congratulations on the occasion of a promotion:

> I just learned of your promotion to the post of vice-president of Security, Inc. Please accept my warmest congratulations and best wishes for every success.

When a colleague wins an award or is elected to office, a congratulatory note is a lift for both the one who sends it and the one who receives it:

> Congratulations on your receipt of the Realtor of the Month award. I could see it coming. Realtors and clients applaud your energy, sincerity, and expertise. Best wishes.

How many times a year do you overlook an opportunity to congratulate someone?

What is your preference—handwritten or typewritten notes?

People don't get too old or too successful to feel good when their contributions are recognized by others.

For an engagement, the letter may take a warm and enthusiastic tone, as in the following example:

> Your good news just arrived, and I wish you and Stephen every possible happiness. He has always seemed to me like a wonderful person, and now he's also a lucky one. Please congratulate him for me.

• Replying to Congratulations

In almost all cases, letters of congratulations should be answered. An acknowledgement might take the following form:

> Many thanks for your nice words about my promotion and for the good wishes. I look forward to continuing to work with you at the Chamber of Commerce. I always enjoy it.

Some replies take a tongue-in-cheek tone, particularly when the promotion is to a rather high-pressure position:

> Thank you for your good thoughts about my promotion. I'm not certain whether congratulations or condolences would have been appropriate!
>
> The job is going to be demanding, especially as I make the transition. I'm going to give it my all, however; and your thoughtfulness is going to help ease the burden. Again, I truly appreciate your support.

Letting a congratulatory message go unanswered is somewhat like failing to say "You're welcome" when someone has said "Thank you." Of course, the message and words used to convey it are important; but the act of responding conveys a positive metacommunication. Impact is reduced, though, if the tone implies self-confessed unworthiness or egotism:

I'm not sure I have the qualities you mentioned.	Unworthiness
Others were more deserving than I.	Unworthiness

> Thanks for your note about my receiving   Ego
> Realtor of the Month award and for
> recognizing my energy, sincerity, and
> expertise.

A direct expression of appreciation is sufficient. It will be recognized as a response without including a sentence to label it as such:

> I appreciate your note. You made me feel very good about my work and those who work with me.

Note the friendliness displayed in letters of congratulations. Because they are usually sent to friends and acquaintances, congratulations messages and acknowledgments are casual, warm, and sometimes witty. We should not delay our message until it is too late to take advantage of the immediacy of the accomplishment.

Evaluations

Even though evaluation is not our purpose, we can hardly escape noticing when the attitudes and performances of others are especially good or especially bad. For those who deserve high marks, letters can encourage; for those who deserve low marks, letters can alert.

• Positive Qualities

When someone has performed exceptionally well or exhibited a commendable attitude, a tangible reward may not be possible or even advisable. From the bestower's point of view, an intangible reward (such as a letter) is easy and inexpensive. From the recipient's point of view, the value of an intangible reward can be much greater than any reasonable tangible reward. (Recall Maslow's hierarchy of needs.)

How can a compliment be worth more than money?

Especially effective are letters that recognize positive qualities or performances. People are not usually reluctant to say "Thank you," "A great performance," "You have certainly helped me," etc. Yet, because people seldom bother to *write* them, such messages are especially meaningful—even treasured. Compared with those who merely *say* nice

Why are *written* compliments so effective?

things, people who take time to *write* them are more likely to be perceived as sincere.

Although a letter of commendation is intended to recognize, reward, and encourage the receiver, it also benefits the sender. Contributing to another's happiness, paying tribute to one who deserves it, encouraging that which is commendable—such feelings can contribute to the sender's own sense of well-being and worth. Such positive thinking can have a salutary influence on the sender's own attitude and performance.

In an intangible way, how do letters of commendation benefit their writers?

Yet some of the potential value (to sender and receiver) is lost if a letter is perfunctory, such as the following example:

> Your speech to our Business Breakfast Club was very much appreciated.
>
> You are an excellent speaker, and you have good ideas. Thank you.

Should a letter that commends be couched in general terms?

To a speaker who has worked hard preparing and who has not been paid, such a letter may have *some* value. After all, the author cared enough to write. Yet, such a letter could have been sent to any speaker, even if its author had slept through the entire speech. A note closed with *sincerely* does not necessarily make the ideas seem sincere. Because the following revision is more specific, it is more meaningful:

> Before noon today, I found myself applying some of the principles you discussed at this morning's Business Breakfast Club.
>
> I jotted down each of your three suggestions on the Money Market. Thanks to all the supporting figures you presented, I am convinced of their validity.
>
> Thank you for an interesting, thought-provoking talk.

The revision does not sound so much like a form letter. At least its author was aware of the three points made and that each was supported. The letter conveys gratitude, an intangible reward. However, a different approach could result in a tangible reward as well—a letter of commendation to the speaker's employer:

> Mr. Will Jones (financial analyst at your Lockwood office) gave a very interesting, informative speech at this morning's Business Breakfast Club.

> In a well-organized and witty presentation, he offered three suggestions on the Money Market (along with supporting facts and figures). From members' reaction during the question-and-answer period that followed, I sensed that his ideas were clearly understood and appreciated.
>
> Possibly Mr. Jones has let you know that he was to give a talk this morning, but I just want you to know that he gave an outstanding speech--totally consistent with the image your bank projects.

With such letters in his file, Mr. Jones's chances for promotion or other tangible rewards are increased. But the intangible reward alone makes the effort worthwhile.

Such letters should be written for the purpose of commending deserving people; they should not be written for the purpose of possible self-gain. Sometimes, however, those who take time to write such letters receive some unexpected benefits.

As an undergraduate student, Henry Kissinger wrote a letter of appreciation to a Prussian general who had spoken at his university. Touched by such thoughtfulness, the general invited Mr. Kissinger to dinner. Concluding that the young man had unusually keen insights into international affairs, the general was instrumental in getting Kissinger admitted to graduate study.

Although generous praise is seldom objectionable, a letter or memo of commendation may not fully achieve its purpose if it reaches the point of exaggeration or uses language that is hardly believable:

> Mr. Combs, who conducted the 10-week seminar that was concluded this week, is by far the best and most informed discussion leader we have had.
>
> He was fantastic. I learned more from him than from all the others combined. Thanks for selecting him.

(As an interoffice communication, the message would be typed as a memorandum.) In the writer's mind, the statements may be true; but in the reader's mind, they may seem unbelievable. Because the language is strong and the statements are not supported, the memo could arouse thoughts about how bad other leaders were; or it could arouse questions about the writer's motives. The training director would probably be more impressed with the following memo:

Why write to an employer about an employee who has gone beyond the call of duty?

Is self-gain a legitimate motive for writing a letter that commends?

Are exaggerations advisable?

Might the superlatives appear to be overstatements?

I commend Mr. Frank Combs for his effectiveness in the 10-week seminar that concluded this week.

In the first session, he began by defining a problem and pointing out relevant factors. Then he formed small groups for specific discussion. After collecting a "solution" from each group, he synthesized the groups' thoughts and helped us derive a sensible solution. In sessions 2 through 10, he always began by reemphasizing principles from the preceding session.

Because he gave us credit for being able to think and because he was willing to listen, we were willing to listen. From his wealth of knowledge and experience, we learned much that we can apply on our jobs.

Does strong language strengthen a compliment?

Although the preceding message does not employ strong language, it conveys a stronger compliment than the other message did. Without the words "best" and "fantastic," it reveals *why* the participant's reaction was favorable.

Who benefits from a commendation letter sent to the subject's employer?

The net effects of the preceding memorandum are positive: (1) the writer feels good for having passed on a deserved compliment, (2) management gains some assurance that a training program is effective, (3) the person about whom the letter was written is encouraged to continue an effective technique, and (4) subsequent trainees may have an increased likelihood of exposure to a similar program. Even when communications point out negatives, however, the intent should be to get results that are positive.

• Negative Qualities

Why are people hesitant about writing letters that point out negatives?

A person who has had a bad experience as a result of another's conduct may be reluctant to write about that experience. Assume, for example, the discussion leader in the preceding illustration had been ineffective. Before writing about the problem, a trainee would recognize the following *risks:* (1) being stereotyped as a complainer, (2) being associated with negative thoughts and thus thought of in negative terms, or (3) appearing to challenge one of management's prior decisions (choice of the leader). Yet such risks may be worth taking because of the benefits: (1) the writer gets a feeling of having exercised a responsibility, (2) management learns of changes that need to be made, (3) the person about whom the letter is written modifies techniques and is thus happier and more successful, and (4) present and future trainees may be exposed to programs that are more beneficial.

When another person has made or is making mistakes, what can be gained by writing a letter?

In the decision to write about negatives, the primary consideration is *intent*. If the intent is to hurt or to get even, the message should not be written. False information would be unethical and illegal.

Are letters that seek revenge advisable?

In a written message that reports negative evaluation results, evaluative words are discouraged. Instead of presenting facts, the following message judges:

> Mr. Frank Combs, discussion leader in our seminar, is positively the worst of all our leaders.

> Because of his lack of promptness, his ineffectiveness in presenting concepts, and his negative attitude, I consider the seminar a complete waste of time.

In the mind of the trainee, the first sentence may be fair and accurate; but in the mind of the reader, "worst" may seem overly harsh. It may convey the tone of a habitual fault-finder. Without details, the charges made in the second sentence lack force. If "complete waste of time" strikes the receiver as an exaggeration, the whole message loses impact. Overall, the memo is short, general, and negative. By comparison, the following revision is long, specific, and positive:

1 Looking back over the last 10 weeks of seminars, I realize I have had exposure to the excellent leaders you spoke about in our orientation.

1 Introduces a discussion of seminar leadership.

2 Of the four leaders, three are just as good as or better than you said they would be. However, some aspects of Mr. Combs's performance need to be called to your attention:

2 Tries to convey fair-mindedness and establish credibility by acknowledging good points in a memo that discusses bad points.

What is the effect of including a positive in a letter that points out and stresses negatives?

1. **3** On three occasions (May 1, May 8, and May 22), he arrived 20 minutes late without apology or explanation.

3 Presents a statement of fact without labeling it in negative terms. Judgment is left to the reader.

What is the effect of assigning a number to each point?

2. **4** His presentations consist of rapid-fire

4 Includes another verifiable fact. A training director

lectures. In all sessions combined, about 15 minutes were devoted to discussion of ways in which principles can be <u>applied</u> in the work we will be doing.

3. **5** Written case analyses submitted on May 22 were scheduled for return and discussion the following week. Now, six weeks later, the papers have yet to be returned.

6 I see Mr. Combs as a well-informed person who could become an excellent discussion leader.

7 Overall, the seminars have been very helpful to me. In the spirit of helpfulness, I am passing this confidential information to you.

who had promised give-and-take discussions does not need to be told how bad the lecture technique is.

5 Continues with a verifiable statement. If such conduct is deplorable, outrageous, or insulting, the reader will be aware of it without the writer's use of such terms.

6 States a positive and thus seeks to add credibility to the preceding negatives.

7 Ends on a pleasant note. Employs "confidential" as a safeguard; the information is intended for professional use only, not designed to hurt and not to be thought of as gossip.

Because one person took the time to write a memo, many could benefit. Although not always easy or pleasant, writing about negatives can be thought of as a civic responsibility. For example, a person who returns from a long stay at a major hotel might, upon returning home, write a letter to the management commending certain employees. If the stay had not been pleasant and weaknesses in hotel operation had been detected, a tactful letter pointing out the negatives would probably be appreciated. Future guests could benefit from the effort of that one person.

Why should you avoid use of judgmental terms?

Whether negative evaluations are presented in writing or in conversation, the same principles apply: have a positive intent, be factual, use positive language, and leave judgment to the recipient.

Invitations

Like most other special letters, invitations are deductive and relatively short. Responses to invitations should be handled similarly.

• Writing Invitations

An informal invitation resembles a business letter. When sent from a business office, the letter is sometimes typed on executive stationery, which is smaller than the regular business letterhead. Wording should be conversational, as though the writer were extending the invitation orally. As a matter of style, the inside address may be placed at the end of the letter. For example:

> We are pleased to invite you to be our guests at the Installation Ball of the Chamber at the Beachrider Hotel on January 5.
>
> As was recently announced, Robert Dodson, our executive vice-president, will be installed then as president of the Chamber of Commerce for the coming year. A cocktail reception at seven o'clock will be followed by dinner and dancing.
>
> Will you please let me know by December 29 whether you will attend. I will be glad to see you there.
>
>   Cordially
>
> Mr. and Mrs. Theodore Smith
> 444 Commonwealth Drive
> Beverly Hills, CA 90037

• Replying to Invitations

All invitations should be acknowledged promptly. When a telephone R.S.V.P. is not mentioned, either a typed or handwritten reply is satisfactory and should use the same conversational style as used in the invitation.

What is the meaning of R.S.V.P.?

Although many formal invitations are handwritten, especially for smaller groups, formal invitations are generally printed and follow formats provided by the printer (Fig. 9.1). When the affair includes formal wear, the invitation should include the notation "black tie."

Replies to such invitations should follow a similar pattern:

> Mr. and Mrs. Charles Longworth accept with pleasure the invitation of the Board of Directors of the Massachusetts Investment Company for dinner on Saturday, the twelfth of June, at seven-thirty o'clock.

The Board of Directors

Massachusetts Investment Company

request the company of

_____

at dinner

on Saturday, the twelfth of June

at seven-thirty o'clock

744 North New York Avenue

Chicago, Illinois

Black Tie   R.S.V.P.

FIGURE 9.1
Formal invitation format.

A simple, one-paragraph letter is satisfactory, particularly when the invitation is from a business concern and contains a fill-in line for the names of those invited. At the most formal level, however, the reply should be prepared in longhand and arranged in the same format as the invitation.

The refusal of an invitation is like the acceptance:

> Mr. and Mrs. Charles Longworth regret they are unable to accept the kind invitation of the Board. . . .

Although formal etiquette calls for handwritten replies to invitations, business protocol permits use of typewritten messages.

News Releases

Through newspapers, magazines, radio, and TV, businesses can inform communities on topics of mutual interest. In preparing news (press) releases, remember these points:

1. Use company letterhead paper (individuals should include a return address and phone number).
2. Include the current date and the preferred date on which the message is to appear.
3. Include the name of the company official responsible for the release (or the name of the individual if the release is not from a company).
4. Give sufficient information (thinking of who, what, when, where, why, and how will help to ensure good coverage).
5. Write deductively with concern for brevity and clarity.

Why begin with the main idea?

The following example illustrates these points:

> March 15, 1990
> NEWS RELEASE (March 18 preferred)
>   WOODSIDE TO BUILD NEW SUBDIVISION
> On June 1, Woodside Homes will begin construction of new homes on a forty-acre tract at the northeast corner of Bell and Ray roads.
>
> The project, expected to be completed in about two years, will feature stucco walls and tile roofs. The four different floor plans range in size from 2,000 to 3,000 square feet.
>
> According to Vince Wilford, vice-president of Woodside, models should be ready for viewing in early September.

Knowing that brevity is important to the media, submitters need to be very conscious of it, too. If a release has to be shortened, the media may eliminate the most important portion (to the submitter). If the phone number appears on the release sheet, the news media may take time to call about possible deletions or ask for more information.

Regrets

The best way to handle an apology is to avoid the need for it. Sometimes, though, events don't turn out as planned and it's our fault. Looking back, our own conduct is regrettable, or some circumstance has prevented us from doing our best. In such cases, apologies are in order—for our own peace of mind and for good future relationships with an offended person.

Whether to apologize face to face, over the phone, or in writing is a personal matter. The nature of the business, custom, seriousness of the infraction, personalities, and other factors are considerations. Regardless of the medium selected, the principles are the same: (1) be sincere, (2) be direct, and (3) be brief. The following memorandum is better than no apology at all, but it has some weaknesses:

Should the main idea be in the final sentence?

❶ I missed yesterday's meeting of the Planning Committee.

❷ I am terribly sorry. I was scheduled to give my report on tax considerations, and I wanted to hear the other scheduled reports and participate in a discussion of them.

❸ If I had known before boarding the plane in Denver that it would not be departing for 45 minutes, I would have called. ❹ Again, I am very sorry for any inconvenience caused by my absence.

❶ States a fact that is already known.

❷ Employs words (terribly sorry) that seem overly strong and unnecessarily negative. Note four uses of "I" in the first two sentences.

❸ Offers an explanation; continues with an "I" orientation.

❹ Presents a second apology; unnecessarily accents negative words.

Addressed to the committee's chairperson, the memorandum could have been more direct, shorter, and less writer centered:

❶ Please accept my apology for missing yesterday's meeting of the Planning Committee.

❷ If the plane from Denver had arrived on schedule, I could have attended. ❸ The report on tax considerations is ready, if you want to include it on next week's agenda.

❶ Presents the apology in the first sentence. Subordinates "apology" and "missing."

❷ Explains, using the subjunctive mood, and thus employs positive language.

❸ Ends with a look to the future meeting.

In apologizing, people who have made mistakes are inclined to condemn themselves too severely or describe the mistake too vividly:

Apologize, but don't be too self-condemning.

① I would like to apologize for two stupid errors I made in introducing you at yesterday's luncheon.

① Begins with a useless—and misleading—expression (would like to). Before the errors were *labeled* "stupid," they may have been thought of in less harsh terms.

② Looking at the tape this morning, I watched in horror as I pronounced your name as "Peabody" instead of "Peaberry" and stated your alma mater as "Northwest" instead of "Northwestern."

② Emphasizes the errors by use of specific language. Until now, the recipient may not have categorized the error as horrible.

③ Please forgive me for making these terrible blunders.

③ Emphasizes the errors by using a negative word as the final word.

Mr. Peaberry probably had noticed the errors in pronunciation but quickly dismissed them as rather common human errors, but suppose he *had* been irritated by them. Labeling them as "stupid" and using "horror" in talking about them (along with actual restatement of the incorrect words) would reinforce his irritation. That reinforcement would work against the purpose of the apology. The revision is better:

① I apologize for the way I pronounced two words when introducing you at yesterday's luncheon--your name and your alma mater's name!

② You deserved--and I wanted you to have--a memorable introduction.

③ My tongue could have cooperated better, but it always has positive things to say when your name is mentioned.

① Apologizes directly. To avoid reinforcing an unpleasant thought, uses general terms instead of repeating the incorrect pronunciations.

② and **③** Seek to make amends.

Beyond apologizing,
do something to
make amends—if
you can.

Of course, an apology without appropriate action is of little value. (Meeting Mr. Peaberry again and saying "Hello, Mr. Peabody" would be fatal.) Without stooping to pick up a classmate's books, an apology for causing them to fall is of little value. Again, empathy is the key: people who have the right attitude have the best chance of finding the right words.

Sometimes, an unsolicited letter of apology removes a barrier or even preserves a business relationship. For example, at the home office of a major firm, a client's representative parked in a space designated for the firm's officers only. Before reaching the entrance, the representative was stopped by a security officer who asked that the car be moved to the visitor's lot. According to the vice-president of finance (who happened to observe the incident), the security officer was obviously angry and used vulgar language in asking that the car be moved. Cheerfully, the representative returned to his car and drove away (perhaps with the intent of terminating the business relationship). The VP addresses a letter of regret to the representative:

❶ In the parking lot this morning, I overheard the discussion between you and the security officer. ❷ For him and for our firm, I apologize for his vulgar language.

❸ He has been reprimanded, and we assure you that his conduct is regrettable. ❹ Please accept our apology.

❶ Begins inductively.
❷ Employs negative language. Emphasizes "vulgar language" by placing it at the end of a short paragraph.

❸ Employs negative language. Some details of the reprimand could make the statement more convincing.
❹ Apologizes a second time. Emphasizes the word "apology" (and its negative connotations) by placing it at the end of the last sentence.

The revision is more direct, more positive, and more detailed:

❶ I apologize for the manner in which our

❶ Emphasizes the apology by placing it in the first

security officer spoke to you this morning.

2 He had been instructed to keep certain parking spaces open for company officers, but he should have remembered his obligation to show genuine respect for you.

3 The chief of security has already assigned the officer to (a) restudy his security manual and (b) attend the human-relations seminars now required of all newly hired employees.

4 When you call at our offices again, you can expect efficiency and courtesy, which have been our goals for the past twelve years.

sentence. Reveals the purpose of the letter. "Manner" of speaking is more positive than "vulgar language."

2 Confirms the officer's right to ask that the car be moved and (through the subjunctive mood and positive words) condemns the officer's methods.

3 Reports measures taken to avoid repetition of such incidents. By reporting something that has been *done,* the letter strengthens credibility of the apology *statement.*

4 Closes with a positive look to future transactions.

If something is done to remedy a situation, an apology is strengthened.

By apologizing quickly, the VP may have avoided the necessity of responding to a strongly worded letter reporting the incident.

Reservations

The practice of making hotel reservations by letter is becoming less and less common. Telephoning usually is more practical in terms of both cost and time. Whether by letter or by phone, a reservation needs to include (1) dates and times of arrival and departure, (2) the number of people who will be staying, (3) the type of room or rooms desired, and (4) a request for confirmation. An organization that has scheduled a convention at a hotel will send its members a blank reservation card. Those who plan to attend simply fill out the card and mail it in to register.

Seasonal Messages

Many businesses send messages to their clients, customers, or employees at certain times of the year: Thanksgiving, Christmas, Yom Kippur, birthdays, the beginning of a new concert season, the anniversary of an active account's opening, etc. The intent is to demonstrate goodwill through an expression of good wishes or appreciation. Such messages remind recipients that they are important to the business, that they are remembered at a special time. For that reason, sales material (even very low-pressure sales messages) should not be included. It would reduce the impact of the primary message. Thinking they had been trapped into reading a sales pitch, readers might be resentful.

Such messages may be stored in the computer, recalled, and sent on letterhead paper with the recipient's inside address and a salutation. More frequently, they are mass produced and written as though they were addressed to members of a group:

> ABC appreciates your efforts in 1990. Thanks to you, every goal has been reached or exceeded. As a token, a gift certificate will be included in your next pay envelope.
>
> May your holiday season be the most enjoyable one you have ever had.

To a valued customer, the following letter would be encouraging:

> One year ago today, you opened an account with us. Thank you for buying your building materials from us during the past year. Your promptness in paying has certainly been noticed, and we want you to know it has been appreciated.

Compared with the goodwill generated by such letters, the cost is likely to be very small.

Telegrams

Telegrams are often an acceptable alternative when people cannot be reached by telephone, or when a written record of transmitted information is needed. For example, your boss is scheduled to arrive at a certain hotel in a distant city, and you want to communicate with her immediately upon arrival. If a telegram is waiting, it will be delivered at check-in:

> New information. Call before issuing contract.

In telegrams, sentences rely on the understood subject. Nonessential words can be omitted but not at the expense of clarity. For immediate delivery during the day, choose *full-rate* telegrams. To get lower rates, send *overnight* telegrams. Their delivery by 2 P.M. the next day is guaranteed. For low rates on more lengthy messages, consider *mailgrams*. The message will be transmitted by the local telegraph office to the post office in the receiving city. The post office will deliver the message (along with the other mail) on the next day.

Delivering telegrams by messenger is no longer a standard practice. Upon receipt of the message at the receiving office, a clerk tries to reach the recipient by phone. The receiver can request that the message be mailed (or, having served its purpose, it can be discarded.) For transmission overseas, cablegrams, radiograms, and lettergrams can be transmitted from the local telegraph office.

Sending a telegram does not require a trip to the telegraph office. It can be transmitted by telephone to the telegraph office. Of course, it should be carefully written first. The charge is based on the number of words, so brevity (without sacrificing clarity) is a consideration. (Names of sender and receiver, addresses, and punctuation marks are not counted in determining the number of words.)

Thank Yous

Following the receipt of a gift, attendance as a guest, an interview, or any of the great variety of circumstances in which a follow-up letter of thanks might be desirable, a thoughtful person will take the time to send a written message. As with all other special-letter situations, our message should reflect our sincere feelings of gratitude. When couples have been guests, one person usually sends the thank-you message for both. The message should be informal; a simple handwritten message is sufficient. When written in a business office to respond to a business situation, the message may be typed on office stationery. Here's a message of thanks for a weekend visit. Rather than the routine, thank-you-for-a-lovely-weekend thought, the letter includes something specific that the writer enjoyed:

> We had a wonderful time this weekend, and Jack and I still have our rosy glows from the swimming and sunshine. The Barkers were as charming as you said they'd be. You were kind to invite us. Thanks again for everything.

A thank-you note covering a business situation might have the following tone:

> Thank you for your letter of introduction, which enabled me to see Albert Jenkins in San Diego. He said some nice things about you, by the way.
>
> We were able to lay the groundwork for future relationships that could be very profitable. I very much appreciate your taking the time to help me and look forward to an opportunity to return the favor.

In cases such as those covered by these two letters, thanks could be conveyed as well by telephone calls. However, the notes seem much more thoughtful.

All gifts received should also be acknowledged by a thank-you note. In longhand, we should identify the gift, tell why we like it, and describe how we'll use it:

> Bill and I are delighted with the beautiful silver candy dish you sent us. We plan to use it on our coffee table where everyone will see it first thing. Thanks so much for your kindness.

Such letters are easy to write, and they require little time. Yet, too many people find themselves doing each day only that which *must* be done. Anything that can wait will wait. The letter waits until tomorrow, then tomorrow, and is never sent.

Welcomes and Farewells

Why *write* a note welcoming a new employee?

For most new employees, the first day on a job is trying—new tasks, new responsibilities, and new people. When introduced, many will extend an *oral* welcome. Those who bother to drop a *written* welcome into the mail box will make a special impact:

> Welcome to the Accounting Department!
>
> On this your first day, George has plans for a thorough orientation. Afterwards, if you have any questions about our facilities or procedures, just stop by Room 121. As soon as schedules permit, let's have lunch together. Best wishes for a long and happy tenure with us.

Positive as the impact of the *words* may be, the *thoughtfulness* demonstrated by taking time to write may have an even greater impact.

For those who are leaving a job, many colleagues and friends will *say* some things that will make the departing employee feel good; but not many will bother to *write*. The written message is likely to have a stronger impact; it may be kept or shared with family members. To identify ideas that might be included, reflect on experiences with the departing person. Brief reference to special interests, skills, accomplishments, or mutual problems may be appropriate. One who has demonstrated an appreciation for humor may enjoy a touch of it. Regardless, the message ought to be brief, sincere, and personal:

Will a *written* farewell have a strong impact?

> I will miss you, but still I am glad to see you get the professional advancement you have earned.
>
> You leave an unmatched reputation for efficiency, punctuality, and integrity. But give me a little time; I'll find someone who can match your skills at pinochle during the lunch hour.
>
> Best wishes for success and happiness on the new job.

What to say in farewell letters (as well as other letters discussed in Chapter 9) is important. For most people, though, *taking time to write them* is the major problem.

Summary

Although routine business affairs dominate most of our time, special situations provide opportunities for us to put our best foot forward. The way in which we display our sensitivity to human relationships marks the kind of people we are. Special letters provide one way to demonstrate that sensitivity.

About Language and Usage

Both: Do not use *both* with *alike, at once, equal, equally,* or *between.*

    Incorrect: *Both equally* deserve the credit.
    Correct: *Both* you and I deserve the credit.
                   John and Joan deserve the credit *equally.*

Else: Do not use *else* with *but* or *except.*

    Incorrect: No one *else but* me was there.
    Correct: No one *but* me was there.
                   No one *else* was there.

In a possessive idea, use *else's* to follow words like *everybody* and *somebody: Somebody else's* paper was ready.

Check Your Writing

To check your writing of a message in one of the twelve categories, first check the points listed under *special letters*. Then check the points listed under the category you're interested in. For example, check a letter of regret against the six qualities listed under special letters *and* the three listed under regrets.

Special Letters

_____ Convey the *right* message.
_____ Use the right *words* to convey the message.
_____ Employ acceptable format.
_____ Achieve correctness in grammar, spelling, punctuation, and key-boarding.

(continued)

———— May be handwritten.
———— Are characterized by directness, brevity, and sincerity.

Condolences

———— Begin with a statement of condolence.
———— Refer to mutual experiences or relationships.
———— Close with words of comfort or affection.

Congratulatory Letters

———— Are short.
———— Are sincere.

Responses to Congratulatory Letters

———— Do not sound egotistical.
———— Do not seem to deny worthiness.

Evaluations

———— Are written for the right purpose.
———— Are deductive if written about positives, inductive if written about negatives.
———— Are factual (not judgmental) if written about negatives.

Invitations

———— Informal invitations have conversational tone.
———— Formal invitations are generally printed.
———— Replies to formal invitations have tone similar to the invitations.

News Releases

———— Are written deductively.
———— Give sufficient information (who, what, when, where, why, and how). (continued)

Regrets

_____   Apology appears only once in the message.

_____   Should not be overly self-critical.

_____   Should not describe a mistake too vividly.

Reservations

_____   Include dates and times of arrival and departure, number of people staying, type of room desired, and a request for confirmation.

Seasonal Messages

_____   Do not include sales-promotional words.

Telegrams

_____   Achieve brevity without losing clarity.

Thank Yous

_____   Are specific about that which is appreciated.

Welcomes and Farewells

_____   Welcome letters try to convey an attitude of friendliness and willingness to help with adjustment to a new job.

_____   Farewell messages are tailor-made to the individual—a reference to a common experience, special skills and interests, accomplishments, or mutual problems.

Exercises

Review Questions

1. Compared with persuasive messages, are messages in the "special" category longer or shorter?

2. For most letters in the "special" category, which is preferred: (a) deductive presentation or (b) inductive presentation?

3. In expressing condolence, what determines whether to send a printed card or a personalized letter?

4. In expressing congratulations, which is more likely to have a strong impact: (a) an interoffice phone call or (b) a memorandum?

5. List two common pitfalls in the writing of responses to congratulatory messages.

6. How are writers rewarded for the time they spend in writing letters of commendation?

7. What are the disadvantages of using superlatives and other strong adjectives and adverbs in a letter that commends someone for a job well done?

8. By writing a letter or memorandum that reports someone's failure to do a job well, what risks does a writer take?

9. In reporting someone's failure to do a job well, why should judgmental terms be avoided?

10. Which is better for writing news releases: (a) deductive sequence or (b) inductive sequence?

11. When the purpose of a message is to apologize, should it begin and end with the apology?

12. Which is the better expression? (a) "I apologize for. . . ." or (b) "I would like to apologize for. . . ." Why?

13. In an apology, should a writer use strong adjectives to describe the mistake for which an apology is presented?

14. Why should sales messages be omitted from seasonal messages?

15. In thanking someone for a gift, which is better: (a) a handwritten message or (b) a typewritten message? Why?

Activities

In the following letter-writing activities, supply names, addresses, and specific facts for each. Although you have freedom to use your imagination, be especially careful to apply the principles discussed in the preceding chapter.

Condolence

1. A friend with whom you had taken several classes suffered a fatal accident. Write a letter of condolence to the friend's parents.

Congratulation

2. One of your friends (a student who has a very high scholastic average and has been active in student government) has been appointed to serve a year on the school's board of regents. Write your friend a letter of congratulation.

Response to Letter of Congratulation

3. As the student who was appointed to serve a year on the board of regents (Activity 2), write a response to a fellow student's letter of congratulation.

Positive Evaluation

4. The semester is almost over. One of your professors taught an outstanding course. Write a letter to that professor's department head. Your purpose is to commend and encourage.

5. As department head, write a response to the student's positive evaluation (Activity 4).

Negative Evaluation

6. Your semester will be concluding two weeks from now. One of your professors (use a fictitious name) has been exceedingly ineffective. Write a letter to that professor's department head. Your purpose is to help the department, students who may be in that professor's class later, and the professor.

7. As department head, write a response to the student's negative evaluation (Activity 6).

News Release

8. Assume your fraternity or sorority is sponsoring a dance. Proceeds will go to a local children's home. Prepare a news release.

9. As president of Beta Gamma Sigma (honorary fraternity for business majors), you were responsible for having pins engraved and

certificates ordered. After the initiation ceremonies, you got a call from an irate parent. John Stedman's (pronounced with a short "e") name was mispronounced at the ceremony, and "John Steedman" was printed on the certificate. Write an apology to Mrs. Stedman. In less than a month, you will be able to mail John a certificate with the name spelled correctly.

Thank You

10. While crossing the desert on an extremely hot day, your car's engine failed. For 15 minutes, dozens of cars roared by; finally, one stopped. The driver diagnosed the problem as "vapor lock," gave you and each of your two children a cold soft drink, worked under the hood for about 10 minutes, and started the car. For you, he solved a major problem; to him, it seemed like a very small favor. He did accept your expression of gratitude and handed you his business card when you asked if he had one. Write a letter of appreciation.

11. On a tax-reform bill, your representative in Congress voted as you had hoped he would. The bill was eventually defeated, but you appreciated his stand and hope he will continue to work for tax reform. Write a letter of appreciation and encouragement.

12. A personnel director was invited to talk to your class about résumé writing. Trying to incorporate suggestions given, you prepared a résumé and submitted it to your school's career-services division. In subsequent interviews, you have been highly commended for having prepared an outstanding résumé. Write a letter of appreciation to the personnel director.

13. Attending a convention in a distant city, you happened to remember that a former classmate lives in that city. You would have been satisfied with a short phone conversation, but the classmate insisted on taking you to dinner—in one of the city's fanciest restaurants. The food was outstanding; reminiscence was a genuine pleasure. After returning home, write a thank-you letter.

14. Write a letter to your parents or to a special relative to thank them for something special they have done for you while you have been in college.

Welcome or Farewell

15. As president of a sorority or fraternity, write a message of welcome to new members.

16. Assume an elderly, eminent ophthalmologist removed a tissue growth from your eyeball. The operation was very delicate; results were perfect. Your last trip to the physician's office was routine. Upon paying your account before leaving, you were told that Dr. Sooter-Smith was retiring. You were the last patient in a career that spanned more than fifty years. Write a letter that she will treasure.

17. For thirteen years, Charlene has been an outstanding receptionist in a personnel office. But now she needs to return to her hometown to be near her parents who are confined to a rest home. As a clerk who has worked in the office for five weeks, you have been very grateful to Charlene for helping you adjust to your job. Write her a farewell letter.

Memoranda

18. As president of the Markens Art Company, you have very much appreciated your employees' conduct during the Summer Arts Festival. With huge crowds attending, the days seemed hectic. Many employees worked overtime in the evenings and on weekends. The box score: no accidents, no complaints from any source, sales much larger than anticipated. Now that the heavy work season is over, write a memorandum to all employees. Express your appreciation.

19. Vinita Clark (operations manager for MAC) attended one of Ruth Hutchinson's lectures on the history of American Sculpture. Vinita liked the ideas presented, Ruth's subtle sense of humor, and the emphasis given to Maynord Jenkins' work. As Vinita, write a memorandum to Ruth. Commend her for a job well done.

20. As a part-time salesperson at MAC, you have become reasonably well acquainted with Ruth Hutchinson. You are well aware of her lectures, her success as purchasing manager, and her plans to write a book on the history of American Sculpture. Now that you have learned that she will be retiring within two weeks, write her a farewell message.

When you have finished studying Part 4, you should be able to

- Undertake the job-search process.

- Compile an effective personal résumé.

- Reveal your personal strengths through letters related to employment.

- Engage in constructive employment interviews with knowledge about both the interviewer and interviewee roles.

COMMUNICATING ABOUT WORK AND JOBS

Preparing Résumés

Not failure, but low aim, is a crime.

JAMES RUSSELL LOWELL

On his regular morning walk, an elderly counselor spoke to a man who was raking leaves: "Good morning. How's it going today?" The response: "Hi. Well, I'm not getting anywhere raking these leaves." Responded the counselor: "Not getting anywhere? Where do you want to get?" Reflecting for a moment, the raker said "I have never thought much about that." "I'll be walking by here tomorrow at this same time," said the counselor, "and between now and then, why don't you do some thinking about it?"

Setting Goals and Planning

As a result of the conversation, the leaf raker began to do some serious thinking about his life's goals—about what he wanted to get from life and the price he was willing to pay. Through subsequent encouragement from the counselor, the leaf raker analyzed himself, the careers in which he had some interest, and some specific jobs that would be better than raking leaves. Eventually, the man had a rewarding career in the computer field.

Have you set *your* goals? Do you have a plan for reaching them?

Vital to his success were (1) setting a goal and (2) developing a plan for reaching it. For many years, another counselor conducted seminars for people who had very high economic aspirations. He asked participants to ponder the question, "How rich do I want to be?" He asked each person to write that figure on a small card, place it in his or her billfold, and look at it each night and morning. These daily reminders of the goal increased the likelihood of its attainment.

Goal-setting does for individuals what management-by-objectives does for businesses. It forces consideration of these questions: *What* is to be accomplished? *How* is it best accomplished? How is progress measured? Are decisions congruent with goals? Important as such questions are, they sometimes do not get the attention they deserve. Many college seniors have confided to advisers, "I'm scared. About all I've ever done is go to school. Now, I'll have to earn a living. How do I find a suitable job?"

Life's happiness is directly related to life's work.

Because the answer to that question can mean the difference between a pleasant life and an unpleasant one, it deserves careful attention. A suitable job satisfies needs at all of Maslow's needs levels—from basic economic needs to self-actualizing needs. During your working lifetime, you will spend about one-third of your nonsleeping time on a job (and probably much additional time thinking about your work). The *right* job for you will not be drudgery; the work itself will be satisfying. It will give you a sense of well-being; you can see its positive impact on others. The satisfaction derived from work has a positive influence on enjoyment of nonworking hours.

Career decisions, then, have a major influence on a person's enjoyment of life. Yet students (like the leaf raker) tend to devote too little time and thought to career decisions, or they unnecessarily postpone decisions. Of the 40 to 45 courses required to achieve your B.S. degree, how much time is devoted to *one* course? (Think of the daily reading assignments, research, preparation for tests, writing a term paper, etc.) Are you willing to spend that much time gathering, recording, and analyzing information that will lead to a satisfying career? Would you be willing to start putting together a notebook of information that would guide you to the best career?

Research and analyze before choosing a career.

Just as finding the right career is important for you, finding the right employees is important for the employer. Before offering you a job, employers will need information about you—in writing. The résumé, as the written document that provides a basis for judgment about you, is of vital importance. Major concerns in its preparation are (1) getting essential information, (2) planning your résumé, and (3) constructing your résumé.

Getting Essential Information

Recall from the discussion of sales letters that becoming informed about the product is a prerequisite to writing. Likewise, becoming informed is a prerequisite for preparing a résumé. Beneficial as reading and thinking are, they are not enough. Career-related information should be *written* in your personal career notebook. Just as an accountant uses a worksheet when preparing a profit and loss statement and a balance sheet, job seekers can use a career notebook in preparation of a résumé. Keeping such a notebook (1) encourages the gathering of pertinent and sufficient information, (2) makes review and summary easy, and (3) assists in analysis. The act of putting thoughts on paper helps in clarifying, remembering, and analyzing. Self-analysis, career analysis, and job analysis precede résumé preparation.

Why make a written record of career information?

• Self-Analysis

Do you know
yourself as well as
you could?

Before analysis can take place, questions need to be asked and answered. A good way to proceed is, using double or triple spacing, to type the following questions on a sheet for inclusion in your career notebook:

The kind of person I am

1. Do I have a high level of *aspiration*?
2. Do I *communicate* well?
3. Am I *dependable*?
4. Am I *energetic*?
5. Am I free of personal *habits* that would interfere with my work?
6. Am I *financially* independent?
7. Am I a *leader*?
8. Am I *people oriented* (or would I like to work alone)?
9. Am I *self-confident* (without being egotistical)?
10. Do I spend *time* wisely?

My aptitudes (results of psychological tests)

Aptitudes: inborn
traits

1. Do I have a high quantitative aptitude?
2. Do I have high verbal aptitude (written and oral)?
3. Do I have high aptitude for learning foreign languages?
4. Do I have a high mechanical aptitude?
5. Do I have a high aptitude for problem solving?

My achievements

Achievement:
acquired knowledge
and skills

1. What is my overall grade-point average?
2. What is the grade-point average in my major?
3. In which courses have I excelled?
4. Which courses have been most difficult?
5. Have I done well in problem-solving courses?
6. What have been my achievements in extracurricular activities, in jobs I have held, or in volunteer work?

My interests

1. What are my favorite *academic* interests (the courses I *liked* best, not necessarily the ones in which I made the best grade).
2. Which *professional* magazines or journals are most appealing?
3. What type of books or magazines do I read for pleasure?

4. To which campus and off-campus organizations do I belong?
5. How do I prefer to spend leisure time?
6. Do I like to travel?

My education

1. From which high school and in what year was I graduated?
2. What is my declared major in college and when do I expect to graduate?

My experience

1. What summertime jobs have I held?
2. What part-time jobs have I held?
3. What full-time jobs have I held?

After preparing these questions (and others you may want to add) for your notebook, write your answer beneath each question. The notebook is for *you,* so either typing or handwriting would be all right. Typing requires less space and will probably look neater. (Why not take pride in something you're doing solely for yourself?) Thoughtful answers to such questions will almost certainly point out some strengths (about which you can feel good) and some weaknesses (about which you can begin to make corrections).

Make the career notebook thorough and neat; it's for you.

The thinking required for answering the preceding questions is excellent preparation for writing a résumé. Having written thoughtful answers to these questions, you will have a good chance of providing ready answers for questions asked during an employment interview.

Making the notebook is good preparation for writing a résumé and facing an interview.

• Career Analysis

Just as the act of asking and answering questions about yourself is helpful, the same technique is helpful in career analysis. Seek answers to questions such as these:

Type of career (such as accounting, finance, food distribution, sales, etc.)

Ask these questions about your first, second, and third choices of career.

1. Which aptitudes (quantitative, verbal, mechanical) would be most beneficial?
2. Is the occupation considered a "pressure" occupation?
3. Are there significant health hazards?
4. Is relocation or frequent travel expected?
5. Is the field crowded, or is it short of workers?

Preparation

1. What are the academic requirements (degree, major)?
2. What are the professional requirements (certificates)?
3. Are continuing education or training programs expected and available?
4. What experiences are considered prerequisite?

Rewards

1. What is the standard salary of beginning workers?
2. Are there significant opportunities for advancement in salary and responsibility?
3. What are the fringe benefits?
4. What are the intangible rewards?

Future of the field

1. Is the field expected to expand or contract?
2. Will the field be strongly influenced by changes in technology?
3. Is competition in the field increasing?
4. Will changes in political administrations or governmental regulation have a significant impact on the field?

In providing answers to the preceding questions, the following sources are especially helpful:

Bolles, Richard N. *What Color Is Your Parachute? A Practical Manual for Job Hunters and Career Changers,* 2nd ed. Berkeley, Calif.: Ten Speed Press, 1984.

Career Opportunities. Chicago, Ill.: J. G. Ferguson, (published monthly).

Bureau of Employment Security, U.S. Department of Labor, *Dictionary of Occupational Titles.* Washington, D.C.: U.S. Government Printing Office.

Bureau of Labor Statistics, U.S. Department of Labor, *Occupational Outlook Handbook.* Washington, D.C.: U.S. Government Printing Office, (published yearly).

Powell, C. Randall. *Career Planning Today.* Dubuque, Ia.: Kendall-Hunt, 1981.

Available in school or community libraries, these sources also are usually available in college and university career service centers.

After writing answers to the career-oriented questions suggested for your notebook, you almost certainly will have either an increased enthusiasm for the career or a feeling that other careers should receive your consideration. Either way, the effort has been worth while. Reasonably well satisfied that you have selected the right field for your career, you can now begin to examine a specific job in that field.

• Job Analysis

Most college graduates with little or no experience would expect to take what is commonly referred to as an "entry-level" position. Many businesses provide training or orientation programs for such newly hired employees. Before preparing a résumé, students need to ask and answer questions such as these:

1. What are the specific duties and responsibilities? (Good sources: the firm's personnel office, local public and private employment offices, the college or university's career services office, and *The Dictionary of Occupational Titles.*)

2. Do my personal characteristics seem compatible with the specified duties and responsibilities? (Aptitudes? Interests? Others—dependability, leadership, aspirations, etc.?)

3. Does my education satisfy requirements for the position (degrees earned or in progress, special training programs, directly related courses)?

4. Are my experiences directly related to the job's specified duties and responsibilities? (List related summer jobs, part-time jobs, or full-time jobs. If experience is scant, what aspects of the academic program, school-related activities, volunteer work, or other jobs are related to the job in which you are interested?)

With answers to the preceding questions recorded in your career notebook, you can quickly review. Use the notebook for other job-related information, too. Add pertinent questions and answers to the preceding lists. Occasionally review and update. Reserve some pages for clippings of career- and job-related information. Record addresses and phone numbers of firms for which you would consider working, employers and supervisors for whom you have worked (along with specific dates on which employment began and ended), and references. Include a copy of a transcript or a list of courses taken. Record notes taken during interviews.

Making a career notebook requires discipline; job success also requires discipline.

• Interview with a Career Person

Before making the decision to embark on a certain career, you can profit greatly from interviewing someone who is already pursuing it. The interview is to your advantage, regardless of whether it increases your

If possible, interview more than one person in the career.

enthusiasm or reveals that the career is definitely not for you. For maximum benefit, prepare beforehand a set of questions:

> When did you become interested in this field?
>
> What do you see as ideal preparation for entry?
>
> What was your first job in this field?
>
> Are there reasonable opportunities for advancement?
>
> Does the field have great potential for growth?
>
> What tasks do you perform on a typical day?
>
> What do you like best about your career?
>
> What do you dislike?
>
> What is your advice to someone who is considering entry into this field?

By recording answers in the notebook, you reinforce them in your mind and preserve them for reference. By reviewing the notebook, you can easily identify information that should be included on your résumé.

Planning Your Résumé

In format, content, and style, your résumé will in some respects resemble the résumés illustrated on pages 354–356. It *must* include your name, address, phone number; the job (or type of work) sought; and your qualifications (primarily your education and experience). It *may* include career goal, personal information, and references. Whether you include these items is a matter of personal preference and your assessment of whether the receiver will want or need them. The goal of the résumé is to get an interview, so ask yourself this question: "Does inclusion of this information increase my chances of getting an interview?" If the answer is "Yes," include it; if the answer is "No," omit it and use the space to develop your qualifications.

What purpose does a résumé serve?

• Career Goals

If the job sought is clearly a step toward your career goal, state your goal.

If the job for which you are applying is clearly a logical step toward a certain career goal, stating the career goal on the résumé seems advisable. For example, a person majoring in fashion merchandising eventually would like to become a buyer but is now applying for a selling job in a department store. By revealing long-range goals, the applicant connotes ambition, farsightedness, and orderliness—positive qualities that should increase the chance of getting an interview. However, an applicant for a job in retail clothing sales would gain little by putting "Career goal: lead singer in a rock group" on the résumé. Even though the career goal may to the reader seem commendable, retail selling is not recognized as a logical step toward it. By implying strong interest in music, the applicant could be stereotyped as having insufficient interest in selling (and not be invited for an interview).

• Personal Information

If personal information is included, it must be carefully selected. Under the 1964 Civil Rights Act (and subsequent amendments), employers cannot make hiring decisions based on gender, religion, age, marital status, handicap, or national origin. If such information *appears* on a résumé, subsequent questions could be raised about whether it were *used*. Most employers would counsel against inclusion of such information. Its absence leaves more space for development of qualifications.

What type of personal information is best omitted?

However, you may *want* to reveal certain personal information. When it is to your advantage, do so. For example, an applicant for a job with a religious or political organization may benefit from revealing affiliation with such an organization. An unmarried person could benefit from revealing marital status, especially if a job requires relocation or frequent travel. A married person may want that status to be known. Or a nonsmoker may want to reveal that fact. To some employers, it may be a favorable factor in the decision to interview. To others, it may be unfavorable, raising the question of the applicant's compatibility with present employees. Yet, for the person who really wants a nonsmoking work environment, "nonsmoker" on the résumé will restrict the number of interviews with employers who condone smoking and increase the number of interviews with employers who don't.

Would you reveal that you don't smoke, drink, or use drugs?

Such personal information as height, weight, color of hair and eyes are not normally worthy of inclusion. Photographs are discouraged because they convey information about gender, age, and national origin—criteria employers are forbidden to *use* as a basis for hiring. Applicants, however, are not forbidden to *provide* such information. Reveal ethnic background or physical handicap if doing so is to your advantage. For example, certain businesses may be actively seeking employees in certain ethnic groups. For such a business, ethnic information would be useful and appreciated.

Should a picture be attached?

What type of
personal information
is appropriate for
inclusion?

In making a decision about whether to include certain personal information, consider three criteria: (1) How closely is it related to the job sought? (2) Does it portray me as a well-rounded, happy individual off the job? and (3) Is it controversial? If not included under some other heading in the résumé, the following items are possibilities for inclusion under the "Personal Information" heading: oral and written communication skills, machine-operating skills, foreign or computer languages skills, military service, community service, scholastic honors, job-related hobbies, and professional association memberships. Favorite sports may be included, but be cautious. To an employer who plays a lot of golf, your enthusiasm for it may be a plus. To one who does not, it could be a small but eliminating factor. Listing a sport that is stereotyped as dangerous or overly time consuming would be risky. Ideally, the personal information list should be selective. If it's too long, it will compete for attention with more important information (education and job experience).

• References

Advantages and
disadvantages of
including references

A list of references (people who have agreed to supply information about you when requested) may be included. Inclusion of names, addresses, and telephone numbers of people who can provide information about you adds credibility to the résumé. Employers, former employers, teachers, and former teachers are good possibilities. Friends, relatives, and neighbors aren't (because of their bias in your favor).

Recommendation
letters include mostly
positive information.
Why?

In recent years, legislative acts and court decisions have diminished the value of recommendations from references. Employees in certain industries and businesses have the legal right to look at information in their personnel folders. People who write recommendations recognize the possibility of legal action (or ruined professional relationships) if negative information is given. Thus, recommendation letters are inclined to concentrate on positives only, which restricts their value to employers.

An applicant with good qualifications that are well presented will probably be invited to an interview, even if references are omitted completely. Practices vary; but in many businesses, interviews are conducted before communicating with references. A list of references can be provided after a successful interview. By withholding references until they are called for, an applicant may avoid unnecessary or untimely requests sent to the present employer. The interview gives an applicant a chance to assess the desirability of the job. Until then, the applicant may not want the present employer to receive inquires (which may be interpreted as dissatisfaction with the present job).

Instead of supplying a list of references on the résumé, an applicant can include a statement "References will be supplied on request." To someone who has seen those words hundreds of times, it may seem like a cliché. With a little imagination, the résumé writer can find a less worn way of expressing the idea. Or include a statement such as "For reference information, call or write to (give address and phone number of the career services center of your college or university)."

Why register with your school's career services center?

College students who are serious about finding a job will have registered with their career services center. It will have collected recommendation letters and reproduced sets of them for mailing to employers.

As a unique individual, you do not want your résumé to look just like another person's or to contain the same information. Make *your* decisions about whether to include a statement of long-range career goals, which personal information is worthy of inclusion, and whether to include references.

Like any theme, letter, or memorandum you have written, your résumé will need to meet high standards of *content*. Previously discussed parts are important, but the most important portion of all is your qualifications. If they seem compatible with job requirements, you have a good message to present. Confident that you have a good message, you are now ready to put it on paper—to construct a résumé that will impress the employer favorably.

The career notebook helps provide the résumé's content.

Constructing a Résumé

Résumés may be constructed in a variety of ways. Instead of making a résumé to suit *you,* try to make one that you think will suite *the person who will read it*. Although acceptable résumés are illustrated later in this chapter, they are not intended to restrict your own creativity. Your goal is to produce a résumé that will emphasize the compatibility of *your qualifications* and *the prospective employer's job requirements*. You seek to achieve it through organization, style, and mechanics.

Use empathy; the résumé is designed to impress the employer.

• Organization

Organization is fairly standard:

Name, address, and telephone number

Job objectives

Qualifications

Personal information

References

The primary organizational challenge is in dividing the qualifications section into parts, choosing labels for them, and arranging them in the best sequence. Reviewing their self-, career-, and job-analysis data, applicants usually recognize that their qualifications stem mainly from their *education* and their *experience*. Those words traditionally appear as headings on the résumé. Which appears first depends on which is perceived as more impressive to the employer, with the most impressive appearing first. Working with pencil and paper, make a trial outline.

Should the education section precede the experience section?

Chronological résumé   Two headings normally appear in the portion that presents qualifications:

Education

(Under which would appear your major and your degree or a report on your progress toward it. Any special training programs, or specific courses—if not sufficiently implied by identifying your major—and favorable results of aptitude tests could be reported under this heading.)

Experience

(Under which would be listed your present job and the jobs that preceded.)

Why list jobs held in reverse chronological order?

Look at the two headings from the employer's point of view and reverse their positions if doing so would be to your advantage. Under the "Experience" division, jobs are normally listed in reverse order. Assuming normal progression, the latest job is likely to be more closely related to the job sought than is the first job held. Placing the latest job first will give it the emphasis it deserves. For each job, beginning and ending dates are usually included. From these dates, this traditional résumé gets its name—a *chronological* résumé. Yet, listing jobs in chronological order is not a requirement. If listing jobs in order of their *relatedness* to the job sought or the *value of experience provided* is to your advantage, deviate from the time sequence. Begin with the job that will make the best impression. Including the dates is not a requirement.

Why list first the experience most closely related to the job sought?

The person who reads your résumé will likely look at résumés of others competing for the same job. About 70 percent will employ "Education" and "Experience" as major headings. Listing experience is easy, and use of those headings is common. Yet, while you are still working with pencil and paper, try constructing an outline with a different basis for division (and a different set of headings).

Functional Résumé   A functional résumé requires some analysis. However, preparation of your career notebook has already forced you to analyze yourself, the career, and the job.

Review the notebook and envision an employer who has a stack of résumés, a limited amount of time for reviewing them, and plans to select two for invitations to an interview. Looking through the résumés, the employer is trying to answer the question: "Who has what we're looking for?" The same question may be phrased in different ways: "Who can do best what we want done?" or "Who has qualifications that match our requirements?" The major headings (Education and Experience) of chronological résumés do not answer this last question. Rather, it is answered in the typewritten lines that appear beneath the headings. Thus, the answer is subordinated. If the answer could be incorporated into the major headings, it would be emphasized—more likely to be seen and more likely to make a vivid impression. In functional résumés, the points of primary interest to employers appear in major headings.

Assume, for example, that a person seeking a job as an assistant hospital administrator wants to emphasize qualifications by placing them in major headings. From the hospital's advertisement of the job and from accumulated job-appraisal information, the applicant sees this job as both an administrative and a public-relations job—one that requires skill in communicating and knowledge of accounting and finance. Thus, headings in the qualifications portion of the résumé could be

Administration
Public Relations
Communication
Budgeting

These headings highlight what the applicant can *do* for the employer—the *functions* that can be performed well. A résumé that uses such headings (instead of Education and Experience, which appear on chronological résumés) is called a *functional* résumé. Under each heading,

Do functional résumés report experience and education?

Do functional résumés employ "Experience" and "Education" as major headings?

the applicant could draw from educational and/or work-related experience to provide supporting evidence. Under "Public Relations," for example, the applicant could reveal that a public relations course was taken at State University, from which a degree is to be conferred in June, and that a sales job at ABC Store provided abundant opportunity to apply principles learned. With other headings receiving similar treatment, the qualifications portion reveals the significant aspects of education and experience.

Should major headings be presented in alphabetic order?

Order of importance is probably the best sequence for functional headings. Assuming accurate job analysis and self-analysis, the selected headings will highlight points of special interest to the employer. Glancing at headings only, an employer could see that you have qualities needed for success on the job. By carefully selecting headings, you reveal knowledge of the requisites for success on that job.

Having done the thinking required for preparing a functional résumé, you are well prepared for a question that is commonly asked in interviews: "What can you do for us?" The answer is revealed in your major headings. They emphasize the functions you can perform and the special qualifications you have to offer.

Do functional résumé headings emphasize qualifications?

If you consider yourself well qualified, a functional résumé is worth considering. If your education or experience is scant, a functional résumé may be best for you. Using "Education" or "Experience" as a heading (as would be done in a chronological résumé) works against your purpose if you have little to report under that heading. The *absence* of education or experience would be highlighted.

A résumé that *combines* features of chronological and functional résumés may serve your purpose well. The qualifications portion could have headings such as these:

Combination of chronological and functional résumés can give quick assurance that educational and experience requirements are met and still use other headings that emphasize qualifications.

Education
(List the school, major, degree, and graduation date.)
Experience
(Briefly list jobs held and previously held.)
Administration
(Give details drawn from education and/or experience.)
Public Relations
(Give details drawn from education and/or experience.)
Communication
(Give details drawn from education and/or experience.)

Budgeting
    (Details drawn from education and/or experience.)

These headings illustrate the type of headings that *could* be used. Of course, functional headings would vary for different jobs. Moreover, two people applying for the same job would not be likely to choose the same headings or list them in the same sequence. Select headings that are appropriate for *you* and that the employer will see as directly related to the job.

    In planning the résumé, take note of specific job requirements. They are good possibilities for functional headings. For example, for a job that requires bonding, "Top Security Clearance" would get deserved attention as a heading. Each of the following conditions, if it applies to the job sought, could be the basis for a heading: the work is in small groups, the work requires much overtime in certain seasons, a non-smoker is preferred, travel is frequent, overseas assignments are a possibility, adaptability to rapid changes is desirable, ability to take criticism is essential, long and detailed reports are required, or lateral transfers can be expected. Choosing appropriate headings is the most critical decision in résumé preparation. Expressing the ideas, however, is also vital.

> In résumés as in outlines, choice of major headings is critical.

• Style

On some résumés, information appears in the form of lists (lists of courses taken, jobs held, etc.). For them a discussion of style is hardly worthwhile. More commonly, though, résumés employ sentences to help employers see the value of applicants' education and experiences. To save space, and to emphasize what you've *done* as preparation, consider these stylistic techniques: omit pronominal references to yourself, use subject-understood sentences, begin sentences with action words, and select adjectives carefully:

Instead of	Use
I had responsibility for. . . .	*Had* responsibility for. . . .
I wrote computer programs. . . .	*Wrote* computer programs. . . .
I supervised 27 operators. . . .	*Supervised* 27 operators. . . .

> What is the advantage of using subject-understood sentences and verbs as first words?

    Because employers are looking for people who will *work,* action verbs are especially appropriate. As first words in these subject-understood sentences, action words are emphasized. The following list illustrates verbs that would be useful in résumés:

accomplished	developed	planned
administered	drafted	presented
analyzed	established	proposed
assisted	expanded	recruited
compiled	implemented	researched
completed	initiated	scheduled
computed	invented	sold
controlled	maintained	studied
counseled	managed	supported
created	organized	wrote

To give the employer a vivid picture of you as a productive employee, you may find some of the following adjectives helpful:

adaptable	efficient	reliable
analytical	forceful	resourceful
conscientious	independent	sincere
consistent	objective	systematic
dependable	productive	tactful

To avoid a tone of egotism, don't use too many adjectives or adjectives that seem overly strong. Plan to do some careful editing after writing your first draft.

• Mechanics

Can poor mechanics nullify superior content, organization, and style?

Compared with *what the message is,* its *arrangement on the page* may seem rather insignificant. Yet, if the page is arranged unattractively or in poor taste, the message may never be read. Errors in keyboarding, spelling, and punctuation may be taken as evidence of a poor academic background, lack of self-respect, lack of respect for the employer, carelessness, or haste. Try hard for perfection; then ask someone to check it carefully for you.

For most students, a résumé can be arranged on *one* page.

Employers seem to agree that one page is usually sufficient for including all needed information. A one-page résumé that includes irrelevant information is too long. A two-page résumé that omits relevant information is too short. As significant experiences accumulate, you may need two or more pages.

Allow decent margins and systematically place headings. Emphasize headings or lists by surrounding them with white space. However, leaving too much unused space can suggest wastefulness.

Use modern equipment. A résumé typed on a manual typewriter with a fabric ribbon will look distracting. Regardless of whether the machine is electric, electronic, or a computer printer, use carbon ribbon for sharp, clean-looking characters. Under most circumstances, a dot matrix printer is inadvisable. Laser printers are excellent. Some professionals in résumé preparation are now using laser printers. To locate such professional agencies, look under "Résumés" in the Yellow Pages.

If the page is keyboarded on a computer and few copies are needed, each copy could be printed individually. If reproduction equipment is used, only high-quality reproduction should be considered.

Use high-quality paper, nothing less than 16-pound paper. Unless you have a special reason for using colored paper, use white. In a stack of résumés on an employer's desk, a colored page may get attention; but the attention has a chance of being unfavorable. In the reader's experience, such attention-getting techniques may be the trademark of poorly qualified candidates. On the other hand, colored paper *could* be favorably received. If color is considered, it should be one of the pastel shades.

Advantages and disadvantages of using colored paper.

Use standard-sized ($8\frac{1}{2} \times 11$) paper. Since the résumé will accompany a cover letter, use the large (No. 10) envelope. Or you may want to consider using a brown envelope large enough to accommodate the résumé unfolded. Unfolded on the reader's desk, it may get favorable attention. Or the reaction could be "I'm wise to that trick"; if so, chances of an interview may be reduced.

Exemplars

On pages that follow, three different types of résumés are illustrated. Note the differences in the use of periods and commas and straight versus ragged right margins in these résumés. Until recently, style manuals and secretarial handbooks recommended use of a period after an abbreviation and a comma after the name of a city. Typewriters weren't equipped to adjust space between words and letters to make straight right margins. The U.S. Postal Service and vastly increased computer use are changing all that. The U.S. Postal Service recommended omission of all punctuation marks in envelope addresses, which has carried over to usage in letters, memoranda, résumés, and similar written material.

Computer considerations also favor omission of punctuation; computer use allows straight right margins. To some readers, omission of punctuation would be disturbing; to others, use of punctuation would seem old-fashioned. Use the method that you're most comfortable with or think that the reader would approve. Figures 10.1, 10.2, and 10.5 reflect the new style; Figures 10.3 and 10.4, the traditional.

Laura Lindholm
Sunstate Apartments #113
317 W Fourth Street
Winiford CA 91002
Telephone: (214) 987-6543

Professional Goal

A career in fashion merchandising, beginning in retail clothing sales.

Education

Pursuing a Bachelor of Science degree at West State University, Winiford, California. Now enrolled in Accounting, Computer Information Systems, and Microeconomics. Anticipated graduation date: June, 1991.

Major: Marketing, with a specialty in fashion merchandising.

Grade average: 3.6 (on a 4.0 scale).

Business courses completed: Quantitative Analysis, Introduction to Business, Macroeconomics, and Interpersonal Communication.

Business courses planned for the junior year: Retailing, Marketing Environments, Public Relations in Business, and Seminars in Fashion Merchandising.

Sales and Other Experience

August 1985 to May 1986. Sold sandwiches and soft drinks for Winiford Quickburger, 20 hours per week.

Summers 1984, 1985, and 1986. Served as unpaid assistant (candy striper) at Winiford Community Hospital, 15 hours per week. Was president of candy stripers' group in 1986.

Personal Data

Determined to compile a superior academic record and qualify for membership in Alpha Gamma Sigma (honorary fraternity open to juniors and seniors). Subscribe to Retail Selling and Fashions of the Year. Have strong interest in health and physical fitness. Exercise regularly. Earning 25 percent of my college expenses.

References

Ms Sharon Wells RN	Dr May Hart Adviser	Mr Tom Holt Manager
Community Hospital	Marketing Department	Winiford Quickburger
1123 N Lake Street	West State University	151 W Warren Street
Winiford CA 91003	Winiford CA 91002	Winiford CA 91002
(214) 345-6789	(214) 345-9876	(214) 456-1234

FIGURE 10.1

Chronological résumé, for part-time job early in a person's college career.

The name, address, and telephone number are placed in the horizontal center, with each line centered.

The five headings could be placed at the left margin instead of being centered. Note the spacing above and below each heading: two blank lines above each heading and one below.

From the statement of goals, the employer learns the type of work applied for and the career to which it is to lead.

With limited experience, Ms. Lindholm assumes that her education would impress an employer more than her work experience. Thus, she presents education first. Her major directly relates to the work applied for. The grade index (since it is high indicates that Ms. Lindholm takes her school work seriously and learns quickly—attributes that probably would carry over to her on-the-job performance. The classes most closely related to fashion merchandising are upper-division classes (which as a sophomore she is not yet eligible to take). She therefore lists pertinent business courses already taken and some related courses she plans to take.

Because the résumé is submitted for a sales job, the word "sales" appears in the experience heading. Note use of the active verb "sold" in presenting the fast-food experience. By listing her volunteer work, Ms. Lindholm gives some indication of her service attitude. Like selling clothing, her volunteer work is a people-oriented experience.

Personal data are positive, related to job success, and noncontroversial.

References are presented in easy-to-use address form.

LAURA LINDHOLM
Sunset Apartments #113
317 W Fourth Street
Winiford CA 91002   Telephone: (214) 987-6543

Objectives

To begin work in retail clothing sales and later to advance in fashion merchandising, possibly to become a buyer.

Sales-Oriented Career

Have since childhood had a strong interest in fashions. Have had three years' part-time experience in selling fast foods. Currently a sophomore majoring in marketing (with specialty in fashion merchandising) at West State University. Subscribe to Retail Selling and Fashions of the Year. To graduate in May 1991.

Public-Relations Skills

Saw the value of tact in taking and filling orders in the fast-food business (Winiford Quickburger, part-time from August 1985 to May 1986). Commended by manager for diplomacy with patrons and staff. Received an A in Interpersonal Communication and will be taking Public Relations next year. Volunteer work (as a candy striper at Winiford Community Hospital for three summers) provided experience in coping with various personality types.

Record-Keeping Skills

Used cash register and balanced receipts against records each day at Quickburger. Now taking two classes (accounting and computer science) that emphasize keeping records electronically.

Dependability

Was always on the job when scheduled for work. In three years, was never late for work. Responsible, occasionally, for opening, closing, and taking cash to bank. Attend classes regularly.

Learning Capacity

Commended for learning work procedures quickly. On the dean's list for the last two semesters. Achieved 3.6 grade average (on a 4.0 scale) in the last two semesters.

Interests

Developed strong interest in health and physical fitness while serving at the hospital. Exercise regularly. Earn 25 percent of college expenses. Now enrolled in the third Spanish course.

References

Ms Sharon Wells RN	Dr May Hart Adviser	Mr Tom Holt Manager
Community Hospital	Marketing Department	Winiford Quickburger
1123 N Lake Street	West State University	151 W Warren Street
Winiford CA 91003	Winiford CA 91002	Winiford CA 91002
(214) 345-6789	(214) 345-9876	(214) 456-1234

FIGURE 10.2

Functional résumé, for part-time job early in a person's college career.

Note placement of headings: all begin at the left margin and are underscored. Using all-capital letters and omitting the underscore would have been an acceptable alternative. Note that the white space above each heading is slightly more than the space below it.

With so many words on the page, it may appear to be overly long—even a little forbidding. Remember, though, that the reader is a serious person who wants to select the best applicant available. A detailed résumé would not be objectionable to an employer who is being led to see the relationship of education and experience to the job.

Compare and contrast the headings with the headings employed in Figure 10.1. The headings in Figure 10.1 identify portions of the page in which information about education, experience, and personal matters is presented. The headings in Figure 10.2 emphasize the qualities the applicant offers as a solution to the employer's problem. For a sales position, an employer should be impressed with someone who has a long-standing interest in sales and plans to make sales a career (Sales-Oriented Career). Likewise, the employer would like someone who can get along with people (Public-Relations Skills), who can handle cash transactions (Record-Keeping Skills), who is dependable, who can adjust quickly to a new job, and who has interests compatible with the job. A quick look at the headings suggests that this applicant knows important requisites for success in sales.

In the material under each heading, note that the applicant draws from either education or experience (or both) for support.

DELBERT ASHWORTH

School Address	Address after May 1
Rothberg Hall 601	417 W. McClean Avenue
Alton State College	Worthington, LA 65431
Alton, LA 65432	
Phone (315) 123-4567	Phone (315) 345-6789

CAREER OBJECTIVES

Immediate: to enter a management-trainee program.

Eventual: to specialize in personnel or industrial management.

MANAGEMENT-ORIENTED EDUCATION

B.S. degree, Alton State College, Alton, Louisiana. To be conferred on May 1, 1990.

Major: management, with a specialty in personnel management. Degree program includes 24 units in management at the upper-division level, 33 units in other functional fields in business, 57 units in liberal arts, and 12 units of electives. Nine of the elective units have been taken in computer sciences.

Honors: Beta Gamma Sigma (College of Business honorary society), selected as a junior with grade average in the top 5 percent. Sigma Iota Epsilon (national honorary society for management majors), admitted as a senior with a 3.8 grade average (on a 4.0 scale). On the Dean's list for seven semesters.

MANAGEMENT-RELATED EXPERIENCE

May 1988 to present

Desk manager (part time). Domeview Hotel in Alton. Make room reservations, register guests, keep computerized records, and supervise bellhops.

January 1986 to April 1988

Administrative assistant (part time). Keyboarded letters, reports, and memos for the head of the Management Department, Alton State College. Reproduced tests for professors, proctored examinations, and showed management films in seminars.

ADDITIONAL INFORMATION

Letters from references and personal data may be obtained by calling (315) 123-8765, Alton State's Career Services Center, or by writing to the Center at Alton State College, Alton, LA 65432.

FIGURE 10.3

Chronological résumé, for a full-time job at the conclusion of a person's college career.

Planning to move to a new address after graduation, Mr. Ashworth presents both the old and new address—along with phone numbers.

Knowing that the corporations he has been considering have trainee programs designed for recent graduates, he applies for acceptance. From the school's career services center, and from talking with seniors who have had interviews already, he knows that academic background is a significant factor in selection. Hence, he gives details about degree requirements he will have completed. By devoting space to honors, he gives some evidence of ability to succeed in a rigorous training program and his willingness to exert the effort required. Applicants with lower grade averages could (instead of devoting space to honors) devote space to activities in which they had been involved or to special projects in which they had participated.

Because the résumé seeks acceptance into a *management*-trainee program, the word "management" is included in the headings for the education and experience sections.

In the decision to exclude personal information, Mr. Ashworth considers these factors: space is limited, personal information would compete for attention with education and experience (which are more important factors), personal data appear on the career services center's sheets (assuming they are requested), and the application letter will include a small amount of personal information.

These factors contributed to the decision to exclude a list of references: professors and employers have already submitted letters to the career services center (no need to burden them with writing a second letter), space is limited, and the list may not be needed until after the interview (when it could be supplied).

DELBERT ASHWORTH

Rothberg Hall 601
Alton State College
Alton, LA 65432
   Phone (315) 123-4567

Address after May 1:
   417 W. McClean Avenue
   Worthington, LA 65431
   Phone (315) 345-6789

CAREER PLANS — To enter a management-trainee program and later specialize in personnel or industrial management.

MANAGEMENT EDUCATION — To receive B.S. degree in Business with a major in Management, May 1, 1990. Specialty is Personnel Management. Grade average to date, 3.8 (on a 4.0 scale). Member of Beta Gamma Sigma (honorary for business majors) and Sigma Iota Epsilon (honorary for management majors).

MANAGERIAL EXPERIENCE — Domeview Hotel in Alton. Worked part-time as a desk manager since May 1988. Supervise bellhops, reserve rooms, register guests, and keep computerized records.

Management Department, Alton State College. For five semesters, served as administrative assistant. Keyboarded messages, reproduced tests, proctored exams, and showed management films.

COMMUNICATION SKILL — Participated in group discussions and listening drills. Wrote memos, letters, and business reports. Writing was thoroughly critiqued and returned. Gave speeches and researched corporate communication problems. Wrote term papers for most of the business courses. "Case" studies provided abundant opportunity for oral exchange of ideas.

APPRECIATE CRITICISM — Benefited from criticism of written materials and from critiques of oral presentations. Sensitive at first, came to recognize criticism as intent to help. Improved oral presentations after self-criticisms of taped presentations. Appreciate the need for tact in giving criticism.

COMPUTER LITERATE — Elected to take three computer courses (beyond the two required for management majors). The most recently studied languages (PL/1 and RPG) are especially useful in producing written reports.

Letters from references and personal data may be obtained from Alton State's Career Services Center, Alton State College, Alton, LA 65432. Phone (315) 123-8765.

FIGURE 10.4

Combination chronological and functional résumé, for full-time job at the conclusion of a person's college career.

The physical arrangement of major headings (all caps, white space above and below, and placed at the extreme left margin) emphasizes them.

Glancing at the headings only, a reader can see that the résumé covers points vital to success in a trainee program. For acceptance into the program, a degree with a management major is required; some managerial experience is helpful. Knowing that a trainee program involves communication from beginning to end, Mr. Ashworth emphasizes his communication skills by using "Communication" in a heading and reviewing educational experiences that helped to develop his skill.

During the career-analysis phase, Mr. Ashworth had interviewed a successful manager who had been through a trainee program five years previously. According to that manager, a major weakness of trainees is inability to accept criticism. The same manager lamented his own lack of a computer background. Because these comments seemed to be consistent with viewpoints expressed in his classes and in management literature, portions of the résumé are devoted to criticism and computer literacy.

If references are needed before an interview, a call to the career services center will produce them.

Figure 10.4 combines features of the chronological and functional résumés. "Education" and "Experience" are traditional headings on a chronological résumé. "Communication," "Appreciation of Criticism," and "Computer Literacy" are functional résumé headings. Yet, all five major divisions have one common denominator: each is a factor in managerial success.

FRANKLIN E. JOHNSON
1129 E Wentworth Road
Braxton OR 90112

Residence: (502) 345-0987   Work: (502) 345-6543

GOAL

Senior loan officer in a major banking firm

EXPERIENCE

Commercial Loan Officer, Westgate Bank (May 1987 to present). Manage a $25 million loan portfolio, make substantial credit decisions (for loans averaging $800,000 each), and strive to achieve realistic lending goals. Arrange loans primarily for importers and exporters, wholesalers, and manufacturers with sales of $2 million to $90 million.

Prior to becoming a loan officer, completed Westgate Bank's training program for commercial loan officers. It was a 9-month program of classroom training. Passed an intermediate accounting examination as a condition of admittance; passed a rigorous loan officer's examination upon completion.

Intern at Sunbelt Bank (October 1985 to April 1987). Was selected from a group of more than 50 applicants for the internship. Designed to prepare interns for executive responsibilities in managing retail branches, the program included most facets of managerial development in retail banking. Worked primarily as a branch manager's assistant, solving personnel problems and approving consumer loans.

Teller, Saguaro Bank (May 1983 to September, 1985). Working 20 hours per week, progressed from Teller I to Teller III.

EDUCATION

Bachelor of Science in Business, Westbrook University, May 1987. Major: Finance and Real Estate.

Grade average in Finance and Real Estate: 3.6 (4.0 scale).

Honors: Dean's list, four semesters
           Du Bois Foundation Scholarship
           Beta Gamma Sigma, Business Honorary
           Phi Kappa Phi, University Honorary

FIGURE 10.5

First page of two-page chronological résumé, after three years of full-time experience.

Providing residence and work phone numbers enables callers to reach Mr. Johnson while he is at work or during evenings and weekends.

Now that three years have passed since graduation, experience is considered to be a much stronger recommendation than it was earlier. "Experience," therefore, precedes "Education" on the first page. As the years pass and Johnson moves upward, the experience section of his résumés would become longer, and the education section would be condensed.

By presenting figures in describing present responsibilities, he gives an impression that superiors have confidence in his judgment.

Franklin E. Johnson, page 2

Activities: Council member, College of Business for two years
Student representative on the Faculty Curriculum Committee, senior year

PERSONAL DATA

Married. Two sons, ages 2 and 4. Excellent health. Homeowner. Nonsmoker. Member, Kiwanis. Fundraiser in Braxton's Food-for-the-Hungary program.

REFERENCES

Mr Calvin West
President
Westgate Bank
110 North Central
Braxton OR 90113
   (502) 345-1111

Mr Roger Madison
Vice-President Training
Sunbelt Bank
14 East Ranch Avenue
Colton NM 80115

Mrs Ruth Corban
Vice-President Loans
Westgate Bank
110 North Central
Braxton OR 90113
   (502) 345-1134

FIGURE 10.5 (*continued*)
Second page of two-page chronological résumé, after three years of full-time experience.

Note the heading for the second page of the résumé (name of *applicant* and page number). For business *letters,* the heading for the second page lists the name of the *addressee,* the page number, and the date.

Inclusion of "nonsmoker" could endear Mr. Johnson to some employers; to others, it could be a turnoff. Normally, controversial points should be excluded. Revealing an attitude toward smoking, however, seems less risky than revealing an attitude toward religion, politics, or abortion.

The reference section *could* be omitted, but including references may save an employer's having to ask for them. Their inclusion demonstrates that the applicant is secure in his present position.

Finding Prospective Employers

For organizing information about job opportunities, the career note-book is especially helpful. Under the name, address, and phone number of each employer who has a job in which you have an interest, leave some space for recording additional data. Record the date of each call (along with what you learned from the call), the date of each returned call, the name of the person who called, the date of sending a résumé, and so on. By listing each prospective employer on a separate sheet and alphabetizing the sheets, you can find a name quickly and respond effectively to a returned phone call.

Why alphabetize your list of prospective employers?

Information about career and job opportunities is available from many different sources. Among these sources are career services centers, employers' offices, employment agencies and contractors, help-wanted ads, libraries, and professional organizations.

• Career Services Centers

Don't wait until your last semester to learn about the services provided by your college or university's career services center. It may be listed under such names as "Career Services Department," "Career Services Division," or "Placement Center." Typically, the unit has a browsing room loaded with career information and job-announcement bulletins. Career counseling is usually available. Through the center, students can schedule on-campus interviews with company recruiters who make regular visits to the campus.

Register with your career services center.

The career services center can be especially helpful to students who are looking for a job. Students fill out a form, giving information about academic major, progress toward a degree, graduation date, career goals, and so on. Students then invite three to five people (professors, employers, or others who could provide valid information) to send letters of recommendation to the center. The form and letters are reproduced for sending to prospective employers when requested. With this arrangement, a reference submits only one letter of recommendation; but it can be sent to many different employers. By making one call to the career services center, an employer can get three or more recommendations plus additional data.

If you're registered, the career services center can provide an employer with *several* letters of recommendation—in response to *one* call.

• Employers' Offices

Employers who have not advertised their employment needs may respond favorably to a telephoned or personal inquiry. The receptionist may be able to provide useful information, direct you to someone with whom you can talk, or set up an appointment.

• Employment Agencies and Contractors

Telephone directories list city, county, state, and federal employment agencies. The service is free or inexpensive. Some agencies provide a recorded answering service; by dialing and listening, callers can get information about job opportunities and the procedure for using the agency's services. Private agencies charge a fee for assistance in finding a job. The fee is normally based on the first month's salary and paid off within a few months. Some agencies specialize in finding high-level executives or specialists for major firms. Employment "contractors" specialize in providing temporary employees. Instead of helping you to find a permanent job, a contractor may be able to use your temporary services until you do find a full-time job.

How can employment contractors help in finding a job?

• Help-Wanted Ads

Responses to advertised positions should be made as quickly as possible after the ad is circulated. If your résumé is received early and is impressive, you could get a favorable response before other applications are received.

Remember that many good jobs are not advertised in help-wanted ads.

If an ad invites response to a box number without giving a name, be cautious. The employer could be legitimate but doesn't want present employees to know about the ad. However, you have a right to be suspicious of someone who wants to remain obscure while learning everything you reveal in your résumé.

• Libraries

The following library sources are useful in identifying firms in need of employees:

Annual reports from major firms

Black Enterprise (each year's June issue)

Career, The Annual Guide to Business Opportunities

College Placement Annual

Company house organs (newsletters)

Directory of American Firms Operating in Foreign Countries

Dun and Bradstreet's *Million Dollar Directory*

Encyclopedia of Careers and Vocational Guidance

Engineering Index

Forbes ("Annual Directory Issue," published May 15 each year)

Fortune

Moody's *Manuals*

Science Research Associates' Occupational Briefs

Standard and Poor's *Register of Corporations, Directors, and Executives*

Trade or professional journals

United States Civil Service Commission

Wall Street Journal

• Professional Organizations

Officers of professional organizations, through their contacts with members, are sometimes very good sources of information about job opportunities. Much job information is exchanged at meetings of professional associations. In response to help-wanted and position-wanted columns in journals of some professional organizations, interviews are sometimes arranged and conducted at hotels or schools in which the organization holds its annual meeting.

In addition to the professional growth that comes from membership in professional organizations, active participation is a good way to learn about job opportunities. Visiting lecturers sometimes provide job information. In addition, employers are favorably impressed when club membership is listed on the résumé. They are even more impressed if the applicant is (or has been) an officer in the club (implied leadership, willingness to exert effort without tangible reward, social acceptance, or high level of aspiration). By joining and actively participating in professional, social, and honorary clubs for their majors, college students increase their opportunities to develop rapport with peers and professors. One of the benefits is sharing job information.

A student who expects to graduate in May should begin the search for prospective employers weeks or months beforehand. Waiting until late to begin and then hurrying is hazardous, whether searching for names of prospective employers or developing the résumé that is to be mailed to them.

Summary

Because life's enjoyment is strongly influenced by success on the job, planning and preparing for a career are vital. Like other important decisions, career decisions are preceded by gathering information. Preferably, it is recorded in a career notebook for easy reference. About *yourself,* ask questions such as these: What kind of person am I? What are my aptitudes? What have I achieved? What are my interests? Is my education pointed toward a career? About a possible *career,* ask questions such as these: Is it compatible with my aptitudes and interests? Is the field overcrowded? How much academic preparation is required? What are the rewards? About a specific *job* in the chosen field, raise questions about duties and responsibilities. Interview people already working at the job. Recording and analyzing results will assist you in selecting a satisfying career and preparing an effective résumé.

Like other written documents, résumés should reflect high standards of content, organization, style, and mechanics. If errors are detected in any of these categories, an interview will probably not be granted.

Chronological résumés employ "Education" and "Experience" as headings and list experiences in a time sequence. Functional résumés employ *functions you can perform* or *attributes you have* as headings. Choose the one with which you feel most comfortable.

Names and addresses of possible employers may be obtained from career services centers at schools, employers' offices, employment agencies and contractors, help-wanted ads, libraries, professional organizations.

About Language and Usage

Among words we often hear and may not know are these:

Machiavellian	Politically cunning, power politics; "The *Machiavellian* actions of some legislators are astounding."

| *Narcissism* | Self-love or admiration of one's appearance; "Her *narcissism* was enough to drive away potential friends." |
| *Tacit* | Unspoken, silent, implied but understood; "We obtained *tacit* approval for the project." |

Check Your Writing

Résumés

Content

_____ Is based on self-, career, and job analysis.
_____ Qualifications and requirements seem compatible.
_____ Includes only ideas that are relevant.

Organization

_____ Headings are arranged in appropriate sequence.
_____ Significant ideas are in emphatic position.
_____ Experiences (on chronological résumés) are listed consistently, either in time sequence or order of importance.

Style

_____ Shows absence of personal pronouns.
_____ Uses active verbs.
_____ Uses past tense for previous jobs; present tense for present job.
_____ Places significant words in emphatic positions.

(Continued)

_____ Uses parallelism in listing multiple items.
_____ Uses positive language.
_____ Uses simple words (but some jargon of the field is acceptable).
_____ Uses correct grammar.

Mechanics

_____ Is keyboarded on paper of good quality.
_____ Is well balanced on the page.
_____ Has consistent margins.
_____ Has headings consistently centered or at the left margin.
_____ Shows perfection in keyboarding, spelling, and punctuation.

Exercises

Review Questions

1. For a college student, what are the advantages of developing a career notebook?
2. If you want to learn about the duties and responsibilities of a certain job, what would be a good library source?
3. What headings typically appear on a chronological résumé?
4. What are the advantages and disadvantages of including a "personal information" section?
5. Under what conditions might you choose not to include references?
6. If you had little or no experience, which résumé would probably be better: (a) chronological or (b) functional?
7. What are the advantages of using "subject understood" sentences in résumés?
8. For mailing a résumé, what size envelope is preferred?
9. Five years after graduation, which would probably appear first on a résumé: (a) "Education" or (b) "Experience"?

10. List five sources from which prospective employers' names and addresses may be obtained.

Activities

1. Turn to the questions listed under the discussions of self-, career, and job analysis. Answer the questions as though they were directed to you.

2. Prepare a résumé for a job you would like to have.

Writing Letters About Employment

*Do your work with your whole heart, and you will succeed—
there is so little competition! The best preparation for good work
tomorrow is to do good work today.*

ELBERT HUBBARD

W hen employers invite you to send a résumé, they expect you to include an application letter. When they invite you to send an application letter, they expect you to enclose a résumé. The two go together. Other employment-related letters are written to follow application letters, express gratitude for interviews, accept or refuse job offers, ask that recommendation letters be sent, recommend others for employment, and resign from the present job.

Application Letters

What is the purpose of an application letter?

The résumé summarizes information related to the job's requirements and the applicant's qualifications. The application letter (1) seeks to arouse interest in the résumé, (2) introduces it, and (3) interprets it in terms of employer benefits. One of its functions is to introduce, so the application letter is placed on top—where it will be seen first.

Is an application letter a *sales* letter?

As an instrument that seeks to arouse interest and to point out employer benefits, the application letter is persuasive. Written inductively, it is designed to convince an employer that qualifications are adequate (just as a sales letter is designed to convince a buyer that a product will satisfy a need). Like sales letters, application letters are either invited or uninvited. Job advertisements *invite* applications. Uninvited letters have greater need for attention getters; otherwise, invited and uninvited letters are based on the same principles.

Advantages and disadvantages of sending "prospecting" application letters

Uninvited application letters are sometimes referred to as "prospecting" letters. The same basic letter (perhaps with slight modifications) can be sent to many prospective employers. Sending uninvited letters (1) increases the possibility of finding employers who have employment needs, (2) competes with fewer applicants than invited letters, and (3) alerts employers to needs not previously identified. Impressed by the qualities described in an uninvited letter, an employer could create a job for the applicant. The author of an uninvited letter has demonstrated initiative, a quality most employers appreciate. However, sending uninvited letters has some disadvantages: (1) because the employer's specific needs are not known, the opening paragraph is likely to be more general than the opening paragraph in invited letters; and (2) depending on the ratio of responses to letters sent, the process could be expensive.

Because satisfaction derived from work plays a major role in life's total enjoyment, and because the decision to interview is based primarily on reaction to the application letter and résumé, these documents may be among the most important you will ever write. Even after an interview, the application and résumé could receive further scrutiny and turn out to be deciding factors in your favor.

One of the most important letters you will ever write

They represent *you*. They should be different from any other person's. Copying or paraphrasing someone else's résumé or application letter would be a serious mistake, but you can benefit from seeing letters in which others have applied or violated principles. In evaluating application letters written by others (and in thinking about your *own* letter to be written later), keep in mind the criteria by which any writing can be evaluated.

• Content

If content is satisfactory, the letter will contain the *right ideas;* that is, the *message* will be appropriate. Do you think the following letter is effective?

Are application letters expected to persuade?

> Wishing to be considered for a sales position in your children's apparel department, I submit the attached résumé.
>
> After you have studied it, I shall appreciate your calling me to set up an interview.

The letter identifies the job sought, introduces the résumé, and encourages action—but what is missing? Does it attempt to arouse the manager's interest? Does it lead the manager to expect something positive in the résumé? Does it include anything that might cause the manager to think, "I'm eager to see *this* résumé; it may lead to the solution of my employment problem"?

Length   Did you recognize the preceding letter as being too short to serve well as a sales letter? Recall that persuasive messages have to be long enough to give supporting evidence. Some personnel managers favor short letters, pointing out that only a few seconds can be spared for reading each letter. A short letter that is *read*, they argue, will do an applicant more good than a long one that is merely *skimmed*. They see brevity as a virtue that can be demonstrated in an application letter.

Employers are very busy. Is that a valid argument for keeping application letters short?

Others favor longer letters. They point out that good employees are hard to find and that longer letters provide (1) more information and (2) more opportunity to evaluate. If the first lines arouse interest, employers will thoroughly and eagerly read additional paragraphs if doing so will possibly resolve an employment problem.

By making paragraphs long enough to include interpretation of experiences on the present or previous job, you can give an employer some confidence that you are well prepared for (or at least know what to expect) on your next job. For example, the following paragraph from an applicant whose only work experience was at a fast-food restaurant is short and general:

> For three months last summer, I worked at Quickburger. Evaluations of my work were superior. While the assistant manager was on vacation, I supervised a crew of five on the evening shift.

As the only reference to the Quickburger experience, the paragraph does convey one employer's apparent satisfaction with performance. Superior evaluations and the responsibility of some supervision are evidence of that satisfaction, but added details and interpretation could make the message more convincing:

To be convincing, include details.

> In my summertime job at Quickburger, I could see the value of listening carefully when orders were placed, making change quickly and accurately, offering suggestions if customers seemed hesitant, and keeping a cheerful attitude. Supervising a crew of five while the assistant manager was on vacation, I appreciated the need for fairness and diplomacy in working with other employees.

Apparently, the applicant's experience has been meaningful. It called attention to qualities that managers like to see in employees: willingness to listen, speed, accuracy, concern for clients or customers, a positive attitude, fairness, and tact. As a *learning* experience, the Quickburger job has taught or reinforced some principles that the employer will see as vital on the job applied for.

Write about a previous job as a *learning* experience.

For graduating students entering the world of full-time work for the first time, their educational background is more impressive than their experience background (see Chapter 10). They can benefit from interpreting their education as a meaningful, job-related experience. An applicant for acceptance into an auditor's trainee program should do more than merely report having taken auditing theory and practice:

Write about school as a *learning* experience.

> In my auditing theory and practice class, I could see specific application of principles encountered in my human relations and psychology classes. Questions about leadership and motivation seemed to recur throughout the course: What really motivates executives? Why are auditors feared at many

levels? How can those fears be overcome? How can egos be salvaged? "Consider the human element" was a frequent admonition. That element was the focus of my term paper, "The Auditor as a Psychologist."

Because the preceding paragraph included questions discussed in a class, don't assume that your application letter should do likewise. Or because this paragraph gives the title of a term paper, don't assume the same technique is a must for your letter. The techniques are commendable, though, in that they help to portray the educational experience as meaningful and related to the job sought. Recognizing that auditors must be tactful (a point on which the one reading the letter will surely agree), the applicant included some details of his class. That technique is a basic in persuasion: don't just say a product or idea is good; say what makes it good. Don't just say that a certain educational or work experience was beneficial; say what made it so.

<aside>To be convincing, be specific.</aside>

Your letter is approaching a desirable length if it succeeds in arousing interest and helps the reader to see ways in which your services would be beneficial. Consensus is that one page is usually enough, especially for students and graduates entering the job market. Yet, if circumstances seem to justify a longer letter, two- or three-page letters are not taboo.

Source of Job Information   Sometimes, referring to your source of job information may be to your advantage. For example, if a person well known in a large business spoke to your class and indicated a need for employees in a certain category, revealing that person's name in the first paragraph could serve as an attention getter. Or referring to the newspaper or magazine in which a job was advertised is an easy way to identify the job sought. The reference is easy to include in a beginning sentence.

<aside>Sometimes, using the name of a person the employer knows is a good way to begin.</aside>

Knowledge of Employer's Activities   A thorough job search may have identified current trends in the industry you're entering. The company to which you are applying may have had a recent stock split, announced the upcoming opening of a new branch, or introduced a new product. Sentences that *imply* your knowledge of such matters may make a favorable impression. They imply that you really are interested in the field, read widely, do more than you are required to do, gather information before making decisions, and so on.

<aside>Be informed, but don't sound like a sleuth.</aside>

Knowledge of Job Requirements   Such statements as "The requirements of this job are. . . ." or "I understand that this job requires. . . ." are seldom necessary. Your knowledge of job requirements is usually assumed. They need not be stated directly (doing so would take up space and repeat what is known already). If a certain job, though, is known to place special emphasis on certain requirements, your awareness of that emphasis could be a point in your favor. For example, a certain accounting job requires frequent and complicated written reports. Instead of writing "I understand the job requires frequent reports" (which is already known), you could refer to writing experiences you have had or your preference for work that requires writing (if that's true). Your understanding is revealed without direct statement.

Why not state job requirements directly?

Some ads for employment force respondents to include certain information: "Must provide own transportation and be willing to travel. Give educational background, work experience, and salary expected." In the responding letter, these points must be discussed. Preferably, the question of salary is left until the interview; but if an ad should request a statement about it, the letter should include that statement. Whether to give a minimum figure, indicate willingness to accept a figure that is customary for work of that type, or indicate preference for discussing salary at the interview is a personal decision.

Should a prospecting application letter mention salary?

Unless an ad requests a statement on salary, an application letter should not mention it. Like the price of a product in a sales letter, salary in an application letter is a negative. To discuss it is to discuss money with which the employer parts. Instead, the emphasis should be on what you can contribute. Until after the interview, neither the employer nor the applicant knows whether the two are compatible. If they aren't, a discussion of salary would be pointless. Like salary, the following ideas (sometimes found in application letters) should be omitted.

Discussing Your Own Problems   Your need for more income, to be closer to your work, for more pleasant surroundings, or for greater advancement opportunities are of little interest to the firm. The excitement you experienced upon learning about a job opportunity isn't worth mentioning. The possible implication is that, for you, jobs are really hard to find, perhaps because of your shortcomings. With empathy, concentrate on reporting that which will meet the employer's needs.

Use empathy. Think in terms of the employer's interests.

Making Statements of the Obvious   "This is an application," "I read your ad," and "I am writing to apply for" are sufficiently understood without making direct statements. With the letter *and* résumé in hand, a reader learns nothing from "A résumé is enclosed." Already aware of job requirements and requisites for success in a certain job, managers need not be told again. Such sentences as "An auditor should be able to. . . ." and "Sales personnel should avoid. . . ." seem to lecture. Although they may reveal familiarity with matters important to the job, they may be resented.

Discussing Current Employer's Shortcomings   Regardless of how negatively you perceive your present employer, that perception has little to do with your prospective employer's needs. Also, if you knock your present employer, you could be perceived as someone who would do the same for the next employer.

Making Self-Deprecating Statements   Your need and right to concentrate on reporting your strengths are well recognized. Surely, you would not apply for a job you thought you could not do. Just tell the aspects of your background that have prepared you for that job. Reporting failure or lack of aptitude at some other endeavor only weakens your case. Mentioning it could raise questions about your self-esteem. Instead of apologizing for some shortcoming, look for positive aspects of your education or experience. Reporting them may be to your advantage.

Making Boastful Connotations   Self-confidence is commendable, but overconfidence (or worse still, just plain bragging) is objectionable. Like unsupported or unsupportable superlatives in sales letters, some self-judgmental terms can do more harm than good. Instead of labeling your performance as "superior" or "excellent," give supporting facts. A manager may think of them as evidence of superiority or excellence and react favorably.

> Sound confident without sounding overconfident.

Using Flattery   If a firm is well known for its rapid expansion, currently successful advertising campaign, competitive advantage, superior product, etc., conveying your awareness of these positive achievements is to your advantage. On the other hand, deliberate attempts at flattery will almost surely be detected. They are more likely to be resented than appreciated. For example, referring to the employer as "*the* leader in the field," "the best in the business," or "a company with an outstanding record" is risky. If such labels are inaccurate, they will be so recognized. If they are accurate, their use is still risky. They could be taken as an attempt to get a favorable decision as a reward for making a complimentary statement.

> Subtle, deserved compliments may help. Flattery won't.

Why avoid the
narrative approach?

Giving a Biographical Discourse In certain situations, chronology is the best order in which to arrange items. Listing jobs in the order in which they were held is one legitimate sequence, but an application letter should not sound like a history of a job seeker's life. The narrative approach is likely to emphasize the individual too much and the employer's needs too little. For organizing an application letter, chronology is seldom the best sequence.

• Organization

As a persuasive letter, an application letter employs the same sequence of parts as a sales letter:

Sales Letter	Application Letter
Gets attention	Gets attention
Introduces product	Introduces qualifications
Presents evidence	Presents evidence
Encourages action	Encourages action

Like a well-written sales letter, a well-written application letter employs a central selling feature—a theme. It is introduced in the first or second paragraph and stressed in paragraphs that follow. Two to four paragraphs are normally sufficient for supporting evidence. Consider order of importance as a basis for their sequence, with the most significant aspects of your preparation coming first.

Should the first
paragraph introduce
the résumé?

A persuasive letter is designed to get action, which in this case is to get the reader to (1) read the attached résumé and (2) invite you to an interview. Preferably, reference to the résumé comes near the end of the letter. If you refer to it in the first or second paragraph, readers may wonder whether they are expected to put the letter aside at that point and look at the résumé. Because your purpose in writing is to get an interview, the final paragraph is the logical place for making reference to it. Now that your message is complete, the next move is the reader's. The organizational decision about where to *place* reference to the interview is easy; the stylistic decision about how to *express* it is more challenging.

• Style

Should the action be
forcefully worded?

Stylistic principles that apply in other writing (especially in sales writing) also apply in application-letter writing. Some stylistic matters, though, deserve special attention:

Using Language Used on the Job   If the letter employs terminology commonly used by accountants, an applicant for an accounting job implies familiarity with the job and the language used. An applicant for a computer job would benefit from use of acronyms and other terms well known in the computer field but not altogether meaningful to others. Such language would communicate clearly, save space, and imply a computer background. The same principle applies to writing about other occupations.

Are acronyms acceptable?

Avoiding Overused Words and Expressions   Some words that are useful in talking *about* letters of application are often used too frequently *in* them:

Try to avoid using words and sentences that have been overused by other applicants.

Applicant	If the letter shows how you are suited for the job sought, you need not label yourself as an "applicant." Obviously, you are.
Application	As a page that introduces a résumé and discusses your preparation for a job, your letter is obviously an application.
I	Because the letter is designed to sell *your* services, some use of "I" is natural and expected; try to restrict the number of times "I" is used. Empathy for the employer will help. "I" is especially noticeable if it is the first word of consecutive paragraphs.
Interview	This word is very commonly used in the final paragraph. It connotes a formal question-and-answer session. The *idea* of a face-to-face meeting can be introduced without using "interview." "Talk with you," "discuss the work," and "come to your office" are possibilities.
Opening	Meaning "an unfilled position," the term is readily understood; but it seems abstract, is overused, and usually unneeded.
Position	A "position" may be thought of as a title that someone *holds;* it does not necessarily apply to *work.* Compared with "job" or "work," it may sound more formal than you want your letter to sound.

| Qualifications | Employers will recognize training, education, and experience as "qualifications" without such a label. Either leave the word to implication or use such words as "background," "preparation," or "record." |
| Vacancy | Like "opening," the word seems abstract, overused, and usually unnecessary. |

Using some of the preceding words would not be an *error,* but they could take up space and make your letter sound too much like competitors' letters. The following examples illustrate overused sentences and phrases:

Consider me an applicant for the position.	The letter and résumé sufficiently imply desire for consideration.
I would like to apply for....	"Would *like* to" connotes desire to apply if conditions were different. Application is evident without use of "apply."
...to become associated with....	The phrase seems vague, formal, and even condescending. The goal is to get a job, not to associate with an employer.
...your organization [your firm, your company].	Avoid these terms or use the *name* of the unit instead.
...interview at your earliest convenience.	Avoid, or find other words to express the idea.

Because an invitation to interview is the object of the letter, the reader needs to be motivated to extend the invitation. Encouraging action is a delicate matter.

Tactfully Encouraging Action The desired action is for the reader to (1) *write a letter* or (2) *place a phone call* inviting you to come for a face-to-face discussion. The choice (write or call) is best left to the employer. Asking for a written response when the employer prefers to call (or vice versa) could result in no response. The goal is to introduce the idea of action without seeming to apologize for doing so and without seeming to be demanding or "pushy." Find *your* words for achieving it, and try to avoid some frequently made errors:

An applicant with strong qualifications need not press forcefully for action.

1. *Setting a date.* "May I have an appointment with you on March 14." Grateful to have any appointment at all, you are better off to

let the employer set the date. The date you name could be inconvenient; or even if it is convenient for the employer, your forwardness in setting it could be resented.

2. *Giving permission to call.* "You may call me at 987-6543." By making the call sound like a privilege (*may* call) you could alienate the reader. Implied meaning: you are very selective about the calls you take, but the employer does qualify.

3. *Reporting capability of response.* "You can call me at 987-6543." When a number or address is given, employers are well aware that they are capable of using it ("can" call).

4. *Expressing doubt.* "*If* you agree," "I *hope* you will," and "*should* you decide" employ subjunctive words in which your awareness of possible negative results is implied. By showing lack of confidence, you may reduce reader confidence.

5. *Suggesting a one-way conversation.* ". . . when I can talk to you about the job." Use of "*with* you" (instead of "*to* you") would imply a two-way conversation.

6. *Sounding overconfident.* "I know you will want to set up an appointment." If the writer doesn't know, the statement is inaccurate; if the writer does know, it seems unnecessary and egotistical.

7. *Sounding apologetic.* "May I take some of your time" or "I know how busy you are" may seem considerate, but the hoped-for interview should be thought of as advantageous to both people involved. Apology is totally out of place in a letter that discusses way in which the employer *benefits* from hiring you.

If the final paragraph (action ending) of your letter is preceded by paragraphs that are impressive, you need not press hard for a response. Just mentioning the idea of a future discussion is probably sufficient. Compared with the action endings of sales letters, the endings of application letters have less need for forceful statements that define specific action. Surely, an employer who has just finished reading an impressive application would know what to do about it. Forceful statements about *when* and *how* to respond are unnecessary and could arouse resentment.

As closing sentences that refer to an invitation to interview, the following sentences are free of the weaknesses pointed out in preceding illustrations. They are not intended as model sentences that should appear in *your* letter. When the time comes to write your own closing sentence, write it, analyze it carefully, and rewrite it if necessary. Because finding the right job is so important to you, you will be well rewarded for the time and thought invested.

About Language and Usage

Coupled with roots of words, prefixes and suffixes are among the important builders of words and word power. When placed either before or after roots, prefixes and suffixes create words of different meaning. Here are some common prefixes:

Prefix	Meaning	Example
anti	against	antisocial
ante	before	antecedent
hyper	excessively	hyperactive
il	not	illiterate
im	not	impossible
in	not	indecent
ir	not	irrelevant
un	not	unnecessary
post	after	postgraduate

How did we develop so many prefixes meaning "not"?

When a date and time can be arranged, I would like to talk with you.

Passively constructed, "can be arranged" does not indicate *who* will do the arranging. If the work of extending the invitation is performed by an assistant, the employer's part is fast and easy—just tell the assistant to schedule an interview and inform the applicant. If the employer's needs have been satisfied already, or if the letter and résumé are not impressive, the date and time for an interview are irrelevant; no action is requested or expected. In the independent clause—"I would like to talk with you"—the

I would appreciate an opportunity to discuss the loan officer's job with you.

meeting place and the subject of the conversation are understood.

Reference to action is not direct. If the opportunity arises, it will be as a result of the reader's action. Assuming preceding sentences have not overused "I," use of first person is appropriate. Appreciation is more emphatic when expressed in first person.

With two days' notice, I could meet with you at any hour of your working day.

The indirect reference to action is not forceful; but assuming impressive qualifications, the reader will want an interview and will not need to be pushed. How the notice is given is the reader's choice. Intended to show consideration for the employer's time schedule, "at any hour" could imply an overabundance of free time or even lack of concern for getting the present employer's work done. Yet, the résumé will show whether the applicant now has a job. The "two days' notice" could indicate a flexible working schedule. Or the applicant may need time to arrange for a replacement while the interview is being conducted.

To discuss your employment needs and my production-scheduling experience, I would appreciate an appointment.

When and if the appointment occurs is up to the employer. For an applicant who has had significant experience related to the job and has made that experience a central selling feature, incorporating it into the action ending adds unity and stresses the applicant's strongest qualification. To increase emphasis on the word "experience," the independent clause could be moved to the beginning of the sentence. As the last word in the final paragraph, "experience" would stand out vividly.

Analysis of the preceding sentences illustrates, to some extent, how much thought is involved in preparing a satisfactory letter. Too often, it is written in haste. Too little time is allowed for reconsideration; for getting others' suggestions; and for making corrections in content, organization, style, and mechanics.

• Mechanics

Before the letter is read, its appearance has already communicated something about the applicant.

Compared with superior qualifications, physical arrangement on a page may seem insignificant. Yet, before the letter is read, it communicates something about you. If it conveys a negative impression, it may not be read at all. The size, color, and quality of paper have their influence; so do margins, letter format, keyboarding, and paragraphing.

Unless you have a special reason for doing otherwise, use standard $8\frac{1}{2} \times 11$ white paper. If a 500-sheet ream weighs less than 4 pounds, the paper is too flimsy. Paper with some rag content (preferably as much as 25 percent) is recommended.

Use margins of at least an inch. Since your letter is personal, your present employer's stationery cannot be used. If you have your own letterhead (or if your computer puts your letterhead on the sheet for you) use it; otherwise, type your return address in the position illustrated in the personal business letter shown in the Appendix.

Strive for mechanical perfection.

The same principles of paragraphing and keyboarding that apply in other letters also apply in application letters. Errors in grammar, spelling, and punctuation are especially damaging. They could imply that you pay little attention to detail, get behind schedule and do your work hastily, have shortcomings in basic education, lack pride, or lack respect. Because the letter represents you and will be thought of as the best you can do, allow yourself time to do it well. Get opinions of others and make revisions where necessary.

Acronyms (such as OSHA and NASA) and abbreviations (such as FDIC and CPA) are sometimes very appropriate; they save space and are well known by business people. An application addressed to a specialist in finance may profitably use CFA (for certified financial analyst), or one addressed to an insurance executive could use CLU (for certified life underwriter). Use such space savers only when you are confident they will be understood.

Like other letters in which an enclosure is mentioned in the body of the letter, an application letter includes "Enclosure" a double space beneath the typewritten name.

• Exemplars

The first part of this chapter has given you an opportunity to think *separately* about content, organization, style, and mechanics. Analyzing some *entire letters* will enable you to synthesize, to understand why some practices should be avoided, and to see how principles can be applied. An analysis of a substandard example precedes an analysis of an improved example. Proceed in this manner: (a) read sentence number 1; (b) identify principles *you* think it applies or violates; (c) read the statement about sentence number 1 (which appears at the right); and (d) proceed in the same manner with other sentences. The thinking involved in such letter analyses will pay dividends when you later compose your own letter of application.

The following letter is designed to accompany the résumé in Figure 10.1:

1 Please consider me an applicant for the part-time position in retail clothing sales, as advertised in this morning's paper.

2 I am currently a sophomore at West State University.

3 Because I am planning a career in fashion

1 Employs a cliché. Commendably identifies the job sought. Should give the name of the paper.

2 Emphasizes "I" by using it as the first word in a paragraph. Directly states the same information that appears on the résumé.

3 Employs "I" for the second and third time.

merchandising, I have declared marketing as my major. **4** Although I have not previously worked in retail clothing sales, I have sales experience: nine months in fast-food sales at Quickberger. **5** It gave me experience in getting along with fellow workers, in dealing with the public, and handling money.

6 With this background of experience and my marketing major, I feel qualified for the sales position you advertised. **7** A résumé is enclosed.

8 May I have an interview at your earliest convience.

Sentence is writer centered.
4 Continues to use "I" in a self-oriented sentence. Confesses lack of direct experience (dependent clause should be omitted).
5 Commendably attempts to interpret experiences as beneficial and related to the job sought.

6 Passes judgment on her own qualifications. Judgment is best left to the employer.

7 Repeats the obvious, but does call attention to the résumé.

8 Uses a cliché in the action ending. Misspells "convenience."

In the following revision, note that "I" is not entirely eliminated; but it is used less frequently. It does not directly restate information that appears on the résumé; rather it attempts to point out ways in which educational and work experiences are directly related to the job sought.

1 My college and work experiences have been preparing me for the clothing-sales job advertised in last night's Gazette.

2 With plans for a career in fashion merchandising, I included business courses in my first year's classes.

1 Identifies the job sought and the source of information. Introduces a discussion of the applicant's background.

2 Includes *career* idea early—to set the applicant apart from others whose interests may be less serious. Leads to a presentation of ways in which courses taken have served as preparation for a job in selling clothing.

3 They have stressed principles directly related to success in selling: empathy in working with customers, accuracy and speed in keeping records, and determination in reaching goals.

4 Junior and senior classes will explore such topics as advertising, display, clothing design, fabrics, sartorial arts, and public relations.

5 Selling at a fast-food restaurant taught me the value of cooperating with other workers, listening carefully to customers, working fast without seeming to rush, and being cheerful even in rush hours.

6 In hospital volunteer work, helping patients was a real pleasure. **7** A similar satisfaction would come from helping shoppers select clothing.

8 After you have seen the attached résumé, I would welcome an opportunity to talk with you about a career in selling.

3 Points to ways in which courses listed on the résumé (such as accounting and interpersonal communication) have contributed to job preparation. Reveals an awareness of qualities essential for success.

4 Mentions future courses—to emphasize definite plans for a career in the field. Employs words commonly used in retail selling. A part-time employee who would be concurrently taking such courses would have more appeal to an employer than an applicant who did not have such plans.

5 Points out experiences on the previous job that would be encountered on the sales job.

6 and **7** Seek to connect volunteer work with sales work. The employer may associate the *satisfaction* derived from work with *success* and *enthusiasm* for it.

8 Introduces the résumé. Uses an action ending, without sounding pushy or apologetic. No preference is expressed about whether a call or a letter is preferred in responding.

To illustrate arrangement on a keyboarded page, the preceding letter is shown in Figure 11.1.

From reading the letter of application and the accompanying résumé, the employer should be able to see the commonality of the applicant's experiences and the job's requirements. That commonality needs to be emphasized in either the application letter or the résumé. In this case the letter of application (Figure 11.1) attempts to interpret experiences because its accompanying résumé (Figure 10.1) does not.

Look back at Figure 10.2, a functional résumé. It does point out the commonality of experiences and job requirements. The application letter, therefore, need not do so. The letter (Figure 11.2) identifies the job applied for, gives just enough highlights to generate interest in the résumé, refers the reader to it, and makes an allusion to action.

Comparing Figure 11.1 with 11.2, note the differences in punctuation and format (for the reasons given in Chapter 10). Figure 11.1 is more traditional: conventional return address, commas and periods in the return and inside addresses, "Dear" in the salutation, mixed punctuation (colon after salutation and comma after complimentary close), and an irregular right margin. Figure 11.2 is less traditional: a personal letterhead that has been stored in a personal computer, no commas or periods in the letterhead and inside address, no "Dear" in the salutation, open punctuation (no punctuation marks after the salutation and complimentary close), and a right margin that is straight. The techniques used in either Figure 11.1 or 11.2 are acceptable. In choosing, (1) be consistent, (2) consider the image you want to project, and (3) use the technique you think would be most acceptable to your reader.

In the résumés and letters illustrated, applicants have high grade indexes. They suggest willingness to work hard, ability to learn quickly, and (possibly) skill in human relations. Compared with other professions, the accounting profession is reportedly most influenced by a high grade index. Its reasoning is that knowledge of accounting principles and techniques is vital, and graduates who have the highest grades will know the most. Because students with 4.0 indexes are sometimes stereotyped as "bookworms" or socially insensitive, such students should present personal information that depicts them as being well rounded. The résumé or the application letter could—by reporting special interests, activities, and accomplishments—counter the stereotype.

Most students who have a grade average between a 2 and a 3 (on a 4.0 scale) choose not to report the grade average. Readers (most of whom are likely to be graduates themselves) are well aware that degrees are awarded only to students who have at least a 2 average. Applicants

Sunstate Apartments, #113
317 West Fourth Street
Winiford, CA 91002
October 10, 1990

Mr. Robert Johnson, Director
Sales Personnel
Watson's Department Stores, Inc.
Greenwood Mall
Winiford, CA 91003

Dear Mr. Johnson:

SUBJECT: JOB IN RETAIL CLOTHING SALES

My college and work experiences have been preparing me for the
clothing-sales job advertised in last night's Gazette.

With plans for a career in fashion merchandising, I included business
courses in my first year's classes. They have stressed principles
directly related to success in selling: empathy in working with
customers, accuracy in keeping records, and determination in
reaching goals.

Junior and senior classes will explore such topics as advertising,
display, clothing design, fabrics, sartorial arts, and public relations.

Selling at a fast-food restaurant taught me the value of cooperating
with other workers, listening carefully to customers, working fast
without seeming to rush, and being cheerful even in rush hours.

In hospital volunteer work, helping patients was a real pleasure. A
similar satisfaction would come from helping shoppers select
clothing.

After you have seen the attached résumé, I would welcome an
opportunity to talk with you about a career in selling.

Sincerely,

Laura Lindholm

Enclosure

FIGURE 11.1
Application letter to accompany a chronological résumé.

LAURA LINDHOLM
Sunstate Apartments #113
317 W Fourth Street
Winiford CA 91002

October 10, 1990

Mr Robert Johnson Director
Sales Personnel
Watson's Department Stores Inc
Greenwood Mall
Winiford CA 91003

Mr Johnson

SUBJECT: EMPLOYMENT APPLICATION, CLOTHING SALES

"Part-time sales, retail clothing. Submit résumé." That ad in last night's Gazette prompted me to review my background in sales.

My major in college is fashion merchandising. Some courses have been directly related to sales. More are planned.

Restaurant and volunteer work have provided sales and sales-related experiences. They helped me to select sales as my life's work.

The grade average shown on the attached résumé gives some indication of the energy devoted to my school work. The references will be glad to comment on my efficiency and my human-relations skills.

When an appointment can be arranged, I would like to talk with you.

Sincerely

Laura Lindholm

Enclosure

FIGURE 11.2
Application letter to accompany a functional résumé.

who choose not to report grade average can, instead, emphasize note-worthy school activities, offices held, volunteer work, or part-time work.

Either on the résumé or in the application letter, students who have earned all (or a portion of) their school expenses are well advised to report it. Employers tend to react favorably (evidence of hard work, thrift, organization, determination, etc.).

Follow-Up Letters

When an application and résumé do not elicit a response, a follow-up letter may bring results. Sent a few weeks or months after the original letter, it includes a reminder that an application for a certain job is on file, presents additional education or experience accumulated, points out its relationship to the job, and closes with a reference to desired action:

Could a follow-up letter imply perseverance?

> Having applied for a sales-analyst job at the ABC Company in April, I now have additional education and experience to report.
>
> The attached up-dated résumé now includes a course in advanced statistical analysis taken this summer and the part-time experience in the Marketing Department's research division.
>
> The course and the job have expanded my knowledge, increased my speed and skill in using the computer, and confirmed my interest in work as a sales analyst.
>
> When ABC needs to add another sales analyst, I would appreciate your calling or writing to me.

In addition to conveying new information, follow-up letters can imply persistence (a quality that impresses some employers).

Thank-You Letters

After the job interview, a letter of appreciation is a professional cour-tesy. Even if during the interview you decided you did not want the job or you and the interviewer mutually agreed that the job is not for you, a thank-you letter is appropriate. It expresses gratitude, refers to some

Even though "thank you" was *said* at the close of the interview, *write* a "thank-you" letter?

point that was discussed in the interview, and closes pleasantly. It may mention the possibility of applying again after qualifications have been improved:

> Thank you for taking time with me to discuss the possibility of my working for Riley-Smith.
>
> Partly as a result of your suggestions, I plan to continue my present job and take night courses in hotel administration. Afterward, I would welcome another opportunity to talk with you about a career in hotel management.

Why refer to a point discussed in the interview?

After an interview has gone well and you think a job offer is a possibility, include these ideas in the letter of appreciation: express gratitude, identify the specific job applied for, refer to some point or points discussed in the interview, and close by making some reference to the expected call or letter that conveys the employer's decision:

> Thank you for taking time to talk with me on Tuesday.
>
> Your description of your management-trainee program really made me appreciate the case-method approach used in my advanced management classes. You made me very glad I had taken courses in human relations and communications.
>
> The program is very appealing, and I am eager to receive the call from your office next week.

A tardy thank-you letter has less impact.

If the thank-you letter confirms that your enthusiasm for a job increased during the interview, the impact on the decision could be favorable. For maximum impact, send a thank-you letter as quickly as possible after an interview—the day of the interview or the following day.

Job-Acceptance Letters

A job offer may be extended either by phone or by letter. Even though a job has been accepted by phone, the firm may also want a written acceptance. Note the deductive sequence: acceptance, details, and closing that confirms the report-for-work date:

> I accept your employment offer as a market analyst.
>
> Thank you for responding so quickly after our discussion on Thursday.
>
> As requested, the forms (enclosed) have been filled out in detail. If you should need to communicate with me before I report for work on the 14th, please leave a message at 987-6543.

When a job search results in more than one offer, only one can be accepted. Others may be refused by phone or by letter.

Job-Refusal Letters

Like other messages that convey bad news, job-refusal letters are written inductively: a beginning that reveals the nature of the subject, explanations that lead to a refusal, the refusal, and a pleasant ending. Of course, certain reasons (even though valid in your mind) are better left unsaid: you question the firm's goals or methods of operation, negative attitude of present employees, possible bankruptcy, unsatisfactory working conditions, etc. In the following letter, the applicant prefers not to be specific about the reason for turning a job down:

Should job-refusal letters be organized like bad-news letters?

> I appreciated your spending time with me discussing the loan officer's job.
>
> After thoughtfully considering job offers received this week, I have decided to accept a job in the actuarial department of an insurance company.
>
> Thank you for sharing your thoughts about careers in the world of finance.

When your attitude toward the offering firm is positive, or when you recognize the possibility that at some later time you may want to reapply, you may want to be more specific about your reasons for refusal:

> Meeting with you to discuss the loan officer's job was one of my most memorable job-seeking experiences.

> Thank you for your candid comparison of my background and opportunities in finance and insurance. Having received job offers in both fields, I am now convinced that a career in insurance is more consistent with my aptitudes and goals. Today I am accepting a job in the actuarial department of States Mutual.
>
> Thank you for the confidence demonstrated by the job offer. When I read reports of Earnabank's continued success, I will think of the dedicated people who work for it.

Letters of acceptance and refusal employ the personal business format illustrated in the Appendix. Letters of resignation, though, require a different format.

Resignation Letters

By the time you have reached the point of resignation, you will know whether your employer expects it to be in writing. Use the memorandum format illustrated in the Appendix. Plan to give enough advance notice to allow the employer time for finding a replacement.

Why emphasize positive ideas?

Just as a summary paragraph brings your themes to an end, so does a resignation letter bring your job to an end. Even if your job has made you unhappy, or if some unpleasant circumstance is causing you to leave, you still can find something positive to say. A resignation letter is hardly an appropriate instrument for telling executives how a business should be operated. Harshly worded statements could result in immediate termination or cause human-relations problems during the remaining working days. Remember, too, that your boss may subsequently review the resignation letter just before writing a recommendation letter for you.

Thinking positively, treat a resignation letter as a bad-news letter. Because your employer has had confidence in you, has benefited from your services, and will have to seek a replacement, your impending departure *is* bad news. As such, the letter is written inductively. It calls attention to your job, gives reasons for leaving it, conveys the resignation, and closes on a positive note:

> My job as manager of Women's Apparel for the last two years has been a rewarding experience. It has taught me much

about the marketing of clothing and changing preferences in style.

For me, predicting public acceptance of certain styles has been fascinating. From the time when I declared a major in fashion merchandising, I have wanted to become a buyer. Before accepting my present job in management, that goal was discussed. Now, it is becoming a reality: I have accepted a job as buyer for Belton's.

It begins one month from today; if satisfactory with you, I would like May 31 to be my last day as manager here.

This job has allowed me to grow professionally. Thanks to you and others, I've had the privilege of trying new ideas and selecting sales personnel who get along well with one another and with customers. Thank you for having confidence in me, for your positive rapport with the sales staff, and for your expressions of appreciation for my work.

Looking forward to my job as a buyer for Belton's, I shall always recall pleasant memories of my job at Roscoe's.

Of course, the preceding letter is not likely to come as a complete surprise to its reader. The new employer has probably already asked the old employer for a letter of recommendation.

Recommendation Letters

Usually, letters of recommendation are written in response to a request. The request may come from the applicant or from the prospective employer.

• Applicant's Request for Recommendation

When prospective employers tell applicants to have recommendation letters sent, the normal procedure is to place a call to each reference. As the applicant, you would identify the job for which you are applying, give a complete address to which the letter is to be sent, and indicate a date by which the employer needs the letter.

In the conversation, you may need to remind the reference of a previously expressed willingness to supply employment information about you. By sharing some information about job requirements and reporting recent job-related experiences that are relevant, you may assist

Don't apologize for asking someone to spend time writing about you.

the reference in writing an effective letter. Indicate your gratitude, but don't apologize for making the request. (The reference has already agreed to write such a letter and will likely take pleasure in assisting a deserving person.)

Similar information is included when the request for a recommendation is made by letter:

> As one step in my application for a loan officer's job, Earnabank has asked me for letters of recommendation.
>
> Since receiving permission to use your name as a reference, I have completed the B.S. degree with a major in finance and real estate. If a job offer is made, I would enter Earnabank's loan-officer trainee program and later specialize in real-estate loans.
>
> The attached résumé will give you a quick summary of my academic and work-experience preparation for a job in a loan department.
>
> The recommendation is needed by October 4. The address:
>
>> Mr. Lyle Richardson
>> Personnel Division
>> Earnabank and Trust Company
>> 3740 N. Central Avenue
>> Edgewood, OR 99041-3447
>
> I certainly appreciate your willingness to spend time in my behalf.

Sometimes, people who have applied for jobs can greatly assist their references by alerting them to imminent requests for information (especially if considerable time has elapsed since the applicant and reference have last seen each other):

References like to know that a request is forthcoming.

> Almost two years have passed since I received permission to use your name as a reference, but you may be receiving a request for recommendation soon.
>
> Weston Chemical Company is considering my application for a job as sales representative. A copy of the attached résumé has been submitted to Weston.
>
> When you were my supervisor at Spensor's, my name was Linda Eldridge. It's now Linda Edwards.
>
> The experience at Spensor's was an ideal start in a selling career. Thanks for all the encouragement you gave me.

By alerting the recipient to the possibility of a request and by enclosing a recent résumé, the applicant may enable the reference to write a letter that is specific and convincing.

• Employer's Request for Recommendation

When businesses request information about prospective employees, use of forms is fairly standard. The forms normally allow space for responding to specific questions, and they either provide space for respondents to express themselves or invite them to attach a letter. When the request is by letter (instead of a form), the letter needs to identify the specific type of information wanted. Numbering and tabulating assist the writer in emphasizing, and they assist the reader in responding:

> Mr. Walter Wilson has given your name as someone who could provide information about his background for a job as head of security at the Tripod Hotel.
>
> We would appreciate your candid and confidential comments on his
>
> 1. dependability,
> 2. tact (with the public and with security personnel),
> 3. knowledge of law-enforcement practices,
>
> and any other information you think would assist us in predicting his performance in security work.
>
> We would appreciate your comments by April 24.

What is gained by tabulation?

The word "confidential" implies that the response will be seen only by the person or persons who have responsibility for the hiring decision. Yet, after taking the job, the employee may have a legal right to inspect the personnel folder. Recognizing the possibility of hurt feelings, ruined friendships, and legal action, respondents are inclined to omit negatives or present them with extreme care.

Protect yourself against possible suits.

• Negative Recommendations

Almost everyone who asks permission to use your name as a reference will expect your recommendation to be favorable. For a person whom you couldn't favorably recommend, you have the option of (1) saying "No" when asked for permission to use your name, (2) letting the request go unanswered, (3) responding with an objective appraisal, or (4) responding by letter and inviting a phone call.

Refusing permission may be difficult; but, for you, it is easier than writing a negative letter. For the applicant, your refusing to serve as a reference may be preferable to your accepting and subsequently sending a negative letter.

Failure to answer a request for information is in effect a negative response, even though the employer does not know whether you received the request. Nonresponse is legal and it requires no effort; but (recognizing your responsibility to the applicant, the employer, and yourself) this option would probably be totally unacceptable to you.

Responding with an objective appraisal will give you the satisfaction of having exercised a responsibility to both applicant and employer. Because of your letter, an employer may escape some difficulty encountered after hiring an ill-qualified person. Your letter could spare an applicant the agony of going to work on a job that leads to failure. Keep these cautions in mind:

1. Include some positives, even though your overall recommendation is negative. By including both positives *and* negatives, you show your objectivity.

2. Report facts, not judgments. For example, the number of workdays missed without prior communication with the boss is a verifiable fact. To label it as "a terrible record" or "irresponsible" is to pass judgment (which is best left to the reader). Avoid such defaming and judgmental words as these: corrupt, crook, dishonest, hypocrite, incompetent, and swindler.

3. Use an inductive sequence and stylistic techniques of de-emphasis (unless your feelings are strong and you think emphasis of the negative is justified). Normally, the inductive sequence with de-emphasis techniques will seem considerate.

4. Label your letter as confidential and indicate that it is written in response to a request. These precautions are legal safeguards; they indicate that intent was not to defame but to give an honest answer to a legitimate request for information.

Note application of the preceding points in the following letter:

As requested in your letter dated June 1, WEBCO provides confidential employment information about James Wilson.

He worked from October 1 to December 13 as a meat cutter in one of our retail stores. As a cutter, he had above-average

> skills. At the sales counter, he seemed to have good rapport with customers.
>
> On three occasions (each on a Monday morning), he did not report to work as scheduled; and he had not given the department any notice of his absence. He left the department at WEBCO's request.
>
> While he was on the job, his work was satisfactory.

Responding by letter and inviting a phone call enables a reference to avoid putting negative ideas in writing. The letter is short, positive, and easy to write:

> Subject: John Smith's employment record
>
> John Smith worked as a systems analyst for WEBCO from August 15, 1989, to October 30, 1989.
>
> The confidential information you requested will be provided by telephone: (601) 876-5432.

Recognizing the possibility of negatives the reference didn't want to state in written form, the recipient might not call. In response to such a call, abide by the same precautions that apply to writing letters of recommendation.

• Positive Recommendations

Fortunately, most people who invite you to write a recommendation are confident you will report positive information. Designed to help a deserving applicant, your message should be believable. Believability may be questioned, though, if the letter includes unsupported superlatives and adjectives or adverbs that are overly strong.

How could strong adjectives be detrimental?

Before requesting a recommendation, the employer has almost certainly seen the applicant's résumé, application letter, and (possibly) application forms. Although the effect of your letter may be to *confirm* some of the information already submitted, do not devote all your space to *repeating* it. Instead, concentrate on presenting information the employer probably doesn't have. Of special interest will be your statements about proficiency and capacity to interact with others.

Regardless of whether a recommendation is for promotion within the firm or for work in another firm, the same principles apply. For promotion within a firm, use the memorandum format, as shown in Figure 11.3. A recommendation letter is shown in Figure 11.4.

MEMORANDUM

To   Tom Gray, Chair, Promotion Committee

From   Harold Mead, Chief Loan Officer

Date   May 1, 1990

Subject   Frank Johnson's Promotion to Senior Loan Officer

Frank Johnson would be an ideal Senior Loan Officer. For the following reasons, I recommend his promotion:

Note the impact of a short sentence following each number.

(1) He is efficient. Beginning with a $14 million loan portfolio, he now manages $25 million. In three years, the number of clients has grown from 16 to 26. Clients are astonished at the speed with which his paperwork is completed.

(2) He stays informed. Daily, he spends time on the financial monitor and reads financial journals. Because his information was current, he has frequently made loans that would otherwise have gone to our competitors.

(3) He works well with the staff. Colleagues and office personnel can communicate easily with him. His friendly, positive disposition contributes to our pleasant office atmosphere.

(4) He helps maintain Westgate's public image. Active in Kiwanis and in fund raising for the needy, he has frequent contacts with clients, possible clients, and competitors in social situations. To me, he is an ideal person for reflecting the bank's image.

A promotion would reward him for the part he has played in expanding our loans and help us to keep him on our team.

FIGURE 11.3

Recommendation memorandum.

TULSA DENTAL GROUP, INC.

7335 S. LEWIS • SUITE 206
TULSA, OK 74136-5450
(918) 496-1051

February 10, 1990

Frederick Woodburn DMD
Woodburn Dental Clinic
913 E Carlson Street
Holbrook CA 90311

Dr Woodburn

I heartily recommend Cynthia Moore as a dental hygienist.

She started working for us three years ago, soon after receiving her B.S. degree and her R.D.H. certificate. By the following standards, she has been an outstanding member of our periodontal team:

1. Proficiency. Her scaling and root planing are always thorough. She manages to maintain a tight schedule while sharing with patients some techniques of self-care in preventing periodontal diseases.

2. Versatility. Holding certificates in nitrous oxide, local anesthesia, and analgesia, she frequently assists in procedures many hygienists are not certified to perform.

3. Congeniality. Her patient empathy is natural. Cheerful and friendly with patients and staff members, she has had a very positive influence on our office atmosphere.

4. Professionalism. As a Registered Dental Hygienist, she is active in local, state, and national organizations. Last year she was responsible for editing the Oklahoma Dental Hygienists' Quarterly Bulletin.

If Cynthia should ever come back to live in the Tulsa area, I would welcome an opportunity to reemploy her.

Sincerely

Karl Williams DDS

blb

FIGURE 11.4
Recommendation letter.

Application Forms and Form Letters

Before going to work on a new job, you will almost certainly fill out the employer's application and employment forms. Some words of caution:

1. *Follow instructions.* If the form calls for last name first and you write your first name first, the damage could be fatal. If instructions clearly say "Print" and you write cursively instead, you could be stereotyped immediately as a bungler. When the form has multiple copies (NCR sheets or sheets with carbon paper between), place the form on a hard surface and put enough pressure on the pen to make the last copy clear. If instructions are "Do not fold," honor them.

2. *Fill in forms neatly.* If erasing is necessary, do it cleanly. Marking through an original answer and squeezing another, printing in all-capital letters in some blanks and in capital-and-lowercase letters in others—such techniques may imply indecisiveness, carelessness, lack of respect, or haste. Unless instructions or circumstances forbid, consider using a typewriter instead of a pen.

3. *Respond to* all *questions.* For any questions that do not apply, write "NA" in the blank. If the form provides space for you to add additional information or make a comment, try to include something worthwhile. Competitors, especially those who habitually do no more than is required of them, will probably leave such space blank.

4. *Answer questions accurately.* If you have developed an employment notebook (as described in Chapter 10), it will contain much information that would be called for on an employment form: transcripts of courses taken, dates of employment on other jobs, names and addresses of references, and so on. Carry it in a briefcase or satchel and take it with you to employment offices and interviews. With a copy of the résumé and application letter in the notebook, you can make sure all factual statements are consistent with statements on the form. Of course, falsification would be unethical and impractical. It could result in your being hired for a job you could not do well or termination in disgrace when the falsehood is discovered.

A well-organized employment notebook assists in giving quick, accurate information.

Some application forms, especially for applicants who apply for jobs with a high level of responsibility, are very long. They may actually appear to be tests, on which applicants give their answers to hypothetical questions and write defenses of their answers. If you fill out and submit the employer's application form before the job interview, keep-

Why keep a copy of an application form that has been filled in?

ing a copy may be to your advantage. By reviewing it prior to the interview, you may be able to anticipate some questions and give more polished answers.

The résumé, application letter, and thank-you letter can be retained in a personal computer and adapted for submission to other firms when needed. Many job seekers keep a record of their efforts on a computer: dates on which letters and résumés were sent to certain firms, answers received, names of people talked with, facts conveyed, and so on. When a call is received, that firm's record can be recalled and seen on the monitor while the conversation is taking place. If the purpose of the call is to arrange an appointment, an employer has been impressed already with your résumé and application letter.

Is your personal computer useful in the job search?

Summary

An application letter accompanies a résumé. The purposes are to introduce the applicant and the résumé, arouse interest in the information given on it, and assist an employer in seeing ways in which the applicant's services would be desirable. As such, it is a persuasive letter—beginning with an attention getter and ending with a reference to action.

Length is influenced by the type of résumé. If it is detailed enough to point out ways in which the employer benefits from the applicant's education and experience, the letter can be relatively short. If it lists degrees earned and jobs held without pointing out employer benefits, the letter will need to be relatively long.

The major portion of an application letter is devoted to evidence of compatibility between an applicant's qualifications and the employer's job requirements. Employers sometimes appreciate (at least they do not resent) a statement about the source of job information. They are pleased if the letter reveals some familiarity with the firm's goals, services, products, or procedures. They react negatively to statements of the obvious, discussion of the applicant's problems, comments about the present employer's shortcomings, bragging, flattery, and a biographical emphasis. The following words are sometimes overused: applicant, I, interview, opening, position, qualification, and vacancy.

Assuming an impressive background that is well presented in preceding paragraphs, the final paragraph (action ending) need not be worded forcefully. Sounding neither apologetic nor pushy, it refers to future action. Whether it is by phone or letter is left to the employer's preference.

Follow-up letters either add information that has been accumulated since an application was sent or ask that an application be kept in the active file. After an interview, a thank-you letter is sent as a matter of courtesy regardless of whether a job offer is expected. Acceptance letters are written deductively; refusals, inductively.

Resignation letters normally satisfy a firm's requirement that resignations be submitted in writing; they confirm that termination plans are definite. Assuming a satisfactory employer–employee relationship, resignations are usually bad news for an employer. As such they are written inductively, with emphasis on positive aspects of the job.

For job seekers with good qualifications, recommendation letters are written deductively; otherwise, inductively. Principal concerns are fairness and legality.

Instructions on application forms should be followed carefully. Neatness, completeness, and accuracy are expected. If these qualities are evident, if the résumé and application letter show a good match of qualifications and job requirements, the employer may be eager to schedule an interview.

Check Your Writing

Application Letter

Content

_____ Ideas are valid (statements are true).
_____ From the first sentence, a reader can identify the letter as an application for a certain job.
_____ Nonessential ideas are excluded.
_____ Significant qualifications are emphasized.
_____ Makes reference to attached résumé.
_____ Action ending is neither apologetic nor pushy.

(continued)

Organization

_____ Begins by revealing the job sought in the attention getter.

_____ Presents paragraphs in most appropriate sequence (order of importance is possibly best).

_____ Ends with a reference to action employer is to take (call or write and extend an invitation to an interview).

Style

_____ Employs simple language (no attempt to impress with a sophisticated vocabulary; some professional jargon is justified).

_____ Uses relatively short sentences with sufficient variety.

_____ Places significant words in emphatic positions.

_____ Employs correct grammar.

Mechanics

_____ Has consistent margins.

_____ Is well balanced on the page.

_____ Is typed on paper of good quality.

_____ Has first and last paragraphs that are relatively short; others are held to fewer than six or seven lines.

_____ Achieves perfection in typing, spelling, and punctuation.

Exercises

Review Questions

1. Should an application letter and a résumé contain the same information? Explain.
2. What do application letters and sales letters have in common?
3. In application letters, is flattery appropriate?

4. As a sales letter, what action does an application letter seek?

5. List some words that are frequently overused in application letters.

6. In application letters, are acronyms appropriate? Explain.

7. What ideas are included in a follow-up letter?

8. In a thank-you letter, what is the advantage of referring to some point or points discussed in the interview?

9. Which would be written deductively: (a) an acceptance letter or (b) a refusal letter?

10. Describe the format recommended for a resignation letter.

11. Professor Adams agreed to serve as one of your employment references, but you have not talked with her for two years. Today, you listed her name on an application form. Should you write to her? Explain.

12. An employee whom you fired last year has given your name as a reference. In the responding letter, would you include some positives *and* negatives? Explain.

13. In a negative recommendation, what is the advantage of labeling your letter "confidential" and reminding the reader that the information was requested?

14. List some suggestions for filling out employment forms.

15. How may a personal computer be useful in the job-seeking process?

Activities

1. Write an application letter to accompany your résumé. Make the assumption you prefer:

   a. You are applying for an immediate part-time job.

   b. You are applying for a full-time job for next summer.

   c. You are applying for a full-time job immediately after your graduation. Look at the list of courses you plan to take and write as though you had taken them and satisfied the requirements for a degree.

After you have submitted the letter to your professor and she or he has commented on it and returned it, you could revise and mail the letter or retain it until needed. If you had such a letter in your file, you could bring it up to date and get it into the mail on short notice.

2. Assume a $1,500 scholarship for students in your major field of study has been advertised in *Business Week*. The money comes from a national honor society in your discipline. The recipient must (a) have a B or higher grade average, (b) have more than 60 hours of college credit, (c) be free to attend a week-long, expenses-paid convention in Houston during the second week of May, and (d) write a satisfactory letter of application. Address your letter to The Scholarship Foundation, 301 Skinker Boulevard, St. Louis, MO, 63132.

3. Assume the student council in your college has invited students to participate in the selection of a "teacher of the year." Write a letter addressed to your student council. Recall the professors who taught your classes last year and write a recommendation letter for one of them.

Study the following application letters. As directed by your professor (a) write a sentence-by-sentence critique, (b) make a list of ways in which the letter applies and violates principles discussed in this chapter, (c) rewrite the letter in such a way as to overcome its principal weaknesses, or (d) be prepared to discuss the letter in class.

4. ❶ Please consider me as an applicant for the buyer's position you advertized in last nights issue of the Gazette.

❷ The primary advantage I would have as a buyer is my heavy educational background. ❸ Among the courses I have taken are buyer behavior, retailing, marketing, public relations in business, and advertizing. ❹ I am sure you realize the many ways in which these courses can prepare one for a career in marketing.

❺ In addition to my classes, my educational background includes work in the university bookstore, service on the school yearbook, and president of my fraternity.

❻ I will be receiving my degree on May 5, 1990. ❼ If you can use an energetic young man with my educational background, I will appreciate you studying the résumé which you will find inclosed. ❽ May I have an interview at your earliest convience. ❾ So I can put my educational background to work for you.

5. ❶ Please consider me for the insurance position you advertized in yesterday's paper.

❷ As you can see from the attached résumé, I have worked for a real estate firm for the last fifteen years. ❸ As you know, real estate experience is very similiar to insurance experience.

❹ An insurance man needs (above all else) dependability. ❺ He needs to be accurate, courteous, and understanding. ❻ He needs to be able to communicate, both orally and written. ❼ I have written many letters in conection with my work in real estate. ❽ Actually, I do most of the correspondence for the other people in this office. **9** As a student in college, you will observe that I have been exposed to Marshall McLuhan's theories in various courses. **10** I have observed the influence of his thinking in all the writing I do.

11 While in school (where I compiled a 3.621 average as a business major) I took some very valuable courses in insurance. **12** Work in real estate has kept me in constant contact with insurance matters.

13 References (and details of my qualifications) are presented in organized form on the enclosed résumé which is attached for your convenience.

14 I shall look forward to the opportunity of meeting you personaly and discussing my qualifications.

Interviewing for Success

He has occasional flashes of silence that make his conversation perfectly delightful.

SIDNEY SMITH

T he word *interview* comes from Latin and Middle French words meaning to "see between" or to "see each other." Interviews occur whenever two people meet to converse, both in work and nonwork situations.

Types of Interviews

Interviewers and interviewees may meet "to see between" for a variety of purposes: for hiring, firing, teaching, evaluating and appraising job performance, exchanging factual information, attempting to solve personal problems, or handling customer complaints. Here are examples of interview twosomes:

Interviews are interpersonal communication. (See Chapter 1.)

Seller and prospective buyer

Employment interviewer and job prospect

Boss and subordinate

Marketing researcher and product buyer

Political pollster and voter

Instructor and student

Doctor and patient

Police officer and traffic violator

Newsmaker and reporter

Talk-show host and celebrity guest

Parent and child

Interviews fall into several broad categories based on their purposes. Within each category, interviews may be further classified by subject.

• Employment Interviews

Of special importance to you, perhaps, is the employment interview; it receives intensive attention later in this chapter. As a special category, it combines several interview purposes. It also involves the interviewer's goal of selecting someone who matches the employer's work needs and who will fit effectively into the organization.

• Informational Interviews

Informational interviews are essentially factually oriented meetings. In a doctor–patient meeting, the patient reveals information, which the doctor processes as part of the diagnostic function. The patient obtains information from the doctor about how to treat the diagnosed condition. Even though the exchange is primarily factual, both participants must listen for both *facts and feelings*.

Review Chapter 2 for a refresher on listening.

• Personnel Interviews

Interviews between superiors and current employees cover a wide range of purposes. An appraisal interview is one usually conducted to inform the employee about a performance evaluation for whatever time is covered—usually semiannual or annual periods. The gist of these interviews is to develop a mutually agreed-on evaluation and course of action for the next evaluation period. Obviously the appraisal interview is a sensitive one.

Other personnel interviews conducted frequently are those devoted to disciplining an employee, counseling an employee about personal problems, terminating an employee, promoting an employee, and seeking advice or information about work and working conditions.

• Sales or Persuasive Interviews

Talk to many salespeople and you'll find that interviewing is the lifeblood of their business. Depending on the nature of the product or service offered, a salesperson may also have to be a problem solver for the potential customer. The appeals used in sales interviews are the same as those used in sales letters.

The key to persuasion in interviewing is in accepting, challenging, and rebutting the other person's arguments. Keep in mind that arguments are not quarrels; arguments involve exchanges of opinion and facts with each party attempting to win. If winning means making a sale, or in the case of a resistant buyer avoiding a purchase, that is the goal. Here are some suggestions:

1. Listen to detect a difference of opinion or an objection.
2. Restate the objectionable item in your own words. Debaters claim that such paraphrasing often causes the objection to sound less convincing. When you provide this feedback, the listener is able to analyze his or her own statements.
3. Use facts as evidence. Facts are provable items; misrepresentation can't be backed by facts.
4. In persuasive interviews, keep cool, don't raise your voice, don't rub it in when you win, and lose gracefully when you lose—your turn will come.

Effective feedback

Structure of Interviews

The structure an interview may take depends most on the goals of the interviewer. Note that each of the following structures may apply to any of the styles of interviews.

• Structured Interviews

Structured interviews follow rather formal procedures. The interviewer follows a predetermined agenda, including a checklist of items or a series of questions and statements designed to elicit the necessary information or interviewee reaction.

• Unstructured Interviews

Unstructured interviews are freewheeling exchanges and may shift from one subject to another, depending on the interests of the participants. Some experienced interviewers are able to make a structured interview seem like an unstructured one. The goal of many unstructured interviews is to explore unknown areas in search of new ideas.

• Stress Interviews

Some interviewees create their own stress.

Stress interviews are designed to place the interviewee in a stressful situation so an evaluation of the interviewee's performance under stress may be made. Both structured and unstructured interviews may also become stress interviews.

In all cases, interviewees should attempt to assess the nature of the interview quickly and attempt to adjust behavior accordingly. As the following discussion of the role of the interviewer reveals, you, as an interviewee, can perform much better when you understand what the interviewer is doing.

Job Interviewer's Role

The success of any interview depends on the communication skills of the participants and how strongly each wants to practice them. As a guide, the following four steps apply to almost all interviewing and will vary with the types of interviews:

1. Preparation
2. Interchange
3. Evaluation
4. Action

An interview: The ultimate in interpersonal communication

• Preparing for the Interview

Preparation may be the most neglected of the four steps, yet it may be the most important. Preparation involves the following elements:

1. *Purpose.* What is the purpose of the interview? What are the expected outcomes? What style is most appropriate, and what atmosphere is best—relaxed or stressful?

2. *Physical arrangements.* Is the physical setup consistent with the purpose? Is privacy adequate? What distractions should be eliminated?

3. *Self-understanding.* Does the interviewer have an awareness of his or her own strengths and weaknesses, prejudices, biases, perceptions, and other possible barriers to effective communication?

4. *Understanding the other.* What is known or should be known about the interviewee? What are her or his values, aspirations, motives, and background?

Through effective preparation, the interviewer can set the stage for whatever kind of interview desired. If the interview is to be structured, have items to be discussed been arranged in proper sequence? Will the nature of the questions elicit information-revealing responses? Will the sequence lead to a relaxed interview or to a stressful one? When you, as a job applicant, plan for your interview, keep in mind that most personnel interviewers have probably gone through these preparatory steps. This reminder will help you determine the interview style, so you can adapt your behavior appropriately.

• Meeting Face to Face—The Interchange

During the interview, both the interviewer and the interviewee should pay particular attention to the following factors:

1. *Rapport.* How well have you reached a common ground to establish a climate consistent with the purpose of the meeting? Does an air of mutual respect exist?

2. *Flexibility.* Can the interviewer redirect the flow of discussion when it strays from the purpose and disrupts the original plan?

Does a first impression last long?

3. *Two-way flow.* Are the participants engaged in two-way communication, or is one or the other turning it into a one-way situation?

As either the interviewer or the interviewee, you can become far more effective than the usual participant if you develop some simple techniques for providing feedback and for clarifying issues. Listening in the classroom, for example, is relatively easy to do because you assume a listening role as your primary activity. In an interview, however, you will be both a listener and a speaker; and some of your listening time will be spent preparing what you will say when it is your turn to speak. Interviewing as a process is much like ordinary one-to-one conversation, differing primarily in the higher degree of tension that normally goes with interviewing. Thus, you should work to make your shift from listener to speaker as smooth a transition as possible. If you haven't listened thoroughly enough to understand completely, your response to the other person will probably be inadequate. Effective, active listening involves mental concentration and good physical posture. It is not a passive activity as many people believe.

Feedback makes the interview!

Questioning is one technique used by good conversationalists and interview participants to gain more information before making a complete response. It can also encourage a shy person to participate more fully. An example of a question to get more information:

Bob: I had no idea I would be invited to run for office.
Jane: What did you say to them after being invited?

A question to clarify word meaning:

Mariette: Jerry has been pusillanimous about this.
Bill: How can you tell? (pusillanimous = cowardly)

A question to seek feeling:

George: Then I was promoted to a job I didn't like.
Mac: How did you adjust to that?

Questions are effective feedback forms and tend to keep the interview moving when it might otherwise fall flat. *Direct* questions can be answered easily and briefly. They ask for *yes* or *no* answers or for factual information. *Do you like to fly? When will you graduate? Have you traveled overseas?* Because they call for factual information, direct questions don't help much in encouraging the dialogue of the interview. *Indirect* questions, however, do contribute to dialogue because they call for answers that require thought on the part of the receiver. *Why do you feel accounting is the career for you? What experience have you had in working as part of a team or group?*

Questions or statements are often a form of paraphrasing—restating the content or the intent of the sender's message to check your own understanding.

Tamara:	I'm looking forward to the Christmas vacation.
Alice:	You'll get caught up on your school work.
Tamara:	No, I'm caught up on that. I'll have time to spend with my parents.

Alice received meaning clarification.

We use the techniques of questioning and paraphrasing most of the time in conversation. The thoughtful use of these techniques can contribute much to interviewing situations and to two-way flow.

• Evaluating the Interview

Decision-making time arrives at the close of the interview. Is the interviewer prepared to analyze alternative actions? Should the decision be made or postponed? Should the interviewee be invited for further interviews? Should the interviewee be told a letter will be sent at a later time? The interviewer should know what action to take simply because arriving at some kind of decision or outcome was considered in the preparation step. Does each of the two participants know exactly what is to be done? Has a mutual understanding been developed?

Should an interviewee ask, "What happens next?"

• Some Interviewer Guidelines

The interviewee should be told the interviewer's guidelines because they can help both parties in the meeting. If the interviewer plans to take notes during the interview, for example, the interviewee must be forewarned. Otherwise, the interviewee might freeze when the interviewer takes notes. On the other hand, if notes are not made, the job applicant in a personnel interview might feel that he or she is not receiving fair consideration. The interviewer should introduce the note-taking idea with a statement such as: "I like to take a few notes during the interview to jog my memory later and to make sure we cover everything we should. We can also use them near the end of the interview to make sure your comments and my understanding are in agreement. Do you mind?" Following agreement, note taking will not be a barrier of consequence, particularly if the notes are not considered secret and if they are for the interviewer's use only. Even leaving the notes in a visible place will help assure the interviewee. Of course, the interviewer can always add personal impressions to the notes after the interviewee leaves.

The interviewer can help establish the style of the interview by proper use of voice tone and volume. A friendly tone may put the applicant at ease. A harsh, aggressive tone may frighten the applicant and result in a stress situation. In the same way, the interviewer can set the stage for a relaxed or stressful interview simply by organizing questions. Asking the most difficult question first, for example, may throw the applicant into a frenzied state. Body posture is also an important element. By paying attention through eye contact and by appearing interested through the use of acknowledging head motions and a general body posture indicating concern, the interviewer has a better opportunity to pursue the goals of the interview.

> **Some of these techniques must be practiced by both participants.**

These guidelines have much to do with the effectiveness of the interview, but the kinds of questions asked can determine its success or failure. Questions that can be answered with a simple "yes" or "no" don't contribute much and may leave interviewees in a position of having to stray from the subject to put themselves in a better light. Questions that ask how, what, or why provide openings for genuine discussion.

• Interviewer Prohibitions

In general, interviewers must describe all working conditions to *any* job candidate. The candidate must then decide whether he or she is willing and able to meet those conditions. From Equal Opportunity Commission and Fair Employment Practices Guidelines, items that may be considered sexually, racially, or religiously discriminatory should not be introduced in job interviews:

1. To turn down an applicant because customers would not want to deal with a particular gender or ethnic group, because co-workers might object, because the position requires travel with members of the opposite sex, because working hours are unusual, or because restroom facilities are lacking is illegal.

2. To offer a lower salary than is offered to other applicants of equivalent background is illegal.

3. During an interview, questions, statements, or actions such as the following are considered discriminatory.

   a. Questions about marriage plans, child-bearing plans, and marital status asked of a woman applicant and not of a man.

b. Any statement showing hiring preference for married or unmarried individuals.

c. Discussing a stereotyped woman's job with a woman applicant, especially if the applicant is applying for a different job.

d. Job benefits or conditions that pertain only to heads of households or principal wage earners.

e. Company literature that refers to all employees by the outdated generic masculine pronouns as well as comments about the *girls* in the office.

Therefore, employment interviewers must be well prepared and must use appropriate language in their meetings with women candidates. These discriminatory actions apply equally to racial minorities.

For you as an interviewee, these guidelines indicate that the professional personnel interviewer must be thoroughly prepared for the interview. No matter how casual or how formal the interview may seem to be, you can rest assured that considerable effort went into planning it. Obviously, interviews can never be identical. Participants change as a result of each interview experience, and each experience gives them greater self-confidence. Competent interviewing is one of the most satisfying and rewarding management skills.

> As an interviewee, use discretion in discussing discrimination.

Job Interviewee's Role

Just as the interviewer proceeds through a step-by-step process, so should the interviewee. As the interviewee, you'll want to engage in some pre-interview activities, prepare to perform well during the interview, and take appropriate action after the interview.

College students generally schedule on-campus interviews with representatives from various business organizations. Following the on-campus interviews, successful candidates are often invited for further interviews on the company premises. The purpose of the second interview is to give executives and administrators, other than the personnel interviewer, an opportunity to appraise the candidate. Whether on campus or on company premises, interview methods and practices apply to the situation. When the interview is with company executives, the candidate will probably encounter a wide variety of interview styles. Preliminary planning can pay rich dividends.

• Preparing for the Interview

Pre-interview planning involves learning something about the company or organization, doing some studying about yourself, and making sure your appearance and mannerisms will not detract from the impression you hope to make.

Study the Company Nothing can hurt the candidate more than knowing little about the organization. No knowledge probably indicates insincerity, and the interviewer doesn't want to waste precious interview time providing the candidate with information that should have been gathered long before.

Those with publicly traded stock are required to publish annual reports. Many business-school libraries have a file of annual reports and several financial service reports. Other information can be obtained from brokerage houses, from periodicals, and from financial newspapers. Employees of the company or other students who have been interviewed may be of particular help to the interviewee. Some major schools have prepared videotape interviews with various company recruiters and make the tapes available to students. Attempt to prepare a guide similar to that shown in Figure 12.1 for each company with which you interview.

Use your public library, too.

Study Yourself When you know something about the company, you'll also know something about the kinds of jobs or training programs they have to offer. Next, assess your own interests and abilities:

1. Are you a "people" person or a "loner"?
2. Are you an extrovert?
3. Do you like detailed work?
4. Do you have an achievable career plan?
5. Is job-related travel a problem for you?

Your answers to these and similar questions will help prepare you for an interview. If you can't see a relationship between you and the job or company, you won't be able to demonstrate the interest or sincerity to sell yourself!

A good method of approaching the know-yourself problem is to attempt a match between you and the potential job as in

Company and Job Requirements	My Qualifications and Needs	
Detailed or broad		Psychological services administer interest tests.

Detailed or broad
Inside–outside
People orientation
On a career path
High or low pay
Educational requirements
Travel requirements
Job security
Prestige level

Of course, you'll probably never find the job and the organization that will satisfy all your needs and meet all your requirements. Additionally, you'll personally place greater weight on some factors than on others. In any case, the analysis you give such factors before you embark on each interview may avoid problems later.

Company Information

Name. Know that *IBM* stands for *International Business Machines,* for example.

Status in the industry. Know the company's share of the market, its Fortune 500 standing if any, its sales, its assets, and its number of employees.

Latest stock market quote.

Recent news items and developments.

Scope of the company. Is it local, national, or international?

Corporate officers. Know the names of the chairperson, president, and chief executive officer.

Products and services.

Job Information

Job title. Know what the typical entry-level positions are called.

Job qualifications. Understand the specific knowledge and skills desired.

Probable salary range.

Career path of the job.

FIGURE 12.1

Interviewee's guide for studying the company.

Many companies
have "images" to
maintain—do you fit?

Plan Your Appearance   An employment interviewer once said that if the job applicant did not meet her *extremities* test, the interview might as well not take place. She went on to explain that the extremities were the candidate's fingernails, hair, and shoes. The fingernails had to be clean and neat, the shoes shined, or at least clean, and the hair clean and well groomed. Long hair on men met the standard, incidentally, if clean and well groomed. She simply felt that if the candidate did not take care of those items, the candidate could not really be serious about, or fit into, her organization. Another interviewer turned down an otherwise outstanding applicant because the applicant could not look him in the eye when he answered a question. Interviewers are subject to personal perceptions and biases, just as others are.

The job applicant, of course, cannot be prepared for everything but must be adequately groomed and attired. Not being so calls negative attention to something that may or may not be job related. In terms of appearance, then, the applicant should

1.   Be as clean and well groomed as possible.
2.   Wear appropriate footwear.
3.   Select appropriate clothes for the interview.

If you must, borrow clothes from a friend. Avoid gaudy colors. Research the company dress code—real or implied—ahead of time. And remember that if you *look* and *dress* like the people who already work at the company, the interviewer will be able to visualize your working there. Your college placement officer may be able to provide helpful hints.

Plan Your Time   One of the worst things you can do is be late for an interview. Another is to miss the interview entirely. Therefore, plan your time so you will arrive early. This planning allows you to unwind and mentally review the things you plan to accomplish. At the same time, don't just sit in a waiting room making yourself nervous. Move around some to keep loose. But by *all* means, be on time. Should something happen to prevent your doing so, telephone an apology.

• Meeting Face to Face—The Interchange

Now that you have gone through the planning stages, you are ready for the interview. Your job is to sell yourself so successfully that you are invited to proceed to whatever the next step in the hiring process might be. If the first step was an on-campus interview, the next step will be an interview with company executives. You should not expect to receive a firm job offer in the first interview, but one may be made.

Opening Formalities   When you meet the interviewer, use the interviewer's name if you are sure you know how to pronounce it correctly. You may ask how to pronounce the name if necessary. Usually, the interviewer will initiate the handshake, although you may do so. In either case, apply a firm handshake. You don't want to leave the impression that you are weak or timid. At the same time, you don't want to overdo the firm grip and leave an impression of your being overbearing. Once the introduction is over, wait for the interviewer to invite you to be seated. These common courtesies—using the correct name, applying a firm handshake, and waiting to be seated—can contribute to a favorable first impression. Use your body language to add to that impression. Sit erect with a slight forward lean to express interest. A slouchy posture can do nothing for your image—nor can smoking or gum chewing.

The interviewer will begin the conversation and effectively set the stage for the interview. You might expect either some nonbusiness talk or a direct opening into the business of the interview.

Research supports the conclusion that a positive or negative impression is created during the first four minutes of an interview; this impression often determines, albeit unconsciously, the outcome of that interview. You should be able to determine quickly whether the interview will be structured or unstructured, nonstressful or stressful.

During these early minutes, make appropriate eye contact with the interviewer and be conscious of the nonverbal messages the two of you are sending. Some professional interviewers may look out the window while you are talking, stand up and stretch, or do other things early to detect your reaction. You can usually tell whether these actions are genuine; quite probably, they are acts. Retain your composure!

As you proceed into the interview, keep in mind the barriers to communication in interviews as revealed by a survey of 164 employment interviewers after they had interviewed undergraduate seniors at a major state university. Most barriers are attitudinal, as shown in Figure 12.2.

Interviewing Guidelines   Much of the information about you will appear on your résumé or company application form, already available to the interviewer. Thus, the interviewer will most likely seek to go beyond such things as your education, work experience, and extracurricular activities and attempt to assess your attitudes toward work and the probability of fitting you successfully into the organization.

The best way to prepare for the interview discussion is to study the company and yourself, of course. Additionally, though, you can prepare

Repeating the interviewer's name will help you remember it.

Can you smile under pressure?

Know your résumé thoroughly. It's a source for interviewer questions.

Rank	Barrier
1	Tendency not to listen
2	Lack of credibility
3	Lack of interest in subject discussed
4	Hostile attitudes
5	Use of profanity
6	Poor organization of ideas
7	Resistance to change
8	Know-it-all attitude
9	Lack of trust
10	Lack of feedback

FIGURE 12.2

Rank order of interview communication barriers. (*Source:* Steven P. Golen and David H. Lynch, "The Seriousness of Communication Barriers in the Interviewer–Interviewee Relationship," *The Delta Pi Epsilon Journal,* XXIX(2), Spring 1987, pp. 47–55.)

to answer questions such as those listed in Figure 12.3. Having thoughtfully answered such questions *before* the interview, you can give smooth and confident answers *during* the interview.

Your education is your *major asset* if you are a student. You should point out its relationship to the job for which you are being considered. Even more important, the fact that you have succeeded in school indicates that you have the ability to learn. Because most companies expect you to learn something on the job, your ability to learn and, thus, to become productive quickly may be your greatest asset. So your most important response to the interviewer's questions may be about your ability to learn. Even no work experience may be an asset. You have acquired no bad work habits that you will have to unlearn!

Your *interpersonal skill*—skill in getting along with others—may be an important attribute. What did you do in college that helped you get along with others? Were you a member, an officer, or president of an organization? What did you accomplish? How did others perceive you? Were you a leader? The extracurricular activities listed on your résumé give an indication of these traits, but how you talk about them in your interview helps. "I started as corresponding secretary and was subsequently elected to higher office for four semesters, eventually becoming

Do you have special training or out-of-the-ordinary background?

FREQUENTLY ASKED TOUGH INTERVIEW QUESTIONS

Universal Questions for Students and Employed Job Changers

1. What do you know about our company?
2. Why do you want to work for us?
3. Why should we hire you?
4. What are your greatest strengths?
5. What weaknesses do you have that we should know about?
6. What do you think are the real qualifications for this job?
7. How do you compare to the job qualifications?
8. What is important to you in a job?
9. How do you spend your spare time?
10. What are your salary expectations?
11. What other firms do you plan to interview?
12. What are your career plans?

Additional Questions for Employed Job Changers

13. Why do you want to leave your present job?
14. What opportunities do you have for promotion with your present employer?
15. What salary are you making and what do you hope to get on your next job?
16. What is your opinion about your present co-workers and your boss?
17. Are you willing to take some psychological tests before we discuss employment offers?

FIGURE 12.3
Frequently asked interview questions.

president" may be a statement that proves your leadership qualities. If at the same time your organization went on to greater heights, all the more power to you.

Humility pays off in all interviews. If you are being interviewed by a representative of General Motors, don't suggest that you can turn the company around. A candidate for the presidency of a university was not considered further when he said he could turn the university around when the university was already successful. Incidentally, he had been president of another university for only six months and claimed he had

Can humility and confidence be combined?

turned that university around. Obviously, the candidate hadn't become familiar with the problems of the university. The candidate had failed to take even the first step toward a successful interview: study the company.

"*Why do you want to work for us?*" is really not a difficult question to handle if you do some planning. In addition to your study of the company from the literature, you can usually locate someone who works for the company to tell you about it. You can often visit a local office of the firm, as well. Then you can make a favorable impression simply by referring to the people you have talked with about the working conditions, company achievements, and career paths. You'll also show you are strongly interested in the company and not just taking an interview for practice. The interviewer not only attempts to develop an impression of you but also evaluates you in comparison with others being interviewed for the position. Your responses can indicate your sincere interest in getting a job with this company rather than just any company.

Your response to inquiries about why you should be hired will be a composite of some of the things already discussed. You have the proper education, you have proved you have the ability to learn, and you are enthusiastic about working for the company. If you really understand the job requirements, you should have little difficulty relating your skills and knowledge to the job. If the immediate job will lead to supervisory or management responsibilities later, make certain that you stress your skill in getting along with others and working successfully as part of a team.

A question about whether the company can offer you a career path is probably best answered with a question such as "I believe someone like me has a future with your company, but I would like to discuss the normal progression with the company. Can you tell me about it?" Most candidates for positions with public accounting firms are familiar with the steps from staff accountant to partner; but the steps are not so clearly defined in marketing, finance, and management paths. An open discussion can provide you with new information.

Everyone has a weakness. Thus, when asked about your greatest strengths and weaknesses, you can make an impression by acknowledging a weakness. To do otherwise may display a lack of appropriate humility. You may indicate that you occasionally become overcommitted to extracurricular activities, particularly if your résumé shows a high level of extracurricular participation. But use this response only if you also have a strong academic record. Don't confess that your overcom-

Get across the idea of "I like your company."

Do you get the hint that weaknesses should border on being desirable traits?

mitment resulted in a failure to pursue your education properly. Thoughtless answers can sometimes screen you out of further consideration. Your greatest strength probably is easy to identify: (1) the ability to learn, (2) the ability to work with others and to assume leadership roles, (3) the ability to organize your time in such a way that you can achieve academically while still participating in nonclass activities or work, and (4) skill in problem solving. Because the question asks for your *greatest* strength, you should focus on a single point rather than brag about all your strengths.

Questions about how you spend your spare time and about how your extracurricular activities have added to your education are designed to make you elaborate on résumé items. Give some thought to these items so you can appear to have broad, balanced interests rather than a single, time-consuming avocation.

What's important in a job goes beyond financial reward. Although we are all interested in a paycheck, any job satisfies that need—some will pay more, some less; but the paycheck is a part of the job and should not be your primary concern. Intrinsic rewards such as personal job satisfaction, the feeling of accomplishment, and making a contribution to society are things you should think about discussing in the interview. You should like what you are doing. You should look forward to a challenge. A job that will satisfy these needs is important to almost everyone.

Develop a sincere, straightforward answer!

One of the major reasons for college graduates' changing jobs is lack of challenge and the resulting dislike for the job. Research has shown that most of us change jobs two or three times before finding our career occupation. So, as you engage in the interview, look for things that will satisfy your immediate needs and lead to future challenges. Job changes usually involve hardships of some sort, and careful consideration of how the job and the company will meet your needs can prevent later problems.

Handling Salary Discussion   For most entry-level positions, the beginning salary is fixed. However, if you have work experience, excellent scholarship records, or added maturity, you may be able to obtain a larger salary. The interviewer should initiate the salary topic. What you should know is the general range for candidates with your qualifications so that your response to a question about how much you would expect is reasonable. If your qualifications are about average for the job, you can indicate that you would expect to be paid the going rate or within the normal range. If you have added qualifications, you might say "With my two years of work experience, I would expect to start at the upper end of the normal salary range.''

If you have other job offers, you are in a position to compare salaries, jobs, and companies. In this case, you may suggest to the interviewer that you would expect a competitive salary and that you have been offered X dollars by another firm. If salary hasn't been mentioned, and you really want to know about it, simply ask courteously how much the salary would be for someone with your qualifications. In any case, though, if you really believe the job offers the nonmonetary things you seek, don't attempt to make salary a major issue.

Should you stress opportunity over salary?

Normally, an interviewer will introduce the subject of benefits without your asking about them. In some cases, a discussion of total salary and "perks" (perquisites) is reserved for a follow-up interview. If nothing has been said about certain benefits, you should take the liberty of asking, particularly when an item may be especially important to you. Medical insurance, for example, may be very important when you have children. Retirement planning, however, is inappropriate for a new graduate to discuss.

Closing the Interview   The interviewer will provide the cues indicating that the interview is completed by rising or making a comment about the next step to be taken. At that point, don't prolong the interview needlessly. Simply rise, accept the handshake, thank the interviewer for the opportunity to meet, and close by saying you look forward to hearing from the company. The neatness with which you close the interview may be almost as important as the first impression you made. Be enthusiastic. If you really want the job, you might ask for it!

• Following Up the Interview

After the interview, don't take too long to send a thank-you letter to the interviewer. The letter should be similar to the thank-you letter described in Chapter 11. If you were asked to submit some statement or further information, the prompt follow-up action becomes all the more important.

Is the letter of thanks a reminder of your interest?

• Practicing for Interviews

Essential to presenting yourself favorably is your display of sincerity. Although most of us tend to be nervous during our first interview, we gain confidence with experience. Therefore, practice and rehearse your own interviewing style. Work with someone else in mock interviews, alternating roles as interviewer and interviewee. Then follow each practice interview with a constructive critique of each other's performance. A few such mock interviews will give you some experience and will make the first real interview more effective.

The job interview may be the most important face-to-face interaction you will have. You will be selling yourself in competition with others. How you listen and how you talk are characteristics the interviewer will be able to measure. Your actions, your mannerisms, and your appearance will combine to give the total picture of how you come across. Added to the obvious things you have acquired from your education, experience, and activities, your interview performance can give a skilled interviewer an excellent picture of you. Practice leads to perfection, so the time you devote to preparing for the interview may determine the payoff by making you stand a little higher than your competition.

You might use a third person as an observer.

Summary

Job interviews, in many cases the graduate's final steps in getting the first job and beginning a career, are the focus for the discussion of interviewing in this chapter. Interviewers and interviewees can be looked at as buyers and sellers: Interviewers want to know whether job candidates can meet the needs of their firms before making a "purchase"; interviewees want to sell themselves based on sound knowledge, good work skills, and desirable personal traits. When interviews fail, the reason usually lies in attitudinal shortcomings.

Good interviews seldom occur by accident. Both interviewers and interviewees have responsibilities for the success of the meeting. Just as actors practice their lines and roles, those engaged in interviews should plan and practice for their performances, too.

About Language and Usage

Some words with foreign roots have become frequently used terms in English. Unfortunately, their meanings are often interpreted incorrectly or their pronunciation is not understood.

(continued)

Some examples:

dilettante   A dilettante is one who pursues the arts as a hobbyist, a dabbler, an amateur. The antonym is *expert* or *professional*. The preferred pronunciation omits the final *e*, but pronouncing the *ē* is acceptable.

gauche   Pronounced "gōsh," gauche comes from French meaning "left-handed," hence clumsy. It also means uncultured, tasteless, ill-bred, socially awkward, plebeian, proletarian. To tell someone his or her manner or dress is *gauche* is not a compliment.

forte   Forte means a special gift, strength, or natural talent and is pronounced "fort."

Watch for these in interviews.

Exercises

Review Questions

1. How do employment interviews differ from other personnel interviews?
2. How do structured and unstructured interviews differ?
3. What is meant by paraphrasing?
4. How do responses to direct and indirect questions differ?
5. Compose three statements or questions that might be considered discriminatory in employment interviews.
6. List some possible sources of information about a company.
7. What posture and body movements can an interviewee use to impress an interviewer?
8. If your education is your foremost attribute, how can you stress what it says about you and your potential value to an employer?
9. List four leading barriers to communication in employment interviews.
10. What is a good strategy to use when you are asked about your major weakness?

Activities

1. Indicate whether each of the following items is a direct or an indirect question:
   a. When did you move to Missouri?
   b. What would be your feeling if you were asked to travel for long periods?
   c. What is your grade-point average?
   d. Why do you want to work for us?
   e. What was your favorite college subject and why?
   f. How did you benefit from your membership in the business fraternity?

2. Prepare questions to clarify each of the following statements addressed to you as the interviewer:
   a. I prefer to work with things rather than with people.
   b. A job in a bank would be perfect for me.
   c. I think I'd rather stay in school for a couple of years and obtain an M.B.A.
   d. I'm scared when I meet someone at the executive level.
   e. I hate coffee.

3. Prepare paraphrases (reflecting sentences rather than questions) as responses for the items in Activity 2.

The following activity may be used as described or adapted for television taping and review.

4. Form groups of four to practice job interviews. Each person should have available a copy of his or her résumé. Alternatively play the roles of interviewer and interviewee, with the two additional people serving as critical observers. Change places until all four have had an opportunity to serve as interviewer and interviewee. You may assume the jobs being applied for are the ones you have selected and designed applications for. Or you may use one of the following positions:
   a. A part-time job visiting high schools to sell seniors on the idea of attending your school.
   b. A full-time summer job as a management intern in a local bank.

When you have finished studying Part 5, you should be able to

- Approach problem-solving situations analytically.
- Collect, manage, and organize quantitative and written material for use in reports.
- Prepare short reports and proposals in a professional way.
- Use an objective, nonpersonal writing style when necessary.
- Prepare reports in formal style.

COMMUNICATING THROUGH REPORTS

The Report Process and Research Methods

In expanding the field of knowledge, we but increase the horizon of ignorance.

HENRY MILLER

nstitutions of all types—business, governmental, service, and charitable—are faced with daily problem-solving and decision-making tasks. Whether at the policy-making executive level or at the operational management level, decision makers and problem solvers require a steady supply of information on which they can rely. This information may be supplied orally or in written form. The term used to describe the body of information is a *report*. The process of developing the information, preparing it for presentation, and presenting it is *reporting*.

Knowing the Characteristics of Reports

Hello, Pete. This is Walters in customer services. The boss wants to know how things are going with the 400-case Sleepwell order. Are we going to make the 4 P.M. shipping deadline?

Oh hi, Walt. We are going to make the deadline, with time to spare. We have about 250 cases on the loading dock, another hundred on the box line, and fifty going through the labeling process. They'll all be ready for the loader at 2 o'clock.

This brief exchange illustrates a simple reporting task. A question has been posed; the answer given (along with supporting information) satisfies the reporting requirement. Although Pete may never have studied report preparation, he did an excellent job; so Walters, in turn, can report to his boss. Pete's oral report is a very simple illustration of five main characteristics of reports:

1. Reports are generally requested by a higher authority. In most cases, people would not generate reports unless requested to do so.

Is a report feedback to downward communication?

2. Reports typically travel upward in the organization structure. The upward direction of reports is a result of their being requested by higher authority.

3. Reports are orderly. Orderly, in this sense, means that reports are logically organized. In Pete's case, he gave Walt an answer to his question first and then supported the answer with evidence to justify it. Our study of the organization of letters showed us the difference between deductive and inductive organization. Pete's report was deductively organized. If Pete had given the supporting evidence first and followed that with the answer that he would meet the deadline, the organization of his reply would have been inductive and would still have been logical.

4. Reports stress objectivity. Because reports contribute to decision making and problem solving, they should be as objective as possible; when nonobjective (subjective) material is to be included, the reporter should make that known.

5. Reports are generally prepared for a limited audience. This characteristic is particularly true of reports traveling within an organization and means that reports, like letters, can be prepared with the receiver's needs in mind.

• What Is a Report?

Based on those five characteristics, a workable definition of a report is "an orderly, objective message used to convey information from one organizational area to another or from one institution to another to assist in decision making or problem solving." Reports have been classified in numerous ways by management and by report-preparation authorities. The form, direction, functional use, and content of the report are used as bases for classification. However, a single report might be included in several classifications. The following brief review of classifications helps explain the scope of reporting and establishes a departure point for studying reports and reporting.

What is the ultimate purpose of reports?

Formal or Informal Reports   The formal–informal classification is particularly helpful because it applies to all reports. Formal reports are carefully structured; they stress objectivity and organization, contain much detail, and are written in a style that tends to eliminate such elements as personal pronouns. Informal reports are usually short messages with natural, casual use of language. The internal memorandum generally can be described as an informal report. All reports lie on a continuum as shown in Figure 13.1. Later chapters will explain more fully the distinction among the degrees of formality of various reports.

See the dictionary definition of "formal."

Short or Long Reports   "Short-or-long" can be a confusing classification for reports. A one-page memorandum is obviously short, and a term paper of twenty pages is obviously long. What about in-between lengths? One important distinction generally holds true: as a report becomes longer, it takes on more characteristics of formal reports. Thus, the formal–informal and short–long classifications are closely related.

Informational or Analytical Reports   Informational reports carry objective information from one area of an organization to another. Analytical reports present attempts to solve problems. The annual re-

Formal ⟵⎯⎯⎯⎯⎯⎯⟶ *Informal*

Scientific Research

Routine Business Research

Informational Messages

FIGURE 13.1
Report formality continuum.

port of a company is an informational report as are monthly financial statements, reports of sales volume, and reports of employee or personnel absenteeism and turnover. Reports of scientific research, real-estate appraisal reports, and feasibility reports by consulting firms are analytical reports.

Do you recall organizational control and coordination from Chapter 1?

Vertical or Lateral Reports   The vertical–lateral classification refers to the directions reports travel. Although most reports travel upward in organizations, many travel downward. Both represent vertical reports and are often referred to as upward-directed and downward-directed reports. The main function of vertical reports is to contribute to management *control.* (See Figure 13.2.) Lateral reports, on the other hand, assist in *coordination* in the organization. A report traveling between units of the same organizational level, as between the production department and the finance department, is laterally directed.

Internal or External Reports   Internal reports travel within the organization. External reports, such as annual reports of companies, are prepared for distribution outside the organization.

Periodic Reports   When reports are classified as periodic, they are issued on regularly scheduled dates. Periodic reports are generally upward directed and serve management-control purposes. Daily, weekly, monthly, quarterly, semiannual, and annual time periods are typical of those covered by periodic reports. Preprinted forms and computer-generated data contribute to uniformity of periodic reports.

Functional Reports   The functional classification includes accounting reports, marketing reports, financial reports, personnel reports, and a variety of other reports that take their functional designation from the

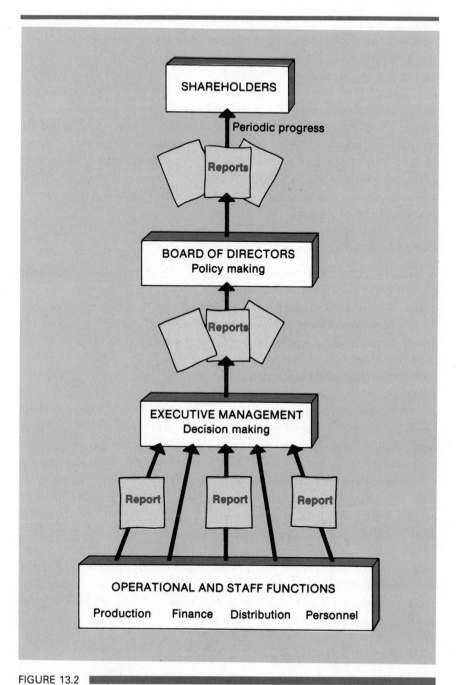

FIGURE 13.2
The general upward flow of reports.

ultimate use of the report. For example, a justification of the need for additional personnel or for new equipment is described as a justification report in this classification.

Aren't these report classifications based on flow, time, and use?

As you review these report classifications, you will very likely decide that almost all reports could be included in most of these categories. If this thought does cross your mind, you are correct. A report may be formal or informal, short or long, informational or analytical, vertically or laterally directed, internal or external, periodic or nonperiodic, functionally labeled, or any combination of these classifications. Although authorities have not agreed on a universal report classification, these report categories are in common use and provide a nomenclature for the study and use of reports.

• Proposals as Special Reports

A variation of problem-solving reports is the proposal, a document prepared to describe how one organization can meet the needs of another. Whenever you shop for a particular item, a salesperson may "sell" you on his or her merchandise by describing how it will meet your needs. If you are a conscientious shopper, you'll probably visit more than one store before making a purchase. In effect, you are receiving oral proposals, weighing one against another, and finally making a selection.

Are newspaper ads proposals?

On a broader scale, most governmental agencies advertise their needs by issuing "requests for proposals," or RFPs. The RFP specifies a need, such as for architectural services. Potential suppliers, then, prepare proposal reports telling how they can meet that need. Those preparing the proposal create a convincing document that they hope will result in their obtaining a contract. In addition, both public agencies and most private businesses issue "calls for bids" that meet the specifications established for proposed major purchases of goods and certain services.

In our high-technology environment, proposal preparation is a major activity for many firms. Chapter 15 presents proposal preparation in considerable detail. Although that chapter also discusses preparation of short reports, keep in mind that a proposal to build a space station would perhaps require many volumes.

• Basis for a Report: A Problem

The upward flow of reports provides management with information to use in problem solving and decision making. If problems did not exist, reports would be unnecessary. Some problems are recurring and, hence, call for a steady flow of information; other problems may be unique and call for information on a one-time basis. If we can accept the idea that a problem is the basis for a report, the preparation, organization, and writing of the report all become much easier.

Whatever the problem—business or otherwise—human reason has developed the following steps for finding a solution:

1. Recognize and define the problem.
2. Select a method of solution.
3. Collect and organize the data.
4. Arrive at an answer.

These steps form the report skeleton.

Only after all four steps have been completed is the report written for presentation. Reports represent an attempt to communicate how a problem was solved and what the solution was. Let's take a closer look at the four steps in problem solving and in successful report preparation. Keep in mind that these problem-solving steps are completed *before* the report is written in final form.

Recognizing and Defining the Problem

Problem-solving research cannot ever begin before those doing the research define the problem. Frequently, those requesting a report will attempt to provide a suitable definition. Nevertheless, researchers should attempt a paraphrase to ensure they will be on the right track.

Research studies often have both a statement of the problem and a statement of the purpose. For example, a real-estate appraiser accepts a client's request to appraise a building to determine its market value. The problem is to arrive at a fair market value for the property. The purpose of the appraisal, however, might be to establish a value for a mortgage loan, to determine the feasibility of adding to the structure, or to assess the financial possibility of demolishing the structure and erecting something else. Thus, the purpose may have much to do with determining what elements to consider in arriving at an answer.

Pinpoint your purpose.

In other words, unless you know why something is wanted, you might have difficulty knowing what is wanted. Once you arrive at the answer to the *why* and *what* questions, write them down. You'll be on your way to solving the problem.

• Using Hypotheses and Statements of Purpose

A *hypothesis* is a statement to be proved or disproved through some type of research. For example, a study of skilled manufacturing employees under varying conditions might be made to determine whether production would increase if each employee were part of a team as opposed to being a single unit in a production line. For this problem, the hypothesis could be formulated in this way: "The productivity will increase when skilled manufacturing employees are members of production teams rather than as single units in a production line." Because the hypothesis tends to be stated in a way that favors one possibility or a prejudice toward a particular answer, many researchers prefer to state hypotheses in *null* fashion: "No significant difference will exist in productivity between workers as team members and workers as individual production line units." The null hypothesis tends to remove the element of prejudice toward an answer.

Does the null form seem more objective?

Whether you develop hypotheses statements is not of great importance. But you should be familiar with the use of hypotheses and their statement in null style.

To restate the hypothesis as a problem and purpose statement, you might say "The purpose of this study is to determine whether production will increase when employees are organized as teams as compared to their working as individuals in a production line." You have the option of using the hypothesis approach or the problem–purpose approach. In many ways, the purpose of a study is determined by the intended use of its results.

• Limiting the Problem

One of the major shortcomings of research planning is the failure to establish or to recognize desirable limitations. Assume, for instance, that you want to study clerical salaries. Imagine the scope of such a task. Millions of people are employed in clerical jobs. And perhaps a thousand or so different types of jobs fall into the clerical classification. To reduce such a problem to reasonable proportions, use the *what, why, when, where,* and *who* questions to limit the problem. Here's what you might come up with as the personnel manager at a metropolitan bank:

The "W" words help narrow report scope.

What:	A study of clerical salaries.
Why:	To determine whether salaries in our firm are competitive and consistent.
When:	Current.

Where: Our metropolitan area.
Who: Clerical employees in banks.

Now you can phrase the problem this way: "The purpose of this study is to survey clerical salaries in local banks to determine whether our salaries are competitive and consistent." Note that this process of reducing the problem to a workable size has also established some firm limits to the research. You've limited the problem to current salaries, to the local area, and to a particular type of business. Note, too, how important the *why* was in helping establish the limitations. Limiting the problem, to use a cliché, is "zeroing in on the problem."

• Defining Terms Clearly

Vague terms contribute greatly to faulty communication. Clearly in the study of clerical salaries, a comparison of one bank's salaries with those paid by others would be meaningful only if the information gathered from other banks relates to identical jobs. A job description defining the duties performed by a clerk-typist, for example, would help ensure that all firms would be talking about the same job tasks regardless of the job title.

Additionally, the term *salary* requires definition. Is it hourly, weekly, monthly, or yearly? Are benefits included? A conversion table would probably be necessary to provide consistency in converting amounts to appropriate pay periods. In all research, terms must be defined if they could be misleading.

Definition: A statement of what something is.

Selecting a Method of Solution

After defining the problem, the researcher will plan how to arrive at a solution. One or a combination of the following recognized research methods can be used to collect necessary information:

1. Library research
2. Survey research
3. Observational research
4. Experimental research

Library research uses *secondary* sources—material already created. Surveys, observational studies, and experiments also rely on methods designed to create their own information—*primary* sources.

• Doing Library Research

Does library research save time and effort?

Library research, as a part of all research studies, provides information about what others previously have done in the same field. It saves researchers the wasted time and effort of duplicating things that have already been undertaken. For example, computer-program indexes, periodicals, and books provide information about available programs, making creation of those programs unnecessary. A scientist working in the area of airborne navigation systems knows others have been and are working in the same area. By engaging in library research, the scientist can determine the boundaries of knowledge before proceeding into the unknown.

Figure 13.3 illustrates the constant development of knowledge. Within the confines (white area) of a field of knowledge, certain truths have been established. These truths are treated as principles and reported in textbooks and other publications. However, because knowledge is not static and is constantly expanding, the researcher knows that new information is available. The job, then, is to become familiar with the library, canvass the literature of the field, and attempt to redefine the boundaries of knowledge (shaded area). This redefinition is the function of library research. Researchers then explore the unknown (dark area). Through redefinition of boundaries, library research accomplishes the following objectives:

1. It establishes a point of departure for further research.
2. It avoids needless duplication of costly research efforts.
3. It reveals areas of needed research.

Why do universities have huge libraries?

One other point should be made: library research makes a real contribution to a body of knowledge.

Applied to business problems, library research involves the investigation of books, periodicals, and any records stored by the business because they might be needed for future information.

When beginning to collect data for a study, beware of one of the major deterrents to good reporting—the problem of collecting too much information. Although you want to be thorough, you don't want to collect and record such a large amount of information that you'll hardly know where to begin in your analysis. Try these suggestions to keep the volume at a minimum:

Good advice: protect yourself against too much material!

1. Use suggestive or cue notes.
2. Develop a card system.
3. Learn rather than accumulate.

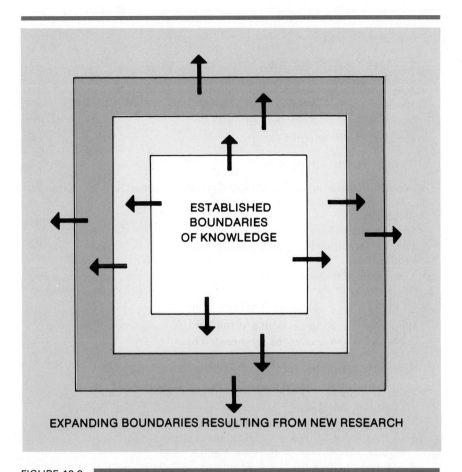

FIGURE 13.3
The constant expansion of the boundaries of knowledge.

Suggestive Note or Cue Note A suggestive or cue note is a reminder to yourself of something you wanted to recall. Whether you put these reminders on a single sheet of paper or on separate sheets or cards, the goal is to reduce bulky material to small, convenient-to-use data. Develop a system that satisfies your own needs.

Card System The card system is particularly useful for library work. Standard 3×5 or 5×8 cards are helpful. When library information is needed, go first to catalogs and readers' indexes to compile a basic bibliography. Become familiar with sources such as those shown in Figure 13.4. By making a complete bibliographical entry, you may save a return trip to the library. Note how the essential items are included in Figure 13.5.

On Locating Information

Business Periodicals Index
Education Index
New York Times Index
Readers' Guide to Periodical Literature
Social Science and Humanities Index
Wall Street Journal Index

General Factual Information

Statistical Abstract of the United States and other Bureau of the Census publications
Dictionary
Encyclopedia (*Americana* or *Brittanica*)
Fortune Directories of U.S. Corporations
World Atlas
The World Almanac and Fact Book

Biography

Who's Who in America (and a variety of sub–who's who's by geographic areas, industries, and professions)

Report Style and Format

Form and Style: Theses, Reports, Term Papers, by William Giles Campbell and Stephen V. Ballou, Houghton Mifflin Company
A Manual of Style, University of Chicago Press
MLA Handbook for Writers of Research Papers, Theses, and Dissertations, Modern Language Association
A Manual of Style for the Preparation of Papers and Reports, by Irwin M. Keithley, South-Western Publishing Company
A Manual for Writers of Term Papers, Theses, and Dissertations, by Kate L. Turabian, University of Chicago Press
Style Guide: Publications Manual of the American Psychological Association
Style Manual for Written Communications, by Arno Knapper and Loda Newcomb, Grid, Inc.

FIGURE 13.4
Useful reference and source books.

Definitions   423.166

Flexner, Stuart B. (ed.). Family Word Finder. Pleasantville,
N.Y.: The Reader's Digest Association, 1975. pp. 896.

p. 161--communicate (verb). make known, inform of, announce,
apprise of, tell, notify, advise, pass on, convey, disclose,
divulge, reveal, relate, bring word, proclaim, broadcast,
publish, publicize; state, declare, say, mention; show, exhibit,
signify. . . . Antonyms: keep secret, hush up, suppress,
repress, withhold, hold back, cover up.

FIGURE 13.5

Cue card showing classification, bibliographical reference, and noted material.

You can make notes from each reference in the form of direct quotes or as paraphrases (putting the information in your own words). Put quoted material in quotation marks as a reminder. When paraphrasing, be extremely careful not to change the author's intended meaning. Also indicate on your card the page numbers from which cited material is taken. This step may save you another trip to the library. The call number of the reference is a time saver, incidentally, when you must return to the reference.

If you work with numerous references, develop a subject classification as a help in keeping like materials together. You might even begin a card file to be built over time.

As an admonition, give credit where credit is due when using the work of others. Many students who have been accused of cheating because of plagiarism can vouch for the benefits of documenting the work of others. Giving footnote and bibliography credit demonstrates integrity and a sense of scholarship. Not to do so is foolish.

Goal of Library Research   The primary purpose of library research is to *learn*, not to accumulate. The following technique is especially effective: (1) read an article rapidly, (2) put it aside, (3) list main and supporting points *from memory*, and (4) review the article to see whether all significant points have been included. Rapid reading forces concentration. Taking notes from memory reinforces learning and reduces the temptation to rely heavily on the words of others. If you really learn the subject matter of one source, you will (as research progresses)

Summarizing is a special ability.

see the relationship between it and other sources. You will see yourself growing toward mastery of the subject.

• Doing Normative Survey Research

Normative survey research determines the status of something at a specific time. It uses survey instruments such as questionnaires, opinionnaires, checklists, and interviews to obtain information. Election-time opinion polls represent one type of normative survey research. The term *normative* is used to qualify surveys because surveys reveal "norms" or "standards" existing at the time of the survey. An election poll taken two months before an election might have little similarity to one taken the week before the election.

Is the Census used to establish allocation of Representatives in Congress?

Surveys can help verify the accuracy of existing norms. The U.S. Census is conducted every decade to establish an actual population figure, and each person is supposedly counted. In effect, the census tests the accuracy of prediction techniques used to estimate population during the years between censuses. A survey of what employees consider a fair benefits package would be effective only for the date of the survey. People retire, move, and change their minds often; these human traits make survey research of human opinion somewhat tentative. Yet, surveys remain a valuable tool for gathering information on which to base policy making and decision making.

Validity and Reliability   Whether a survey involves personal interviewing or the distribution of items such as checklists or questionnaires, some principles of procedure and preplanning are common to both methods. These principles assure the researcher that the data gathered will be both valid and reliable. Data are *valid* (said to possess *validity*) when they measure what they are supposed to measure. Data are *reliable* (said to possess *reliability*) when they give assurance that they are reasonably close to the truth; that is, when they measure accurately.

Is the Census both reliable and valid because everyone is counted?

Validity generally results from careful planning of questionnaire or interview questions (*items*). Cautious wording, preliminary testing of items to detect misunderstanding, and some statistical techniques are helpful in determining whether the responses to the items are valid.

Reliability results from asking a large enough sample of people so that the researcher is reasonably assured the results would be the same even if more people were asked to respond. For example, if you were to ask ten people to react to a questionnaire item, the results might vary considerably. If you were to add ninety more people to the sample, the results might tend to reach a point of stability, where more responses would not change the results. Reliability would then be assured.

Use of Sampling   In all surveys, the research assumes that the people asked to respond are either representative of a larger group or constitute the entire group that is to be surveyed and about whom generalizations are to be made. The researcher normally can't survey everyone in the population. However, through sampling techniques, the researcher can be confident that only a small part of the total population can fairly represent the total population. *Sampling,* then, is a survey technique that saves the time and trouble of questioning 100 percent of the population.

The sampling process is based on the principle that a sufficiently large number drawn at random from a population will be representative of the total population; that is, the sampling group will possess the same characteristics in the same proportions as the total population. For example, public-opinion polls actually survey only a few people; but they are considered valid if the sample of people surveyed has the same percentage of butchers, housewives, Democrats, Republicans, cabdrivers, schoolteachers, retired persons, mothers, and so on, as the entire population does.

Sampling is thus a vital part of effective surveys. If, for example, you survey the members of the class on the value of this course, you will have surveyed the entire population—all the members of the class. Results would be reliable because you would not plan to make generalizations about a larger population from this limited information.

When sampling methods may be necessary because of the size of the population involved, several options are available. These include (1) random sampling, (2) stratified random sampling, and (3) systematic random sampling.

1. Random sampling is perhaps the most desirable technique. To determine the career plans of a college student body, a researcher could use random sampling by putting the name of each student on a small piece of paper, tossing all the names into a container, mixing them, and drawing out a preselected number to include in the survey. Of course, the registrar's computer could be programmed to provide a random list as well. Because the entire student body is included, each name would have an equal opportunity to be drawn.

2. Stratified random sampling is the method public-opinion poll organizations should use. In surveying the student body using this method, you would continue to draw names at random until you

> How large is the Census population? Would sampling be effective?

> Does random imply chance?

have the same percentage of seniors, juniors, sophomores, and freshmen as are in the total student population. If 1,000 students in the total student body of 10,000, composed of 30 percent freshmen, 27 percent sophomores, 23 percent juniors, and 20 percent seniors, are to be included, you should draw names until you had 300 freshmen, 270 sophomores, 230 juniors, and 200 seniors. You could program other characteristics into your sample as well.

3. Systematic random sampling is a form of random sampling in which, to use our college survey as an example again, every tenth name might be drawn from the files of the registrar. To ensure randomness, you would place in a hat numbers 0–9 and then draw one. If 7 is drawn, for example, you would use the seventh name in the files, then the 17th, 27th, 37th, and so on until you have the number you wanted to include.

These techniques are used in surveys that attempt to determine shopper preferences, buying habits, attitudes, and similar marketing studies. Again, of course, the researcher must be cautious about drawing conclusions from a sample and applying them to a population that might not be represented by the sample. For example, early-morning shoppers may differ from afternoon or evening shoppers, young ones may differ from old ones, men may differ from women. The good researcher defines the population as distinctly as possible and uses a sampling technique to ensure that the sample is representative.

Achieving sophistication in surveys requires considerable study of the field. Findings are only as reliable and valid as are the methods of selecting and surveying the sample.

Why are public opinion polls often inaccurate?

Even when the sampling technique results in a representative sample, the construction of the survey instrument—usually a questionnaire or interview guide—is critical to the process. Special attention is given to development of questionnaires and other survey instruments later in this chapter.

• Doing Observational Research

Observational, or statistical, research describes research involving statistical analysis of one or more sets of data. Suppose we wanted to know whether scores on college aptitude tests really had any relationship to grades made in a college history course. We would gather the grades of students in the history class, obtain the college aptitude scores of those same students, and perform statistical correlations of the two sets of data to seek information about the relationship.

Frequently, businesses use both observational and survey methods to solve problems. Market analysts may use survey methods to determine buying habits of certain income groups. Then statistical analyses are used to determine the most desirable markets.

The name *observational research* is used because this type of analysis involves observing certain phenomena to assist in establishing new principles. Several studies have used the observational method to determine the differences between "good" or "bad" business letters. One study used a random sample of 500 letters obtained from the files of various companies. Copies of the 500 letters were sent to five experts in written communication who served as a rating jury. Each jury member was asked to sort the letters into five sets. The first set was to include the 100 best letters in the jurist's opinion; the second set, the second-best 100; the third set, the middle 100; and so on. The reports of the five jury members were then combined to determine the 100 letters with the highest ratings and the 100 with the lowest ratings. Three hundred letters fell in the middle and were discarded. Thus only the best and worst 100 remained. Then, the two groups of letters were analyzed in terms of planning, writing style, tone, sentence length, spelling, punctuation, and length. Statistical tests of significant differences between the two groups were used to determine the characteristic differences between good and bad letters. In this study, the observational method was used because certain phenomena were observed, counted, and analyzed statistically to help establish principles.

Are traffic-flow studies observational?

• Doing Experimental Research

Experimental research is familiar to most of us as the test-tube research conducted in a laboratory by a scientist wearing a white smock. Scientists are conducting experimental research when they put exactly the same materials into two test tubes and then add one new ingredient to only one of the two original tubes. After the new ingredient is added to one tube, the changes that take place in that tube are measured. Any change is due, of course, to the addition of the new ingredient.

Basically, then, *experimental research* involves two samples that have exactly the same ingredients before a variable is added to one of the samples. The differences observed are due to the variable.

Comparing results of treatment with medicines to results using placebos is experimental.

How is experimental research used in business? As a simple example, assume an office has a great number of clerk-typists doing the same routine job. Management decides to make a study of the effects of incentive pay (extra pay for production in excess of a minimum standard). It separates the clerk-typists into two groups about equal in experience, skill, and previous productivity rates. Then one group is placed on an incentive-pay basis. During the period of the study, the difference in the two groups is noted. Because the incentive pay is assumed to be the only variable, any difference is attributed to its influence. Of course, we can criticize such a study; but the point is that the business used the experimental research method just as the laboratory scientist used it.

Collecting Data Through Surveys

Although selecting an appropriate population sample may seem difficult at times, obtaining responses to questionnaires and other survey instruments may seem even more difficult. For surveys conducted by mail, responses often represent only a small percentage of the total mailings. In some cases, a return of 3 to 5 percent is considered adequate and is planned for by researchers. In other cases, depending on the population, the sample, and the information requested, a return of considerably more than half the mailings might be a planned result. Here are some of the problems with which researchers must cope in conducting surveys:

Why is a 5% response sometimes adequate?

1. Questionnaire surveys by mail are inexpensive and not limited geographically. Respondents may remain anonymous, which might result in honest answers, and a mailed survey removes difference-in-status barriers—a corporation president may respond readily when the researcher might never succeed in getting a response by phone or by personal interview. At the same time, mail survey instruments must be concise or they'll end in the wastebasket. Most people who respond have strong feelings about the topic, so this group of respondents might not be representative of the intended population. Researchers must prepare persuasive transmittal messages that indicate how the respondent can benefit by answering. That persuasion often takes the form of a gift for answering.

2. Personal interviews allow the interviewer to obtain answers in depth and perhaps to explore otherwise sensitive topics. But interviews are expensive in terms of time and money if interviewers are to be paid, and many people simply don't want to be interviewed.

3. Telephone interviews are inexpensive as a rule. But like mailed questionnaires, a low percentage of total phone calls will actually provide wanted information.

4. Participant observation is frequently used in consumer research with the observer simply noting how people seem to make selections. A problem, of course, is that observation is sight only and does not give clues about judgment or analytic processes.

No matter which survey technique or combination of techniques is used, the way in which the survey instrument is designed and written has much to do with response validity and reliability, percentage of response, and quality of information received.

• Designing Questionnaires

Before formulating items for a questionnaire or opinionnaire, a researcher should attempt to visualize the ways in which responses will be assembled and included in a final report. Here are some suggestions for effective questionnaires:

1. The sequence of items should be logical; if possible, the sequence should proceed from easy-to-answer to difficult-to-answer items. A difficult opening question might result in a wasted mailing; easy items get respondents involved and encourage them to finish.

2. Items that concern the same subject should be grouped for easy answering and tabulation. For example, demographic data such as name, age, gender, family size, and income are often requested. They are easy to answer and often provide background for analysis of other responses. If these items are not necessarily critical, you should indicate that answers to certain ones are optional.

3. Ask for factual information whenever possible. Opinions may be needed in certain studies, but opinions may change from day to day. As a general rule, too, the smaller the sample, the less reliable are conclusions based on opinions.

4. Short-answer items are easy to tabulate. Make answering easy, then. Respondents like items that may be answered by merely making a check mark or circling a response.

   Ease your own workload by making tabulating easy.

5. Provide enough space for respondents to answer essay-type questions. "What effect would an additional tax on oil and natural gas have on the economy?" may require a lengthy answer.

6. Ask for information that can be recalled readily. To ask for information going back in time may not result in sound data.

7. Test the wording of items with others before preparing a final survey instrument. Test for clarity, ease of answering, and quality of answers.

8. Mailed questionnaires have higher percentages of returns when a return envelope with postage paid is included.

Gathering Demographic Data   Researchers often find their studies require information about groups of respondents. For example, a survey of prospective buyers of Mercedes Benz automobiles would certainly be strengthened if the respondents all could afford luxury cars. Should you find yourself in need of such information as income and age, arrange your questionnaire items so you can arrive at an average age and income for the total population. For example, the following questionnaire item asks for household income:

Please check the blank that best describes your household income:

Could these items also be listed from high to low?

1. $10,000–19,999 _____
2. 20,000–29,999 _____
3. 30,000–39,999 _____
4. 40,000–49,999 _____
5. 50,000–59,999 _____
6. 60,000–69,999 _____
7. 70,000–79,999 _____
8. 80,000–89,999 _____
9. 90,000–99,999 _____
10. 100,000 and over _____

Ten possible answers are included only for discussion purposes; normally a few with broader ranges would be adequate. By using ranges such as $50,000–$59,999, all the replies falling into that category could be assumed to be distributed equally throughout the range. In this case, the midpoint of the range—$55,000—could represent all incomes in the range.

People prefer to reply with check marks and within ranges simply because doing so is easy. Questions about age might be arranged in the following manner:

Please check the blank for your age group:

20–29   _____
30–39   _____
40–49   _____

50–59	_____
60–69	_____
70–79	_____
80 and over	_____

In this example, people whose ages are between 20.0 and 29.99 years would check 20–29, and the assumed age for everyone in that group would be the midpoint, 25.0.

Wording of Items Items requiring yes–no or agree–disagree responses should provide an opportunity for those who are undecided to respond, as in

Should the city have a sales tax? Yes _____ No _____

Undecided _____

Items should be tested to avoid wording that might put people in awkward positions, as in

Have you stopped abusing your spouse? Yes _____ No _____

Undecided _____

Should items also be tested for clarity?

Avoid "skip-and-jump" instructions; such as, "If you answered yes to 4, skip directly to 9; if you answered no, explain your reason under 5 and 6." Note how the portion of a questionnaire shown in Figure 13.6 makes responding easy.

• Designing Rating Scales

Rating scales are similar to questionnaires because they pose problems or questions that can be responded to simply. Suppose you want to determine the most pressing problems facing employees in a production line. You could ask them to list the problems, but the responses might be so ambiguous that tabulating them would be impossible. A rating scale such as the following one would be an improvement.

For each of the following problems, please circle the degree to which the problem affects you:

Acceptance by others

1	2	3	4	5	6

| Little effect | | Moderate effect | | Great effect | |

MARKETING SURVEY OF STEREO
PURCHASING PREFERENCES

Please check the appropriate space in each of the items:

Your Age Group (1)

a. under 20 _____

b. 20–29 _____

c. 30–39 _____

d. 40–49 _____

e. 50–59 _____

f. Over 59 _____

Your Occupation (2)

a. Student _____

b. White Collar _____

c. Blue Collar _____

d. Professional _____

e. Retired _____

f. Unemployed _____

g. Other _____

Your Gender (3) a. Female _____ b. Male _____

Marital Status (4) a. Married _____ b. Single _____

Household Income Group (5)

a. Below $10,000 _____

b. $10,000–19,999 _____

c. $20,000–29,999 _____

d. $30,000–39,999 _____

e. $40,000–49,999 _____

f. $50,000+ _____

Do you presently own a stereo? (6) a. Yes _____ b. No _____

If not, do you plan to purchase one? (7) a. Yes _____ b. No _____
c. Undecided _____

If you have a system, do you plan to add to it within the next year? (8)
a. Yes _____ b. No _____ c. Uncertain _____

If you own a stereo system, please check the appropriate spaces in the
following items:

FIGURE 13.6

Portion of a questionnaire keyed for computer input.

Your Estimate of the Value of Your Present System (9)

a. Under $200 _____

b. $201–400 _____

c. $401–600 _____

d. $601–800 _____

e. $801–1000 _____

f. $1001–1200 _____

g. Over $1200 _____

FIGURE 13.6
(continued)

Interest in the job

1	2	3	4	5	6
Little effect		Moderate effect		Great effect	

Note that six numbers have been used to indicate how respondents feel. When an odd number of choices, such as five, is provided, respondents tend to converge toward the middle number, thus perhaps creating a bias in the responses.

Similar information could be obtained by listing the potential problems and by asking respondents to rank the problems in order of their importance:

Please rank the following problems in order of their importance to you. Place a 1 in the space following the most important problem, a 2 in the space following the second most important problem; proceed in this manner until all have been ranked. Two blank lines have been left for you to write in a problem area that may have been omitted.

Acceptance by others _____

Interest in the job _____

Economic security _____

Concern for health _____

_____ _____

_____ _____

Does convergence toward the middle say something about human nature?

Even though most of us are familiar with ranking scales because we have encountered them both at work and at school, when we do use them in research, we should first test them on a small sample to see if they are clearly understood and produce the kind of information sought.

To determine which of the problems is most critical to the production employee, a *forced answer* question can be used:

Of all the problems listed, which is the <u>single</u> most critical problem for you personally? _____

_____

This question could also have been posed in multiple-choice form, much like the multiple-choice items used in school tests:

Which of the following problems is the <u>single</u> most critical problem for you personally? Please check.

a. Acceptance by others   _____
b. Interest in the job   _____
c. Economic security   _____
d. Concern for health   _____
e. Other   _____

Researchers must select from the several choices available the one best suited to the situation. Criteria for selecting one alternative over the others might include the following: Which format leaves the least chance for misinterpretation? Which format provides information in the way it can best be used? Can it be tabulated easily? Can it be cross referenced to other items in the survey instrument?

Organizing the Data

Having decided on a method, researchers must outline a step-by-step approach to the solution of the problem. The human mind is an inquiring mind. But it is also susceptible to digressions. Although these may be short-lived, they distract from the job at hand; and, if given free rein, they can lead to obliteration of the real object of the study.

Therefore, *keep on the right track*. Plan the study and follow the plan. Question every step for its contribution to the objective. Keep a record of actions. In a formal research study, the researcher is expected to make a complete report. Another qualified person should be able to make the same study, use the same steps, and arrive at the same conclusion. Thus, a report serves as a guide.

Tabulation techniques should be used to reduce quantitative data such as numerous answers to questionnaire items. Suppose we have made a survey and have collected several hundred replies to a twenty- or thirty-item questionnaire in addition to many cards or notes from library sources. What do we do next? As shown in Figure 13.7, the report process is one of reducing the information collected to a size that can be handled conveniently in a written message.

Does tabulating serve the same purpose as cue cards in library research?

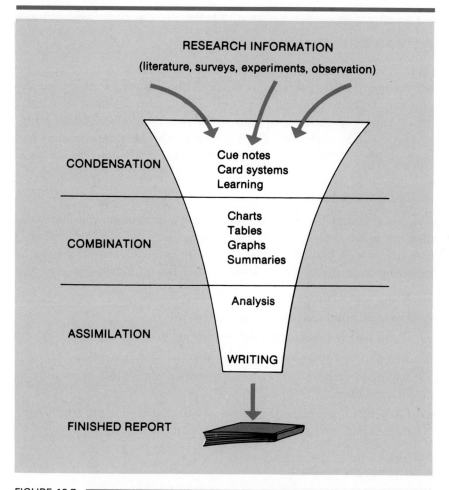

RESEARCH INFORMATION
(literature, surveys, experiments, observation)

CONDENSATION
Cue notes
Card systems
Learning

COMBINATION
Charts
Tables
Graphs
Summaries

Analysis

ASSIMILATION

WRITING

FINISHED REPORT

FIGURE 13.7
The report process.

Visualize the report process as taking place in a huge funnel. At the top of the funnel, pour in all the original information. Then, through a process of compression within the funnel, take these steps:

Is it easier to read 300 separate questionnaires or a few tables?

1. Evaluate the information for its usefulness.
2. Reduce the useful information through the use of suggestive notes, card systems, or learning.
3. Combine like information into understandable form through the use of tables, charts, graphs, and summaries.
4. Report in written form what remains.

Arriving at an Answer

Even if valid and reliable data have been collected, a report can be worthless if the interpretation is faulty. Although success at interpretation may be closely related to mental ability, even the most intelligent person cannot be expected to draw sound conclusions from faulty information. Sound conclusions can be drawn only when information has been properly (1) collected and (2) interpreted.

• Collecting Data

If acceptable data-gathering techniques have been employed, data will measure what they are intended to measure (have validity) and will measure it well (have reliability). Some common errors at the data-gathering stage that seriously hamper later interpretation are

Poor sampling spoils the analysis.

1. Using samples that are too small.
2. Using samples that are not representative.
3. Using poorly constructed data-gathering instruments.
4. Using information from biased sources.
5. Failing to gather enough information to cover all important aspects of a problem.
6. Gathering too much information and then attempting to use all of it even though some may be irrelevant.

• Interpreting Data

If we avoid data-collecting errors, we are more likely to reach sound conclusions. But sound conclusions are unlikely if interpretation is faulty. Some common mental errors seriously handicap the interpretation of data:

1. *Trying, consciously or unconsciously, to make results conform to a prediction or desire.* Seeing predictions come true may be pleasing, but objectivity is much more important. Facts should determine conclusions.

2. *Hoping for spectacular results.* People often need ego satisfaction. But an attempt to astonish our superiors by preparing a report with revolutionary conclusions can only have a negative effect on accuracy.

3. *Attempting to compare when commonality is absent.* Concluding that a certain product would sell well in Arizona because it sold well in Massachusetts would be risky. Because of differences in geography, climate, and economic factors, relationships might not be at all comparable.

4. *Assuming a cause–effect relationship when one does not exist.* A company president may have been in office one year and sales may have doubled. But the sales might have doubled *in spite* of the president rather than *because* of her.

5. *Failing to consider important factors.* A college professor returned from a tour of the educational institutions in Mexico. Speaking to a group of high school teachers, he cautioned against modifying the school curriculum to include four years of science and math, four years of foreign language, four years of social studies, and four years of English. That curriculum, he said, is Mexico's curriculum, and in Mexico last night two-thirds of the babies went to bed hungry. He apparently neglected to consider the influence of such factors as geography, climate, natural resources, tradition, and politics.

6. *Basing a conclusion on lack of evidence.* "We have had no complaints about our present policy" does not mean that the policy is appropriate. And, conversely, lack of evidence that a proposed project will succeed does not necessarily mean that it will fail. The old adage that "No news is good news" is not applicable in research.

7. *Assuming constancy of human behavior.* A survey indicating 60 percent of the public favors one political party over the other in March does not mean the same thing will be true in November. Because some people paid their bills late last year does not mean a company should refuse to sell to them the next year. The reasons for slow payment may have been removed.

The women's basketball team has won every game since you began attending. Is it a coincidence or your influence?

Keep in mind the differences in some research terms as you analyze your material and attempt to seek meaning from it. A *finding* from a research study is a specific, measurable fact:

. . . *67 percent of those interviewed preferred steel-belted, white-wall tires.*

. . . *average daily temperature in July is 89° in New Orleans and 70° in San Francisco.*

A *conclusion* is derived from findings:

. . . *steel-belted, white-wall tires are preferred.*

. . . *the temperature of San Francisco meets the needs of XYZ Company.*

When you select one item from among several, you may have findings about each related to cost, weight, manufacturer service after the sale, and any number of other criteria. Your conclusion from these findings may be "Item G meets my needs best."

A *recommendation* is simply a suggested action based on your research. Recommendations are not a part of every report and should be included only when requested or when they seem to be a natural outcome of the research. In effect, a finding is factual, a conclusion is drawn from findings, and a recommendation evolves from the conclusions and the nature of the problem.

Summary

In arriving at an answer (a conclusion), report writers must have the results of their research before them. They should be able to see the problem as a whole. If they carefully defined the problem, selected an appropriate method of research, and gathered and analyzed the data, they can arrive at a sound conclusion. Throughout the entire process, however, researchers must protect themselves not only against their own human failings but also against their material. This process is the essence of objectivity. As you approach the report-writing task, your success will rest primarily on your ability to retain your objectivity.

About Language and Usage

Note how the following suffixes can expand on or change the meaning of root words:

Suffix	Meaning	Example
-ful	filled or full	thankful
		spoonful
-hood	condition or character	childhood
		likelihood
-less	without	faultless
		painless
-ly	like, similar	saintly
		godly
-meter	measure	thermometer
		speedometer
-ship	condition or skill	friendship
		marksmanship
-some	tendency or trend	bothersome
		winsome

Exercises

Review Questions

1. Why do reports generally travel upward in an organization?
2. How do informational and analytical reports differ?
3. In a bank, the internal auditing division performs semiannual audits of each branch. Then the audit reports are sent to the bank's chief executive officer and chief financial officer and to the manager of the audited branch. The purpose of the audits is to determine whether policies and practices are properly followed. Into what report classifications might the audit report fall? Explain.
4. How do the four steps in problem solving apply when the driver of an automobile realizes a tire is going flat rapidly?
5. How might a null hypothesis be stated for a research study attempting to determine whether television or newspaper advertising has greater influence on cereal sales?
6. How does library research make a contribution to all studies?

7. Gathering so much information that the researcher is "snowed under" by the amount is often a barrier to good reporting. How might researchers protect themselves against the possibility?

8. Distinguish between "reliability" and "validity."

9. What is meant by "random sampling"?

10. What type of research is characterized by efforts to measure the effect of a variable added to one of two samples?

11. What questions might you ask of someone who wants assistance in planning a questionnaire survey to determine automobile-owner satisfaction with certain after-the-sale services provided by dealers?

12. Why is an even number of rating scale responses supposedly better than an odd number?

13. Of the data-collection errors, which are directly related to construction of data-gathering instruments?

14. How does the assumption that human beings behave in consistent manners over time present a danger in data interpretation?

Activities

1. For each of the following research topics, write a positive hypothesis and then restate it as a null hypothesis. Thus, you have two items to write for each topic. Solutions to topic (a) are given.

   a. A study to determine the relationship existing between the FOG Index readability rating of business textbooks and student interest in courses using the textbooks.

   Hypothesis: Students show more interest in courses using textbooks with low FOG Indexes than in courses using textbooks with high FOG Indexes.

   Null Hypothesis: Readability levels of course textbooks have no relationship to student interest in those courses. *Or:* No relationship exists between readability of textbooks and student interest in courses using those textbooks.

   b. A study to determine whether people's net worth at age 50 is directly related to education.

   c. A study to determine functional business areas from which chief executive officers advanced in their organizations. Functional areas are legal, financial, accounting, marketing, production, and other.

2. What factors might limit or influence your findings in any of the studies in Activity 1? Could you apply the findings of Activity 1 studies to a broader population than those included in the studies? Why or why not?

3. What research method would you use for each of the research problems included in Activity 1?

4. If you were to conduct a survey of the 14,000 homeowners in a community of 40,000 people, describe how you might construct a sampling procedure to avoid having to survey the entire population.

5. "A course in economics should be taken by every college student" is a statement frequently made and also frequently challenged. Could this statement be tested through research? If so, what kind of research? Comment.

For the research studies in Activities 6 to 10, prepare a one-page description of your attack on the problem. Use the following headings for the problem assigned:

Statement of the Problem

Research Method and Sources of Information

Nature of Data to Be Gathered and Analyzed

Hypothesis or Hypotheses to Be Proved or Disproved (if feasible)

Think ahead to the nature of the questionnaire or other type of research instrument or technique you might use.

6. As research director of Glow-Stern, a stock brokerage firm, you have the task of determining investment practices for your clients. Your goal is to learn how different age groups manage their investment or savings dollars. Because this subject could be quite sensitive to many clients, your survey is to be anonymous. You've also decided that your age groups should be adults under the age of 30, people between 30 and 50, and those over 50.

7. As marketing director of Club Carib, proprietor of a chain of resort hotels in the Caribbean, you want to determine what former customers liked and disliked about their vacations at your resorts.

8. McDonald's fast-food company plans to open a new outlet in one of three possible locations: (1) on an interstate highway, (2) in a downtown shopping district, (3) in a neighborhood shopping mall. All locations are within a 3-mile radius of the center of a city. You are to submit a recommendation.

9. As marketing promotion director for the Ajax Cosmetics Company, you are planning to advertise your new line of high-priced cosmetics in either *Vogue* or *Cosmopolitan* magazine. Only one can be selected because of budget. You plan to run ads of a full page in color for the next 12 months.

10. As promotion-advertising director of City First Thrift and Loan, you have the job of determining whether the firm should give gift certificates or actual gifts (of items such as calculators, pens, or hand kitchen mixers) as incentives to encourage people to open accounts. In either case, the incentives cannot exceed a value of $5 for each $1,000 deposited in the new account.

CHAPTER 14

Managing Data and Using Graphics

We must think things, not words, or at least we must constantly translate our words into the facts for which they stand, if we are to keep the real and the true.

OLIVER WENDELL HOLMES

fter the problem has been defined, the method of research re-
fined, and the data gathered, the next step is to prepare the
written research report. In many cases, putting the research
study in written form may be quite simple; in others, however, the
amount of data gathered may present a major problem for the researcher. To analyze voluminous amounts of data requires some techniques and approaches that "protect" researchers against being overwhelmed by data.

Managing Quantitative Data

In many studies, particularly those involved with surveys, many of the
data gathered lend themselves to statistical analysis. A number of people
respond "yes," another number respond "no," and another number
respond "no opinion" to a questionnaire item. Whether these responses
are counted manually or by computer, the counting process is called
tabulation; and tabulation must precede analysis. Assume for example
that you have been given a stack of 200 or 300 questionnaires containing people's responses to several items. To tabulate the responses manually, you would probably make a list of the items, go through each
questionnaire visually, and make a pencil mark to show the response to
each item.

Tabulating would provide you with a single page showing total
responses for each possible response to each item. For example, responses for a preferred color might appear like this following the tabulation of 300 questionnaires:

Red	75
Blue	60
Yellow	54
Green	42
Orange	30
Brown	24
Others	15
	300

This breakdown reduces 300 responses to a manageable size. The
tabulation shows only seven items, each with a specific number of responses from the total of 300 questionnaires. Because people tend to
make comparisons during analysis, the totals are helpful. But people

generally want to know proportions or ratios, and these are best presented as percentage parts of the total. Thus, convert the number tabulations to percentages, as follows:

Color	Number	Percent
Red	75	25
Blue	60	20
Yellow	54	18
Green	42	14
Orange	30	10
Brown	24	8
Others	15	5
	300	100

Does the percent
column simplify your
analysis?

Now analyzing the data becomes relatively easy. One of every four
people preferred red; five out of eight preferred red, blue, or yellow.
Another observation could be that almost half selected either red or
blue, depending on how exactly you intend to interpret the percentages.

This analysis first reduced 300 questionnaire responses to seven
tabulated categories. The total response of 300 was reduced to 100
percent, and the 100 percent was further talked about in terms of ratios
or fractions such as one out of four or three out of four. In research
about people's opinions, likes, preferences, and other subjective items,
rounding off statistics to fractions helps paint a clear picture for readers.
In actuality, if this question were asked again a day or two later of the
same group of people, a few would probably have changed their minds.
If someone who had indicated red as the preferred color was ticketed the
next day for going through a red light, that person might well develop a
dislike for red.

• Common Language

Fractions, ratios, and percentages are often called examples of common
language. In effect, they reduce difficult figures to the "common denomi-
nators" of language and ideas. Although "60 out of 300 prefer the color
blue" is somewhat easy to understand, "20 percent prefer the color
blue" is even easier, and "one out of five prefers the color blue" is really
understandable.

Common language also involves the use of indicators other than
actual count or quantity. The Dow-Jones industrial averages accurately
describe stock market performance and are certainly easier to understand than the complete New York Stock Exchange figures for 2,000

Are school letter
grades common
language?

stocks. "Freight car loadings" are weight measurements used in railroad terminology rather than "pounds carried," and oil is counted in barrels rather than in the quart or gallon sizes purchased by consumers. Because of inflation, dollars are not very accurate items to use as comparisons from one year to another in certain areas; for example, automobile manufacturers use "automobile units" to represent production changes in the industry. The important thing for the report writer to remember is that reports are communication mediums and everything possible should be done to make sure communication occurs.

• Measures of Central Tendency

Measures of central tendency are simple statistical treatments of distributions of quantitative data that attempt to find a single figure to describe the entire distribution. The three most commonly used measures are the mean, the median, and the mode.

The mean is the arithmetic average.

The Mean   The *mean* is the figure obtained when all the values in a distribution (table of values) are totaled and divided by the number of values. If, for example, eight people score values of 60, 65, 70, 75, 80, 85, 90, and 95 on a test, the total of these values is 620. Dividing 620 by 8 gives a mean of 77.5. Most people would call 77.5 the average score, but *mean* is a more accurate term. When material is tabulated by classes, such as "10 people scored between 80 and 89," statisticians would take the midpoint—84.5—and multiply it by 10 to get a total score for that class. Doing the same for other classes would provide a total for all those in the tabulation. Dividing the total of all classes by the number of scores would provide a group mean. Placing scores in classes is not much different from totaling them separately. To determine the mean is simply a process of totaling all values and dividing by the number whether totaled by classes or by individual scores.

The median is the middle or midpoint.

The Median   The *median* is the middle value in a distribution. For example, values of 20, 65, 70, 75, 80, 85, and 100 in a distribution would have 75 as the median. In this case, using the median might be more descriptive than would a mean because the very low score of 20 would not influence the measure of central tendency. In a case, for example, where nine people each earn $10,000 and a tenth person earns $110,000, the median is $10,000—a far better descriptive value for the ten people than a mean of $20,000.

When values are counted in classes, find the middle score or value by counting from the top down or from the bottom up to the class containing the middle value. Roughly speaking, that class could then be described as the median class.

The Mode   The *mode* is the value found most frequently in a distribution. For example, ten test scores of 65, 70, 75, 75, 75, 80, 85, 90, 90, and 100 would have a mode of 75—the most frequent score. The mean would be the total 805 divided by 10, or 80.5. The median would be halfway between 75 and 80—the fifth and sixth scores of the ten—or 77.5. In this case, either the mean or the median would be an acceptable and more desirable measure than the mode.

The mode is the most common value.

In general, the mean is the most stable of these three measures and will usually fluctuate less than the other two. As a result, the mean is used in calculating standard deviations and is extremely reliable when distributions are large. Even a person 150 years of age or with an income of $1,000,000 would not affect the mean very much in a distribution of several hundred people. In small distributions the median is often a good indicator, especially when some very high or very low extreme values would influence the mean.

These simple statistical measures help report writers describe the content and meaning of their tables and graphs. These measures are part of the common language of statistics and are especially efficient and effective in reporting to people who understand their meanings. Good judgment on the part of the report writer should determine which measure to use or whether to use one at all.

The Range   When researchers first glance at a distribution, they probably look for the *range*—the difference between the lowest and highest values. For example, test scores of 20, 30, 75, 75, 75, 80, 85, 90, and 95 would have a range of 20 to 95, or 76 points (95 − 20 + 1, to count both the 20 and the 95).

High minus low plus one = range.

The range helps a researcher determine how many classes should be used in tabulating large numbers of values. In general, a first glance at the range reveals the extremes of values and assists in data analysis.

Some researchers use the *interquartile range*—the spread of the middle 50 percent of the values—as a form of central tendency measurement. For example, in a distribution such as 7, 19, 21, 23, 24, 25, 29, and 41, the interquartile range is 21 to 25. Because eight items are included, two are in each quarter of the distribution. The two middle quartiles, the middle half, has the figures 21, 23, 24, and 25. Even though the total range is 7 to 41, the interquartile range shows that most figures are grouped tightly. Thus, the extreme values of 7 (the low) and 41 (the high) become less important.

Using Tables and Graphics

Managing data effectively protects a report writer from being overwhelmed by the data collected. To protect readers from also being overwhelmed, report writers must select appropriate means of presenting the data. "One picture is worth a thousand words" is an old but meaningful saying. Material that can be reported in a table, picture, graph, or chart will make your written analysis of it clearer to the reader. Imagine trying to put in composition style all the information available in a modern financial statement. Several hundred pages might be necessary to explain all the material that could otherwise be contained in three or four pages of balance sheets and profit and loss statements. And even then, the reader would no doubt be thoroughly confused! Graphics go hand in hand with the written discussion to achieve clarity. As you proceed through the remainder of this chapter, ask yourself if the discussion would be effective if the accompanying graphic figures were not included.

• Tables

A *table* is a presentation of data in column form. Very simply, 2 plus 3 plus 5 plus 6 plus 11 equals 27 is better represented

Is the addition format also common language?

$$
\begin{array}{r}
2 \\
3 \\
5 \\
6 \\
\underline{11} \\
27
\end{array}
$$

Typically, the preparation of tables is concerned with labeling techniques to make the content clear. Here are some helpful practices in table preparation:

1. Number tables and all other graphics consecutively throughout the report. This practice enables you to refer to "Figure 1" rather than to "the following table" or "the figure on the following page."

Incidentally, the term *figure* should be used to identify all tables, graphs, pictures, and charts. In this chapter, for example, note that all illustrations are identified as figures.

2. Give each table a title that is complete enough to clarify what is included without forcing the reader to review the table. Table titles may be quite long and even extend beyond one line. A two-line title should be arranged on the page so that neither line extends into the margins. The second line should be shorter than the first and centered under it. Titles may contain sources of data, numbers included in the table, and the subject; for example, "Base Salaries of Chief Executives of the 200 Largest Financial Institutions in the United States." Titles may be written in either uppercase or lowercase letters.

    Detailed titles improve communication.

3. Label columns of data clearly enough to identify the items. Usually, column headings are short and easily arranged. If, however, they happen to be lengthy, use some ingenuity in planning the arrangement.

4. Labels for the rows (horizontal items) in a table are easy to arrange with two exceptions. First, if the label requires more than one line, indent the second line two or three spaces. Labels that are merely subdivisions of more comprehensive labels should be indented, and summary labels such as *total* should also be indented. The sample table shown in Figure 14.1 illustrates effective layout. Figure 14.2 illustrates this effective layout in actual use.

A major problem for amateur typists is arranging a great amount of data on one page. Keep in mind that two-page tables are often necessary, that scissors and paste are fair to use in making large tables, and that when the material won't fit on the page vertically, it might very well fit horizontally. In other words, a little creativity helps. Note in Figure 14.3 that the table is "turned" on the paper, its width running from the bottom of the page to the top. And note that because the table was copied in its entirety from another source, the source is included; it is shown a double space after the last line in the table.

• Graphics

In reports, the most commonly used graphic forms are bar charts, line charts, pie charts, pictograms, maps, flowcharts, and actual pictures. These graphic presentations are also often used as aids during oral reports. But, whether the report is written or oral, several guidelines can

Figure Number TITLE			
Line Identification	**Caption Head**		
	Subcaption	**Subcaption**	**Subcaption**
Line caption	xxxx	xxxx	xxxx
Line caption	xxxx	xxxx	xxxx
Line caption	xxxx	xxxx	xxxx
Line caption	xxxx	xxxx	xxxx
Line caption	xxxx	xxxx	xxxx
Line caption	xxxx	xxxx	xxxx
Summary or total caption	xxxx	xxxx	xxxx
Footnote or source placement			

FIGURE 14.1

Effective table layout with identifying captions and labels.

Figure 1
COMBINED FIRST-YEAR COSTS FOR THREE SITES

Cost	Location		
	Main	Linden	Palmeran
Lease	$ 90,000	$ 75,000	$ 72,000
Property Tax	14,000a	22,000	22,000
Trucking	64,000	60,000	64,000
Preparation	30,000	50,000	30,000
Totals	$198,000	$207,000	$188,000

a. Real property in Main is to be reassessed in March. A 50 percent increase to about $21,000 is anticipated.

FIGURE 14.2

Effective table layout.

Figure I

COMPARISON OF PEBBLE AND JORDAN PROCESSES

Item	Process--Pebble Mill	Process--Jordan
Power consumption per ton of rubber	127.2 KW	9.06 KW
Recovery of rubber	65 percent	95 to 100 percent
Dirt in rubber (insolubles)	10 to 11 percent	1 percent or less
Rubber tensile strength	3,720 psi	5,200 psi
Aging-resistance to oxygen	Poor	Excellent
Elongation	Good	Excellent
Shrub condition for milling	Seasonal, must be preconditioned for one to eight months	Use any time, no preconditioning
By-products	None	Paper pulp, resin for industrial uses
Resin content before deresination	20 to 24 percent	12 to 15 percent
Deresination	Costly batch process	Continuous process
General operation	Intermittent batch with much "down" time	Little "down" time, continuous operation, faster

Source: Hugh H. Anderson, Pacific Rubber Growers, to Dr. John Hatchett, U.S. Department of Agriculture, Pacific Rubber Growers' Correspondence File.

FIGURE 14.3
Effective table layout.

be used to determine whether a graphic presentation should be used at all and to make the graphic effective. We can ask ourselves these questions:

1. Does the graphic presentation contribute to the overall understanding of the subject? Would a graphic assist the reader?

2. Can the material be covered adequately in words rather than in visual ways? Graphics, both in written and oral reports, should be saved for things that are difficult to communicate in words alone.

3. Will the written or spoken text add meaning to the graphic display?

4. Is the graphic easily understood? Extreme use of color, complicated symbols, confusing art techniques, and unusual combinations of typefaces only detract from the impact of the material presented.

5. Is the graphic honest? The hand is often quicker than the eye; as we will discover later in this chapter, data can be distorted rather easily.

6. If the visual presentation is part of an oral report, can it be seen by the entire audience? Flip charts, poster boards, and overhead-projector transparencies are the visual means most often used to accompany oral reports.

> A picture may be worth a thousand words.

Perhaps the most recent computer innovation to have an effect on business is computer graphics. With the proper software programs, managers may now produce at their desks almost any of the graphics discussed in this chapter. The graphics may be either in black and white or in multicolored, three-dimensional style. Printing of computer graphics may require plotters and/or dot matrix printers, and special computer programs.

The greatest advantage of computer graphics at this stage is in their value to the individual decision maker who formerly had to battle through a maze of computerprinted output. Now the computer can produce a graphic after performing the data-management functions discussed at the beginning of this chapter. For written reports, instantaneous creation of graphics is unnecessary. However, when the computer graphic is completed it may be reproduced in a variety of ways for inclusion in reports. The great range of graphics available in the personal computer field is illustrated in Figure 14.4.

Bar Charts   The *simple bar chart* is perhaps the most effective graphic device for comparing quantities. The length of the bars, whether they are horizontal or vertical, indicates quantity, as shown in Figure 14.5. The quantitative axis should always begin at zero, and the grada-

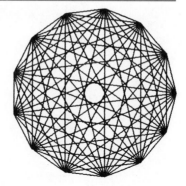

```
For The Mathematically Inclined:

FOR I= 1 TO S
X1=R*COS(I*2*PI/S)*2
Y1=(7*R/8)*SIN(I*2*PI/S)
FOR N= I TO S
X2=R*COS(N*2*PI/S)*2
Y2=(7*R/8)*SIN(N*2*PI/S)
LINE (X1+320,Y1+100)-(X2+320,Y2+100),1
NEXT N
NEXT I

S=13 R=100 PI=3.1416
```

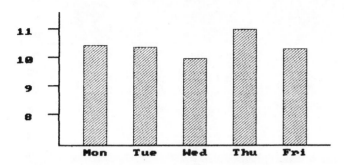

Daily Work Hours

FIGURE 14.4

Unretouched graphics produced on IBM® Proprinter.

tion spaces should be equal. Also, of course, the width of the bars should be equal, or the wider bar will imply that it represents a larger number than the narrower bar. Here are further suggestions:

1. In bar charts, shadings, cross-hatchings, or variations in color can be used to distinguish among the bars.

2. Even though the bars present relationships, readers will get even a clearer picture when the specific dollar or quantity amount is printed at the top of each bar. Readers tend to skim the text and rely on graphics for details. Use your good judgment in listing specifics in graphics.

    Bars emphasize relationships!

3. The figure number and title of the graph may also be placed at the top of the graphic (upper left in Figure 14.5) if the placement seems better than following the graphic, as shown.

4. Without making the graphic appear so complicated that readers will

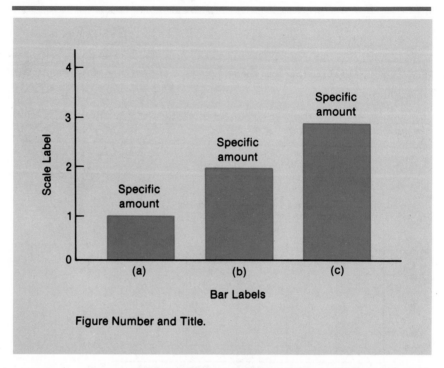

FIGURE 14.5
Simple bar-chart layout.

skip it, include enough information in your scale labels and bar labels to be understandable. If Figure 14.5 represents sales figures for three years, amounts would appear in the vertical scale labels and years in the bar labels.

5. If some quantities are so large that the chart would become unwieldy, the bars may be broken to indicate omission of part of each bar, as shown in Figure 14.6.

The *component bar chart,* also called a segmented or subdivided bar chart, is shown in Figure 14.7. When we want to show how different factors (components) contribute to a total figure, the component bar chart may be desirable. This graphic is particularly useful when components for two different periods are being compared. Note how the components carry percentage figures to indicate the composition of the total student body indicated at the top of each column. Additionally, different colors or cross-hatchings may be used to distinguish the different com-

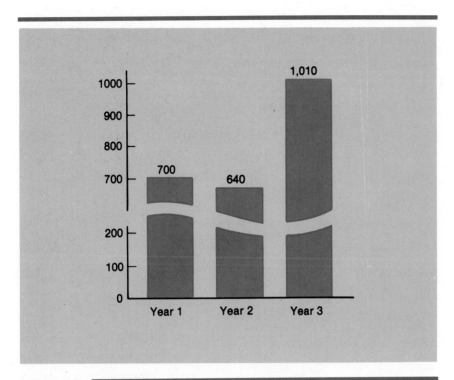

FIGURE 14.6
Broken-bar chart.

ponents, with a key included at the bottom of the chart. To avoid confusing figure numbers in examples with figure numbers used for the text, figure numbers are omitted from the examples.

Sometimes negative quantities show up in data. In the *positive–negative bar chart*, as shown in Figure 14.8, both positive and negative amounts can be illustrated and relationships shown clearly.

Line Charts   Line charts, such as the one shown in Figure 14.9 depict changes in quantitative data over time and illustrate trends. When constructing line charts, keep these general guides in mind:

1. Use the vertical axis for amount and the horizontal axis for time.
2. Begin the vertical axis at zero. When the height of the chart may become unwieldy, break it in the same way the vertical scale was broken in Figure 14.6.
3. Keep all vertical gradations equal, and keep all horizontal grada-

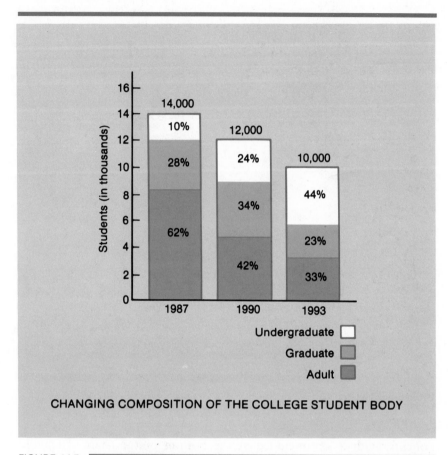

FIGURE 14.7

Component bar chart with key.

Lines emphasize changes over time.

tions equal. The vertical or amount gradations, however, need not be the same as the horizontal or time gradations. In any case, use your judgment in determining the size of gradations so the line or lines drawn will have reasonable slopes. (By using unrealistic gradations, you would develop startling slopes that could mislead readers.)

Cumulative line charts are similar to component bar charts, because they show how different factors contribute to a total, as shown in Figure 14.10. This chart might represent the components that make up the assets of a savings institution. The cumulative total of net worth, borrowings, and savings is illustrated by the top line on the chart.

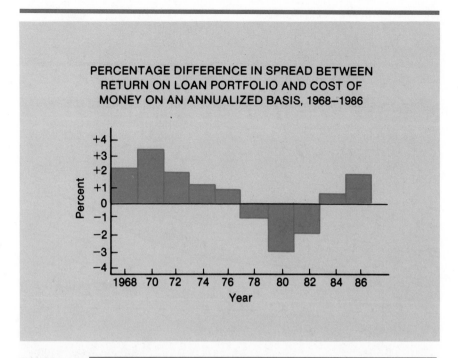

FIGURE 14.8
Positive–negative bar chart.

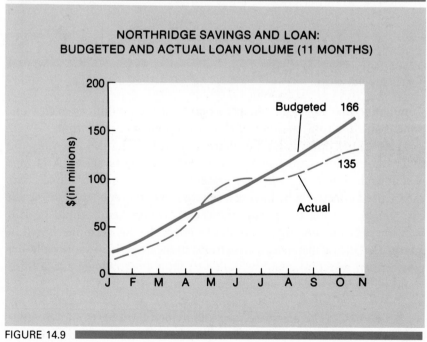

FIGURE 14.9
Line chart.

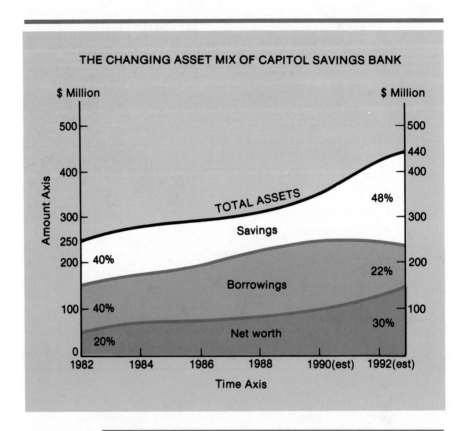

THE CHANGING ASSET MIX OF CAPITOL SAVINGS BANK

FIGURE 14.10
Cumulative line chart.

Cumulative line charts enable us to represent the amount of each component and the total amount of those components at any time.

Line charts differ from bar charts in that bar charts show only the total amount for a time period, whereas line charts show variations within each time period. In oral presentations, a cumulative line chart can be used effectively by having a separate transparency made for each component. During the presentation, each transparency could be laid over the previous one for a cumulative effect. In the example shown in Figure 14.10, for instance, a first transparency may show only the net worth; then a second could be added to show borrowings; and a third could be added to show savings and complete the chart.

Pie Charts Like component or subdivided bar charts and cumulative line charts, pie charts show how the *parts of a whole* are distributed.

As the name indicates, the whole is represented as a pie, with the parts becoming slices of the pie, as shown in Figure 14.11. These two charts are taken from an annual report of a savings bank. Although the total amounts represented by the two charts might be different, the pies are the same size. Pies are effective in showing percentages (parts of a whole), but they are ineffective in showing quantitative totals or comparisons. Bars are used for those purposes.

Here are some generally used guides for the construction of pie charts:

1. Begin slicing the pie at the 12 o'clock position and work clockwise.

2. Slice the largest piece first and continue slicing in descending order of size.

3. Try to label each slice and include information about the quantita-

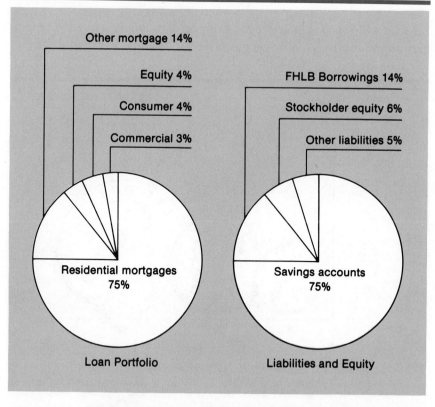

FIGURE 14.11
Pie charts.

tive size (percentage, dollars, acres, square feet, etc.) of each slice. Note the labeling in Figure 14.11.

For dramatic effect, perhaps, or even lack of knowledge, periodicals and other journalistic forms often violate these rules.

Pictograms   A pictogram uses pictures to illustrate numerical relationships. Pictograms are frequently used in newsmagazines. Unfortunately, pictograms can be more dramatic than meaningful if they aren't planned properly, because doubling the height and width of a picture increases the total area four times. Note that the relative sizes of the coins in Figure 14.12 are misleading and make the actual amounts and relationships hard to understand. On the other hand, using the same size figures, as in Figure 14.13, makes both amounts and relationships instantly clear.

Maps might even help people learn something about geography!

Maps   Maps are effective as graphics, particularly when the reader may not be able to visualize geographic relationships. The map shown in

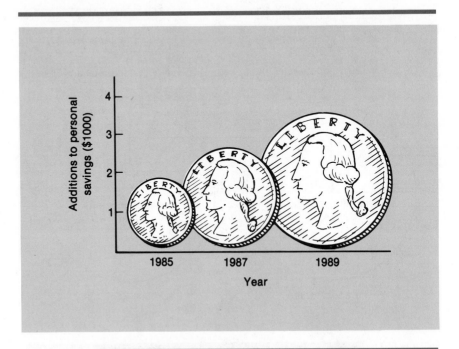

FIGURE 14.12
Pictogram with misleading symbols.

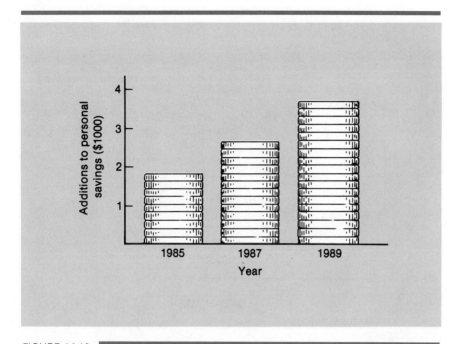

FIGURE 14.13
Pictogram with same-size symbols.

Figure 14.14 is taken from an annual report; it effectively presents geographic material for shareholders who are scattered across the country and perhaps are not familiar with the geography discussed in the report.

Flowcharts   A variety of problems can be resolved through the use of charts to support written analysis. For example, most companies have procedures manuals to instruct employees on how to accomplish certain work tasks. As shown in Figure 14.15, the routing of copies of a form can be made clearer through the use of a flowchart. If the same information were presented only in a series of written steps, we would have to rely not only on the employee's reading ability but also on the employee's willingness to read and study. When the chart accompanies written instructions, chances of errors are lessened.

Organization charts are widely used to provide a picture of the authority structure and relationships within an organization. They

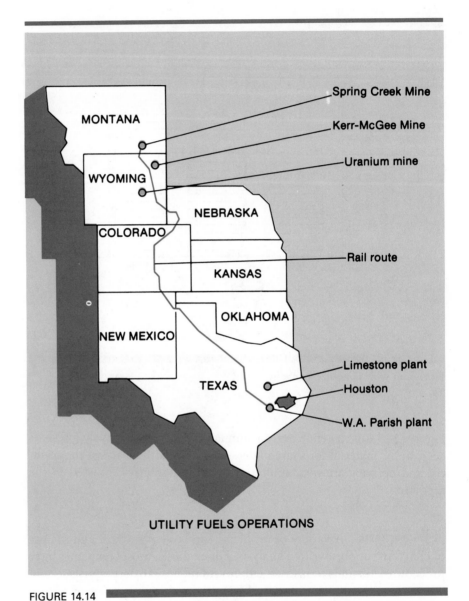

FIGURE 14.14
Map presentation. (*Source:*   courtesy of Houston Industries, Inc.)

provide employees with an idea of what their organization looks like in terms of the flow of authority and responsibility.

Other Graphics   Other graphics such as floor plans, photographs, cartoons, blueprints, and lists of various sorts, may be included in re-

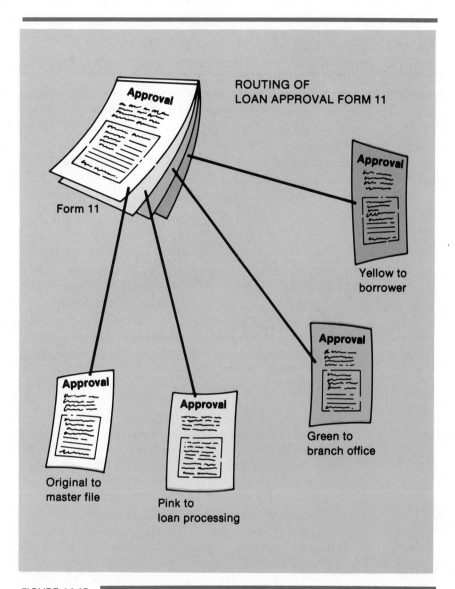

FIGURE 14.15
Flowchart.

ports. Frequently you will find that some material must be included in the report but that its inclusion in the narrative discussion would make the report unwieldy. In this case, the material might be placed in an appendix and only referred to in the report, as explained in Chapters 15 and 16.

Graphics assist narrative but do not replace it.

Introducing Tables and Graphs in the Text

Under no conditions should a table or graph be included in the report without being referred to in the textual material. Text and graphics are partners in the communication process. If readers come to tables, graphs, or pictures in the text before they have been told about them, they will begin to study them and draw their own inferences and conclusions. But if the reader is told about the graphic and its implications, the graphic will supplement what has been said.

Note how the language used in these sentences introduces graphic or tabular material:

Poor:	Figure 1 shows reader preferences for shopping locations.	This sentence is poor because it tells the reader nothing more than would the title of the figure.
Acceptable:	About two-thirds of the consumers preferred to shop in suburban areas rather than in the city. (See Figure 1.)	This sentence is acceptable because it does the job of interpreting the data, but it puts the figure reference in parentheses rather than integrating it in the sentence.
Improved:	As shown in Figure 1, about two-thirds of the consumers preferred to shop in suburban areas rather than in the city.	Although improved over the previous examples, this sentence puts reference to the figure at the beginning, thus detracting from the interpretation of the data.
Best:	About two-thirds of the consumers preferred to shop in suburban areas rather than in the city, as shown in Figure 1.	This sentence is best for introducing figures because it talks about the graphic and also includes introductory phrasing, but only after stressing the main point.

Does the reader get the point before turning to the graphic?

Ideally, graphics should be integrated within the text material immediately after their introductions. If a graphic occupies an entire page, it should appear on the page following the page on which it was introduced. In this chapter, figures are placed as closely as possible to their introductions in accord with these suggestions. However, in some cases, several figures may be introduced on one page, making perfect placement difficult and sometimes impossible.

Should you face a similar problem in your reports, simply arrange material as correctly as possible. Because you probably will prepare your graphics *before* you write, you might try preparing your graphics in finished form, cutting the paper to just fit the graphic, and pasting the graphic on the typing page after its introduction. Then you can continue typing your narrative material.

Throughout the discussion of tables and graphics, the term "graphics" has been used to include all illustrations. Although your report may include tables, graphs, maps, and even photographs, you'll find organizing easier and writing about the illustrations more effective if you label all items as "Figure" followed by a number and number them consecutively. Some report writers like to label tables consecutively as "Table 1," etc., and graphs and charts consecutively in another sequence as "Graph 1," etc. When this dual numbering system is used, readers of the report may become confused when they ultimately come upon a sentence saying, "Evidence presented in Tables 3 and 4 and Graph 2 supports. . . ." Both writers and readers appreciate the single numbering system, which makes the sentence read, "Evidence presented in Figures 3, 4, and 5 supports. . . ."

Multiple labeling systems detract from communication.

Summary

How difficult would it be to drive across the country for the first time without the aid of a road map? We'd probably have to ask directions frequently. And in a large city, finding a specific street address without assistance would be almost impossible. Tables and graphics add clarity to reports just as a map aids a traveler. Protecting ourselves against a deluge of data through good data management and use of tables and graphs has a great deal to do with effective report preparation.

Fortunately, we live in an age in which much of what we have discussed can be aided by computers. If you plan to make a study involving the collection and analysis of considerable quantitative data, talk to an expert in your computer facility. Questionnaires and other data-gathering devices can be designed so that a respondent's answers can be fed to computers through optical scanning equipment directly from the answer sheet. A variety of easy-to-use programs are available for doing much of the data-management mathematics described earlier. Properly designed, the work of data management can be reduced hundreds, even thousands, of times. Many computers also have graphic capability; they can produce the tables and other graphic figures so important to reports.

For many reports, you'll find it an easy task to prepare the tables and graphics on your own. The important thing in terms of your study of this chapter is that you must know what you want and how to construct it. Then you can either do the work on your own or tell the computer what to do.

The skilled report writer knows not only what graphics to use but also when to use them. When people read about number relationships and ratios, they understand only when they have visualized in their minds what is involved. Your use of tables and graphics to complement your written words makes the visualization easy.

Although this discussion has emphasized the use of graphics in written reports, you'll also make use of them to support oral presentations. Often the writer of a report will be called on to make oral presentations about the written report. Many times, of course, graphic materials used in oral presentations will not have a research basis. Speeches designed to inform, to entertain, and to persuade are often built around the use of visual materials.

About Language and Usage

Forming plurals of words is normally done by adding -s or -es, and this method could be described as *regular*. But variations abound. Some words change spelling before adding the plural ending: *half, halves; wolf, wolves; elf, elves.* Others provide two ways: *calf, calves* or *calfs; wharf, wharves* or *wharfs.* Others have different spellings: *ox, oxen; child, children.*

Still others, primarily animals, have the same form for both singular and plural: *bison, moose, deer, sheep,* and *cattle.* The following words from Latin with their English plural and Latin plural are interesting; take your pick of plurals: *antenna, antennas, antennae; appendix, appendixes, appendices; datum,* no English plural, *data* (often used as either plural or singular); *index, indexes, indices; radius, radiuses, radii; stadium, stadiums, stadia.*

These plurals are correct: *chambers of commerce, sisters-in-law, cupfuls.* Finally, names ending in -ese that are derived from place names are the same for singular and plural: *Chinese, Japanese, Portuguese, Balinese, Taiwanese.*

Exercises

Review Questions

1. In what ways does "managing data" help protect researchers against their material?

2. What is meant by "common language," and what are some examples?

3. Why should vertical gradations be equal in a graphic? Can variation in the sizes of horizontal gradations create the same problem?

4. What is meant by a "broken chart"?

5. Why can't pie charts do the same thing as simple line charts?

6. What is the difference between a component bar chart and a cumulative line chart? Give an example of how each might be used.

7. Why does a lack of consistency in size of pictures create misleading pictograms?

8. If a distribution consists of the amounts 12, 65, 68, 72, 73, 79, 81, 85, and 85, which measure of central tendency would be most appropriate? Why?

9. Which measure of central tendency do most people describe as the "average"? How is it calculated?

10. Where should a graphic be placed in a report?

Activities

1. Select what to you is the most effective graphic means of presenting each of the following sets of data. Then prepare the graphic and write a sentence that would introduce the graphic effectively in a report.

   a. The registration of voters in a community is 45 percent Democratic, 38 percent Republican, 12 percent uncommitted, and 5 percent minor political parties.

   b. Interest rates on home mortgage loans for the decade of the 1980s (fictitious) averaged:

1980	12.2 percent	1985	12.0 percent
1981	14.2 percent	1986	11.5 percent
1982	15.0 percent	1987	11.0 percent
1983	13.0 percent	1988	10.5 percent
1984	12.0 percent	1989	11.0 percent

   c. Grades received by students in a beginning accounting course showed 12 A's, 22 B's, 40 C's, 14 D's, 8 F's, and 4 In's (incompletes) for the 100 students enrolled.

2. In thousands of dollars, the following figures represent salaries earned by chief financial officers of 25 local high-tech firms. Compute the mean, median, and mode.

36	48	66	74	82
38	49	68	74	87
38	53	70	78	90
42	57	74	80	92
42	62	74	82	96

3. To discover the differences in computing central tendencies from an array of individual items, as in Activity 2, and from grouped data, tally the scores in Activity 2 in seven classes beginning with 30–39, 40–49, 50–59, and so on to 90–99. When you have tallied the scores, compute the mean and the median and indicate the modal class. How do you account for the differences between the answers here and those in Activity 2?

4. Prepare a simple table for the data used in Activity 3 and indicate the appropriate percentages for each class.

5. Obtain a copy of a corporate annual report. Prepare a one-page memorandum to your instructor telling how effectively the report incorporated graphics.

6. Prepare an introductory sentence for the table developed in Activity 4.

7. Improve the following statements taken from reports:

   a. As can be seen in Table 5, the correlation between verbal scores on admissions tests and achievement in English was .57.

   b. Land values in the southern part of the state have increased about 32 percent while those in the northern portion have increased 19 percent. (See Figure 6.)

   c. Take a look at Figure 3, where a steady decline in the price of farm products during the past quarter is shown.

   d. The data reveal (Figure 4) that only one of seven voters is satisfied with the performance of the City Council.

8. Prepare a graphic or tabular presentation for the following paragraph:

CONSUMER CREDIT

Total consumer credit at the end of March was $184.3 billion, of which $32.8 billion was noninstallment. The $151.5 billion of installment credit was composed of $51.6 billion for personal loans, $50.5 billion for automobiles, and $49.4 billion for other consumer goods.

9. Prepare whatever graphic or tabular presentations you think would be desirable for the following discussion involving fictitious information:

URBAN FAMILY BUDGETS

Costs of three hypothetical family budgets for an urban family of four rose about 16 percent from the autumn of 1987 to the autumn of 1988, according to the Bureau of Labor Statistics. An urban family consisting of a 38-year-old husband employed full time, his nonworking wife, a boy of 13, and a girl of 8 could expect the average cost of an intermediate budget to amount to about $25,866. Average cost of the lower budget amounted to $16,080, with the higher budget $33,412.

Family-consumption items comprised 76 percent of the intermediate family budget with the remaining 24 percent composed of gifts and contributions, occupational expenses, life insurance, and social security and personal income taxes. Total family consumption at the lower- and higher-budget levels comprised 82 percent and 70 percent of the family budget, respectively. During the year, consumption costs rose by approximately 11.4 percent for all three budgets. Food costs accounted for 38 percent of total family consumption at the lower level, 33 percent at the intermediate, and 28 percent at the higher level. Food costs represented the largest single component for the lower and intermediate budget levels, but the largest component of consumption at the higher level was housing expenditures.

10. Prepare graphic or tabular presentations for the following fictitious information:

JOB GROWTH RATE

The rate of government jobs opened and filled in the last decade was almost two times that in private industry, according to the Tax Foundation. Between 1978 and 1988 the number of federal, state, and local government workers increased 50 percent from 10.6 million to 15.9 million compared to a 27 percent job growth rate in private industry. Total nonfarm payroll employment in the U.S. rose from 62.0 million to 80.0 million in the ten-year period. Of this increase, 12.7 million jobs were added by the private sector and 5.3 million by the government.

11. Prepare graphic or tabular presentations for the following fictitious information:

COSTS OF HIGHER EDUCATION

Median expected educational expenses for full-time college students in September 1989 varied from about $1,300 for those in community colleges to $11,000 for those in private universities. These costs cover tuition and fees, books and supplies, and transportation. For public institutions, the estimated medians were about $2,400 for four-year colleges, $3,200 for universities, $1,900 for vocational schools, and $1,300 for two-year colleges. For students attending private universities, median expenses were considerably higher than for those attending public schools: $11,000 for private universities compared to $3,200, $8,700 for four-year colleges compared to $2,400, and $9,000 for two-year colleges compared to $1,300. Board-and-room costs varied widely, but the median for those living at home and commuting was estimated at $4,200 a year. For those living at school, the median was $6,100.

12. Prepare a graphic for the following fictitious information:

HOW THE WEALTHY INVEST

For families with net worths over $1 million in addition to residence equities, their assets were divided as follows: rental real estate, 15 percent; retirement savings programs, 10 percent; stock market equities, 30 percent; savings accounts, 5 percent; tax-exempt bonds and funds, 25 percent; government securities other than tax exempt, 15 percent.

CHAPTER 15

Organizing and Writing Short Reports and Proposals

Thinking things through—finding answers to knotty problems—is perhaps best done in writing. Refinement demands that we visualize what is in the mind. Whatever cannot be made clear in writing probably is not clear in the mind.

LEONARD READ in *The Freeman*

Suppose that, using one or more of the established research methods, we have followed the four steps of

1. Defining the problem,
2. Selecting a method of solution,
3. Collecting and analyzing data,
4. Arriving at a conclusion

to solve a problem or to gather information to assist in problem solving. For everyday use, these four steps may be called simply (1) problem, (2) method, (3) findings, and (4) conclusion. For many research studies, a suitable report could be written using only these four terms as headings for the written content.

The type of research employed has little influence on the use of headings in a report. However, the length of the report has a strong influence. As reports grow longer, they are more likely to need headings.

Growth of a Report

Obviously, the difference between a short and a long report is length. The differences between a formal report and an informal report lie in format and possibly in writing style. The type of report you prepare depends on the subject matter, the purpose of the report, and the readers' needs. At the short, informal end of the report continuum described in Chapter 13, a report could look exactly like a brief memorandum. At the long, formal extreme of the continuum, the report might include most or all of the following parts:

Might a short report also be formal?

I. Preliminary parts
    A. Letter of transmittal
    B. Title page
    C. Contents page and list of tables
    D. Synopsis or summary (when not included in the letter of transmittal)
II. Body of the report
    A. Purpose
    B. Method
    C. Findings (in as many sections as necessary)
    D. Conclusions (and recommendations if requested)

III. Addenda
   A. Bibliography
   B. Appendix material
   C. Index

All these parts are rarely found in a business report. They are listed here simply to name all the possible parts. The preliminary parts and addenda are mechanical items that only support the body of the report. The body contains the report of the research and covers the four steps in the research process. The organization of the body of the report leads to the construction of the contents page.

Because we usually write to affect or influence others favorably, we often add parts as the number of pages increases. When a report exceeds one or two pages, we might add a cover or title page. And when the body of the report exceeds four or five pages, we might even add a finishing touch by placing the report in a plastic cover or ring binder. Reports frequently take on the characteristics of the formal end of the continuum simply by reason of size. Note how the number of preliminary parts and addenda items increases as the report increases in size, as depicted in Figure 15.1.

Memo and letter reports (Figure 15.1) are seldom longer than a page or two, but they can be expanded into several pages. As depicted, long reports may include some special pages that do not appear in short reports:

Title page. A title page is often added when the writer opts to use it rather than a memorandum heading format or a letter arrangement. The title page includes the title, author, date, and frequently the name of the person or organization that requested the report.

Transmittal. As the report becomes more formal, the writer may prepare and attach a letter or memorandum that "transmits" the report to the reader.

Table of contents. Usually simply called "contents," this table is an outline of report headings with page numbers listed. A report heavy with graphics and tables might also include a "List of Figures" separate from the contents table.

Summary. A brief summary of the highlights of the report may be added at the beginning for the reader's benefit. It provides an overview and simplifies understanding of a long report. This summary may be called a synopsis, epitome, precis, résumé, brief, or abstract. Of these, abstract is most used professionally.

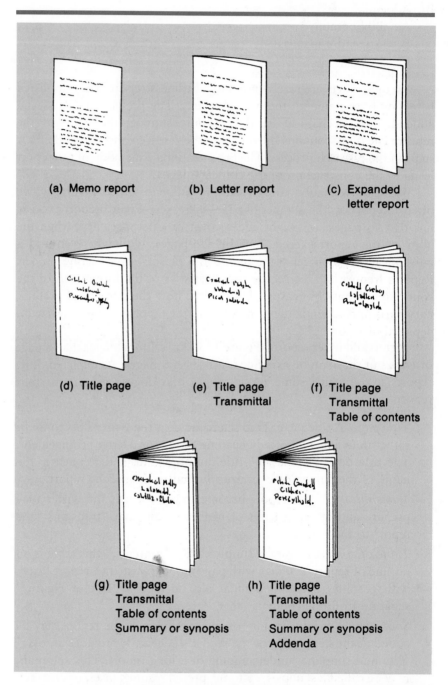

(a) Memo report

(b) Letter report

(c) Expanded letter report

(d) Title page

(e) Title page
Transmittal

(f) Title page
Transmittal
Table of contents

(g) Title page
Transmittal
Table of contents
Summary or synopsis

(h) Title page
Transmittal
Table of contents
Summary or synopsis
Addenda

FIGURE 15.1

As the size of a report increases, so does the number of assisting items.

Addenda. The addenda to a report may include all materials used in the research but not necessary inclusions in the report body. Addenda items may include bibliographies, lists of footnotes, an index, copies of survey instruments, complex mathematical computations and formulas, legal documents, and a variety of items the writer presents to support the body of the report and the quality of the research.

Inclusion of many of these items tends to make a formal report repetitious. In addition to the formal presentation in the body of the report, the title page, the synopsis, the transmittal, and the contents outline will repeat report content in various ways.

Because the body of the report discusses the four steps in problem solving—usually the items of most interest to readers—it represents the core of the presentation. Within the body, the purpose and method of solution steps are minor items in terms of space and are considered part of an introduction to a report. But the findings leading to the conclusion or conclusions will consume the major portion of space.

Repetition is one way of learning.

Organizing Findings

Assume that you have the task of selecting a personal computer from among three alternative models—the Strad, the Amati, and the Beta. The purpose of your study is to select the computer that will best serve the record-keeping and word-processing needs of a small office.

You gather all the information available from suppliers of the three machines; you try each one personally and have two other people use them; and finally you compare the three against a variety of criteria. Your final selection is the Beta. Why did you select it? What criteria served as decision guides? When you write the report, you'll have to tell the reader—the one who will put out the money to buy the machine—how the selection was made in such a way that the reader is "sold" on your conclusion.

If you organize your report in such a way that you tell the reader everything about the Strad, then everything about the Amati, and follow with everything about the Beta, the reader may have trouble making comparisons. Your content outline might look like this:

I. Introduction
    A. The Problem
    B. The Method Used

    II. Strad
  III. Amati
  IV. Beta
   V. Conclusion

Note that this outline devotes three of the Roman numeral sections to the findings and only one to the problem and method. This division is appropriate because the most space must be devoted to the findings. But the reader has difficulty comparing the storage of the computers because the information is in three different places. Would it be better to discuss storage capacity of the three in the same section of the report? Would prices be compared more easily if they were all in the same section? Most reports should be divided into sections that reflect the criteria used rather than into sections devoted to the "things" compared.

If you selected your computer based on cost, storage, service warranty, keyboarding ease, and availability of software programs, these criteria might better serve as divisions of the findings. Then your content outline would appear this way:

With page numbers added, the outline could be a contents page.

     I. Introduction
        A. The Problem
        B. The Method Used
    II. Cost Favors Strad
  III. Storage Capacity Points to Beta
  IV. Service Warranties Are Equal
   V. Keyboard Is Best on Beta
  VI. Software Is Plentiful for Beta
 VII. Beta Is the Best Buy

The four-part outline now has seven major sections and two subsections, with five of the major sections devoted to the findings. When the report is prepared in this way, the features of each machine are compared in the same section, and the reader is led logically to the conclusion.

Note the headings used in sections II–VII. These are called "talking headings" because they talk about the content of the section and even give a conclusion about the section. Page numbers following each outline item convert the outline into a table of contents. Interestingly, the headings justify the selection of Beta. As a result, a knowledgeable reader who has confidence in the researcher might be satisfied by reading only the content headings.

Might logical order take several forms?

In addition to organizing findings by criteria, report writers can use other organizational plans. The comparison of three computers was an analytical process. But when the report is only informational and not analytical, you should use the most logical organization. Treat your material as a "whole" unit. A report on sales might be divided up by geographic sales region, by product groups sold, by price range, or by time periods. A report on the development of a product might use chronological order. By visualizing the whole report first, you can then divide it into its major components and perhaps divide the major components into their parts. Remember, a section must divide into at least two parts or it cannot be divided at all. Thus, in an outline you must have at least an "A" subsection and a "B" subsection following a Roman numeral or you may not have any subsections.

A final caution: beware of overdividing the sections. Too many divisions might make the report appear disorganized and choppy. On the other hand, too few divisions might create a reading problem for the reader. Note how the four steps have been developed through headings to the Roman numeral outline and to a contents page for the report, as shown in Figure 15.2.

When developing content outlines, some report writers believe that readers expect the beginning of the body to be an introduction, so they begin the outline with the first heading related to findings. In our example, then, section I would be "Cost Favors Strad." Additionally, when

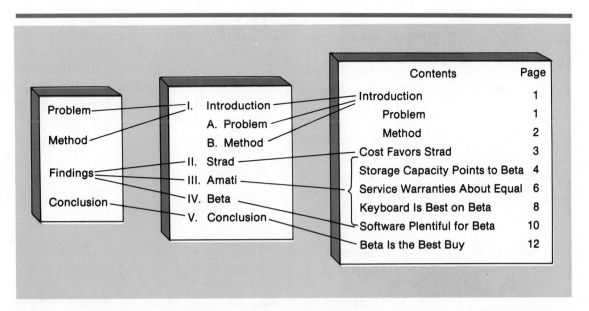

FIGURE 15.2

The basic outline grows to a contents page.

they reach the contents page, they may eliminate the Roman numeral or other outline symbols. A contents page for a report without the introduction–problem–methods headings would look like this:

Contents

	Page
Cost Favors Strad	3
Storage Capacity Points to Beta	4
Service Warranties About Equal	6
Keyboard Is Best on Beta	8
Software Plentiful for Beta	10
Beta Is the Best Buy	12

The research process consists of inductively arranged steps:

Inductive is indirect: conclusion last.

1. Problem
2. Method
3. Findings
4. Conclusion

When the report is organized in the same order, its users must read through the body to learn about the conclusions—generally the most important part of the report to users. To make the reader's job easier, report writers may organize the report deductively inasmuch as the report is obviously written after the research has been done. In a deductive arrangement, the conclusions would appear at the beginning of the report. This sequence is usually achieved by placing a synopsis or summary at the beginning:

Deductive is direct: conclusion first.

1. Conclusion reported in the synopsis.
2. Body of the report
   a. Problem
   b. Method
   c. Findings
   d. Conclusion

This arrangement permits the reader to get the primary message early and then to look for support in the body of the report. The deductive arrangement contributes to the repetitious nature of reports, but it also contributes to effective reporting.

After you conclude the research process, putting the report in final form is the next step. The format you select—long or short, formal or informal—may help determine how many of the supporting introductory and addendum items to include.

Report writers have an opportunity to be creative and to use their own good judgment!

Benefits of Form Reports

An excellent example of meeting a demand for numerous, repetitive reports is the *form* report. As a short report, form reports have the following benefits:

1. When designed properly, form reports tend to increase clerical accuracy by having designated places for specific items. College registration forms, applications for credit, airline tickets, bank checks, and perhaps hundreds of other written documentary items are simple form reports.
2. Forms save time by telling the preparer where to put each item and by having the elements common to all preprinted so the person filling in the form need not do any narrative writing.
3. In addition to their advantages of accuracy and time saving, forms make tabulation of data relatively simple. The nature of the form is uni*form*ity.

Most form reports, like the bank teller's cash sheet in Figure 15.3, are informational. At the end of the teller's work period, cash is counted and totals entered in designated blanks. All teller cash reports are then totaled to arrive at period totals and perhaps verified by computer records.

Do forms also tend to improve the quality of routine reports?

In addition to their informational purpose, form reports also assist in analytical work. A residential appraisal report, the first page of which is shown in Figure 15.4, assists real-estate appraisers in analyzing real property. With this information, the appraiser is able to determine the market value of the property using the cost and the sales comparison approaches; and in the case of rental property, a third method—the income approach—is presented. For commercial and industrial properties, appraisers prepare narrative appraisal reports in letter form for small properties and in long, formal formats for major properties.

Teller's Cash Sheet

Currency

	VAULT (Double Custody)		VAULT (Single Custody)		WRAPPED		LOOSE		TOTAL
$1									
$2									
$5									
$10									
$20									
$50									
$100									
MISC.									
MUT.									
MARKED									
TOTALS										(A)

Coin

	VAULT (Double Custody)		VAULT (Single Custody)		WRAPPED		LOOSE		TOTAL
1¢									
5¢									
10¢									
25¢									
50¢									
$1.00									
TOTALS										(B)

Grand Total

A + B = [   ] (C)

Cash Proof

Cash on hand from previous day	$
Cash received/paid over counter	$
Net cash should be	$
Actual cash to vault (C)	$
Short	$
Over	$

Teller's Signature   Date

Check In Performed By

Actual Count By (Teller Differences and Certifications)

Date

Each item checked below was verified and checked in:

☐ Counter & Reserve Currency   ☐ Cashier's Checks
☐ Food Coupons   ☐ Money Orders
☐ Foreign Currency   ☐ Int'l Money Orders
☐ Traveler's Cheques

Teller's Stamp

TEL-20X 1-87

FIGURE 15.3

Teller's cash sheet.

UNIFORM RESIDENTIAL APPRAISAL REPORT File No. [ ][ ][ ]

SUBJECT

Property Address 8812 Salesian	Census Tract
City Parkside County Cook State IL Zip Code 60061	
Legal Description Lot #8 of Block 24 of Sunset Park	
Owner/Occupant John Doe	Map Reference
Sale Price $ 105,000 Date of Sale June 14, 1981	PROPERTY RIGHTS APPRAISED
Loan charges/concessions to be paid by seller $ none known	
R.E. Taxes $ 2100 Tax Year 1987 HOA $/Mo. NA	
Lender/Client Michael Beach/William Hester	

LENDER DISCRETIONARY USE

Sale Price	$
Date	
Mortgage Amount	$
Mortgage Type	
Discount Points and Other Concessions	
Paid by Seller	$
Source	

PROPERTY RIGHTS APPRAISED
- [x] Fee Simple
- [ ] Leasehold
- [ ] Condominium (HUD/VA)
- [ ] De Minimis PUD

NEIGHBORHOOD

LOCATION	[ ] Urban	[x] Suburban	[ ] Rural
BUILT UP	[ ] Over 75%	[x] 25-75%	[ ] Under 25%
GROWTH RATE	[ ] Rapid	[x] Stable	[ ] Slow
PROPERTY VALUES	[ ] Increasing	[x] Stable	[ ] Declining
DEMAND/SUPPLY	[ ] Shortage	[x] In Balance	[ ] Over Supply
MARKETING TIME	[ ] Under 3 Mos.	[x] 3-6-Mos.	[ ] Over 6 Mos.

NEIGHBORHOOD ANALYSIS	Good	Avg.	Fair	Poor
Employment Stability	x			
Convenience to Employment		x		
Convenience to Shopping	x			
Convenience to Schools	x			
Adequacy of Public Transportation		x		
Recreation Facilities		x		
Adequacy of Utilities		x		
Property Compatibility	x			
Protection from Detrimental Cond.	x			
Police & Fire Protection		x		
General Appearance of Properties	x			
Appeal to Market	x			

PRESENT LAND USE %
Single Family	60
2-4 Family	10
Multi-family	10
Commercial	20
Industrial	
Vacant	

LAND USE CHANGE
- Not Likely
- Likely [x]
- In process
- To: _____

PREDOMINANT OCCUPANCY
- Owner [x]
- Tenant
- Vacant (0-5%)
- Vacant (over 5%)

SINGLE FAMILY HOUSING
PRICE $ (000)	AGE (yrs)	
80	5	Low
130	7	High
100	6	Predominant

Note: Race or the racial composition of the neighborhood are not considered reliable appraisal factors.

COMMENTS: The subject is located near schools and churches in a neighborhood consisting of well-maintained residences of similar quality and age.

SITE

Dimensions 70 x 125	Topography	Level
Site Area 8750 Sq. ft.	Size	Typical
Zoning Classification Residential Corner Lot No	Shape	Rectangular
HIGHEST & BEST USE: Present Use x Zoning Compliance Yes	Drainage	Appears adequate
	Other Use No	View	Northward

UTILITIES	Public	Other	SITE IMPROVEMENTS	Type	Public	Private
Electricity	x		Street	Asphalt	x	
Gas	x		Curb/Gutter	Concrete	x	
Water	x		Sidewalk	Concrete	x	
Sanitary Sewer	x		Street Lights		x	
Storm Sewer	x		Alley	None		

Landscaping	Typical
Driveway	Concrete
Apparent Easements	None
FEMA Flood Hazard	Yes* ___ No x
FEMA* Map/Zone	

COMMENTS (Apparent adverse easements, encroachments, special assessments, slide areas, etc.):
No survey was furnished. All dimensions are approximate.

IMPROVEMENTS

GENERAL DESCRIPTION
Units	1
Stories	1+
Type (Det./Att.)	Detached
Design (Style)	Split Level
Existing	x
Proposed	
Under Construction	
Age (Yrs.)	6
Effective Age (Yrs.)	3-5

EXTERIOR DESCRIPTION
Foundation	Poured concrete
Exterior Walls	Brick/frame
Roof Surface	Asph. Shingle
Gutters & Dwnspts.	Aluminum
Window Type	Casement
Storm Sash	Yes
Screens	Yes
Manufactured House	No

FOUNDATION
Slab	On grade
Crawl Space	Yes
Basement	No
Sump Pump	No
Dampness	No
Settlement	No
Infestation	No

BASEMENT
Area Sq. Ft.	0
% Finished	
Ceiling	
Walls	
Floor	
Outside Entry	

INSULATION
Roof	[ ]
Ceiling	[x]
Walls	[x]
Floor	[ ]
None	[ ]
Adequacy	[ ]
Energy Efficient Items:	

ROOM LIST

ROOMS	Foyer	Living	Dining	Kitchen	Den	Family Rm.	Rec. Rm.	Bedrooms	# Baths	Laundry	Other	Area Sq. Ft.
Basement LL					1	1			1	1		
Level 1	1	1	1	1								
Level 2								4	2			

Finished area **above** grade contains: 7 Rooms; 4 Bedroom(s); 3 Bath(s); 1786 Square Feet of Gross Living Area

FIGURE 15.4

Form appraisal report.

SURFACES	Materials/Condition	HEATING		KITCHEN EQUIP.		ATTIC		IMPROVEMENT ANALYSIS	Good	Avg.	Fair	Poor
Floors	Carpet/good	Type	Forced air	Refrigerator	x	None	x	Quality of Construction	x			
Walls	Drywall/good	Fuel	Gas	Range/Oven	x	Stairs		Condition of Improvements	x			
Trim/Finish	Wood/good	Condition	Good	Disposal	x	Drop Stair		Room Sizes/Layout	x			
Bath Floor	Ceramic	Adequacy	Good	Dishwasher	x	Scuttle		Closets and Storage	x			
Bath Wainscot	Ceramic	COOLING		Fan/Hood		Floor		Energy Efficiency	x			
Doors	Wood	Central	x	Compactor		Heated		Plumbing-Adequacy & Condition	x			
		Other		Washer/Dryer		Finished		Electrical-Adequacy & Condition	x			
		Condition	Unk	Microwave				Kitchen Cabinets-Adequacy & Cond.	x			
Fireplace(s)	#	Adequacy	Unk	Intercom				Compatibility to Neighborhood	x			
CAR STORAGE:	Garage x	Attached		Adequate		House Entry		Appeal & Marketability	x			
No. Cars 2+	Carport	Detached		Inadequate		Outside Entry		Estimated Remaining Economic Life			50	Yrs.
Condition	None	Built-In		Electric Door		Basement Entry		Estimated Remaining Physical Life			60	Yrs.

Additional features: ___Lower level includes laundry room, family room, den, and full bath.___ ___A fireplace is in the family room. Patio in rear.___

Depreciation (Physical, functional and external inadequacies, repairs needed, modernization, etc.): _____
___No inadequacies noted.___

General market conditions and prevalence and impact in subject/market area regarding loan discounts, interest buydowns and concessions: _____
~~Market conditions are good in general and especially for the neighborhood.~~

Freddie Mac Form 70 10/86 **10Ch.** **AE**   Fannie Mae Form 1004 10/86

**FIGURE 15.4
(continued).**

Characteristics of Short Reports

Most short reports include only the minimum supporting materials to achieve effective communication. The heading format for memoranda, for example, does the job of a transmittal letter and a title page; therefore, these preliminary parts of a formal report are unnecessary. The enclosure would be an appendix item in a formal report, as shown in Figure 15.5. Short reports focus on the body—problem, method, findings, and conclusion.

Additionally, short reports might incorporate any of the following features:

Some short report elements apply to long, formal reports.

1. Personal writing style using first- or second-person style. Contractions are appropriate when they contribute to a natural style.

2. Use of graphics to reinforce the written portion.

3. Use of headings and subheadings to delineate portions of the body and to reflect organization. Note how the two headings in Figure 15.5, an informational report, highlight the critical information.

MEMORANDUM

To   Philip Brierly
From   Arthur Frahm
Date   April 15, 199___

Subject   Training Department Activity
          Report for Third Quarter

During the third quarter of our fiscal year, January 1 to March 31, the Training Department engaged in the following activities:

Programs Conducted by Departmental Staff

18 Orientation seminars. Total participants: 143.
   Total classroom time: 148 hours.
3 Preretirement seminars. Total participants: 32.
   Total classroom time: 72 hours.
6 Written communication courses. Total participants: 120.
   Total classroom time: 72 hours.
4 Leadership and supervision courses. Total
   participants: 32. Total classroom time: 80 hours.

Programs Conducted by Consultants

1 Tax law changes presentation. Total participants: 54.
   Total time: 3 hours.
8 Computer system orientation programs. Total
   participants: 320. Total time: 64 hours.

Additionally, we prepared teaching-learning materials and video tapes for the training sessions that will take place during the next two quarters to bring the entire staff up to date on the new computer information and communication system. Copies of these materials are enclosed.

Enclosure

FIGURE 15.5

Short report in memorandum form.

4. Use of memorandum and letter formats when appropriate. The letter report in Figure 15.6 uses "Performance of the CPT Equipment" as the title of the report and places it where the subject line would appear in a letter. Following the title is an introductory paragraph followed by four sections, each with a heading.

Of particular interest because of its persuasive organization is the report of a reading-improvement program conducted by a consultant, as shown in Figure 15.7. Apparently, the program would be expanded to include more people in the firm if the experimental (trial) program succeeded. Examine the report and note the following features:

1. The letterhead, inside address, and subject line serve as a title page and a transmittal.

2. The headings within the report reveal the organization and the conduct of the experimental program:

   Purpose and Method
   Beginning Speed and Comprehension
   Ending Speed and Comprehension
   Conclusions and Recommendations

3. The inductive organization of the report is used as a means of *convincing* the vice-president that continuation of the program is advisable.

4. All figures are introduced in the narrative *before* the reader comes to them.

5. Means, medians, and percentages are used as common language in the interpretation of the quantitative data.

6. Table titles and column headings are clear.

7. The success of the program is developed in the logical analysis. Subtly, the writer lets the results speak for themselves.

8. Evidence from an outside source was used to support the significance of the ending scores.

9. The recommendation on page 3 includes the writer's offer (proposal) to continue the work for the company.

As a special kind of short report, the executive summary contains a condensation of a complex or lengthy subject. For example, the executive summary in Figure 15.8 represents an abstract of a 150-page real-estate appraisal report covering a large office building. The summary concisely presents the major elements from the report. It gives clients

June 15, 199__

Ms. Martha Weston
Word Processing Supervisor
ABC Company
Post Office Box 7190
Ventura CA 93888

Dear Ms. Weston

SUBJECT: CPT PERFORMANCE

I'm pleased to tell you about our experience with the CPT Word
Processor as you requested recently. We are pleased with its
performance and versatility. I assume you have looked at several
machines and have narrowed down your choices. Here are my
observations.

An approach to adopting word processors

Eighteen months ago we adopted CPT equipment on a limited scale
with the idea in mind that we could phase out our reliance on
electric typewriters a little at a time as we became familiar with the
potential of word processing. We began with two work stations and
now have four. The stations are actually in pairs so each pair can
share a common printer. The Rotary VIII printer with a speed of 45
characters a second can easily handle two input stations.

We use the equipment as dedicated word processors, although we do
have the ability to link up with our computer installation.

The step-at-a-time development of our word-processing center has,
we think, saved us money and training time and has lessened the
confusion that exists about buying software packages.

Performance

In terms of performance, the CPT equipment is excellent. We have not
experienced mechanical problems, and our service contract and
warranty have covered all maintenance costs.

We have software packages that check spelling and signal when a
typo occurs. Our routine letters are prepared from disc-stored
masters. Using both printers, we recently prepared 1200 individually
typed form letter mailings in under four hours. We have no
complaints about our preparation of executive reports.

FIGURE 15.6
Letter report (continued on next page).

Ms. Martha Weston
June 15, 199—
Page 2

Versatility

When we installed our equipment as dedicated word processors, we
did not anticipate its application to different areas of our business.
We now process all customer billing on an after-hours basis through
a specially designed program. All customer and supplier address lists
are maintained in our department, and we can update them regularly
as changes occur.

General Satisfaction

As you can tell, we are satisfied with our CPT installation. In
eighteen months we've learned a lot, and we learn more every day.
The equipment can do far more than we have asked it to do, I'm sure.

Although this is a brief and generalized commentary on our use of
CPT, I hope it will be of help to you in making your selection. Please
call on me again if you'd like; and if you'd like to visit our office,
please let me know.

Sincerely

Martin Sloan

Martin Sloan
Director, Word Processing

FIGURE 15-6.
(continued).

Johnson and Associates
Suite 2410, Wilton Towers
440 North Michigan Boulevard
Chicago IL 60611-4088

October 1, 199___

Ms Jean Tobler
Executive Vice-President
Noble Oil Company
P.O. Box 4521
Stillwater OK 36363

Dear Ms Tobler

SUBJECT: READING IMPROVEMENT PROGRAM

Sixty middle-management officials of Noble Oil have now completed the reading-improvement program which began on September 1. I am pleased to report the successful results of this experimental phase of the program.

Purpose and Method

The company's purpose for the program was to attempt to improve the critical reading speed and comprehension skills of its management and supervisory personnel. In the program, each participant spent 15 one-hour sessions over a four-week period at the Controlled Reader, a machine that flashes printed material on a small video screen at varying speeds.

My role was that of instructor of reading techniques and how to adapt them to use with the Controlled Reader at their individual study stations. Reading tests were administered to each member of the group at the beginning and at the end of the program. The tests consisted of material specially designed to include and reflect business and industrial language and difficulty. The effectiveness of the program was evaluated from comparisons of beginning and ending test scores.

Beginning Speed and Comprehension

At the beginning of the program, the median reading speed of the group was 385 words a minute; and two of every three participants were reading at less than the 450 words-a-minute rate that is considered good, as shown in Figure 1.

FIGURE 15.7
Short report (continued on next page).

Ms Jean Tobler
October 1, 199__
Page 2

Figure 1. Beginning Reading Speeds

Rate in Words a Minute	Number of Readers at This Rate	Percentage Readers
600–699	3	5
500–599	8	13
400–499	14	23
300–399	32	54
200–299	2	4
100–199	1	1
	60	100

Comprehension scores in percentages of correct answers produced a median of 63, as shown in Figure 2. Ninety percent of the participants scored lower than the 80 that is considered acceptable.

Figure 2. Beginning Comprehension Scores

Score	Number of People	Percentage
90–99	2	3
80–89	4	7
70–79	6	10
60–69	27	45
50–59	16	27
40–49	5	8
	60	100

Ending Speed and Comprehension

Both reading speed and comprehension increased significantly during the program. The reading speed median at the end of the program was 625 words a minute, and the median score for comprehension was 90, as shown in Figures 3 and 4.

FIGURE 15.7
(continued).

Ms Jean Tobler
October 1, 199__
Page 3

Figure 3. Ending Reading Speeds

Rate in Words a Minute	Number of Readers at This Rate	Percentage of Readers
900–999	4	7
800–899	7	11
700–799	10	17
600–699	12	20
500–599	18	30
400–499	6	10
300–399	3	5
	60	100

Figure 4. Ending Comprehension Scores

Score	Number of People	Percentage
90–99	31	52
80–89	27	45
70–79	2	3
	60	100

Conclusions and Recommendations

Using mean values, rather than medians, reading speeds increased from 408 to 645 words a minute; comprehension scores increased from 64 to 90 percent. The ending mean scores are both in the top 5 percent nationally for the adult population according to Science Research Limited in its report of December last year.

I found some participants doubled and tripled their reading speeds. The one person whose beginning rate was under 200 words a minute read at a 620-word rate on the ending test and scored 80 percent on comprehension.

FIGURE 15.7
(continued).

Ms Jean Tobler
October 1, 199__
Page 4

The program proved to be successful, and I received very complimentary comments from many participants. Should you decide to offer the program on a wider basis, as you had indicated you might, I will be glad to continue our relationship.

Sincerely

Roger M. Johnson

Roger M. Johnson

FIGURE 15.7
(continued).

EXECUTIVE SUMMARY

Property Location:	2450 Market Avenue—east side between 51st and 52nd Streets.
Interests Appraised:	Condominium estate in fee simple including 100% of the basement, 1st, 2nd, and 20th through 38th floors, all land and all common elements.

Current Assessment:

Land	$ 7,250,000
Building	18,250,000
Total	$25,500,000

Site:	58,110 square feet
Building Description:	Modern, high-density office building with an efficient interior layout and a fairly attractive facade.
Economic Status of Central City:	(a) Former fiscal crisis seems manageable. (b) Corporate relocations have slowed. (c) Capital investment is increasing reflecting investor confidence. (d) City encourages business with favorable tax rates. (e) Employment appears to be on the rise.
Marketing Background:	Approximately 3.5 million square feet of modern midtown office space is available in contiguous blocks, so competition for tenants exists. Some 2.5 million square feet is expected to be absorbed within the next year. Two years may be required to rent 92% of the available net rentable area of the subject property.

FIGURE 15.8

Executive summary (continued on next page).

Page 2

Financial Data: (a) About $4 million may have to be spent to bring the property up to normal physical and operational standards. (b) Both standard and above standard tenant installations may cost $8 million over three years. (c) Estimated cash flows are estimated to be approximately

    $5.8 million in year 1
    $4.2 million in year 2
    $0.1 million in year 3
    $3.8 million in year 4
    $4.3 million in year 5

Capital value in five years is estimated to be $48 million and the pretax yield over ten years at 11.5%.

FIGURE 15.8
(continued).

what they are looking for in a two-page report that may be attached at the beginning of the complete report. When clients accept the appraiser's abstract, they may omit reading the total report.

The purpose of abstracts is to give busy people the gist of books, articles, conferences, and other meetings. Some executive assistants may find preparing abstracts a major part of their job assignments. These abstracts help keep executives up to date professionally and on conferences and meetings they are unable to attend. An effective way to assemble abstracts is to pay special attention to topic sentences and to concluding sentences in paragraphs or within sections of reports. In many cases, this technique yields abstracts based on major ideas and reduces the use of supporting details.

Abstracting: a step up the corporate ladder?

Preparing Proposals

A proposal is a report form rapidly becoming prevalent in business, particularly in businesses engaged in high-technology activities and in producer relationships with governmental agencies.

A proposal is generated as the result of a potential buyer's "request for a proposal" (RFP). The request describes a problem to be solved and invites respondents to describe their proposed solution. The proposal includes (a) details about the manner in which the problem would be solved and (b) the price to be charged. By naming the price, the proposal "bids" on the project. Governmental agencies as well as major suppliers to the Department of Defense place most of their orders and contracts on the basis of the most desirable proposals. Therefore, proposals receive intense attention as a critical part of the successful operation of many companies in a variety of industries.

The response to a proposal request often results in a lengthy report designed to "sell" the prospective buyer on the ability of the bidder to perform. However, a simple price quotation (RFQ), such as that shown in Figure 15.9, also constitutes a proposal in response to a request for quotation. In this case, the supplier is in the United States and the prospective buyer is in France, with facsimile transmission being the means of communication.

• Parts of a Proposal

The format of a proposal will be a memorandum report when the proposal travels within the organization; a letter report when it is short and

FELDSCO   QUOTATION

Feldsco Products, Inc.
1001 Astralka Avenue
Marvel, CA 94011–6003

TO: M. B. Electronique   Date: Sept. 15, 199__
     606 rue Fourny-Zac de Buc
     B.P. 34, 87540 BUC, France   Customer No: TLX 88, 9789

     Attn: D. Zarazoga
            FAX NO. 011-33-158-554462

We are pleased to provide the following quotation in response to your
request above:

Item	Quantity	Feldsco P/N	Customer P/N—Description	Unit Price	Delivery
1	2	905R901	Switch	$270.00	150 days ARO
2	2	153C906	Switch	$703.00	150 days ARO
3	2	705C011	Switch	$852.00	150 days ARO

Note: THE QUOTED DELIVERY IS FELDSCO'S STANDARD
       SCHEDULE FOR THIS PRODUCT TYPE. IF THIS
       SCHEDULE DOES NOT MEET YOUR REQUIREMENTS,
       PLEASE REQUEST FELDSCO TO MAKE A DELIVERY
       REVIEW.

Note: COMPLETE EXPORT STATEMENT INFORMATION ON
       END USE AND END USER REQUIRED UPON ORDER
       PLACEMENT.

TERMS: NET 30 DAYS F.O.B. MARVEL, CALIFORNIA

        This quotation is valid for a period of 60 days
        and subject to the conditions stated on the reverse
        side.

                    Feldsco Products, Inc.

        By   D. Wybrand   D. Wybrand
             International Contracts Administrator

FIGURE 15.9
Simple price quotation.

518

travels outside the organization; and a formal report when it is long, whether it travels outside or remains within the organization. A variety of parts may be used in proposal preparation, and you may use these general ones or their variations as headings in a proposal:

Problem	Personnel/recommendations
Purpose	Follow up/evaluation
Scope	Cost or budget
Method/procedures	Summary
Material	Addenda items
Equipment	

These parts, of course, are in addition to any of the normal preliminary report parts such as title page, transmittal message, content outline, and synopsis, and any items added at the end of the report such as bibliography, appendix, and index.

Writers have much flexibility in preparing proposals. When they find a particular pattern that seems to be successful, they no doubt will adopt it as their basic plan. The ultimate test of a proposal is its effectiveness in achieving its purpose. The writer's task is to assemble the parts of a proposal in a way that "sells" the reader.

To put the proposal together expeditiously, determine the parts to include, select one part that will be easy for you to prepare, prepare that part, and then go on to another. When you have completed the parts, you can arrange them in whatever order you like, incorporate the transitional items necessary to create coherence, and then put the proposal in finished form. As with most report writing, you will first prepare the parts that you will later assemble as the "whole" report. Trying to write a report by beginning on line one, page one and "plowing" through to the end may prove to be frustrating and time consuming. Keep in mind that you should have done the research and planning before you begin to write.

Should you become involved as part of a "team" to produce a proposal of major size, you will probably be responsible for only a small portion of the total report. Someone will have the responsibility for putting all the parts together and creating the finished product. Simply to provide you with a picture of the scope of a major proposal, Figure 15.10 represents the headings taken from the content pages of a proposal prepared by a supplier to a military aircraft manufacturer. The proposal team consisted of sixteen executives, managers, and engineers. One page from the proposal, shown in Figure 15.11, illustrates the format and descriptive thoroughness used. Let's examine a few of the

Synergism at work

Introduction

Program Personnel Organization

Company and Program Organization
Company Management and Key Program Personnel
Program Schedule

Program Planning and Control

Planning
Contract Requirements
Task Performance Statement
Work Breakdown Structure
Functional Assignment Matrix
Schedules
Job Order Release Scheduling
Contract Authorization
Work Authorization
Job Orders
Control
Time Card Control
Vendor Audit
Management Review
Purchasing and Subcontracting
Schedule Monitoring
Project Management
Measurement
Design Reviews
Performance Standards
Management Audits
Contract Compliance
Personnel Loading

Production Program Plan

Organization
Production Management System
Manufacturing Engineering
Production Planning and Scheduling
Manufacturing

FIGURE 15.10
Technical proposal contents (continued on next page).

Page 2

Quality Assurance Plan

General
Applicable Documents
Procurement Control
Quality Control
Handling, Storing, Marking, Labeling, Packaging
Test and Measurement Calibration System
Nonconforming Material Control
Corrective Action and Customer Source Inspection

Logistics Support

Company Capabilities

Primary Physical Facilities

Quality Assurance Test Laboratory
Environmental Test Laboratory
Manufacturing Capability
Antenna Testing Facilities

Proposal Summary

* The body of this proposal is 87 pages.

FIGURE 15.10
(continued).

FELDSCO

The Production Scheduler is responsible for the part numbers in his product line from the time an order or contract is received until it is delivered. The Scheduler, with his manager, plans the end item to determine indentured breakdown, make or buy, and lead items. He writes the shop orders and purchase requisitions and does the follow up to ensure schedule attainment. He coordinates with shop supervision, production control, purchasing, inspection, test, and engineering personnel to ensure that no problems hinder the progress of his work. Upon shipment, the order is closed out and deleted from the backlog.

Work orders released for either fabrication or assembly are controlled in a kit package that includes the blueprint, parts list showing required and issued, operation card, assembly instructions, and the component dates. The hard copy is retained in the area where the job is working in due-date sequence.

The Material Requirements Planning System provides access to a large in-plant, Feldsco-owned, Prime central computer system through terminals and printers. Subprograms or reports, utilizing the database as programmed, are obtained by programming through the terminal.

4.5.2 In-Process Inspection

All fabricated parts will be inspected as applicable for conformance to Engineering Drawings, Operation Cards, Historical Record Cards, and other Quality Assurance approved instructions.

Subassembly and assembly inspection will be performed as applicable for conformance to Engineering Drawings, Operation Cards, Assembly Instructions, Special Inspection Instructions, Historical Record Cards, and other Quality Assurance approved instructions.

Visual inspection for workmanship and conformity to applicable drawings, documents, and Quality Assurance approved instructions will be performed prior to closure or covering of the unit.

Preliminary functional test will be performed as deemed desirable by quality Assurance Department and/or customer quality requirements.

39

FIGURE 15.11
Page from a technical production proposal.

parts from a variety of proposals to see how they might eventually fit into a total proposal.

Problem and/or Purpose   *Problem* and *purpose* are often used as interchangeable terms in reports. Here is the introductory statement called "Project Description" in a proposal by a firm to contribute to an educational project:

Project Description

Mainline Community College has invited business and industry to participate in the creation of Business Communication, a television course and video training package. These materials will provide effective training in business communication skills to enhance the performance of individuals in business and contribute to organizational skills and profitability. In our rapidly evolving information society, skill in communication is integral to success.

Note how the heading "Project Description" has been used in place of "Purpose." In the following opening statement, "Problem" is used as the heading:

Problem

The Board of Directors of Heatherington Village Association has requested a proposal for total management and operation of its 1,620-unit permanent residential planned housing development. This proposal demonstrates the role and advantages of using Central Management Corporation in that role.

The purpose of the proposal may also be listed as a separate heading when the proposal intends to include objectives of a measurable nature. When you list objectives such as "To reduce overall expenses for maintenance by 10 percent," attempt to list measurable and attainable objectives and list only enough to accomplish the purpose of selling your proposal. Many proposals have been shunted aside simply because they promised more than they could ever actually achieve.

Scope   When determining the scope of your proposal, you can place limitations on what you propose to do or on what the material or equipment you sell can accomplish. The term *scope* need not necessarily be the only heading for this section. "Areas Served," "Limitations to the

Study," and "Where XXX Can Be Used" are examples of headings that describe the scope of the proposal. Here is a "scope" section from a consulting firm's proposal to conduct a salary survey:

Are problem, purpose, and scope related and introductory?

<u>What the Study Will Cover</u>

To assist ABDEC, Inc., for formulating its salary and benefits program for executives, Smith and Smith will include an analysis of compensation (salary and benefits) for no fewer than twenty of ABDEC's contemporaries in the same geographic region. In addition to salaries, insurance, incentives, deferred compensation, medical, and retirement plans will be included. Additionally, Smith and Smith will make recommendations for ABDEC's program.

Another statement of scope might be as follows:

<u>Scope</u>

Leading figures in business and industry will work with respected academicians and skilled production staff to produce fifteen 30-minute television lessons that may be used in courses for college credit or as modules dealing with discrete topics for corporate executives.

After scope tells "what," method tells "how" it will be done.

Method and Procedures   The method used to solve the problem or to conduct the business of the proposal should be spelled out in detail. In this section, simply think through all the steps necessary to meet the terms of the proposal and write them in sequence. When feasible, you should include time schedule or framework material to indicate when the project will be completed.

Materials and Equipment   For large proposals, such as construction or research and development, indicate the nature and quantities of materials and equipment to be used. In some cases, several departments will contribute to this portion. When materials and equipment constitute a major portion of the total cost, include prices. Much litigation arises when clients are charged for "cost overruns." When contracts are made on the basis of "cost plus XX percent," the major costs of materials, equipment, and labor/personnel must be thoroughly described and documented.

Personnel and Recommendations   Assuming your proposal meets with acceptance in terms of services to be performed or products to be supplied, the prospective customer will buy if the "conviction" part of your proposal really convinces. As in a sales message, conviction plays a role in proposals. If everything outlined is acceptable, the "who" and "how much" sections may be critical. Conviction in proposals is based on past records of the bidder, the recommendations of its past customers, and the proposed cost.

A brief biography of the principal members in the proposal plays a strong part in conviction:

Following "what" and "how," proposals describe "who."

Principals

Engagement Principal: Harold M. Jones, M.B.A., M.A.I.
Partner in Miller, Jones, and Smith, consulting appraisers,
since 1966. Fellow of the American Institute of Appraisers.
B.A., M.B.A., Harvard University. Phi Kappa Phi and Beta
Gamma Sigma honorary societies. Lecturer and speaker at
many realty and appraisal conferences and at the University
of Michigan.

In another related section, the proposal might mention other work performed:

Major Clients of Past Five Years

City of Denver, Colorado; Dade County, Florida; City of San
Francisco, California; City of Seattle, Washington; Harbor
General Corporation, San Francisco; Gulf and Houston,
Incorporated, Houston, Texas. Personal references are
available on request.

Follow Up and/or Evaluation   Although your entire proposal is devoted to convincing the reader of its merit, clients are frequently concerned about what will happen when the proposed work or service is completed. Will you return to make certain your work is satisfactory? Can you adjust your method of research as times change?

If your proposal is for a research grant, don't promise more than you can do. If your study is to explore a promising new approach to medical cures for serious diseases, don't promise to solve all the world's problems. Not all funded research proves to be successful.

Follow up and evaluation provide feedback.

If you propose to make a study in your firm's area of expertise, you may be more confident. A public accounting firm's proposal to audit a firm's records need not be modest. The accountant follows certain audit functions that are prescribed by the profession. However, a proposal that involves providing psychological services probably warrants a thoughtful follow-up program to evaluate the service.

Budget, Cost, and Summary   The budget or cost of the program should be detailed when materials, equipment, outside help, consultants, salaries, and travel are to be included. A simple proposal for service by one person might only consist of a statement such as "15 hours at $200/hour, totaling $3,000, plus mileage and expenses estimated at $550." Present the budget or cost after the main body of the proposal.

In addition to a cost or budget, you might conclude the proposal with a summary. This summary may also be used to open the total proposal to put it in deductive sequence.

Most work resulting from proposals is finally covered by a working agreement or contract to avoid discrepancies in the intents of the parties. In some cases, for example, users of outside consultants insist that each consultant be covered by a sizable general personal liability insurance policy that also insures the company. Many large firms and governmental organizations use highly structured procedures to assure understanding of contract terms.

Addenda Items   When certain supporting material may be necessary to the proposal but would make it too bulky or would detract from it, include the material as an addendum item. A bibliography and an appendix are examples of addendum items. References used should appear in the bibliography or as footnotes. Maps, questionnaires, letters of recommendation, and similar materials are suitable appendix items.

In selling, do you introduce price after you've convinced?

• Sample Short Proposal

A short, informal proposal that includes several of the parts we've discussed is shown in Figure 15.12. It consists of three major divisions: The Problem, A Proposed Course of Instruction, and Cost. The Course of Instruction section is broken into five subdivisions.

Summary

As they increase in length from one page to several pages, reports also grow in formality with the addition of introductory and addenda items. As a result, reports at the formal end of the continuum tend to be repetitive. Title pages, transmittal messages, summaries, and content tables all mention or discuss some elements included in the body of the report.

Dear_____

As a follow-up to our discussion of the need for training in the area of oral and interpersonal communication for your supervisory and middle-management personnel, I am pleased to present the following proposal.

The Problem

Management has perceived a need for improved communication performance on the part of supervisory and middle-management personnel to strengthen relationships between them and their subordinates.

A Proposed Course of Instruction

Based on our experience, the following broad concept should be effective in producing better understanding and improved performance:

Teaching-Learning Method. The acquisition of interpersonal skills results from an activity-oriented training program in which students have an opportunity to apply theory through role playing, case discussion, and critical feedback.

In this approach, the instructor is a learning facilitator rather than a lecturer. Frequent use of our video playback accompanied by instructor and group feedback reinforces learning.

Content. The following topics constitute the content core of the program:

1. Perception and self-concept
2. A positive communication climate
3. Sending skills
4. Receiving skills
5. Nonverbal skills
6. Reducing communication barriers
7. Resolving conflict
8. Interviewing
9. Small-group communication
10. Power and persuasion

Learning Materials. Because students seem to feel more comfortable when they have a textbook to guide them, we use the Verderber book, Interact. Additionally, case-problem handouts are provided for role playing and discussion.

FIGURE 15.12

Short proposal (continued on next page).

<u>Length of Course</u>. The course consists of twelve 2-hour sessions over a six-week period.

<u>Number of Participants</u>. Because of the activity orientation of the program, a maximum of 12 students (participants) is desirable.

<u>Cost</u>

All teaching-learning materials will be provided by us and include textbooks, handouts, video camera and playback equipment. Based on a 12-session, 12-participant program, the total cost is $1,800. When two courses are offered on the same days, the total cost is $3,300.

Should you like to discuss implementation of the program, I will be pleased to meet with you at your convenience.

Sincerely

R. M. McNitt

R.M. McNitt

Enclosures: Biographical sketches of instructional staff.

(2)

FIGURE 15.12
(continued).

Organizing the content of a report involves the ability to see the report problem in its entirety and then break it into its parts. Because reports are written after the research or field work has been completed, writers may begin writing with any of the report parts and then complete the rough draft by putting the parts in logical order.

Short reports are usually written in memorandum or letter form. They are called "short" because they simply are not long enough to require the many supporting preliminary and ending parts of longer reports. Nevertheless, short reports require the same organizing and writing skills of preparers as do long reports.

Proposals represent a bridge between short and long reports inasmuch as they may be either short or long, call for thorough organization, and require writing methods that will be not only informative but convincing in a selling way. Proposals are often written by teams; in this way, they typify the nature of reports as having discrete parts that writers can prepare in any order and then assemble into whole reports.

About Language and Usage

Here are some words frequently heard and often not understood:

implacable (im-'plak-e-bel)
Not capable of being appeased or changed. Opponents of the oil drilling were implacable.

irenic (ī-'ren-ik)
Conducive to peace and conciliation. The irenic meeting bode well for the future.

malevolent (ma-'lev-o-lent)
Showing intense, even vicious ill will. The malevolent attacks were unwarranted.

pariah (pa-'rī-a)
A social outcast. His past was kept secret to prevent his being treated as a pariah.

penultimate (pe-nŭl-'ti-mate)
Next to the last. He was the penultimate choice for the role.

supernumerary (sū-per-nū-'me-ra-ri)
A person serving no function; one only used as needed; an actor in a minor role. Most of John's career was spent as a supernumerary on Broadway.

Exercises

Review Questions

1. What four terms could probably be used as headings for many reports?
2. What is meant by the concept that as reports become longer they grow in formality?
3. What are some synonyms for "summary"?
4. How do criteria for judging things fit into report organization?
5. How does an inductive organization become deductive when applied to reports?
6. How do form reports increase accuracy of information?
7. What determines whether memorandum or letter format should be used for short reports?
8. What is the primary purpose of a proposal? What is meant by RFQ?
9. When a long, complex proposal is prepared in industry, who does the original writing?
10. What factor or factors make it possible to begin writing a report or a proposal with any part of the report?

Activities

1. Visit a computer store that handles more than one line or three stores that emphasize only a single line. Examine three brands of personal computers and select the one that you believe best serves the dual purpose of personal computer and word processor. Use whatever criteria you believe will enable you to make a selection. Prepare a short report to your instructor.

2. For a proposal, make whatever assumptions you want to make about your background. A franchise for a fast-food outlet will be assigned in your community, and proposals have been requested. You'd like the franchise because it should yield about $50,000 a year for an owner who does not work actively in the operation and about $100,000 for one who does. Capital required is $150,000; you have $50,000 and have made arrangements for the remainder from financing sources. The franchiser, Frenchies, will supply initial staff training, the additional financing for the physical structure, and financial management advice.

Frenchies is a solid organization, similar to McDonalds, and has had few franchise failures. The firm operates on a percentage of the gross income of each franchise. Prepare a proposal to the Consumer Service Division of Frenchies.

3. Prepare a short report on the selection of one of three automobiles to be used as home-delivery vehicles for a food service. No trips are more than five miles from the company's food-preparation facility.

Cases

Prepare short reports or proposals as solutions for each of the following.

Stock Selection Case Select ten stocks listed on the New York Stock Exchange and reported in your daily paper or in the *Wall Street Journal*. Assume you will purchase 100 shares of each of the ten stocks at the prices listed at the market close on a particular day. You are going to keep a record of changes in the stocks for a one-week period—five trading days. Submit a memorandum to your instructor on the purchase date reporting your ten stocks according to the following format:

Name of Stock   Price per Share   Total Cost (×100)

At the end of the five-day period, submit another memorandum to your instructor detailing how your investment fared during the week. Record the Dow-Jones Industrial Average of thirty stocks for both your purchase date and the end of the five-day period. Compare your total performance—percentage gain or loss—with that of the Dow-Jones average. Prepare a summary report for your instructor.

Perception of Occupations and Professions Case As vice-president of Demographic and Social Research, Inc., you are the principal investigator for a study sponsored by your state society of Certified Public Accountants. The society is interested in determining what perceptions the general public has of CPAs compared with other occupations or professions. They would like to improve whatever image they present so more college students would investigate careers in public accounting.

The society contracted with your firm to make a study that could be used by a public relations firm to promote accounting as a career. Your job, therefore, is simply to determine how accountants are viewed by the general public. You are not hired to make recommendations about a public relations program, nor are you to study how the profession of accounting is viewed. The primary task is to get a view of how an accountant is perceived when compared with other professionals or practitioners of an occupation.

In particular, the society has asked you to assess how an accountant compares on four qualities: (1) honesty, (2) personality, (3) intelligence, and (4) physical appearance. The CPA society has consulted with public relations firms and determined these four qualities lend themselves to effective image changing. Based on your results, the public relations firm will design a program to improve the perception of the professional accountant.

Using a stratified national sample of 6,000 people originally designed for national surveys by your firm, you obtained opinions on the public's perception of ten occupations/professions. These are listed on the left side of the following tabulation. The four qualities assessed are the column heads, and the columns contain the final ranking of each occupation/profession on each trait. Because you had used a weighted, computerized method of arriving at the ranks, you should assume that you will attach the computer printouts in the appendix of your report. As you review the tabulation, note that some ties exist. These occur because the difference in the weighted perceptions was not significant enough to distinguish between or among ranks. For example, "honesty" shows a four-way tie among business executives, dentists, engineers, and

Rank Order Perceptions of Professions by 6,000 People

	Honesty	Personality	Intelligence	Physical Appearance
Public Accountants	2	9	5	6
Airline Pilots	8	2	8	2
Business Executives	6	4	6	1
Clergy	1	5	7	9
Dentists	6	7	4	7
Elected Officials	10	1	9	4
Engineers	6	9	2	5
Lawyers	9	3	2	10
Medical Doctors	6	6	2	8
Postal Employees	3	9	10	3

medical doctors. They were all given rankings of 6 because ranks 4, 5, 6, and 7 were not significantly distinguishable.

Think about each of the four traits as a separate part of the findings. In this way, you can develop four separate simple tables as the basis for your discussion. You might point to similarities among rankings and professions on certain traits. These similarities, for example, could raise the question: "Does stereotyping play a part in public perceptions?" Prepare a short report in letter form. Use your own address or a fictitious one for your company. Address your report to J. J. Adams, Executive Director, State CPA Society, the capital city of your state.

Food Service Case   Preptech University is located in a community of 60,000 and has an enrollment of 8,500 students. As a private school with relatively high tuition, Preptech enrolls many students from upper-level income groups. At the same time, about 60 percent of the students receive some form of financial aid in the form of government loans, work-study funds, and university grants. Of the 8,500 students, about 6,000 live in campus dormitories, fraternities and sororities, and nearby off-campus apartments. The remainder are commuters living within about 25 miles of the campus.

The University Food Service operates a cafeteria, a deli shop, and a restaurant with a combined capability of serving about 3,000 people at each of the three daily meals. Meals at fraternities and sororities accommodate about 1,200 students. For those living in dormitories, the university has three board-and-room plans and a room-only plan. The room-only plan is $180 a month, and monthly board-and-room plans are as follows:

A. Room with 3 cafeteria meals daily, Monday–Friday: $360
B. Room with a cafeteria meal ticket worth $100 monthly: $280
C. Room with one meal daily—lunch or dinner, Monday–Friday: $260

During the past four school terms (semesters), the number of people selecting the plans has been as follows:

	Room Only	Plan A	Plan B	Plan C
This Term:	685	285	700	1280
Last Term:	520	405	770	1140
1 Year Ago:	450	560	840	960
$1\frac{1}{2}$ Years Ago:	385	836	950	880

The University Food Service manager, Carla Perkins, is concerned about the decline in use of campus food facilities and has been pressured from higher university administrators to do something about the problem. Overall, the total university enrollment has remained stable in the neighborhood of 8,500 during the four terms.

Although off-campus eating facilities have been around for a number of years, two years ago a McDonald's, a Taco Bell, a Joe's Pizza Parlor, and a full-service restaurant (the University Club) opened within a short walk of the campus.

Ms. Perkins asks your business communication instructor for a group from your class to assist her by making a study of student opinion about the university food services compared with the off-campus eating facilities. The university will pay $1,200 for the study. Because your class is organized in four-person teams, your instructor decides that the teams should compete for the job by submitting proposals.

Your study plan is to determine the cost of meals for board-and-room plans A, B, and C and the cost of average meals in the four new eating facilities. Additionally, you then plan to conduct a survey of student opinion using a rating scale for the eating facilities. You will sample about 20 percent of the student body during meal hours in the various eating facilities. The rating scale will make use of a 5-point scale. Your team has decided to obtain student opinion about these items:

Cost of meals
Convenience
Variety
Food quality
Atmosphere

Prepare a proposal to compete for the project. You may make any assumptions you like in preparing the proposal.

Nickle Savings Bank Case   As assistant vice-president of the Nickle Savings Bank, you are the second in command of a department whose job is to dispose of real estate the Bank may acquire through foreclosure, purchase, or trades. One property owned is at 4312 Main Street, a vacant corner lot. According to real-estate appraisers from your staff, the best use of the property would be for construction of a restaurant. Your job is to survey the people in the community to determine whether an effort should be made to interest a fast-food chain, an enclosed sit-down restaurant, or a specialty restaurant in the location. Your findings will be combined with other aspects of feasibility in a presentation to the bank's executive committee. You have conducted an interview survey of families in the area, of workers in nearby businesses, and of a sample of passersby.

You believe the 400-person sample is representative of potential users of a dining facility. Prepare a short report for your boss, G. J. Jenks, vice-president of real estate. Here are the results of your survey:

1. What kind of prepared-food service should be located at 4312 Main Street?
    - 36   Enclosed sit-down restaurant
    - 152 Fast-food chain restaurant
    - 212 Specialty restaurant

2. On average, how often do you eat out each week?
    - 32   0 or 1 times
    - 244 4 or 7 times
    - 112 2 or 3 times
    - 12   8 or more times

3. What meal would you most often have outside the home?
    - 96   Breakfast
    - 248 Lunch
    - 56   Dinner

4. When you eat out, how much per person would you usually spend?
    - 10   Under $2
    - 72 $2–3
    - 80 $3–4
    - 84 $4–5
    - 92 $5–6
    - 39 $6–7
    - 15 $7–8
    - 8   Over $8

During your interviews, you asked people to estimate the amounts they spent as "$2 to $3, $3 to $4," etc. If you were to do mathematical computations, you'd probably use midpoints such as $2.50, $3.50, and $4.50 for values for each class. In this case, however, write in generalities simply using percentages. Measures of central tendency are not necessary.

Payroll Mistake Case As a member of the internal audit department of your firm, you have found that hourly-rate employees often believe their paychecks are incorrect. Misunderstandings and timecard mistakes are usually responsible. The current method is haphazard. Employees go to the payroll office during working hours and stand around waiting for the error to be checked and corrections to be made. Employees on hourly rates are paid every two weeks. In cooperation with the payroll department manager, you have come up with a procedure similar to the following. When a payroll error is suspected, the employee should see the department head or supervisor to determine whether a mistake has been made. If so, the department head will fill out a Payroll Claim Form to be signed by the employee and the supervisor. The supervisor will send it to the payroll office by messenger. Small adjustments will be paid in checks for the next pay period. Special checks will be issued the next day for amounts exceeding $50 or more. Sort through the information presented and prepare a report presenting the new procedure. The memorandum will be distributed to all departments and supervisors. Steps in your procedure should be numbered in sequence and should be written for *employee* understanding.

CHAPTER 16

Writing the Formal Report

If we value the pursuit of knowledge, we must be free to follow wherever that search may lead us. The free mind is no barking dog to be tethered on a ten-foot chain.

ADLAI STEVENSON

Although reports also grow in formality as they grow in size, the determination about whether a report should be prepared in formal style and format is made by researchers before the preparation–writing process begins. In the process of organizing and making tentative outlines, writers learn quickly the format and style of report best able to do the communication job needed. As you review the writing procedures, techniques, and documentary methods in this chapter, keep in mind that they also apply to reports in general and should be used when necessary or desirable in short reports and proposals.

Procedures for Writing

A writing procedure that works well for one person may not for another, but consider the following general suggestions:

1. Begin writing only after you have reached a conclusion and prepared a suitable outline.
2. Select a good writing environment. Avoid distractions. Some people can be creative in an environment that might be distracting to others.
3. Start planning early. "Burning the midnight oil" is sometimes necessary, but it doesn't always produce your best work. Give yourself more time than you anticipate using.
4. Sometimes beginning with an easy section helps prepare you for more difficult ones later on.

Is uninterrupted time more important than long periods?

5. Set aside long, uninterrupted blocks of writing time.
6. Write rapidly and plan to rewrite later. Do not attempt to edit as you go—you only waste time and lose your train of creative thought.
7. Skip difficult places when composing and return to them later. Usually they aren't as difficult then.
8. When you have finished the draft, let it sit for a day or two. To edit or rewrite immediately may not pay off. Something you have just written may look great. Tomorrow it may look as though it needs some work.
9. Review for possible improvement. Some points might need more supporting evidence. Reading your writing aloud reveals awkward grammatical construction and poor wording. Silent reading often misses these errors.

10. Rewrite where necessary. Rewriting is more than editing; sometimes you may have to rewrite weak material completely without reference to the original.

Techniques of Conviction and Style

Of all the qualities a report should possess, none is more important than conviction. If a report is convincing, readers will accept it as valid and reliable. You will write more convincingly if you have been careful in conducting the research and in interpreting the data. But these writing aids will also add to conviction:

1. *Avoid emotional terms.* "The increase was fantastic" doesn't convince anyone. "The increase was 88 percent—more than double that of the previous year" does convince.

2. *Identify assumptions.* Assumptions are things or conditions taken for granted. When you make an assumption, state that clearly. Statements such as "Assuming all other factors to remain the same, . . ." let the reader in on the writer's starting point.

3. *Label opinions.* Facts are preferred over opinion, but sometimes the opinion of a recognized professional is the closest thing to fact. "In the opinion of legal counsel, . . ." lends conviction to the following statement and lends credence to the integrity of the writer.

   Use sound sources; readers may check your references.

4. *Use documentation.* Footnotes and bibliographies indicate the writer's scholarship and honesty. These methods acknowledge the use of secondary material in the research.

For a more thorough treatment of stylistic techniques, refer to Chapters 4 and 5. Some more stylistic problems common to formal report writing are summarized as follows:

1. *Avoid first-person pronouns as a rule.* In formal reports, the use of *I* is generally unacceptable. Because of the objective nature of research, the fewer personal references you use the better. However, in some organizations the first person is acceptable. Certainly, writing is easier when we can use ourselves as subjects of sentences. People who can change their writing by avoiding the use of the first person will develop a genuine skill.

   Does first-person use the writer as sentence subjects?

2. *Use concrete nouns.* "Authorization was received from the IRS" might not be as effective as "The IRS granted authorization." Subjects that can be visualized are advantageous, but you should also

attempt to use as subjects things most important to the report. If "authorization" were more important than "IRS," the writer should stay with the first version.

3. *Use tense consistently.* Because you are writing about past actions, much of your report writing is in the past tense. However, when you call the reader's attention to the content of a graphic, remember that the graphic *shows* in the present tense. If you mention where the study *will take* the reader, you will use a future-tense verb.

Transitions build bridges.

4. *Use transition sentences.* Because you are writing a report in parts, you can show the connection between those parts by using transition sentences. "Although several advantages accrue from its use, the incentive plan also presents problems" may be a sentence written at the end of a section stressing advantages and before a section stressing problems.

5. *Use tabulations and enumerations.* When you have a series of items, don't hesitate to give each a number and to list them consecutively. This list of writing suggestions is easier to understand because it contains numbered items.

6. *Define terms carefully.* When terms might have specific meanings in the study, define them. Definitions should be written in the term-family-differentiation sequence: "A dictionary (*term*) is a reference book (*family*) that contains a list of all words in a language (*point of difference*)." "A sophomore is a college student in the second year."

7. *Use a variety of coherence techniques.* Just as transition sentences bind portions of a report together, certain coherence techniques bind sentences together: repeating a word, using a pronoun, or using a conjunction. If such devices are employed, each sentence seems to be joined smoothly to the next. The words and phrases here are particularly useful:

Time Connectors	Contrast Connectors
finally	although
further	despite
furthermore	however
initially	in contrast
meanwhile	nevertheless
next	on the other hand
then	on the contrary
thereafter	yet
while	
at the same time	

Similarity Connectors	Cause-and-Effect Connectors
for instance	but
for example	conversely
likewise	as a result
in the same way	because
just as	consequently
similarly	hence
	since
	therefore
	thus

These words and phrases keep you from making abrupt changes in thought.

8. *Check for variety.* While you write, most of your attention should be directed toward presenting the right ideas and support. Later review may reveal that certain portions have a monotonous sameness in sentence length or construction. Changes are easy and well worth the effort.

The preceding stylistic techniques become habitual through experience. Without much awareness of them, you can simply use them while concentrating primarily on presenting and supporting ideas at the first-draft stage. Necessary improvements can be made later.

Documenting Reports

In footnotes and bibliographies, the key word is consistency. Documentation should be complete enough that another person could locate the material footnoted or listed in a bibliography. Therefore, as you review the following suggestions, look on them simply as guides rather than rules.

Documentation is done for several reasons:

1. Citations give credit where it is due—to the one who created the material. People who document demonstrate a responsibility to scholarship.

   Why use documentation?

2. Documentation protects writers against plagiarism, which occurs when someone steals material from another and claims it as his or her own writing. It is said, "Not documenting a source is plagiarism, but documenting it is scholarship."

3. Documentation supports statements. If recognized authorities have said the same thing, your work takes on credibility; and you put yourself in good company.

• Using Footnotes

Footnotes should be used to refer readers to sources of quotations, paraphrases, and quantitative data used in the report. Several footnote citation methods are available, and you may use any of them. When you select one method, use it consistently throughout the report. Note the differences among the following methods.

Bottom-of-the-Page Method   Placing footnotes at the bottom of the page on which they are cited might be called the traditional method because of its long use.

The citation: "Comparisons between countries are always tendentious to some extent and thus suspect."[1]
The footnote following a 1½-inch line at end of page:

―――――――――――
[1] Edwin J. Feulner, Jr., Congress and the New Economic Order (Washington, D.C.: The Heritage Foundation, 1976), p. 53.

Traditional footnote styles for a variety publications are shown in Figure 16.1. Spacing between parts of footnotes may vary between typewritten and printed material. Because most people know the final item in a footnote is the page or pages on which the reference is located, the "p." or "pp." before page numbers is optional and may be omitted.

End-of-Report Footnote List   The end-of-report footnote style lists all footnotes in a list called "Notes" or "List of Footnotes" at the end of the report. The footnotes are listed in the order in which their citations appear in the report. Citing the material to be footnoted is done by placing the superscript above the line as in the bottom-of-the-page method or by placing the citation figure in parentheses on the line of writing:

The citation: "... some extent and thus suspect."[1]
       or: "... some extent and thus suspect." (1)
The footnote at the end of the chapter for either citation:

(1) Edwin J. Feulner, Jr., Congress and the New Economic Order (Washington, D.C.: The Heritage Foundation, 1976), 53.

GUIDES TO FOOTNOTE CONSTRUCTION

1. For a book reference with one or two authors:

William C. Himstreet and Wayne Murlin Baty, Business Communications, 9th ed. (Boston: PWS-KENT Publishing Company, 1990), p. 201.*

2. For three authors:

Harold R. Jones, Michael Smith, and Thomas Brown, Tomorrow (Chicago: Western Press, 1986), p. 335.

3. For more than three authors use et al. ("and others") after name of first author:

Alex Hales et al., Secrets of Hispanola (San Francisco: Golden Gate Press, 1923), p. 54.

4. For an edited book:

Brent D. Rubin, ed., Communication Yearbook 1 (New Brunswick, N.J.: Transaction Books, 1977), pp. 48–50.

5. For a magazine or journal article:

Betty R. Ricks, "The Neglected Managerial Communication Skills: A Critical Analysis," The A.B.C.A. Bulletin, December 1981, pp. 22–25.

6. For unpublished speeches, interviews, and letters:

Wayne L. Miller, Personal letter to Mary Ellen May, July 31, 1988.

Ronald R. Reagan, Radio address to the nation, May 14, 1988.

7. For unpublished papers:

Homer Lawrence, "Behavior Patterns in Rigid Organizations" (Doctoral dissertation, Arizona State University, Tempe, June 1986), p. 145.

8. For a government publication:

United States Department of Agriculture, Dry-Farming Possibilities for Guayule in California (Washington, D.C.: U.S. Government Printing Office, 1988), p. 75.

* The p. or pp. before page numbers is optional.

FIGURE 16.1

Traditional footnote styles.

Footnote Citation-to-Bibliography Link   A method that ties foot-notes to the bibliography and does away with the need for a separate list of footnotes is the citation-to-bibliography link. The citation number in the text is followed by any page reference as in the following example:

The citation: "... some extent and thus suspect." (4:53)

In this case, the reader can locate the original source by turning to the bibliography. It will be listed as number 4 in the bibliography:

4. Feulner, Edwin J., Jr., <u>Congress and the New Economic Order</u>, Washington, D.C.: The Heritage Foundation, 1976.

The figure 4 indicates the reference is fourth in the alphabetic listing of bibliography items. By using the numerical listing and page numbers in the citation, the writer makes the bibliography serve also as a list of footnote references.

Author–Date Reference Link   A relatively new footnoting method places the author's name and the date of publication in the footnote citation. This author–date reference link enables the reader to turn to the bibliography, locate the author's name and the date of publication, and look up the original source. Use of the method and/or variations of it is advocated by the originator, the American Psychological Association. The Modern Language Association has a similar method; both are often required for scholarly publications. Here are some examples of that type of footnote citation:

a.   ... is illustrated in a new text (Ruch & Rye, 1988).

b.   ... and thus suspect (Feulner, 1976).

c.   ... is illustrated by Ruch and Rye (1988).

d.   Marshall McLuhan (1965) coined the phrase....

e.   ... as the reward (Reardon, 1981; Smith, 1984).

f.   Jones, Smith, and Brown (1986) concluded....

g.   A study of motivation ... (Hansen et al., 1989).

In each of these citations, reference is made to a book, article, or other publication included in the bibliography or list of references (one or the other is used). Note that when the name or names of authors is used as a subject or object in the sentence, only the date is placed in the parentheses. When not used in the sentence, the name or names are included in the parentheses along with the date to avoid repetition. In (e), two sources are cited in the same parentheses. In (g), the citation indicates that more than *six* authors collaborated in the cited work. When six or fewer are involved, all names are listed; otherwise, list only the first name and the "et al." abbreviation to indicate "and others."

A useful reference for the method is the following:

American Psychological Association. (1986). Publication manual (*3rd ed.*) *Washington, D.C.: Author.*

Note the word "Author" is used in the last position when the author and the publisher are the same—in this case, the American Psychological Association. Although the title is italicized (underscored in typescript), only the first letter of the first word is capitalized. More about this method will be presented in the discussion of bibliographies.

Footnotes may also be included for reasons other than documentation. These are called explanatory footnotes. For example, a footnote to support a statistical table might describe the mathematics involved, as in

> * The weighted opinion was arrived at by assigning responses from high to low as 5, 4, 3, 2, 1; totaling all responses; and dividing by the number of respondents.

In this case, the asterisk (*) was used rather than a number to identify the footnote both in the text and in the footnote citation. This method is often used when only one or two footnotes are included in the paper and, in the case of two, they do not fall on the same page.

The primary concern for the report writer is to maintain consistency. Footnotes are designed to permit the reader to locate the original source if desired. Here are some suggestions for handling footnotes:

1. If in doubt about whether to include certain information, follow the rule that it is better to include more than enough rather than too little.

2. Place explanatory information in footnotes when the information is not easily incorporated as part of the text.

3. Be consistent. Simply because our examples may include a comma or period to separate parts of the footnote citation does not necessarily mean that is the only way to prepare the entry. Any good style manual will have its own method.

   Pick a method and stay with it.

4. Become familiar with many of the Latin abbreviations used in documentation work. Here are a few of the most common ones:

Abbreviation	Latin Word(s)	Meaning
et al.	et alibi	and elsewhere
et al.	et alii	and others
ibid.	ibidem	in the same place; from the same work
id.	idem	the same
loc. cit.	loco citato	in the place cited; in the message last referred to
op. cit.	opere citato	in the work cited

• Using Bibliographies

Note the differences between the traditional footnote and bibliographic entries in the following examples:

Footnote: [1] Edwin J. Feulner, Jr., <u>Congress and the New Economic Order</u> (Washington, D.C.: The Heritage Foundation, 1976), p. 53.

Bibliography: Feulner, Edwin J., Jr., <u>Congress and the New Economic Order</u> (Washington, D.C.: The Heritage Foundation, 1976).

Bottom-of-the-page and end-of-report footnotes use given names of authors first; bibliographies use surnames first. In the American Psychological Association (APA) method surnames come first; but initials only are used rather than given names; i.e., Feulner, E. J., Jr. Additionally, this method places the date after the author's name to coincide with the footnote citation:

Feulner, E. J., Jr. (1976). <u>Congress and the new economic order</u>. Washington, D.C.: The Heritage Foundation.

In scholarly journals, the APA method predominates. In business reports and college papers any of the methods is suitable. As a reader of professional literature and a writer and user of business reports, you should be familiar with all methods.

How do footnotes and bibliographic entries differ?

Bibliographies differ from footnotes in other respects. First, bibliographic entries refer to the entire work cited and not simply to the specific page or pages from which material came. Thus, a footnote might cite a specific page, but the bibliographic entry would include the entire book without page references. A magazine article in a bibliography would include the beginning and ending pages of the article. Second, bibliographic entries are written with the author's last name first; footnotes with the given name first.

Just as footnotes provide references to specific quotes, paraphrases, and information sources, bibliographic entries give evidence of the nature of sources from which the author has obtained information. All footnote sources are included in the bibliography as well; however, informational, explanatory footnotes that do not refer to literature or other verbal sources would not appear. In addition, a researcher often uses sources that provide broad information but do not result in footnote citations. Your judgment should tell whether to list them in the bibliography; when in doubt, include them.

The bibliography shown in Figure 16.2 contains both book and article references in separate sections. When the bibliography contains only five or six references, division isn't necessary; simply combine books, articles, and other citations in a single alphabetic listing. However, extremely long bibliographies may contain several headings, such as books, articles, publications of learned societies, unpublished documents and papers, government publications, newspaper articles, interviews, and personal letters.

When should books and articles be listed separately?

When more than one bibliographic entry is by the same author, the second entry substitutes an underscore for the author's name or names, as in

Jones, Joseph J., <u>The New Communication</u>, . . .

———, "Hearing Is No Good Without Listening," . . . .

Several variations are acceptable in the internal mechanics of bibliographic entries. For example, some authorities place the location of the publisher before the name of the publisher and others reverse them. When the city is well known, the state need not be indicated. Rather significant changes from the traditional bibliography are evident in the format and style of the American Psychological Association bibliography, portions of which are shown in Figure 16.3.

Using Headings Effectively

Headings are signposts along the way, informing readers about what is ahead. Headings take their positions from their relative importance in a complete outline. For example, in a Roman numeral outline, "I" is a

BIBLIOGRAPHY

Books

Aronson, Elliott, The Social Animal, San Francisco: W. H. Freeman and Company, 1972.

Clark, Virginia, Language, New York: St. Martin's Press, Inc., 1972.

Gay, Kathlyn, Body Talk, New York: Charles Scribner's Sons, 1974.

Harris, Thomas A., I'm OK--You're OK, New York: Avon Books (published by arrangement with Harper & Row, Publishers), 1973.

Lewis, Phillip V., Organizational Communication: The Essence of Effective Management, 2nd ed., Columbus, Ohio: Grid Publishing, Inc., 1980.

Williams, Frederick, The Communications Revolution, Beverly Hills, Calif., Sage Publications, 1982.

Articles

"Body Language: Student and Teacher Behavior," Saturday Review of Education, 1(5) (May 1973), pp. 78–84.

Cater, Douglass, "The Communications Revolution--What Social-Political Consequences?" Current, 3(155) (October 1973), pp. 36–40.

Davis, Keith, "The Care and Cultivation of the Corporate Grapevine," Dun's Review, 102(7) (July 1973), pp. 44–47.

James, Muriel, and Dorothy Jongeward, "Born to Win," Family Circle Magazine, June 1975, pp. 18–28.

Swift, Marvin H., "Clear Writing Means Clear Thinking Clear ...," Harvard Business Review, 51(1) (January 1973), pp. 59–62.

FIGURE 16.2
Format of a bibliography.

REFERENCES

Blake, R., & Mouton, J. (1964). The managerial grid. Houston: Gulf.

Deal, T. E., & Kennedy, A. A. (1982). Corporate cultures. Reading, MA: Addison-Wesley.

Himstreet, W. C., & Baty, W. M. (1990). Business communications (9th Ed.). Boston: PWS-KENT.

McDermott, V. (1975). The literature on classical theory construction. Human Communication Research, 5, 83–103.

Maslow, A. H. (1954). Motivation and personality. New York: Harper & Row.

Sharpe, W. F. (1985). Investments (3rd Ed.). Englewood Cliffs, NJ: Prentice-Hall.

Szilagy, A. D., Jr., & Wallace, M. J. (1987). Organizational behavior and performance (4th Ed.). Glenview, IL: Scott, Foresman & Co.

FIGURE 16.3

List of references in American Psychological Association Format.

first-level heading, "A" is a second-level heading, and "1" is a third-level heading:

I. First-level heading

    A. Second-level heading

    B. Second-level heading

        1. Third-level heading

        2. Third-level heading

II. First-level heading

Two important points about the use of headings also relate to outlines:

If an outline contains an "A," must it also contain a "B"?

1. Because second-level headings are subdivisions of first-level headings, you should have at least two subdivisions (A and B). Otherwise, the first-level heading cannot be divided—something divides into at least two parts or it is not divisible. The same logic applies to the use of third-level headings following second-level headings.

2. All headings of the same level should appear in the same physical location and print, as shown in Figure 16.4.

As you review Figure 16.4, note that two lines have been skipped preceding first-degree headings and only one line omitted preceding second-degree headings. This method is by no means universal, and you may follow any format you like. The important thing is to select a format and follow it consistently to aid communication with the reader. A further suggestion, as you will observe in Figure 16.4 and in the sample report that follows, is to avoid having two headings appear consecutively without any intervening text. For example, always write something following a first-degree heading and before the initial second-degree heading.

Two consecutive headings with no intervening text is a "no-no."

With computers and word processors, you can develop fourth- and fifth-level headings simply by using boldface and varying type fonts. In short reports, however, organization rarely goes beyond third-level headings; thoughtful organization can limit excessive heading levels in formal reports.

The Complete Report

Following a brief description and discussion of its makeup, a complete report is presented. Because it contains the following parts and tends to avoid first-person pronouns, the report may be called formal:

Double-Spaced Copy

FIRST-DEGREE HEADING

xxxxxxxxxxxxxxxxxxxxxxxxxxxxxxxxxxxxxxxxxxxxxxxxxxxxxxx
xxxxxxxxxxxxxxxxxxxxxxxxxxxxxxxxxxxxxxxxxxxxxxxxxxxxx.

Second-Degree Heading

xxxxxxxxxxxxxxxxxxxxxxxxxxxxxxxxxxxxxxxxxxxxxxxxxxxxxx
xxxxxxxxxxxxxxxxxxxxxxxxxxxxxxxxxxxxxxxxxxxxxxxxxxxxx.

Second-Degree Heading

xxxxxxxxxxxxxxxxxxxxxxxxxxxxxxxxxxxxxxxxxxxxxxxxxxxxxx
xxxxxxxxxxxxxxxxxxxxxxxxxxxxxxxxxxxxxxxxxxxxxxxxxxxx.

Third-degree heading.   xxxxxxxxxxxxxxxxxxxxxxxxxxxxxxxxxxx
xxxxxxxxxxxxxxxxxxxxxxxxxxxxxxxxxxxxxxxxxxxxxxxxxxxx.

Third-degree heading.   xxxxxxxxxxxxxxxxxxxxxxxxxxxxxxxxxxx
xxxxxxxxxxxxxxxxxxxxxxxxxxxxxxxxxxxxxxxxxxxxxxxxxxxx.

FIRST-DEGREE HEADING

FIGURE 16.4
Suggested heading formats (continued on next page).

Single-Spaced Copy

FIRST-DEGREE HEADING

XXXXXXXXXXXXXXXXXXXXXXXXXXXXXXXXXXXXXXXXXXXXXXXXXXXXXXXXXX
XXXXXXXXXXXXXXXXXXXXXXXXXXXXXX.

<u>Second-Degree Heading</u>

XXXXXXXXXXXXXXXXXXXXXXXXXXXXXXXXXXXXXXXXXXXXXXXXXXXXXXXXXX
XXXXXXXXXXXXXXXXXXXXXXXXXXXXXX.

<u>Second-Degree Heading</u>

XXXXXXXXXXXXXXXXXXXXXXXXXXXXXXXXXXXXXXXXXXXXXXXXXXXXXXXXXX
XXXXXXXXXXXXXXXXXXXXXXXXXXXXXX.

<u>Third-degree heading</u>.   XXXXXXXXXXXXXXXXXXXXXXXXXXXXXXXXXXXXXX
XXXXXXXXXXXXXXXXXXXXXXXXXXXXX.

<u>Third-degree heading</u>.   XXXXXXXXXXXXXXXXXXXXXXXXXXXXXXXXXXXXXX
XXXXXXXXXXXXXXXXXXXXXXXXXXXXX.

FIRST-DEGREE HEADING

FIGURE 16.4
(**continued**).

1. Transmittal letter
2. Title page
3. Summary
4. Contents and list of figures
5. Body of sample report
6. Reference list
7. Questionnaire in appendix

The report demonstrates several presentation and writing techniques discussed earlier. It should not be considered the only way to prepare reports, but it is a satisfactory model. Following the sample report—in the Chapter Summary—is a comprehensive checklist for use in report writing.

As you review the report, note the following items and features:

1. *Transmittal letter.* The transmittal is in first-person and attempts to stress friendship and a desire to help, as shown in Figure 16.5. Note the similarity between the transmittal and the summary.

2. *Title page.* Four essential items are shown on the title page: title, person or organization for whom the report was prepared (called the authority for the report), identification of the preparer, and the date, as shown in Figure 16.6.

3. *Summary.* The summary contains an abstract of the complete report, including comments about the purpose, method, findings, conclusions, and recommendations, as shown in Figure 16.7. In practice, summaries are frequently called abstracts or synopses.

4. *Contents and list of figures.* The content outline and the list of figures are included on one page, as shown in Figure 16.8, but they could be placed on separate pages if the writer desired. Because people usually expect the beginning of a report to be an introduction, the headings for "Introduction," "Purpose," and "Method and Procedures" could be omitted from the report and from the content outline. In that case, the first item in the content outline would be "America's Role and the Park Manager." The first page of the body of the report would not carry any headings, but the writer might choose to head page one with the title of the report.

Note that all tables and graphics are numbered consecutively and labeled as figures, as shown in Figure 16.8. If the report contained tables only, you could choose to label the items as "Table 1, Table 2, etc." However, when reports contain a variety of tables, graphics, maps, photos, and other illustrations, labeling them all as figures and numbering them consecutively aids readers.

Logic and consistency lead to formats.

How many items on a title page?

Must an introduction be labeled?

When separate labels such as "Figure" for graphics, and "Table" for tables are used, reports may contain sentences confusing to readers, such as "The evidence presented in Figure 4 and Table 1. . . ." When illustrations are numbered consecutively and labeled as figures, the sentence would be simpler as "The evidence presented in Figures 4 and 5. . . ."

5. *Body of sample report.* The body of the report, Figure 16.9, covers eleven pages. The placement of headings in the body is consistent with those in the content outline. Additionally, figures are introduced in sentences preceding them, which may tend to seem somewhat repetitious. For example, "as shown in Figure 1" is almost immediately followed by the heading "Figure 1" on page 3 of the report.

   Communication is improved by reader involvement when the sentence introducing the figure says something interpretive about the data in the figure. Good report writers make certain their comments in the introductory sentences say something more than a mere restatement of the title. A poor introductory sentence for Figure 1 of the report would be "Figure 1 shows ages of park managers," a statement that adds nothing to meaning.

   The documentation style of the American Psychological Association (APA) is used in the body of the report to show how it appears in practice.

   Because the investigation was to result in recommendations as well as conclusions, the report's concluding major section is titled "Conclusions and Recommendations." Although conclusions are often placed under one heading and recommendations under another, they are combined in this report because each conclusion leads directly to a recommendation. Note the active voice headings that also emphasize the recommendations.

6. *Reference list.* All references in Figure 16.10 were used as footnotes and represent the bibliography as well. The list of references is in the recommended APA style, but full given names of authors are used rather than initials. This variation seems to be an improvement.

7. *Questionnaire in appendix.* The appendix item is the questionnaire used to acquire data from residents, as shown in Figure 16.11. When more than one item is included in the appendix, the items are labeled "Appendix A," "Appendix B," etc. For lengthy appendices, a page title "Appendices" might be used to separate that section from the preceding parts of the report.

MARION AND ASSOCIATES

SUITE 330
1227 MONMOUTH AVENUE
DENVER CO   88888

April 15, 199__

Mr. Robert L. Kamden
President
American Mobile Home, Inc.
P.O. Box 441
Scottsdale AZ   85286-0441

Dear Mr. Kamden

I'm pleased to send you our report of the park management study
you authorized in your letter of February 5.

The report reaffirms some of your observations and presents
conclusions and recommendations you should find useful. To gather
information, we surveyed 2,400 residents for opinions about the
weaknesses and strengths of park managers. In addition, audits of
management performance were conducted in 40 parks.

Management weaknesses centered around interpersonal
communication problems with residents and in certain office and
record-keeping functions. Their strengths were primarily in the
maintenance of park physical facilities. Our recommendations
include, among others, focusing training programs on the areas of
weakness.

When you have reviewed the report, Mr. Kamden, I'll be glad to
discuss it further with you.

Sincerely

Lucille Marion
President

lm:ss

FIGURE 16.5
Transmittal letter.

IMPROVING PARK MANAGEMENT

Prepared for
Robert L. Kamden
President
American Mobile Home, Inc.
Scottsdale, Arizona

Prepared by
Marion and Associates
Suite 330
1227 Monmouth Avenue
Denver, Colorado 88888

April 199_

FIGURE 16.6
Title page.

SUMMARY

American Mobile Home, Inc., owns and operates 76 mobile home parks. Because of rapid growth, American has found it necessary to employ and install, as park managers, people who may not have had adequate preparation or skills in all areas of their jobs. This study attempts to identify areas of less-than-adequate managerial performance and to recommend ways in which improvement may be made. The study was authorized by Robert L. Kamden, President of American Mobile Home, Inc.

Research was conducted in two ways: (1) A questionnaire survey of 2,400 park residents was designed to determine park managers' strengths and weaknesses as viewed by residents. (2) Two-person audit teams from Marion and Associates visited 40 parks to interview managers and to examine practices.

Residents indicated managerial weaknesses lay primarily in interpersonal communication skills and in knowledge of and enforcement of rules. Strengths, on the other hand, were managers' abilities to maintain physical facilities.

The audit teams found office work of managers inadequate in cost control, record keeping, and cash management. Additionally, managers were not as active nor as effective in community involvement as American desired them to be.

The study concluded that current managers should be given an opportunity to benefit from training programs designed to meet their needs and corporate needs. In addition to new training programs, recommendations included preparing procedures manuals, underwriting costs of certain community activities for managers, and creating a method for better face-to-face interaction between individual managers and corporate representatives.

FIGURE 16.7
Summary.

CONTENTS

LIST OF FIGURES

FIGURE 16.8
Contents and list of figures.

INTRODUCTION

In the past, zoning laws and citizens' groups have discriminated against the mobile home in much the same way the automobile was legislated off the highway and out of the cities when it first appeared. But these laws were not enforceable because the automobile provided a service that could not be given by the horse and buggy. Mobile and modular housing is essentially doing the same thing ... as more people find their housing needs are harder to satisfy ... they will begin to look for better solutions (Condon, 1976).

As a leader in the residential mobile home park industry, American Mobile Home, Inc., relies heavily on the managers of its residential parks. American's rapid growth in the "sun belt" region has forced it to employ park managers who may not have had the preparation to assume managerial responsibilities.

Purpose of the Study

This study was requested by American Mobile Home, Inc., (American) and conducted by Marion and Associates to determine the adequacy of park managers and to recommend ways in which their job performance might be enhanced. Answers were sought to the following questions:

(1) What are the strengths and weaknesses of managers as viewed by residents of the parks?

(2) How effective is the performance of managers in the technical aspects of their work and in their relationships in local communities?

1

FIGURE 16.9

Body of sample report. (*Note:* To promote readability and to conform to textbook page size, this sample report contains longer typed lines and fewer lines to a page than on 8 1/2 x 11″ paper. Top and bottom margins are reduced. In other ways, the report conforms to the report checklist.)

Methods and Procedures Used

A questionnaire survey was conducted by mail to gather information from residents. Mailings were sent to every odd-numbered lot in each of the 76 mobile home parks operated by American, a total of 4,560. Of these questionnaires, 2,400 were returned and also found usable. The relatively high return of over half of the questionnaires may be attributed to the anonymity provided respondents and to the mention that a response would not jeopardize their own park managers but would help improve service to them and to other residents. A copy of the questionnaire is included in this report appendix.

To gather information about technical performance and community relations, four two-person management audit teams each spent a full day at 10 parks; thus, a total of 40 audits provided data that were considered representative of all 76 parks. Conclusions and recommendations were developed from an analysis of survey and audit data and are presented at the end of this report.

AMERICAN'S ROLE AND THE PARK MANAGER

American Mobile Home, Inc., began business in 1965 with two parks in Phoenix, Arizona. Today it owns and operates 76 parks located in Arizona

FIGURE 16.9
(continued).

(16), California (16), Texas (12), Florida (12), New Mexico (10), Nevada (7), and Utah (3). According to <u>Woodall's Mobile Home and Park Directory</u> (1988), all of American's parks rate either four or five stars, the top ratings given. One of the requirements for these ratings is that management must be available on a full-time basis.

American's managers and their families (spouse and children over 18 years of age) live in the parks. Their homes double as offices in several smaller parks; separate offices are provided in the 58 parks having over 100 homes. American has attempted to eliminate the landlord-tenant concept and uses <u>manager</u> and <u>resident</u> as modern terms. Irwin (1986) says that landlords and tenants are medieval terms. Progressive managers refer to present-day tenants as occupants, residents, or lessees.

The modern manager may play several roles in addition to being the day-to-day manager of facilities and records. The manager may have to be a counselor, financial advisor, home decorator, arbitrator, psychologist, confession hearer, and friend.

The median age of managers is about 58 years; and a fourth are under 50, as shown in Figure 1.

FIGURE 16.9
(continued).

4

Figure 1

Ages of 40 Park Managers

Age	Number	Percent
30–39	4	10
40–49	6	15
50–59	13	32
60–69	17	43
	40	100

Over half of the managers can serve for some time before reaching 70, a usual retirement age; however, American does not practice mandatory retirement.

Despite their seeming maturity, managers have limited experience in the mobile home park industry. Over a third are in their first three years as managers, and the median tenure is about five years, as shown in Figure 2.

FIGURE 16.9
(continued)

5

Figure 2

Park Management Experience of 40 Managers

Years	Number	Percent
1–3	14	35
4–6	10	25
7–9	8	20
10–12	6	15
Over 12	2	5
	40	100

Most managers are able to relate to the residents of mobile home parks, who are generally their age peers. At the same time, younger managers in the 30–49 age range possess the potential to contribute continuity to American's operations. As this study shows, managers still have much to learn; fortunately, they are capable of learning and of benefiting from meaningful experiences on the job.

RESIDENTS' VIEWS OF WEAKNESSES AND STRENGTHS

The survey questionnaire was designed to elicit responses from resident experiences with the manager. The weaknesses and strengths were indicated

FIGURE 16.9
(continued).

6

by residents simply by check mark responses to listed items. Space was left

for "other" items that may have been important to residents.

<u>Weaknesses Involve People Skills</u>

Most leading weaknesses of managers, in the view of residents, center

around problems of an interpersonal nature and a lack of personal

knowledge, as shown in Figure 3.

Figure 3

Top 5 Weaknesses as Viewed by 2,400 Residents

Weakness	Number	Percent
1. Not readily available	1,425	59
2. Not consistent in rule enforcement	1,216	51
3. Doesn't seem to listen to residents	1,009	42
4. Unsure of laws and restrictions	828	435
5. Weak in settlement of disputes	658	27

FIGURE 16.9
(continued)

Lack of availability to residents, failure to listen or seemingly not listening, weakness in resolving disputes, and inconsistent rule enforcement indicate that managers need better communication with the corporation and with residents. Criticizing management for lack of availability is a common complaint inasmuch as all residents want to talk to the "top" authority. Unanswered telephone calls accumulate simply through volume and become cause for complaints.

Some of these problems could be eased by developing residents' associations in all parks. Eight parks now have such associations. As Rejnis (1974) said, "Whatever the practical/altruistic ratio in organizing (residents), the management that starts a resident organization is to be commended. Resident associations spot trouble before it explodes, develop friendships, help build morale, and can be effective sales tools."

Strengths Involve Things

Although weaknesses involved "people" aspects primarily, the leading strengths of managers, as viewed by residents, involved "things." Managers were complimented for their abilities to maintain facilities, as shown in Figure 4.

FIGURE 16.9 (continued).

8

Figure 4

Top 5 Strengths as Viewed by 2,400 Residents

Strength	Number	Percent
1. Maintenance of recreational facilities	2,100	87
2. Maintenance of streets and grounds	1,935	81
3. Concern for security and safety	1,550	65
4. Advice on appliance repairs	960	40
5. Attitude toward visitors	650	27

Following the maintenance strengths of management, only one other strength of the 14 possible areas listed on the questionnaire received mention by more than half of the residents. This concentration on the three leading strengths is significant. Weaknesses, on the other hand, received less concentrated emphasis with no weakness being selected by as many as 60 percent of the residents. Strengths were related to visible actions, and weaknesses were identified as somewhat intangible people skills.

"Interview the manager, learn about management empathy for residents, ask about landlord (management)-resident legislation; see if management is

FIGURE 16.9
(continued).

9

informed; ask for opinions; and check park rules" is the advice given prospective residents by Condon (1976). This advice is pertinent today and pinpoints some of the very items residents found wanting in their park management.

THE MANAGEMENT AUDIT

In addition to the questionnaire survey of residents, the study included audit team analysis of management performance in 40 parks. In the areas of cost control, record keeping, and cash management, the audit teams rated management performance in half or more parks not satisfactory, as shown in Figure 5.

Figure 5

Audit Analysis of 5 Activities in 40 Parks

Activity	Good		Satisfactory		Not Satisfactory	
	No.	Percent	No.	Percent	No.	Percent
Supplier relationships	18	45	15	38	7	17
Supplies control	12	30	16	40	12	30
Cost control	6	15	14	35	20	50
Record keeping	3	7	12	30	25	63
Cash management	1	2	9	23	30	75

FIGURE 16.9
(continued).

In the opinion of the audit teams, managers do a commendable job of working with suppliers and an adequate job of supplies control. In cost control, record keeping, and cash management, park managers have difficulty because of lack of training. An additional reason not articulated was that the record-keeping function was not considered particularly important when compared with maintenance of facilities.

American wants its managers to play active roles in the communities where parks are located. This type of involvement occurs in such areas as church and service club membership, attendance at city council meetings, assistance to youth groups, and participation in such community affairs as celebrations, parades, anniversaries, and fund-raising benefits. Managers tend to be familiar with local suppliers and services, mildly knowledgeable about their communities, and less than satisfactory participants in community activities, as shown in Figure 6.

FIGURE 16.9
(continued).

11

Figure 6

External Relations of 40 Managers

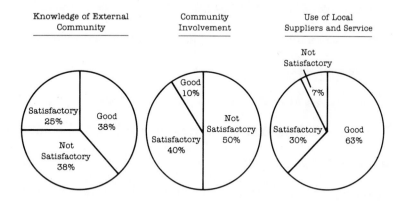

Knowledge of External Community

Satisfactory 25%
Good 38%
Not Satisfactory 38%

Community Involvement

Good 10%
Not Satisfactory 50%
Satisfactory 40%

Use of Local Suppliers and Service

Not Satisfactory 7%
Satisfactory 30%
Good 63%

CONCLUSIONS AND RECOMMENDATIONS

Based on the findings of the resident survey and the audits of management performance, the following conclusions were drawn:

1. In general, current managers are young enough to be with American for several years.

2. Park managers are "new" to their jobs and relatively untrained for their tasks.

3. Major weaknesses of park managers, as perceived by residents, are in the practice of interpersonal relations and in the understanding and enforcement of laws and restrictions.

FIGURE 16.9
(continued).

12

4. Major strengths of park managers, as perceived by residents, lie in their abilities to maintain the physical facilities, streets, and grounds.

5. Park managers, as revealed by the audit analysis, are inadequately prepared to handle record-keeping, cost control, and cash management tasks.

6. Park managers are familiar with local suppliers and services. They are not as knowledgeable about their surrounding communities nor as involved in community affairs as American would like them to be.

The following recommendations follow logically from the conclusions; and, if adopted, they should contribute to the development of a capable staff of managers:

Train Managers

Two types of training programs are recommended. The first focuses on office work and should emphasize cost and supplies control, record keeping, and cash management. The program should be built around a corporate park operations manual, with specific procedures included for various tasks. The second program should be devoted to improving the human relations and interpersonal communication skills of managers.

FIGURE 16.9
(continued).

13

Bernhard and Ingols (1988) suggest that training programs are successful when corporations do the following:

1. Articulate a vision. Let participants in training programs know about goals such as "Our goal is industry leadership through quality parks and quality park management."

2. Analyze needs. Be honest by letting participants know why they are in the program rather than having them ask one another "Why are we here?"

3. Involve top management to a degree that reveals corporate support.

Develop Resident Associations

Residents want good parks, and they like to be heard. Many of the criticisms of managers' failures to listen can be allayed through resident associations. Association leaders could meet regularly with the manager and thereby reduce the number of individual resident-manager meetings.

Encourage Community Involvement

Park managers are currently inactive in community affairs to a large degree. Park residents contribute to the economy of the community; and as an economic force, the parks should be represented just as are other

FIGURE 16.9
(continued).

business concerns in affairs of community interest. American should

consider underwriting the costs of manager membership in chambers of

commerce and/or service clubs.

<u>Organize Regionally</u>

In addition to considering other recommendations, American should

consider creating regional supervisors who would work closely with park

managers.

Implementation of these recommendations should be done with the idea

that education and training for managers will be a continuing program. "The

world of the 90s will be recognizable--no colonies on the moon--but different

enough to require shifts in thinking and tactics" (Kupfer, 1988).

FIGURE 16.9
(continued).

BIBLIOGRAPHY

Bernhard, Harry B., & Ingols, Cynthia A. (1988 September–October).
    Six lessons for the corporate classroom. Harvard Business
    Review, 66(5), 40–48.

Condon, Kaye. (1976). Guide to mobile homes. Garden City, NY:
    Doubleday & Co.

Irwin, Robert (Ed.). (1986). Handbook of property management. New
    York: McGraw-Hill Book Co.

Kupfer, Andrew. (1988 September). Managing now for the 90's.
    Fortune, 118(8).

Rejnis, Ruth. (1974). Everything tenants need to know to get their
    money's worth. New York: David McKay Co. 163.

Woodall Publishing Co. (1987). Woodall's mobile home and park
    directory. Highland Park, IL: Author.

15

FIGURE 16.10
Reference list.

Dear Resident of an American Mobile Home Park

We have been requested by American Mobile Home, Inc., to study the management of its residential parks. A part of that study is to ask residents for their opinions about the strengths and weaknesses of their park managers. Your opinion will help identify areas that may be improved through training programs or through better assistance from the corporation. Your response will be held confidential and will be included in group data so no reference will be made to your park manager.

Please help by taking just a few minutes to check your manager's strengths and weaknesses as listed below. *Leave blank all items about which you are in doubt.* When you have finished, slip this page into the enclosed postage-paid envelope and drop it in the mail. We will be grateful for your help.

	Please Check (√)	
	Strength	*Weakness*
1. Availability	_____	_____
2. Consistency in rule enforcement	_____	_____
3. Listening ability or willingness	_____	_____
4. Speaking ability or conversation ability	_____	_____
5. Concern for security and safety	_____	_____
6. Attitude toward visitors	_____	_____
7. Recreation leadership	_____	_____
8. Knowledge of city, state, and county laws and restrictions	_____	_____
9. Maintenance of streets and grounds	_____	_____
10. Maintenance of recreational facilities	_____	_____
11. Appliance help to residents	_____	_____
12. Settlement of disputes	_____	_____
13. Attention to detail	_____	_____
14. Creativity	_____	_____
15. Other_____	_____	_____

16

FIGURE 16.11

Questionnaire in appendix.

Summary: A Formal Report Checklist

The following checklist provides a concise, handy guide for your use as you prepare a report. It covers in condensed, outline form many of the principles and practices suggested in the last few chapters.

I. The Transmittal Memorandum or Letter
    (Use the following points for a letter-style transmittal in reports going outside the organization. For internal reports, use a memorandum transmittal.)
    A. Let the letter of transmittal carry a warm greeting to the reader.
    B. Open quickly with a "Here is the report you requested" tone.
    C. Establish the subject in the first sentence.
    D. Follow the opening with a brief summary of the study. Expand the discussion if a separate summary is not included in the report.
    E. Acknowledge the assistance of those who helped with the study.
    F. Close the letter with a thank you and a forward look.

II. The Title Page
    A. Include on the title page
        1. The title of the report.
        2. Full identification of the authority for the report (the person for whom the report was prepared).
        3. Full identification of the preparer of the report.
        4. The date of the completion of the report.
    B. Use an attractive layout. If the items are to be centered, leave an extra half-inch on the left for binding. In other words, make sure the point from which the items are centered is a little to the right of the actual center of the paper.

III. The Contents Page
    A. Use *Contents* or *Table of Contents* as the title.
    B. Use a tabular arrangement to indicate the heading degrees used in the report.
    C. If many graphs or tables are used, list them in a separate *List of Figures*. Otherwise, the graphs or tables should *not* be listed because they are not separate sections of the outline but only supporting data within a section of the report.

    D. Center the entire contents outline horizontally and vertically on the page.

IV. The Synopsis

    A. Use a one-word title, such as *Synopsis, Summary, Epitome, Brief, Abstract,* or *Précis.*

    B. Prepare the synopsis as a condensation of the major sections of the report.

    C. Concentrate on writing effective, generalized statements that avoid detail available in the report itself. Simply tell the reader what was done, how it was done, and how it all ended.

V. The Body of the Report

    A. In writing style, observe the following rules:

        1. Avoid the personal *I* and *we* pronouns. Minimize the use of *the writer, the investigator,* and *the author.*

        2. Use active construction to give emphasis to the *doer* of the action; use passive voice to give emphasis to the *results* of the action.

        3. Use proper tense. Write naturally about things in the order in which they happened, are happening, or will happen. Try to write the report as though the reader were reading it at the same time it was written.

        4. Avoid ambiguous pronoun references. If a sentence begins with *This is,* make sure the preceding sentence employs the specific word for which *This* stands. If the specific word is not used, insert it immediately after *This.*

        5. Avoid expletive beginnings. Sentences that begin with *There is, There are,* and *It is* present the verb before presenting the subject. Compared with sentences that employ the normal subject-verb-complement sequence, expletive sentences are longer.

        6. Enumerate lists of three items or more if the tabulation will make reading easier. For example, a list of three words such as *Ivan, George,* and *Diana* need not be tabulated; but a list of three long phrases, clauses, or sentences would probably warrant tabulation.

        7. Attempt to incorporate transition sentences to ensure coherence.

    B. In physical layout, observe the following rules:

        1. Use headings to assist the reader by making them descrip-

tive of the contents of the section. Talking headings are preferred.

2. Maintain consistency in the mechanical placement of headings of equal degree.

3. Use parallel construction in headings of equal degree in the same section of the report.

4. Try to incorporate the statement of the problem or purpose and method of research as minor parts of the introduction unless the research method is the unique element in the study.

5. Use the picture-frame layout for all pages. Recommended margins are *top* = 1 inch; *right* = 1 inch; *bottom* = $1\frac{1}{2}$ inches; *left* = $1\frac{1}{2}$ inches (the extra half-inch is for binding).

6. Number all pages, with the first page of the body of the report being page 1. For pages, such as page 1, that have a major title at the top, omit the number or place it in the center of a line a double space below the last line on the page. For all other pages, place the number in the center of the top line, or in the upper-right corner a double space above the first line on the page, or centered a double space below the last line on the page.

C. In using graphics or tabular data, observe the following rules:

1. Number consecutively the figures used in the report.

2. Give each graph or table a descriptive title.

3. Refer to the graph or table within the text discussion that precedes its appearance.

4. Place the graph or table as close to the textual reference as possible and limit the text reference to analysis. It should not merely repeat what can be seen in the graph or table.

5. Use effective layout, appropriate captions and legends, and realistic vertical and horizontal scales that help the table or graph stand clearly by itself.

D. In reporting the analysis,

1. Question each statement for its contribution to the solution of the problem. Is each statement either descriptive or evaluative?

2. Reduce large, unwieldy numbers to understandable ones through a common language such as units of production, percentages, or ratios.

      3. Use objective reporting style rather than persuasive language; avoid emotional terms. Identify assumptions and opinions. Avoid unwarranted judgments and inferences.

      4. Document the report wherever necessary.

      5. Tabulate or enumerate items when it will simplify the reading or add emphasis.

  E. In drawing conclusions,

      1. State the conclusions carefully and clearly, and make sure they grow out of the findings.

      2. If it seems necessary, repeat the major supporting findings for each conclusion.

      3. If recommendations are called for, make them grow naturally from the conclusions.

VI. Documentation

  A. When using footnotes,

      1. When in doubt, footnote the material or the source.

      2. Plan the placement of the bottom-of-the-page footnote in advance so it doesn't run off the page or below the bottom margin.

  B. When preparing the bibliography or list of references,

      1. If in doubt about whether a reference should be included, make the entry.

      2. If in doubt about what to include for an entry, include more information than you believe might be necessary.

      3. Prepare the bibliography in alphabetic sequence by author from index cards.

      4. If the bibliography is lengthy, include separate sections for books, articles, governmental publications, and unpublished references.

VII. Appendix Material

  A. Include cover letters for survey instruments, the survey instruments, maps, explanations of formulas used, and other items that should be included but are not important enough to be in the body of the report.

  B. Label each item beginning with *Appendix A, Appendix B,* and so on.

  C. Identify each item by giving it a title.

About Language and Usage

English has absorbed about half of the Latin language, much of it via Norman French after 1066. The contributions of Latin are all around us. Note these word families:

Latin *signum* means "sign"	Latin *portare* means "to carry"
insignia	porter
design	import
signal	export
significant	portable
insignificant	deport

Latin *facere* means "to do" or "to make" (base is *fac*)	Latin *dicere* means "to say" "to tell" (base is *dic*)
fact	dictate
factor	dictaphone
factory	predict
factual	diction
manufacture	malediction

Exercises

Review Questions

1. When using a word processor, a writer should always expect to prepare final copy without working with a rough draft. Is this statement true? Discuss.

2. Why is reading your writing aloud an effective way to review?

3. Give two or three examples of emotional terms. Why should they be avoided?

4. Why is the use of the pronoun "I" generally unacceptable in formal report writing?

5. What is meant by "transition" in composition? By "coherence"?

6. Using the term–family–differentiation method, write definitions of "highway patrol," "Senator," and "elm."

7. Identify each of the following as time, contrast, similarity, or cause-and-effect connectors: because, for example, then, although.

8. How can a writer eliminate bottom-of-the-page footnotes?

9. What is the difference in the way an author's name is presented in traditional footnote and bibliographic formats?

10. How does documentation serve a report writer or an author? List three ways.

11. Explain the relationship between the content outline of a report and the placement of headings within the body of the report.

12. The body of a formal report is usually organized inductively. Does the placement of a summary before the body modify that organization? If so, how?

13. May formal reports be organized in only one way? Must they contain all the beginning and ending parts?

14. Should the contents outline and the list of figures always be placed on separate pages?

15. Is the heading "Introduction" essential on the first page of the body of a report? Why or why not?

Cases

Report the following cases in formal style. Include preliminary and ending parts as you believe appropriate. Even though survey results are included in some of the cases, prepare a questionnaire in appropriate form. Sequences in questionnaire results and the discussion in the cases are purposely random. You must analyze and sort the data as part of the report process.

Homeowner Association Investments Case   As a client executive of Marshall Property Management, Inc., you, along with other members of the firm, serve as consultants to boards of directors of several condominium associations in your community. Additionally, a member of your firm serves full-time as general manager in many large associations. Boards of directors in these homeowner associations have the responsibility of making and enforcing policies and overseeing the funds of the associations.

Several of your client associations have from 300 to 1,200 members, each owning a condominium or residence. As part of their membership initiation fees and monthly dues or assessments, associations set aside funds for replacement of roofs and improvements or repairs of other property common to all members. Because boards of directors must oversee their reserve funds—often amounting to several million dollars—they seek sound advice from your firm.

Legally most boards of directors are restrained in their investment of reserve money by documents called Covenants, Conditions, and Restrictions (CC&Rs) effective upon formation of the associations. The restrictions generally require that money not be invested in risk ventures, such as common stocks, real-estate syndications, and corporate bonds. Rather, the money should be invested in secure, insured investments where the return would be less but the principal would be secure. Prepare a report on possible investments of this nature in banks; thrifts, such as savings banks and savings and loan associations; and insured funds of brokerages or other institutions.

The report should be addressed to one association, Marlboro Country Homes; in your transmittal letter, however, you will say the report is also being sent to other client boards. Your report should be informational—a comparison of the amount of investments possible, the rates of return for varying amounts, the maximum amounts insured, the time restriction on accounts, and the availability of money if needed. Because most associations can space their needs for money, they can invest some amounts of $100,000 for as much as five years. Homeowners' associations must pay tax on taxable interest paid to them.

Photocopying Machine Case As office administrator at the Wilmoth Company, you must make a recommendation for the selection of a single photocopying machine, or a variety of machines, for use throughout the organization's seven offices—one home office and six branch offices.

Each branch has 30 employees, and the home office has 210 employees. Copying load for work orders, incoming and outgoing invoices, checks, and typewritten materials is about 600 pages a day in all six branch offices. In the home office, the number of copies a day is about 4,000. In the branches, copies may be made on any kind of paper. About 10 percent of the copies made in the home office must be on bond paper.

All employees in the home office are located on two floors of a large office building. Letters and reports are prepared in a word-processing center, which uses bond paper for some of its work. The word-processing center is within easy walking distance of any department.

Investigate the products of three different copy machine manufacturers and prepare a report making a recommendation to the operations vice-president, Ellen Bondesson. You know Ms. Bondesson likes formal reports with adequate supporting evidence for whatever recommendations are made.

Office Equipment Case Using the information in the preceding case, conduct a similar study and prepare the report for any of the following types of office equipment:

a. Selection of a word processor.

b. Selection of a personal computer.

c. Selection of a heavy-duty electronic typewriter.

Make the selection from a choice of three major brands. You are the office administrator; and your report will be prepared for Ellen Bondesson, the operations vice-president for your firm, the Wilmoth Company.

Far East Tour Case As summer-tour coordinator for the Beverly Hills Travel Bureau, you have to plan and promote vacation travel tours. The tours are usually made by charter flight to reduce travel costs. The Beverly Hills Travel Bureau is one of the largest firms of its kind in the nation. Before you can promote a tour, you submit a report to Mr. Sidney Rosenfeld, president, for consideration by the executive committee. Once approval is given, you then work out the details of specific dates, travel itinerary, meal and hotel arrangements, and final costs. Prior to submitting the report, you survey a selected list of former tour customers about their desires. The survey helps establish interest in tours and the broad guidelines for specific travel. For the coming year, a tour of the Far East has been proposed. As a result, you surveyed by mail 600 former tour customers; 300 replied. Following are the cover letter, the questionnaire material, and the tabulated results of the 300 respondents:

Dear Traveler:

Because you have traveled with us before, we would greatly appreciate your taking the time to complete the following questionnaire. Your ideas will help us plan a charter trip to the Far East. As a seasoned traveler, your ideas are valued even though you may not be planning such a trip. Please simply respond as if you could plan your own trip.

When would you most like to leave on a tour of the Far East?

Late spring   75
Midsummer   200
Late summer   25

Which countries would you like to visit? Check all that apply.

Philippines   33   Mainland China 279
Vietnam   56   Taiwan   180
South Korea 234   Thailand   115
Maylasia   78   Borneo   54

Which do you prefer?

Air—sea tour   78   Air—land tour 222

Which cities would you prefer to visit? Check all that apply.

Seoul   234   Bangkok   115   Tokyo   283
Taipei   180   Singapore   60   Manila   30
Hong Kong 300   Beijing   276   Shanghai 144

Which hotel type would you prefer?

Luxury hotels   75   First-class hotels 180   Local tourist hotels   45

How many meals would you prefer the tour to have together each day?

1 meal   45   2 meals 225   3 meals   30

How would you like your evenings?

Planned   45   Open   90   Some planned, some open 165

Which would you prefer?

Only American tour leaders   42
Native, English-speaking guides   36
A combination   222

What length trip would you prefer?

10—11 days   60   14 days   66   21 days 135   One month   39

Which price range is most acceptable to you for the trip you visualized in your responses?

	10—11 days	14 days	21 days	One month
$2,000—2,999	50	12	6	0
$3,000—3,999	10	54	16	0
$4,000—4,999	0	0	110	0
$5,000—5,999	0	0	3	39
	60	66	135	39

Foreign Travel Package Tour Case Using the design of the study in the preceding case as a guide, prepare your own questionnaire for a tour of any one of the following areas: Europe, the Mediterranean, South America, Scandinavia, Australasia, or Africa. You may select either of these options to gather data: (1) survey members of your class and multiply responses by 10 to obtain a larger assumed sample, or (2) make up your own distribution of 300 assumed responses. Prepare a report for Mr. Rosenfeld. You might do some outside research by visiting a couple of travel agencies.

Product Advertising Case Assume you are involved in selecting advertising outlets and preparing advertisements for the Ajax Cosmetic Company. Your supervisor is Mr. Brian McDermott, director of sales promotion. He has asked you to select a national magazine from three magazines of your choice as a probable place to purchase advertising space for an initial new-product sales campaign. The product is a new line of women's competitively priced cosmetics. Ajax has long been a leader in low-priced facial cosmetics, but this new product represents an attempt to break into the high-style field. Your new product line consists of skin, eye, and lip cosmetics.

Although you have been told to select from three magazines of your choice, you know that for proper exposure you should select from magazines such as *Vogue, Harper's Bazaar, McCall's, Mademoiselle, Cosmopolitan,* and other fashion-oriented magazines including some of the newer publications such as *New Woman* and *Working Woman.* From the three magazines you select for study, your final choice will be based on the nature of appeals used in advertisements in each magazine, the kinds of products advertised, and the cost of advertising. You can find information about cost of ads and circulation of all national magazines in the most recent issue of *Consumer Magazine* and *Farm Publication Rates and Data.*

Your plan is to use three recent issues of each of your three magazines to analyze the nature of advertisements. Ajax plans to use only full-page color or black-and-white ads. You plan to begin your study of each magazine with the inside cover and to analyze the first 30 or 40 ads of each of three issues until you have at least 100 ads in your total sample. Thus, you'll analyze at least 300 ads by the time you have covered three issues of each of the three magazines.

A couple of assumptions must be made here. First, you are an expert in determining the basic appeal of an advertisement; second, a sample of

100 ads is adequate to determine the nature of products advertised and appeals used in each magazine.

Here are some of the product categories you may find convenient in tabulating your count of ads:

Automobiles	Travel
Cosmetics and beauty aids	Personal services (nonproduct)
Office equipment and	Household appliances
supplies	Furniture
Convenience items	Food
Clothing	

You may add others, of course. Some of the suggested product groups may not apply in certain magazines. If you find only a small number of ads in a product area, you may want to combine two or more areas such as household appliances and furniture. Should some ads not fit in any category, you could have a *Miscellaneous* or *All Other* grouping.

Advertising appeals typically fall into one or more categories:

Security	Quality
Love	Sex
Safety	Elegance
Beauty	Economy
Health	Comfort
Pride	Goodwill

Again, these are suggested appeal groupings only. You may find it convenient to combine closely related ones, such as safety and security or pride and quality.

After selecting your magazine, make a trial analysis to test the nature of the categories you'll want to use. Keep in mind that the purpose of your study is to determine the products most advertised and the appeals most used for those products. For instance, your findings should indicate that the four or five most advertised product groupings were. . . . At the same time, you'll report that the four or five most used advertising appeals were. . . . To keep a record of which appeals were used for each product, you'll find it helpful to make a chart similar to the one shown on page 586 for your initial tabulation of each magazine. All three issues of each magazine may be included in one chart.

Your charts will be much larger, no doubt. Using them will simplify your analysis and lead to better information for your written report. For example, an automobile advertisement using an appeal to quality would

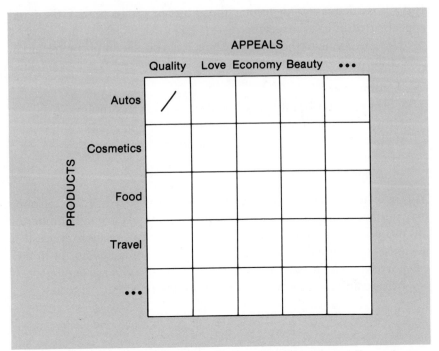

be recorded by making a slash mark (/) in the counting cell, as shown. After you have tabulated all the advertisements on the chart, you can total across each row to get the number of automobile ads, the number of cosmetic ads, the number of food ads, etc. By totaling down the columns, you can determine the total number of each appeal used. And by inspecting the cosmetic ads across the chart, you can determine the frequency with which each appeal was used in cosmetic advertisements.

Neat revisions of your three tabulating charts would be appropriate appendix items. You'll also use the totals in the charts for construction of tables and other figures to be used in the body of your report. For example, a figure showing the percentage of total ads devoted to cosmetic products from each of your three magazines would be an excellent table in the body of your report. As you study your tabulation charts, you'll find an almost endless combination of items that lend themselves to tabular and graphic presentation.

You hope to be able to recommend a magazine and a major appeal or appeals to be used in the advertising campaign. The magazine and its readership should be compatible with your product. Prepare a formal report.

Communications Center Case   A major manufacturer of typewriters and related equipment, M.B.I., has made a presentation to your boss, Ms. A. J. Wainwright, executive vice-president of the American Automobile Association Club in your area. The presentation encouraged the club to establish a communications center (or word processing center), which would bring all but five of the current twenty-three secretaries together in one area. Each of the eighteen departments that previously had personal secretaries would simply pick up a telephone, push the dictation button, and dictate material to the center where a supervisor would distribute dictated tapes to typists for transcription.

Additionally, at their own interoffice terminals, writers could produce rough drafts that could be transmitted to the center for final production.

The manufacturer has claimed that twelve of the eighteen secretaries moved to the center could handle the entire work load, thus creating a savings of six secretarial salaries if the six were released or assigned to other clerical duties in the organization. The cost of installing the system is about $75,000. The total yearly salaries of six secretaries are about $120,000. The manufacturer points out that replacement of the equipment would be necessary only about once every five years. Thus, the savings would be significant; quality control over secretarial production would be improved because individual secretaries would then be working in a common area under one supervisor; morale too, it is claimed, would be high once the secretaries adapted to the idea of working in the center.

The morale problem is one that bothers Ms. Wainwright. Rumors about the proposed center have started, and the grapevine message is that the secretaries are up in arms and several plan to quit if the center becomes a reality. Additionally, several of the departments and executives who have private secretaries are very upset about having their routines changed. Ms. Wainwright has asked you to take a survey of the secretaries involved and their supervisors to determine just what their attitudes are.

You have developed a questionnaire that you fill out yourself following an interview with each of the twenty-three secretaries. To open each interview, you describe briefly what the center will be like in terms of physical facilities. If it comes to reality, the center will include soundproofing, air conditioning, music, plush carpet, and all-new secretarial desks and chairs. Here's the questionnaire with the responses of the twenty-three secretaries as you subjectively recorded them after each interview:

1. Do you believe you'll be one of those moved to the center?
   Yes: 19
   No: 4

2. Do you think the work load will be greater in the center than it is for you now?
   Yes: 22
   No: 1

3. Have you talked with other secretaries about the center?
   Yes: 23
   No: 0

4. Do the ones you talked with like the idea of the center?
   Yes: 0
   No: 23

5. Have you thought about leaving if the center becomes a reality?
   Yes: 9
   No: 14

6. Would you definitely leave if transferred to the center?
   Yes: 5
   No: 18

7. Miscellaneous sample comments:

   "We'll certainly lose a lot of our present harmony with our bosses."

   "Will we get a raise if we're assigned to the center?"

   "Who'll be fired if we reduce the number of secretaries?"

   "Aren't we doing a good job now?"

   "Who'll answer the phone in here when the executives are out of the office? That seems terrible--letting the phone ring and all that, you know."

   "With all the money you'll spend, why can't we just put better stuff in our present offices?"

   "I'll bet those secretaries who work for Wainwright and her crowd don't get transferred. They aren't all that good either."

   "Have you asked the executives about this? I'll bet some of them can't dictate to a machine and most can't type at all."

   "Sure sounds great to me. I'd like to work in a nice place."

   "Wearing those earphones all day is a sure way to drive someone crazy."

"I suppose we'd really be regimented--like punching time clocks and lacking freedom to move about as we have now."

"Can you see my boss typing his own rough drafts!"

Your interviews with executives were a little more direct, and you tabulated their responses as follows:

1. Do you like the idea of the center?
   Yes: <u>5</u>
   No: <u>10</u>
   Undecided: <u>8</u>

2. Are you satisfied with the current arrangement?
   Yes: <u>11</u>
   No: <u>12</u>

3. If the answer to item 2 was "no," what is not satisfactory? (Several listed more than one unsatisfactory item.)
   a. Quality of work: <u>4</u>
   b. Secretary is often busy with others when needed: <u>4</u>
   c. Answering the phone keeps the secretary busy when other work is pending: <u>7</u>
   d. Secretarial hours of 9 to 5 are such that I have to write my letters in longhand at night and in the early morning and leave them for typing on days when I am out in the field (out of the office): <u>7</u>

4. How would your office be affected if the secretary were moved to the center?
   a. Need a clerk-typist for the office: <u>18</u>
   b. Need a receptionist for the office: <u>12</u>
   c. Need a system to make sure we'd always have an open line to the center: <u>18</u>
   d. Need a system to permit dictation outside of normal office hours: <u>7</u>

Prepare a report for Ms. Wainwright outlining your findings and making recommendations for her consideration.

Apartment Complex Facilities Case   You have been hired by a major building firm, Watt Construction Company, to make a survey of what college students would prefer in nearby apartment complexes. The following data were developed as a result of your study, which included 200 students selected at random. The figures in parentheses following each item are the numbers of women's responses. Men's responses are covered in the figures preceding the parentheses. Thus, you have the data covering the responses of men and women separately; by combining them, you have the total response. Prepare the report for R. A. Watt, President.

I. Personal Data (check one alternative in each part of this section)

    A. Gender:
       Men: 112
       Women: 88

    B. Marital status:
       Married: 27(2)
       Single: 85(86)

    C. Age:
       18 & less: 4(6)
       19–21: 63(47)
       22–25: 27(17)
       26–30: 8(12)
       31–40: 6(6)
       41 & more: (10)

    D. Current residence:
       Dormitory: 23(24)
       On-campus apartment: 16(7)
       Fraternity or sorority: 38(26)
       Off-campus apartment: 13(11)
       With parents: 22(20)
       Other (specify): 0(0)

    E. School standing:
       Graduate: 16(8)
       Undergraduate: 96(80)

II. Recreational Facilities

    A. Outdoor facilities (check all that you would like to have provided)
       Pool: 85(80)
       Jacuzzi: 51(70)
       Tennis courts: 78(53)
       Badminton-volleyball courts: 40(37)
       Barbecue area: 25(67)

    B. Indoor facilities

       1. Recreation room (check one)

          Should be provided: 84(50)

          Should not be provided: 28(38)

If you think that a recreation room should be provided, check all recreation room facilities that you would want:

Billiards tables: 37(10)
Ping-pong tables: 25(15)
Television sets: 10(27)
Lounging area: 55(36)
Fireplace: 31(48)
Cocktail area: 70(50)
Party area: 78(50)
Kitchen: 52(21)

2. Gymnasium (check one)

Should be provided: 60(30)
Should not be provided: 52(58)

If you think that a gymnasium should be provided, check all gymnasium facilities that you would want:

Weights: 45(15)
Conditioning machines: 20(30)
Ropes or rings: 50(2)
Slant boards: 42(30)

3. Sauna (check one)

Should be provided: 75(31)
Should not be provided: 37(57)

C. Organized recreation (check one)

Should be provided: 32(20)
Should not be provided: 80(68)

III. Parking Facilities
   A. Number of parking spaces per apartment that should be provided:
      1. Spaces per one-bedroom apartment (check one)
         One: 57(31)
         Two: 54(55)
         Three: 1(2)
      2. Spaces per two-bedroom apartment (check one)
         One: 18(16)
         Two: 88(71)
         Three: 6(1)

B. Type of parking lot that should be provided (check one)
Conventional: <u>75(38)</u>
Underground: <u>37(50)</u>

If you chose underground, check one:

Secured: <u>28(40)</u>
Unsecured: <u>9(10)</u>

IV. Security Facilities (check all that you would like to have provided)
None: <u>0(2)</u>
Locks on all doors to complex: <u>93(80)</u>
Watch dog: <u>16(27)</u>
Security guard: <u>79(75)</u>

Shopper Survey Case As part of a team selected from your class, make a one-hour survey of the nature of shoppers in your school bookstore. Each member of your team will also survey shoppers during a one-hour period, and you'll pool your data to provide a comprehensive sample. The purpose of your study is to determine (a) what kind of people shop in the bookstore during certain hours, (b) what items seem to sell to certain categories of shoppers, and (c) what services or products not now offered would be desirable additions. In other words, your team will make a survey to determine how to provide better services. Organize your team in any way you like. Keep in mind sampling techniques. Don't survey only between 8 and 9 A.M. each day of the week. And don't limit your study to Friday afternoons. Outline the kinds of information you'll need and can get. Your team will make an oral presentation to the class in addition to a written presentation to the instructor.

Communication Analysis Case Following is a brief list of studies concerned with communication. Each may be completed individually or in teams and should be presented in formal report form.

a. Collect sixty copies of letters written by business firms. You will have to ask for them personally to explain why you want them. You can also offer each donor of letters a copy of your report when it is finished. Naturally, the letters will be held confidential; if they prefer, you'll be happy to take copies with no identifying information on them. For example, the inside address and the name of the writer may be deleted. When you have the copies, analyze them according to whatever criteria you can establish from earlier chapters in this book. For example, you might use planning, grammar and usage, spelling, consideration of the reader, Fog Index, and adequacy of detail as criteria. Keep track of the kinds of exceptions you find that would violate writing principles. Another approach would be to have a knowledgeable jury—a team of students in your class—select the fifteen best and the fifteen worst letters. Forget about the thirty letters that fall in the middle. Then attempt to determine what distinguishes good from bad letters. Prepare a report for your instructor.

b. Collect several samples of news items and analyses from *Time, Newsweek,* and a local newspaper that discuss the same topic. Analyze each in terms of readability, pictorial presentation, and quality of writing. You might again use the jury approach. Attempt to use some quantitative basis—for example, a rating scale as described in Chapter 16—to determine which publication is best in terms of your study.

c. We are bombarded constantly with sales slogans and the use of personalities to promote products and services advertised on television. Develop a list of slogans and personalities with a matching list of products. Then attempt to determine from people in your age group which seem to be best known ads by having people attempt to match the products with the advertising theme or personality. Analyze why some are better recognized than others. You may find help in advertising or marketing textbooks and periodical literature. You can also ask respondents to indicate the amount of time they watch television each week, which television shows, games, and news reports they watch most, and whether they are really conscious of television advertising.

Research Report Case   Here are some topics for research reports. Previous report assignments in this section have provided data for report preparation. For the following topics, you will be required to develop an entire report from your own research findings. Your report may be based on interviews and library research. This list is only suggestive, of course. In the process of reviewing it, you may discover other topics simply by adapting the general theme as you see fit.

General Topics

College Bookstore Traffic and Desirable Reorganization

Student Political Attitudes

Items for a Student Handbook

Student Evaluation of Teachers

Campus Parking and Traffic

How Students Spend Their Out-of-Class Time

Readability of Popular Books vs. Textbooks

Career Ambitions of Students

How to Select a Photocopy Machine

Personal Profile of a Typical Student

Part-Time Employment Opportunities

Communicating on Campus

Student Opinion of Campus Eating Facilities

Teachers' Views of Their Profession

Characteristics of Student Leaders

Risk and Investments

Savings Opportunities in Commercial Banks, Savings and Loans, and Thrift Institutions

The Most Desirable Small Car

Campus Housing

What Students Want in Housing

Library Services and Problems

Survey of First-Year Accountants

The Legalization of Marijuana

Consumer Tax Burdens

Merit Rating as a Form of Employee Evaluation

Organization of a Textbook Exchange

Real Estate Markets in the County (or City)

Job Opportunities in the County (or City)

Price Depreciation of Various Automobile Makes and Models

Topics Related to Careers

Real Estate Appraising

Personal Financial Planning

Property Management

Property Custodial Services

Selling Insurance

Museum and Fine Arts Management

Travel Agent and Consulting

Recreation Management

O B J E C T I V E S

When you have finished studying Part 6, you should be able to

- Use much of the vocabulary of electronic communication tools and applications.

- Cope with some problems of selection and use of electronic communication hardware and software.

- Relate to the problems of cross-cultural communication.

- Work with foreign employers or employees with greater appreciation for cultural differences.

- Apply your communication skills in multiculture environments.

COMMUNICATING ELECTRONICALLY AND CROSS-CULTURALLY

Electronic Tools for Business Communication

Business is being revolutionized by science and technology. The future belongs to those who understand.

STANLEY M. DAVIS in *Future Perfect*

Each day, millions of shares of stock are purchased and sold on the national and regional stock exchanges. Billions of transactions are made at record stores, clothing stores, bookstores, and many other retail businesses. Banks move money from one account to another—or from one bank to another—hundreds of thousands of times a day. All of these varied transactions, and many more, are facilitated by the use of computers.

We now live in "the information age." Success in business is based in large part on how much information someone has and how he or she is able to use that information. Managers need to have available to them large amounts of data. They must be able to understand those data, analyze them, and manipulate them.

Computers, the basic tools of electronic information processing, can facilitate such work. Their capacity to store huge amounts of data can make information readily accessible. Compact discs, for instance, are used to store data for access by computer as well as to produce high-quality music recordings. A single compact disc smaller than five inches in diameter holds the entire editorial content of a 21-volume encyclopedia—over 9 million words. Data storage is not the only benefit that derives from using computers, though. Knowing how to use computers gives a manager an edge in analyzing and manipulating data as well. A budget prepared using a computer can be recalculated in seconds, far less time than that required to refigure a budget calculated on a calculator and written out by hand.

You can probably still function in the working world without using these electronic tools, but not very effectively. Information continues to accumulate; and without electronic tools, you have little access to it and a lessened ability to use it. In turn, your ability to communicate with others diminishes.

Electronic tools have not eliminated the need for the basic communications skills you have learned in previous chapters. If anything, these electronic tools—like all new tools and techniques—create new obstacles or barriers to communication that must be overcome. These tools, however, also create opportunities, which extend from the kinds of communications that are possible to the quality of the messages themselves. Among the benefits of electronic tools for communication, they can help people

1. Communicate quickly and efficiently with others who are distant.
2. Locate information for messages.
3. Communicate in a timely way.
4. Shape their messages to be more clear and effective.

Have you ever used a computer?

Can a computer do all the work of communicating?

We cannot, in one chapter, explain all aspects of computers in detail. We can, however, describe those features of these machines that permit communication. We can outline some of the problems that may arise in messages fashioned using these electronic tools and describe some steps to take to avoid these pitfalls. First, however, we give a brief overview of what computers are and what makes them tick.

The Basics of Computers

Computers have two elements: equipment, called *hardware,* and the instructions for how to manipulate data, called *software.* Think of a computer as a manager's staff. The equipment, the hardware, is the staff itself. It represents capability, but not volition; it is essentially in a state of potential, ready to perform as instructed but unable to initiate action. The instructions come from the software. These instructions can lead the computer to take a number of actions—find the address of a client, say, or figure out the commissions earned by the sales staff, or send a message from headquarters to a field office.

This manager–staff relationship has three key factors:

1. Unlike a staff of human workers, the computer cannot act without orders. It does not have the ability to make independent judgments about what to do.

2. The instructions must be given in specific ways, using a special vocabulary and grammar, or they will not be carried out.

3. Hardware and software must both be capable of performing a task for the computer to get the job done. For instance, while some graphics-generating programs are capable of creating slides, you can only make an actual slide if the computer is connected to a piece of equipment that can make slides. Just as the equipment is only a potential until the software instructs it in what to do, so the software is only a potential without the proper hardware to carry out its instructions.

• Types of Hardware

Although many different kinds of computer equipment exist, a basic computer system includes these components:

1. *Central processing unit (CPU).* The CPU, the brain of the computer, is the circuitry that allows the computer to process data. The CPU

also contains silicon chips that serve as memory; they retain the information that is entered into the computer for use later.

2. *Keyboard.* An expanded version of a typewriter keyboard, the keyboard is connected to the CPU by a cable and is used to place information into the CPU. This task is called *inputting.*

3. *Monitor.* The monitor is the screen by which the operator can *monitor* the information input into the computer and the results of the computer's manipulation of that information.

Monitors are sometimes called *video display terminals* (VDTs).

These three pieces of equipment are essential to any computer; without them, no electronic data processing could be done. Other pieces of equipment can be added as well to increase a given system's capabilities. These include a printer; a *mouse,* which allows the user to move information around more efficiently than a keyboard; and a *modem,* a device that acts like a telephone for data rather than voices, allowing someone to send messages from one computer to another.

Of all the additional pieces of equipment, perhaps the most important are data storage devices. While the CPU has memory, there's a catch—once the machine is turned off, the memory is no longer active and the information stored in it is lost. Suppose you start to write a report for your boss and, three pages into it, decide to break for lunch. You turn off the computer and leave for your meal. When you return and turn the computer on again, you would find no report. Once you hit the off switch, not one word would still exist in the computer's memory. The data would have been erased from that memory.

A sudden loss or surge of power can have this effect as well.

Clearly such a machine is of limited usefulness. It would be uneconomical to leave it turned on at all times, day and night, and yet otherwise all work is lost. The solution is data storage devices. Called *disk drives,* these components have the ability to take the information in the computer and encode it onto a thin plate coated with a magnetic film, where it can be stored and be available for retrieval later. Disk drives, and the disks onto which they write the data, expand the computer's ability to use data from one day to the next.

• What Software Does

What are the data used for? How are the bits of information manipulated? What determines the answers to these questions is the computer's software. The CPU is capable of many tasks; the software tells it exactly which ones to perform. These instructions are called *programs.*

Some programs control the actual operation of the computer, telling it how to interpret the information entered at the keyboard or how to

These programs are called *utilities.*

store that information on disks. The most familiar group of programs, though, is the one that encompasses the different tasks that the computer will perform. Called *applications,* these programs tell the computer how to process data. We will be studying three broad groups of applications:

1. *Software for manipulating data.* This group includes what may be the three main uses of computers—word processing, used to write letters, memos, and reports; spreadsheets, used to organize and analyze numbers; and databases, used to store and access large amounts of data.
2. *Software for presenting data.* This category of applications includes programs aimed at making communications as effective as possible. It includes programs that run printers, the new field of desktop publishing, and applications that allow the creation of graphs and charts.
3. *Software for sharing data.* This growing category of applications provides the capability of sharing data from one computer to another.

These are not the only kinds of software available. Some programs have been developed to handle an organization's accounting functions. Others are used to design new products on screen rather than using pencil and paper. Many others exist as well, each offering a specialized tool aimed at the specific needs of a group of businesspeople. We will study the three broad categories just outlined because they are common to the tasks faced by most managers, whatever their industry or special concerns.

Manipulating Data

Businesses run on words, numbers, and data. The three main categories of applications—word-processing programs, spreadsheets, and databases—facilitate the varied and efficient manipulation of those three kinds of information.

• Word Processing

Many different word-processing systems are available, but each performs similar functions. *Word processing* allows you to

Word processing enables you to see what you'll print before printing.

1. Enter text by keyboarding the copy, similar to the way you enter text on a typewriter.
2. Make changes to the text.
3. Save the document for future use.
4. Print the document.

In a sense, a word-processing system is an advanced typewriter that permits the creation, editing, and printing of text.

Normally what is meant by word processing is hardware that uses instructions (software) to perform these four functions. The computer may be capable of performing only word processing and no other electronic functions, in which case it is called a *dedicated* word processor. Alternatively, the machine could be a general-purpose computer that can run all the variety of programs discussed here and that, for this particular function, uses any one of a number of popular word-processing programs such as *Displaywrite, Microsoft Word, Multimate, Word-Perfect,* or *Wordstar.* The general-purpose computer may be a small personal computer (or PC) or a large mainframe computer. It may have the capability of being used by one or by many individuals.

Will word processing do away with the need to write well?

Using word-processing software to create business communications has many benefits. Some features of these programs permit the easy formatting of text with **boldfacing** or underlining for emphasis. Others allow rapid movement within a document to review or revise the text. Reports and longer documents become much less tedious to produce because of many features that facilitate writing and editing:

In the past, this was done with scissors and paste.

1. *Insert and delete.* The insert feature allows you to enter new copy—from one character to several paragraphs—anywhere in the document. The delete feature, quite simply, allows you to remove text, from a single character to many pages.
2. *Block.* The block feature allows you to identify any portion of the document as a block, which can then be deleted, moved to another location, or copied from one spot to another. You could create a block and use the move feature if, after keyboarding a long report, you decide that a paragraph makes more sense in another location. You could use block along with the copy feature to repeat a complicated table in more than one part of a report.
3. *Search and replace.* The search and replace feature is helpful when you have consistently misspelled a word throughout a document. To replace "microeconomics" with "macroeconomics" in a report, for example, is a simple matter of a few keystrokes.

4. *Mail merge.* One feature that facilitates large-scale mailings is mail merge. You can produce multiple letters addressed to different individuals by combining a standard letter with lists of client or customer names and addresses. Thus, instead of sending each client a photocopy of the letter with his or her name individually typed in— a laborious task that creates a less favorable impression—you can give each individual his or her own original letter, as in Figure 17.1.

5. *Automatic table of contents and index.* Most of the sophisticated word-processing programs available include a special feature that can generate a table of contents and an index automatically. This feature saves time in the initial creation of these pages and also in their updating if pagination should change during editing.

6. *Spellcheck and thesaurus.* Other beneficial features are such stored references as dictionaries and thesauruses. With spellcheck, you can automatically check the spelling of every word in a document against the program's dictionary. The words misspelled or not in the dictionary are highlighted, to be automatically corrected or to be changed by you. Some programs allow you to add words to the dictionary. A thesaurus feature automatically generates a list of synonyms for any word you wish. You then choose one from the list to substitute for the original, and the computer does the rest.

Direct mail marketing

Spelling ability is still necessary!

• Spreadsheets

For preparing reports containing any analysis of numbers, an electronic spreadsheet is invaluable. An *electronic spreadsheet* is a forecasting and decision-making tool that can be thought of as a replacement for—and enhancement of—a calculator. As with a calculator, you can add, subtract, multiply, and divide using a spreadsheet; but you can also do more, making the manipulation and analysis of data easy. A spreadsheet provides the ability to forecast, allowing the user to ask, for instance, how profits would change if costs and sales were reduced by 10 percent or increased by 5 percent. The ability to calculate quickly these variable forecasts—called "what-if" questions—is one of the main benefits of spreadsheets.

To understand how such a program works, think of a spreadsheet as an arrangement of columns and rows, as shown in Figure 17.2. Where columns and rows intersect is called a *cell.* The letter at the top of the column and the number to the left of the row are used to identify the cell; the location is called the *cell address.* For example, in Figure 17.2 cell address E9 contains the amount $18,440.

Spreadsheets can be used with computers but not with dedicated word processors.

PERSONAL TRACKER, INC.

October 22, 199__

Mr. Bill Rolf
President
SPECIAL DATA SERVICES, INC.
728 Hyde Park Circle
Huntington Beach, CA 99223

Dear Bill:

As a follow-up from the DEMA conference, I am sending you the information you requested. I am also enclosing my itinerary for the next three weeks. If you are planning to be at any of these data entry conferences, please visit our booth.

I will be able to show you some new features that will be added to our software in the next release.

Sincerely,

Jennifer Evans

Jennifer Evans

18888 Airport Circle • Irvine • CA 92222 • (714) 555-5555

FIGURE 17.1

Can you tell whether this is a form letter?

	A	B	C	D	E	F	G
1			Tracker Product Line				
2			Weekly Sales Report				
3			October 22, 19--				
4							
5	Salesperson		Years	Training	Sales		Commission
6			Employed	No. of Hrs.			
7	==						
8	Allen, Robert		2	84	20460.00		5115.00
9	Barry, Jane		2	80	18440.00		4610.00
10	Simms, Allen		4	100	22840.00		5710.00
11	White, Sharon		1	20	420.00		105.00
12							
13							
14							
15							
16							
17							
18							
19							
20							

FIGURE 17.2
Spreadsheet application.

A cell can contain a label, text (as in cell A9, which contains the name Jane Barry), a number (cell E9), or a formula, which is hidden. Cell G9, for instance, contains the formula "E9 × .25," which calculates a 25 percent sales commission based on whatever level of sales is shown in cell E9. Once a value is entered in cell E9, the corresponding value of cell G9 is automatically computed. Such formulas are the key to "what-if" analysis. By supplying a new number in E9, you cause the spreadsheet automatically to recalculate the commission and fill in a new result in G9.

Can this capacity help the report writer?

The spreadsheet can transform a vast amount of numerical data into information that can be used for decision making. By condensing data into organized tables, the spreadsheet greatly assists the manager in using the data. Once it has been created, a spreadsheet can be inserted into a document by using a word-processing program. The result can be invaluable for getting a point across quickly, as shown in Figure 17.3. Although it isn't absolutely necessary to know how to create a spreadsheet, you should know how to use it to emphasize and analyze important information. Popular spreadsheet programs include *Lotus 1-2-3,* *Microsoft Excel,* and *Quattro.*

• Databases

Lists are important in business. All businesses have a number of lists that must constantly be created, updated, and maintained. The information in them is often vital to the production of certain reports. Because the best report is useless if it isn't timely, the information in the lists must be easy to retrieve and accurate to be useful.

Database software allows the creation of useful lists. It organizes the data, permits them to be updated, and allows them to be retrieved in a variety of report formats. The reports can in turn be used for decision making or other purposes. Well-known database programs include *dBase, R:base,* and *Q&A.*

Data are stored in a hierarchical structure—progressing from the smallest unit (field) to the largest (database). Just as the words *city, county, state,* and *nation* describe progressively broader units of territory, the words *field, record, file,* and *database* describe progressively broader units of information. Think of a college's database of students. Each student's name, address, phone number, total credits, and so on, make up the field of his or her record. The records for each student in a class make up the file for the entire class. The files of all classes of all teachers make up the database for the school.

MEMO

To: Victoria Wilson, Director of Operations
From: Bob Larson, Sales Manager
Date: Oct. 22, 19--

You asked why I am so adamant about requesting that
Sharon spend more time with the sales trainer.

Salesperson	Years Employed	Training No. of Hrs.	Sales	Commission
Allen, Robert	2	84	20460.00	5115.00
Barry, Jane	2	80	18440.00	4610.00
Simms, Allen	4	100	22840.00	5710.00
White, Sharon	1	20	420.00	105.00

Do I need to say more?

FIGURE 17.3
Does the spreadsheet make a point?

Is this electronic file
cabinet more
convenient than a
metal one?

Think of a database as a large electronic file cabinet where all data, such as names and subjects, are cross-referenced. Because data are cross-referenced, needed information can be located quickly and easily. Suppose you had a business with 10,000 customers and wanted the names of all those who purchased $5,000 to $10,000 worth of products during January and February. With a database, you can compile the list far more quickly—and accurately—than you could manually.

Besides the ability to organize large amounts of data, databases offer two other advantages:

1. *Data integrity.* There is some assurance that the data will be accurate and complete.
2. *Data security.* The data are secure because access to a database is controlled through several built-in data security features.

Data integrity is possible because—short of machine failure—data stored in a database will not be lost or misplaced, as a file folder might be. Because updating is relatively easy, the database is more likely to be up-to-date. In fact, some updating can even be automatic. For example, a system can be established that automatically checks a customer's address against the existing database of customers when an invoice is issued. If the search reveals that the address differs from that in the database, the program will automatically change the address that is stored to the new one.

Security problems
exist for all computer
systems.

Data security exists because users must enter an identification code or a password to gain access to the database, thus protecting it from unauthorized personnel. A system can also be devised that permits only certain authorized workers to change information in the database even though a broader range of workers can actually access the data.

Types of Databases   Databases are classified as internal or external. *Internal databases* contain intracompany information such as financial, sales, or production data. An internal database for a wholesaler, for example, might contain all the possible retailers in different geographic locations. From these data, a list of retailers in the Midwest could be compiled and printed in a few minutes.

Other databases
allow users to access
major newspapers.

External databases are libraries of information that can be accessed using a modem to obtain more broadly applicable information. The Dow-Jones Retrieval Service, for example, may be accessed for up-to-the-minute stock and bond information. Databases can provide important business information quickly and relatively inexpensively. Some external databases charge a membership fee and others simply charge for each call.

Database Searches   To use the information in a database, you must conduct a database search, which requires knowing the search procedures and how to construct a search strategy.

Database searching, once a complicated task successfully done only by research librarians, has become more "user-friendly," meaning that the process is easier to learn and use. For some database systems, you may need 30 to 45 minutes to master retrieval techniques; some of the more complicated systems may require a few hours.

In the past, to obtain information from a database required complex questions worded in difficult-to-learn languages. Now users can more easily communicate with a database by using English-like query languages such as Structured Query Language (SQL). Commands such as SELECT NAMES FROM STUDENTS WHERE MAJOR EQUALS MARKETING might be used to retrieve the names of all students with a major in marketing. Modern database technology may also use artificial intelligence (AI) software that enables the user to communicate with the database in even simpler English. For example, the command previously stated in query language might be as simple in an AI language as WHAT STUDENTS HAVE A MAJOR IN MARKETING? As you can see, database query languages are becoming more accessible, enabling almost everyone to communicate with databases.

> What does "user-friendly" mean?

> Doesn't this seem easy?

Presenting Data

It is not enough to be able to access and manipulate data; the course of daily business often requires that these data be communicated to others. Computers can be used in this work. Various kinds of software, along with some specialized hardware, make very effective tools for creating convincing presentations.

• Printing

One of the main vehicles for business communications remains the printed page. The quality of appearance of a printed document depends not only on the software but also on the printer. A number of different types of printers are available, but most can be grouped into two categories, based on the quality of the characters they print: letter quality and near letter quality. Most printers of either type form letters in essentially the same way by printing a concentrated mass of dots in the shape of the letter. The closer together the dots are—and the higher is the number of dots in the same space—the better is the quality of the printed character.

Letter-quality printers produce letterforms in one of three ways. The first group uses the impact of a print wheel against an inked ribbon. These printers are the exception to the rule that letters are formed by printing dots on paper. Instead they use wheels or elements with preformed letters much as a typewriter does.

Can colors add to meaning?

In the second group of letter-quality printers, tiny jets of ink are sprayed onto the paper. These printers have the benefit of allowing color printing by changing the color of the ink employed.

The third group produces characters of the highest quality available for printers that are commonly used in businesses. These printers use lasers and a process similar to photocopying to produce a page of characters at a time. Because the characters can be shaped in the form of the letters traditionally supplied by professional typesetters for publishing, these printers are considered near typeset quality.

Whichever of the three methods is employed, these three groups of letter-quality printers offer high-quality characters. They are generally the most expensive. Some, especially the laser printers, add the benefits of speed and the capability of handling sophisticated graphic images.

What is an advantage and a disadvantage of dot matrix printers?

The second category of printers, those of near letter quality, is an affordable alternative to the letter-quality group. These printers have a mechanism called a *printhead* with a number of points called *pins* that strike the ribbon in various combinations to create characters on the paper. Because characters are created by patterns of dots, these printers are called *dot matrix printers*. They can also be used to print certain graphic images, making them versatile. Dot matrix printers are the workhorses of the office.

• Desktop Publishing

Traditionally most communications intended for use within an organization were prepared using typewriters or, more recently, word processors connected to letter-quality printers. Even reports, however formal, generally had a typewriter-quality look. Some materials, primarily important publications such as prospectuses and annual reports, however, were prepared using the standard methods of publishing, including high-quality typesetting that produced clear, sharp letters such as the type you are reading in this book.

In recent years, the growing capabilities of personal computers have changed all that. Now one person or a work group within an organization can use sophisticated page-layout software to drive a personal computer and a laser printer to create near-typeset-quality documents at lower cost than was possible in the past. This phenomenon, called *desktop publishing,* helps managers and other workers surpass simple word processing by using typography, design elements, and even graphic images to create communications that are persuasive and professional looking.

In the typical flow of desktop publishing, a document—or a number of documents—is created, edited, and proofread in a word-processing program. It is then brought into a page layout, or desktop publishing, program such as *Ventura Publisher* or *PageMaker,* where the text can be styled with different typefaces, sizes, and other enhancements, such as rules, boxes, and boldface or italic type. If desired, graphic images can be brought into the document as well. The images can range, for example, from a pie chart showing the distribution of total sales among six regions to the picture of a new building to supplement a newsletter article announcing the opening of a new division. The text and graphics are combined electronically to make a complete presentation. When printed on a laser printer, the result can be a convincing report or newsletter.

Using desktop publishing, you can create a company or corporate image at a fraction of the cost once required. This software can be used to create business cards, letterheads, forms, in-house newsletters, direct-mail advertising, catalogs, manuals, sales reports, and countless other publications. Some of these documents can even be created through the use of top-of-the-line word-processing programs. (See Figure 17.4 for an example.)

• Graphics Programs

Images can often convey a message more effectively than words. Pie charts, bar graphs, and line graphs can be generated by graphics software to help people grasp a point more readily than they can interpret a narrative or even a table. Look at the increasing use of graphics in newspapers and television news reports; the communications professionals who create these messages are well aware of the direct impact that pictures can have on the reader or viewer.

As more and more information becomes circulated, graphics take on even greater importance. Decision makers, who don't have the time to wade through pages of written text searching for key information, are

What is easier to understand, the weather map or the meteorologist's description?

Acacia Hills College
Information Systems Center

WORD PROCESSING PROCEDURES GUIDE

Compiled by: Information Systems Center Staff
October 1989

FIGURE 17.4
Title page created using WordPerfect.

among the primary beneficiaries of graphic presentations. A manager may win the day by supporting her case for expansion with a line graph showing the resulting increase in profits. A salesperson could close a deal by backing up his proposal with five bar graphs illustrating the superiority of his product over the competition's.

The use of graphics in presentations has grown greatly in recent years because of the development of increasingly capable programs for generating graphs on personal computers. Such packages as *Harvard Graphics, Freelance Plus,* and *Microsoft Chart* create standard graph types that work as shells within which data is placed to produce a polished, professional-looking image. The images can be produced quickly and efficiently, as well. The graph shown in Figure 17.5 was created in less than two minutes with the use of *Harvard Graphics.*

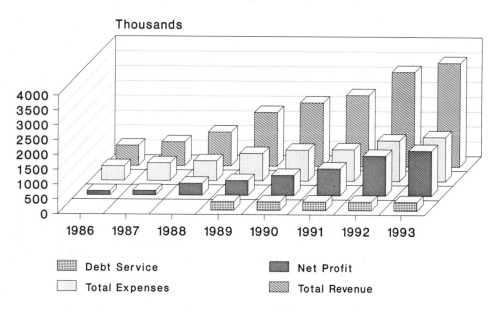

FIGURE 17.5

A computer graphic can be easily created, changed, and printed.

Transfer a graphic to a transparency for an oral report.

Once generated, the graphs can be printed separately in black and white or given more elaborate treatment. Most graphing programs allow the user to create color images that can either be printed on paper using special color printers or turned into slides to form part of an oral presentation. The image may be converted into a transparency as well. It could also be brought into a document being produced using desktop publishing software to serve as a graphic highlight to a story.

Sharing Data

The rise of computers has added another kind of communications to the practice of business—electronic communications. We have already seen that a modem can link someone with a personal computer to a large database, allowing the computer user to access important and up-to-date information such as stock and bond prices. Computerized communications can also link individuals in other ways.

• Electronic Mail

Offices use a number of traditional methods for sending a document, depending on the time constraints and the cost of the method. The U.S. Postal Service can be relied on for two-to-four day delivery or overnight service within the United States. Many private carriers provide overnight or second-day service. Sometimes, though, a message must be sent faster than those methods can manage. In that case, electronic mail is used.

Electronic mail is most commonly defined as person-to-person communication in which the transmission and receipt of the message takes place through a computer. Electronic mail, or *e-mail*, as it is sometimes called, can be categorized as either internal or external.

Internal E-mail   Within a company, electronic mail can be used to distribute memos, reports, and documents without sending them through the mailroom. Suppose that the sales manager completes a report and wants the division chiefs to review it before they all meet that afternoon. Before electronic mail, he or she would have to get a messenger to hand deliver the document to the various recipients. Using the company's internal electronic-mail system, however, the manager can now deliver the report to each of the others almost instantly.

Two basic systems handle the flow of information within a company: (1) microcomputers wired for networking and (2) multiuser systems. In a network, a number of individual personal computers are linked using wires or cables, a modem, and communications software. In a multiuser system, each user, rather than having a separate computer with its own processor, simply has a keyboard and a monitor attached by cable to a large mainframe computer. In either system, communications software can enable one user to send messages to others almost instantly.

These systems attack another problem often encountered in business. Approximately 70 percent of business phone callers do not reach the person they called on the first try. The result is "telephone tag," as the caller and the person called keep trying to reach the other unsuccessfully. Electronic mail removes the problem; the caller simply keys in a message and sends it to an electronic mailbox. Receivers are notified that a message awaits them, and they respond to the caller as soon as the message is read.

What is telephone tag?

External E-mail   With external electronic mail, the message is transmitted over telephone lines by using a modem and communications software. The caller keys in a telephone number, connects with another party, and the two can "talk" from their keyboards, with the messages displayed on their monitors. As with internal communications, messages can be stored in the recipient's computer if he or she is not there when the call comes through. The benefit is that less time is lost when a caller doesn't connect with the recipient.

Another form of external communications involves connecting to a system of information exchange called an *electronic bulletin board*. A bulletin board is organized by individuals interested in a particular topic or area of study; by dialing the number of the bulletin board from their computers, individuals can, for instance, share tips for using software or learn how to solve a problem with a printer.

Voice mail is another recent development in electronic communications. With this method, you use your telephone to dial a voice-mail service and store an oral message; it is then delivered to the person you're calling. The audio quality of the message is similar to the actual voice. Since virtually everyone has a telephone, this service is not limited to owners of specialized equipment.

Some individuals use electronic mail not just to send short messages but to transmit their work from their home, which is their workplace, to the office. Memos, reports, even whole books can be transmitted in this way.

News reporters can send their stories this way.

A growing form of electronic mail is *facsimile transmission,* or fax. Fax machines are becoming more and more common, with 82 million documents being sent daily in 1989 from and to over 3.5 million machines. Now some entrepreneurs are putting faxes that take credit cards into airport lounges, hotel lobbies, and convention centers. To use them, you simply insert your credit card in the machine, dial the number you want to reach, and send your document.

Should a fax machine be used to send advertisements?

The advantage of fax transmission is its speed. For example, a high-speed fax machine can transmit a page in about 20 seconds. Improved machines offer higher quality of print, comparable to that of a copy machine. Because fax machines can be programmed, the cost of transmission can be cut by sending the message in evening hours when telephone rates go down.

• Teleconferencing

Electronic mail offers an alternative to sending written and oral messages, memos, letters, or reports. Teleconferencing, on the other hand, is an alternative to face-to-face meetings that can reduce the high costs of travel, hotels, food, and time lost in transit. With teleconferencing, several people at different locations can communicate electronically almost as effectively as in a face-to-face meeting.

The three main types of teleconferencing are audio teleconferencing, audiographic teleconferencing, and audiovideo teleconferencing. A fourth, educational teleconferencing, is usually a combination of the three main types.

Audio Teleconferencing   Telephone companies have offered teleconferencing facilities for business use for many years. The telephone conference call, in which the phone company arranges for several people in different geographic locations to be on the same line at the same time, is an example of this type of teleconferencing. Modern phones, with their electronics, are capable of establishing the necessary connections from the console itself.

Audiographic Teleconferencing   In addition to the voice portion of the teleconference, graphics may be transmitted using facsimile devices. The audiographic teleconference might take place in a room specifically designed for the purpose, with hand-held microphones for each participant and with machines sending images of documents or still photos of conference participants.

Audiovideo Teleconferencing   The audiovideo teleconference takes advantage of all media—audio, graphics, and video. A specially equipped room is necessary for an audiovideo teleconference: speakers provide the audio feedback, facsimile devices send graphics, and cameras transmit the video portion of the conference. Participants can engage in group discussions while observing one another's facial expressions and gestures, which aids the communication process. Major television news programs frequently use two-way video equipment to show both the interviewer and interviewee; audiovideo teleconferencing is a similar process.

Psychologically, the distance factor exists.

Educational Teleconferencing   Educational programs on television bring the class to the student rather than the student to the class. With closed-circuit television and feedback audio equipment, actual campus classes can be sent to remote classrooms or even to a business organization's educational facility. Students in remote classrooms can contact the actual classroom when they have questions or answers. The same system can be used with ill or disabled students in elementary and secondary schools. Although the possibilities of teleconferencing in education are almost boundless, the intellectual, social, and psychological growth that occurs when students attend school with one another argues against sole reliance on this technique.

Putting It All Together: The Executive Workstation

Executive workstations bring to one place all the electronic tools previously described. The *executive workstation* consists of a personal computer or a keyboard and monitor linked to a mainframe. In either case, the workstation has the ability to draw upon a number of computerized tools.

You'll probably have your own workstation.

Because of the diversity of the executive's duties, the workstation needs capabilities for word processing, spreadsheet analysis, and database management. With these programs, the workstation provides the executive with flexibility in writing and revising written material, analyzing data, interacting with databases, and preparing reports based on the accumulated information.

Some software programs, called *integrated programs,* include all three of these main applications in one common form. They share similar key combinations to initiate commands for manipulating data or formatting reports. By creating common structures for files, integrated programs facilitate the use of one kind of data—for example, a spreadsheet—in another, such as a report being prepared on the word processor.

Some executive workstations, of course, add to these core applications other of the software programs that have been discussed. Depending on the manager's area of responsibility, his or her workstation could be equipped with desktop publishing or graphics-generating programs. Providing these workstations with electronic communications programs is typical.

Executives can use their workstations not only to carry out these important functions but also to plan their days. Scheduling or calendaring programs allow managers to query the computer about their schedules and plan conferences accordingly. In a shared system, such as a network or multiuser system, the computer system can even scan the calendars of a number of people to determine the best meeting time for all individuals involved.

Another software tool that can aid the executive is a newer development called the *personal information manager*. These programs facilitate scheduling and the organization of random notes. They use very sophisticated methods of linking disparate bits of information through key words and phrases to allow the executive to thumb electronically through scores of notations in search of, for instance, all references to a particular client.

An added benefit of such programs is the fact that they can prevent time conflicts when assistants are making schedules for their superior. By making up-to-the-minute schedule information available to both executive and assistant, they prevent duplicate booking of time.

Although the executive workstation allows executives and assistants to work more efficiently by communicating through the computer, some executives are hindered by the fear of new technology. Many who start out feeling uneasy about their new machine, however, soon learn that the equipment can liberate them by performing boring and repetitive tasks quickly, as well as by significantly helping them do their jobs through the provision of easy and rapid access to vital information.

To take advantage of these tools, an executive must be able to do the following:

1. Type the letter and number keys at a speed of 40 to 50 words per minute.
2. Create or revise text using a word processor.

3. Analyze data from spreadsheets.
4. Access and retrieve database information.
5. Plan and schedule activities.
6. Use the electronic mail system to send and receive messages.

Computers and Barriers to Communication

Like all communication tools, computers both help and hinder good communication. In some respects, the requirements or capabilities of the machine can lead the user astray when creating or interpreting a message. We will examine how this can occur in each of the areas previously studied.

• Barriers Caused by Systems

The very nature of computers—the way they record, move, and manipulate data—can create barriers to communication. First, keep in mind that all computers do not work in exactly the same way. The engineering of the CPU channels the way programs work and data are recorded, but different computers are engineered differently. Some systems have certain important core structures in common, in which case data stored on one system can be retrieved on another. But with other systems, that is not the case. System incompatibility, then, is one barrier to communication between computers. Large companies often have a department that focuses on the organization's computer systems. The staff of that department, which has special expertise in the area, can advise you on whether you would be able to share data or make contact with another computer at another location.

A second systemic barrier to communication stems from the way people use computers. These machines follow a rigid and inexorable logic. They are very structured, and the person using one must be very structured as well, or else he or she will become lost in the rigor of the machines. Ignoring the proper sequence for leaving a program and turning off the machine, for instance, could result in the loss of some data. Forgetting to issue the commands to store a report on a disk loses the report.

While computers must be commanded in a logical and structured way, this does not mean that you should be afraid of the computer or afraid of making a mistake. It only means that you must be careful to

> Compatibility with existing systems must be analyzed before purchasing computer hardware or software.

perform tasks, when necessary, in a step-by-step fashion and not try to skip ahead.

• Barriers to Manipulating Data

Word Processing   The rigidity of the computer's logic can cause problems as well when using an application program such as a word processor. Because computers are able to perform so many tasks so rapidly, people form the mistaken notion that they are infallible, not realizing that they carry out instructions without hesitation and without judgment.

Using the automatic search and replace feature, for instance, may cause undesired results. Read the following paragraph:

> Each person present at the demonstration was given a list of word-processing commands. The office manager later reprimanded the man who raised the question about the reliability of the software.

Suppose that the search and replace feature was used to replace the word *man* with *woman*. This seemingly innocent change causes the following incoherence:

> Each person present at the demonstration was given a list of word-processing comwomands. The office womanager later repriwomaned the woman who raised the question about the reliability of the software.

The computer changed *every* instance in which the letters *man* appeared in sequence to the word *woman*. Computers do not exercise judgment; they carry out commands. Users must be sure to construct their commands in such a way as to get the results they really want.

Another potential barrier to communication stemming from word-processing programs is overreliance on spellcheckers. Documents must still be proofread to avoid errors such as those in the following example, in which words were spelled correctly but used incorrectly. The sentences as input and checked for spelling read as follows:

> He was complemented on his choice _ office manager, paralegal, and son. The attorney's hardly approved.

Unfortunately, what was intended was the following:

> He was complimented on his choice of office manager, paralegal, and so on. The attorneys heartily approved.

What can be done to prevent this problem?

The mail merge feature, too, can lead to barriers to communication. The most frequent complaint about this feature is that form letters are impersonal. Many people simply refuse to read such letters for that reason. Constructing a good standard letter that doesn't sound like a form letter can circumvent this problem. To make a form letter more personal,

1. Add more variables to the standard letter so you have more opportunity to tailor it to the individual.
2. Use personalized envelopes instead of mass-produced mailing labels.
3. Be sure to spell names correctly.
4. Produce a higher quality document by using better grade paper and better quality printers.

Spreadsheets   The main barrier to good communication with a spreadsheet is the use of incorrect formulas for manipulating data. Whenever a template for a particular spreadsheet is created, the validity of the formulas should be checked by running a sample test with some data.

Another barrier stems from the confidence that people develop in the results produced by a spreadsheet. Because the computer has such vast capabilities, users assume that a computer-generated report must be correct. Remember, though, that the results are only as good as the data that are entered in the first place. Data entered into the spreadsheet should be double-checked against the source from which it came. The assumptions behind "what-if" projections should be checked to ensure that they are reasonable.

Databases   A problem may arise with databases if they are not properly designed. A database usually has a limit on the number of fields per records that can be used. When constructing a database, you need to decide which fields are necessary and which are not. Inexperienced database designers will try to create fields for all possible data about a customer or client, rather than identifying and omitting unnecessary data. The result is a poorly designed database that is difficult and time-consuming to use.

• Ineffective Presentations

Working with type, design, and graphics introduces new considerations that were once the concern of only the graphic artist or typesetter.

How does too much variety get in the way of communicating?

Desktop publishing puts a very useful tool in the hands of the untrained user; the results, unfortunately, often show the lack of training. Having the opportunity to design does not mean being capable of designing. Newcomers to desktop publishing, enchanted with the effects that can be created with type, rules, shadows, and boxes, clutter documents with too many changes of type style or with too many lines. The result is not an effective presentation but a jumble of words and graphic elements that confuse and alienate the reader.

By following some simple principles of design, however, the budding desktop publisher can effectively use the tools at his or her disposal:

1. *Keep it simple.* The worst thing to do is everything. The more variety there is on the page, the more difficulty the reader will have in following the message. Restricting the document to no more than two or three typefaces and just a few special effects is often the best approach. Other variations are still available to be used in another publication.

Emphasis should be given to the main points in the communication.

2. *Keep it consistent.* Treat comparable elements in comparable ways. All the headlines in a newsletter with five stories should be in the same typeface and style. Save special treatments for material that is special.

3. *Let form follow function.* The document should be styled in such a way that it looks like what it is. A purchase order need not be elegant; the menu of an expensive restaurant should look more dignified than the price list of a dry-cleaning service.

A problem that may arise with graphics-generating programs is similar; a person may be so eager to create eye-catching graphics that the actual relationships of data are distorted. The purpose of graphs is to emphasize points, not to obscure them. Be careful to use graphics reasonably.

• Barriers to Electronic Communications

Electronic mail is a handy way to communicate quickly and conveniently with another worker or with a database. It is not, however, a toy to be used for entertainment. The messages put on an electronic mail system should be related to business and not supplied to give the recipient a good laugh.

Summary

Some people mistakenly think of electronic tools for business communication as substitutes for basic communication skills. Rather, they are merely tools—tools that augment and enhance the communication process.

The main categories of these tools are

1. Tools for manipulating words, numbers, and data, called word processing, electronic spreadsheet, and database programs.
2. Tools for presenting information, including desktop publishing and graphics-generation programs.
3. Tools for communicating electronically from one computer to another.

These tools may be used individually or in combination. Executive workstations bring many tools together in one place.

As with all tools, computer programs must be used properly to effect communication. Even spellchecking, an apparently straightforward use of computers, can result in errors if not used properly. Although the electronic tools described in this chapter can make communication easier or the presentation of a message more effective, they are no substitute for the basic communications skills the user must possess.

About Language and Usage

As a highly technical field, computer science has its own terminology. Although nothing is wrong with specialized usage, barriers to communication can arise if people use the terms inappropriately in another context. Here are some terms and their meanings when used in reference to computers:

backup	Second, identical, copy of a program or of data, prepared in case some damage should occur to the original.
bug	Problem in a program that makes it work incorrectly.
DOS	Disk Operating System, the programs that instruct the computer how to interpret the inputs

(continued)

	from the keyboard, how to connect with various pieces of equipment, and how to use stored data.
file	Name of a group of data that are stored together, whether they be a memo, a report, or a spread-sheet.
format	Prepare a new disk to be able to receive data for storage; also, to establish the way a file will appear when printed.
hard copy	Printed files, as opposed to the same file stored electronically on a disk.
import	Bring information from one computer or program to another.
input	Information placed into the computer, whether by keyboard, mouse, or other piece of equipment.
output	Results of the computer's processing, whether sent to the monitor or to a printer.
save	Instruct the computer to store data on a mass storage device.

Exercises

Review Questions

1. What is more important, the computer equipment or the software that makes it work?

2. Review the following word-processing features: spellcheck, thesaurus, search and replace, block and move, block and copy, insert, and delete. Which feature would you select for each example?

   a. Two lines of copy were omitted.

   b. Words were misspelled.

   c. One sentence needs to be removed.

   d. The company name was misspelled twelve times.

   e. Three paragraphs on the first page need to be on page 10.

   f. A complicated table on page 2 needs to be used on page 14.

   g. You cannot think of a word to use in place of "advent."

3. Explain how a form letter can be made more personal.

4. Describe the types of activities you can do using an electronic spreadsheet. Give an example of how an electronic spreadsheet can be used to improve your communications.

5. Why are lists important in business? Identify a number of different types of lists a company might have. Give an example of a list that would help you in your personal life.

6. Give an example of how desktop publishing or graphics-generating software can actually be a barrier to communication.

7. Describe some advantages of electronic mail.

8. Identify the category of electronic tool that best describes the following:
   a. Desktop publishing
   b. Automatic table of contents
   c. Databases
   d. "What-if" feature
   e. Data integrity
   f. Teleconferencing
   g. Electronic mail
   h. Scheduling and planning
   i. Query language
   j. Artificial intelligence

9. Explain what is meant by "personal information management."

10. What is meant by the statement "Electronic mail eliminates telephone tag"?

Activities

1. Perform an automatic search and replace procedure on any word in a one-page document created using any word-processing package. Discuss any problems that occur as a result of the automatic search and replace feature.

2. Keyboard a one-page document and perform a spellcheck using any word-processing package. Proofread the document and compare your results. Report your findings to the class.

3. Consult advertising and design books and periodicals and write a two-page report on the use of different type styles.

4. Bring to class a sample of a document produced on different quality

printers or typewriters. Discuss the effect the quality of print has on the message.

5. Describe a communication obstacle you have encountered when using an electronic communication tool. If you do not have a personal experience, imagine one that could happen.

6. Go to the library and request or perform a database search, going back two years, on one of the topics in this chapter. Locate one of the articles on microfilm and print a copy. Hand in the list and the copy of the article.

7. Management has asked you to suggest ways to improve office productivity. You conduct interviews with several employees. What are your solutions to the following problems?

   a. A memo takes two or three days to get from one department to another.

   b. Sales executives are very frustrated about the excessive time spent in air travel for regional product information meetings.

   c. "Telephone tag" is a problem for many employees.

   d. Space is not available to add file cabinets of any kind. File clerks are constantly harassed about lost or misplaced documents.

   e. Administrative assistants become very upset when asked to make changes or revisions in documents because they have to spend hours retyping entire documents.

   f. Compiling reports is a major time-consuming task. For example, someone wants to know the names of all customers who purchased $2,000 to $5,000 worth of Brand X last year. An employee complains that it will take months to pull this information from the company files, it may not be accurate, and it may be impossible to find this information for other states.

   g. The company seems to be falling behind in market share because of a lack of knowledge of some recently developed products that its customers want. If sales reps had known more about some of these developments, they could have made the sale.

Cross-Cultural Communication at Home and Internationally

CHAPTER

Somehow everyone must respect the dignity and worth of human personality, and ultimately people must be judged not on the basis of the color of their skin but on the content of their character. Somewhere we must learn to live together as brothers (and sisters) or we will all perish together as fools.

MARTIN LUTHER KING, JR.

Since United States corporations face ever fiercer competition abroad, and their own power has diminished, the leaders of these enterprises have only one choice—to get smarter about the world.

LOUIS KRAAR, *Fortune*, March 1980

Although this book is not the place for a complete coverage of international or cross-cultural communication, the two opening quotes provide adequate incentive to explore a few of the communication problems of our shrinking world.

Following World War II, the United States—through its European Recovery Program (the Marshall Plan) and the occupation and rebuilding of Japan—played a major role in getting the world back on its economic feet. Today Canada, Western Europe, and Japan are our major trading partners. In time, other Western Hemisphere nations are likely to become major partners. The free-trade agreement signed with Canada and approved by the Senate in late 1988 opens the door for greater, mutually satisfying trade with that nation. Doors to mainland China have opened along with that nation's desire to incorporate a touch of Western "capitalism" into its economy, and whatever changes occur in the U.S.S.R. may further expand international business.

During the past four decades, U.S. firms have established plants in Europe, Central and South America, and Asia. More recently, Asians (primarily Japanese) and Europeans have built plants in the United States. Additionally, periods of a weakened dollar on international markets have encouraged foreigners to buy a piece of the United States by acquiring banks, manufacturing firms, publishing houses, food-processing plants, and real estate—homes, resorts, and office buildings. More than 2 million North Americans work for foreign employers. Growing business contacts with those from other countries is happening in reverse as well; the number of Mexican and other Central American workers in the United States grows daily.

Chances are great that you'll be involved either in international business activities or in some activity in which you'll have to communicate across cultural gaps. How about being manager of a McDonald's in Beijing, of a Ford plant in Moscow, or of a resort hotel in Dubrovnik! What if you find yourself managing a clothing manufacturing operation in the Southwest with no English-speaking production employees? As technology continues to make our world more compact, business is becoming international business, whether at home or abroad.

As a result, you will have to confront problems created by cultural differences. The reason is that business communications happen in the context of a society. How messages are decoded and encoded is not just a function of the experiences, beliefs, and assumptions of the person sending or receiving those messages. Equally vital is how those attributes of the individual are shaped by the society in which he or she lives.

Each of us learns patterns of behavior from our society. These pat-

Portions of the Volvo automobile are made in as many as nine countries!

terns affect how we perceive the world, what we value, and how we act. They can create barriers to communication if we encounter another person whose behavior follows different patterns. In the past, the potential communication problems arising from such situations were not so great because cross-cultural contacts were fewer. In an era of global economies, mutual economic interdependence, multinational corporations, and multiculturalism, however, these contacts are frequent—and often awkward. Understanding how culture can erect barriers to communications—and knowing ways to break down those barriers—are keys to success in this modern world.

Nature of Culture

The *culture* of a people is the sum total of their living experiences within their own society. It could be described as "the way of life" of a people and includes a vast array of behaviors and beliefs.

Can you describe your own culture?

• Elements of Culture

Culture reaches into all aspects of our lives, touching the most basic dimensions of human interaction. While the forms or content of these elements vary from place to place, each culture is built on a foundation of the following elements:

- *Values*—what people consider important concerning such phenomena as time, work, change, spirituality, and materialism. Values are the culture's underlying assessment of what is good or bad, acceptable or unacceptable.
- *Norms*—values find their expression in norms, the guidelines for action within the culture. Norms can be unwritten customs, such as the proper way to introduce one person to another or the accepted kind of dress for a date. Norms may also be codified as laws.

Are the norms of students the same as the norms of businesspeople?

- *Symbols*—each culture has certain objects, gestures, sounds, or images that contain special meaning for that culture. The American flag symbolizes our nation's independence and strength; a package using the colors of that flag tries to associate itself with those meanings. Advertising, which in some respects is the use of cultural symbols, requires sensitivity to the specific cultural meaning of the symbols employed.

- *Language*—how people communicate in speaking and writing as well as nonverbally is shaped by culture. Language is the medium through which culture is passed from one generation to the next. It also reflects cultural values and norms. Spanish, for instance, has two second-person pronouns, one formal and the other more informal. The formal "you" is a sign of respect used when addressing a superior or a new acquaintance, whereas the informal "you" is reserved for family and friends. American English does not have this fine distinction. An American businessperson, unfamiliar with the distinction in Spanish, could unintentionally offend a Spanish-speaking client by employing the incorrect form.

What kinds of things are part of cultural knowledge?

- *Knowledge*—the last element of culture is the body of facts and information that a people accumulate over time. A cliché of American movies set in the European theater of World War II was the scene in which an apparent American soldier was discovered to be a German spy by his failure to know a fact about baseball. While overused, the episode reveals a truth about culture: the members of a culture share a common pool of knowledge that influences how they view the world.

Culture has three key characteristics. First, it is learned by people over time—they are not born knowing their culture but acquire it through interactions with others. The family; schools; social institutions such as churches, clubs, and businesses; and the media all play a part in teaching each member of a society the expectations and norms of behavior.

Second, the various components of culture are interrelated. In the United States, for instance, the high value placed on material goods is related to the use of economic well-being as a measure of success and happiness. These values provide support for the approval placed on independence of mind and action, which in turn is connected to the existence of a relatively fluid class structure. The list of connections could go on, but these examples alone make it clear that each of these components of American culture is connected to others.

The third main characteristic of culture is that it is shared. In other words, the various aspects of culture are common to many individuals. No country has a monolithic culture, however. Human societies are so large and diverse that many different cultures can exist within them; these are called *subcultures*. While each subculture differs from others, they often share some traits that derive from the main or dominant culture.

• Manifestations of Culture

Each society exhibits its culture in many ways. Certainly customs, the accepted way of interacting with others, are expressions of the culture. The American practice of shaking hands upon meeting reflects the value that is placed on the individual. Indians greet each other with a slight bow to honor the divine spark that they believe resides in each person.

Institutions also manifest culture. The structure and role of churches, schools, social organizations, businesses, and governments all reflect the way the people of that culture see the world. These institutions, in turn, shape how the people see the world by passing the culture on.

Ways of thinking are another way that culture shows itself. Americans have a culturally supported belief in progress. They interpret developments in light of this belief, always looking for the evidence that progress has occurred or will eventually take place. Faith in progress combines with faith in rationalism to produce an optimistic, problem-solving approach to difficulties. After all, if things tend toward progress, a difficulty must be temporary. It's simply a matter of using your head to find the solution.

Finally, culture is manifested in language. Culture enables us to acquire a language, which we may use in common with others of the same culture. But language is an outgrowth of culture and not the reason for culture. English is the language of Australia, Jamaica, and South Africa, as well as Great Britain, Canada, and the United States; but all these cultures are very different—in fact, even their languages differ.

What other language is used differently in different countries?

In sum, culture provides us with the standards for behavior and gives us a feeling of identification and belongingness; we feel a part of something larger than ourselves. Problems occur between people of different cultures primarily because people tend to assume that their own cultural norms are the right way to do things. They believe—incorrectly—that the specific patterns of behavior desired in their cultures are really universally valued.

Cross-Cultural Contacts

That awareness of other cultures is of growing importance to anyone in business is clear simply from watching the news or reading the paper. Stories about the balance of trade, competition from foreign businesses, the possible loss of jobs, and the growing number of immigrants looking for work abound.

What is the level of foreign investment today?

What may not be clear from these stories is the extent to which international contacts take place. Such major corporations as Dow Chemical, Gillette, Black & Decker, and IBM saw more than 40 percent of their total sales coming from foreign operations in a recent year; Coca-Cola, Johnson & Johnson, ITT, Avon, and Xerox were not far below that level. Foreign investment in the United States is growing. In 1987, the level of foreign investment was over $260 billion a year, about 80 percent of the value of U.S. investment abroad.

• Foreign Businesses Entering the United States

The growth of foreign ownership of U.S. businesses introduces new factors to American business, and Japan is a major source of that growing ownership. For 3,000 years, Japan existed in isolation, with virtually no immigration and little emigration. The scene has now changed. With its economic strength, Japan has been forced to expand beyond isolation. The Japanese success in world markets produced a high standard of living that can be sustained further only by selling worldwide. The drive to trade and keep the economy growing is vital to Japan's economic survival. As one Japanese leader said, "If we close up, we die."

Overseas expansion means that Japan faces the same problems of cross-cultural contact that other world powers confronted in the past. Japanese companies are likely to expand to the United States with increasing frequency. They will employ more and more Americans and both foreign company and domestic workers will have to learn to adapt and adjust to the new situation.

• The Foreign Firm's American Employee

The strain that arises during this process of adaptation is the result of the clash between two distinct cultures. It may be particularly acute in the case of Japanese-American employees of a Japanese firm; with the physical attributes of a Japanese worker or manager, they may be mistakenly assumed to be part of the Japanese culture. But the culture that shaped their values and behavior was different.

Douglas Kitani is Japanese-American, born and raised in the Pacific Northwest and college educated; as a U.S. export representative for Mitsui and Company, a Tokyo-based firm, he often deals with Japanese citizens. He is frequently confusing to them. "They're not used to someone being so independent, who cooks for himself, lives on his own," the 26-year-old said. "They wonder why I don't live with my parents to save money."

Another Japanese-American employee of a Japanese firm feels the strain in a different way. "You're supposed to act like an insider, but you don't get the perks," he said. "They expect too much without giving rewards." On the other hand, some Japanese firms that have been in the United States for some time, such as banks, provided executive opportunity for Japanese-Americans in an earlier time when educated Japanese often could find work only in factories and in agriculture.

Other firms are experiencing a similar problem—one found at one stage or another by most multinational corporations. The question is how to treat nationals with managerial ability. Mitsubishi International Corporation (MIC) does more than half its trading volume in the United States; and it made good sense to hire Americans, who now fill 80 percent of the workforce of the American subsidiary. From 1970 until just recently, however, those American employees found promotion extremely difficult. A study of MIC by the Business Research Institute at St. John's University found that many Japanese believed Americans could not handle leadership positions.

Each year, more Americans attain top-level positions with foreign-owned firms.

The study confirmed that cultural differences do play a role in how we observe others. Perhaps Americans were seen as unable to lead simply because they hadn't adopted Japanese leadership styles. Whatever the cause of the problem, MIC recognized its existence and has begun to initiate promising American traders into the idiosyncrasies of the company. By 1988, three Americans served as members of the board of directors, one American was an executive vice-president, and nine Americans were vice-presidents. A few Americans are spending two-year stints with Mitsubishi in Japan, working side-by-side with key contacts in the company and building effective personal networks. Additionally, the firm sponsors week-long retreats in New York during which Americans and Japanese work together on simulated business projects in an effort to foster closer relationships.

• Multiculturalism and Demographic Trends in the United States

The United States has always accepted individuals from other lands; it is a commonplace that everyone came here from somewhere else. For many decades, the flow of immigrants was reduced. At the same time, descendants of the last immigrants were intermarrying, breaking down the barriers between subcultures and creating a sense that the dominant culture was more dominant than in truth it was.

As the "melting pot," the United States developed a reputation for melding disparate groups into one common culture, thus bridging cultural gaps. Such blending did take place to an extent; as they lived their new lives in the new land, immigrants did adopt key elements of the dominant culture. To perceive this blending as the major aspect of the new nationals' experience, however, may be misleading.

The United States, rather than being a melting pot, created an environment in which people of varying cultures could live. People with common heritage generally collected together, formed their own neighborhoods—or ghettos—and worked intently at retaining their original culture, while still sharing in the common culture to an extent.

In the 1970s, with the influx of large numbers of immigrants from Southeast Asia and Latin America, Americans began to confront the fact that the melting pot was an unfortunate metaphor for the immigrant experience. The new immigrants—as had immigrants in the past—gathered together when possible. They tried, as best as possible, to retain their traditional customs and language, looking for some familiarity in their new world. As a phrase made popular in another context put it, "You can take the boy out of the country, but you can't take the country out of the boy."

The rise in new immigrants is not the only recent demographic trend that affects business, however. The maturing of the "baby-boom" generation, a relatively low birth-rate, and increasing life spans have led to a higher average age in the population. The flood of women entering the job market has substantially changed the American workforce. The increase in the number of women workers, along with black, Hispanic, and Asian workers, is graphically shown in Figure 18.1. The traditional makeup of the workforce is changing. The proportion of women is projected to increase until, in the year 2000, they become the single largest demographic group in the workforce.

With each percentage change in the composition of the workforce, some aspect of cross-cultural communication becomes increasingly important. Whether you are a man or a woman, the member of a racial minority or not, a native or an immigrant, or the member of any other demographic group, your ability to reach out to the members of other groups will have much to do with the success of cross-cultural communication throughout the world.

What have you learned from your ancestry?

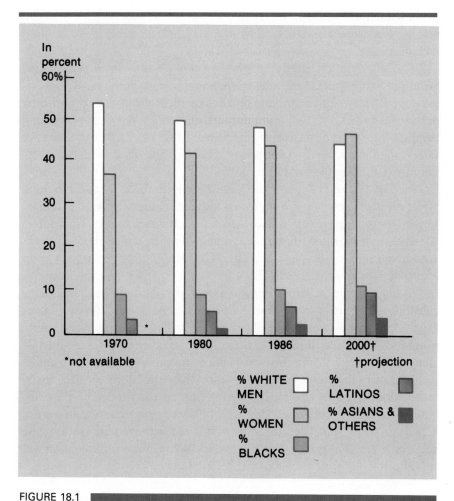

FIGURE 18.1

Share of the workforce by demographic group. (*Source:* Data from U.S. Census and Bureau of Labor Statistics.)

• The American Firm's Minority Employee

With these changing demographics, American-owned firms have been forced to deal with ethnic diversity in the workplace. A *Los Angeles Times* article related a story similar to the following one.

The photograph projected on a classroom screen at Northern Tele-com's semiconductor components plant in Rancho Bernardo showed a farmer piling hay into a wagon drawn by two plow horses. "Where do you think this picture was taken?" the instructor asked her fifteen stu-

Cultural stereotyping?

dents. China, one called out. Texas, said another. Indiana, Mississippi, and Russia were also guessed by the class of assembly workers and technicians.

The answers reflected the global span of the employees' backgrounds. Seven were American-born Anglos, four Filipinos, two Latinos, one African-American, and one Pakistani. No one was correct. The photo was taken in Ohio, and the point was clear. We view everything through the prism of our own experience. "Just because of the way we were brought up, we can see how we have problems communicating" the instructor summarized.

Openness based on trust?

As part of the class, workers discuss how their cultural differences affect the attitudes they bring to work. Privately, they reported that they formed snap impressions about other nationalities in the workforce. When these preformed notions are presented to the entire class, students are encouraged to discuss the differences frankly and relate them to improving work practices.

Many American firms are addressing the issues raised by multiculturalism. Because more than half its employees were foreign born, Esprit de Corp., a women's clothier, added English classes to its training program. At times, limited knowledge of English creates problems. Slang and hurried instructions can make immigrants' lives miserable. Cultural customs can interfere as well. A Korean administrative assistant nodded her head as her supervisor gave instructions about a computer spreadsheet program. Her nod indicated only that she had been *listening*. When she failed to do as instructed, she was crestfallen. She had not *understood* what had been said. When miscommunication occurs, both sides are frustrated and often angry.

What elements of the dominant American culture have been adopted from an immigrant group's subculture?

Several generations will undoubtedly be required to "Americanize" the ethnic minority workforce. As these changes evolve, subtle changes will probably occur in the dominant culture as well. Such changes have occurred throughout America's history as people of different backgrounds have joined—and contributed to—our culture.

Barriers to Cross-Cultural Communication

Because cultures give different definitions to such basics of interaction as values and norms, people raised in two different cultures may clash. It is time to explore some of the main areas in which those clashes take place.

We will identify the following barriers to communication:

- Stereotypes
- Time as language
- Space as language
- Body language
- Ethics
- Translation problems

• Stereotypes

One group often forms a mental picture of the main characteristics of another group, creating preformed ideas of what people in this group are like. These pictures, called *stereotypes*, color the way members of the first group interact with members of the second. When they observe a behavior that conforms to that stereotype, the validity of the preconceived notion is reinforced. The other person is no longer viewed as an individual, but as a representative of a class of people.

Are stereotypes fair?

All cultures have stereotypes about the other cultures they have encountered. These stereotypes can get in the way of communication when people interact on the basis of the imagined representative, and not the real individual. One way of exploring the force of stereotypes is by reviewing those held about Americans.

The American stereotype does exist, although it may undergo drastic change as our previously unchallenged world dominance in international trade fades. The abundance of natural resources, our industrial strength, and our consumer economy have made us appear affluent and wasteful in the eyes of some foreigners. "Visiting foreigners are often astonished to see cars less than ten years old heaped in junkyards. These cars would probably still be on the road in most countries because other cultures seem more inclined to foster an awareness of the need for conserving resources and preserving material goods" (Phatak, 1983).

We attempt to control nature; many other cultures worship it as part of their religions. We also seem to seek status through the acquisition of material things—automobiles, imported shoes, designer jeans—while many other cultures can get along with mass transportation, ordinary footwear, and a pair of pants. That this material orientation can create a rich irony is clear from the following anonymous piece.

Much of the world also likes our shoes and jeans.

Only in America

He drove his German car made of Swedish steel and interior of Argentine leather to a gasoline station, where he filled up with Arab oil shipped in a Liberian tanker and bought two French tires, composed of rubber from Sri Lanka.

At home, he dropped his Moroccan briefcase, hung up his Scottish tweed wool coat, removed his Italian shoes and Egyptian cotton shirt, then donned a Hong Kong robe and matching slippers from Taiwan.

More comfortable now, he poured a cup of hot Brazilian coffee into an English coffee mug, set a Mexican placemat on an Irish linen tablecloth atop a Danish table varnished with linseed oil from India. Then he filled his Austrian pipe with Turkish tobacco, lit it, and picked up a Japanese ballpoint pen with which he wrote a letter to his congressman demanding to know why the United States has an unfavorable balance of trade.

This piece was done "tongue in cheek."

Americans are also looked upon by many others as strong individualists, aggressive, and "macho" in the case of men. These traits have been fostered and reinforced by the movies we export and by our taking on the role of an international police force.

Can you list your need preferences in 1, 2, 3 order?

Additional elements in the American stereotype are our attitudes toward formality, time, and change. We generally act informally, perhaps in keeping with our reputation of rugged individualism. Many other cultures place a high value on formality, rituals, and social rules. They also place the family, group, and organization before individuals. To Americans, "time is money." In certain other cultures, though, time is the cheapest commodity and an inexhaustible resource. It represents the person's life span on earth, which is only part of eternity. Americans look on change as inevitable but also attempt to initiate it and control it. In many other cultures, change is seen as inevitable; but no attempt is made to initiate it.

If much of the world looks at us as just described, how do we look at the rest of the world? Rather than attempting to describe the American stereotypes of all world peoples, let it be said that each of us does some stereotyping, just as we probably do so collectively. We have our good guys, bad guys, and so-so guys. If we have no personal experience on which to draw, we may use popular news sources to develop second-hand judgments.

What is stereotyping? How does it develop?

Stereotyping is a pervasive activity. Yet, it is a barrier to communication in international relations—political, economic, and social. The problems of being seller or buyer, of being employee or employer, of being superior or subordinate, or of being based at home or in a foreign location are all affected by each person's culture and the stereotypes of other cultures that he or she learns from that culture.

• Time as Language

In our own hemisphere, Latin Americans have a different attitude toward time. Anyone who has visited Mexico and arranged taxi service to arrive at a certain time can attest to the two time frames of Mexico—clock time and "Mexican" time.

This observation is not made to denigrate Mexicans. It simply explains the different values the two cultures place on time. Americans, like some northern Europeans who are also concerned about punctuality, make appointments, keep them, and don't waste time completing them.

In some cultures—such as Latin America—the language of time says that important things take longer than unimportant ones. An interesting thing about cultures that pay little attention to appointment keeping is that once the appointment begins, the host will probably spend more than the agreed-on time and show more hospitality and generosity than Americans generally expect. The next visitor may be kept waiting interminably—the nearest American parallel is the wait in a doctor's office—but that visitor will also receive the same cordial, considerate treatment.

How do you value time?

The language of time is based on cultural factors often not understandable to others. In the Middle East and in many countries of Asia, life on earth is only a tiny portion of a person's total time, including life after death. In that perspective, what difference does an hour or so make?

• Space as Language

Space operates as a language just as does time. In America, large offices are frequently reserved for executives as status symbols. In many parts of the world, large offices are for clerical workers and smaller ones for executives. Not much space is required for thinking and planning, so large areas are reserved as working spaces.

The distance between people functions in communication as "personal space" or "personal territory" in all cultures. In America, for example, for intimate conversations with close friends and relatives, we are willing to stay within about a foot and a half of others; for casual

Watch for examples of personal space.

conversations, up to two or three feet; for job interviews and personal business, four to twelve feet; and for public occasions, more than twelve feet. The next time you are on an elevator in a public building notice how uncomfortable most people appear. They usually stare either at the floor or at the ceiling because their personal territory has been invaded and they must stand shoulder to shoulder with strangers.

But in many foreign cultures, close personal contact is accepted. Men customarily kiss each other on the cheek when they are introduced or when they meet. To the American "macho," this is normally an embarrassing situation; to the foreigner, it is no more personal than shaking hands. As a rule, we tend to move away when someone enters our personal territory. By observing the behavior of others, we can gain some idea of their concepts of personal territory, which can assist us in our own attempts to communicate.

• Body Language

The familiar American symbol for "okay" or "everything is all right" is made by forming a circle with the thumb and forefinger. In other cultures the same gesture may mean zero, as in France; money, as in Japan; or a vulgarity, as in Brazil. The familiar symbol of "V" for victory formed by the index and middle fingers is an insulting sign in much of Europe, particularly in Britain, unless the palm faces the receiver of the message.

We nod our heads up and down to indicate agreement or "yes." In other parts of the world, the nod indicates only that the person heard what was said. In Bulgaria and some other Eastern European countries, the up-and-down head motion means "no" and the side-to-side motion "yes"—just the opposite of our meanings. Other cultures indicate "no" by a jerk of the head or a back-and-forth waving of a finger, as we sometimes do when saying "no-no" to a child.

You can have your appointment or interview cut short in most Arabian countries if you sit in such a way that the sole of your shoe is visible—an insulting symbol. The solution is to sit with feet flat on the floor.

The "business lunch" is an American tradition; much business is transacted on the golf course, on tennis courts, and at social functions as well. However, in most parts of the world, dining and recreation are social functions and not the place or time to conduct business. So, "when in Rome. . . ."

• Ethics

In the last few years, considerable attention has been focused in the media on the apparent decline of ethics in American business. The savings and loan crisis, junk bonds and leveraged buyouts, stock manipulation, environmental abuse, insider trading, and commodity frauds reflect negatively on American business institutions and management. Here are some observations made by distinguished panelists in a recent news column called "Are Business Ethics Slipping?" (*Los Angeles Times*, 1989).

Richard Lamm, former governor of Colorado and director of the Center for Public Policy and Contemporary Issues at the University of Denver: "There are lots of problems in the American business community, but outright corruption is certainly not at the top of the list. In Mexico and South America and a number of other countries, corruption is a way of business. In the United States, corruption is the exception, not the rule."

Kirk O. Hanson, business ethics expert: "I suspect that corruption on Wall Street and in the commodities business and the defense industry has always existed. The highly publicized incidents . . . are evidence in part of more aggressive enforcement and better reporting."

Father Theodore Hesburgh, president emeritus of the University of Notre Dame and a prominent corporate director: "In general, I find the level of ethical conduct quite high in American business. I wish I could say the same for European business . . . some of our toughest competitors overseas are the worst."

Apparently, we have a problem, but a relatively small one. The United States has always professed high ethical standards for conduct in business, and a rationale that "everyone is doing it" cannot be a reason for lowering the standards.

How can we keep low-level ethics from becoming culturally embedded?

• Translation Problems

Words in one language do not always have an equivalent meaning in other languages, and the concepts the words describe are often different as well. A study of how Japanese and American business students understood the concept of profit concluded this way: "It is important for the American to understand that his definition of *profit* as solely corporate gain—involving as it will the maximization of short-term gains—conflicts with the Japanese definition, which necessarily involves a long-term view of things" (Sullivan & Kameda, 1982). When the meaning of a word is not agreed on in advance, later misunderstanding is a strong possibility.

In a humorous and helpful book about marketing overseas, David A. Ricks (1983) highlights the problems of translating with several examples of American advertising and product labels that resulted in different meanings when translated. General Motors promoted its cars in Belgium with "Body by Fisher," a phrase familiar to Americans; but in Flemish, the translation was "Corpse by Fisher." "Come alive with Pepsi" became "Come out of the grave . . ." in German and "Bring your ancestors back from the dead" in parts of Asia. Some products didn't succeed: Pet milk failed in France because *pet* means, among other things, to break wind. In Mexican slang, *fresca* means lesbian. An American product failed in Sweden because its name translated to enema, which the product was not.

Even within English-speaking countries, words can vary greatly in meaning. In England and in our own dictionaries, *homely* refers to someone who is plain, unpretentious, and warm. Yet, we often hear it used to identify someone who is unattractive, even ugly.

Studying foreign languages involves a similar process.

Translators can be helpful, but keep in mind that a translator is working with a second language and must listen to one language, mentally cast the words into another language, then speak them. This process is difficult and opens the possibility that the translator will fall victim to one or more of the cultural barriers.

Guides to Good Cross-Cultural Communication

With so many barriers to communication, is it possible for people of one culture to understand those of another? The very existence of international business argues for the affirmative; were understanding not the case, no agreements could be reached between firms from different countries. Nevertheless, it is clear that pitfalls exist. Anyone who enters the business world today must be aware of these potential trouble spots and of possible ways of avoiding them.

• General Principles

A good guideline for someone about to engage in business with a person from another country is to learn about that person's culture. Many sources of useful information are available. Experienced businesspeople write books recounting some of the subtle but important ways that people in other countries communicate. Simple networking can generate the names of other businesspeople who have made contact with another culture; a phone conversation or a lunch may provide pointers on what to do and what not to do. Large corporations with frequent and extensive dealings in other lands often establish workshops in which employees receive briefing and training before entering the field. Learning the language is an invaluable way of becoming more familiar with another culture.

Another basic guide to communicating is to have patience—with yourself and the other person. Conversing with someone from another country, when one of you is likely to be unfamiliar with the language being used, can be difficult and time-consuming. It is not the same as the free-and-easy way you have of talking with your roommate. By being patient with mistakes, making sure that all questions are answered, and not hurrying, you can make the outcome of the conversation more likely to be positive.

The third basic rule of communicating is to get help when you need it. If you aren't sure what is being said—or why something is being said in a certain way—ask for clarification. If you feel uneasy about going into a conversation with someone from another culture, try to bring along someone you trust who understands that culture. Then you have a resource if you need help.

• Written Communications

When writing for intercultural consumption, keep in mind some of these suggestions:

1. Write naturally but avoid slang, idioms, acronyms, and other devices that may cause confusion to those unfamiliar with American usage.
2. Use the message-planning principles you learned in this course. Rely primarily on deductive paragraph organization.
3. Use simple terms but attempt to be specific as well. Some of our simplest words—for example, the word *fast*, with several meanings—must be interpreted within the context of each situation in which they are used.
4. Attempt to limit sentences to one idea.
5. Use graphics when possible.

Should you write "down" to another?

6. Use numbers for figures. The number system is almost universal. Keep in mind, however, that most people in the world use the metric system.

• Oral Communications

In face-to-face communication, attempt to be natural while at the same time being aware of cross-cultural aspects. Rely on some of these suggestions:

1. Attempt to minimize your stereotype of a people and to focus on the other person as an individual.
2. Try to understand some of the cultural elements that distinguish you from others in the communication process.
3. As with writing, avoid slang, idioms, and other devices peculiar to American usage.
4. When you have advance notice about a meeting, do some research about the participants' country or countries. A 1988 study by the National Geographic Society found Americans—youths and adults—unable to locate countries on a world map. Americans ranked below both Asians and Europeans in simple place geography. Nothing would be more embarrassing than to reveal total ignorance about others.

Ask questions, but don't needlessly interrupt.

5. Do not hesitate to provide feedback or ask whether the other person understood. Develop a technique of verifying your understanding by asking if you or the listener might restate something in another way.
6. Attempt to conclude a meeting with a clear understanding of what has been agreed on and what further actions are necessary.
7. Watch the other person throughout. When a message is not clear, you will know by watching and be able to rephrase the statement.

Summary

Language, values, attitudes, and other cultural traits change only very slowly. Therefore, communicating interculturally calls for recognition of the cultural elements that cause people to view things differently and thus create barriers to communication.

A relatively new factor in intercultural communication in business and industry has been created by foreign-owned businesses establishing American plants and hiring American workers to work for foreign managers. Older patterns dealt with international trade and American-owned firms employing ethnic minority workers. Under all three conditions, communication may be difficult.

Instead of attempting to forget about or ignore cultural factors, workers and employers may improve communication by recognizing them and by considering people as individuals rather than as members of stereotypical groups. Suggestions for improving written and oral communication include many of the same practices recommended for communication within a culture. An important difference, however, is to avoid the use of terms peculiar to a language or terms open to several interpretations.

The business school graduate of today will almost certainly work for a multinational firm or have to interact with one. For many people, the growing area of international business will require them to work overseas as their careers progress; their success or failure will very much depend on skill in communicating in an intercultural environment.

About Language and Usage

Although the use of words of Spanish origin occurs primarily in the American West and Southwest, many of these words are known generally in the United States:

bravado	swaggering courage
caballero	horseman or gentleman
bronco	unbroken horse
enchilada, taco, tostado, tortilla, garbanzo, tamale	all are foods or types of food
macho	aggressively male
plaza	public square
patio	interior courtyard
siesta	afternoon nap
fiesta	festival or celebration

References

Los Angeles Times. (1989). Are business ethics slipping? January 29, Part IV.

Phatak, Arvind V. (1983). *International dimensions of management*. Boston: PWS-KENT.

Ricks, David A. (1983). *Big business blunders*. Homewood, IL: Dow Jones–Irwin.

Sullivan, Jeremiah H., & Kameda, Naoki. (1982). The concept of profit and Japanese-American business communication problems. *Journal of Business Communication*, 19(1).

Exercises

Review Questions

1. How does a culture benefit a people?

2. What factors have caused and are causing the decline in the dominance of the white man in leadership roles in business?

3. What dangers are inherent in the stereotyping of a people?

4. What effect might religion have on "the language of time"?

5. The United States seems to have difficult problems in dealing with relatively small countries such as Vietnam, Iran, and Nicaragua. Suggest some ways or some cultural differences that lead to such problems.

6. What is meant by "We view everything through the prism of our own experience"?

7. How do slang expressions and idioms endanger cross-cultural communication?

8. Stereotyping is considered both bad and good. What are some helpful or good aspects of stereotypes? What precautions can you take about stereotyping as you prepare for a communication?

9. How can you elicit feedback in cross-cultural communication?

Activities

1. Make a list of foreign job opportunities available in the *Wall Street Journal* or in a leading city newspaper.

2. Go to a world map and locate the following: The Persian Gulf, Hong Kong, Taiwan, South Korea, New Zealand, Iraq, South Yemen, Indiana, Delaware, Chile, South Africa, Yugoslavia, and Tasmania.

3. Interview a student for whom English is not the first language. Prepare a report of not more than one page on the student's perceived language problems and on your own observation of possible problems.

4. Make a list of the foreign-made products you might find in any home or apartment. Are similar products manufactured in the United States?

Appendix A

I f messages do not meet high standards of grammar and mechanics, they have negative consequences. The receiver may (1) misunderstand the message, (2) lose time by stopping to review the message, (3) think more about the error than the message, or (4) think negatively about the sender's background or respect for the receiver.

The following pages review some of the common problems that confront business writers. The subject matter is basic. Regardless of job level (from the lowest entry level to the highest managerial level), a knowledge of basics is beneficial. Mastery of the following pages is exceedingly beneficial for those engaged in (or associated with) word processing. For both administrative personnel and correspondence personnel, knowledge of basic English usage is considered a necessity.

The following review of basics seeks to answer frequently encountered questions about grammar, spelling, punctuation, and typing. For more thorough reviews, consult standard reference books on grammar or transcription.

Pretest

Grammar and Mechanics

The following test is designed to measure your knowledge of grammar, spelling, and punctuation. Proceed in this manner:

a. Place a cover sheet over the indented sentence that follows sentence 1.

b. As you read sentence 1, look for errors in grammar, spelling, and punctuation.

c. With pen or pencil, make necessary corrections. Do not attempt to revise a sentence and state its idea in an entirely different way. Do not divide a sentence into two sentences.

d. Move the cover sheet downward and check your answers against the corrected (indented) sentence. Making an unnecessary change is a mistake; failing to make a necessary change is a mistake. If a sentence can be corrected in more than one way, two corrected sentences appear beneath it. Either is acceptable.

e. Record the number of mistakes in the space provided at the left.

f.   Continue this procedure for the remaining sentences.

———   1. Only one of our assistants have applied for promotion; but four have applied for transfer.

> Only one of our assistants has applied for promotion, but four have applied for transfer.

———   2. Our tanks' were empty, theirs were full.

> Our tanks were empty; theirs were full.
>
> Our tanks were empty, but their tanks were full.

———   3. When discussion began, Frank and Karen were present, but they left before a vote was taken.

> When discussion began, Frank and Karen were present; but they left before a vote was taken.

———   4. The supervisor was enthused about the suggestion, it was very unique.

> The supervisor was enthusiastic about the suggestion; it was unique.
>
> The supervisor was enthusiastic about the suggestion because it was very unusual.

———   5. While the primary criteria for promotion is competence personality receives some consideration.

> Although the primary criterion for promotion is competence, personality receives some consideration.
>
> The primary criterion for promotion is competence, but personality receives some consideration.

———   6. One applicants' interview was postponed for two hours, this may have affected his performance.

> One applicant's interview was postponed for two hours; this delay may have affected his performance. (Some other noun—such as *postponement*—could be used instead of "delay.")

———   7. One news media has proposed a face to face debate between you and I.

(continued)

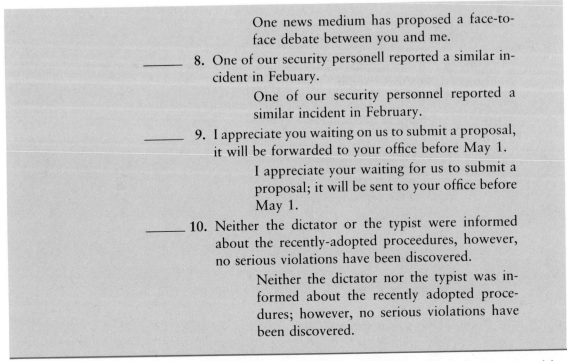

One news medium has proposed a face-to-face debate between you and me.

_____ 8. One of our security personell reported a similar incident in Febuary.

One of our security personnel reported a similar incident in February.

_____ 9. I appreciate you waiting on us to submit a proposal, it will be forwarded to your office before May 1.

I appreciate your waiting for us to submit a proposal; it will be sent to your office before May 1.

_____ 10. Neither the dictator or the typist were informed about the recently-adopted proceedures, however, no serious violations have been discovered.

Neither the dictator nor the typist was informed about the recently adopted procedures; however, no serious violations have been discovered.

The preceding test provides approximately thirty-five opportunities for error. The more errors you made, the more profitably you can study the following pages.

As the following review is intended for *study* or for *reference,* the terminology found in English textbooks is employed. For those who have forgotten, many of the basic grammatical terms are defined. Principles are followed with illustrations. For best results, (1) read the principles, (2) examine the illustrations that follow, and (3) *then read the principles again.* Returning to the principle after seeing the illustrations increases the clarity of the principle and reinforces learning.

In the following pages, principles fall conveniently into two categories: grammar and mechanics.

Grammar and Mechanics

For a *complete* review of grammar, other sources would be needed; but knowledge of the words frequently misused, the parts of speech, and sentence structure prevents a high percentage of errors that appear in business writing.

• Words Frequently Misused

1. *Above* and *below.* In referring to material that comes before or after, avoid use of *above* and *below.*

   Not: The <u>above</u> statement. . . .
   But: The <u>preceding</u> statement. . . .

   Not: The graph <u>below</u>. . . .
   But: The <u>following</u> graph. . . .

   Above and *below* are especially distracting when they appear in unfortunate positions on a typewritten page. Too often, *below* appears in the last paragraph of a page and the reference is *not* in fact below (it's at the top of the next page); or *above* appears in the first paragraph of a page and the reference is *not* in fact above (it's at the bottom of the preceding page).

2. *Accept, except.* Accept means "to take what is offered," "to accede," "to assent"; *except* means "to leave out," "to exclude."

   All columns have been added <u>except</u> one.

   I <u>accept</u> your offer.

3. *Accompanied by, accompanied with. Accompanied by* is used when *people* are involved. *Accompanied with* is used when *objects* are involved.

   She was <u>accompanied by</u> her secretary.

   The letter was <u>accompanied with</u> a check.

4. *Affect, effect. Affect* is a verb meaning "to influence"; *effect* is a noun meaning "result"; *effect* is also a verb meaning "to bring about."

   The change does not <u>affect</u> his pay.

   What <u>effect</u> will the change have?

   The manager wants to <u>effect</u> a change in the schedule.

5. *Aid, aide. Aid* is verb that means "to assist"; it is also a noun that means "assistance" or "help." *Aide* is a noun that means "a person who serves as an assistant."

   The potion will <u>aid</u> digestion.

   The potion serves as an <u>aid</u> to digestion.

   The governor's <u>aide</u> made a statement to the press.

6. *All right, alright.* Alright is considered substandard usage.

The answers were <u>all right</u>.

That's <u>all right</u> with me.

7. *All together, altogether.* *All together* means "in one group"; *altogether* means "completely" or "wholly."

The answer is <u>altogether</u> correct.

The employees were <u>all together</u>.

8. *Already, all ready.* *Already* means "at a previous time"; *all ready* means "inclusively ready."

The employee had <u>already</u> left for home.

The machines are <u>all ready</u> for use.

9. *Among, between.* Use *among* to discuss three or more, *between* to discuss two.

Divide the earnings <u>among</u> the six workers.

Divide the earnings <u>between</u> the two workers.

10. *Amount, number.* Use *amount* when speaking of money or of things that cannot be counted; use *number* when speaking of things that can be counted.

The <u>amount</u> of grumbling has been troublesome to the supervisors.

The <u>number</u> of workers has been increased.

11. *Anxious, eager.* Use *anxious* only if great concern, doubt, worry, or anxiety is involved.

The manager is <u>eager</u> to participate.

He is <u>anxious</u> about the lack of security.

12. *Anyone, any one.* Use *anyone* if the *any* is to be accented; use *any one* if the *one* is to be accented. *Any one* will usually be followed by *of*.

Does <u>anyone</u> have a pencil?

<u>Any one</u> of our machines will be satisfactory.

13. *As to, about,* and *on.* Use *about, on,* or some other single-word preposition instead of *as to*.

Do you have any remarks <u>about</u>   Not "as to."
the contract?

May we have your comments <u>on</u>   Not "as to."
the proposal?

14. *Bad, badly.* As an adjective, *bad* modifies a noun. *Bad* also follows a sense verb (touch, sight, smell, sound, taste). As an adverb, *badly* modifies a verb, adjective, or adverb.

> We received a <u>bad</u> report.
>
> Fred feels <u>bad</u> about the outcome.
>
> The fender was bent <u>badly</u>.

15. *Balance, remainder.* Use *balance* to refer to the difference between the debit and credit sides of a ledger account or when referring to an amount of money owed. Use *remainder* to refer to that which is left over.

> The unpaid <u>balance</u> is $60.
>
> Our staff can complete the <u>remainder</u> of the work in an hour.

16. *Biannual, biennial. Biannual* is the label for an event that happens twice in a year; *biennial* is the label for an event that happens once in two years.

> Your <u>biannual</u> payments are due in January and July.
>
> Congressmen are eager to adjourn for their <u>biennial</u> campaigns.

17. *Can, may. Can* indicates capability or power. *May* indicates permission.

> We <u>can</u> do this work easily.
>
> You <u>may</u> talk with the superintendent now.

18. *Capital, capitol. Capital* is money, property, or a city in which state or national government is located. A *capitol* is a building in which the government meets.

> One business partner provided the <u>capital</u>; the other provided the expertise.
>
> The <u>capitol</u> is at the intersection of Jefferson Street and Tenth Avenue.

19. *Coarse, course. Coarse* means "lacking in fineness," "rude," or "rough." *Course* means "a school subject," "the ground designated for a race," "a portion of a meal served at one time," "a series of successive proceedings."

> The gravel was too <u>coarse</u> for use in the concrete mixture.
>
> She is taking a <u>course</u> in mathematics.
>
> That issue has now run its <u>course</u>.

20. *Compare to, compare with.* Use *compare to* in pointing out similarities; use *compare with* in pointing out differences as well as similarities.

He <u>compared</u> Kennedy <u>to</u> Lincoln.	He pointed out similarities.
He <u>compared</u> Kennedy <u>with</u> Lincoln.	He pointed out differences as well as similarities.

21. *Complement, compliment. Complement* means "to complete" or "that which completes or suits another." *Compliment* means "words of praise."

The clerk was <u>complimented</u> for his success.

This shipment is a <u>complement</u> to our latest series of orders.

22. *Consensus of opinion. Consensus* means "general opinion"; therefore, *of opinion* is redundant.

The <u>consensus</u> was that we should withdraw.

23. *Continual, continuous.* If an action is *continual,* it will have planned-for breaks in continuity; if an action is *continuous,* it will be constant, without breaks.

The clock has run <u>continuously</u> for four years.	It has not stopped.
The mechanism for raising and lowering the garage door has given <u>continual</u> service for four years.	It provided service over a four-year period, but it did not raise and lower the door constantly.

24. *Correspond to, correspond with.* If one thing *corresponds to* another, it matches or has a similarity. To *correspond with* is to write, to exchange letters.

His recommendations <u>correspond to</u> mine.

Mr. Woods has <u>corresponded with</u> us about a job.

25. *Council, counsel. Council* means "an advisory group." *Counsel* means "advice," "one who gives advice," or "to advise."

<u>Council</u> members will meet today.

First, seek legal <u>counsel</u>.

The defendant and his <u>counsel</u> were excused.

An attorney will <u>counsel</u> the suspect.

26. *Credible, creditable. Credible* means "believable." *Creditable* means "praiseworthy" or "worthy of commercial credit."

The explanations were <u>credible</u>.

Mr. Jones did a <u>creditable</u> job for us.

27. *Criteria, criterion.* A *criterion* is a standard for judging, a yardstick by which something is measured. The plural form is *criteria*.

The most important <u>criterion</u> was cost.

Three <u>criteria</u> were developed.

28. *Data, datum. Datum* is a singular noun meaning "fact," "proposition," "condition," or "quantity" from which other facts, etc., may be deduced. *Data* is the plural form.

This <u>datum</u> suggests....

These <u>data</u> suggest....

Use of *data* as a singular form is gaining some degree of acceptance. Some people use the word in the same way in which they would use *group*. Although composed of more than one, *group* is singular:

The group <u>has</u> decided.

Until (and if) *data* becomes generally accepted as a singular, the word should be used carefully. Because *data is* may sound incorrect and distracting to some and *data are* equally incorrect and distracting to others, an alternative expression may be preferred. Instead of "This data is," or "These data are," such expressions as "This *set* of data is," "These facts are," "This information is," or "These figures are" can be used to avoid the risk of alienating certain readers or listeners.

29. *Deal. Deal* is not a good substitute for *transaction* or *exchange.*

We reaped a profit from the   Not "deal."
<u>transaction</u>.

30. *Decent, descent, dissent. Decent* means "respectable" or "good." *Descent* means "a movement downward." *Dissent* means "to disagree."

We were served <u>decent</u> meals.

Fasten your seat belts; the plane is beginning its <u>descent</u>.

The motion passed; only one member <u>dissented</u>.

(*Words Frequently Misused* continues after Exercise 1.)

Exercise 1

Select the correct word.

1. If you agree with the (preceding, above) statement, please write your initials in the space provided.
2. The governor was accompanied (by, with) two body guards.
3. All questionnaires were returned (accept, except) one.
4. Exactly how will the change (affect, effect) us?
5. The governor brought two of his (aids, aides) to the hearing.
6. Is the proposal (alright, all right) with you?
7. Do you think these figures are (all together, altogether) correct?
8. The committee has (all ready, already) decided to accept.
9. The commission is to be divided equally (among, between) the three sales agents.
10. We were astonished by the (amount, number) of complaints.
11. The hod carriers were (anxious, eager) for a raise in the hourly wage.
12. Does (anyone, any one) have a suggestion?
13. Do you have a question (about, as to) procedures?
14. The waitress felt very (bad, badly) about the way the meal was cooked.
15. Most of the work is finished; the (balance, remainder) will be completed next week.
16. Members of the U.S. House of Representatives are elected (biannually, biennially).
17. You (can, may) take your coffee break now.
18. The (capital, capitol) will be repainted before the legislature convenes in January.
19. Because of conflicting instructions, the employees hardly knew which (coarse, course) to pursue.
20. In this research, the scores of smokers will be compared (with, to) the scores of nonsmokers.
21. Thank you. I consider that remark a (compliment, complement).
22. The (consensus, consensus of opinion) is that you should reapply.
23. Sam was (continually, continuously) asking for a raise.
24. Because your information corresponds exactly (with, to) mine, the decision will be easy.

25. The suspect declined to accept legal (council, counsel).
26. Because the suspect's statements were (credible, creditable), no charges were filed.
27. The conclusion was based on only one (criteria, criterion).
28. This (data, set of data) will be fed into our computer.
29. We are eager to bring this (deal, transaction) to a conclusion.
30. The measure was passed without (descent, dissent).

- ## Words Frequently Misused (continued)

31. *Differ from, differ with.* Use *differ from* in discussing characteristics; use *differ with* to convey the idea of disagreement.

    This machine <u>differs from</u> that machine.

    The manager <u>differs with</u> the president.

32. *Different from, different than.* *Different from* is correct; *different than* is to be avoided.

    That machine is <u>different from</u> mine.

33. *Disinterested, uninterested.* Use *disinterested* to convey neutrality or impartiality; use *uninterested* to convey lack of interest or lack of concern.

    Both employees agreed to accept the decision of a <u>disinterested</u> colleague.

    Because of severe financial pressures, the owner was <u>uninterested</u> in the discussion of social problems.

34. *Each other, one another.* Use *each other* when referring to two people; use *one another* when referring to more than two.

    The two typists competed with <u>each other</u>.

    The members of the group helped <u>one another</u>.

35. *Eminent, imminent.* *Eminent* means "well known." *Imminent* means "about to happen."

    An <u>eminent</u> scientist will address the group.

    A merger seems <u>imminent</u>.

36. *Enthused, enthusiastic.* *Enthusiastic* is preferred. *Enthused* is colloquial.

    The gentleman is <u>enthusiastic</u>   Not "enthused."
    about his work.

37. *Envelop, envelope. Envelop* is a verb meaning "to surround" or "to hide." *Envelope* is a noun referring to a cover for a letter.

A fog was about to envelop the island.

Just use the enclosed envelope for your reply.

38. *Equable, equitable. Equable* means "uniform throughout," "steady," "even," or "without variation." *Equitable* means "just," "fair," or "impartial."

For an equable mixture, use an egg beater.

The wage-scale proposal was considered equitable; therefore, it was accepted.

39. *Farther, further.* Use *farther* when referring to distance. Use *further* when referring to extent or degree.

Let's go one mile farther.

Let's pursue the thought further.

40. *Fiscal, physical. Fiscal* means "financial" or "pertaining to revenue." *Physical* pertains to nature or to the parts of the human body.

The budget director stressed the need for fiscal responsibility.

Ten minutes were devoted to physical exercise.

41. *Following, preceding.* These words are not nouns; they are adjectives and should be followed by nouns. Avoid "the following is" or "the preceding is." Instead, write

The following list is up to date.

The preceding idea is ascribed to the president.

42. *Formally, formerly.* Use *formally* in discussing that which is ceremonious or done according to an established method. Use *formerly* in discussing that which has preceded in time.

The award will be formally presented at tomorrow's convocation.

Tom formerly worked for the department of revenue.

43. *Forward, send.* Use *send* to convey the idea of *initiating* movement of an item toward its receiver; use *forward* to convey the idea of *redirecting* an item that has already been sent on its way to the receiver.

After the contract is signed, I shall send it to you.

The package came to my address, but I forwarded it to you.

44. *Impact.* Use *impact* as a noun, not as a verb.

The cost increase had a serious impact on our decision.

Avoid expressions such as "cost will *impact* our decision," or "the decision will seriously *impact* performance."

45. *In, into.* Use *in* to denote location. Use *into* to denote action.

The keys are in the vault.

He fell into the water.

46. *Infer, imply.* *Infer* means "to draw a conclusion"; readers or listeners infer. *Imply* means "to hint" or "to set forth vaguely"; speakers and writers imply.

I infer from your letter that conditions have improved.

Do you mean to imply that conditions have improved?

47. *Ingenious, ingenuous.* An *ingenious* person is clever or skillful in inventing. An *ingenious* device has been cleverly conceived or designed. An *ingenuous* person is honorable, frank, or free from disguise.

The superintendent is ingenious; he can always find a way to solve such problems.

The superintendent is ingenuous; he never makes excuses.

48. *Insure, ensure.* To *insure* is to contract for payment of a certain sum in the event of damage or loss. To *ensure* is to make certain that a specified event or result will occur.

We plan to insure the house for $150,000.

To ensure a passing score, study systematically.

49. *Irregardless.* Avoid this word. Use *regardless* instead.

50. *Its, it's.* *Its* is a possessive pronoun; *it's* is a contraction for "it is."

The phrase has lost its meaning.

It's time to quit.

51. *Kindly.* Avoid using *kindly* for "please."

Please fill out the attached form.   Not "Kindly."

52. *Later, latter.* Use *later* as an adverb or as an adjective; use *latter* only as an adjective that precedes a noun.

The minutes will be read later.   Adverb

| The frost will be <u>later</u> than usual this year. | Adjective |
| Our first frost usually comes in the <u>latter</u> part of October. | Adjective |

53. *Latest, last.* Use *latest* to refer to something that is still in effect; use *last* to refer to something that came after all the others.

| The <u>latest</u> model has a twelve-inch carriage. | The series has not necessarily ended; other models could follow. |
| The <u>last</u> model had a ten-inch carriage. | The series has ended; no other models will follow. |

54. *Less, fewer.* *Less* refers to things that cannot be counted; it also refers to money. *Fewer* refers to things that can be counted.

He concentrates more on accuracy, <u>less</u> on speed.

We can now do work with <u>fewer</u> mistakes.

55. *Lie, lay.* In the present tense, *lie* means "to rest" and *lay* means "to put."

Lie	Present:	He <u>lies</u> on the sofa.
	Past:	He <u>lay</u> down for an hour.
	Perfect participle:	He <u>has lain</u> there for an hour.

Lay	Present:	She <u>lays</u> the book on the table.
	Past:	She <u>laid</u> the book there yesterday.
	Perfect participle:	She <u>has laid</u> it there many times.

56. *Lose, loose.* *Lose* means "to fail to keep"; *loose* means "not tight."

Don't <u>lose</u> the moneybag.

The cap on the fountain pen is <u>loose</u>.

57. *Majority.* Avoid use of *majority* in referring to a singular.

Not: The <u>majority</u> of the contract is acceptable.
But: The <u>major portion</u> of the contract is acceptable.
Or: The <u>majority</u> of the provisions are acceptable.

58. *Marital, martial.* *Marital* pertains to marriage; *martial* pertains to the military (army, navy, air force, marines).

After years of <u>marital</u> problems, the couple divorced.

For two years after its defeat, the country was governed by <u>martial</u> law.

59. *Media, medium.* A *medium* is a means for transmitting a message.

Letter, telephone, radio, newspaper, and telegraph are examples. The plural form is *media*.

The best <u>medium</u> for advertising this product <u>is</u> the radio.

The news <u>media</u> are very objective in <u>their</u> coverage.

60. *Moral, morale.* A *moral* person meets generally accepted high standards of personal conduct; such a person is considered virtuous or ethical. *Morals* is often used as a noun to mean "principles of ethical conduct." *Morale* is a level of cheerfulness or confidence.

The applicant has high <u>moral</u> standards; I would trust him completely.

People enjoy working there; <u>morale</u> is high.

(*Words Frequently Misused* continues after Exercise 2.)

Exercise 2

Select the correct word.

1. Late in the discussion, the manager and supervisor differed (from, with) each other over the wage issue.
2. Your answers are different (than, from) mine.
3. As an accounting major, Ruth was (disinterested, uninterested) in a thorough study of poetry.
4. The three panelists were constantly interrupting (each other, one another).
5. Completion of Project A is six months away, but completion of Project B is (eminent, imminent).
6. The president was (enthused, enthusiastic) about the proposal.
7. Remember to include return (envelops, envelopes) with your questionnaires.
8. Union members rejected the proposal because it was not considered (equable, equitable).
9. The issue will be discussed (further, farther) at our next meeting.
10. Our finance department will check the report from a (fiscal, physical) point of view.
11. The trend is depicted in the (following, following graph).
12. Stan (formerly, formally) worked for the health department.
13. Please (send, forward) a copy of your report to me.

14. That decision will (impact, have an impact on) our collection procedures.

15. Insert the key (in, into) the lock.

16. From his statements to the press, I (infer, imply) that he is optimistic about the proposal.

17. Production has increased 300 percent since we adopted this (ingenious, ingenuous) labor-saving device.

18. Fred forgot to (ensure, insure) his car.

19. (Regardless, Irregardless) of weather conditions, we should proceed.

20. The storm seems to be losing (its, it's) force.

21. If you agree, (kindly, please) sign and return the enclosed form.

22. We planned to incorporate (latter, later) in the year.

23. The story appeared in the (last, latest) issue of *Time*.

24. We've had (less, fewer) cancellations this month than last month.

25. Perhaps you should (lie, lay) down and rest for a while.

26. Do not (loose, lose) sight of your primary objective.

27. I agree with the (majority, major portion) of his argument.

28. If your (marital, martial) status is single, turn immediately to page 3.

29. Only one news (media, medium) was present for the announcement.

30. Employees were complaining; (moral, morale) seems to be very low.

- ## Words Frequently Misused (continued)

61. *Miner, minor. Miner* means "one who works in mines." *Minor* means "inferior in importance or size" or "one who has not reached adulthood."

    Our <u>miners</u> struck a rich lode at 2,000 feet beneath the surface.

    Too much time was spent discussing <u>minor</u> points.

    As a <u>minor</u>, Steve was ineligible to vote.

62. *Myself, me. Myself* is used to intensify *I* or *me*. It should not be used in place of these words.

    I <u>myself</u> would like to have a vacation.

    The manager and <u>I</u> have investigated this plan.   Not "myself."

    Give the report to Ms. Smith and <u>me</u>.   Not "myself."

Use of such pronouns as *myself, herself,* and *themselves* is appropriate when the pronoun has been used already in the sentence.

I taught <u>myself</u> to type.

She sees <u>herself</u> as a perfectionist.

They were criticizing <u>themselves</u>.

63. *Nor, or.* Use *nor* with *neither;* use *or* with *either.* (*Or* is also used in sentences that don't contain *either.*)

Use <u>neither</u> pen <u>nor</u> pencil.

Use <u>either</u> pen <u>or</u> pencil.

You may pay now, <u>or</u> you may wait until January.

64. *Only.* Place *only* as close as possible to the word it is intended to modify.

<u>Only</u> Carol takes dictation.	No one else takes dictation.
Carol <u>only</u> takes dictation.	She does nothing more than take it; she does not transcribe.
Carol takes dictation <u>only</u>.	Dictation is the only thing she takes.

65. *Party.* Except in legal documents, do not use *party* as a synonym for *person.* Technically, a *party* is a group of people.

Another <u>person</u> (not <u>party</u>) is interested in buying this house.

66. *Passed, past. Passed* is the past tense of the verb *pass. Past* is an adjective when used to describe a time period that has ended; it is also used as a noun to identify time that has gone by.

Mary <u>passed</u> her test. A car <u>passed</u> us on our right.

We had several inquiries in the <u>past</u> week.

In the <u>past</u>, the system worked beautifully.

67. *Personal, personnel. Personal* means "concerned with a person" or "private." *Personnel* means "people" or "employees."

Omit the questions about family background and musical preference; they're too <u>personal</u>.

All advertising <u>personnel</u> are invited to participate in the workshop.

68. *Practical, practicable. Practical* means "useful" or "not theoretical." *Practicable* means "capable of being put into practice." Do not use *practicable* in describing a person.

The manager is a <u>practical</u> person.

This is a <u>practical</u> tool.

The plan appears to be <u>practicable</u>.

69. *Principal, principle. Principal* means "main" or "primary"; *principle* means "rule" or "law."

The <u>principal</u> runs the school.

The <u>principal</u> purpose is to gain speed.

The <u>principal</u> plus interest is due in thirty days.

The theory is based on sound <u>principles</u>.

70. *Quiet, quite. Quiet* means "silent"; *quite* means "entirely" or "completely."

This room is <u>quiet</u>.

The instructions are <u>quite</u> clear.

71. *Raise, rise. Raise* means "to lift up" or "to move something upward." *Rise* means "to go up" or "to come up."

Raise	Present:	We do not want to <u>raise</u> prices.
	Past:	We <u>raised</u> our prices last year.
	Perfect participle:	Our prices have been <u>raised</u> this year.

Rise	Present:	I do not expect prices to <u>rise</u>.
	Past:	Prices <u>rose</u> slightly last year.
	Perfect participle:	Prices have <u>risen</u> this year.

72. *Reason is because.* Since *because* means "for the reason next presented," *reason is because* constitutes a form of redundancy.

Not: The <u>reason is because</u> losses from bad debts tripled.

But: The reason is <u>that</u> losses from bad debts tripled.

Or: Profits decreased <u>because</u> losses from bad debts tripled.

73. *Respectfully, respectively. Respectfully* means "with respect." *Respectively* means "in the sequence presented."

The speaker is eminent; please listen <u>respectfully</u>.

The highest scores were made by Ruby, Gil, and Carrie, <u>respectively</u>.

74. *Set, sit. Set* is "to place"; *sit* is "to rest one's body on the buttocks."

Set	Present:	<u>Set</u> your briefcase on the counter.
	Past:	She <u>set</u> the briefcase there yesterday.
	Perfect participle:	She <u>has set</u> the briefcase there previously.

Sit   Present: Please <u>sit</u> on the bench.
         Past: He <u>sat</u> there yesterday.
         Perfect participle: He <u>has sat</u> there for ten minutes.

75. *Shone, shown. Shone* is the past and past participial form of *shine.*
    Shown is the past participial form of *show.*

    The sun had <u>shone</u> for two hours.

    This article was <u>shown</u> in last week's exhibit.

76. *Sometime, some time.* Use *sometime* to refer to a point of time on
    the clock or calendar. Use *some time* to refer to an indefinite number
    of time units.

    Come to the office <u>sometime</u> this afternoon.

    Try to pay the account <u>sometime</u> next month.

    We have not seen him for <u>some time</u>.

    <u>Some time</u> has elapsed since we saw him.

77. *Stationary, stationery. Stationary* means "without movement" or
    "remaining in one place." *Stationery* is writing paper.

    The machine is to remain <u>stationary</u>.

    Order another box of <u>stationery</u>.

78. *Statue, stature, statute.* A *statue* is a molded or sculptured figure.
    Stature means "height" (with respect to the human body), "rank,"
    "reputation," or "status." A *statute* is a law.

    A <u>statue</u> of the king stands in the park.

    <u>Stature</u> was a primary consideration in the recruitment of basket-
    ball players.

    Because of Mary's <u>stature</u> in the insurance field, she was invited to
    testify.

    According to the judge, only one <u>statute</u> had been violated.

79. *Steal, steel. Steal* means "to commit theft." *Steel* is iron in modified
    form (contains a certain amount of carbon).

    A vagrant tried to <u>steal</u> from the supply room.

    The concrete is to be reinforced with <u>steel</u> rods.

80. *Suit, suite.* A *suit* is a set of garments to be worn together; it is also
    the act or process of bringing a disputed matter to court. A *suite* is a
    group of connected rooms; it is also a set of furniture.

    The players will soon receive warmup <u>suits</u>.

The <u>suit</u> will be heard by Judge Jones.

We leased a <u>suite</u> in the Medical Arts Building.

We ordered a dining-room <u>suite</u>.

81. *Sure, surely. Sure* is an adjective; *surely* is an adverb.

I am <u>sure</u>.
We <u>surely</u> appreciate that atti-   Not "sure."
tude.

82. *Suspicion. Suspicion* is a noun; it should not be used in place of the verb *suspect*.

Her actions aroused <u>suspicion</u>.

We <u>suspect</u> her.   Not "suspicion."

83. *That, which.* Use *that* when a relative clause is essential in conveying the basic meaning of the sentence. Use *which* when a relative clause is not essential in conveying the basic meaning of the sentence.

The books <u>that</u> were on the shelf have been sent to the bindery.

The apparent purpose of the sentence is to identify certain books as having been sent to the bindery; therefore, "that were on the shelf" is essential. Because the clause restricts the discussion to certain units, it is called a *restrictive* clause.

Multigrade oil, <u>which</u> is only slightly more expensive than one-grade oil, will serve your purpose better.

The apparent purpose of the sentence is to convey the superiority of multigrade oil; therefore, "which is only slightly more expensive than one-grade oil" is not essential. Because the clause does not restrict the discussion to certain units, it is called a *nonrestrictive* clause. Note that nonrestrictive (*which*) clauses employ punctuation; restrictive (*that*) clauses do not. Note the difference in meaning:

Return the papers <u>that</u> are   Return "passing" papers only;
marked "passing."   keep the others.

Return the papers, <u>which</u> are   Return all papers; incidentally,
marked "passing."   they are marked "passing."

84. *Unique, complete, perfect.* These adjectives have neither comparative nor superlative forms. *Unique* means "the only one of its kind"; therefore, something that is unique is not comparable. Anything is either unique or not, complete or not, perfect or not.

Her score is <u>perfect</u>.   Not *more perfect* or *most perfect*.

The plan is <u>unique</u>.   Not *very unique* or *more unique*.

His report is <u>complete</u>.   Not "fairly complete."

85. *Very, real. Very* is an adverb; *real* is an adjective. Do not use *real* to modify verbs, adjectives, or adverbs.

The report was <u>very</u> effective.   Not "real."

86. *Wait for, wait on. Wait for* means "to await." *Wait on* means "to serve."

We are <u>waiting for</u> the report.

The waitress will <u>wait on</u> us next.

87. *Was, were.* Use *was* with the singular and *were* with the plural. However, use *were* with the singular when the mood is subjunctive (when the sentence speaks of doubt, probability, sorrow, wishfulness, or conditions that do not actually exist).

She <u>was</u> present.

They <u>were</u> present.

I <u>wish</u> the story <u>were</u> true.   Not "I wish the story *was* true."

If I <u>were</u> old enough, I <u>would</u> apply.   Not "If I *was* old enough. . . ."

88. *Weather, whether.* Use *weather* in discussing conditions of the atmosphere. Use *whether* in discussing alternatives.

In January, <u>weather</u> conditions made construction difficult.

I don't know <u>whether</u> to invest in stocks or bonds.

89. *While. While,* meaning "at the same time that," should not be used as a synonym for such conjunctions as *but, though, although, and,* and *whereas.*

You do the worksheet <u>while</u> I type a stencil.   Concurrent activities.

One man likes his work, <u>but</u> the other doesn't.   Not "while."

<u>Although</u> we realize your account is overdue, we think you should not pass up this opportunity.   Not "while."

90. *You.* Do not use *you* to mean "I" or "people in general." "You can scarcely interpret these data" is incorrect if it is intended to mean "I

can scarcely interpret these data" or "People can scarcely interpret these data." Such misuses of *you* can make a reader think his or her abilities have been underestimated.

Exercise 3

Select the correct word.

1. Except for a few (miner, minor) points, the contract is acceptable.
2. The contract must be signed by a notary public and (me, myself).
3. Neither the morning shift (nor, or) the afternoon shift will be affected.
4. Which sentence, (a) or (b), reveals that John makes deliveries in no area other than the south side?
   a. John makes deliveries on the south side only.
   b. Only John makes deliveries on the south side.
5. One (party, person) spoke under conditions of anonymity.
6. The incident occurred three times in the (past, passed) month.
7. This employee is entitled to examine her (personal, personnel) folder.
8. For our purposes, this machine is very (practical, practicable).
9. The system's (principal, principle) advantage is monetary.
10. Will you please be (quite, quiet).
11. The college plans to (raise, rise) entry standards.
12. The reason is (because, that) legislative appropriations have been stalled.
13. The supervisor listened (respectfully, respectively) to operator's complaints.
14. Before turning on the switch, (set, sit) the dial at 12.
15. The device will be (shone, shown) to the committee on May 13.
16. You will need (some time, sometime) to relax before the demonstration begins.
17. Please have (stationary, stationery) printed for our new address.
18. The jury decided no (statue, statute) had been violated.
19. Construction is to be of (steal, steel) and concrete.
20. Because of the dispute, a (suit, suite) will soon be filed in superior court.
21. The attorney (sure, surely) appreciates the information I provided.
22. I (suspect, suspicion) the data are faulty.

23. We sold only the mowers (that, which) were in the demonstration booth.
24. Your demonstration was very (unique, unusual).
25. Your demonstration was (very, real) effective.
26. We are waiting (on, for) our accountant to verify the figures.
27. If the story (was, were) true, I would resign.
28. When (weather, whether) conditions improve, construction will begin.
29. (Although, While) my findings are similar, my conclusions are dissimilar.
30. From my seat in the large lecture hall, (you, students) could hardly hear the speaker.

• Nouns

Nouns (words that indicate people, places, or things) may be either specific or general, concrete or abstract, proper or not proper.

1. **Specific Versus General.** For most business writing, use *specific* nouns because they let a reader see exactly what is meant. "The dean objected" gives a clearer picture than "An administrator objected"; "A $2\frac{1}{2}$-ton truck is missing" is clearer than "One vehicle is missing."

   When you do not want (or need) to convey a vivid mental picture, you can use general words. "I appreciated your letting me know about the accident" is less vivid (and better) than ". . . about your sprained ankle, your broken ribs, and the smashed-up car."

2. **Concrete Versus Abstract.** *Concrete* nouns are word labels for that which is solid—something that can be seen, touched, and so on. *Abstract* nouns are word labels for that which is not solid—something that cannot be seen, touched, and so on. *Tree* is a concrete noun. *Thought, confrontation,* and *willingness* are abstract nouns.

   As sentence subjects, concrete nouns are normally preferred because they help to present ideas vividly. "Joe explained the procedure" is more vivid than "Explanations were given by Joe." As "explanations" are harder to visualize than "Joe," the idea in the second sentence is more difficult to see. However, if a writer does not want an idea to stand out vividly, an abstract noun can be used as the subject of a sentence: "His weakness was well known" is less vivid than "He was known to be weak."

3. **Proper Versus Common.** A proper noun begins with a capital letter; other nouns do not. Capitalize special names of geographic locations: the *Near East*, the *South*, the *Great Plains*.

Do not capitalize words that simply indicate direction: *southern* Arizona, *west* of Kansas City, an *easterly* direction.

Exercise 4

For each pair of sentences, (1) select the better sentence and (2) give your reason for thinking it is better than the other sentence.

1. a. Mr. Edwards called me yesterday.
   b. Mr. Edwards contacted me yesterday.
2. a. George was driving 40 mph in a 25-mph zone.
   b. George was exceeding the speed limit.
3. a. We appreciate the explanation of your financial circumstances.
   b. We appreciate the information you gave about your losses from bad debts and your shrinking markets.
4. a. An explanation of the procedures was presented by Mary Lewis.
   b. Mary Lewis explained the procedures.
5. a. This column of figures was not added correctly.
   b. You made a mistake in adding this column of figures.
6. a. The plant will be constructed about 30 miles South of St. Louis.
   b. The plant will be constructed about 30 miles south of St. Louis.

• Pronouns

Pronouns (words used in place of nouns) enable us to make our writing smoother than it would be if no pronouns were used. For example, compare these versions of the same sentence:

Without pronouns: Mr. Smith had some difficulty with Mr. Smith's car, so Mr. Smith took Mr. Smith's car to the corner garage for repairs.

With pronouns: Mr. Smith had some difficulty with his car, so he took it to the corner garage for repairs.

Grammatically, selecting pronouns of the appropriate gender is simple. Socially, the problem is more complicated (see Chapter 4). Pronouns do present three grammatical problems: (1) how to get agreement in *number,* (2) how to use the appropriate *case,* and (3) how to use *relative* and *interrogative* pronouns.

1. **Agreement in Number.** (*Number* indicates whether a pronoun involves one or more than one. An *antecedent* is the specific noun for which a pronoun stands.)

   a. When a pronoun represents two or more singular antecedents connected by *and,* the pronoun must be plural:

The secretary <u>and</u> the treasurer will take <u>their</u> vacations.	The article "the" before the word "treasurer" indicates that the sentence is about two people.
The secretary <u>and</u> treasurer will take <u>his</u> vacation.	Lack of the article *the* before the word "treasurer" indicates that the sentence is about one person who has two sets of responsibilities.

   b. Parenthetical remarks (remarks that can be omitted without destroying the basic meaning of the sentence) that appear between the pronoun and its antecedent have no effect upon the form of the pronoun:

The manager, <u>not the secretaries</u>, is responsible for <u>his</u> correspondence.	Because "his" refers to manager and not to "secretaries," "his" is used instead of *their.*

   c. *Each, everyone, no,* and their variations are singular and take singular pronouns:

   <u>Each</u> student and <u>each</u> teacher will carry <u>his or her</u> own equipment.
   <u>Everyone is</u> responsible for <u>her or his</u> work.

   d. When two or more singular antecedents are connected by *or* or *nor,* the pronoun must be singular:

   <u>Neither</u> David <u>nor</u> Bill can complete <u>his</u> work.

   Ask <u>either</u> Mary or Sue about <u>her</u> in-service training.

   e. When a noun represents a *unit* made up of more than *one* person or thing, use a singular pronoun:

   The <u>company</u> stands behind <u>its</u> merchandise.

   The <u>group</u> wants to retain <u>its</u> goals.

   f. Collective nouns take pronouns that agree in number with the intended meaning of the collective noun:

The accounting <u>staff</u> has been asked for <u>its</u> contributions.	Here the staff is thought of as a *unit;* thus, the singular *its* is appropriate.

The accounting <u>staff</u> have been asked for <u>their</u> contributions.	Here the *staff* is thought of as more than one individual; the plural pronoun *their* is appropriate.

2. **Pronouns and Case.** *Case* tells whether a pronoun is used as the subject of a sentence or as an object in it.

   a. Use nominative-case pronouns (*I, he, she, they, we, you, it*) as subjects of a sentence or clause:

   The manager and <u>he</u> are working on the report.

   <u>You</u> and <u>I</u> must work together.

   b. Use objective-case pronouns (*me, him, her, them, us, you, it*) after transitive verbs (active verbs requiring an object):

   Mrs. Kellegher telephoned <u>him</u>.

   Mrs. Kellegher telephoned Mr. Horn and <u>me</u>.

   I wish she had assigned the problem to <u>you</u> and <u>me</u>.

   c. Use objective-case pronouns after prepositions:

The information is valuable only to <u>you</u> and <u>me</u>.	*You* is still *you* regardless of whether it is used in the nominative or objective case.
This is a secret between <u>you</u> and <u>me</u>.	
The increase in salary is for the manager and <u>her</u>.	

   d. When forms of the linking verb *be* require a pronoun to complete the meaning, the pronoun should be in the nominative case.

   It was <u>he</u> who received credit for the sale.

   It is <u>she</u> who deserves the award.

   Because "he" and "she" in these sentences are equal in meaning with the subject "It," these pronouns are correctly expressed in nominative case. Yet, the correct constructions "It was he," "It is she," etc., may to some people sound just as distracting as the incorrect constructions "It was him," and "It is her." To avoid error or distraction, express the ideas in a different way:

   He was the one who received credit for the sale.

   She deserves the award.

   e. Use the possessive form of a pronoun before a gerund (a verb used as a noun):

Incorrect: We were delighted at <u>him</u> taking the job.

Correct: We were delighted at <u>his</u> taking the job.

"Taking the job" is used here as a noun. "His" in this sentence serves the same purpose it would serve in "We are delighted at *his* success."

Incorrect: I shall appreciate <u>you</u> helping me.

Correct: I shall appreciate <u>your</u> helping me.

Problems with possessive pronouns involve apostrophes, so possessive pronouns are discussed in the punctuation section.

3. **Interrogative and Relative Pronouns.** An *interrogative* pronoun is used to form a question.

<u>Who</u> is there?

<u>Which</u> is correct?

A *relative* pronoun joins a subordinate clause to its antecedent.

The woman <u>whom</u> we choose must have experience.

"Whom we choose" is the subordinate clause; it is less significant than "The woman must have experience." "Whom" is the relative pronoun that joins "woman" and "we choose"; it is "whom" because it is the object of the choosing.

a. Place relative pronouns as near their antecedents as possible.

Incorrect: The <u>members</u> were given receipts <u>who</u> have paid.

Correct: The <u>members who</u> have paid were given receipts.

Incorrect: The agreement will enable you to pay <u>whichever</u> is lower, 6 percent or $50.

Correct: The agreement will enable you to pay <u>6 percent or $50, whichever</u> is lower.

b. Use *who* as the subject of the sentence; use *whom* as an object:

<u>Who</u> does the work?

Those <u>who</u> work will be paid.

Although "who" is not itself the subject, "who" refers to the subject.

We are working for <u>whom</u>?

To <u>whom</u> shall we send the report?

"We" is the subject; "whom" is the object of "for" in the preceding question and of "to" in this question.

c. To determine which pronoun to use, restate the subordinate clause introduced by *who* or *whom*:

She is the type of secretary <u>whom</u> we can promote.

Restating "whom we can promote" gives the proper form of the pronoun: "We can promote *her* (*whom*)."

She is the type of secretary <u>who</u> can be promoted.

Restating "who can be promoted" gives the proper form of the pronoun: "*She* (*who*) can be promoted."

Note in the first example the pronoun is the object; in the second example, the pronoun is the subject.

d. To determine the correct form of an interrogative pronoun such as *who, whom, which,* or *what,* change the question to a statement:

<u>Whom</u> did you call?

You did call *whom.*

<u>Whom</u> did you select for the position?

You did select *whom* for the position.

e. Use *who* or *whom* to refer to persons; *which* to refer to things or animals; and *that* to refer to things, animals, or persons.

f. Instead of risking a vague pronoun reference, restate a noun:

Vague: The patrolman captured the suspect even though <u>he</u> was unarmed.

Clear: The patrolman captured the suspect even though <u>the patrolman</u> was unarmed.

Or: Even though the patrolman was unarmed, <u>he</u> captured the suspect.

g. Do not use a pronoun to refer to a phrase, clause, sentence, or paragraph. (*A pronoun should stand for a noun, and that noun should appear in the writing.*)

Incorrect: He expects to take all available accounting courses and obtain a position in a public accounting firm. <u>This</u> appeals to him.

Correct: He expects to take all available accounting courses and obtain a position in a public accounting firm. This plan appeals to him.

Exercise 5

Select the correct word.

1. The copy editor, not the keyboarders, (were, was) at fault.
2. In the boys' class, everyone was asked to share (his, their) opinion.
3. Of all the ladies who took the test, only one had brought (her, their) calculator.
4. Carol and Helen were recognized for (her, their) contribution.
5. Neither Carol nor Helen was recognized for (her, their) contribution.
6. Our company is revising (their, its) statement of purpose.
7. Elaine asked me to take a picture of her husband and (her, she).
8. The instructor asked Dan and (I, me) to leave the room.
9. Lucille requested that proceeds be divided equally between Calvin and (her, she).
10. These supplies were intended for James and (me, I).
11. I shall appreciate (you, your) returning the form by June 1.
12. The speaker did not notice (me, my) leaving early.
13. We were surprised about (him, his) leaving so soon.
14. To (who, whom) should we appeal?
15. (Who, Whom) is calling?
16. She is an employee in (who, whom) we have great confidence.
17. He is the one (who, whom) arrived twenty minutes late.
18. (Who, Whom) will take her vacation first?
19. (Whom, Who) shall we invite?
20. (Whom, Who) was invited last year?
21. He is the one (that, who) applied last year.
22. We are betting on the horse (that, who) won last week's race.
23. Mr. Smith forgot to retain his expense vouchers; (this, this oversight) caused a delay in reimbursement.
24. The inspector was two hours late; (this, this tardiness) was inexcusable.
25. Interest rates have been steadily declining. (This, This decline) resulted in our reconsideration of the venture.

• Verbs

Verbs present problems in mood, number, person, tense, and voice.

1. **Mood.** *Mood* reveals the writer's attitude toward the idea expressed, indicating whether the idea is to be thought of as a fact; a command; or a supposition, desire, or possibility.

    The *indicative* mood makes a statement of fact or asks a question:

    The merchandise <u>arrived</u> today.

    When <u>is</u> the delivery date?

    The *imperative* mood states a request or a command:

    <u>Send</u> us your check today.

    <u>Wait</u> until the end of the month.

    The *subjunctive* mood talks of conditions that do not necessarily exist. It suggests doubt, supposition, probability, wishfulness, or sorrow.

    a. In the subjunctive mood, use *were* for the present tense of *to be*:

        Incorrect: I wish the story <u>was</u> true.
        Correct: I wish the story <u>were</u> true.

        Incorrect: If I <u>was</u> he, I would try <u>again</u>.
        Correct: If I <u>were</u> he, I would try <u>again</u>.

    b. Consider the subjunctive mood for communicating negative ideas in positive language:

I wish I <u>were</u>.	In response to someone who asks if you are going to the company picnic, the sentence sounds better than "No, I am not."
We <u>would</u> make a refund if the merchandise had been used in accordance with instructions.	The sentence conveys "Since the merchandise has *not* been used in accordance with instructions, we are *not* making a refund" but avoids negative words.

2. **Number.** *Number* is used to describe how many people, things, items, and so on are being discussed.

    a. Do not switch unnecessarily from singular to plural:

        Incorrect: <u>We</u> shall appreciate your returning the contract to me. <u>I</u> am glad you are joining Burdon's.

Correct:	I shall appreciate your returning the contract to me. I am glad you are joining Burdon's.	Both "I" and "we" are frequently overused, but changing from one to the other just for variety may cause confusion about whether one is speaking for oneself only or for oneself and others.

b. If the subject is singular, use a verb form that fits the singular; if the subject is plural, use a verb that fits the plural:

Incorrect:	Good material and fast delivery is essential.
Correct:	Good material and fast delivery are essential.

Incorrect:	The gentleman and his son is in charge of the business.
Correct:	He and his son are in charge of the business.

c. Remember that parenthetical words coming between the subject and the verb have no effect on the verb used:

Incorrect:	You, not the carrier, is responsible for the damage.
Correct:	You, not the carrier, are responsible for the damage.

Incorrect:	The manager, as well as her three secretaries, were inclined to agree with the statement.
Correct:	The manager, as well as her three secretaries, was inclined to agree with the statement.

d. When *or* or *nor* comes between two subjects, determine the verb form by inspecting the number of the noun closer to the verb:

Incorrect:	Only one or two questions is necessary.
Correct:	Only one or two questions are necessary.

Incorrect:	Several paint brushes or one paint roller are necessary.
Correct:	Several paint brushes or one paint roller is necessary.

e. Determine the verb by the subject, not by modifiers that come between the verb and subject:

Incorrect:	The attitude of these people are receptive.	
Correct:	The attitude of these people is receptive.	"Attitude" is the subject; "of these people" is simply a phrase coming between the subject and the verb.

Incorrect:	One of the clerks were dismissed.	
Correct:	One of the clerks was dismissed.	"One" is the subject; "of the clerks" is simply a phrase coming between the subject and the verb.

f. Use singular verbs with plural nouns that have a singular meaning:

The news is good.

Economics is a required course.

Mathematics is to be reviewed.

g. Use a singular verb with plural subjects that are thought of as singular units:

Twenty dollars is too much.

Ten minutes is sufficient time.

h. Even if titles of articles, firm names, and slogans are plural, use a singular verb:

"Understanding Computers"
is an interesting article.

Stein, Jones, and Baker is the
oldest firm in the city.

"Free lunches for all" is our   In each sentence, the subject is
campaign slogan.   singular: one article, one firm, and
                                       one slogan.

3. **Person.** *Person* is used to describe the quality of the verb that indicates whether the subject is (1) speaking, (2) being spoken to, or (3) being spoken about:

First person:	I am, we are.	Writer or speaker
Second person:	You are.	Receiver of message
Third person:	He is, she is, they are.	Person being discussed

a. Choose verbs that agree in *person* with their subjects:

Incorrect:	She don't attend class regularly.
Correct:	She doesn't attend class regularly.
Correct:	They don't attend class regularly.

b. For vivid, emphatic writing, choose second person instead of third person:

Less vivid:	Next, the operator takes the film in his right hand, swings the gate open with his left, and....
More vivid:	Next, you take the film in your right hand, swing the gate open with your left, and....

   c. Try to avoid second person in formal reports.

> Poor: <u>You</u> would have difficulty interpreting such data.
> Improved: Such data would be difficult to interpret.

To the reader, "you" could have three different meanings: the one who asked for the report, all readers of the report, or the writer of the report.

   d. Try to avoid third person in referring to yourself. In business letters, *I* is preferable to *the writer* or *the undersigned*. However, *I* should be used sparingly because its overuse usually places too much emphasis on the one who writes. In business reports, *I* is almost always avoided; it has the effect of emphasizing the writer and thus taking emphasis away from the subject matter.

4. **Tense.** *Tense* indicates time. Tenses are both simple and compound.

   a. Simple tenses:

Present:	I <u>see</u> you.	Tells what is now happening.
Past:	I <u>saw</u> you.	Tells what has already happened.
Future:	I <u>shall see</u> you.	Tells what is yet to happen.

   b. Compound tenses:

Present perfect:	I <u>have seen</u> you.	Tells of past action that extends to the present.
Past perfect:	I <u>had seen</u> you.	Tells of past action that was finished before another past action.
Future perfect:	I <u>shall have seen</u> you.	Tells of action that will be finished before a future time.

   c. When something *was* and *still is* true, write about it in present tense:

> Incorrect: The speaker reminded us that Rhode Island <u>was</u> smaller than Wisconsin.
> Correct: The speaker reminded us that Rhode Island <u>is</u> smaller than Wisconsin.

   d. Avoid unnecessary shifts in tense:

> Incorrect: The deliveryman <u>brings</u> my package but <u>left</u> without asking me to sign for it.
> Correct: The deliveryman <u>brought</u> my package but <u>left</u> without asking me to sign for it.

Verbs that appear in the same sentence are not required to be in the same tense. For example, "The contract that *was prepared* yesterday *will be signed* tomorrow."

5. **Voice.** *Voice* is the term used to indicate whether a subject *acts* or whether it *is acted upon*. If the subject of a sentence acts, the verb used to describe that action is called an *active verb:*

The typist made an error.
The woman asked for an adjustment.

If the subject of the sentence is acted upon, the verb used to describe that action is called a *passive verb.*

An error was made by the typist.
An adjustment was asked for by the woman.

For most business writing, active voice is preferred. But sometimes passive voice is more appropriate. Use passive voice in the following situations:

a. To emphasize the receiver of action more than the doer:

Say: Dinner is now being served.
Not: The waiters are now serving dinner.

b. To avoid an accusing tone:

Say: Three errors have been made on this page.
Not: You made three errors on this page.

c. To avoid revealing names:

The procedure has been criticized severely.   The sentence is appropriate if the writer does not want to reveal who has been criticizing.

Exercise 6

Change each sentence from passive to active voice.

1. The booklet was edited by Susan Woodward.
2. The figures have been checked by our accountant.
3. Miss Jackson was recommended for promotion by the supervisor.
4. The applications are being screened. (In revising, assume that a committee is doing the screening.)
5. Your request for a leave has been approved. (In revising, assume the manager did the approving.)

Exercise 7

In revising each sentence, (a) use passive voice and (b) conceal the doer.

1. Wesley made three computational mistakes on this page.
2. Meredith reported Tom's absence to the personnel office.
3. The committee has denied Willard's application for promotion.
4. You should have proofread the report more carefully.
5. Students have handed in their reports.

Exercise 8

Select the correct word.

1. Mrs. Walls and her son (was, were) invited.
2. If he (was, were) over 18, he would have been hired.
3. Only one of the graphs (was, were) usable.
4. The typesetters, not the editor, (was, were) responsible for these errors.
5. The typesetter, not the editors, (was, were) responsible for these errors.
6. Neither the players nor their coach (was, were) invited.
7. Neither the coach nor the players (was, were) invited.
8. Both John and Steven (was, were) promoted.
9. Only one of the statements (was, were) audible.
10. The news from the rescue mission (is, are) encouraging.
11. *Ten Steps to Greatness* (has, have) been placed in the company library.
12. Two of the booklets (has, have) been edited.
13. Kelley & Smith (was, were) the only firm to submit a bid.
14. Apparently, "Do unto Others" (is, are) John's motto.
15. About one child in ten (inherit, inherits) left-handedness.
16. A child reminded me that the earth (rotates, rotated) on its axis.
17. Only one of the issues (has, have) been discussed.
18. Tim (don't, doesn't) ask for favors.
19. The president studied the page for a minute and (starts, started) asking questions.
20. Sally wrote rapidly and then (revises, revised).

• Adjectives and Adverbs

Adjectives modify nouns or pronouns. *Adverbs* modify verbs, adjectives, or other adverbs. Although most adverbs end in *ly,* some commonly used adverbs do not end in *ly: there, then, after, now, hence,* and *very.* Most words that end in *ly* are adverbs; but common exceptions are *neighborly, timely, friendly, gentlemanly.* Some words are both adjective and adverb: *fast, late,* and *well.*

1. **Adjectives**

   a. Use an adjective to modify a noun or pronoun:

   She wrote a <u>long</u> letter.
   I prefer the <u>little</u> one.

   b. Use an adjective after a linking verb when the modifier refers to the subject instead of to the verb. (A linking verb connects a subject to the rest of the sentence. "He *is* old." "She *seems* sincere.")

The salesperson seemed <u>enthusiastic</u>.	The adjective "enthusiastic" refers to "salesperson," not to "seemed."
The president looked <u>suspicious</u>.	The adjective "suspicious" refers to "president," not to "looked."

   c. Use comparatives and superlatives carefully:

Incorrect:	She is the <u>fastest</u> of the two workers.
Correct:	She is the <u>faster</u> of the two workers.
Correct:	She is the <u>fastest</u> of the three workers.

Incorrect:	He is the <u>best</u> of the two operators.
Correct:	He is the <u>better</u> of the two operators.
Correct:	He is the <u>best</u> of the three operators.

   d. Exclude a person or thing from a group with which that person or thing is being compared.

Incorrect:	He is older than <u>anyone</u> in his department.	As a member of his department, he cannot be older than himself.
Correct:	He is older than <u>anyone else</u> in his department.	
Correct:	He is older than <u>any other person</u> in his department.	

"The XD600 is newer than any machine in our department" is illogical if the XD600 is in "our" department. It can't be newer than itself. It can be newer than any *other* machine in our department or newer than any machine in some *other* department.

2. **Adverbs**

   a. Use an adverb to modify a verb:

The salesperson looked <u>enthusiastically</u> at the prospect.	The adverb "enthusiastically" refers to "looked," not to "salesperson."
The president looked <u>suspiciously</u> at the cash register.	The adverb "suspiciously" refers to "looked," not to the "president."

   b. Use an adverb to modify an adjective:

The committee was <u>really</u> active.	The adverb "really" describes the adjective "active." Because it is an adjective, "real" could not be used to modify "active" or any other adjective.

   c. Use an adverb to modify another adverb:

Worker A progressed <u>relatively faster</u> than did worker B.	The adverb "relatively" modifies the adverb "faster."

Exercise 9

Select the correct word.

1. Our supply is being replenished (frequent, frequently).
2. Chester works (enthusiastic, enthusiastically) and never asks for time off.
3. Chester looked (angry, angrily).
4. Chester looked (eager, eagerly) for help.
5. Help arrived (real, very) quickly.
6. The lecture seemed (really, real) long.
7. Of the two people who were interviewed, Jane made the (better, best) impression.
8. Hazel is the (youngest, younger) of the three daughters.
9. The waitress moved (quick, quickly) from table to table.
10. Of the two keyboarders, John was the (fastest, faster).
11. John is faster than (any, any other) keyboarder in his department.
12. Although John is in the accounting department, he is faster than (any, any other) keyboarder in the presentation department.

• Sentence Structure

1. Be sure to state the subject of each sentence (unless the sentence is a command):

   Incorrect: <u>Received</u> the foreman's request today.
   Correct: <u>I received</u> the foreman's request today.

   In such imperative sentences as "Return the forms to me," the subject (*you*) is understood and therefore appropriately omitted.

2. Rely mainly on sentences that follow the normal subject-verb-complement sequence:

   <u>We</u> <u>withdrew</u> <u>for three reasons.</u>
   (subject) (verb) (complement)

   People are accustomed to sentences that employ this sequence. Sentences that expose the verb *before* revealing the subject have three disadvantages: they slow down the reading, they present less vivid pictures, and they employ more words than would be required if the normal sequence were followed:

   Original: There are <u>two reasons</u> for our withdrawal.
   Better: <u>Two reasons</u> for our withdrawal are....
              <u>We</u> withdrew for two reasons.

   Original: <u>It</u> is important that we withdraw.
   Better: <u>Our withdrawal</u> is important.
              <u>We</u> must withdraw.

   There and *it* are called *expletives*—filler words that have no real meaning in the sentence.

3. Do not put unrelated ideas in the same sentence:

The <u>coffee break</u> is at ten o'clock, and the company plans to purchase additional <u>parking space</u> for its employees.	These ideas appear to have little relationship. Therefore, they should certainly not be introduced in the same sentence; they should be discussed in different paragraphs or even in different messages.

4. Put pronouns, adverbs, phrases, and clauses near the words they modify:

   Incorrect: I saw his <u>performance</u> at the Christmas party, <u>which</u> I certainly enjoyed watching.
   Correct: I saw his <u>performance, which</u> I certainly enjoyed watching, at the Christmas party.
   Correct: I certainly enjoyed watching his performance at the Christmas party.

Incorrect:	He <u>only</u> works in the toy department for $3.25 an hour.
Correct:	He works in the toy department for <u>only $3.25</u> an hour.
Incorrect:	The <u>secretary</u> stood beside the mimeograph machine <u>in a white dress</u>.
Correct:	The <u>secretary in a white dress</u> stood beside the mimeograph machine.
Incorrect:	He put a new type of <u>oil</u> on his hair, <u>which</u> he had just purchased at the drugstore.
Correct:	He put a new type of <u>oil, which</u> he had just purchased at the drugstore, on his hair.

5. Do not separate subject and predicate unnecessarily:

Incorrect:	<u>He</u>, hoping to receive a bonus, <u>worked</u> rapidly.
Correct:	Hoping to receive a bonus, <u>he worked</u> rapidly.

6. Attach an introductory phrase to the subject of an independent clause. Otherwise, the phrase dangles. Remedy the dangling phrase in one of two ways: change the subject of the independent clause, or make the phrase into a subordinate clause by assigning it a subject:

Incorrect:	<u>When</u> a little boy, <u>my mother</u> took me through a milk-processing plant.	Implies that the mother was once a little boy.
Correct:	<u>When</u> a little boy, <u>I</u> was taken through a milk-processing plant by my mother.	
Correct:	<u>When I was a little boy,</u> my mother took me through a milk-processing plant.	
Incorrect:	<u>Working</u> at full speed every morning, <u>fatigue</u> overtakes me in the afternoon.	Implies that "fatigue" was working at full speed.
Correct:	<u>Working</u> at full speed every morning, <u>I</u> become tired in the afternoon.	
Correct:	<u>Because I work</u> at full speed every morning, <u>fatigue</u> overtakes me in the afternoon.	
Incorrect:	<u>After working</u> four days on the financial statements, <u>they</u> were finally completed.	Implies that "financial statements" were "working four days."

Correct: <u>After working</u> four days
on the financial state-
ments, the <u>accountants</u>
finally completed the task.

Correct: <u>After the accountants</u> had
worked four days, the
<u>financial statements were</u>
finally <u>completed.</u>

Incorrect: <u>To function</u> properly, <u>you</u>   Implies that if "you" are "to
must oil the machine   function properly," the ma-
every hour.   chine must be oiled hourly.

Correct: <u>To function</u> properly, the
<u>machine</u> must be oiled
every hour.

Correct: <u>If the machine</u> is to function properly, <u>you</u> must
oil it every hour.

7. Express related ideas in similar grammatical form (use parallel construction):

Incorrect: The machine operator made three resolutions: (1) <u>to
be punctual</u>, (2) <u>following</u> instructions carefully, and
<u>third, the reduction</u> of waste.

Correct: The machine operator made three resolutions: (1) <u>to
be punctual</u>, (2) <u>to follow</u> instructions carefully, and
(3) <u>to reduce</u> waste.

Incorrect: The personnel manager is concerned with <u>the selec-
tion</u> of the right worker, <u>providing</u> appropriate indoc-
trination, and <u>the worker's</u> progress.

Correct: The personnel manager is concerned with <u>selecting</u>
the right worker, <u>providing</u> appropriate indoctrina-
tion, and <u>checking</u> the worker's progress.

8. Do not end a sentence with a needless preposition:

Incorrect: Where is the plant to be located <u>at</u>?
Correct: Where is the plant to be located?

Incorrect: The worker did not tell us where he was going <u>to</u>.
Correct: The worker did not tell us where he was going.

9. End a sentence with a preposition if for some reason the preposition
needs emphasis:

I am not concerned with what he is paying <u>for</u>. I am concerned
with what he is paying <u>with</u>.
The prospect has everything—a goal to work <u>toward</u>, a house to
live <u>in</u>, and an income to live <u>on</u>.

10. Avoid clumsy split infinitives. (Two words are required to express an infinitive: *to* plus a *verb*. The two words belong together. An infinitive is split when another word is placed between the two.)

Incorrect: The superintendent used <u>to</u> occasionally <u>visit</u> the offices.
Correct: The superintendent used <u>to visit</u> the offices occasionally.

Incorrect: I want <u>to</u> briefly <u>summarize</u> the report.
Correct: I want <u>to summarize</u> the report briefly.

Exercise 10

For each sentence, write an answer to the question "What weakness in structure does the sentence illustrate?" Then write an improved version of the sentence.

1. Have reconsidered your proposal.
2. It is essential that you sign and return the enclosed form.
3. There is no need to refurnish this room.
4. When a small girl, my brother taught me to play basketball.
5. Mary only works on Sunday; Ruth works Monday through Friday.
6. I am submitting an article to *Time,* which I wrote last summer.
7. Almost all of my time is spent in planning, organizing, and the various aspects of control.
8. While driving 30 miles an hour, my dog jumped out the window.
9. Where is the personnel department at?
10. We want to quickly bring the project to a conclusion.

Dictating

Effective letters, memos, and reports meet high standards of content, organization, style, and mechanics. Knowledge of ways to achieve these qualities greatly assists in successful dictation.

Most dictation now involves speaking the message into a machine. The recorded message may be transcribed (converted to a typewritten page) by someone in the executive's office or by a keyboarder who works in another room and does little but transcribe. The practice of dictating directly to a secretary who writes the words in shorthand is fast disappearing.

Regardless of whether a message is to be the *initial* link in a chain of correspondence or a *response* to another's message, success in dictating is greatly influenced by prior planning. Suggestions for getting ready to dictate:

1. Underline or highlight significant points in incoming mail and make notations in margins.
2. Arrange mail in order, with those in most urgent need of reply on top.
3. Gather the information needed and decide what the content (major idea and supporting details) is to be.
4. Make an outline.

Having taken these preliminary steps thoughtfully, a dictator generates a positive feeling about the upcoming dictation: the ideas are valid, and they are arranged in a sensible order.

Feeling successful in having taken the *preliminary* steps, the dictator has increased chances for success in the *next* step—dictating. Suggestions for dictating:

1. Begin by telling who you are. (Of course, this identification can be omitted if you are the *only* one who dictates into a machine, or if standard procedure is that a certain employee transcribes *your* messages but no one else's.) Indicate whether you are about to dictate a letter, a memo, or a report. If the office has not adopted a standard letter format (as it probably should have), indicate the format you want. (See the letter formats in the "Keyboarding" section of this appendix.)
2. Dictate the inside address (unless the person doing the keyboarding will have a copy of the letter being answered).
3. Speak clearly and much slower than in normal conversation. In addition to the pause at the end of each sentence, insert some pauses within long sentences.
4. Be sensitive to words or letters that may not be clearly understood when a transcriber hears them. When the following letters are used as initials, speak slowly and overemphasize the pronunciation: B, F, H, M, N, P, T, V, and Z. Ordinal numbers with the "th" ending are sometimes difficult to hear: fifth, sixth, seventh, fifteenth, and seventeenth.
5. Use the phonetic alphabet employed by telephone operators to clarify the letters used in difficult-to-understand names or words:

A	Alice	N	Nellie
B	Bertha	O	Oliver
C	Charles	P	Peter
D	David	Q	Quaker
E	Edward	R	Robert
F	Frank	S	Samuel
G	George	T	Thomas
H	Henry	U	Utah
I	Ida	V	Victor
J	James	W	William
K	Kate	X	X-ray
L	Lewis	Y	Young
M	Mary	Z	Zebra

For example, *Orvil* is spelled "O as in Oliver, R as in Robert, V as in Victor, I as in Ida, and L as in Lewis."

6. Insert necessary instructions to the operator, but let them *sound* a little different from the message. For example, if the word "Supervisor" is to begin with a capital letter, change voice tone or pitch and say "*Capital* Supervisor." Or change voice and say "Quote" to introduce a quotation and (changing to the same voice in which "Quote" was said) say "Unquote" at the end of it.

7. Insert punctuation marks (unless you are willing to accept the keyboarder's judgment instead of your own). Like other instructions, punctuation marks are best given in a voice tone that is different from that used in speaking the words of the message. Voice inflection is almost always sufficient to indicate the ends of sentences; thus, dictating "period" is unnecessary. "Paragraph," though, *is* necessary.

8. Let instructions *precede* dictation of items that are to be arranged in some special way. For example, instructions to indent a quoted paragraph five spaces from left and right margins should be given *before* dictating the paragraph. Otherwise, it would have to be keyboarded again. Obviously, instructions to type the *next* heading in all caps and centered on the page are preferable to *rearranging* a heading already dictated.

9. Make your own corrections where possible. Unhappy with a sentence or paragraph, a dictator can back the machine up to the point at which revision is needed and begin to dictate the revision.

10. Prepare a rough draft of tabulated material and transmit it to the keyboarder along with the tape.

11. Dictate closing instructions (unless the closing is standard). When you know who the keyboarder will be, and when that person has prepared many letters for you previously, dictating the complimentary close, name, and job title is hardly necessary. If an enclosure is to be included, or if certain people are to receive copies, so indicate.

12. Become thoroughly familiar with the equipment being used. Study the operations manual and make maximum use of the machine's features.

If transcription is done in a separate word-processing room, dictators can profitably visit the room to become acquainted with the equipment and those who use it. Transcribed pages will be returned to you for approval and signature.

Proofreading

Writers who compose at the console (instead of dictate) have a definite advantage: they can make needed corrections on the screen. Likewise, keyboarders should proofread carefully. An error corrected on the screen is much less costly than an error detected (on paper) by the dictator and returned to the keyboarder for correction. Regardless of who caused an error, catching it is the responsibility of the person who dictates and signs the message.

Preferably, a written message should be proofread twice—once to make sure the ideas are what the dictator intended and once to make sure those ideas are expressed on paper in an acceptable manner. Sometimes for long messages, two people do the proofreading. One reads aloud and the other follows the copy. Usually, though, proofreading is done by one person. Those who have done much proofreading soon learn to check for errors in the following categories:

Spelling in proper names
Correctness of addresses
Correctness of abbreviations
Hyphenation
Completeness of sentences
Omitted, transposed, or added letters
Punctuation
Capitalization

Enclosure notations

Homonyms

To speed the process of proofreading and call attention to needed changes, publishers long ago developed a set of symbols, as shown in Figure A.1. Most keyboarders and proofreaders have at some time been exposed to them; they can be quickly relearned and effectively used in

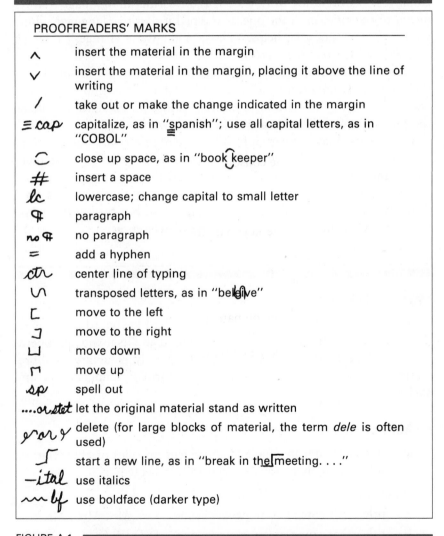

PROOFREADERS' MARKS

∧	insert the material in the margin
∨	insert the material in the margin, placing it above the line of writing
/	take out or make the change indicated in the margin
≡ *cap*	capitalize, as in "spanish"; use all capital letters, as in "COBOL"
C	close up space, as in "book keeper"
#	insert a space
lc	lowercase; change capital to small letter
¶	paragraph
no ¶	no paragraph
=	add a hyphen
ctr	center line of typing
∩	transposed letters, as in "bellive"
[	move to the left
]	move to the right
⊔	move down
⊓	move up
sp	spell out
....*or stet*	let the original material stand as written
or	delete (for large blocks of material, the term *dele* is often used)
⌐	start a new line, as in "break in the meeting. . . ."
—*ital*	use italics
∼∼ *bf*	use boldface (darker type)

FIGURE A.1

Common proofreaders' marks.

business. Note the use of proofreader's symbols in the original copy and its subsequent revision, as shown in Figure A.2.

Proofreading introduces a potential human-relations problem. Having been asked to retype a page to correct errors in the first draft, keyboarders may get the feeling that they are being "picked on" or that the proofreader's primary purpose was to "catch" them in an error. Such reactions may be avoided by orientation training for the job. From the beginning, all workers should be convinced that the firm and all its employees benefit when work is done right. Criticism of a page is never meant to be criticism of the one who typed it. Positive language, along with a positive attitude, helps. "Please make these changes" is much better than "Correct these errors."

For maximum efficiency, keyboarders need to be convinced that their service is important and that *others* think it is important, too. Sometimes, heavy work loads and the pressure of deadlines can make the job stressful. When basic knowledge is weak, stress is intensified. Time pressures may not permit frequent use of references, but questionable points must be verified in such sources as dictionaries, style manuals, handbooks, and so on. For a student, the easy way is to think "Why bother now? If I ever need to know, I can always look it up." Actually, the best way is the easiest way: *learn* the basics of keyboarding and thus avoid the need for frequent use of references.

Keyboarding

Basic skill in "touch" typewriting on a standard keyboard is assumed. So is familiarity with the equipment being used and its manual of operation. Some keyboarding problems that frequently recur are in abbreviation, capital letters, division of words, formats, punctuation, and spelling.

• Abbreviation

Style manuals are not in complete agreement on rules of abbreviation, but the following conventions are generally accepted:

1. Abbreviate
    a. titles that come before proper names: *Dr., Mr., Mrs., Ms.*
    b. titles that come after proper names: *D.D.S., Esq., Jr., M.D., Ph.D., Sr.*

Original Copy:

Today, due to societal change, ~~there is~~ a wide variety of magazines ~~that~~ concentrates ~~its~~ circulation appeal on women in the 18–34 age group. These magazines talk specifically to women who work, women with children, women vitally interested in good health. Three womens magazines that fall into this category are Glamour, Mademoiselle, and Cosmopolitan. ~~It is~~ these ③ printed media selections ~~that~~ will be evaluated by this study. All evaluations are based on the assumption that the Star Cosmetic company will continue to advertise using one, page four, color ads.

Retyping with the changes results in this copy:

Today, due to societal change, a wide variety of magazines concentrates circulation appeal on women in the 18-34 age group. These magazines talk specifically to women who work, women with children, and women vitally interested in good health. Three women's magazines that fall into this category are Glamour, Mademoiselle, and Cosmopolitan. These three printed media selections will be evaluated by this study. All evaluations are based on the assumption that the Star Cosmetic Company will continue to advertise using one-page, four-color ads.

FIGURE A.2

Proofread and marked copy with revised copy.

c. commonly known government agencies: *FDIC, FCC, FHA, TVA*

d. commonly known organizations, businesses, or institutions: *AAUP, NEA, UN, GE, IBM, MIT, UCLA*

e. commonly used business expressions: *f.o.b., C.O.D., A.M., or P.M.* (Note: Use A.M. and P.M. only when a specific time is mentioned. Small letters—a.m. and p.m.—are acceptable.)

Incorrect: Come to the office this A.M.

Correct: Come to the office at 10:15 A.M.

Correct: Come to the office this morning.

f. the names of businesses when their own letterheads contain abbreviations: Smith & Company; Jones and Smith, *Inc.;* The John C. Andrews *Co.*

g. the word *number* when it is used with a figure to designate something:

Go to room No. 7.

May we have a carton of No. 10 envelopes.

Refer to Policy No. 384862.

h. the names of states when they appear as parts of envelope addresses or inside addresses. The post office prefers the following abbreviations for states:

Alabama	AL	Kentucky	KY	Oklahoma	OK
Alaska	AK	Louisiana	LA	Oregon	OR
Arizona	AZ	Maine	ME	Pennsylvania	PA
Arkansas	AR	Maryland	MD	Puerto Rico	PR
California	CA	Massachusetts	MA	Rhode Island	RI
Canal Zone	CZ	Michigan	MI	South Carolina	SC
Colorado	CO	Minnesota	MN	South Dakota	SD
Connecticut	CT	Mississippi	MS	Tennessee	TN
Delaware	DE	Missouri	MO	Texas	TX
District of		Montana	MT	Trust	
Columbia	DC	Nebraska	NE	Territories	TT
Florida	FL	Nevada	NV	Utah	UT
Georgia	GA	New		Vermont	VT
Guam	GU	Hampshire	NH	Virgin Islands	VI
Hawaii	HI	New Jersey	NJ	Virginia	VA
Idaho	ID	New Mexico	NM	Washington	WA
Illinois	IL	New York	NY	West Virginia	WV
Indiana	IN	North Carolina	NC	Wisconsin	WI
Iowa	IA	North Dakota	ND	Wyoming	WY
Kansas	KS	Ohio	OH		

2. Do Not Abbreviate
   a. the names of cities, states (except in envelope and inside addresses), months, and days of the week.
   b. the words *avenue, boulevard, drive,* and *street* (except in envelope and inside addresses where abbreviations will make line lengths more uniform):

   Send to our Main Street office
   Go south on Mill Avenue.

   MR CY WOOD
   230 LOMA VISTA BLVD
   TEMPE AZ 85282

   c. points on the compass (except on envelopes and in inside addresses).

   Tom has been in the West for seven years.
   Go east one block and turn south.

   MR HENRY LOPEZ
   1150 W ADAMS STREET
   ATLANTA GA 30305

   d. the word *Christmas.*
   e. names of school subjects.

Use	Instead of
physical education	phys. ed.
corporation finance	corp. fin.
vocational agriculture	vo. ag.
economics	econ.

   f. a person's name (unless you know that he or she abbreviates it):

Use	Instead of
Charles	Chas.
Barbara	Barb.

• Capital letters

Style manuals are in general agreement on the rules of capitalization.
1. Capitalize
   a. names of people, animals, places, geographic areas, days of the week, months of the year, holidays, deities, publications, and other special names.

b. the first word of a direct quotation:

The sales representative said, "We leave tomorrow."

c. the first word of a title (book, magazine, article, theme) and all other words of a title or heading except conjunctions (*and, for, but*), articles (*a, an, the*), and short prepositions (*in, on, of, to*):

"The Story of My Life"   Article

The Prince and the Pauper   Book

"Cost of the Land"   Heading in a report

d. the first word following a colon when a formal statement or question follows:

Here is an important rule for report writers: Plan your work and work your plan.

Each sales representative should ask himself or herself this question: Do I really look like a representative of my firm?

e. pronouns that refer to the deity:

The clergyman asked His guidance.

f. father, mother, brother, sister when used as names:

Make the suggestion to my father.
Make the suggestion to Father.

g. only the first and last words in salutations and only the first word in complimentary closes:

My dear Madam:
Sincerely yours,

h. the names of documents and historical events:

The Missouri Constitution
Battle of Bunker Hill

i. titles that come before or after a name:

Editor Smith
President King
Mr. John Smith, Editor
Dr. John King, President

Used with a person's name, such words as "editor" and "president" are capitalized when they are used as *titles;* they are not capitalized when they are used as *explanations:*

Helen Platt, <u>President</u>, Broadmor PTA	Her title in the organization.
Helen Platt, <u>president</u> of a local speakers' club, offered to serve as MC.	Explanation of her credentials.
Eugene Jenkins, <u>Editor</u>, <u>Sun City Daily</u>	His title.
Eugene Jenkins, a newspaper <u>editor</u>, will serve as judge in the essay contest	An explanation.

j. a one-word sentence.

<u>Yes</u>!
<u>Certainly</u>.

k. the word *number* when used with a figure to designate something:

Policy <u>No</u>. 8746826

2. Do Not Capitalize

a. the first word of an indirect quotation.

He said that <u>it</u> was time to part.

b. such words as father, mother, uncle, or cousin when they are preceded by a possessive pronoun:

He has taken the position formerly held by his <u>father</u>.
Please mail the check to my <u>mother</u>.

c. the names of school courses that are not proper nouns:

The student is taking French, <u>mathematics</u>, <u>science</u>, and English.

d. the names of seasons (except when they are personified):

We make most of our profits during the <u>winter</u>.

Note: When a season is used to designate a school term or semester, the season is ordinarily capitalized.

<u>Summer</u> session
<u>Spring</u> semester

e. the first word in the last part of an interrupted quotation:

"We shall proceed," he said, "<u>with</u> the utmost caution."

f.   the first word of a parenthetical sentence:

The president said (you will probably agree) that production
could be increased by 10 percent.

Exercise 11

Recopy each of the following sentences, making essential changes in
abbreviation and capitalization.

1. In the spring semester, my mother will be teaching a course in
   general science.
2. When I was interviewed on monday, the first question was "why do
   you want to work for us?"
3. Was *The Power Of Ethical Management* advertised in the Sept. 7
   issue of *Time*?
4. We paid by check no. 627 on December 10.
5. The P. T. A. meeting will be moderated by Carl Smith, jr.
6. At 8:30 P.m., Mister Raferty will address the assembly.
7. The NCAA will meet in Boston in 1990 and in N. Y. in 1991.
8. Mister and Mistress Smith plan to spend Xmas. in MO.
9. The first question was "when do we eat?"
10. A retirement ceremony is being planned for president Schwada.

• Word Division

With word-processing equipment, straight right margins are easily
achieved; but irregular right margins are still common. If one line is a
few spaces shorter or a few spaces longer than the lines above and below
it, no harm is done; but if a line is exceedingly long or short, it detracts
from the overall appearance. A divided word at the end of the line
would be less distracting.

Try to avoid dividing words at the end of a line. Too many lines that
end with divided words will be just as distracting as lines that extend too
far into the right margin. If words *must* be divided, the following rules
apply:

1. Divide words between syllables only. (Words with only one syllable
   cannot be divided: *through, hearth, worked.*)
2. Do not divide a word if it has fewer than seven letters. (Lines on a
   typewritten page can vary as much as six or seven letters in length;
   therefore, division of such short words as *letter* or *report* is pointless.)

3. Do not separate the following syllables from the remainder of a word:

   a. A syllable that does not include a vowel: would/*n't*.

   b. A first syllable that contains only one letter: *a*/greement.

   c. A last syllable that contains only one or two letters: pneumoni/*a*, apolog/*y*.

4. Divide a word after a single-letter syllable, unless the word contains successive single-letter syllables: sem*i*-nary, congrat*u*-late, exten*u*-ate, sem*i*-aquatic.

5. Try to avoid dividing hyphenated words at any place other than the hyphen: self-employed, semi-independent.

6. Avoid dividing proper names.

7. Try to avoid dividing a word at the end of a page.

• Footnotes

To achieve acceptable form and consistency in keyboarding footnotes, use the style manual recommended by your company, college, or professor. For acceptable footnote layout, see Chapter 16.

• Formats

Just as a speaker's appearance has an impact on an oral message, arrangement on the page (format) has an impact on a written message. Typically, letters and memoranda are single spaced with a space between paragraphs. Paragraph indentions are not employed. Looking at the formats illustrated in Figures A.3–A.9, note that the content gives pertinent information about the format of that page.

    If the letters were longer, page balance could be achieved by reducing the space between the date and the first line of the inside address. Or, if the letters were shorter, the number of spaces could be increased. Also, balance can be achieved by increasing the margins when the letter is short, by decreasing them when it is long. Because changing margins requires machine adjustments, and because word processors commonly have preset margins (12 on the left and 72 on the right when the type is ten characters per inch), the most common practice is to use the preset margins for both long and short letters.

    The pages shown in Figures A.3–A.9 were typed on a word processor. Some have straight right margins (called "justified" right margins). They assist in achieving a page arrangement that is attractive, but the uneven spacing between words can be distracting. Justified right

January 4, 1990

Mr. John L. Smith
1234 South Welch Avenue
Northwood, NE 65432

Mr. Smith:

This letter is arranged in the block format. It is very commonly used in business writing.

Every line begins at the left margin. The page looks a little heavy on the left side, but keyboarding is easy.

Pay special attention to the vertical spacing. The date is placed two lines below the letterhead. On this page, the first line of the inside address is on the sixth line below the date line. The number of vertical spaces following a date line can vary--more if the letter is short, fewer if the letter is long. One blank line (single vertical space) is left after the inside address, the salutation, each paragraph, the writer's title, and the reference initials. After the complimentary close, three lines are left blank to allow room for the signature.

Reference initials (initials of the keyboarder) are included only when the keyboarder and the writer are not the same person. See the enclosed booklet for further explanations.

Sincerely,

Sally Ingram
Supervisor

lcw

Enclosure

"one stop for quality printing at reasonable prices"

1801 East Baseline, Suite 103 • Tempe, Arizona 85283 • 602-897-1909

FIGURE A.3
Block format.

January 4, 1990

Mr. John L. Smith
1234 S. Welch Avenue
Northwood, NE 65432

Dear Mr. Smith:

This letter is arranged in the modified block format. Like the block format, it is very commonly used.

The date, complimentary close, dictator's name, and title of the dictator begin at the horizontal center of the page. The arrangement gives the page a more balanced appearance than does the block format.

Lowercase letters and punctuation marks in the inside address are acceptable. Omission of the punctuation and use of all-capital letters would be acceptable also, especially if the letter were to be mailed in a window envelope.

The inside address, salutation, paragraphs, reference initials, and enclosure line are in the same position as in the block format (begin at the left margin). Vertical spacing is the same. Because the right margin has not been "justified," the space between words is consistent. Whether to justify right margins is a matter of personal preference.

In both block and modified block formats, punctuation after the salutation and complimentary close is optional. Either "open" punctuation (no punctuation) or "mixed" punctuation (colon after salutation and comma after complimentary close) is acceptable.

Sincerely,

Edward Higgins
Manager

lcw

"one stop for quality printing at reasonable prices"

1801 East Baseline, Suite 103 • Tempe, Arizona 85283 • 602-897-1909

FIGURE A.4
Modified block format.

January 4, 1990

Mr. John L. Smith
1234 South Welch Avenue
Northwood, NE 65432

FORMAT OF THE AMS SIMPLIFIED LETTER

This letter is arranged in the simplified format endorsed by the Administrative Management Society. Compared with other formats, it is less commonly used; but it has begun to gain acceptance.

As in the block format, every line begins at the left margin.

A salutation is not included. Instead, a subject line appears. It is keyboarded in all capitals on the third line below the inside address. The first line of the letter is keyboarded on the third line below the subject line.

A complimentary close is not included. On the fourth or fifth line below the final sentence, the writer's name and title are keyboarded in all-capital letters.

Sometimes, the person who is to sign a letter delegates its composition to someone else. Regardless of whether the format is block or simplified, the composer's initials are included (in capital letters) on the line with the keyboarder's initials.

ALICE HAMMOND, SUPERVISOR

BFR/lcw

P.S. Like block and modified-block letters, AMS simplified letters may include postscripts. Use of "P.S." to precede the postscript is optional.

"one stop for quality printing at reasonable prices"

1801 East Baseline, Suite 103   •   Tempe, Arizona 85283   •   602-897-1909

FIGURE A.5

Administrative Management Society simplified format.

221 West 14th Street
Westfield, AZ 87654
January 4, 1990

Ms. Maxine Ragsdale, Compositor
One Stop Print Shop
1801 E. Baseline Road, Suite 103
Tempe, AZ 85283

Dear Ms. Ragsdale

This arrangement of a personal business letter begins with the address of the writer. It begins at the horizontal center of the page, as do the date, complimentary close, and keyboarded name.

The letter also illustrates enumeration and tabulation, which can be used in any letter format. A number appears before each point, the lines are shorter than the lines of paragraphs, and white space appears above and below each item. The arrangement has significant advantages:

1. Simplifies dictation. After the points have been identified, the dictator can present them in the predetermined sequence and express in a similar manner.

2. Emphasizes points. Because each item is separated from others and because the treatment is different from the paragraphs that precede and follow the series, ideas stand out vividly.

3. Facilitates recall and discussion. Items that are separated in this manner are easy to envision; they can be discussed by number.

This arrangement on the page is especially appropriate when a letter asks or answers a series of questions. It is very effective in both business letters and personal letters.

Sincerely

Tiffany Layton

FIGURE A.6
Personal business letter format.

MEMORANDUM

To: Judith Reid, Engineering Section

From: Curt Ralston, Presentation Department

Date: January 4, 1990

Subject: Format for Memoranda

For speed and consistency in keyboarding memoranda, the following guidelines are provided:

1. Use standard-size (8 1/2 by 11) paper for all memoranda, regardless of length.

2. Set the left margin at 12 and the right at 72.

3. Omit courtesy and professional titles on the "To" and "From" lines. After the name, place the name of the unit in which that person works.

4. Spell out the name of the month.

5. Begin the first word of the subject line with a capital letter. Begin all other words with a capital letter except articles, prepositions, and conjunctions.

6. Leave two blank lines between the subject line and the first paragraph.

7. Single space, but leave a blank line between paragraphs and between tabulated items (as is done on this page).

8. Indent tabulated items 5 spaces from the left margin, and end each line about 5 spaces short of the right margin. When enumerated items require more than one line, begin the second line directly beneath the first letter of the first line. (With all tabulated lines beginning at the same point, the preceding number stands out vividly.)

9. If the memorandum is longer than one page, type the number 2 at the right margin on the third line from the top edge of the paper. Begin the second page on the sixth line from the top edge.

Other companies may use somewhat different formats, but these guidelines will help us to be consistent.

FIGURE A.7

Memorandum with tabulation and enumeration.

M E M O R A N D U M

To: Board of Directors

From: Thomas H. Duley

Date: December 15, 1990

Subject: FINANCIAL REPORT FOR NOVEMBER

Net earnings for the month of November were $12.4 million or $.56 a share compared with $13.8 million or $.63 a share a year ago. Net earnings for the eleven months ending November 30 were $125.0 million or $5.60 a share. That was an improvement of 124.6 percent over the $55.7 million or $2.26 a share for the comparable period last year.

Net interest income continues to make substantial improvements, up $17.7 million for the month of November and $181.0 million for the eleven-month period. In addition, the following significant items affected earnings:

--Earnings for the month of November included $2.2 million from the sale of loans and investments, an amount well below the $8.5 million for November of last year.

--The interest rate spread was 2.52 percent for the month of November and remained at 2.45 percent for the eleven-month period--an increase of 72 basis points over the 1.73 percent for the prior comparable period.

--The insurance subsidiary contributed net earnings of $1.4 million for the month and $12.5 million for the year to date with both figures more than double the totals of last year.

Shareholders' equity was $1.015 billion at November 30.

Additional information will be presented at the December board meeting.

FIGURE A.8

Financial-report memorandum.

MEMORANDUM

TO: R. H. McAfee, Vice-President
FROM: Sylvia Glass, Marketing Director
DATE: March 31, 1990
SUBJECT: Marketing Activity Report for March

The marketing division reports the following activities for March:

Advertising

Three meetings were held with representatives of the Bart and Dome agency to complete plans for the fall campaign for Fluffy Buns. The campaign will concentrate on the use of discount coupons published in the Thursday food sections of sixty daily newspapers in the Pacific states. Coupons will be released on the second and fourth Thursdays in June and July.

Estimated cost of the program is $645,000. That includes 2.2 million redeemed coupons at 20 cents ($440,000).

A point-of-sale advertising display, shown on the attached sheet, has been developed for retail grocery outlets. Sales reps are pushing these in the regular and new calls. The display may be used to feature a different product from our line on a weekly basis.

Sales Staff

We have dropped one sales rep from the northern California section and divided the area between southern Oregon and Sacramento reps. We have added a rep to our Arizona section. During the month, our fifty-two reps made 8,320 calls and solicited $6,330,000 in new orders in addition to servicing their continuing accounts.

FIGURE A.9
Marketing-report memorandum.

margins appear to be less popular in business than machine manufacturers originally expected them to be. For a business that wants to project a progressive image, justified right margins may help.

A handwritten memo (see Figure A.10) effectively personalizes a message. Usually addressed to a close friend or associate, it is informal. "To" and "From" lines may include first names (or nicknames) only. Sentences may use contractions, acronyms, abbreviations, and jargon.

The *1989 ZIP Code and Post Office Directory* recommends all-capital letters for envelope addresses. In the interest of work simplification, speed, and consistency, all-cap arrangement of inside addresses may seem logical. It is not required, and it is not altogether popular. If a letter is to be inserted into a window envelope, all-caps for the inside address may assist the post office in processing and delivering it quickly.

When letters and memoranda are longer than one page, the second page needs a heading that identifies it as a continuation of the first page. For pages other than the first, use plain sheets (no letterhead or "Memorandum" appearing at the top). The heading includes (1) the name of the person to whom the message is sent, (2) the page number, and (3) the date. Place the heading one inch from the top edge of the paper; leave two vertical spaces between it and the first line of writing. Various arrangements are acceptable, such as

1. On one line, beginning at the left margin and ending at the right margin.

    Ruth Wilson   -2-   May 1, 1990

2. On one line, beginning at the left margin.

    Ruth Wilson, May 1, 1990, page 2

3. On three lines.

    Ruth Wilson
    May 1, 1990
    Page 2

The same heading (with appropriate page number) would appear on pages 3, 4, etc. On sales letters that are mass produced and mailed, page headings are seldom employed.

• Envelopes

Post offices accept and deliver envelopes that have been addressed by pen or typewritten in the traditional manner (in capital-and-lowercase letters with punctuation). They recommend, however, that capital letters be used exclusively and that commas and periods be omitted.

MEMORANDUM

To: Jerry
From: Chuck
Date: 10/27
Subject: Lunch with Apco on 10/27

I just want to confirm our
date with Apco rep on 10/27.
Please let Charlotte know.
She'll get in touch with me.

Handwritten memorandum.

When addresses are keyboarded as recommended in the *1989 ZIP Code and Post Office Directory*, optical character readers can convert them to a bar code, which is then printed near the bottom edge of the envelope. At the destination post office, the characters are "read" by another machine, which sorts the envelopes for delivery. In the interest of speed and efficiency, those who mail letters should try to comply with the wishes of those who deliver them (the post office): use caps, do not use commas or periods, and type envelope addresses in single-spaced form.

Note that the address in Figure A.11 is not *totally* without punctuation. Periods are used in the abbreviation for "post office" and a hyphen is used in the ZIP code.

1. **Small (No. $6\frac{3}{4}$) envelopes**

Return Address	**Address**
$\frac{1}{2}$ inch from top edge	2 inches from top edge
$\frac{1}{2}$ inch from left edge	2 inches from left edge
Single spacing	Single spacing
All caps with no punctuation, *or* small letters with punctuation.	All caps with no punctuation (preferred by the post office), *or* small letters with punctuation.
2 spaces between state and ZIP code.	2 spaces between state and ZIP code.

```
Calvin Scott
123 E. Ash Street
Waco, TX  76711


              ACE EMPLOYMENT AGENCY
              ATTENTION JOHN C YOUNG JR
              PO BOX 3384
              AMARILLO TX  79011-1234
```

FIGURE A.11

Small-envelope address.

The first digit in a ZIP code represents one of ten national areas. Within these areas, each state is divided into an average of ten smaller geographic areas, identified by the second and third digits. The fourth and fifth digits identify a local delivery area. Some cities (usually larger ones) employ an additional set of four digits. They enable automated equipment to sort mail to a specific carrier. The first two digits of the "plus 4" denote a delivery "sector," which may be several blocks, a group of streets, several office buildings, or a small geographic area. The last two digits denote a delivery "segment," which might be one floor of an office building, one side of a street, a firm, a suite, a post office box, or a group of boxes.

Most businesses use envelopes on which the firm name and address have been printed in the return-address position. In the half inch of space just above the printed return address, the name of the letter writer can be typed (Figure A.12). Note, also, the position of "Special Delivery," "Registered," or other instructions, to the P.O.

In Figure A.12, John Young *could* have printed (instead of

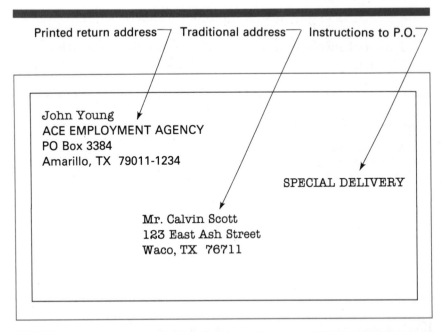

FIGURE A.12

Envelope with printed return address, traditional address, and instructions to P.O.

typed) his name above the printed firm name. The address is written in small letters with punctuation. Note, also, use of the courtesy title (Mr.). The form is illustrated for those who have little enthusiasm for the all-cap address recommended by the U.S. Postal Service. Addresses in the traditional form may look more "normal," but they may also result in slower delivery. "SPECIAL DELIVERY," "PRIORITY MAIL," and "REGISTERED MAIL" are written at least three lines above the inside address in the space directly beneath the stamp. Of course, such instructions to the post office can appear on either a small or a large envelope, as can instructions to those to whom mail is delivered.

2. **Large (No. 10) envelopes**

The only difference between keyboarding addresses on small envelopes and large envelopes is in placement of the address, as shown in Figure A.13. The first line is begun about 2 inches from the top edge and 4 inches from the left edge. If an envelope includes instructions to those to whom mail is delivered (such as "Hold for Arrival" or "Open on May 1"), the words are placed three spaces below the return address and typed in capital letters or underscored.

```
Ruth Johnson
Route 4 Box 123
Barton MO  65713

Hold for Arrival


                    MRS MARY ALICE REDFORD CPA
                    SMITH ELECTRONICS INC
                    154 N HORTON STREET
                    MOUNTAINSIDE CO  84321
```

FIGURE A.13
Large envelope with instructions to receivers of mail.

• Numbers

Business people use quantitative data often, so numbers appear frequently in business writing. *Accuracy* is exceedingly important. The most frequent problem in expressing numbers is whether to write them as figures or to spell them as words.

1. Use Figures
   a. in most business writing (not spelled-out words), because (1) figures are important to get deserved emphasis; (2) figures are easy for readers to locate if they need to reread for critical points; and (3) figures provide economic use of time and space—*12* can be typed faster and in less space then *twelve*.

      Regardless of whether a number has one digit or many, use figures to express dates, sums of money, mixed numbers and decimals, distance, dimension, cubic capacity, percentage, weights, temperatures, and page numbers. (With the preceding exceptions, numbers one to ten are normally spelled out if no larger number appears in the same sentence: "Only *three* people were present." "We need *five* machines." "Send *5* officers and *37* men.")

   b. with ordinals (*th, st, rd, nd*) only when the number precedes the month.

      The meeting is to be held on May 10.

      The meeting is to be held on the 10th of May.

   c. without the ciphers when presenting an even-dollar figure that is not accompanied with a figure that includes both dollars and cents.

      He paid $30 for the cabinet.

      He paid $31.75 for the table and $30.00 for the cabinet.

2. Spell Out
   a. numbers if they are used as the first word of a sentence:

      Thirty-two people attended.

   b. numbers that represent time when *o'clock* is used:

      Please be there at ten o'clock.

      Meet me at 10:15 P.M.

   c. names of streets up to and including twelve:

      Fifth Street, Seventh Avenue

d.   the first number when two numbers are placed together in the same sentence:

We need <u>four 17-cent</u> stamps.

We need <u>seventeen 4-cent</u> stamps.

Note: if one number in a sentence follows another, style manuals agree that *one* of the numbers should be spelled ("4 17-cent" or "17 4-cent" may cause a reader to ponder). Manuals do not agree on *which* number is to be spelled. Be consistent. Note also that a hyphen joins the second number with the word that follows it, thus forming a compound adjective that describes the noun "stamps."

e.   numbers that are indefinite or approximate:

Several hundred boxes were shipped.

The incumbent won by about ten thousand votes.

f.   numbers in legal documents, following them with figures enclosed in parentheses:

For the sum of <u>four hundred dollars ($400)</u>,...

For the sum of <u>four hundred (400)</u> dollars,...

...including <u>forty (40)</u> acres, more or less.

Exercise 12

Assume the following sentences appear in a letter or a report. If a number is presented in appropriate form, copy the sentence as is. If a number is presented in inappropriate form, change the number to correct form as you recopy the sentence.

1. The question was answered by sixty-one percent of the respondents.
2. The meeting will be at 9:30 a.M on February 21st.
3. Three figures appeared on the expense account: $21.95, $30 and $35.14.
4. Go to the service station at 5th Street and Hardy Drive.
5. We ordered five sixteen-ounce hammers.
6. Fifteen minutes were devoted to announcements; 10 minutes were devoted to business.
7. 21 members voted in favor of the motion.
8. The cost will be approximately $1,000,000.00.
9. Mix two quarts of white with 13 quarts of brown.
10. Examine the diagram on page seven.

• Paragraphs

Long, complicated paragraphs look forbidding. Important ideas that appear in the middle receive little emphasis. In reviewing a letter, a reader can easily spot important points if they appear in short paragraphs. Therefore, a writer should rely mainly on short paragraphs; four to six lines is a good *average* for business letters. But, of course, some can be longer; some can be short, even one short sentence. Short paragraphs help achieve emphasis and enable a reader to read rapidly.

• Postscripts

Because we should plan carefully before we write, we should very seldom need to include a postscript as an afterthought. Rather, a postscript is used for emphasis (whatever appears last on a page gets special attention). Leave one vertical space between the reference initials and the postscript if the letter includes no enclosure. If an enclosure is included, leave one blank line space between *Enclosure* and the postscript.

• Punctuation

In business writing, punctuation is basically the same as in other writing. Clarity is a primary consideration. Convention is another.

1. Use an Apostrophe
    a. to form the possessive singular: man, *man's;* firm, *firm's;* worker, *worker's.* (Add an apostrophe and an *s.*)
    b. to form the possessive plural: drivers, *drivers';* players, *players';* dealers, *dealers'.* (Place an apostrophe after the *s.*)
    c. to show possession of a proper noun in which the last letter is not an *s.* Mr. *Wilson's* boss, Mr. *Bostrom's* interview. (Add an apostrophe and an *s.*)
    d. to form the possessive singular when the last letter in a proper noun is an *s.* Determine placement of the apostrophe by the number of syllables in the noun:

        When the singular form of a one-syllable noun ends in *s,* form the possessive by adding *'s*: Jones, *Jones's;* Ross, *Ross's.*

        When the singular form contains more than one syllable and ends in *s* or in an *s* sound, form the possessive by adding an apostrophe only: Miss Richards, Miss *Richards';* Mr. Harris, Mr. *Harris'.*

e. in expressions that indicate ownership. The apostrophe shows omission of a preposition:

Last year's reports....   Reports of last year....

f. when the noun presents time or distance in a possessive manner: an *hour's* visit, three *weeks'* vacation, a *mile's* journey.

g. when a noun precedes a gerund:

Miss Bowen's receiving the promotion caused....

Mr. Green's taking the gavel indicated....

h. to show whether ownership is joint or separate:

To indicate joint ownership, add an *'s* to the last name only: *Olsen* and *Howard's* accounting firm.

To indicate separate ownership, add an *'s* to each name: *Olsen's* and *Howard's* accounting firms.

2. Do Not Use an Apostrophe

a. in the titles of some organizations. Use the name as the organization uses its name:

National Business Teachers Association

National Sales Executives Association

b. to form the possessive of a pronoun (most pronouns become possessive through a change in spelling; therefore, an apostrophe is not employed):

Yours   Not *your's*

Ours   Not *our's*

(*Punctuation* continues after Exercise 13.)

Exercise 13

Which, (a or b), uses the apostrophe correctly?

1. a. Three week's wages were paid.
    b. Three weeks' wages were paid.

2. a. Two service stations were cited: West's and Johnson's.
    b. Two service stations were cited: West and Johnson's.

3. a. The responsibility is our's.
    b. The responsibility is ours.

4. a. I shall appreciate Mary's calling before the 15th.
    b. I shall appreciate Marys calling before the 15th.

5. a. This company's mission-and-scope statement is excellent.
   b. This companys' mission-and-scope statement is excellent.

6. a. October's market decline was severe.
   b. Octobers' market decline was severe.

7. a. Mr. Morris's letter of acceptance had been received.
   b. Mr. Morris' letter of acceptance had been received.

8. a. Mr. Ross' report was late.
   b. Mr. Ross's report was late.

9. a. Miss Ward's status was uncertain.
   b. Miss Wards' status was uncertain.

10. a. These workers' concerns are warranted.
    b. These worker's concerns are warranted.

• **Punctuation** (continued)

3. Use Brackets

   a. to enclose words that are inserted between words or sentences of quoted material:

   "How long will the delay be? No longer than this: [At this point, the speaker tapped the podium three times.] That means no delay at all."

   b. as required in certain mathematical formulas.

   c. to enclose parenthetical material that contains parentheses:

   The motion passed. [The vote (17 for and 4 against) was not taken until midnight.]

4. Use a Colon

   a. to suggest that a list will follow a statement that appears in complete-sentence form:

   For three reasons, we have decided to move to a new location: (1) We need an expanded market. (2) We need an inexpensive source of raw materials. (3) We need a ready source of labor.

   Three factors influenced our decision: an expanded market, an inexpensive source of raw materials, and a ready source of labor.

   We need to (1) expand our market, (2) locate an inexpensive source of materials, and (3) find a ready source of labor.

(A colon does not follow *to* because the words preceding the list do not constitute what could be a complete sentence.)

b. when the verb that would complete a sentence is sufficiently understood and thus omitted

The proposal was rejected. The reasons: (1) no money, (2) no technicians, and (3) no work space.

Verbs such as "are presented," "are given," and "are stated" could be employed after "reasons," but they are not essential. Since the thought is complete without them, a colon is used.

c. to stress an appositive (a noun that renames the preceding noun) at the end of a sentence:

His heart was set on one thing: promotion.
Our progress is due to the efforts of one man: Mr. Keating.

d. after the salutation of a letter (when mixed or closed punctuation is used):

Dear Dr. Gorga:

Dear Miss Campbell:

e. after a word or phrase followed by additional material in ads or signs:

No Parking: Reserved for executives

For Rent: Two-bedroom apartment

f. between hours and minutes to express time in figures:

5:45 P.M.

11:05 A.M.

(*Punctuation* continues after Exercise 14.)

Exercise 14

Of the statements that follow each sentence, which is correct?

1. The program has one shortcoming: flexibility.
    a. The colon after "shortcoming" is appropriate.
    b. "Shortcoming" should be followed by a semicolon.

2. Our meetings are scheduled for: Monday, Tuesday, and Friday.
    a. The colon after "for" is appropriate.
    b. The colon after "for" should be removed.

3. We liked this car because of its: price, durability, and appearance.
   a. The colon after "its" should be removed.
   b. The colon after "its" is appropriate.

4. We liked three features of Miss Cole's résumé: her experience, her education, and her attitude.
   a. The colon after "résumé" is appropriate.
   b. The colon should be changed to a semicolon.

5. We are enthusiastic about the plan because: (1) it is least expensive, (2) its legality is unquestioned, and (3) it can be implemented quickly.
   a. The colon after "because" is appropriate.
   b. The colon after "because" should be removed.

- **Punctuation** (continued)

5. Use a Comma
   a. between coordinate clauses joined by *and, but,* and *for:*

      He wanted to pay his bills on time, <u>but</u> he did not have the money.

   b. after participial phrases or dependent clauses:

      Believing that her earnings would continue to increase, she sought to borrow more money.

      Sentences that begin with prepositions or such words, as *if, as,* and *when* almost always need a comma.

      Under the circumstances, we think you are justified.
      To get the full benefit of our insurance plan, just fill out and return the enclosed card.
      Whatever you do, please explain it to your supervisor.
      As you may know, Mr. Smith has been ill for three weeks.
      If you can meet us at the plane, please plan to be there by six o'clock.
      When I left the building, doors were being closed.

   c. to separate words in a series:

You have a choice of gray, green, purple, and white.	Without the comma after "purple," no one can tell for sure whether there are four choices, the last of which is "white," or whether there are three choices, the last of which is "purple and white."
You have a choice of purple and white, gray, and green.	Choice is restricted to three, the first of which is "purple and white."

d. between coordinate adjectives (two separate adjectives that modify the same noun):

New employees are given a long, difficult examination.	"Long" and "difficult" both modify "examination."
We want quick, factual news.	"Quick" and "factual" separately modify "news" and are separated by a comma.
The supervisor is an excellent public speaker.	Do not place a comma between two adjectives when the second adjective may be considered as part of the noun that follows. Technically, "excellent" and "public" are both adjectives. In this sentence, however, "excellent" modifies the noun "public speaker."

e. to separate a nonrestrictive clause (a clause that is not essential to the basic meaning of the sentence) from the rest of the sentence:

Mr. MacMurray, who is head of the collection department, is leaving for a vacation.	The parenthetical remark is not essential to the meaning of the sentence.
The man who is head of the collection department is leaving for a vacation.	Commas should not be used because "who is head of the collection department" is essential to the meaning of the sentence.

f. to separate parenthetical expressions from the rest of the sentence:

Miss Watson, speaking in behalf of the entire department, accepted the proposal.

g. before and after year dates when the month and day precede:

On July 2, 1977, Mr. Kababik made the final payment.

h. before and after the name of a state when the name of a city precedes:

I saw him in Kansas City, Missouri, on the 12th of October.

i. after a direct address:

John, I believe you have earned a vacation.

j. after the words *No* and *Yes* when they introduce a statement:

Yes, you can count on me.

No, I shall have to decline.

k. to set off appositives:

The group heard a speech from Mr. Matthew Welch, a recruit.
Mr. Herbert Jackson, former president of the Jackson Institute, spoke to the group.

A comma before an appositive is used for neutral emphasis; a dash (instead of a comma) is used for heavy emphasis.

l. between contrasted elements:

We need more money, not less.

The job requires experience, not formal education.

m. to show the omission of words that are understood:

Miss Reno scored 96 percent on the preemployment examination; Mr. Mehrmann, 84 percent.

n. before a question that solicits a confirmatory answer:

It's a reasonable price, isn't it?

Our bills have been paid, haven't they?

o. between the typewritten name and the title on the same line beneath a signature.

ROY MURR, PRESIDENT
CATHRYN W EDWARDS
PRESIDENT OF ACADEMIC AFFAIRS

p. after a conjunctive adverb:

The check was for the right amount; however, it was not signed.

q. Do not place a comma between compound predicates:

We just ate and ran.

The insurance agent inspected the car and recommended total reimbursement.

The group discussed the proposal and referred it to the finance committee.

(*Punctuation* continues after Exercise 15.)

Exercise 15

Insert needed commas; delete unneeded commas. Some sentences may need more than one comma; others, none.

1. The man who came in late, has not been interviewed, but all other applicants have been interviewed.
2. Margie Harrison a new member of the board, remained silent.
3. Ammonium sulfate, which is available at almost all home-supply stores is ideal fertilizer for citrus.
4. This carpet is available in three colors: brown, tan and blue.
5. We had a long bitter discussion.
6. As the following graph illustrates, costs have doubled in the last two years:
7. By the time I arrived at the meeting the issue had been discussed thoroughly and put aside.
8. If you approve of the changes in paragraph three please place your initials in the margin.
9. We surveyed the entire population but three of the responses were unusable.
10. Because only 21 percent of the members were present, the motion could not be considered.
11. John was awarded $25; Bill $40.
12. We have lost our place in the production line haven't we?
13. We should be spending less money, not more.
14. On November 20 1988 all related documents were submitted.
15. Yes, I agree that the meeting in Oxford, Tennessee should be scheduled in April.

• Punctuation (continued)

6. Use a Dash

In typewritten material, the dash is constructed by striking the hyphen key twice with no space before or after. The dash is thus twice as long as the hyphen and has a slight break in the middle. In typeset material it is longer than a hyphen but has no break.

a. to place emphasis on appositives:

His answer--the correct answer--was based on years of experience.

Compare the price--$125--with the cost of a single repair job.

She was concerned with one thing--promotion.

b. when appositives contain commas:

Their scores--Mary, 21; Sally, 20; and Jo, 19--were the highest in a group of 300.

c. when a parenthetical remark consists of an abrupt change in thought:

The committee decided--you may think it's a joke, but it isn't--that the resolution should be adopted.

7. Use an Ellipsis

to indicate that some words have been omitted from a quotation:

Mr. Thomas said, "We believe . . . our objectives will be accomplished."

Mr. Thomas reported, "The time has come when we must provide our employees with in-service training. . . ."   Ellipses at the end of a quotation employ four periods, one of which indicates the end of the sentence.

8. Use a Hyphen

a. in such compound words as *self-analysis* and *father-in-law*.

b. between the words in a compound adjective. (A *compound adjective* is a group of words joined together and used as a single word to describe a noun that follows.)

An attention-getting device

A page-by-page description

An up-to-date record

A technical, hard-to-follow lecture

Observe that each of the hyphenated expressions precedes a noun. Hyphens would not be required in "a lecture that was hard to follow," a "record that is up to date," and so on. Do not use a hyphen in such expressions as "*commonly accepted* principle," "*widely quoted* authority," "*rapidly advancing* leader":

since the first word in each expression ends in *ly,* no compound adjective is involved. *Commonly,* for example, is an adverb modifying *accepted.*

c. to prevent misinterpretation:

A <u>toy-machine</u> man	A man concerned with toy machines
A <u>toy machine</u> man	A toy man of the machine type
<u>Guaranteed used</u> tires	Used tires that are guaranteed
<u>Guaranteed-used</u> tires	Tires that are guaranteed to have been used
Twelve <u>foot-soldiers</u>	Twelve soldiers who travel by walking
<u>Twelve-foot</u> soldiers	Soldiers twelve feet tall
<u>Eight inch</u> blades	Eight blades, each of which is an inch long
<u>Eight-inch</u> blades	Blades eight inches long
<u>Recover</u> a chair	To obtain possession of a chair once more
<u>Re-cover</u> a chair	To cover a chair again

d. to express fractions that precede a noun:

A two-thirds interest
A three-fourths majority

Figures—2/3 and 3/4—are acceptable. Spelled-out fractions not followed by nouns are not hyphenated: *two thirds* of the members.

e. in spelling out compound numbers:

<u>Thirty-one</u>

<u>Ninety-seven</u>

f. to avoid repetition of a word:

<u>First-,</u> second-, and <u>third-class</u> mail

<u>Short-,</u> <u>medium-,</u> and <u>long-range</u> missiles

"Short-range, medium-range, and long-range missiles" would have the same meaning; but repetition of "range" is not necessary. The hyphens after "short" and "medium" show that these words are connected to another word that will appear at the end of the series.

g. to divide words at the end of a line. (See the discussion of dividing words.)

h. in a nine-digit ZIP code: 83475-1247

9. Use Parentheses

   a.   for explanatory material that could be left out:

Three of our employees (Mr. Bachman, Mr. Russo, and Mr. Wilds) took their vacations in August.	Dashes may be used instead of parentheses to precede and follow parenthetical material. Dashes have the effect of emphasizing; parentheses, de-emphasizing.
All our employees (you'll not believe this, I predict) have perfect attendance records.	Sentences within sentences neither begin with a capital letter nor end with a period.

   b.   for accuracy in writing figures:

For the sum of three thousand five hundred dollars ($3,500)....

   c.   To enclose figures when parts of a sentence are enumerated:

The clerk has authority to (1) issue passes, (2) collect membership fees, and (3) sign checks.

   d.   *after* a period when an entire sentence is parenthetical; *before* a period when only the last part of a sentence is parenthetical:

The board met for three hours. (The usual time is one hour.)
Success can be attributed to one man (Earl Knott).

   e.   both before and after that which is parenthetical:

Incorrect: ... authority to 1) issue passes, 2) collect fees.
Correct: ... authority to (1) issue passes, (2) collect fees.

10. Use a Period

   a.   after imperative and declarative sentences:

Complete this report.

We shall attend.

   b.   after a courteous request:

Will you please complete the report today.

May I have your answer this week.

Technically, the sentences are questions; but they do not suggest a verbal answer. They do suggest an *action* answer.

   c.   after an abbreviation:

Dr.

M.D.

Mrs.

Ms.

Miss (not abbreviated when used as a title; it's a complete word)

d. to end a sentence in which the last word is abbreviated:

Incorrect: Send to John Cook, Jr..
Correct: Send to John Cook, Jr.

Two periods look too much like an ellipsis.

11. Use Quotation Marks

a. to enclose direct quotations:

The supervisor said, "We shall make progress."

"We shall make progress," the supervisor said, "even though we have to work overtime."

Note that the period and comma are typed within the quotation marks. All other punctuation is typed outside—unless it is part of the quotation.

b. before the first word and after the last word of a multiple-sentence quotation:

The president said, "Have a seat, gentlemen. I'm dictating a letter. I should be through in about five minutes. Please wait."

c. to enclose titles of songs, magazine and newspaper articles, and themes:

"Home on the Range"

"Progress in Cancer Research"

(Underscore or italicize the titles of books, magazines, and newspapers.)

d. to define terms:

As used in this report, syntax means "the branch of grammar that has to do with sentence structure."

e. to enclose slang expressions:

Gentlemen, we can describe the attacks against our policies with one word--"hogwash."

    f. to enclose nicknames:

And now for some comments by Ray "Skinny" Johnson.

    g. to imply that a different word may be more appropriate:

Our "football" team. . . .	Hints that the team appears to be playing something other than football.
Our football "team". . . .	Hints that "collection of individual players" would be more descriptive than "team."
. . . out for "lunch."	Hints that the reason for being out is something other than lunch.

    h. to enclose quoted material that contains other quoted material:

The budget director said, "Believe me when I say 'A penny saved is a penny earned' is the best advice I ever had."

Note: A quotation that appears within another quotation is enclosed in *single* quotation marks.

    i. before and after a word that is used in an unusual way. The last word in each of the following sentences is used in the usual sense:

The presentation was effective.

May I please have your recommendation.

In the first sentence, the last word conveys the idea of a presentation that accomplishes its purpose; in the second, the last word conveys the idea of a proposed alternative or course of action. No quotation marks are needed. However, the following sentences employ the same words in unusual ways; therefore, quotation marks are used:

The word "effective" was used in describing his presentation.

In this sentence, "effective" is used as an adjective.

He had difficulty learning to spell "recommendation."

In the preceding sentences, the words included in quotation marks could (instead) be presented in italics (if the typewriter is equipped with keys for italics).

    j. in their proper position within a sentence. Place periods and commas *inside* quotation marks:

"Take your time," she said, "and the work will be easier."

Place semicolons *outside* quotation marks:

The foreman said, "That's fine"; his facial expressions conveyed an entirely different message.

Place question marks *inside* quotation marks when the question is within the quotation:

The contractor asked, "When shall we begin?"

Place question marks *outside* quotation marks when the question is not within the quotation:

Did the contractor say, "We shall begin today"?

(*Punctuation* continues after Exercise 16.)

Exercise 16

Pay special attention to use of the dash, ellipsis, hyphen, parentheses, period, and quotation marks. For each pair of sentences, what is the difference in meaning?

1. a. The first speaker will be Red Gaddis.
   b. The first speaker will be "Red" Gaddis.

2. a. Have you read *The Power of Ethical Management*?
   b. Have you read "The Power of Ethical Management"?

3. a. His accomplishments are summarized on the attached page.
   b. His "accomplishments" are summarized on the attached page.

4. a. Tim said the firm plans to establish a sinking fund.
   b. Tim said, "The firm plans to establish a sinking fund."

5. a. Only one attorney (Helen Johnson) is working on the case.
   b. Only one attorney—Helen Johnson—is working on the case.

6. a. Three day passes will be issued this afternoon.
   b. Three-day passes will be issued this afternoon.

7. a. The speaker will be Ms. Mary Thompson.
   b. The speaker will be Mrs. Mary Thompson.

8. a. A party is being planned for the ten-game winners.
   b. A party is being planned for the ten game winners.

9. a. Check to see whether the sofa can be recovered.
   b. Check to see whether the sofa can be re-covered.

10. a. Our accountant said, "Such expenses . . . are not justified."

    b. Our accountant said, "Such expenses are not justified."

- ## Punctuation (continued)

12. Use a Semicolon

    a. when a conjunction is omitted:

> Our workers have been extraordinarily efficient this year, and they are expecting a bonus.

> Our workers have been extraordinarily efficient this year; they are expecting a bonus.

    b. in a compound-complex sentence:

> We prefer delivery on Saturday morning at four o'clock, but Friday night at ten o'clock will be satisfactory.

> As indicated earlier, we prefer delivery on Saturday morning at four o'clock; but Friday night at ten o'clock will be satisfactory.

> We prefer delivery on Saturday morning at four o'clock; but, if the arrangement is more convenient for you, Friday night at ten o'clock will be satisfactory.

    c. before conjunctive adverbs:

> The shipment arrived too late for our weekend sale; therefore, we are returning the shipment to you.

> Other frequently used conjunctive adverbs are *however, otherwise, consequently,* and *nevertheless.*

    d. in series that contain commas:

> Some of our workers have worked overtime this week: Smith, 6 hours; Hardin, 3; Cantrell, 10; and McGowan, 11.

    e. before illustrative words, as in the following sentences:

> We have plans for improvement; for example, we intend to. . . .

> The engine has been "knocking"; that is, the gas in the cylinders explodes before the pistons complete their upward strokes.

(*Punctuation* continues after Exercise 17.)

Exercise 17

In each sentence, place a semicolon where it is needed.

1. Expense tickets were not included, otherwise the request would have been honored.

2. The following agents received a bonus this month: Barnes, $400, Shelley, $450, and Jackson, $600.
3. The bid was not considered, it arrived two days late.
4. This paint does have some disadvantages, for example, its drying time is too long.
5. Soon after the figures have been received, they will be processed, but a formal report cannot be prepared before May 1.

• Punctuation (continued)

13. Use Symbols

    a. for convenience in filling out such forms as invoices and statements, but not in sentences of letters and reports. The dollar sign ($), in contrast with such symbols as %, ¢, @, and #, should be used in letters and reports.

    b. in sentences of letters and reports, spell out:

       31 <u>percent</u> (not "31%")

       80 <u>cents</u> a foot (not "80¢ a foot")

       21 <u>cases</u> at $4 a case (not "21 cases @ $4 a case")

       To policy <u>No.</u> 468571 (not "to policy # 468571")

14. Use an Underscore or Italics

    a. to emphasize a word that is not sufficiently emphasized by other means.

    b. to indicate the titles of books, magazines, and newspapers:

       <u>Gone with the Wind</u>

       <u>The Reader's Digest</u>

       <u>The Evening Star</u>

• Spacing Properly While Keyboarding

These rules of spacing apply to the *keyboarding of business letters and reports*. They do not necessarily apply in the *printing of books, magazines, and newspapers*.

To achieve right margins that are straight, typesetters can vary the amount of space between words, punctuation marks, and sentences. Since this arrangement is not possible with standard typewriters, the following guidelines will help the appearance of letters:

1. Space twice after a period, question mark, or colon at the end of a sentence.

   Step two was completed. Then. . . .

   When will he arrive? Regardless of the time. . . .

   We have three questions: (1) Where is. . . .

2. Space once after a comma and a semicolon:

   When the end of the month comes, we shall be prepared.

   The operator left at three o'clock; he was ill.

3. Space once after a period following an initial:

   Mr. Warren H. Ragsdale

   Mr. W. H. Ragsdale

4. Space once after a period following such abbreviations as No., Co., and Corp.:

   Send a case of No. 6 nails to the Johnson Co. of Chicago.

5. For proper vertical spacing in business letters, leave
   a. one blank line between (1) the inside address and the salutation, (2) the salutation and the first paragraph, (3) paragraphs, and (4) the last line of the last paragraph and the complimentary close.
   b. two blank lines above and two blank lines below the subject line in a letter that employs the simplified letter format.
   c. two blank lines below the inside address when the letter is to be inserted into a window envelope.
   d. at least three blank lines between the complimentary close and the typewritten signature.

6. Leave a 1-inch margin at the top, bottom, and right-hand side of a page in a typewritten report. If the page is to be bound at the left, leave $1\frac{1}{2}$ inches at the left; otherwise, leave 1 inch on each side.

Exercise 18

Write brief answers to each question.

1. How many times should a keyboarder hit the space bar after typing
   a. a period at the end of the sentence?
   b. a question mark at the end of a sentence?

   c. a period following an abbreviation that is somewhere other than at the end of a sentence?

   d. a colon that precedes a list?

   e. a semicolon?

   f. a comma?

2. How many vertical spaces should be left between

   a. an inside address and a salutation?

   b. a salutation and the first line of a letter?

   c. paragraphs?

   d. before and after the subject line in a simplified letter?

   e. the last line of a letter and the complimentary close?

   f. the complimentary close and the typewritten signature?

3. In business reports, how much space should be left for margins?

4. For envelope addresses, does the post office recommend single spacing?

• Spelling

The following words appear often in business letters and reports. To avoid frequent references to the dictionary and to avoid embarrassing errors when a dictionary is not available, study and try to memorize the list.

acceptable	arrangement	collectible
accessible	attorneys	column
accommodations	automatically	commodities
accompanying	available	competent
accumulate	bargain	competitive
accurate	beginning	congratulations
acknowledging	believing	consent
acknowledgment	beneficial	controlled
across	benefited	controlling
advisable	bookkeeper	convincing
allowance	bulletin	deductible
announcement	calendar	deferred
announcing	cancellation	deficiency
apparently	changeable	definite
appealing	changing	describe
argument	chargeable	description

desirable	independent	permissible
developing	indispensable	personnel
development	inquiring	persuade
difference	installation	pleasant
disbursement	interfered	policies
discrepancy	introducing	possibilities
distribute	issuing	precede
distribution	journeys	preceding
efficiency	labeled	predictable
eligible	legible	preferred
embarrassing	leisure	preparing
enclosed	license	prevalent
enforceable	making	privilege
enforcing	management	procedure
equipped	mistake	putting
exceed	modern	quantity
excellent	movable	questionnaire
exchangeable	moving	receive
exhausted	noticeable	recipient
existence	notifying	referred
existent	occasion	reinforcement
extension	occupies	repetition
facilities	occurred	reputable
factories	occurrence	requirement
feasible	offered	research
February	offering	retrieve
finally	officially	separate
forcible	omitting	signature
furniture	organizing	similar
getting	original	suffered
grateful	overestimate*	supersede
guaranteed	pamphlet	surprise
handling	parallel	transferring
helpful	perform	traveling
incidentally	permanent	truly

* Words compounded with "over" and "under" are not hyphenated.

Exercise 19

Grammar and mechanics. Examine each of the following sentences for errors in word usage, spelling, punctuation, and manner of expressing numbers. If a sentence contains no error, copy it as it is. If a sentence does contain one or more errors, make the needed corrections as you copy the sentence. Do not divide a sentence into two sentences.

1. Will you please find out weather first and second-year students are elligible too receive that scholarship.

2. George was formerly in charge of security at the capital building, he is not enthused about our firms security system.

3. The questionaires which were mailed on June 1 have been returned; but only a few of those mailed latter in the month have been returned.

4. This years biennial evaluations will take place during the second week of July and the first week of December.

5. In the passed, only one news media has been invited to attend the meetings.

6. John has submitted more suggestions than anyone in his department, but he has yet to receive an award.

7. While that proceedure has been highly successful it is not popular in our department.

8. The man, who came late to the meeting, was the only one to leave early.

9. The three applicants were waiting to interview for the same job, therefore they had little to say to each other.

10. Only one of my recomendations were considered, this was very disappointing to the superintendant and I.

11. The majority of the discussion was devoted to fiscal policy, but, as I discovered later, that topic had not been listed on the agenda.

12. Because Mister Burris's wife called each morning and afternoon, the couple was suspicioned of having martial problems.

Review Exercises

In Exercises 20 through 25, the first sentence of each pair contains one or more errors. In the second sentence, the errors have been corrected. Parenthetical numbers identify pages where explanations can be found. For maximum benefit, use a cover sheet. After trying to identify errors in the first sentence, slide the cover sheet downward and study the corrected sentence. To review reasons for changes, refer to the parenthetical numbers. Within each set of parentheses, the first number is a page number in the text; the second number or letter identifies a certain place on that page.

Caution: Remember that the sentences have been deliberately designed to reinforce knowledge of word usage, grammar, spelling, punctuation, and manner of expressing numbers. Just make the changes necessary for correctness in these categories. Do not attempt to revise a sentence and present its idea in an entirely different way.

Each exercise is designed to reinforce between twenty and forty principles. For *mastery* of these principles, do exercises 20 through 25 repeatedly throughout the semester. Students who want to form *habits* of correctness will find these exercises (which invite frequent re-exposure to principles) exceedingly beneficial.

Exercise 20

1. I shall appreciate you sending next months report too my home address. (676:e) (719:e)

   I shall appreciate your sending next month's report to my home address.

2. If I were him, I would include second- and third-degree headings in my report. (676:d) (680:1a) (722:5b) (727:f)

   If I were he, I would include second- and third-degree headings in my report.

3. When Miss. Forrest became an aid to the governor her salary was $35,000, but she is now earning $51,000. (722:5b) (755:5) (729:e) (722:b) (732:b) (716:1c)

   When Miss Forrest became an aide to the governor, her salary was $35,000; but she is now earning $51,000.

4. Each of the following words were used several times in the report: greatfull, 7, occassion, 7, separate, 8, recommend, 10, priviledge, 10, recieve, 10, and deductible, 10. (681:e) (720:4a) (722.5c) (732:d) (735) (736)

   Each of the following words was used several times in the report: grateful, 7; occasion, 7; separate, 8; recommend, 10; privilege, 10; receive, 10; and deductible, 10.

5. Our stockbroker has written an article on physical policy, it will appear in the March 21st edition of "Newsweek". (732:a) (716:1b) (733:14b) (662:40)

   Our stockbroker has written an article on fiscal policy; it will appear in the March 21 edition of Newsweek.

6. Only one of the participant's were willing to ask "what do you think?" (718:a) (681:e) (700:b) (730–31:j)

Only one of the participants was willing to ask "What do you think?"

Only one of the participants was willing to ask, "What do you think?"

7. John Hargus's figures are different then mine, therefore I have offered to hire an auditor. (718:d) (661:32) (732:c) (724:p)

John Hargus' figures are different from mine; therefore, I have offered to hire an auditor.

8. If you can complete the survey before July 1, 1990, please procede; otherwise ask the superintendent for a new set of questionaires. (722:5b) (724:g) (732:c) (724:p) (736)

If you can complete the survey before July 1, 1990, please proceed; otherwise, ask the superintendent for a new set of questionnaires.

9. If your martial status is single; you may not be elligible for this $600.00 deductable. (664:58) (722:5b) (736) (716:1c) (735)

If your marital status is single, you may not be eligible for this $600 deductible.

10. The balance sheet does not correspond to the work sheet, please check the figures throughly. (658:24) (732:a)

The balance sheet does not correspond to the work sheet; please check the figures thoroughly.

11. The contracts which have an escape clause, have been submitted to our attorneys; but all others are being prepared for signatures. (670:83) (723:e) (722:5a) (735) (736)

The contracts that have an escape clause have been submitted to our attorneys, but all others are being prepared for signatures.

12. On March 1st, 1990, we moved to a five room suite, it was formally occupied by Woodson Travel Agency. (716:b) (722:5b) (726:8b) (732:a) (662:42) (723:e)

On March 1, 1990, we moved to a five-room suite; it was formerly occupied by Woodson Travel Agency.

On March 1, 1990, we moved to a five-room suite, which was formerly occupied by Woodson Travel Agency.

Exercise 21

1. Irregardless of recent commentary this book is very unique. (663:49) (722:5b) (670:84)

   Regardless of recent commentary, this book is unique.

   Regardless of recent commentary, this book is very unusual.

2. Neither Joe or Phil have planed to attend the three day conference, however, the superintendent has issued instructions to do so. (667:63) (681:d) (726:86) (732:c) (724:p)

   Neither Joe nor Phil has planned to attend the three-day conference; however, the superintendent has issued instructions to do so.

3. The box which was in Room C has been prepaired for mailing; all other boxes are to be wrapped with heavy paper, and returned to Room D. (670:83) (732:a) (736) (725:q) (722:5a)

   The box that was in Room C has been prepared for mailing; all other boxes are to be wrapped with heavy paper and returned to Room D.

   The box that was in Room C has been prepared for mailing, but all other boxes are to be wrapped with heavy paper and returned to Room D.

4. Did the principal really use the words "get out of my office?" (668:69) (700:b) (730:j)

   Did the principal really use the words "Get out of my office"?

   Did the principal really use the words, "Get out of my office"?

5. While Jan's requestion for promotion had been denied three times, her moral was high. (671:89) (718:c) (722:5b) (665:60) (722:5a)

   Although Jan's request for promotion had been denied three times, her morale was high.

   Jan's request for promotion had been denied three times, but her morale was high.

6. We need sometime for evaluation of proceedures, therefore a decision will not be made until November 3. (669:76) (736) (732:c) (724:p) (716:b)

   We need some time for evaluation of procedures; therefore, a decision will not be made until November 3.

7. Each of the following words are to be added to your list of hard-to-

spell words: advisable, bulletin, convenience, definitie, maintenance, occassion, offered, precede, and priviledge. (681:e) (726:8b) (720:4a) (735) (736)

Each of the following words is to be added to your list of hard-to-spell words: advisable, bulletin, convenience, definite, maintenance, occasion, offered, precede, and privilege.

8. If I filled out this long complicated questionaire my time would be wasted. (723:d) (722:5b) (736)

If I filled out this long, complicated questionnaire, my time would be wasted.

9. After you have completed your term, please write to me; we have some highly-important matters to discuss. (722:5b) (732:a) (726:8b)

After you have completed your term, please write to me; we have some highly important matters to discuss.

10. After discussing the problem for a hour, three conclusions were drawn by the committee. (722:5b) (689:6)

After discussing the problem for an hour, the committee drew three conclusions.

11. Your biennial performance evaluations will take place during the third week of January and the first week of Dec. (657:16) (699:d)

Your biennial performance evaluations will take place during the third week of January and the first week of December.

12. In the past, this film was only shone to trainees. (667:66) (722:5b) (669:75) (688:4)

In the past, this film was shown to trainees only.

Exercise 22

1. While the company has lost their first-place position this year, next years predictions are real optimistic. (671:89) (675:e) (726:8b) (722:5b) (719:e) (787:b) (722:5a) (671:85)

Although the company has lost its first-place position this year, next year's predictions are very optimistic.

The company has lost its first-place position this year, but next year's predictions are very optimistic.

2. You should talk with Mister Welch, he made a hard to believe score on last weeks make up examination. (697:a) (732:a) (719:e) (726:8b)

You should talk with Mr. Welch; he made a hard-to-believe score on last week's make-up examination.

3. Consensus of opinion is that this 14-page booklet is writen poorly. (658:22) (726:8b)

Consensus is that this 14-page booklet is written poorly.

4. Please try to quickly review these documents, it's to be returned before October 21st. (691:10) (732:a) (716:1b) (91) (100)

Please try to review these documents quickly; they're to be returned before October 21.

Please try to review these documents quickly because they are to be returned before October 21.

5. On the criteria of speed the machine failed; but on the criteria of eficiency, it succeeded. (659:27) (722:5b) (732:b)

On the criterion of speed, the machine failed; but on the criterion of efficiency, it succeeded.

On the criterion of speed, the machine failed; but, on the criterion of efficiency, it succeeded.

6. The request has been rejected, the reason is because the forms are to long. (732:a) (668:72) (100)

The request has been rejected; the reason is that the forms are too long.

The request has been rejected because the forms are too long.

7. While the committee agreed with Miss. Harris's conclusions; serious questions were raised as to the questionair, which was used as a information-gathering device. (671:89) (728:10c) (718:d) (722:5b) (656:13) (736) (670:83) (726:8b)

Although the committee agreed with Miss Harris' conclusions, serious questions were raised about the questionnaire that was used as an information-gathering device.

The committee agreed with Miss Harris' conclusions, but serious questions were raised about the questionnaire that was used as an information-gathering device.

8. If I was her I would exchange that typewritter for a new one, but she thinks new machines are too expensive. (722:5b) (671:87) (680:1a) (732:b)

If I were she, I would exchange that typewriter for a new one;
but she thinks new machines are too expensive.

9. The president was not enthused about the new stationery, but he
signed the order form. (661:36) (669:77) (722:5a)

The president was not enthusiastic about the new stationery, but
he signed the order form.

10. We ordered four 16 pound hammers, but only one was shipped.
(726:8b) (722:5a) (717:d)

We ordered four 16-pound hammers, but only one was shipped.

We ordered four 16-pound hammers; only one was shipped.

11. Because the gravel was to coarse to meet specifications the inspection engineer halted construction. (722:5b) (657:19)

Because the gravel was too coarse to meet specifications, the inspection engineer halted construction.

12. The committee has been charged with responsibility for a practical
equitable plan. (723:d) (667:68) (662:38)

The committee has been charged with responsibility for a practical, equitable plan.

Exercise 23

1. Two thirds of the members think the statue should be revised because of its ambiguity. (716:2a) (727:d) (669:78) (675:e)

Two thirds of the members think the statute should be revised
because of its ambiguity.

2. For you and I that price seems very low, but for a recently-hired
assistant, it probably seems very high. (676:c) (722:5b) (732:b)
(726:8b)

For you and me, that price seems very low; but for a recently
hired assistant, it probably seems very high.

For you and me, that price seems very low; but, for a recently
hired assistant, it probably seems very high.

3. Only one of the applicant's were well qualified, she was interviewed
immediately. (681:e) (718:1a) (732:a) (722:5a)

Only one of the applicants was well qualified; she was interviewed immediately.

Only one of the applicants was well qualified, and she was interviewed immediately.

4. The word processor was not able to detect all errors, for example, derive was typed incorrectly as drive. (732:e) (730:i) (730:j)

The word processor was not able to detect all errors; for example, "derive" was typed incorrectly as "drive."

5. Their research techniques were different than our's, however, their conclusions were similar. (661:32) (719:2b) (732:c) (736) (724:p)

Their research techniques were different from ours; however, their conclusions were similar.

6. 13 respondents thought the company was loosing sight of it's objectives. (716:2a) (664:56) (675:e) (719:2b)

Thirteen respondents thought the company was losing sight of its objectives.

7. The following have worked a few hours of overtime this week; Welch, 4, Redford, 6, and Woods, 11. (662:41) (736) (720:4a) (732:d) (724:m)

The following employees have worked a few hours of overtime this week: Welch, 4; Redford, 6; and Woods, 11.

8. If I was able to borrow $150,000.00, I would start a business of my own, but I could never borrow that much. (722:5b) (671:87) (716:c) (732:b)

If I were able to borrow $150,000, I would start a business of my own; but I could never borrow that much.

9. One news media is planning to present ten two-hour programs on that subject in February. (664:59) (717:d) (726:8b)

One news medium is planning to present ten 2-hour programs on that subject in February.

10. Helen made a higher score than any one in her work unit but her promotion was denied because of habitual tardiness. (686:d) (722:5a) (656:12)

Helen made a higher score than anyone else in her work unit, but her promotion was denied because of habitual tardiness.

11. Because of our highly advertised expansion program; the need for additional capital is becoming acute. (726:86) (722:5b) (657:18)

Because of our highly advertised expansion program, the need for additional capital is becoming acute.

12. Weather conditions should permit construction to begin in the later part of Febuary. (671:88) (663:52)

Weather conditions should permit construction to begin in the latter part of February.

Exercise 24

1. I suspicion Mistress Russpo is faster than me; but, our performances have not been timed officially. (670:82) (697:1a) (676:a) (722:5a) (736) (732:c)

I suspect Mrs. Russpo is faster than I, but our performances have not been timed officially.

I have a suspicion that Mrs. Russpo is faster than I; however, our performances have not been timed officially.

2. Your payments have been arriving approximately ten days after their due dates; this is causing us some concern. (732:a) (678:g)

Your payments have been arriving approximately ten days after their due dates; this tardiness is causing us some concern.

Your payments have been arriving approximately ten days after their due dates; these delays are causing us some concern.

3. If you will send your rough drafts to Miss. Graff and myself we will edit it throughly. (722:5b) (728:c) (91) (93)

If you will send your rough drafts to Miss Graff and me, we will edit them thoroughly.

If you will send your rough draft to Miss Graff and me, we will edit it thoroughly.

4. Each of our assistants are required to take a short intensive training course. (681:e) (723:d)

Each of our assistants is required to take a short, intensive training course.

All our assistants are required to take a short, intensive training course.

5. After Mr. Childress's draft has been edited, it will be forwarded to this office for printing. (728:c) (718:d) (722:5b) (662:43)

After Mr. Childress' draft has been edited, it will be sent to this office for printing.

6. Of the attorneys interviewed one-fifth thought the revised statute would have no affect on employee theft. (735) (722:5b) (727:d) (655:4) (669:78)

Of the attorneys interviewed, one fifth thought the revised statute would have no effect on employee theft.

7. The amount of purchases returned have been decreasing, however sales in that district has been increasing. (656:10) (681:e) (732:c) (724:p)

The number of purchases returned has been decreasing; however, sales in that district have been increasing.

8. Among the contestants who made superior scores were: Wilson, Brosque, and Martinez respectfully. (720:4a) (722:c) (668:73)

Among the contestants who made superior scores were Wilson, Brosque, and Martinez, respectively.

9. In a speech to sophomores the imminent physician inferred that experimental treatment had been totally effective. (722:5b) (661:35) (663:46)

In a speech to sophomores, the eminent physician implied that experimental treatment had been totally effective.

10. I accept your invitation to participate in the program, it promises to be real beneficial (655:2) (732:a) (671:85) (101)

I accept your invitation to participate in the program; it promises to be very beneficial.

I accept your invitation to participate in the program because it promises to be really beneficial.

11. One of the major issues was whether or not the concrete should be reinforced with steal. (681:e) (81) (669:79)

One of the major issues was whether the concrete should be reinforced with steel.

12. The research techniques are acceptable; however, one of the conclusions seem questionable. (732:c) (724:p) (681:e)

The research techniques are acceptable; however, one of the conclusions seems questionable.

Exercise 25

1. When I compared my results with yours', I found few similiarities. (658:20) (719:b) (722:5b)

When I compared my results with yours, I found few similarities.

2. A short intensive review will be conducted on April 14th. (723:d) (716:b)

A short, intensive review will be conducted on April 14.

3. In rewriting the final draft, please change the word charge to debit. (722:5b) (730:i) (730:j)

In rewriting the final draft, please change the word "charge" to "debit."

4. When the plan was introduced in 1986 it was well received; but, management soon discovered serious weaknesses. (722:5b) (732:b) (736)

When the plan was introduced in 1986, it was well received; but management soon discovered serious weaknesses.

5. Prices began their descent in February, and hit their lowest point in Sept.. (659:30) (725:q) (699:2a) (729:10d)

Prices began their descent in February and hit their lowest point in September.

6. The commission is too be divided equally between Ray, Coleen, and Edith. (656:9) (722:c)

The commission is to be divided equally among Ray, Coleen, and Edith.

7. While the majority of the work has been completed the superintendent has asked for a three week extension of the contract. (671:89) (722:5b) (644:57) (726:8b) (736)

Although the major portion of the work has been completed, the superintendent has asked for a three-week extension of the contract.

Most of the work has been completed, but the superintendent has asked for a three-week extension of the contract.

8. In reviewing Miss. Chambliss's application, the director found errors in: spelling, application of the rules of grammar, and punctuation. (728:c) (722:5b) (718:d) (720:4a) (690:7)

   In reviewing Miss Chambliss' application, the director found errors in spelling, grammar, and punctuation.

9. Only one of the proposals was discussed; but it was placed on the table for further discussion. (681:e) (722:5a) (662:39)

   Only one of the proposals was discussed, but it was placed on the table for further discussion.

10. Almost 85 percent of the questionairs has been returned, it is now being tabulated. (716:1a) (736) (681:e) (91) (732:a)

    Almost 85 percent of the questionnaires have been returned; they are now being tabulated.

11. The company has changed it's policy, three week vacations are no longer permited. (719:2b) (732:a) (726:8b) (675:e)

    The company has changed its policy; three-week vacations are no longer permitted.

12. Neither the manager or his assistants are being invited to attend the two day workshop. (667:63) (681:d) (726:8b)

    Neither the manager nor his assistants are being invited to attend the two-day workshop.

Grading Symbols

In placing comments on students' papers, teachers can save time by using symbols instead of words. By learning the symbols or referring to them when they appear on returned papers, you will discover ways in which your work can be improved.

ACE	Avoid copying examples
ACP	Avoid copying problems
ADE	Avoid doubtful expressions
ADP	Avoid dangling participles
AEB	Avoid expletive beginnings

AOS	Avoid obvious statements
ARW	Avoid repeating words
ASI	Avoid split infinitives
AWE	Avoid worn expressions
BMS	Be more sincere
GRF	Give reasons first
HCA	Hyphenate compound adjectives
ISS	Improve sentence structure
ITI	Interpret this idea (give concrete evidence to illustrate the point)
LC	Lowercase (don't capitalize)
LTI	Leave to implication
MIL	Make introduction logical (action taken or spoken of in an introductory phrase is attributed to the noun that follows)
PRA	Put reader in action
SSQ	Single space quotes
STP	Subordinate this point
UAC	Use antecedents correctly
UAE	Use action ending (an action ending tells what and how, makes action seem easy, and encourages quick action)
UAS	Use appropriate salutation
UAV	Use active voice
UAW	Use another word
UCL	Use capital letters
UCS	Use correct spelling
UDS	Use deductive sequence
UFN	Use firm name
UFP	Use first person
UFW	Use fewer words
UIS	Use inductive sequence
UPC	Use parallel construction
UPL	Use positive language
UPV	Use passive voice
USS	Use shorter sentences
USW	Use specific words
UTS	Use transition sentence

#	Insert space
✐	Delete
∿	Reverse order of letters or words
◌	Close up (leave no space)
←↑↓→	Move copy this direction (up, down, across)
/	Divide word here.

Appendix B

CIPS—IBM PC

COMPUTERIZED
INTERACTIVE
PRACTICE SET

USER
INSTRUCTIONS

For use with the IBM PC
(with 64K Memory or greater
and Color/Graphics Card)

CONTENTS

CIPS Diskette Contents
How to Start CIPS
Prompts
Commands
Types of Frames
Hints for the User

CIPS Diskette Contents

How to Start CIPS

Start the computer with the DOS diskette (PC DOS Version 1.1 or greater). Place a CIPS diskette in drive A. Type A: and press <Enter>. Type CIPS and press <ENTER>. The monitor will automatically display the Kent logo and then the title. Pressing the space bar will advance you to the copyright statement; pressing the <M> key will take you to the menu for the diskette. When you get to the menu, select a section for study and press the letter on the keyboard that corresponds to that section. For example, to view Instructions to the User, press the letter A. If you press a nonfunctional key, the prompt at the bottom of the screen will inform you of the keys that may be pressed. If the display of the menu (or any screen) has been interrupted, press the <D> key.

After you have chosen a section from the menu, respond as indicated by the prompt or use one of the command keys, which are described in these instructions and on each diskette in the Instructions to the User.

You may move from one diskette to the other by replacing the current diskette with the other diskette. Press <M> to get the new menu; or, if you are already at a menu, press <ESC> to get the menu of the new diskette.

Note: If the computer displays the message "Error 5 in line 320," then your computer does not have the required Color/Graphics Card.

Prompts

A prompt is a signal that the computer is waiting for your instructions or input. After each screen is displayed, a prompt appears near the lower left corner of the screen. The following is a list of prompts used by CIPS and their functions:

<Space>	indicates that you are to push the space bar to move to the next frame. To move to frames other than the "next" one, you must press other keys, discussed under Command Keys.
<Space> to continue	indicates that you are looking at one screen in a short sequence of screens. Pressing the space bar will display additional closely related material.

Your choice?	is used at Menu frames and Question frames; indicates that you are to press a letter key to select a topic or a number key to answer the question. When help, principles, or examples are available, the commands for summoning them (H, P, and E) appear to the right of the prompt.
Please stand by . . .	is displayed whenever information must be transferred from the diskette to the computer.
Use only: _____	is displayed if you press a nonfunctional key—that is, a key not on the list; the blank indicates a list of keys that may be pressed.
Press M or B	is used at the end of a section, when the only choices are to return to the menu by pressing <M> or to review that section by pressing <B> to back up.

Commands

These commands are available at all times, whether they appear to the right of the prompt or not:

<Space>	Move to next frame or complete display of current frame after pause
<A>	Advance to next question, skipping over intervening material
<B>	Back up to previous frame
<D>	Display current frame in full (after interruption by user or to view animation again)
<M>	Return to menu
<T>	Select track (choice of track 1, study; 2, review; 3, practice)*
<Q>	Quit

*At the study track, you view all the frames—discussion, example, and question—in normal sequence. At the review track, the examples are omitted, allowing you to view the discussion and then answer the questions. Both discussion and examples are skipped at the practice track, leaving only the questions for you to answer.

These commands are available when the corresponding letters appear to the right of the prompt:

<H>   Help

<P>   Principle (displays principle relevant to current question or discussion)

<E>   Example

Note: From a Wrong-answer frame, <Space>, <B>, and <A> all return you to the incorrectly answered question.

Types of Frames

The word *frame* describes a unit of information or a complete thought. Only a limited amount of information can be displayed at one time on a computer's video screen; thus the information in some frames exceeds the space available on a single screen. We therefore distinguish between a *frame*—the complete thought—and a *screen,* the information visible on the monitor at a given time. Long frames (think of them as long thoughts) use two or more screens of information. You can identify a multiscreen frame by looking in the lower right corner for the word *continued.* The prompt is "<Space> to continue."

You will probably not notice any difference between single- and multiple-screen frames as you move *forward* through CIPS. The difference becomes significant when you wish to back up or redisplay information. The <B>ackup command takes you to the previous *frame;* <D>isplay takes you to the beginning of the current frame, which will be the first screen of a multiscreen frame. If you forget you are in a multiscreen frame and press <B>, it is not a serious problem; you just back up a little farther than you expected.

CIPS contains the following types of frames:

Menu frames	list topics available for selection
Objectives frames	(at the beginning of each section) list the knowledge and skills to be acquired in the section
Discussion frames	present the basic subject matter of each section
Question frames	pose multiple-choice questions to test understanding of the material
Right-answer frames	provide positive reinforcement for correct responses to questions

Wrong-answer frames	explain why a choice is wrong
Help frames	offer further help or review of the concepts
Example frames	provide examples similar to the question
Principle frames	state the principle that applies to the question
Terminal frames	mark the end of each section

Hints for the User

The command keys are operational even while the frame is going on the screen. You do not have to wait until you get the prompt before pushing a key to move on or back up.

A word of caution: If you push the space bar while a question or menu is going on the screen, the frame will stop, and you will get the prompt "Use only: _____." If this happens, press the <D>isplay key and the frame will be completed.

A reminder: From the second or third screen of a multiscreen frame, the <D>isplay key takes you to the first *screen:* the <B>ackup key takes you to the previous *frame.*

It is never necessary to work all the way through a section. If you accidentally select the wrong section, you can return to the Menu frame by using the <M> key. At the menu, you can select a new section from the current diskette. If you wish to work through a lesson on a different CIPS diskette, insert the new diskette and press <ESC>. The menu of the new diskette will be displayed, and you may choose a section from the new menu.

INDEX